Family

Matters

Readings on Family Lives and the Law

Family

Matters

Readings on Family Lives and the Law

Edited by Martha Minow

A New Press "Law in Context" Series Reader

The New Press, New York

Published in the United States by The New Press, New York
Distributed by W.W. Norton & Company, Inc.
500 Fifth Avenue, New York, NY 10110

Library of Congress Cataloging-in-Publication Data

Family matters: readings on family lives and the law / [editor],
Martha Minow.—1st ed.
p. cm.—(The New Press law in context in series)
ISBN 1-56584-017-8   ISBN 1-56584-042-9 (pbk.)
1. Domestic relations—United States. 2. Family—United States.
3. United States—Social conditions—1980- I. Minow, Martha. 1954-
II. Series.
KF505.Z9F34 1993
346.7301'5—dc20
[347.30615]   92-53727
                                                        CIP

First Edition

Book design by Acme Art

Established in 1990 as a major alternative to the large, commercial publishing houses, The New Press
is intended to be the first full-scale nonprofit American book publisher outside of the university presses.
The Press is operated editorially in the public interest, rather than for private gain; it is committed to
publishing in innovative ways works of educational, cultural, and community value, which, despite
their intellectual merits, might not normally be "commercially viable."

◆

ACKNOWLEDGMENTS

Thanks to the following for permission to print or reprint the works listed:

Barrett, Michele and Mary MacIntosh, *The Anti-Social Family* (Verso/NLB: London and New York, 1982),
   pp. 134–59.
Bartholet, Elizabeth, "Where Do Black Children Belong? The Politics of Race Matching," in *Adoption*,
   1 *Reconstruction* no.4 (1992), pp. 22–43.
Becker, Robin, "Into the Badlands," copyright © 1985 Robin Becker. Reprinted with permission from
   The Things That Divide Us, Conlon, de Silva, Wilson, eds. (Seattle: Seal Press), pp. 15–26.
Belkin, Lisa, "As Family Protests Hospital Seeks an End to Women's Life Support," *The New York Times*,
   Jan. 10, 1991. Copyright © 1991 by The New York Times Company. Reprinted by permission.
Bryant, Dorothy, "Blood Relations," from *The Graywolf Annual Eight: The New Family*, Scott Walker, ed.
   (St. Paul, Minn.: Graywolf Press, 1991), pp. 75–80. Dorothy Bryant is the author of eight novels,
   including *The Kin of Ata Are Waiting for You*, and *Confessions of Madam Psyche*.
Burnham, Margaret, "An Impossible Marriage: Slave Law and Family Law," 5 *Journal of Law and Inequality*
   198 (1987).

Acknowledgments continued on page 415.

To my families

Introduction

ONE   **What Is a Family?**

    Images of Family As Haven, Family As Hell

       BLOOD RELATIONS **2**
       Dorothy Bryant

       ROYAL BEATINGS **5**
       Alice Munro

    Definitions of Family: Who's In, Who's Out, and Who Decides

       THE NEW FAMILY **22**
       Bonnie Timmons

       PERSONAL KINDREDS **23**
       Carol Stack

       DANNY IN TRANSIT **31**
       David Leavitt

       FRIENDS AT LAST **42**
       John Corry

TWO   **Entering families: Fact or Law?**

    Becoming a Parent

      Choosing Parenthood

       HAND-ME-DOWN DREAMS **46**
       Carol Peacock

       PREGNANT ON PURPOSE **47**
       Sharon Thompson

      Adoption

       A MARKET FOR BABIES **56**
       J. Robert S. Prichard

       WHERE DO BLACK CHILDREN BELONG?: THE POLITICS OF RACE-MATCHING IN ADOPTION **66**
       Elizabeth Bartholet

       COMMENT ON "WHERE DO BLACK CHILDREN BELONG?" **94**
       Rita J. Simon

New Reproductive Technologies

DO NEW REPRODUCTIVE TECHNIQUES THREATEN THE FAMILY? 96
Martha Field

INSIDE THE SURROGATE INDUSTRY 104
Susan Ince

Foster Care

WHY SHOULD I GIVE MY BABY BACK? 115
Jane Doe

FOSTER CARE AND THE POLITICS OF COMPASSION 117
Nanette Schorr

Mothering vs. Fathering

NIGHT PIECES: FOR A CHILD 125
Adrienne Rich

JUSTICE, GENDER, AND THE FAMILY 125
Susan Moller Okin

PREGNANCY LEAVE DISCRIMINATES AGAINST MEN! 129
Dan Wasserman

THE NEW FATHER 130
Letty Cottin Pogrebin

Who May Marry?

AN IMPOSSIBLE MARRIAGE: SLAVE LAW AND FAMILY LAW 142
Margaret Burnham

SOME COMPLICATING THOUGHTS ON SAME-SEX MARRIAGE 157
Nitya Duclos

MOST LIKE AN ARCH THIS MARRIAGE 169
John Ciardi

Cohabiting Without Marriage

DECONSTRUCTING CONTRACT DOCTRINE . . . 170
Clare Dalton

INTO THE BADLANDS 178
Robin Becker

THREE Violence and Neglect

Violence in Families, Neglect by the State

INTIMATE VIOLENCE **188**
Richard J. Gelles and Murray A. Strauss

VIOLENCE IN INTIMATE RELATIONSHIPS **200**
bell hooks

SOCIAL POLICY AND ELDER ABUSE **206**
Stephen Crystal

**"WORDS AND THE DOOR TO THE LAND OF
CHANGE": LAW, LANGUAGE, AND FAMILY
VIOLENCE, part one** **209**
Martha Minow

Neglect by Families, Violence by the State

I STAND HERE IRONING **216**
Tillie Olsen

**HAVEN IN A HEARTLESS WORLD:
THE FAMILY BESIEGED** **221**
Christopher Lasch

**NO NAME MADDOX, CASE HISTORY
OF CHARLES MANSON** **223**
Kenneth Wooden (1976)

**RACE, GENDER AND VIOLENCE
AGAINST WOMEN** **230**
Kimberlé Crenshaw

MAKING AN ISSUE OF CHILD ABUSE **232**
Barbara Nelson

Responding to Violence and Neglect

FOR SHELTER AND BEYOND **246**
Massachusetts Coalition of Battered Women
Services Groups

WELCOME AND RULES **257**
Waltham Battered Women Support Committee

**WOMEN'S EXPERIENCE AND THE PROBLEM
OF TRANSITION** **261**
Christine Littleton

"WORDS AND THE DOOR TO THE LAND OF
CHANGE": LAW, LANGUAGE, AND FAMILY
VIOLENCE, part two 272
Martha Minow

Debates Over "State Intervention":

THE MYTH OF STATE INTERVENTION
IN THE FAMILY 277
Frances Olsen

Medical Treatment Decisions

A RECKONING 283
May Sarton

AS FAMILY PROTESTS, HOSPITAL SEEKS
AN END TO WOMAN'S LIFE SUPPORT 285
Lisa Belkin

GUARDIANSHIP OF PHILLIP BECKER 288
Superior Court of Santa Clara

PACT ON CUSTODY LEADS TO SURGERY 299
Robert Lindsey

REPRESENTING LESBIANS 301
Anne B. Goldstein

FOUR   Family Break-Up and Reorganization

Why Should the State Care?

EPILOGUE: THE PURSUIT OF HAPPINESS 309
Elaine Tyler May

BUT WHERE ARE THE MEN 314
Ruth Sidel

NEW FAMILY CAR 324
Pamela Painter

CONSIDER THE CONSEQUENCES:
REVIEW OF LENORE WEITZMAN'S
THE DIVORCE REVOLUTION 329
Martha Minow

Child Custody, Visitation, and Support

THE POLITICS OF FAMILY LAW 336
Fran Olsen

CULTURAL PERSPECTIVES ON
CHILD WELFARE 344
Carol Stack

CHILD SUPPORT AND VISITATION:
RETHINKING THE CONNECTIONS 349
Karen Czpanskiy

JUSTIFYING THE CONTINUED USE OF JAIL . . . 353
David Chambers

FAMILY STRUCTURE, BLACK UNEMPLOYMENT,
AND AMERICAN SOCIAL POLICY 361
Kathryn Neckerman, Robert Aponte, and
William Julius Wilson

Access to Lawyers, Access to Court, Access to Law

NORTHSIDE SECRETARIAL SERVICE: CHARGE
OF UNAUTHORIZED PRACTICE 365
Leila Kern and Frank Sander
Harvard Law School Program on the
Legal Profession

LAWYERS AND LEGAL CONSCIOUSNESS: LAW
TALK IN THE DIVORCE LAWYER'S OFFICE . . . 373
Austin Sarat and William L.F. Felstiner

PRO SE DIVORCE: A STRATEGY FOR
EMPOWERING WOMEN 377
Emily Joselson and Judy Kaye

FIVE Alternatives to Court, Alternatives to Law, Alternatives to Family Law

THE NEW MEDIATORS 382
Marilyn Stasie

DIVORCE MEDIATION: A CRITICAL
OVERVIEW 384
Kenneth Kressel

DOMINANT DISCOURSE, PROFESSIONAL
LANGUAGE, AND LEGAL CHANGE IN CHILD
CUSTODY DECISION-MAKING 387
Martha Fineman

THE ANTI-SOCIAL FAMILY 397
Michele Barrett and Mary MacIntosh

LOVE IS NOT THE PROBLEM 412
June Jordan

Introduction

What is family law? People often ask me this question when I say this is what I teach. It would be easy to answer that family law is marriage, divorce and adoption, child custody and support. Certainly, these are part of the story. But conveying the other parts may be more important. First, these topical issues belong to a larger domain. Family law includes all the rules announced and applied by public officials to govern the creation and dissolution of families. Family law also applies to disputes among family members over the control, protection, and custody of children; and over property, income, and support obligations claimed by one family member against another. Family law, in addition, involves the procedures; the courts, including judges and court officers; mediation centers; lawyers; and do-it-yourself practices which provide mechanisms for expressing, resolving, managing, or prolonging these disputes.

Still another layer of family law appears in the rules and practices adopted by varied levels of government that affect people because of their family roles. Consider tax regulations that turn on the taxpayer's marital status or position as a child or parent, or benefits that use an applicant's family relationship to determine eligibility, or that look to the resources held by other family members before granting eligibility. Unemployment benefits, housing and zoning rules, criminal laws, and rules of evidence may each render one's family status critical when asserting a right or a defense.

But even this range of topics understates the subject of family law in the United States. By constitutional principle, religion and government must be separate and yet much of the domain of family law once historically fell within the purview of religious authorities and still for many people involves religious dimensions. In some countries, one's religion (such as Islam, Hinduism, Christianity, or Judaism) determines the body of family laws and institutions that apply. Here, the state may recognize religious actions, for example, concerning marriage, or religious identities in adoption and child custody matters. Yet, the constitutional demand to separate church and state complicates the relationship between religious and governmental family law. Can the legislature condition secular divorces upon the parties' full compliance with religious laws, as New York tried to require in seeking to accommodate the Orthodox Jewish requirement that a husband supply a religious document before a wife obtains a religious divorce?

Should a secular court take into account a parent's sincere religious beliefs in evaluating neglect charges brought in light of the parent's opposition to medical treatment for the child? Not only constitutional law, but also religious sources may be crucial to understanding family law in these instances.

Perhaps less visible, but no less profound, are the sources of family law in opinions and attitudes expressed and shaped by mass media and other cultural sources. Television and radio talk shows, along with situation comedies and great dramas, explore issues about the availability and impact of divorce, interracial adoption, relationships between gay or lesbian couples, child abuse and spouse abuse, and the enforceability of a contract to use a woman's womb to produce a child. Popular music, opera, academic research, and journalism can influence the opinions of judges, the arguments of lawyers, and the behavior of people in families. These cultural sources become especially influential because so many issues in family law depend on interpreting broad concepts. What is the best interests of the child? What amounts to an equitable distribution of assets following divorce? Such general concepts depend on cultural understandings. Poems, cartoons, and short stories capture and also shape ideas people have about families that inform the practices of family law. A wide array of cultural materials mirror and influence the official decisions of judges, legislators, and administrators. The most candid of these actors acknowledge such influences. Judge Fernandez's opinion in the case of Philip Becker, included in this volume, makes reference to a novel by Charles Dickens, to a neighbor of the judge, and to the judge's own life experiences and emotional reactions. Understanding how to influence decision makers in the field of family law, then, requires attention to the sources of their cultural and life experiences. Fiction, social science, and journalism can illuminate themes in family law just as family law can provide cultural critics and historians with raw materials for interpreting society.

This is a longer explanation of what family law is than many people may expect. And in light of this view, I have assembled a range of readings to accompany the course in Family Law I teach at Harvard Law School. The readings can supplement instruction in the law itself; the readings can also provide a basis for more general study of themes in family law and family lives in North America. The materials expose for discussion critical assumptions. What is a family, who may become a parent, who may marry, what kinds of violence or neglect by family members justify state involvement, how should divorce, child custody, and child support be governed, what role does and should family status play in poverty, and do lawyers and courts help or hurt when families disagree? These questions, I suggest, call into play political debates and social contests over meaning; the answers do not lie in a book of judicial opinions or statutes nor in a dictionary or encyclopedia. I am grateful to the authors of the wildly diverse material gathered here for their willingness to participate in this presentation of controversies and nuance behind the issues of family law.

The title, "Family Matters," conveys my own perspective. I think that families matter. Their centrality in great works of literature, in my mind, oddly lacks a counterpart in the hierarchy of American law. Practicing family law is too often considered less important and prestigious than practicing corporate law or tax law, or other fields involving large sums of money. Yet what could be more critical to people's quality of life, and contexts for meaning, and hopes for the future? In addition, for anyone concerned with the effects of class, race, gender, age, sexual orientation, disability, ethnic and religious identities, and technological change, family lives and legal conflicts are a critical arena for study. As materials in this book explore, examinations of families can shed light on the complex relationships between spheres of intimacy and public rules and between private emotions and social institutions. Family matters, then, is any effort to understand the dimensions of our collective lives.

ONE

What Is a Family?

Are families havens of love, care, attention, and affection? Or are they hells of manipulation, guilt, and oppression? Are families natural preserves, where social and legal rules follow biology and passion? Or are they social institutions created and regulated by government to serve specific public purposes? Assumptions about such fundamental questions underlie American family law, yet legal discussions seldom acknowledge them. The readings in this section provide a range of images and evidence to promote richer consideration of the composition and qualities of families defined, affected, or ignored by law.

Images of Family As Haven, Family As Hell

Pop music lyrics suggest that people want each other too much — or not enough. Consider this tiny sample: Bonnie Rait sings, "I Can't Make You Love Me"; Tina Turner sings "You Can't Stop Me Loving You," and Dan Hicks croons, "How Can I Miss You When You Won't Go Away." Relationships premised on love can turn hateful; ties forged by biological connection can become meaningless. At the same time, the idea of family connections can support people as they provide one another mutual aid and a sense of continuity with past and future. Families thus can provide havens from worlds of work and strangers; families can also be private hells with no easy exit. Which images should inform legal rules about families?

This general question assumes considerable significance when images of families inform legal evaluations of such matters as whether medical personnel can or should defer to family members in treatment decisions about an individual who may not be able to speak for herself or himself. For example, recent Supreme Court jurisprudence manifests inconsistent answers to this question. In *Cruzan* v. *Director, Missouri Department of Health*, 110 S.Ct. 2841 (1990), the Court's majority ruled that the Constitution permits a state to refuse deference to parents of an incompetent, comatose patient. In *Ohio* v. *Akron Center for Reproductive Health*, 110 S.Ct. 2972 (1990), the Court construed the Constitution to permit a state to require notification of a parent when a minor daughter seeks an abortion. The very Justices who declined to trust family members in the first case invoked reasons to trust them in the second — and the dissenting Justices also switched arguments in the two cases.

Lawyers can, and do, distinguish these cases; the first involved a patient who had reached adulthood, formed adult desires, but after a tragic car accident could no longer express them while the second involved a minor who had not yet reached adulthood and perhaps could be presumed legally incompetent until proven otherwise. In addition, the first case involved the "right-to-die" question while the second involved abortion, and different substantive and political views on the two issues could explain the divergent results in the Supreme Court. Alternatively, the two cases could be harmonized under the general principle that the fifty states should be given room under the Constitution in both of these sensitive areas — room to experiment, room to protect an individual who faces medical treatment, and room to protect the parent-child relationship.

Yet it may be just as important to consider the ambivalent attitudes toward family members at work in both cases. The Supreme Court's members can flip-flop in their views about whether to trust or distrust family members because both views are plausible and supported by life experiences. Families can be islands of support and comfort; families can also be arenas of conflict and abuse. Each individual within a family may have had both kinds of experiences at different times. Parents, for example, may be sources of solace and at other times may enrage or frighten the child, or burden the child. Children can be a source of enormous joy — and at times, irritation. Siblings, spouses, lovers, cousins — each may arouse intense feelings of appreciation and resentment, and a variety of emotions in between. If this is true, then the source of ambivalence about the family stems not just from the difficulty in estimating how many families are trustworthy and how many are not. The difficulty arises from the experiences each of us — and perhaps even each United States Supreme Court Justice — has had. Family members at times live up to and at times let down the trust we hope to give them, and we at times let down the trust family members place in us.

The readings gathered here explore a range of images and experiences of family connections. They can provide touchstones for considering the sources of ambivalence about families and the variety of emotions evoked by legal disputes, suppressed conflict, or simply day-to-day interactions within families.

◆

BLOOD RELATIONS
Dorothy Bryant

They had their usual season tickets and, when the first play opened, Frank realized that he wanted to go. David, back in the hospital again, encouraged him. "Take Paul, or Jay." But Frank didn't want to see any of their friends.

There were his sisters, his parents, his cousin. No. He decided he wanted his

From Dorothy Bryant, "Blood Relations," in *The Graywolf Annual Eight: The New Family*, Scott Walker, ed. (St. Paul:Graywolf, 1991), pp. 75–80.

grandmother, who had never gone to plays and concerts and was now over eighty, with failing sight, hearing, memory. "Come with me, Nonna. It's a musical, *Sunday in the Park with George*." He knew she would come. The only grandson of a large family, Italian on both sides, he could count on her old unjust preference. For once he was glad of it, shameless.

They drove down Geary Street through gradually thickening traffic. At a long stoplight, he suddenly asked her one of the old questions about his grandfather, whom he knew only through photographs and the stories Nonna told him. It had been years since she'd told this one, his favorite. How he and his grandfather were together all the time in those last months, puttering in the garden until he was too weak. How Frank, barely three years old but talking constantly in either English or Italian (he could not speak a word of Italian now), understood his grandfather perfectly. No one else could, not after seven operations on his cancerous jaw.

Frank's memories began after his grandfather's death, when Nonna became the settled, widowed old lady he knew. He never thought of her as ever having had a husband. He never asked her how she had endured those two years of his grandfather's terrible dying. Frank's mother said that Nonna nursed him day and night, never complained, never cried. Only that by the time he died, she had a slight tremor, an almost imperceptible shaking of her head that still remained after thirty years. It was as if she were constantly whispering inwardly, No, no, no.

Frank dropped her in front of the theater while he parked the car. Alone he felt a stab of guilt. These stabs came regularly now when, absorbed at work, he forgot for a few minutes, then suddenly remembered David sitting at home, probably staring out the garden window. Or when he took a deep breath of cool, foggy air, felt a surge of ordinary well-being and rejoiced in it. And then remembered David with silvery-blue plastic oxygen tubes in his nose. He wondered if Nonna had ever felt guilty for not being able to share each moment of her husband's pain.

He found her just where he had left her, shivering a bit in the crowd. It took them some minutes to inch their way across the jammed, noisy lobby, to squeeze into the elevator, to find their seats. The theater, filling quickly, was already hot and stuffy, and Nonna looked tired. Usually she was in bed by this time. It had been cruel to bring her. She would not enjoy this kind of musical. Even Frank preferred the old-fashioned kind, with tunes you could hum.

She sat silent, beside him, as usual. Living alone all these years, she had no one to talk to. She spent hours working jigsaw puzzles, as she had done with his grandfather during those final months. It had been something they could do without his having to talk. A visitor could join their silence, watching, fitting in a piece or two. When Frank was there, Nonna had told him, his grandfather would hand him a piece and show him how to fit it in, which he did with great concentration and satisfaction. No, he could not remember that either.

Aside from the puzzles, she read an occasional best-seller, watched television, telephoned her grandchildren. Yet even on the phone she said little. There was silence in her eyes, too. They looked, they saw, they expressed nothing. Frank was grateful for that tonight. It would have been a mistake to have brought his mother. Her eyes said everything. Whenever she looked at him, they widened into an abyss of prophecy, full of images of him in David's place. Last week, suddenly infuriated, he had snapped at her, "Don't bury me yet!" It was a strange phrase for him to use, more like something Nonna would say.

A few minutes into the play he was sure they should not have come. He did not want to sit in the dark listening to these tones of abrasive, intellectual sentiment. It would have been better if they had gone to a movie, where he could cry. Like Nonna, he never cried. Except at the movies, where sometimes, at the most banal scenes, tears suddenly spilled down his cheeks. How David laughed at him! But he had not been to a movie these past two months. The flat, simplistic images that usually relaxed and distracted him had become unbearable, torture by stupidity.

Only his job, only work brought him relief. Nonna had had no job during those two years, no break from nursing her husband, using up their savings, then going to work after he died, on night shift for the next twenty years, "not to be alone when the sun goes down." After the first week, Frank realized he was lucky that he had to go to work every day.

Lucky. It was a word he and David used often now. Lucky to have each other, not like some poor bastard all alone. Lucky to have their own house, no panicky roommates or landlord to evict them. Lucky that family, friends, employers, all were behaving well, impeccably, like Nonna who had, as usual in any family crisis, sent jars of soup, ravioli, and her incomparable veal cutlets. David had laughed and said he wondered where on the hierarchy of "luckier than they" he and Frank stood. Surely his former lovers were calling themselves lucky not to be Frank. He and David laughed a lot these days, alone together, or with friends and family. Everyone roared at each other's jokes. They had become the ideal audience for a stand-up comic, all eagerly pitched on the edge of laughter, dreading the silence that followed.

Frank found himself drawn into the play in spite of, or because of the abrasive repetitive music. Maybe he felt in tune with this music that wasn't trying to be sweet and this story that led nowhere. Ragged and hesitant and fragmented, the story lurched from side to side rather than forward, as George, the impressionist artist, conceived his painting from the bits and pieces of his life, fitting them together into beauty no one else could see.

Frank wondered if Nonna was paying attention or day-dreaming. Could she follow the play? Or did she see and hear and then forget a moment later, as she forgot so many things now? How much did she actually understand before she forgot? Did she understand what was happening to David and would possibly — probably — happen to Frank? He stopped that thought, grabbed it, firmly put it aside. Stopping thought was a new process for him, requiring great discipline. Maybe Nonna didn't really forget, but had learned to put aside certain thoughts she must live with.

When the houselights came up for intermission, she nodded, yes, she was enjoying the play. No, she did not want to leave her seat. She sat watching people move about. Frank knew she would not speak again unless he asked her a question. "Did you ever get mad at my grandfather, I mean when he was sick?"

She seemed unsurprised by the question, nodding as if always ready with the answer. "At the end, the last months, when he was leaving me."

Frank nodded. It had come sooner to him, the rage, and to David as well. Anger exploded in small ways, in telephoning from work and yelling when he learned that David would not, could not, eat his lunch. In low, petty ways, like his sulking when David called the AIDS Project to ask for a counselor, someone who would "come between us," Frank whined, flinching at the contempt in David's eyes, in his cutting response, and then, worst of all, in his silence. They apologized, forgave, quarreled again, made up, forgave, wondered at the ignoble form their anguish took. They were not prepared for this, they who had prepared so well.

They had been together five years when the blood test became available, and they took it, glad of the chance to escape the cloud hanging over their friends, confident that their fiercely defended monogamy would be vindicated. They could hardly believe the results. Positive. Each had picked up the virus years ago. Or one had carried it to the other.

They made their wills, took vitamins, went to bed early, stopped drinking even wine, talked about death-with-dignity, quoted statistics. Only ten percent of positives got sick. Twenty percent. Thirty-five to forty percent. The statistics changed as the year slowly passed, until David became one.

Now, their suicide seemed like childish romanticism. Their contempt for heroic measures shriveled and, abjectly, they accepted medical assault. Dignity dissolved in the ocean of petty necessities — the unwashed dishes, the disability application, the mortgage payments — the dozens of reminders that, while everyone must die, life lurches on.

The lights dimmed again. Now the setting was modern, and the great-grandson of George was the artist, still struggling with the same questions, his own life a fragmented puzzle. The baby in the first-act painting was now a grandmother, dozing and drooping in a wheelchair, singing in a weak, piping squeak, "Children and art, children and art." Those were the only things, she sang, that you leave when you die, that are worth anything. "Children and art, children and art."

Frank waited to see if the insistent chant of that simple equation would take him in like a movie and wet his eyes, but it did not touch him. He would never have children, and he didn't make art. Whatever he left would not be so easy to name. What did Nonna think of that song? Not children and art, just children. They were all that mattered to Nonna. That was why she was here with him, why she would sit in the dark through anything with him. So, the force that held them together was, in reality, a huge gap between them. Did she even know him? Did she understand why he needed her tonight, needed to begin to learn what she had known for thirty years?

He reached out to take her hand, gently, respectful of her arthritis. She gave his hand a quick, hard squeeze. Her strength surprised him, hurt him. She had never been so abrupt with him, so rough. He had never felt so grateful. They sat and watched the rest of the play, hand in hand, dry-eyed, two old soldiers in the long war.

♦

ROYAL BEATINGS
Alice Munro

Royal Beating. That was Flo's promise. You are going to get one royal beating.

The word royal rolled on Flo's tongue, took on trappings. Rose had a need to picture things, to pursue absurdities, that was stronger than the need to stay out of trouble, and instead of taking this threat to heart she pondered: how is a beating

From Alice Munro, "Royal Beatings," in *The Beggar Maid: Stories of Flo and Rose* (New York: Vintage Books, 1978), pp. 473–91.

royal? She came up with a tree-lined avenue, a crowd of formal spectators, some
white horses and black slaves. Someone
knelt, and the blood came leaping out like
banners. An occasion both savage and
splendid. In real life they didn't approach
such dignity, and it was only Flo who tried
to supply the event with some high air of
necessity and regret. Rose and her father
soon got beyond anything presentable.

Her father was king of the royal beatings. Those Flo gave never amounted to
much; they were quick cuffs and slaps
dashed off while her attention remained
elsewhere. You get out of my road, she
would say. You mind your own business.
You take that look off your face.

They lived behind a store in Hanratty,
Ontario. There were four of them: Rose,
her father, Flo, Rose's young half brother
Brian. The store was really a house,
bought by Rose's father and mother when
they married and set up here in the furniture and upholstery repair business. Her
mother could do upholstery. From both
parents Rose should have inherited clever
hands, a quick sympathy with materials,
an eye for the nicest turns of mending, but
she hadn't. She was clumsy, and when
something broke she couldn't wait to
sweep it up and throw it away.

Her mother had died. She said to
Rose's father during the afternoon, "I
have a feeling that is so hard to describe.
It's like a boiled egg in my chest, with the
shell left on." She died before night, she
had a blood clot on her lung. Rose was a
baby in a basket at the time, so of course
could not remember any of this. She heard
it from Flo, who must have heard it from
her father. Flo came along soon afterward, to take over Rose in the basket,
marry her father, open up the front room
to make a grocery store. Rose, who had
known the house only as a store, who had
known only Flo for a mother, looked back

on the sixteen or so months her parents
spent here as an orderly, far gentler and
more ceremonious time, with little
touches of affluence. She had nothing to
go on but some egg cups her mother had
bought, with a pattern of vines and birds
on them, delicately drawn as if with red
ink; the pattern was beginning to wear
away. No books or clothes or pictures of
her mother remained. Her father must
have got rid of them, or else Flo would.
Flo's only story about her mother, the one
about her death, was oddly grudging. Flo
liked the details of a death: the things
people said, the way they protested or
tried to get out of bed or swore or laughed
(some did those things), but when she said
that Rose's mother mentioned a hard-
boiled egg in her chest she made the comparison sound slightly foolish, as if her
mother really was the kind of person who
might think you could swallow an egg
whole.

Her father had a shed out behind the
store, where he worked at his furniture
repairing and restoring. He caned chair
seats and backs, mended wickerwork,
filled cracks, put legs back on, all most
admirably and skillfully and cheaply.
That was his pride: to startle people with
such fine work, such moderate, even ri-
diculous charges. During the Depression
people could not afford to pay more, perhaps, but he continued the practice
through the war, through the years of
prosperity after the war, until he died. He
never discussed with Flo what he charged
or what was owing. After he died she had
to go out and unlock the shed and take all
sorts of scraps of paper and torn enve-
lopes from the big wicked-looking hooks
that were his files. Many of these she
found were not accounts or receipts at all
but records of the weather, bits of information about the garden, things he had
been moved to write down.

Ate new potatoes 25th June. Record Dark Day, 1880's, nothing supernatural. Clouds of ash from forest fires.

Aug 16, 1938. Giant thunderstorm in evng. Lightning str. Pres. Church, Turberry Twp. Will of God?

Scald strawberries to remove acid.

All things are alive. Spinoza.

Flo thought Spinoza must be some new vegetable he planned to grow, like broccoli or eggplant. He would often try some new thing. She showed the scrap of paper to Rose and asked, did she know what Spinoza was? Rose did know, or had an idea — she was in her teens by that time — but she replied that she did not. She had reached an age where she thought she could not stand to know any more, about her father, or about Flo; she pushed any discovery aside with embarrassment and dread.

There was a stove in the shed, and many rough shelves covered with cans of paint and varnish, shellac and turpentine, jars of soaking brushes and also some dark sticky bottles of cough medicine. Why should a man who coughed constantly, whose lungs took a whiff of gas in the War (called, in Rose's earliest childhood, not the First, but the Last, War) spend all his days breathing fumes of paint and turpentine? At the time, such questions were not asked as often as they are now. On the bench outside Flo's store several old men from the neighborhood sat gossiping, drowsing, in the warm weather, and some of these old men coughed all the time too. The fact is they were dying, slowly and discretely, of what was called, without any particular sense of grievance, "the foundry disease." They had worked all their lives at the foundry in town, and now they sat still, with their wasted yellow faces, coughing, chuckling, drifting into aimless

obscenity on the subject of women walking by, or any young girl on a bicycle.

From the shed came not only coughing, but speech, a continual muttering, reproachful or encouraging, usually just below the level of which separate words could be made out. Slowing down when her father was at a tricky piece of work, taking on a cheerful speed when he was doing something less demanding, sandpapering or painting. Now and then some words would break through and hang clear and nonsensical on the air. When he realized they were out, there would be a quick bit of cover-up coughing, a swallowing, an alert, unusual silence.

"Macaroni, pepperoni, Botticelli, beans—"

What could that mean? Rose used to repeat such things to herself. She could never ask him. The person who spoke these words and the person who spoke to her as her father were not the same, though they seemed to occupy the same space. It would be the worst sort of taste to acknowledge the person who was not supposed to be there; it would not be forgiven. Just the same, she loitered and listened.

The cloud-capped towers, she heard him say once.

"The cloud-capped towers, the gorgeous palaces."

That was like a hand clapped against Rose's chest, not to hurt, but astonish her, to take her breath away. She had to run then, she had to get away. She knew that was enough to hear, and besides, what if he caught her? It would be terrible.

This was something the same as bathroom noises. Flo had saved up, and had a bathroom put in, but there was no place to put it except in a corner of the kitchen. The door did not fit, the walls were only beaverboard. The result was that even the tearing of a piece of toilet paper, the shifting of a haunch, was audible to those working or talking or eating in the kitchen. They were all familiar with each other's nether voices, not only in their more explosive moments but in their intimate sighs and growls and pleas and statements. And they were all most prudish people. So no one ever seemed to hear, or be listening, and no reference was made. The person creating the noises in the bathroom was not connected with the person who walked out.

They lived in a poor part of town. There was Hanratty and West Hanratty, with the river flowing between them. This was West Hanratty. In Hanratty the social structure ran from doctors and dentists and lawyers down to foundry workers and factory workers and draymen; in West Hanratty it ran from factory workers and foundry workers down to large improvident families of casual bootleggers and prostitutes and unsuccessful thieves. Rose thought of her own family as straddling the river, belonging nowhere, but that was not true. West Hanratty was where the store was and they were, on the straggling tail end of the main street. Across the road from them was a blacksmith shop, boarded up about the time the war started, and a house that had been another store at one time. The Salada Tea sign had never been taken out of the front window; it remained as a proud and interesting decoration though there was no Salada Tea for sale inside. There was just a bit of sidewalk, too cracked and tilted for roller-skating, though Rose longed for roller skates and often pictured herself whizzing along in a plaid skirt, agile and fashionable. There was one street light, a tin flower; then the amenities gave up and there were dirt roads and boggy places, front-yard dumps and strange-looking houses. What made the houses strange-looking were the attempts to keep them from going completely to ruin. With some the attempt had

never been made. These were gray and rotted and leaning over, falling into a landscape of scrub hollows, frog ponds, cattails and nettles. Most houses, however, had been patched up with tarpaper, a few fresh shingles, sheets of tin, hammered-out stovepipes, even cardboard. This was, of course, in the days before the war, days of what would later be legendary poverty, from which Rose would remember mostly low-down things — serious-looking ant-hills and wooden steps, and a cloudy, interesting, problematical light on the world.

There was a long truce between Flo and Rose in the beginning. Rose's nature was growing like a prickly pineapple, but slowly, and secretly, hard pride and skepticism overlapping, to make something surprising even to herself. Before she was old enough to go to school, and while Brian was still in the baby carriage, Rose stayed in the store with both of them — Flo sitting on the high stool behind the counter, Brian asleep by the window; Rose knelt or lay on the wide creaky floorboards working with crayons on pieces of brown paper too torn or irregular to be used for wrapping.

People who came to the store were mostly from the houses around. Some country people came too, on their way home from town, and a few people from Hanratty, who walked across the bridge. Some people were always on the main street, in and out of stores, as if it was their duty to be always on display and their right to be welcomed. For instance. Becky Tyde.

Becky Tyde climbed up on Flo's counter, made room for herself beside an open tin of crumbly jam-filled cookies.

"Are these any good?" she said to Flo, and boldly began to eat one. "When are you going to give us a job, Flo?"

"You could go and work in the butcher shop," said Flo innocently. "You could go and work for your brother."

"Roberta?" said Becky with a stagey sort of contempt. "You think I'd work for him?" Her brother who ran the butcher shop was named Robert but often called Roberta, because of his meek and nervous ways. Becky Tyde laughed. Her laugh was loud and noisy like an engine bearing down on you.

She was a big-headed loud-voiced dwarf, with a mascot's sexless swagger, a red velvet tam, a twisted neck that forced her to hold her head on one side, always looking up and sideways. She wore little polished high-heeled shoes, real lady's shoes. Rose watched her shoes, being scared of the rest of her, of her laugh and her neck. She knew from Flo that Becky Tyde had been sick with polio as a child, that was why her neck was twisted and why she had not grown any taller. It was hard to believe that she had started out differently, that she had ever been normal. Flo said she was not cracked, she had as much brains as anybody, but she knew she could get away with anything.

"You know I used to live out here?" Becky said, noticing Rose. "Hey! What's your name! Didn't I used to live out here, Flo?"

"If you did it was before my time," said Flo, as if she didn't know anything.

"That was before the neighborhood got so downhill. Excuse me saying so. My father built his house out here and he built his slaughterhouse and we had half an acre of orchard."

"Is that so?" said Flo, using her humoring voice, full of false geniality, humility even. "Then why did you ever move away?"

"I told you, it got to be such a downhill neighborhood," said Becky. She would put a whole cookie in her mouth if she felt like it, let her cheeks puff out like a frog's. She never told any more.

Flo knew anyway, and who didn't. Everyone knew the house, red brick with the veranda pulled off and the orchard, what was left of it, full of the usual outflow — car seats and washing machines and bedsprings and junk. The house would never look sinister, in spite of what had happened in it, because there was so much wreckage and confusion all around.

Becky's old father was a different kind of butcher from her brother according to Flo. A bad-tempered Englishman. And different from Becky in the matter of mouthiness. His was never open. A skinflint, a family tyrant. After Becky had polio he wouldn't let her go back to school. She was seldom seen outside the house, never outside the yard. He didn't want people gloating. That was what Becky said, at the trial. Her mother was dead by that time and her sisters married. Just Becky and Robert at home. People would stop Robert on the road and ask him, "How about your sister, Robert? Is she altogether better now?"

"Yes."

"Does she do the housework? Does she get your supper?"

"Yes."

"And is your father good to her, Robert?"

The story being that the father beat them, had beaten all his children and beaten his wife as well, beat Becky more now because of her deformity, which some people believed he had caused (they did not understand about polio). The stories persisted and got added to. The reason that Becky was kept out of sight was now supposed to be her pregnancy, and the father of the child was supposed to be her own father. Then people said it had been born, and disposed of.

"What?"

"Disposed of," Flo said. "They used to say go and get your lamb chops at Tyde's, get them nice and tender! It was all lies in all probability," she said regretfully.

Rose could be drawn back — from watching the wind shiver along the old torn awning, catch in the tear — by this tone of regret, caution, in Flo's voice. Flo telling a story — and this was not the only one, or even the most lurid one, she knew — would incline her head and let her face go soft and thoughtful, tantalizing, warning.

"I shouldn't even be telling you this stuff."

More was to follow.

Three useless young men, who hung around the livery stable, got together — or were got together, by more influential and respectable men in town — and prepared to give old man Tyde a horsewhipping, in the interests of public morality. They blacked their faces. They were provided with whips and a quart of whiskey apiece, for courage. They were: Jelly Smith, a horse-racer and a drinker; Bob Temple, a ballplayer and strongman; and Hat Nettleton, who worked on the town dray, and had his nickname from a bowler hat he wore, out of vanity as much as for the comic effect. He still worked on the dray, in fact; he had kept the name if not the hat, and could often be seen in public almost as often as Becky Tyde — delivering sacks of coal, which blackened his face and arms. That should have brought to mind his story, but didn't. Present time and past, the shady melodramatic past of Flo's stories, were quite separate, at least for Rose. Present people could not be fitted into the past. Becky herself, town oddity and public pet, harmless and malicious, could never match the butcher's prisoner, the cripple daughter, a white streak at the window: mute, beaten, impregnated. As with the house, only a formal connection could be made.

The young men primed to do the horsewhipping showed up late, outside Tyde's house, after everybody had gone to bed. They had a gun, but they used up their ammunition firing it off in the yard. They yelled for the butcher and beat on the door; finally they broke it down. Tyde concluded they were after his money, so he put some bills in a handkerchief and sent Becky down with them, maybe thinking those men would be touched or scared by the sight of a little wry-necked girl, a dwarf. But that didn't content them. They came upstairs and dragged the butcher out from under his bed, in his nightgown. They dragged him outside and stood him in the snow. The temperature was four below zero, a fact noted later in court. They meant to hold a mock trial but they could not remember how it was done. So they began to beat him and kept beating him until he fell. They yelled at him, *Butcher's meat!* and continued beating him while his nightgown and the snow he was lying in turned red. His son Robert said in court that he had not watched the beating. Becky said that Robert had watched at first but had run away and hid. She herself had watched all the way through. She watched the men leave at last and her father make his delayed bloody progress through the snow and up the steps of the veranda. She did not go out to help him, or open the door until he got to it. Why not? she was asked in court, and she said she did not go out because she just had her nightgown on, and she did not open the door because she did not want to let the cold into the house.

Old man Tyde then appeared to have recovered his strength. He sent Robert to harness the horse, and made Becky heat water so that he could wash. He dressed and took all the money and with no explanation to his children got into the cutter and drove to Belgrave where he left the horse tied in the cold and took the early morning train to Toronto. On the train he behaved oddly, groaning and cursing as if he was drunk. He was picked up on the streets of Toronto a day later, out of his mind with fever, and was taken to a hospital, where he died. He still had all the money. The cause of death was given as pneumonia.

But the authorities got wind, Flo said. The case came to trial. The three men who did it all received long prison sentences. A farce, said Flo. Within a year they were all free, had all been pardoned, had jobs waiting for them. And why was that? It was because too many higher-ups were in on it. And it seemed as if Becky and Robert had no interest in seeing justice done. They were left well off. They bought a house in Hanratty. Robert went into the store. Becky after her long seclusion started on a career of public sociability and display.

That was all. Flo put the lid down on the story as if she was sick of it. It reflected no good on anybody.

"Imagine," Flo said.

Flo at this time must have been in her early thirties. A young woman. She wore exactly the same clothes that a woman of fifty or sixty, or seventy, might wear: print housedresses loose at the neck and sleeves as well as the waist; bib aprons, also of print, which she took off when she came from the kitchen into the store. This was a common costume at the time, for a poor though not absolutely poverty stricken woman; it was also, in a way, a scornful deliberate choice. Flo scorned slacks, she scorned the outfits of people trying to be in style, she scorned lipstick and permanents. She wore her own black hair cut straight across, just long enough to push behind her ears. She was tall but fine-boned, with narrow wrists and shoulders, a small head, a pale, freckled, mobile monkeyish face. If she had thought it worthwhile, and had the resources, she might have had a black-and-pale, fragile, nutured sort of prettiness; Rose realized that later. But she would have to have been

a different person altogether; she would have to have learned to resist making faces, at herself and others.

Rose's earliest memories of Flo were of extraordinary softness and hardness. The soft hair, the long, soft, pale cheeks, soft almost invisible fuzz in front of her ears and above her moth. The sharpness of her knees, hardness of her lap, flatness of her front.

When Flo sang:

> Oh the buzzin' of the bees in
> the cigarette trees
> And the soda-*water* fountain...

Rose thought of Flo's old life before she married her father, when she worked as a waitress in the coffee shop in Union Station, and went with her girl friends Mavis and Irene to Centre Island, and was followed by men on dark streets and knew how pay phones and elevators worked. Rose heard in her voice the reckless dangerous life of cities, the gum-chewing sharp answers.

And when she sang:

> Then slowly, slowly, she got up
> And slowly she came nigh him
> And all she said, that she ever
> did say,
> Was young man I think, you're
> dyin'

Rose thought of a life Flo seemed to have had beyond that, earlier than that, crowded and legendary, with Barbara Allen and Becky Tyde's father and all kinds of outrages and sorrows jumbled up together in it.

The royal beatings. What got them started?

Suppose a Saturday, in spring. Leaves not out yet but the doors open to the sunlight. Crows. Ditches full of running water. Hopeful weather. Often on Saturdays Flo left Rose in charge of the store —

it's a few years now, these are the years when Rose was nine, ten, eleven, twelve — while she herself went across the bridge to Hanratty (going uptown they called it) to shop and see people, and listen to them. Among the people she listened to were Mrs. Lawyer Davis, Mrs. Anglican Rector Henley-Smith, and Mrs. Horse-Doctor McKay. She came home and imitated their flibberty voices. Monsters, she made them seem; of foolishness, and showiness, and of approbation.

When she finished shopping she went into the coffee shop of the Queen's Hotel and had a sundae. What kind? Rose and Brian wanted to know when she got home, and they would be disappointed if it was only pineapple or butterscotch, pleased if it was a Tin Roof, or Black and White. Then she smoked a cigarette. She had some ready-rolled, that she carried with her, so that she wouldn't have to roll one in public. Smoking was the one thing she did that she would have called showing off in anybody else. It was a habit left over from her working days, from Toronto. She knew it was asking for trouble. Once the Catholic priest came over to her right in the Queen's Hotel, and flashed his lighter at her before she could get her matches out. She thanked him but did not enter into conversation, lest he should try to convert her.

Another time, on the way home, she saw at the town end of the bridge a boy in a blue jacket, apparently looking at the water. Eighteen, nineteen years old. Nobody she knew. Skinny, weakly looking, something the matter with him, she saw at once. Was he thinking of jumping? Just as she came up even with him, what does he do but turn and display himself, holding his jacket open, also his pants. What he must have suffered from the cold, on a day that had Flo holding her coat collar tight around her throat.

When she first saw what he had in his hand, Flo said, all she could think of was,

what is he doing out here with a baloney sausage?

She could say that. It was offered as truth; no joke. She maintained that she despised dirty talk. She would go out and yell at the old men sitting in front of her store.

"If you want to stay where you are you better clean your mouths out!"

Saturday, then. For some reason Flo is not going uptown, has decided to stay home and scrub the kitchen floor. Perhaps this has put her in a bad mood. Perhaps she was in a bad mood anyway, due to people not paying their bills, or the stirring-up of feelings in spring. The wrangle with Rose has already commenced, has been going on forever, like a dream that goes back and back into other dreams, over hills and through doorways, maddeningly dim and populous and familiar and elusive. They are carting all the chairs out of the kitchen preparatory to the scrubbing, and they have also got to move some extra provisions for the store, some cartons of canned goods, tins of maple syrup, coal-oil cans, jars of vinegar. They take these things out to the woodshed. Brian who is five or six by this time is helping drag the tins.

"Yes," says Flo, carrying on from our lost starting point. "You and that filth you taught to Brian."

"What filth?"

"And he doesn't know any better."

There is one step down from the kitchen to the woodshed, a bit of carpet on it so worn Rose can't ever remember seeing the pattern. Brian loosens it, dragging a tin.

"Two Vancouvers," she says softly.

Flo is back in the kitchen. Brian looks from Flo to Rose and Rose says again in a slightly louder voice, an encouraging sing-song, "Two Vancouvers —"

"Fried in snot!" finishes Brian, not able to control himself any longer.

"Two pickled arseholes —"

"— tied in a knot!"
There it is. The filth.

> Two Vancouvers fried in snot!
> Two pickled arseholes tied in a
>   knot!

Rose has known that for years, learned it when she first went to school. She came home and asked Flo, what is a Vancouver?

"It's a city. It's a long ways away."

"What else besides a city?"

Flo said, what did she mean, what else? How could it be fried, Rose said, approaching the dangerous moment, the delightful moment, when she would have to come out with the whole thing.

"Two Vancouvers fried in snot!/Two pickled arseholes tied in a knot!"

"You're going to get it!" cried Flo in a predictable rage. "Say that again and you'll get a good clout!"

Rose couldn't stop herself. She hummed it tenderly, tried saying the innocent words aloud, humming through the others. It was not just the words snot and arsehole that gave her pleasure, though of course they did. It was the pickling and tying and the unimaginable Vancouvers. She saw them in her mind shaped rather like octopuses, twitching in the pan. The tumble of reason; the spark and spat of craziness.

Lately she has remembered it again and taught it to Brian, to see if it has the same effect on him, and of course it has.

"Oh, I heard you!" says Flo. "I heard that! And I'm warning you!"

So she is. Brian takes the warning. He runs away, out of the woodshed door, to do as he likes. Being a boy, free to help or not, involve himself or not. Not committed to the household struggle. They don't need him anyway, except to use against each other, they hardly notice his going. They continue, can't help continuing, can't leave each other alone. When they seem to have given up they really are just waiting and building up steam.

Flo gets out the scrub pail and the brush and the rag and the pad for her knees, a dirty red rubber pad. She starts to work on the floor. Rose sits on the kitchen table, the only place left to sit, swinging her legs. She can feel the cool oilcloth, because she is wearing shorts, last summer's tight faded shorts dug out of the summer-clothes bag. They smell a bit moldy from winter storage.

Flo crawls underneath, scrubbing with the brush, wiping with the rag. Her legs are long, white and muscular, marked all over with blue veins as if somebody had been drawing rivers on them with an indelible pencil. An abnormal energy, a violent disgust, is expressed in the chewing of the brush at the linoleum, the swish of the rag.

What do they have to say to each other? It doesn't really matter. Flo speaks of Rose's smart-aleck behavior, rudeness and sloppiness and conceit. Her willingness to make work for others, her lack of gratitude. She mentions Brian's innocence, Rose's corruption. Oh, don't you think you're somebody, says Flo, and a moment later, Who do you think you are? Rose contradicts and objects with such poisonous reasonableness and mildness, displays theatrical unconcern. Flo goes beyond her ordinary scorn and self-possession and becomes amazingly theatrical herself, saying it was for Rose that she sacrificed her life. She saw her father saddled with a baby daughter and she thought, what is that man going to do? So she married him, and here she is, on her knees.

At that moment the bell rings, to announce a customer in the store. Because the fight is on, Rose is not permitted to go into the store and wait on whoever it is. Flo gets up and throws off her apron, groaning — but not communicatively, it is not a groan whose exasperation Rose is allowed to share — and goes in and serves. Rose hears her using her normal voice.

"About time! Sure is!"

She comes back and ties on her apron and is ready to resume.

"You never have a thought for anybody but your ownself! You never have a thought for what I'm doing."

"I never asked you to do anything. I wish you never had. I would have been a lot better off."

Rose says this smiling directly at Flo, who has not yet gone down on her knees. Flo sees the smile, grabs the scrub rag that is hanging on the side of the pail, and throws it at her. It may be meant to hit her in the face but instead it falls against Rose's leg and she raises her foot and catches it, swinging it negligently against her ankle.

"All right," says Flo. "You've done it this time. All right."

Rose watches her go to the woodshed door, hears her tramp through the woodshed, pause in the doorway, where the screen door hasn't yet been hung, and the storm door is standing open, propped with a brick. She calls Rose's father. She calls him in a warning, summoning voice, as if against her will preparing him for bad news. He will know what this is about.

The kitchen floor has five or six different patterns of linoleum on it. Ends, which Flo got for nothing and ingeniously trimmed and fitted together, bordering them with tin strips and tacks. While Rose sits on the table waiting, she looks at the floor, at this satisfying arrangement of rectangles, triangles, some other shape whose name she is trying to remember. She hears Flo coming back through the woodshed, on the creaky plank walk laid over the dirt floor. She is loitering, waiting, too. She and Rose can carry this no further, by themselves.

Rose hears her father come in. She stiffens, a tremor runs through her legs, she feels them shiver on the oilcloth.

Called away from some peaceful, absorbing task, away from the words running in his head, called out of himself, her father has to say something. He says, "Well? What's wrong?"

Now comes another voice of Flo's. Enriched, hurt, apologetic, it seems to have been manufactured on the spot. She is sorry to have called him from his work. Would never have done it, if Rose was not driving her to distraction. How to distraction? With her back talk and impudence and her terrible tongue. The things Rose has said to Flo are such that, if Flo had said them to her mother, she knows her father would have thrashed her into the ground.

Rose tries to butt in, to say this isn't true.

What isn't true?

Her father raises a hand, doesn't look at her, says, "Be quiet."

When she says it isn't true, Rose means that she herself didn't start this, only responded, that she was goaded by Flo, who is now, she believes, telling the grossest sort of lies, twisting everything to suit herself. Rose puts aside her other knowledge that whatever Flo has said or done, whatever she herself has said or done, does not really matter at all. It is the struggle itself that counts, and that can't be stopped, can never be stopped, short of where it has got to, now.

Flo's knees are dirty, in spite of the pad. The scrub rag is still hanging over Rose's foot.

Her father wipes his hands, listening to Flo. He takes his time. He is slow at getting into the spirit of things, tired in advance, maybe, on the verge of rejecting the role he has to play. He won't look at Rose, but at any sound or stirring from Rose, he holds up his hand.

"Well we don't need the public in on this, that's for sure," Flo says, and she goes to lock the door of the store, putting in the store window the sign that says BACK

SOON, a sign Rose made for her with a great deal of fancy curving and shading of letters in black and red crayon. When she comes back she shuts the door to the store, then the door to the stairs, then the door to the woodshed.

Her shoes have left marks on the clean wet part of the floor.

"Oh, I don't know," she says now, in a voice worn down from its emotional peak. "I don't know what to do about her." She looks down and sees her dirty knees (following Rose's eyes) and rubs at them viciously with her bare hands, smearing the dirt around.

"She humiliates me," she says, straightening up. There it is, the explanation. "She humiliates me," she repeats with satisfaction. "She has no respect."

"I do not!"

"Quiet, you!" says her father.

"If I hadn't called your father you'd still be sitting there with that grin on your face! What other way is there to manage you?"

Rose detects in her father some objections to Flo's rhetoric, some embarrassment and reluctance. She is wrong, and ought to know she is wrong, in thinking that she can count on this. The fact that she knows about it, and he knows she knows, will not make things any better. He is beginning to warm up. He gives her a look. This look is at first cold and challenging. It informs her of his judgment, of the hopelessness of her position. Then it clears, it begins to fill up with something else, the way a spring fills up when you clear the leaves away. It fills with hatred and pleasure. Rose sees that and knows it. Is that just a description of anger, should she see his eyes filling up with anger? No. Hatred is right. Pleasure is right. His face loosens and changes and grows younger, and he holds up his hand this time to silence Flo.

"All right," he says, meaning that's enough, more than enough, this part is over, things can proceed. He starts to loosen his belt.

Flo has stopped anyway. She has the same difficulty Rose does, a difficulty in believing that what you know must happen really will happen, that there comes a time when you can't draw back.

"Oh, I don't know, don't be too hard on her." She is moving around nervously as if she has thoughts of opening some escape route. "Oh, you don't have to use the belt on her. Do you have to use the belt?"

He doesn't answer. The belt is coming off, not hastily. It is being grasped at the necessary point. *All right you.* He is coming over to Rose. He pushes her off the table. His face, like his voice, is quite out of character. He is like a bad actor, who turns a part grotesque. As if he must savor and insist on just what is shameful and terrible about this. That is not to say he is pretending, that he is acting, and does not mean it. He is acting, and he means it. Rose knows that, she knows everything about him.

She has since wondered about murders, and murderers. Does the thing have to be carried through, in the end, partly for the effect, to prove to the audience of one — who won't be able to report, only register, the lesson — that such a thing can happen, that there is nothing that can't happen, that the most dreadful antic is justified, feelings can be found to match it?

She tries again looking at the kitchen floor, that clever comforting geometrical arrangement, instead of looking at him or his belt. How can this go on in front of such daily witnesses — the linoleum, the calendar with the mill and creek and autumn trees, the old accommodating pots and pans?

Hold out your hand!

Those things aren't going to help her, none of them can rescue her. They turn bland and useless, even unfriendly. Pots can show malice, the patterns of linoleum can leer up at you, treachery is the other side of dailiness.

At the first, or maybe the second, crack of pain, she draws back. She will not accept it. She runs around the room, she tries to get to the doors. Her father blocks her off. Not an ounce of courage or of stoicism in her, it would seem. She runs, she screams, she implores. Her father is after her, cracking the belt at her when he can, then abandoning it and using his hands. Bang over the ear, then bang over the other ear. Back and forth, her head ringing. Bang in the face. Up against the wall, he kicks her legs. She is incoherent, insane, shrieking. *Forgive me! Oh please, forgive me!*

Flo is shrieking too. *Stop, stop!*

Not yet. He throws Rose down. Or perhaps she throws herself down. He kicks her legs again. She has given up on words but is letting out a noise, the sort of noise that makes Flo cry, *Oh, what if people can hear her?* The very last-ditch willing sound of humiliation and defeat it is, for it seems Rose must play her part in this with the same grossness, the same exaggeration, that her father displays, playing his. She plays his victim with a self-indulgence that arouses, and maybe hopes to arouse, his final, sickened contempt.

They will give this anything that is necessary, it seems, they will go to any lengths.

Not quite. He has never managed really to injure her, though there are times, of course, when she prays that he will. He hits her with an open hand, there is some restraint in his kicks.

Now he stops, he is out of breath. He allows Flo to move in, he grabs Rose up and gives her a push in Flo's direction, making a sound of disgust. Flo retrieves her, opens the stair door, shoves her up the stairs.

"Go on up to your room now! Hurry!"

Rose goes up the stairs, stumbling, letting herself stumble, letting herself fall against the steps. She doesn't bang her door because a gesture like that could still bring him after her, and anyway, she is weak. She lies on the bed. She can hear through the stovepipe hole Flo snuffling and remonstrating, her father saying angrily that Flo should have kept quiet then, if she did not want Rose punished she should not have recommended it. Flo says she never recommended a hiding like that.

They argue back and forth on this, Flo's frightened voice is growing stronger, getting its confidence back. By stages, by arguing, they are being drawn back into themselves. Soon it's only Flo talking; he will not talk anymore. Rose has had to fight down her noisy sobbing, so as to listen to them, and when she loses interest in listening, and wants to sob some more, she finds she can't work herself up to it. She has passed into a state of calm, in which outrage is perceived as complete and final. In this state events and possibilities take on a lovely simplicity. Choices are mercifully clear. The words that come to mind are not quibbling, seldom the conditional. Never is a word to which the right is suddenly established. She will never speak to them, she will never look at them with anything but loathing, she will never forgive them. She will punish them; she will finish them. Encased in these finalities, and in her bodily pain, she floats in curious comfort, beyond herself, beyond responsibility.

Suppose she dies now? Suppose she commits suicide? Suppose she runs away? Any of these things would be appropriate. It is only a matter of choosing, of figuring out the way. She floats in her pure superior state as if kindly drugged.

And just as there is a moment, when you are drugged, in which you feel perfectly safe, sure, unreachable, and then without warning and right next to it a moment in which you know the whole protection has fatally cracked, though it is still pretending to hold soundly together, so there is a moment now — the moment, in fact, when Rose hears Flo step on the stairs — that contains for her both present peace and freedom and a sure knowledge of the whole down-spiraling course of events from now on.

Flo comes into the room without knocking, but with a hesitation that shows it might have occurred to her. She brings a jar of cold cream. Rose is hanging on to advantage as long as she can, lying face down on the bed, refusing to acknowledge or answer.

"Oh come on," Flo says uneasily. "You aren't so bad off, are you? You put some of this on and you'll feel better."

She is bluffing. She doesn't know for sure what damage has been done. She has the lid off the cold cream. Rose can smell it. The intimate, babyish, humiliating smell. She won't allow it near her. But in order to avoid it, the big ready clot of it in Flo's hand, she has to move. She scuffles, resists, loses dignity, and lets Flo see there is not really much the matter.

"All right," Flo says. "You win. I'll leave it here and you can put it on when you like."

Later still a tray will appear. Flo will put it down without a word and go away. A large glass of chocolate milk on it, made with Vita-Malt from the store. Some rich streaks of Vita-Malt around the bottom of the glass. Little sandwiches, neat and appetizing. Canned salmon of the first quality and reddest color, plenty of mayonnaise. A couple of butter tarts from a bakery package, chocolate biscuits with a peppermint filling. Rose's favorites, in the sandwich, tart and cookie line. She will turn away, refuse to look, but left alone with these eatables will be miserably tempted, roused and troubled and drawn back from thoughts of suicide or

flight by the smell of salmon, the anticipation of crisp chocolate, she will reach out a finger, just to run it around the edge of one of the sandwiches (crusts cut off!) to get the overflow, get a taste. Then she will decide to eat one, for strength to refuse the rest. One will not be noticed. Soon, in helpless corruption, she will eat them all. She will drink the chocolate milk, eat the tarts, eat the cookies. She will get the malty syrup out of the bottom of the glass with her finger, though she sniffles with shame. Too late.

Flo will come up and get the tray. She may say, "I see you got your appetite still," or "Did you like the chocolate milk, was it enough syrup in it?" depending on how chastened she is feeling, herself. At any rate, all advantage will be lost. Rose will understand that life has started up again, that they will all sit around the table eating again, listening to the radio news. Tomorrow morning, maybe even tonight. Unseemly and unlikely as that may be. They will be embarrassed, but rather less than you might expect considering how they have behaved. They will feel a queer lassitude, a convalescent indolence, not far off satisfaction.

One night after a scene like this they were all in the kitchen. It must have been summer, or at least warm weather, because her father spoke of the old men who sat on the bench in front of the store.

"Do you know what they're talking about now?" he said, and nodded his head toward the store to show who he meant, though of course they were not there now, they went home at dark.

"Those old coots," said Flo. "What?"

There was about them both a geniality not exactly false but a bit more emphatic than was normal, without company.

Rose's father told them then that the old men had picked up the idea somewhere that what looked like a star in the western sky, the first star that came out after sunset, the evening star, was in reality an airship hovering over Bay City, Michigan, on the other side of Lake Huron. An American invention, sent up to rival the heavenly bodies. They were all in agreement about this, the idea was congenial to them. They believed it to be lit by ten thousand electric light bulbs. Her father had ruthlessly disagreed with them, pointing out that it was the planet Venus they saw, which had appeared in the sky long before the invention of an electric light bulb. They had never heard of the planet Venus.

"Ignoramuses," said Flo. At which Rose knew, and knew her father knew, that Flo had never heard of the planet Venus either. To distract them from this, or even apologize for it, Flo put down her teacup, stretched out with her head resting on the chair she had been sitting on and her feet on another chair (somehow she managed to tuck her dress modestly between her legs at the same time), and lay stiff as a board, so that Brian cried out in delight, "Do that! Do that!"

Flo was double-jointed and very strong. In moments of celebration or emergency she would do tricks.

They were silent while she turned herself around, not using her arms at all but just her strong legs and feet. Then they all cried out in triumph, though they had seen it before.

Just as Flo turned herself Rose got a picture in her mind of that airship, an elongated transparent bubble, with its strings of diamond lights, floating in the miraculous American sky.

"The planet Venus!" her father said, applauding Flo. "Ten thousand electric lights!"

There was a feeling of permission, relaxation, even a current of happiness, in the room.

Years later, many years later, on a Sunday morning, Rose turned on the radio. This was when she was living by herself in Toronto.

Well Sir.

It was a different kind of place in our day. Yes it was.

It was all horses then. Horses and buggies. Buggy races up and down the main street on the Saturday nights.

"Just like the chariot races," says the announcer's, or interviewer's smooth encouraging voice.

I never seen a one of them.

"No sir, that was the old Roman chariot races I was referring to. That was before your time."

Musta been before my time. I'm a hunerd and two years old.

"That's a wonderful age, sir."

It is so.

She left it on, as she went around the apartment kitchen, making coffee for herself. It seemed to her that this must be a staged interview, a scene from some play, and she wanted to find out what it was. The old man's voice was so vain and belligerent, the interviewer's quite hopeless and alarmed, under its practiced gentleness and ease. You were surely meant to see him holding the microphone up to some toothless, reckless, preening centenarian, wondering what in God's name he was doing here, and what would he say next?

"They must have been fairly dangerous."

What was dangerous?

"Those buggy races."

They was. Dangerous. Used to be the runaway horses. Used to be a-plenty of accidents. Fellows was dragged along on the gravel and cut their face open. Wouldna matter so much if they was dead. Heh.

Some of them horses was the high-steppers. Some, they had to have the mustard under their tail. Some wouldn step out for nothin. That's the thing it is with the horses. Some'll work and pull till they drop down dead and some wouldn pull your cock out of a pail of lard. Hehe.

It must be a real interview after all. Otherwise they wouldn't have put that in, wouldn't have risked it. It's all right if the old man says it. Local color. Anything rendered harmless and delightful by his hundred years.

Accidents all the time then. In the mill. Foundry. Wasn't the precautions.

"You didn't have so many strikes then, I don't suppose? You didn't have so many unions?"

Everybody taking it easy nowadays. We worked and we was glad to get it. Worked and was glad to get it.

"You didn't have television."

Didn't have no TV. Didn't have no radio. No picture show.

"You made your own entertainment."

That's the way we did.

"You have a lot of experiences young men growing up today will never have."

Experiences.

"Can you recall any of them for us?"

I eaten groundhog meat one time. One winter. You wouldna cared for it. Heh.

There was a pause, of appreciation, it would seem, then the announcer's voice saying that the foregoing had been an interview with Mr. Wilfred Nettleton of Hanratty, Ontario, made on his hundred and second birthday, two weeks before his death, last spring. A living link with our past. Mr. Nettleton had been interviewed in the Wawanash County Home for the aged.

Hat Nettleton.

Horsewhipper into centenarian. Photographed on his birthday, fussed over by nurses, kissed no doubt by a girl reporter. Flash bulbs popping at him. Tape recorder drinking in the sound of his voice. Oldest resident. Oldest horsewhipper. Living link with our past.

Looking out from her kitchen window at the cold lake, Rose was longing to tell somebody. It was Flo who would enjoy hearing. She thought of her saying *Imagine!* in a way that meant she was having her worst suspicions gorgeously confirmed. But Flo was in the same place Hat Nettleton had died in, and there wasn't any way Rose could reach her. She had been there even when that interview was recorded, though she would not have heard it, would not have known about it. After Rose put her in the Home, a couple of years earlier, she had stopped talking. She had removed herself, and spent most of her time sitting in a corner of her crib, looking crafty and disagreeable, not answering anybody, though she occasionally showed her feelings by biting a nurse.

Definitions of Family: Who's In, Who's Out, and Who Decides

Understanding families involves not only consideration of the array of emotions and images produced in a given culture about this social institution; an even more basic question concerns the definition of "family." What constellation of people, connected through what kinds of relationships can and should count as a family?

A common formal legal definition looks to whether official rules of family formation — marriage, birth to a married couple, adoption — have been followed. Yet this definition fails to acknowledge more extended family ties or groups of people who may function like a family even without complying with official legal practices. The tension between official legal forms and functional families has created controversies and accommodations for centuries. In medieval Europe, the practice of clandestine marriage, entered into with only the participation and knowledge of the two parties, persisted despite opposition by church officials. Similarly, in the early part of white frontier life in North America, the requisites of formal marriage, such as finding a minister and recording the marriage officially, were difficult to meet. Therefore, many people — and many courts — concluded that a man and a woman could acquire the legal status of being married if they lived as husband and wife long enough to function like a married couple. This practice acknowledged that legal rules must relate to how people actually live; otherwise it becomes merely a set of beliefs used to distribute status and value rather than rules to guide behavior effectively.

A comparison of legal and even social definitions of family with how people really live in the late twentieth century reveals many gaps. Is a family a nuclear household unit, composed of a male breadwinner, his wife who works inside the home, and their young children? Three-fifths of U.S. households fit that picture during the 1950s and became immortalized in television situation comedies in the 1950s such as "Ozzie and Harriet" and the "Donna Reed Show." As of 1990, only twenty-six percent of U.S. households consisted of a husband, wife, and their children under age eighteen.[1] One estimate claims that only ten percent of households consisted of a married couple with one or more children under eighteen, an employed father and a mother who did not work outside the home.[2] Twenty-five percent of all households are now headed by a single parent; twenty-five percent of all children are born to unmarried mothers.[3] Given high rates of divorce, remarriage, and other kinds of recouplings, one-fourth of all the children born in the last decade will live with a stepparent before reaching age eighteen.[4] Nearly twenty-five percent of the households consist of single persons, which include young people postponing marriage, divorced people, and elderly people.[5] There are also increasing numbers of cohabiting, unmarried adults; many are lesbian or gay couples. Some of these are counted in the census as the eleven percent of American households described as "other" — which also includes siblings living together, other relatives, and roommates.[6]

Statistics and other kinds of empirical evidence may be marshalled to challenge conventional images of family and images used in legal sources. But what if any content should remain in the notion of "family"? Consider local residential zoning rules that often use the term, "single family," to create and preserve areas suitable for residential

---

1. See "Only One U.S. Family in Four Is 'Traditional,' " *New York Times*, Jan. 30, 1991, p. A19, col. 1.

2. See *Los Angeles Times*, Aug. 12, 1990, pp. A1, A26, col.3 (reporting Ford Foundation estimate).

3. Ray Marshall, *Losing Direction: Families, Human Resource Development, and Economic Performance*, (Milwaukee, Wis.: Family Service America, 1991).

4. From David Chambers, "Stepparents, Biologic Parents, and the Law's Perceptions of 'Family' After Divorce," in *Divorce Reform at the Crossroads*, S. D. Sugarman and H. H. Kay, eds., (New Haven:Yale University Press, 1991), p. 102.

5. Marshall, supra, p. 26.

6. James R. Wetzel, "American Families, Seventy-five Years of Change," *Monthly Lab. Rev.* vol. 4, (1990), p.113.

living and shielded from the density, noise, and dangers of other parts of the community. One community defined "family" for this purposes as follows:[7]

"'Family' means a number of individuals related to the nominal head of the household or to the spouse of the nominal head of the household living as a single housekeeping unit in a single dwelling, but limited to the following:

(a) Husband or wife of the nominal head of the household.

(b) Unmarried children of the nominal head of the household or of the spouse of the nominal head of the household, provided, however, that such unmarried children have no children residing with them.

(c) Father or mother of the nominal head of the household or of the spouse of the nominal head of the household.

(d) Notwithstanding the provisions of subsection (b) hereof, a family may include not more than one dependent married or unmarried child of the nominal head of the household or of the spouse of the nominal head of the household and the spouse and dependent child of such dependent child. For the purpose of this subsection, a dependent person is one who has more than fifty percent of his total support furnished for him by the nominal head of the household and the spouse of the nominal head of the household.

(e) A family may consist of one individual."

Mrs. Inez Moore received a notice of violation from the city, based on this ordinance, and when she failed to comply with it, she was convicted and sentenced to five days in jail and ordered to pay a $25.00 fine. With whom was she living? She lived with her son and two grandsons; the two boys were first cousins rather than brothers, and under the explicit terms of the ordinance, this constellation was not a family. Four members of the Court, in *Moore* v. *City of East Cleveland,* 431 U.S. 494 (1977), reasoned that substantive due process protected the tradition of the extended family and the practice of mutual support among close relatives especially in times of adversity. Two of those Justices — Justices Brennan and Marshall — particularly noted the significance of the extended family in the lives of immigrants and black citizens. Justice Stevens wrote a separate opinion concurring in the result but predicated his view on the failure of the city to show a substantial relation between its ordinance and the legitimate purposes of public health, safety, morals or general welfare. The dissenting Justices argued that Mrs. Moore should have sought a variance, or else the Constitution does not protect the kind of association she claimed. The dissenting Justices relied heavily on the prior Supreme Court ruling in *Village of Belle Terre* v. *Boraas,* 416 U.S. 1 (1974), which rejected a challenge brought by six unrelated college students to a zoning ordinance that defined family to exclude any more than two unrelated persons living together in a single housekeeping unit.

Subsequent cases have challenged definitions of family in zoning ordinances that seem to exclude a group home for religious novices; group homes for developmentally

---

7. Section 1341.08 (1966), City of East Cleveland.

disabled adults; and two married couples sharing the same house. Similar issues have arisen under different legal rules, such as rules governing eligibility for low-income housing assistance, occupancy rights to a rent-controlled apartment after the death of the spouse of a deceased tenant, and forfeiture of subsidized housing eligibility by any family member of an individual suspected of engaging in criminal drug-related or violent activity. What definition(s) of family should be permitted and what definition(s) should be rejected? Should the purpose of the regulation make a difference here? Do expansive notions promote a sense of connection, caring, and responsibility or instead dilute those qualities? Who should be empowered to decide any of these questions? These readings, along with others throughout this book, provide varied images of who is, or could be, family.

♦

FAMILY REUNION
Bonnie Timmons

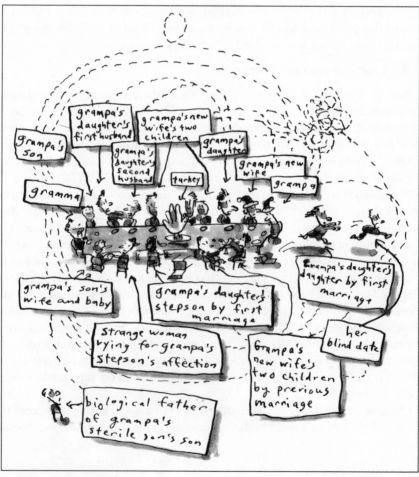

From Bonnie Timmons, *Anxiety*, (New York: Fawcett Columbine, 1992).

◆

PERSONAL KINDREDS
Carol Stack

Billy, a young woman in The Flats,[1] was raised by her mother and her mother's "old man." She has three children of her own by different fathers. Billy says, "Most people kin to me are in this neighborhood, right here in the Flats, but I got people in the South, in Chicago, and in Ohio too. I couldn't tell most of their names and most of them aren't really kinfolk to me. Starting down the street from here, take my father, he ain't my daddy, he's no father to me. I ain't got but one daddy and that's Jason. The one who raised me. My kids' daddies, that's something else, all their daddies' people really take to them — they always doing things and making a fuss about them. We help each other and that's what kinfolks are all about."

Throughout the world, individuals distinguish kin from non-kin. Moreover, kin terms are frequently extended to non-kin, and social relations among non-kin may be conducted within the idiom of kinship. Individuals acquire socially recognized kinship relations with others through a chain of socially recognized parent-child connections. The chain of parent-child connections is essential to the structuring of kin groups.

Although anthropologists have long recognized the distinction between natural and social parenthood, until recently most ethnographic data has not clarified those social transactions involving parental rights. This omission has led to the persis-tent belief that each person is a kinsman of his natural mother and father, who are expected as parents to raise him. Much of the controversial and misleading characterizations of kinship and domestic life can be attributed to this assumption and to the lack of ethnographic data that interprets the meaning people give to the chain of parent-child connections within a particular folk culture.

At birth a child in any society acquires socially recognized kinship relations with others. Who is socially recognized as kin depends largely upon the cultural interpretation of the chain of parent-child connections. Young black children in The Flats are born into personal networks that include some "essential kin," those people who actively accept responsibility toward them, and some "relatives" who do not actively create reciprocal obligations.

My experience in The Flats suggests that the folk system of parental rights and duties determines who is eligible to be a member of the personal kinship network of a newborn child. This system of rights and duties should not be confused with the official, written statutory law of the state. The local, folk system of rights and duties pertaining to parenthood are enforced only by sanctions within the community. Community members clearly operate within two different systems: the folk system and the legal system of the courts and welfare offices.

---

1. The Flats is a fictitious name for the poorest section of a black community in an actual midwestern city [editor's note].

From Carol Stack, "Personal Kindreds," in *All Our Kin: Strategies for Survival in a Black Community* (New York:Harper & Row, 1974), pp. 45–61.

MOTHERHOOD

Men and women in The Flats regard child-begetting and childbearing as a natural and highly desirable phenomenon. Lottie James was fifteen when she became pregnant. The baby's father, Herman, the socially recognized genitor, was a neighbor and the father of two other children. Lottie talked with her mother during her second month of pregnancy. She said, "Herman went and told my mama I was pregnant. She was in the kitchen cooking. I told him not to tell nobody, I wanted to keep it a secret, but he told me times will tell. My mama said to me, 'I had you and you should have your child. I didn't get rid of you. I loved you and I took care of you until you got to the age to have this one. Have your baby no matter what, there's nothing wrong with having a baby. Be proud of it like I was proud of you.' My mama didn't tear me down; she was about the best mother a person ever had."

Unlike many other societies, black women in The Flats feel few if any restrictions about childbearing. Unmarried black women, young and old, are eligible to bear children, and frequently women bearing their first children are quite young.

A girl who gives birth as a teenager frequently does not raise and nurture her firstborn child. While she may share the same room and household with her baby, her mother, her mother's sister, or her older sister will care for the child and become the child's "mama." This same young woman may actively become a "mama" to a second child she gives birth to a year or two later. When, for example, a grandmother, aunt, or great-aunt "takes a child" from his natural mother, acquired parenthood often lasts throughout the child's lifetime. Although a child kept by a close female relative knows who his mother is, his "mama" is the woman who "raised him up." Young mothers and their firstborn daughters are often raised as sisters, and lasting ties are established between these mothers and their daughters. A child being raised by his grandmother may later become playmates with his half siblings who are his age, but he does not share the same claims and duties and affective ties toward his natural mother.

A young mother is not necessarily considered emotionally ready to nurture a child; for example, a grandmother and other close relatives of Clover Greer, Viola Jackson's neighbor, decided that Clover was not carrying out her parental duties. Nineteen when her first child, Christine, was born, Clover explains, "I really was wild in those days, out on the town all hours of the night, and every night and weekend I layed my girl on my mother. I wasn't living home at the time, but Mama kept Christine most of the time. One day Mama up and said I was making a fool of her, and she was going to take my child and raise her right. She said I was immature and that I had no business being a mother the way I was acting. All my mama's people agreed, and there was nothing I could do. So Mama took my child. Christine is six years old now. About a year ago I got married to Gus and we wanted to take Christine back. My baby, Earl, was living with us anyway. Mama blew up and told everyone how I was doing her. She dragged my name in mud and people talked so much it really hurt." Gossip and pressure from close kin and friends made it possible for the grandmother to exercise her grandparental right to take the child into her home and raise her there.

In the eyes of the community, a young mother who does not perform her duties has not validated her claim to parenthood. The person who actively becomes the "mama" acquires the major cluster of parental rights accorded to the mothers in The Flats. In effect, a young mother transfers some of her claims to motherhood without surrendering all of her rights to the child.

Nothing in the conception of parenthood among people in The Flats prevents kinsmen of a child's socially recognized parents from having claims to parenthood. Kinsmen anticipate the help they may have to give to young mothers and the parental responsibilities they may have to assume toward the children of kinsmen. The bond between mothers and children is exceedingly strong, and the majority of mothers in The Flats raise their own children. Statistical data on residence patterns and kin relationships of 1,000 AFDC children in Jackson County was gathered from AFDC case histories. Of the 188 AFDC mothers surveyed, thirty percent were raising their own children, five percent were raising younger siblings, and seven percent were raising their grandchildren, nieces, or nephews.

Just how a "mama" provides a child with concerned relatives can best be viewed in terms of Fischer's (1958) notion of sponsorship. Fischer, in his discussion of residence, calls attention to the questions of who is an individual's immediate sponsor in a residence group. This term refers to the sponsorship of individuals rather than of couples, a flexible means of providing information on residence over an individual's lifetime. The term can also be applied to the creation of personal kinship networks for the newborn child. Determining who becomes one of the immediate sponsors of a child's network clarifies its initial formation, the kinship links that are effective, and the shape of the network.

In The Flats the recognized mother, the "mama" (eighty percent are the natural mother), determines the child's kin-

ship affiliations through females. She is one of the immediate sponsors of a child's personal kinship network. A black child's "mama's" relatives and their husbands and wives are eligible to be members of the child's personal kinship network. How the relationship between a child's natural mother and his or her socially recognized genitor determines a child's kin affiliations through males is described below. When a child is raised by close female relatives of his mother in a more-or-less stable situation, the immediate sponsor of the child's personal network is the "mama." This reckoning of relatives through the immediate sponsor is especially useful when a child's residence changes during his lifetime. Even if a child is raised by a person who is not a blood relative (described below), he usually becomes a part of the network of his "mama."

FATHERHOOD

People in The Flats expect to change friends frequently through a series of encounters. Demands on friendships are great, but social-economic pressures on male-female relationships are even greater. Therefore, relationships between young, unmarried, childbearing adults are highly unstable. Some men and childbearing woman in the Flats establish long-term liaisons with one another, some maintain sexual unions with more than one person at a time, and still others get married. However, very few women in The Flats are married before they have given birth to one or more children. When a man and woman have a sexual partnership, especially if the woman has no other on-going sexual relationships, the man is identified with children born to the woman. Short-term sexual partnerships are recognized by the community even if a man and woman do not share a household and domestic responsibilities. The offspring of these unions are publicly accepted by the community; a child's existence seems to legitimize the child in the eyes of the community.

But the fact of birth does not provide a child with a chain of socially recognized relatives through his father. Even though the community accepts the child, the culturally significant issue in terms of the economics of everyday life is whether any man involved in a sexual relationship with a woman provides a newborn child with kinship affiliations. A child is eligible to participate in the personal kinship network of his father if the father becomes an immediate sponsor of a child's kinship network.

When an unmarried woman in The Flats becomes pregnant or gives birth to a child, she often tells her friends and kin who the father is. The man has a number of alternatives open to him. Sometimes he publicly denies paternity by implying to his friends and kin that the father could be any number of other men, and that he had "information that she is no good and has been creeping on him all along." The community generally accepts the man's denial of paternity. It is doubtful that under these conditions this man and his kin would assume any parental duties anyway. The man's failure to assent to being the father leaves the child without recognized kinship ties through a male. Subsequent "boyfriends" of the mother may assume the paternal duties of discipline and support and receive the child's affection, but all paternal rights in the child belong to the mother and her kinsmen. The pattern whereby black children derive all their kin through females has been stereotyped and exaggerated in the literature on black families. In fact, fathers in The Flats openly recognized 484 (sixty-nine percent) of 700 children included in my AFDC survey.

The second alternative open to a man involved in a sexual relationship with a mother is to acknowledge openly that he is responsible. The father can acknowledge the child by saying "he own it," by telling his people and his friends that he is the father, by paying part of the hospital bill, or by bringing milk and diapers to the mother after the birth of the child. The parents may not have ever shared a household and the affective and sexual relationship between them may have ended before the birth of the child.

The more a father and his kin help a mother and her child, the more completely they validate their parental rights. However, since many black American males have little or no access to steady and productive employment, they are rarely able to support and maintain their families. This has made it practically impossible for most poor black males to assume financial duties as parents. People in The Flats believe a father should help his child, but they know that a mother cannot count on his help. But, the community expects a father's kin to help out. The black male who does not actively become a "daddy," but acknowledges a child and offers his kin to that child, in effect, is validating his rights. Often it is the father's kin who activate the claim to rights in the child.

Fatherhood, then, belongs to the presumed genitor if he, or others for him, choose to validate his claim. Kinship through males is reckoned through a chain of social recognition. If the father fails to do anything beyond merely acknowledging the child, he surrenders most of his rights, and this claim can be shared or transferred to the father's kin, whose claim becomes strengthened if they actively participate as essential kin. By failing to perform parental duties the father retains practically no rights in his child, although his kin retain rights if they assume active responsibility.

By validating his claim as a parent the father offers the child his blood relatives and their husbands and wives as the child's kin — an inheritance so to speak. As long as the father acknowledges his parental entitlement, his relatives, especially his mother and sisters, consider themselves kin to the child and therefore responsible for him. Even when the mother "takes up with another man," her child retains the original set of kin gained through the father who sponsored him.

A nonparticipating father also shares some of his rights and duties with his child's mother's current boyfriend or husband. When a man and woman have a continuing sexual relationship, even if the man is not the father of any of the woman's children, he is expected by the mother and the community to share some of the parental duties of discipline, support, and affection.

A child's father's kin play an active role in the nurturing of children, and as a result they have the right to observe and judge whether a woman is performing her duties as a mother. If a young woman is unable to care for her child, nothing prevents a father's close female relatives from claiming parental rights. When 188 AFDC mothers listed in order of rank who they would expect to raise each of their children (total of 1,000 children) if they died, one-third of the women listed their own mother as their first choice and one-third listed either their child's father or the father's mother as the first choice. The remaining one-third (second through fifth choice) were close kin to the mother (her mother's sister, her own sister or brother, and her daughter). In crisis situations, such as a mother's death or sickness, a child's kin through his mother and father are equally eligible to assume responsibilities of jural parenthood.

The chain of sponsored parent-child connection determines the personal kindreds of children. Participants in active units of domestic cooperation are drawn from personal kinship networks. How a particular individual, say a mother, works to create the active networks which she depends upon for the needs of her children, depends largely on sponsorship or parental links. Commonly, the mother's personal domestic network includes the personal networks of her children, who are half siblings with different fathers. Each child will grow up into a slightly different personal network from his brothers and sisters. Mothers expect little from the father; they just hope that he will help out. But they do expect something from his kin, especially his mother and sisters. Mothers continually activate these kin lines, and since the biological father's female relatives are usually poor, they too try to expand their network. The exchanges and daily dependencies get very complicated, but they constitute the main activity of daily life for these women.

Daily life is also complicated as individuals expand their own personal networks, in part by recruiting friends into their own domestic networks. When friends live up to one another's expectations, they are identified as kin. Friends often participate in the personal networks of others within the idiom of kinship, and some kin exhibit the interactive patterns of friends.

Domestic arrangements and strategies among the black poor in The Flats usually assure that children are cared for and that kin and friends in need will be helped. Participants in cooperative networks are primarily drawn from personal kindreds. R. T. Smith has stated that although there is a tendency among "lower classes" to keep kin links open, this does not mean that large cooperating groups of kinsmen are found among the "lower classes." But I found, to the contrary, stable domestic networks of cooperating kinsmen among the poorest black people. These kinship networks have stability because the needs of the poor are constant. Friendships, on the other hand, change more often, and friends drop in and out of one another's networks while assuming a stable position in their own kinship network. From the individual's viewpoint, he is immersed in a domestic circle in which he can find help.

Similar to patterns found in The Flats, American middle-class children are born into a network of relatives which in principle is infinite. Relatives on both sides of the family are kin, and there is no clear-cut limit to the range of one's kinsmen. But cognatic reckoning by itself cannot distinguish between essential kin and others within the system. The choice of which relatives an individual draws into her personal kindred is by no means mechanical.

How individuals cast their net to create personal kinship networks depends upon the culturally determined perceptions of jural parenthood: the rules and criteria for including and excluding persons connected by blood and marriage to a particular kinsman, and the interpersonal relations between these individuals. These criteria determine which individuals acquire socially recognized kinship relations with others.

Personal kindreds of adults are ego-centered networks of essential kin. These networks are not residential units or observable groups, and they change participants, for example, when friends "fall out" with one another. From the individual's viewpoint personal kindreds comprise the people who are socially recognized as having reciprocal responsibilities. These people become acting and reacting participants for some focal purpose.

Young children exercise little choice in determining with whom they have kinship relations. They are born into a network of essential kin which is primarily the personal kindreds of the kinfolk responsible for them. As children become adults they expand, contract, and create their own personal networks.

Geographical distance, interpersonal relations, or acknowledgment of paternity discourage some relatives from actuating claims of responsibility. These relatives effectively drop out of the individual's personal kinship network, and all of the people linked through them also tend to drop out. Thus, an important criterion affecting the size and shape of the personal kinship network of adults is whether the relative who drops out of the network is genealogically close or distant. Sometimes close kinship links, like that of a parent, are broken. A father, for example, may claim that he doesn't "own the baby," thereby refusing to acknowledge paternity. When a close link such as that of a father is broken, it has a profound effect on the shape of the personal kindred.

. . .

Because any relative can break a link, personal kindreds can take a number of shapes. But the networks are skewed roughly in proportion to the neatness of the kinship links which are ineffective. In principle, the dropping of a father from a network affects the shape of the network in the same way as if other more distant relatives on either side were to drop out. But the effect of dropping a close relative is obviously much more profound.

FRIENDSHIP

Men and women in The Flats know that the minimal funds they receive from low-paying jobs on welfare do not cover their monthly necessities of life: rent, food, and clothing. They must search for solutions in order to survive. They place their hopes in the scene of their life and action: in the closed community, in the people around them, in kin and friends, and in the new friends they will make to get along. Friendships between lovers and between friends are based upon a precarious balance of trust and profit. Magnolia describes this balance, "I don't have nothing great and no more than nobody else. It doesn't matter. I'm happy with my kids and I'm happy with the friends that I got. Some people don't understand friendship. Friendship means a lot, that is if you can trust a friend. If you have a friend, you should learn to trust them and share everything that you have. When I have a friend and I need something, I don't ask, they just automatically tell me that they going to give it to me. I don't have to ask. And that's the way friends should be, for how long it lasts. But sometimes when you help a person they end up making a fool out of you. If a friend ain't giving me anything in return for what I'm giving her, shit, she can't get nothing else. These days you ain't got nothing to be really giving. You can't care for no one that don't give a damn for you."

Even in newly formed friendships, individuals begin to rely upon one another quickly, expecting wider solutions to their problems than any one person in the same situation could possibly offer. As a result the stability of a friendship often depends upon the ability of two individuals to gauge their exploitation of one another. Everyone understands that friendships are explosive and abruptly come to an end when one friend makes a fool out of another. Life, therefore, as Abrahams shows, is "conceived of in terms of a series of encounters with a large number of individuals." As Ruby says, "You got to go out and meet people, because the very day you go out, that first person you meet may be the person that can help you get the things you want."

Individuals in The Flats continually evaluate their friendships by gossip and conversation. They talk about whether others are "acting right" or "doing right by them." They define personal relationships in terms of their dual expectations of friends and kin. When friends more than adequately share the exchange of goods and services, they are called kinsmen. When friends live up to one another's expectations, their social relations are conducted as kin. For example, if two women of the same age are helping one another, they call their friend "just a sister," or say that "they are going for sisters." Anyone in the community with whom a person has good social dealings can be classified as some kind of kin. When a friendship ends because individuals "let one another down," this concludes both their expectations of one another and their kin relationship. In addition, a person defined as a kin, for example, a "sister," does not usually bring to the relationship her own personal genealogical entailments. Her mother is not necessarily her "sister's" mother and her father's father is not her "sister's" grandfather. Losing a fictive relative, therefore, does not dramatically affect the shape of personal networks as does the dropping of a close kinship link.

The offering of kin terms to "those you count on" is a way people expand their personal networks. A friend who is classified as a kinsman is simultaneously given respect and responsibility.

When a mother has a boyfriend, the community expects that he will assume some parental duties toward her children. This is especially true if the couple are "housekeeping," sharing their domestic tasks. A father surrenders many of his rights and responsibilities to the mother's husband or current boyfriend. The attitude and behavior of the boyfriend toward the children defines his relationship to them. Clover compares her last two boyfriends and how they dealt with her children. "I stopped going with Max because he took no time for my kids; he just wanted them out of our way. I took it for a while, 'cause I got things from him, but when he hit my boy I called it quits. If he can't care, he can't bully my kids. But Lee, he was something else. He was so nice to my kids that the babies cried when he left the house. Sometimes I had to yell to keep the kids from bothering him and get some time for myself. After we was housekeeping for about six months, Lee said to the boys that they should call him their 'play daddy.' Lee and I quit last year and I'm sorry we did, 'cause the kids really miss him. But he still comes over, especially when I'm out, and they still call him their 'play daddy.' "

Fictive kin relations are maintained by consensus between individuals, and in some contexts can last a lifetime. If Lee maintains his interest in Clover's boys, he may remain their "play daddy" throughout their adult life.

Children very often establish close and affectionate ties with their aunts and uncles, for example, with their mother's sister's "old man" and their mother's brother's "old lady." These aunts and uncles, on the basis of their original consensual relationship, can remain in a child's personal network for a long time. Personal kinship networks are enlarged by the inclusion of these affines who may keep the relationship active. Ruby recently visited her Uncle Arthur, one of her Aunt Augusta's "old men," in the hospital. "Uncle Arthur and I was always good friends," says Ruby, "even when he and Aunt Augusta weren't getting on. He was staying with Augusta, my grandmother, and me when I was just a kid, and he always treated me like something real special. Now he is just as nice to my kids when he comes over to see them. I really feel sad that he's old and sick; he has high

blood, and I think he may die." Ruby is also attached to her Uncle Lazar, who started going with her mother's youngest sister when her aunt was just fifteen. "My aunt has been married twice since, but Uncle Lazar just remained a part of our family. He's fifty-eight now and he's been a part of our family ever since I can remember. He always has been staying with our family too. Right now he's staying in the basement below Aunt Augusta's apartment and she cooks for him and her old man. He'll always be my uncle and he and my aunt never did get married."

Just as these "aunts" and "uncles" remain in the personal kinship networks of their nieces and nephews, best friends may remain in each other's domestic network on the basis of original friendship even if the friendship has ended. Sometimes when non-kin become a part of a family and are given a fictive kin term, no one remembers just how the tie began. Billy tried to remember how cousin Ola became a part of her family. "My mama once told me," said Billy, "but I hardly remember. I think cousin Ola was my mama's oldest sister's best friend and they went for cousins. When my mama's sister died, Ola took her two youngest children, and she has been raising them up ever since."

In the above examples, social relations are conducted within the idiom of kinship. Members of the community explain the behavior of those around them by allowing behavior to define the nature of the relationship. Friends are classified as kinsmen when they assume recognized responsibilities of kinsmen. Those kin who cannot be counted upon are severely criticized. Harsh evaluation of the behavior of others accounts for some of the constant ups and downs in the lives of friends and kin. Expectations are so elastic that when one person fails to meet another's needs, disappointment is cushioned. Flexible expectations and the extension of kin relationships to non-kin allow for the creation of mutual aid domestic networks which are not bounded by genealogical distance or genealogical criteria. Much more important for the creation and recruitment to personal networks are the practical requirements that kin and friends live near one another.

Members of domestic networks in The Flats are drawn from kin and friends. Of the two, the kin network is more enduring because all of an individual's essential kin are "recognized as having some duties toward him and some claims on him." Friendships end and that is to be expected; new friendships can be formed. But the number of relatives who can be called upon for help from personal kinship networks is limited. As a result a cluster of relatives from personal kinship networks have continuing claims on one another. Some observers of daily life in black communities regard the friendship network as the "proven and adaptive base of operations" in lower-class life. But the adaptive base of operations of the poorest black people can be attributed to personal kindreds as well as to networks of friends.

♦

DANNY IN TRANSIT
David Leavitt

Danny's cousins, Greg and Jeff, are playing catch. A baseball arcs over the green lawn between them, falls into the concavity of each glove with a soft thump, and flies again. They seem to do nothing but lift their gloves into the ball's path; it moves of its own volition.

Danny is lying face down on the diving board, his hands and feet dangling over the sides, watching the ball. Every few seconds he reaches out his hands, so that his fingers brush the surface of the pool. He is trying to imagine the world extending out from where he lies: the Paper Palace, and the place he used to live, and the Amboys, Perth and South. Then Elizabeth. Then West New York. Then New York, Long Island, Italy. He listens to the sucking noise of the wind the ball makes, as it is softly swallowed. He listens to his cousins' voices. And then he takes tight hold of the diving board and tries to will it into flight, imagining it will carry him away from this backyard. But the sounds persist. He isn't going anywhere.

The huge backyard is filled with chilly New Jersey light, elegant as if it were refracted off the surface of a pearl. Carol and Nick, his aunt and uncle, sip tomato juice under an umbrella. Nearby, but separate, Elaine, Danny's mother, stares at nothing, her lips slightly parted, her mouth asleep, her eyes taking account. All that is between them is a plate of cheese.

"We went to a new restaurant, Elaine," Carol says. She is rubbing Noxzema between her palms. "Thai food. Peanut sauce and — oh, forget it."

"Keep that pitch steady, buddy," Nick calls to his sons. "Good wrist action, remember, that's the key." Both of the boys

From David Leavitt, "Danny in Transit," in *Family Dancing* (New York:Knopf, 1983), pp. 95–116.

are wearing T-shirts which say *Coca-Cola* in Arabic.

"What can I do?" Carol asks.

"She's not going to talk. I don't see why we have to force her." Nick turns once again to admire his children.

"Greg, Jeff, honey, why don't you let Danny play with you?" Carol calls to her sons. They know Danny too well to take her request seriously, and keep throwing. "Come on, Danny," Carol says. "Wouldn't you like to play?"

"No, no, no, no, no," Danny says. He is roaring, but his mouth is pressed so tightly against the diving board that his voice comes out a hoarse yowl. Such an outburst isn't hard for Danny to muster. He is used to bursting into tears, into screams, into hysterical fits at the slightest inclination.

Nick gives Carol a wearied look and says, "Now you've done it." Danny bolts up from the diving board and runs into the house.

Carol sighs, takes out a Kleenex, and swats at her eyes. Nick looks at Elaine, whose expression has not changed.

"He's your son," Nick says.

"What?" says Elaine, touching her face like a wakened dreamer.

Carol rocks her face in her hands.

Belle, Danny's grandmother, is in the kitchen, pulling burrs from the dog and cooking lunch, when Danny runs by. "Danny! What's wrong?" she shouts, but he doesn't answer, and flies through the door at the back of the kitchen into the room where he lives. Once inside, he dives into the big pink bed, with its fancy dust ruffle and lace-trimmed pillows; he breathes in the clean smell of the linen. It is Belle's room, the maid's quarters made over for her widowhood, and it is full of photographs of four generations of champion Labrador retrievers. When Danny arrived he was supposed to live with Greg

and Jeff in their room, but he screamed so loudly that Belle — exhausted — said he could sleep in her room, and she would sleep with her other grandsons — at least for the time being. It has been two months, and Danny has not relented.

Belle is pulling burrs from her pants suit. "I'm coming in, Danny," she says, and he buried his face — hard — in the pillow. He has learned that he can usually make himself cry by doing this, even when he is actually feeling happy. The trick is to clench your eyes until a few drops of water squeeze out. And then it just happens.

Danny feels hot breath on his hair, and a soft body next to his on the bed. Belle crawls and eases her way around him, making the bed squeak, until her wet mouth is right at his ear. "What's wrong, sweetie pie?" she whispers, but he doesn't answer, only moans into his pillow.

Belle gets up abruptly. "Oh, Danny," she says, "things would be so much easier if you'd just be nice. What happened to the old Danny I used to know? Don't you know how much happier everyone else would be if you'd just be happy?"

"I hate baseball," Danny says.

Danny is an only child and he looks like the perfect combination of his two parents. His eyes are round and blue, like his mother's, his mouth small and pouting, like his father's, and his wavy brown hair halfway between Elaine's, which is red and packed in tight curls, and Allen's, which is black and straight and dense. Growing up, Danny rarely saw his parents together, and so he doesn't know the extent to which he resembles them. He remembers that his father would come home from work and insist that Danny not disturb him. In those days Belle believed that when a man got to the house in the evening he deserved time alone with his wife as a reward for his labors. Every night

Elaine ate two dinners — Spaghetti-Os or Tater Tots with Danny, at six, and later, after Danny had gone to bed, something elaborate and romantic, by candlelight, with Allen. She would usually talk about the later dinners with Danny during the earlier ones. "Your father's very demanding," she said once, proudly. "He has strict notions of what a wife should do. Tonight I'm making chicken cacciatore." Danny knows that both he and his mother must have been very young when she said this, because he remembers the dreamy deliberateness with which Elaine pronounced "cacciatore," as if it were a magical incantation.

Sometimes, before Elaine put Danny to bed, Allen would pick him up and twirl him around and make sounds like an airplane. Danny slept. Through the open crack in his bedroom door he could see the candles flickering.

As he grew up Danny got to know his mother better. Starting when he was six or seven she lost her enthusiasm for dinner. "I can't manage you, Danny," she'd grumble to him. "I can't manage children. I'm unfit." Danny thought of how she always wrote DANNY G. on his lunchbag (and would continue to do so, even when he entered middle school, where last names matter). He thought of the way she made his lunch each day — peanut butter sandwich, apple, bag of cheese puffs, paper napkin. The candlelit dinners stopped, and Danny, who had never attended any of them, probably missed the ritual more than either of his parents. The three of them ate together, now, usually in silence. In those days, Elaine had a habit of staring darkly at Allen when he wasn't looking. Danny remembers Allen's anxious looks back, when he caught her face full of questions, before she shifted her eyes and changed the subject. In retrospect, Danny knows that his mother was trying to guess something,

and that his father was trying to figure out how much she already knew. "I still wanted to cover my tracks," Allen recently told his son. "I knew it was futile. I knew there was no going back. I don't think I even wanted to go back. But I still covered my tracks. It becomes a habit when you do it your whole life."

One day Danny's mother did not show up to pick him up at day camp. It was getting dark, and he was the only one left. The counselor who had stayed behind began to grow impatient. Watching the sky darken, Danny felt more embarrassment than fear. He was worried that Elaine would be misconstrued as the neglectful mother she believed herself to be, and he knew her not to be.

He lied. "Oh, I forgot," he said. "She had a doctor's appointment. She said I should ask you to drive me home."

"Drive you home?" the counselor said. "Why didn't she send a note?"

"I guess she just thought you would," Danny said.

The counselor looked at him, her face full of confusion, and the beginnings of pity. Perhaps she would call child welfare. Perhaps he would be taken away. But nothing happened. She drove him home. His mother offered no explanation for what she had done, but she did not forget to pick him up again. Danny was relieved. He had feared that she would break down, sobbing, and say to the counselor, "I'm an unfit mother. Take him away."

Somehow they survived the winter. One night at dinner, a few days before spring vacation, Elaine stood up and said, "This is a sham." Then she sat down again and continued eating. Allen looked at her, looked at Danny, looked at his plate. A few nights later she picked up the top of a ceramic sugar bowl which Danny had made her for Christmas and threw it overhand at Allen. It missed him, and shattered against the refrigerator door. Danny jumped, and fought back tears.

"See what I can do?" she said. "See what you've driven me to?"

Allen did not answer her. He quietly put on his jacket, and without a word walked out the back door. He was not home for dinner the next night. When Danny asked Elaine where he'd gone, she threw down her fork and started to cry. "Danny," she said, "there have been a lot of lies in this house."

The next day was the first Monday of vacation, and when Danny came home from playing his mother was still in bed. "It's O.K., Danny," she said. "I just decided to take the day off. Lie in bed all day, since it's something I've never done before. Don't worry about me. Go ahead and play."

Danny did as she said. That night, at dusk, when he got home, she was asleep, the lights in her room all turned out. He was frightened, and he kept the house lights on even after he'd gone to bed. In the morning he knew that his father was really gone. Only his mother was in the bed when he gently pushed open the door. "I'm not getting up again," she said. "Are you all right, honey? Can you go the Kravitzes' for dinner?"

"Don't you want anything to eat?" Danny asked.

"I'm not hungry. Don't worry about me."

Danny had dinner with the Kravitzes. Later, returning home, he heard her crying, but he couldn't hear her after he turned on "Star Trek."

Every afternoon for a week he stood in the threshold of her doorway and asked if she wanted to get up, or if she wanted something to eat. He bought Spaghetti-Os and Doritos with the money in the jar at the back of the pantry he was not supposed to know about. He never asked where his father was. Her room was musty from the closed windows, and even in the morning full of that five o'clock light which is darker than darkness, and in which the majority of car accidents happen. "Leave me alone," she would call out from the dark now. "I'm tired. For Christ's sake, just let me get some sleep. Go play or something."

Then he would close the door and make himself some Campbell's soup and watch forbidden TV all night — variety shows and detective shows and reruns after eleven. Elaine had always allotted him three hours of TV per day; when she came home from shopping she'd feel the TV to see if it was warm, if he'd been cheating. Now there were no rules.

The first day of school — a week after Elaine had gone to bed — Danny woke up to hear her screaming. He ran to her bedroom, and found her sitting up on the bed, streaked in light. She had ripped the curtains open, and the bared morning sun, through the shutters, bisected her face, the mat of her unwashed hair, the nightgown falling over her shoulders. She sat there and screamed, over and over again, and Danny rushed in, shouting, "What's wrong? What's wrong?"

And then she grabbed the ends of her hair and began tearing at them, and grinding her teeth together, and wailing. Finally she collapsed, in tears, onto the bed. She turned to look at Danny and she screamed, "I can't change! Don't you see, no matter how much I want to, I just can't change!"

Danny got Mrs. Kravitz. She came over and hoisted Elaine out of bed and began marching her around the hall. "One, two, three, let's go, let's go," Mrs. Kravitz said. "Danny, go look in the bathroom for empty pill bottles, sweetheart, your mommy's going to be just fine."

Danny didn't find any empty pill bottles, and when he came out of the bathroom some paramedics were coming through the kitchen with a stretcher. "I can't stand up," Elaine was telling Mrs. Kravitz. "I'll be sick."

"Just lie down now," Mrs. Kravitz said. Danny remembered that today was the first day of school, and he wondered whether he should go to his home-room class or not, but when he looked at the clock, he saw that it was already eight o'clock. School had started.

Danny spent the night at the Kravitzes' house, and the next day he want to Nick and Carol's. This was in a different school district but nobody talked about school. That night, when his cousins wanted to watch a different television show from Danny, he threw his first fit.

A few days later, while he was eating his cereal at the kitchen table, Danny's father arrived. Danny didn't say hello. He continued to spoon the sweet milk into his mouth, though the cereal was gone. Belle, who was making pancakes, turned the burner off and quietly slunk out of the room. Allen sat down across from Danny, holding a cup of coffee. He had a new short haircut, and was growing a stubbly beard. They were alone in the room.

"I know you're angry," Allen said. "I know you wonder where I've been and why your mother got sick. I don't know where to begin, and I don't expect instant forgiveness, but I do want you to hear me out. Will you do that for me? I know you'll have a lot of questions, and I'm prepared to answer them. Just give me a chance."

Danny looked at his father and didn't say anything.

On weekends Danny went to visit his father in the city. Allen was living with a man named Gene in an apartment in Greenwich Village, and though he had quit being a stockbroker, he continued to live off his own investments. Each Friday

Danny rode the train up, past the fast-food franchises thrown up around the railroad stations, the muddy Amboys, the rows of tenements in Elizabeth. Allen took him to museums, to the theater, to restaurants. On Sunday he saw his son off at Penn Station. "I used to ride this train every day," he told Danny, as they waited on the platform. "I used to play cards with Uncle Nick on this train. It seems like hundreds of years ago."

"That was when you and Mom had dinner by candlelight," Danny said, remembering how his father twirled him in the air, how his mother pronounced the word "cacciatore" — slowly, and with such relish.

"We were innocent," Allen said. "Your mother and I believed in something that was wrong for us. Wrong for me, I should say."

Danny looked away from his father, toward the train which was now moving into the station.

"You probably think your mother's getting sick is the result of my being gay," Allen said, putting his hand on his son's shoulder. "But that's only partially true. It goes much further, much deeper than that, Danny. You know your mother hasn't been well for a long time."

From where he's lying, his face against the pillow, Danny hears the harsh sound of tires against gravel, and blots up in bed. Through his window he sees a taxi in the driveway, and Allen, dressed in bluejeans and a lumberjack shirt, fighting off Belle's furious barking dog. Elaine, seeing Allen, has crawled up on her haunches, and is hugging her knees. When Allen sees Elaine, he turns to rehail the taxi, but it is already out of the driveway.

"Now, Allen, don't be upset," Nick says, walking out onto the gravel, taking Allen's shoulder in one hand, the dog in the other.

"You didn't tell me she was going to be here," Allen says.

"That's because you wouldn't have come out," says Carol, joining them. "You two have to talk. We're sorry to do this, but it's the only way. Someone's got to take some responsibility."

As if he is a child about to ride a bicycle for the first time without training wheels, Allen is literally pushed by Carol toward his wife.

"What's going on? What's happening here?" shouts Belle. When she sees Allen, she stops dead in her tracks.

"You didn't tell him?" Belle asks.

Allen begins to move uncertainly toward Elaine, who is still rearing, and Carol and Nick push Belle into the kitchen. Danny jumps out of his bed and kneels next to the door.

They whisper. Nick nods and walks outdoors. "Relax, Mom," says Carol. "They've got to talk. They've got to make some decisions."

"Elaine's hospitalized." Belle announces this known fact in a low voice, and looks toward the door to her room.

"She's been hiding her whole life. She's got to face up to the facts. I can't take this much longer." Carol lights a cigarette, and rubs her eyes.

Belle looks away. "He's just a child," she says.

"Their child," Carol says. "Not ours."

"Not so loudly!" Belle says, and points to the bedroom door. "Have some sympathy. She's been through a personal hell."

"I know things were hard," Carol says. "But to commit herself! I'm sorry, Mom, but as far as I'm concerned, that's just self-dramatizing. No one commits themselves these days. You see a psychiatrist on Central Park West once a week. You continue your life, and you deal with your problem."

"Her problem is worse than that," Belle says. "She needs help. All my life I never said so, but I knew she was — not strong. And now I have to admit, knowing she's taken care of, I feel relieved."

"But it's not like she's crazy!" Carol says. "It's not like she's a raving lunatic, or schizophrenic, or anything. She's basically just fine, isn't she? She just needs some help, doesn't she?"

Belle doesn't answer. Carol sits down, lays her head on the kitchen table, and starts to cry.

"Oh, my poor girl," Belle says, and strokes her daughter's hair. "I know you're worried about your sister. And she is fine. She'll be fine."

"Then why can't she just check herself out of that hospital and take her kid and start seeing a goddamned shrink once a week?" Carol says, lifting up her head and turning to face her mother. "I'll pay for it, if that's what she needs."

"Keep your voice down!" Belle whispers loudly. "Let's talk outside."

She pulls Carol out of her chair, and out the screen door. As soon as they've left the kitchen, Danny makes a run for the stairs. He sneaks into his cousins' room, which is full of baseball cards and Star Wars toys, closes the door, and perches on the window seat, which overlooks the swimming pool. Below him, he can see his parents arguing in one corner, while in another, Belle and Carol continue their discussion. Belle is trying to explain that Elaine cannot take care of a household, and this is her problem, and Carol is shaking her head. As for Nick, he has moved out onto the lawn, where he is playing baseball with Greg and Jeff.

Danny can just barely make out his parents' voices. "They arranged this," he hears Elaine saying. "They think Danny's a pain in the ass."

"You know I'd take him if I could," Allen answers.

"I thought you were leading such a model life!"

"There's nothing about my life which would create an unhealthy atmosphere for Danny. I'm just not ready for him yet."

"Good," Elaine says. "He can come live with me."

Danny closes the window. He knows to cover up his tracks. Then he runs back downstairs, through the kitchen, and out the screen door. He runs alongside the pool, past his parents and toward the woods. Allen catches his eye, and waves. Danny waves back, keeps running.

When Danny first arrived at Nick and Carol's, everything was alien: the extra bed in Greg and Jeff's room which pulled out from under, the coloration of the television set, the spaghetti sauce. They were so indulgent toward him, in his unhappiness, that he wondered if perhaps he had leukemia, and they weren't telling him. And then he realized that he did not have leukemia. He was merely the passive victim of a broken home. For months he had held back his own fear and anger for the sake of his mother. Now she had betrayed him. She *was* unfit. He *had* been taken away, as had she. There was no reason to be good anymore.

What Danny didn't count on was Carol and Nick's expectation that somehow he would change, shape himself to their lives. No child with leukemia would be asked to change. Danny decided to become a child with leukemia — a sick child, a thwarted child, a child to be indulged. Nick and Carol asked him if he wouldn't maybe consider trading places with his grandmother and moving into his cousins' room, which would be fun for all three, like camp. Danny threw his biggest fit ever. They never asked him again. They gave him wearied looks, when

he refused to eat, when he demanded to watch what he wanted to watch, when he wouldn't talk to company. They lost patience, and he in turn lost patience: Didn't they understand? He was a victim. And certainly he had only to mention his mother's name, and his own stomach would sink, and Carol's eyes would soften, and suddenly she would become like his grandmother — maternal and embracing. He made himself need her to be maternal and embracing.

The night his mother went to bed forever, Danny learned two things: to be silent was to be crazy, and to be loud was also to be crazy. It seemed to him that he did not have a choice. He knew of no way of living that did not include morose silences and fits of fury. When Carol asked him why he wouldn't just enjoy the life he had, he felt a fierce resistance rise in his chest. He was not going to give himself up.

Now, running from his crazy parents, Danny arrives at a place in the woods — a patch of dry leaves sheltered by an old sycamore — which he has designated his own. Only a few feet away, the neighborhood children are playing Capture the Flag in a cul-de-sac, and he can hear their screams and warnings through the trees. He turns around once, circling his territory, and then he begins. Today he will invent an episode of "The Perfect Brothers Show," the variety show on his personal network. He has several other series in the works, including "Grippo," a detective drama, and "Pierre!" set in the capital city of South Dakota.

He begins. He does all the voices and makes the sound of applause by driving his tongue against the roof of his mouth. "And now," he says, "for your viewing pleasure, another episode of '"The Perfect Brothers Show'!"

The orchestra plays a fanfare. In another voice, Danny sings:

"A perfect night for comedy!
For fun and musicality!
We'll change you!
Rearrange you!
Just you wait and see!
Welcome to The Perfect
   Brothers Show!"

He is in the midst of inventing a comic skit, followed by a song from this week's guest star, Loni Anderson, when Jeff — the younger and more persistently good-natured of the brothers — appears from between the trees. "Can I play?" he asks.

Danny, to his own surprise, doesn't throw a fit. "Yes," he says. "We'll do a comedy skit. You're the housewife and I'm Superman."

"I want to be Superman," Jeff says.

"All right, all right." Now Danny begins to give instructions for the skit, but halfway through Jeff interrupts and says, "This is boring. Let's play baseball."

"If you want to play something like *that*," Danny says, "go play Capture the Flag." He throws up his hands in disgust.

"There are girls playing," Jeff says. "Well, if you won't play, I'll play baseball with my dad!"

"Good," says Danny. "Leave me alone."

Jeff runs off toward the house. Part of the way there, he turns once. "You're weird," he says.

Danny ignores him. He is halfway through his skit — playing both parts — when he is interrupted again. This time it is his father. "How are you, old man?" Allen asks. "Want to go to the Paper Palace?"

For a moment Danny's eyes widen, and then he remembers how unhappy he is. "All right," he says.

They take Carol's station wagon, and drive to the Paper Palace, a huge pink cement structure in the middle of an old shopping center. The shopping center is near Danny's old house.

"You've loved the Paper Palace — how long?" Allen asks. "I think you were four the first time I brought you here. You loved it. Remember what I bought you?"

"An origami set and a Richie Rich comic book," Danny says. He rarely gets to the Paper Palace anymore; Carol shops in the more elegant mall near her house.

"When we lived here, all I wanted to do was to get into Carol and Nick's neighborhood. A year ago today. Just think. All I could think about was getting a raise and buying a house. I might have bought the house next to Carol and Nick's. I wanted you to grow up in that area. All those trees. The fresh air. The great club."

"I am anyhow, I guess," Danny says.

"Don't let it fool you," Allen says. "It all seems so perfect. It all looks so perfect. But soon enough the paint chips, there are corners bitten by the dog, you start sweeping things under the bed. Believe me, under the beds, there's as much dust in Nick and Carol's house as there was in ours."

"Carol has a maid," Danny says.

"Just never trust cleanness. All the bad stuff — the really bad stuff — happens in clean houses, where everything's tidy and nobody says anything more than good morning."

"Our house wasn't like that," Danny says.

Allen looks at him. But now they are in the parking lot of the shopping center, and the colorful promise of the Paper Palace takes both of them over. They rush inside. Danny browses ritualistically at stationery and comic books, reads through the plot synopses in the soap opera magazines, scrupulously notes each misspelling of a character's name. Allen lags behind him. They buy a copy of *Vogue* for Elaine. In front of them in line, a fat, balding man upsets a box of candy on the sales counter as he purchases a copy of *Playgirl*. His effort to avoid attention has backfired, and drawn the complicated looks of all around him. Danny avoids looking at Allen, but Allen's eyes shoot straight to Danny, whose face has a pained, embarrassed expression on it. They do not mention the fat man as they walk out of the store.

Years ago, when Danny was only six or seven, he found a magazine. He was playing in the basement, dressing up in some old clothes of Allen's which he had found in a cardboard box. The magazine was at the bottom of the box. When Elaine came down to check what Danny was up to, she found him sitting on a trunk, examining a series of pictures of young, dazed-looking men posed to simulate various acts of fornication. Elaine grabbed the magazine away from Danny and demanded to know where he'd gotten it. He told her that he had found it, and he pointed to the box.

Elaine looked again at the magazine, and then at the box. She thumbed through the pages, looking at the photographs. Then she put the magazine down on top of the box and wrapped her arms around herself.

"Danny," she said, "for God's sake, don't lie about this. You don't have to. You can tell me the truth. Are you sure that's where you got this thing?"

"Swear to God and hope to die, stick a needle in my eye," Danny said.

"Get upstairs," said Elaine.

"Do you want a Velamint?" Allen asks Danny in the car, as they drive back from the Paper Palace. They are riding down a wide, dark road, lined with sycamores. Danny takes the small blue wafer from his father, without saying anything. He opens the window, sticks his hand out into the breeze.

"You know, Danny, I've been thinking," Allen says. "I know this fantastic place, this school, in New Hampshire. It's great — really innovative — and it's specially for bright, motivated kids like you."

Danny doesn't answer. When Allen turns to look at him, he sees that his son is clutching the armrest so hard his knuckles have turned white, and biting his lip to hold back tears.

"Danny," Allen says. "Danny, what's wrong?"

"I know I've been a problem," Danny says. "But I've decided to change. Today. I've decided to be happy. Please. I'll make them want me to stay."

Allen is alarmed by Danny's panic. "Danny," he says, "this school isn't punishment. It's a great place. You deserve to go there."

"I played with Jeff today!" Danny says. His voice is at its highest register. He is staring at Allen, his face flushed, a look of pure pleading in his eyes.

Allen puts his hand over his mouth and winces. When they reach a stop sign, he turns to Danny and says, as emphatically as he can, "Danny, don't worry, no one's going to *make* you go anywhere. But, Danny I don't know if I *want* you to stay with Nick and Carol. After fifteen years in that world, I don't know if I want my son to be hurt by it like I was."

"I won't become a stockbroker. I won't sweep the dust under the bed. But, please, don't send my away."

"Danny, I thought you didn't like it here," Allen says.

"I'm not unfit."

They are still at the stop sign. Behind them, a car is honking, urging them to move on. Danny's eyes are brimming with tears.

Allen shakes his head, and reaches for his son.

They go to Carvel's for ice cream. Ahead of them in line a flustered-looking woman buys cones for ten black children who stand in pairs, holding hands. Two of the girls are pulling violently at each other's arms, while a boy whose spiral of soft-serve ice cream has fallen off his cone cries loudly, and demands reparations. Allen orders two chocolate cones with brown bonnets, and he and Danny sit down in chairs with tiny desks attached to them, like the chairs in Danny's elementary school. There are red lines from tears on Danny's face, but he doesn't really cry — at least, he doesn't make any of the crying noises, the heaves and stuttering wails. He picks off the chocolate coating of the brown bonnet and eats it in pieces before even touching the actual ice cream.

"I'm glad you haven't lost your appetite," Allen says.

Danny nods weakly, and continues to eat. The woman marches the ten children out the door, and into a small pink van. "Danny," Allen says, "what can I say? What do you want me to say?"

Danny bites off the bottom of his cone. Half-melted ice cream plops onto the little desk. "Jesus Christ," Allen mutters, and rubs his eyes.

When they get back to the house, Allen joins Nick and Carol under the umbrella on the patio. Elaine is still lying on the chaise, her eyes closed. Danny gets out of the car after his father, walks a circle around the pool, biting his thumbnail, and resumes his position on the diving board. Nearby, Greg and Jeff are playing catch. "Hey, Danny, want to throw the ball?" Allen shouts. He does not hear Carol hiss her warning, "No!" But Danny neither does nor says anything.

"Danny!" Allen shouts again. "Can you hear me?"

Very slowly Danny hoists himself up, crawls off the diving board and walks back toward the house.

"Oh, Christ," Carol says, taking off her sunglasses. "This is more than I can take."

Now Belle appears at the kitchen door, waving a batter-caked spatula. "What happened?" she asks.

"The same story," Carol says.

"I'll see to him," Allen says. He casts a parting glance at Elaine, and walks into the kitchen. "The same thing happened this morning," Belle tells him as they walk toward Danny's room.

But this time, the door is wide open, instead of slammed shut, and Danny is lying on his back on the bed, his face blank, his eyes tearless.

At first Belle thinks he is sick. "Honey, are you all right?" she asks, feeling his head. "He's cool," she tells Allen.

Allen sits down on the bed and arcs his arms over Danny's stomach. "Danny, what's wrong?" he asks.

Danny turns to look at his father, his face full of a pain too strong for a child to mimic.

"I can't change," he says. "I can't change. I can't change."

In the kitchen, Belle is wrathful. She does not keep her voice down; she does not seem to care that Danny can hear every word she is saying. "I see red when I look at you people," she tells her children. "In my day, people didn't just abandon everything to gratify themselves. In my day, people didn't abandon their children. You're so selfish, all you think about is yourselves."

"What do you want from me?" Allen answers. "What kind of father could I have been? I was living a lie."

"See what I mean?" Belle says. "Selfish. You assume I'm talking about you.

But I'm talking about all of you. And you, too, Carol." ˅

"For Christ's sake, Mother, he's not my son!" Carol says. "And he's wrecking my sons' lives. And my life."

Elaine has been fingering her hair. But now she suddenly slams her hand against the table and lets out a little moan. "He really said that?" she says. "Oh, Christ, he really said that."

"I've had it up to here with all of you," Belle announces. "It's unspeakable. I've heard enough."

She turns from them all, as if she has seen enough as well. Allen and Elaine and Nick look down at the table, like ashamed children. But Carol gets up, and walks very deliberately to face her mother. "Now just one minute," she says, her lips twitching with anger. "Just one minute. It's easy for you to just stand there and rant and rave. But I have to live with it, day in and day out, I have to take care of him and put up with his crap. And I have to listen to my kids say, 'What is with that Danny? When's he going away?' Well, maybe I am selfish. I've worked hard to raise my kids well. And now, just because Elaine screws everything up for herself, suddenly I'm expected to bear the brunt of it, take all the punishment. And everything I've been working for is going down the tubes because she can't take care of her own kid! Well, then, I will be selfish. I am selfish. I have had enough of this."

"Now just a minute, Carol," Allen says.

"You take him," Carol says, turning around to confront him. "You take him home, or don't say a word to me. There's not one word you have a right to say to me."

"Damn it!" Allen says. "Doesn't anybody understand? I'm doing my best."

"You've had two months," Nick says.

Belle, her arms wrapped around her waist, begins to cry softly. Sitting at the table, Elaine cries as well, though more loudly, and with less decorum.

Then, with a small click, the door to Danny's bedroom opens, and he walks into the kitchen. Allen and Nick stand up, nearly knocking their chairs over in the process. "Danny!" Carol says. Her voice edges on panic. "Are you all right!"

"Yes, thank you," Danny says.

Elaine lifts her head from the table. "Danny," she says. "Danny, I —" She moves her lips, struggling to form words. But nothing comes out. Danny looks down at her, his eyes full of a frightening, adult pity. Then he turns away and walks outside.

Everyone jumps up at once to follow him. But Allen holds up his hand. "I'll go," he says. He scrambles out the door, and after Danny, who is marching past the swimming pool, toward the patch of woods where he likes to play. When he gets there, he stops and waits, his back to his father.

"Danny," Allen says, coming up behind him. "You heard everything. I don't know what to say. I wish I did."

Danny has his arms crossed tightly over his chest. "I've thought about it," he says. "I've decided."

"What?" Allen says.

"About the school," Danny says. "I've decided I'll go."

A few days later, Danny boards the train which snakes along the Jersey coast to New York. He is riding to visit his father. An old couple is sitting across the way from him, a gnarled little man and his taller, white-haired wife, her white gloved hands clasped calmly around each other. Like Danny, the couple is not reading the paper, but looking out the green-tinted windows at yellow grass, small shops, warehouses.

"You'd better get your things together," the husband says. "We're almost there."

"No," the wife says. "We don't want South Amboy. We want Perth Amboy." The husband shakes his head no. "South Amboy. I'm sure she said South Amboy."

The wife is quiet for a few seconds, until the conductor shouts, "South Amboy, South Amboy next!" Now she cannot control herself. "I'm *sure* it's Perth Amboy," she says. The husband is buttoning his jacket, reaching for his hat. "Will you listen to me for once?" he says. "It's South Amboy." The wife shakes her head. "I'm sure," she says. "I'm sure."

Gradually, and then with a sudden grind, the train comes to a halt. The husband lumbers down the aisle, knocking past Danny, shaking his head. "I'm getting off," he says. "Are you coming?" The wife stands, hesitates, sits down. "It's not this stop," she says. He makes a violent motion with his hands, and walks out the door, onto the station platform. She stands to follow him, but the doors close suddenly. His fist appears, as if disembodied, rapping on the window. The train is moving again.

For a moment, she just stands there, shocked. Then the train's lurching forces her to sit down. A look comes over her face first of indignation, then of fear and confusion, then finally, of weariness — with her husband, with the train, with their lives which will go on like this. She bends over and pulls herself into the corner of her seat, as if trying to make herself as small as possible, and picks at a loose thread of her dress with one of her white-gloved hands.

Then she comes to consciousness. She realizes that she is not alone on the train. Her eyes narrow, and focus on Danny. Late afternoon, almost dark. He is singing a song about comedy and fun and musicality. He tells her it's going to be a perfect night.

◆

FRIENDS AT LAST
John Corry

The last thing my ex-wife wrote to me was "Did you get your work done?" The next day she died. She had been too weak to talk, but the handwriting was firm and her spiral notebook contained not a wasted word. Actually, there wasn't much to say those final days, and it was a comfort just to hold hands. It had taken us such a long while to do that.

Irmie and I had been divorced in the 1970s, and while divorce is never easy, ours was worse than most. Much of what happened then is shadowy now. I remember far better when we met. Irmie was an aspiring actress and I an aspiring reporter, and neither of us was equipped for what lay ahead. We married, perhaps, because that was what one did.

We were together twelve years, suffering all the usual problems as well as the ones that leave you changed. Two babies died. Irmie became sick. I began to drink. We should have separated before we did, but we stayed together, or so we thought, because of our two daughters. The night I finally left, we solemnly told them my departure was all for the best. My older daughter cried.

Our amicable separation, however, turned sullen and soon gave way to spite.

From John Corry, "Friends at Last," *New York Times Magazine*, May 10, 1992, p. 12.

Incidents stick in my memory like shards of broken glass, although their chronology now escapes me. First one daughter and then the other left Irmie and came to live with me. The years were full of doctors, therapists and lawyers. I saw my ex-wife only in court or when we both showed up at a school function for one of the girls. We were careful not to speak.

Years passed that way, a dead marriage marked only by alimony checks. Irmie and my daughters gradually repaired their breach. She and I, however, did not. The anger was too great, and, besides, I was afraid even to go near her. What I was afraid of I do not know, although I thought of Irmie as some kind of monster, which is how she also thought of me.

Indeed, she had made that wonderfully explicit. As a therapeutic exercise a few years after we were divorced, she wrote her "autobiography," a copy of which she gratuitously sent me. It was literate and intelligent, and painted a venomous portrait of the unsuitable man she had married. I read just enough to get the gist. Then I put it aside. A year or so later, I went back and read it straight through. Surely Irmie could not think those things about me.

But she did, and in my mind I gave no quarter, either. I carried my resentment like baggage, although scarcely aware of its weight. When I thought of my ex-wife at all, it was only to count myself fortunate I did not have to see her again. Once or twice, I thought I glimpsed her on the street and fled to avoid an encounter. God forbid we should ever meet.

We did meet, though, at the college graduation of our younger daughter. An attractive woman walked up to my second wife. "Mrs. Corry," she said, and extended her hand. "I'm Janet's mother." The attractive woman, of course, was Irmie, but I didn't recognize her at first. Irmie was a

harridan, and this woman seemed so nice. "John," she said anyway, "how are you?"

I do not remember what I said to my ex-wife then, but I remember talking to her later. She thanked me for putting the girls through school, and I surprised myself by thinking I would cry. What I was feeling was relief. A great burden was breaking up and falling in clumps at my feet. That day our daughters took pictures. In one, Irmie and I have our arms around each other. We look like two boxers who just fought a draw.

It would be pleasant to think we simply put the past behind us then, but that would have been too much. We had to feel our way. There was a phone call here, another there, and once we met on the street. We walked together and talked about our daughters. We were both reassured we could do that. We knew at least something had survived those dead years.

We became, once again, parents, or, perhaps, confidants, sharing thoughts about our children in a private parental way. When Irmie got cancer soon after, we talked about that, too. There was a turning point when she had the mastectomy and I visited her in the hospital. She was propped up against pillows and smiling. "John," she said, "you were the only one I wanted to see."

We stayed in touch regularly after that. I would call her, or she would call me, and I discovered things about my ex-wife I never knew. Once, she talked a long while about Edith Wharton and Henry James. She was fascinated by Wharton and distrustful of James, and knowledgeable in her opinion. In my imaginings about Irmie all those years, I had never imagined her reading a book. How well, I wondered, had I known her?

That last year, I know, she wondered about me, too. My daughters told me about it, although they really didn't have to. I understood what was happening full well. My ex-wife and I simply wanted to like each other. The years we had been together could not have been wasted; they had to have more meaning than that.

I visited the hospital quite often the last time Irmie was there. One visit fell on my birthday. At the hospital, my daughters suggested we celebrate with balloons and cake, which was how Irmie and I had celebrated with them when they were children. I thought balloons and a cake would be out of place now, but Irmie smiled and said she would like them.

That evening we had a party. Our daughters talked and fussed, while Irmie and I looked on benignly. Then she told me how happy she was that we had two children. She sounded quite thoughtful, and it was as if she was forgiving us both for what we long ago had done to each other. That night, I think, we reclaimed those lost years.

One day not long after, a new nurse came into the room while I was there and Irmie whispered, "How should I introduce you?" I said it did not matter, and that I thought ex-husband would do. Irmie smiled at the nurse then and told her my name. "He's my best friend," she added. Irmie had just given me a great gift, and I knew it. A few days later, she died.

Two

Entering Families: Fact or Law

What starts a family? Sometimes, a biological event initiates a family — notably, the birth of a child. Sometimes, a decision by legal officials is crucial to the initiation of a family — as with adoption. A range of actions taken by individuals and responses by legal and religious officials can initiate a family through marriage; contemporary American culture ambiguously treats other initiating events, such as cohabitation by two adults, and informal foster care. Does a family start with acts within the control of the individuals involved, or instead as moments of legal decision, within the control of legal officials? Private, individual desire itself may not be enough to accomplish the creation of a family. A heterosexual couple may want a child but face infertility or barriers to adoption. A gay or lesbian couple may want a child and confront even more difficulties.

At the same time, "control" or "intent" may also inadequately describe the range of social factors and conditions that lead one person to become pregnant, another to agree to serve as a gestational-mother-by-contract but then find herself unable to relinquish the child, and a third to seek community acceptance for a relationship the law does not recognize. Should law facilitate the private choices of individuals to form families, through any means possible? Should law restrict family formation, for example, by screening candidates for adoption, limiting access to new reproductive technologies, or refusing marriage to some people who want it?

Sometimes, the formation of one family may involve the termination of or separation from another. Once again, law may play varied roles. Adoption of a child could involve terminating any ties with the biological parent — but it does not have to; this is a policy decision. Foster care could involve only a temporary placement — and place the government under an obligation to reunite the child and the biological parents as soon as possible — or foster care could promote the development of stable and permanent ties between foster child and foster parents. Legal policies about family formation can reinforce or challenge historic meanings of race, gender, and sexual orientation. Adoption rules can promote racial matching or reject it; visitation following divorce, work and unemployment policies, and other practices can rely on or resist traditional gender roles in childrearing; marriage, foster care, and adoption regulations can exclude or include gays and lesbians. What images and values should influence decisions on these issues?

Becoming a Parent

These readings explore the complexities of choice and constraint in becoming a parent through sexual intercourse, adoption, "surrogate" or contract motherhood, *in vitro* fertilization, and foster care. They also involve special issues for teens who face parenthood, drug-exposed infants who need parents, and mothers and fathers who struggle with the inheritance of gender-based parenting presumed by social and legal practices. Should parenthood be deregulated, and governed by the market? Should people who want to be parents be steered away from new reproductive technologies and toward adoption — or vice versa? Should one's marital status have anything to do with becoming a parent or enjoying parental prerogatives? What background rules — of law, workplaces, social conventions — would make it more likely that parents develop close and nurturing relationships with their children?

Choosing Parenthood

◆

HAND-ME-DOWN-DREAMS
Carol Peacock

Drinking iced coffee in her kitchen that May of 1974, Anna said she had something to tell me. Lisa had skipped her period and might be pregnant. Wrinkling my forehead anxiously, I told her not to worry, girls Lisa's age were often irregular.

Well, Anna pointed out, Lisa saw a lot of this new fellow, Victor. "I wouldn't want my daughter havin' a baby outta wedlock, Carol," said Anna, looking at me, hard.

The next day, Lisa, tanned and wearing Victor's little gold chain around her neck, leaned over and said she'd just gotten her period. But she'd thought she was pregnant. Scared her half crazy, she told me.

Birth control, I repeated. We'd talked about it often over the past year.

"But, Ma —," Lisa protested.

I suggested that maybe Lisa should talk with her mother. After all, she had been young once, too. Lisa looked down, terrified. Would I come to talk, too, she asked.

Early that following Friday, the three of us sat tensely at the kitchen table. Anna asked me if I'd seen the sale at Stop 'n Shop, hamburg was only sixty-nine a pound. Crossing her long legs, Lisa picked at her ruffled white halter top and asked what we were going to do for group next Wednesday.

"Lisa thought she was pregnant this month," I stated. I continued, saying that since most girls had sex before they were married nowadays, it was important they didn't have babies.

From Carol Peacock, Hand-Me-Down-Dreams (New York:Schocken Books, 1981), pp. 65–67.

Anna looked across at me encouragingly.

I mentioned contraception, listed the different methods, and said Lisa should be using some form of birth control. Then I sipped my coffee and watched the mother and the dark-haired adolescent beside me.

"What — what do *you* think, Ma?" Lisa asked.

"Well, Lisa," said Anna, breathing deeply. "A' course, I never thought I'd see the day when I was saying this to a daughter a' mine. But I feel, as a precaution, you should do it, Lisa, the oral concepts. You wouldn't want to have a baby now, 'cause you're still so young yourself. An' raisin' a baby without a man," Anna said, "Especially when you are young, is very hard, Lisa, very, very hard."

"So —," Lisa urged.

"So I want it to be different for you," finished Anna.

It was a statement of separation, of different choices open to different women. Lisa gazed at her mother in respect. I think she saw her mother for the first time, a woman who'd lived her own life, borne her own struggles. The morning's earlier tension dissolved. I sensed that the mother and daughter at the table had begun to view each other in a new manner, woman to woman.

◆

PREGNANT ON PURPOSE
Sharon Thompson

My daughter was wanted. You know, she was no mistake. We don't think our babies are a problem because they came to us when we were young.

— Fifteen-year-old mother

Do you know anybody who thinks teenage girls under seventeen should have babies? Adults for adolescent chastity occasionally mutter that teens should rot in the fecund beds they make, and charges of "genocide" hiss through the debate, but the battle against prescribing or dispensing contraception in New York schools has centered on sex — not reproduction. No group has campaigned explicitly *for* teen reproduction.

Outside New York, educators and counselors who work with young mothers have moved toward a perspective on teen pregnancy closer to their clients'. This modified view, which stresses helping teenage mothers over prevention, falls between the right-to-life and family planning movements — an interesting niche. In communities with strong teen mother constituencies, empathy and shrewd PR have turned teen moms from bad girls to good faster than a condom bursts — an amazing reversal for the most frightening bad girl: the one who doesn't get away with it.

It's hard to decide how to take the turnaround. Is the acceptance of teen mothers a point for bad girls or madonnas, feminism or antifeminism? (Wasn't the Virgin Mary a teen mom?) If your litmus test for feminist consciousness is abortion, it's a close call.

Sharon Thompson, Pregnant on Purpose, *Village Voice,* Dec. 23, 1988, p.31.

The names of those interviewed in this article have been changed for confidentiality.

At the closing luncheon of a state-wide conference on adolescent pregnancy in New Mexico last year, a drama club of college-bound teenage girls presented a prize-winning one-act, purportedly on the perils of teenage pregnancy. When the happy ending portrayed the pregnant heroine deciding against the "evil of abortion," spoons dropped in shock. Maybe fifty people clapped. The other 100 or so stared rigidly at their sorbet. The performers looked dazed and disoriented. Good girls, they hadn't had abortions or babies. They stumbled off the dais like beauty show contestants, blinded by the light of controversy.

Maybe some teenage girls should have children, and maybe they should not. In part, the answer depends on the experience itself: To what degree are teenage mothers "made"? In what sense do they "make" themselves? How do gender relations affect this choice? Do most teen moms really have no other option? Are they really worse off when they choose pregnancy than when they don't? And how about their babies? I'm going to approach these questions mainly through life-history evidence, culled from interviews with about 100 teenage mothers and almost 300 other teenage girls about sex, romance, and pregnancy. The subjects include white, Puerto-Rican, Chicana, and black girls from the East Coast, Southwest, and the Midwest. Most of these young mothers grew up poor or in downwardly mobile working-class families.

The majority of teenage mothers describe themselves the way most girls do, as "good," explaining their motherhood as an accident ("I was swept away"; "I didn't know what I was doing"; "I didn't think I could get pregnant"). Only a few argue that they got pregnant on purpose, but all insist they would do it over again. This doesn't mean they would. When a different rhetorical context — advice for a girl who isn't pregnant yet — is proposed,

their sense of responsibility shifts. Regrets and realism surface. Most wouldn't counsel another girl to follow in their tracks. "Take birth control," they say.

Why don't more use contraception themselves in the first place, then? "It never crossed my mind," answer most teen mothers. How can that be? Are teens unable to think about the future? Has crack killed their ability to connect cause with effect? The evidence is: they've got other things on their minds.

Sex, for one thing. Love, lust, even sensual inclination can be a knockout punch. Girls frequently explain they didn't take birth control because intercourse took place "spontaneously." According to the generally accepted reading, spontaneity rationalizes badness (sexuality). True and not true. While teenage girls can plan for spontaneity with a thoroughness that would get them far in engineering, their reports of surprise are also genuine. If sexual desire ambushes adults, how much more likely is passion to catch the young unprepared.

Many teenage mothers report that they have never tried a tampon and few say they masturbate. It makes sense that penetration stuns girls so reticent about their bodies. But even girls who have undergone intensive sex education from progressive schools and liberated parents report astonishment at sex.

> I was on his handlebars. And — and then we started talking and then all of a sudden we started kissing.... It was weird, I mean, because I didn't expect to kiss him! I didn't even expect to be with him!... But then we got off, and we just sat there, and we started kissing....

Teen motherhood evolves in the course of two complex negotiations: bargaining with lovers for intimacy and support and worming out of the family — or into an improved position in family hierarchy.

Q: What were you thinking about if not birth control and sexual pleasure?

A: ...At the time, I felt like I was in love. And so, I guess it was...all I was thinking about

Love means too many things even to surface-mine its permutations here, and teenage mothers don't talk as much about falling in love as other girls do. Their histories are *prüfungsromans* — narratives of trial — not romances. Love comes in as a secondary plot, a precondition or context. Having a baby — initiation — is the real story, which occurs mainly within love affairs that have jelled enough for girls to call them "ongoing." (A study by sociologist Raye Hudson Rosen showed that eighty-nine percent of teenage pregnancies occur in relationships with an average length of fifteen months.)

Teen pregnancy is related to educational disadvantage, according to a recent report from the Children's Defense Fund. My interviews show that many girls turn to pregnancy as a way out of school, or become pregnant as a side effect of truancy. A less common pattern involves a comparatively good student — a girl — who begins to "care" for a boy with "problems." Maybe he has dropped out of school, has a drug problem or family difficulties. They get involved, mainly, through two scenarios. One: He rushes her assiduously. (It's almost as if he has picked her out because of her talents — to stop her, to throw her off track.) At least as often she picks him out. She begins to mother him, and that responsibility overwhelms her fealty to herself. The caring lauded in some quarters as girls' special gift becomes a "good girl's" reason to cut school, break with family, and become a young mother.

Bernadette, for example. The youngest of four children, she didn't want to be "a baby" anymore. She wanted independence and responsibility. She did well in high school through the first semester of her sophomore year, when she met a boy at the mall where she worked. Her Hispanic family was comfortably working class; his, poor and troubled. His tenuous situation, fragility, and neediness moved her. She broke up with her boyfriend, whose "mama's boy" tendencies had annoyed her anyway.

And we went out and we started talking, and we just really talked that whole night.

Q: What did you talk about, do you remember?

A: Uhm, mostly about him. He had a very hard child life. Very hard. His dad's an alcoholic and his mom's not a mom. Like, my mom stays home and cooks and bakes, and his mom is very young, because she got pregnant when she was, well, 16, 17. And she's — right now, she wants to be free. And she has — well, she had eight kids. One recently just died, so she has seven now, but she can't escape. ... So mostly we just talked about things he'd done and things he shouldn't do.

Q: Like what things had he done?

A: Uhm, he used to not go home for two, three weeks. And you know, his parents didn't really care.

Far from being a mama's boy, vassal to another woman, Johnnie needed her care and support — an important point to a girl who was tired of dependency and overprotection. When she came home at 7:30 A.M. from her first date with a boy they didn't know, Bernadette's family was up and waiting.

Q: What happened when you went home?

A: Not too good. I have a big brother. And when I say big, I mean big.... And Johnnie is six-two but he's only 135. He's very skinny and very tall.... My brother just picked him up and told him, "If you ever touch my little sister, I'm going to can your face." And my father also. He said, "You want to die young, don't you?" And my mom and dad — they didn't hit me. They didn't tell me anything. They just said, "You've lost it all. You've lost your reputation. You've lost everything you've worked for." And I said, "Why could I lose it if I didn't do anything?"

Her parents grounded her.

It was the beginning of August and my parents were asleep and he used to get off at 10 from work and he used to go home and wait for my call. And I would call at exactly 10:30 and he would wake up — well, he would get up and get the phone and we would talk till like five in the morning.

But when school started, her parents had to let her leave the house.

And I didn't go to school a lot of times, because I wanted to see him but... I couldn't after school, so we would ditch school — to be together. There was only one class I really ditched, and that was geometry.

Q: I knew it was going to be math.

A: Well, it wasn't so much math. I love math... but it was the class right after lunch.

A series of the dire coincidences that happen so often to teenagers led Bernadette's parents to discover her deception. They gave her a strategically ill-chosen ultimatum: him or us.

And I went and I thought about it for a while and he had already asked me to live with him, and I had told him — you know, "I can't. I'm still in school." And I called him back and I told him, "I'll be there in a minute."

Johnnie's mother was on the lovers' side. (Perhaps she thought having Bernadette in her house might facilitate the liberty her eight children impeded.) She began inquiries about getting custody of Bernadette. Bernadette's parents responded with threats of a private school in a distant state. The pair decided, "they best way to do it is just to get pregnant. They can't touch me."

Almost ten percent of teen mothers say that they and their lovers wanted their pregnancy equally; their pregnancy decisions were intentional, however influenced by circumstances. Most of these girls recalled a childhood and adolescence centered around courting and wedding games. In talking about her relationship with her best friend, for example, Linda, who married at fifteen, said:

We used to play a lot about when we were older. My mom's wedding dress, we used to always try it on and say we were going to get married in it. I got married in it, too. And we used to promise each other, "When you get married, I'll... stand in your wedding, and when I get married, you'll do the same." And she came down for my wedding, too.

These girls forcefully assert a right to teenage motherhood. Pregnancy is a plan they made with their lovers, and it is consonant with their advocacy of children having children. Chicana girls, in particular, argue for a close temporal relation between the generations — and against the concept of adolescent development. Adolescence, they have guessed, it a construct, a notion that seems to them synonymous with a waste of ripe time. They are anxious to be grown. It's not just the freedom of adulthood that lures them: It's the seriousness, responsibility, and prestige. Other girls describe a process in which lovers elicit their agreement to a pregnancy with sweet talk and long-term promises. They resist, they say, but then give in.

Why do boys go to the trouble of talking girls into pregnancy? Don't enough girls get pregnant by chance? There's evidence that boys yearn for the status of fatherhood to make up for low self-esteem caused by school failure. The Children's Defense Fund reports boys with low academic skills are three times more likely to be parents by age eighteen or nineteen than those with average skills — even more likely than girls. This persuasion and bargaining has a long history, of course, and so does girls' surrender. Through sex and pregnancy, girls expect to exchange themselves for men — that is, to get themselves taken up, possessed by a man, and to get a man in return. In this sense — I am borrowing from anthropologist Joyce Canaan here — sex and pregnancy are currencies, subject to rises and falls in the rates of exchanges. Boys set the market, and right now the exchange rate on sex is at a record low; reproduction goes somewhat higher. He gets two for one, in effect. Often this exchange is couched in terms of gifts.

> And he said, "Let's have one." And I go, "But are we ready for it?" And he goes, "Yeah." And we always tried to plan it for his birthday — to come on his birthday.

Girls also claim that once they are pregnant, boys go to extreme lengths to convince them to have their babies. Two-timing, low-down snakes transform into ideal lovers in the first few months of pregnancy. A few continue in that mode: This is really what they want. More begin to act on ambivalence and self-interest, once it seems clear she will have the baby. Bernadette's lover began to see someone else. The boy whose girlfriend planned to have a baby for "his birthday" refused to promise to drive her to the hospital when she went into labor. The Rosen study indicated that while sixty-six percent of teen couples were still "close" when the pregnancy was confirmed; the figure dropped to thirty-three percent after either abortion, miscarriage, or delivery.

When I interviewed teen mothers in their homes, their babies' fathers sometimes turned up for a few minutes. But their brief appearances didn't seem to denote either "relationship" or "support." They flirted and dodged away, often studiedly ignoring the teen mothers' requests for money. Ironic, jiving, these fathers almost seemed to perform for me, but I wasn't sure of their intent. Had they come to charm me? To satisfy their curiosity? Or out of the important self-hatred that generates some forms of reflexive parody: You think I'm a scoundrel? I'll show you a scoundrel!

Pregnancy is a good bet for girls in another sense, though. Girls seldom view their babies — as much commentary on this subject assumes — as big rocks around their necks. You love a guy, maybe he'll love you back, maybe he won't. Maybe he'll keep on loving you. Probably he won't. You love a baby:

> Sometimes she grabs me and hugs me and kisses me and makes me feel really good.

When it's over, a girl has more than she started with. That can't be said about sex without reproduction.

At the same time these girls are trying for love and male (generally) support, they are also negotiating for safer or better deals within their families. These negotiations often backfire. Many parents go berserk when a daughter becomes visibly — not necessarily actively — sexual. It's crucial to recognize this in thinking about parental consent for abortion and contraception and related issues. The histories of girls who maintain they chose pregnancy contain disturbing episodes of parental intrusion — sometimes subtle, sometimes violent — in contraceptive and abortion decisions. Of course, teenagers have a rhetorical practice of blaming adults for their problems; but parents also tell these stories on themselves.

When I asked Angelica, who was seven months pregnant, whether she had ever considered contraception, her mother answered for her:

> Well, that was my fault. [laughs]... She had went to the clinic... and she said she was going to get her some birth control pills. So I said, "Oh no, you're too young for birth control pills." But what she was trying to tell me was, "Mama, I am already having sex. I need the pills." But at the time I didn't understand that. So I told her no, she couldn't have them. So — she ended up pregnant.

Q: How long a period of time was that? Between the first time she brought it up and when you got the pill?

D: I asked you for them earlier, didn't I?

M: Yeah, mmhmm, it was a long time before she got pregnant.

Some parents react calmly at first to the news that a daughter has become sexually active. Then it really hits them and they go nuts. Three months after first intercourse,

long after she broke up with her boyfriend, Terry told her mother she'd had sex.

> She started telling me... "Well, we got to go to the doctor's. See if you're pregnant." And I knew I wasn't, because I did it three months ago, you know, before I told her.... The doctor gave me birth control.... She was all for it until she got home and then she started talking to her boyfriend and her boyfriend told her, you know — I guess he just told her a bunch of stuff to make her say well, she doesn't need it, you know.

That night Terry and her cousin, who had also gone to the clinic, had to bring all their birth control paraphernalia into the living room. Her mother's boyfriend confiscated it:

> And then he went and he took 'em outside and he did somethin' with them. See, and she tore up our cards, and everything for the health center. You know, she was — she really got weird about it.

When Terry became sexually involved again, she didn't tell her mother until she had to — until she was pregnant. Terry clearly meant the moral in this story: she blamed her mother for her pregnancy. I'm with her, except: She didn't give up sex because her mother "got weird." Why did she stop using birth control?

This isn't a fair question, really. Since contraception is not embedded in peer or family culture, it's always more surprising that a girl uses birth control than that she doesn't. Terry had sex again, for example, because she met another guy she liked, and he wanted to, and she wanted to. She didn't use birth control mainly because he didn't ask her to and nobody else brought it up. But there are other reasons why she didn't think of birth control again.

When she was a child, Terry — like many girls — got the idea she was infertile. Possibly she confused her own body with that of her mother, who had a hysterectomy, or misunderstood a comment about having not reached menarche as a diagnosis of infertility. When she managed to have sex for quite a while without getting pregnant, she became convinced that she never would. Secondly, Terry wasn't so much obeying her mother when she surrendered on the birth control issue as resorting to sabotage — saying to her mother: You refused a chance to be a good parent. You refused me the help I needed. You also tried to keep me from pleasure, from adulthood — from what you have — and you let your lousy boyfriend demean me. This is my revenge.

At the same time, Terry's mother may have intended her daughter's pregnancy. Some parents view pregnancy for daughters as they do the army for sons: as remedial training in responsibility. Angelica's mother remarked approvingly: "Since she's got pregnant, she's really matured. She thinks a lot and better than she used to."

My blood turns into Freezone at the thought of family scenes like the one Terry endured, but in comparison with others her story is mild. Not that all these tales are true. When a teenager relates how she hit the streets or moved in with a junkie, she probably feels she'd better come up with a convincing explanation. But under the best of circumstances, family life bears little relation to *The Brady Bunch*.

The dissonance between actual family life and the normative wholesome-family illusion of the Reagan years can make it difficult for individuals to articulate their family experiences — even to themselves. A young mother will talk as though she grew up in a nuclear family, for example, until she finds it impossible to go any further without filling in a few gaps. To explain that her mother's boyfriend molested her, one narrator had to slip in that she had never laid eyes on the wonderful father she'd described earlier — the one with a steady job who was always there for her. She did this without marking the contradiction.

Even the right wing has noticed the gap between profamily rhetoric and everyday life, as its denunciations of drugs, homosexuality, and divorce for "tearing the fabric of the American family apart" signal. To help girls like Terry live good family lives, conservatives would rescind divorce or — Reagan's latest bright idea for welfare — force mothers under 21 years of age to stay with their parents or lose AFDC (he assumes, among many things, that their parents have places to stay). But fathers are not naturally better than stepfathers, and first marriages have as many problems as second and third. What's needed is to cut out the wishful nostalgia about Victorian marriage and the cozy nuclear family and come to terms with the tensions that real families give rise to.

The biggest secret about adolescence and family life is anger. Fights between parents and teenagers have deep psychological as well as everyday causes, scarcity and overcrowding, for example. "My mother wouldn't even give me a plate of food," said one teen mother. Most come up with food as well as every other variety of assistance, but the strain tries their patience. In addition, adolescents and parents experience tensions so new they haven't yet surfaced in public consciousness. Competing in the same sexual marketplace for boyfriends and lovers, for example, exacerbates Oedipal tensions between single mothers and daughters, who often find themselves in deadly states of fury. Among some fundamentalists, puberty is still taken as a biological proof that a girl has gone bad — plenty of excuse for a crackdown. (A study by demographer

Susheela Singh indicates that state adolescent birth rates correlate with the size of the fundamentalist population.)

When domestic violence escalates, girls often take off. Milly moved first to an apartment shared by two guys, both of whom she slept with (which, by her account, she didn't mind) and then to the apartment of a previous lover. His wife resented her presence. Milly didn't seem to understand why, an indication that she still thought of herself as a daughter, not a lover. but when the wife tried to push Milly off the roof, Milly finally moved on.

> From there I just kept on sleeping anywhere I could.... Not nowhere great. Just in the slums.... I used to walk in the street at four o'clock in the morning. I used to be in the streets all alone, walking... where, you know, they had raped and killed girls.

Thinking over what she had told me, Milly reached a conclusion that many girls' histories point to. In the context of their futures — their life options, as the jargon has it — pregnancy constitutes a richer, more workable alternative than most others:

> Come to think of it, I got pregnant as an escape from my family, and plus I wanted somebody, you know, to love and somebody to love me back, and I thought this guy was the right man for me, so I wanted his child, and — mainly those reasons. Those three reasons. So I got pregnant on purpose.

To read the life histories of teenage mothers solely as tragedies is to miss the meaning this material has for them. They regard their pregnancies as fresh starts, second chances, renewals, reforms, awakenings. In the subplot of romance, teenage mothers can present themselves as lovelorn victims but in the broader frame of initiation, they figure as courageous, persistent, and cunning combatants against life's challenges. These are "how I went from there to here" stories. "There" is childhood, which isn't always innocent, but is not fertile. "Here" is motherhood, generally a reform state, but sometimes defiantly, jubilantly transgressive, a liberated zone for sexual adventure and learning. Motherhood, in other words, is almost never depicted as the happy ending portrayed by the teenage actors described earlier, but it doesn't represent the tragedy implied in the family planning version either. Pregnancy is not death.

These narrators have thrown their pitons into the next generation, and they live on the hope that act implies. Pregnancy sometimes gives a girl just what she needs: a reason to live, someone to love and work hard for.

It's one thing to say that teen mothers may be making the best life they can for themselves. But does the luxury of their mothering condemn another generation to the same narrow range of options? Until recently, most literature on teen mothers indicated that teen childbearing entailed severe adverse consequences. Virtually all risks looked higher — from complications in pregnancy and delivery through child abuse. In the past few years a counterpicture has taken shape. The risks of teen childbearing now appear associated more with socioeconomic factors than with age. At the moment, because of the federally supported vogue for pregnant teen and teen mother programs, socioeconomic factors are mitigated in some places by social services, and there's evidence that girls who get that kind of help may do better mothering than older mothers who get no help at all.

Still, most of the teen mothers I've interviewed are not well prepared academically for working lives; their futures — are probably not as bright as they expect on good days. When most of these girls find work, it is on the outer edge of the economy. With meager credentials and fledgling skills, they are the first to be fired, among the last hired, and it's terrifying to think what could happen to them and their babies if social welfare programs were cut further or erode more by inflation. Already the shelters house many teenage girls whose babies have never known another home, and the subtext of hunger in these life histories is chilling.

> I'm not saying she [my mother] has enough room for me and my baby, but I mean, I don't want to leave my mother's house and go somewhere where there's no heat, there's no hot water, we freezing. Because I've been to a girlfriend's house and I say this don't make no sense.... I eat every day."

It doesn't take a wild imagination to envision different outcomes. Suppose Milly hadn't needed to escape from her family, or there'd been somewhere else for her to go, or someone to love who didn't need her pregnancy to lift his self-esteem, or she hadn't needed love so much, or had understood gender relations better. Suppose counseling, housing alternatives, good remedial education, and career guidance. Then how many teenagers would get pregnant? Go to term? Probably about as many as would choose to have their first child after forty if motherhood weren't penalized on the upper rungs of career ladders, and 24-hour child care were a basic social service. The question is: How to go from conditions that lead girls and women to make reproductive decisions in extremis to a reasonable social arrangement?

Obviously, accessible contraception is a basic necessity, like tampons. Girls need them both, and they shouldn't have to ask their parents. But contraception is not enough by a long shot. I am as critical as Dr. Gwendolyn Baker about the singlemindedness of the school health clinic approach. It's not genocide, as she has charged, but it is inhumane to pour money into family planning clinics while ignoring other needs. And it isn't smart.

Dispensing or prescribing contraception through schools will reduce the number of girls in school who get pregnant but make no difference at all to the many girls outside the easy reach of the school system.

What will reach these girls? When the Perry Pre-School study results — indicating that enriched preschool reduced truancy, drug use, pregnancy, and crime — were first published in 1984, family planning veterans joked that short of making a revolution, they might as well forget about girls over age five. The evidence made the cynical joke a realistic assessment. At that time, enriched preschool reduced teen pregnancy more successfully than any family planning program. Now there's little question that girls in good enough shape to stay in school can benefit from contraceptive services, but reaching truants and dropouts is far more difficult.

For girls to genuinely choose their lives, they first need to feel that they have a chance — and this means they really have to have one. A revolution wouldn't hurt. The evidence is increasing — thanks to institutional shifts in research goals — that social and economic conditions are crucial factors in teenage pregnancy decisions. School desegregation, for example, lowers teenage birth rates, and the Singh report shows significantly high teenage pregnancy rates among the urban poor. Racism and poverty are the long-range targets, then.

In the shorter term, education is both the best indicator of who needs help—and the best cure. Low-income students with basic-skills deficits get lost on the assembly line when teacher-student ratios are too high. They key is to pay attention to students at the first sign they are troubled. Dropout prevention programs are fine as far as they go, but as Janet Price, director of Advocates for Children's High School Project, argues, they aren't sufficient.

Teenagers need alternative places to live that don't have shelter limits or operate like miniprisons or religious indoctrination centers. They also need chances to see the world beyond their block, school, and family and to talk in groups about their lives. (To hear spokespeople from the Center for Population Options tell it, comprehensive health clinics are the ideal locale for talk like that, but a little medicalization goes a long way, as feminist analysis has proven.)

Consciousness-raising, counseling, field trips: It's not an original program, but it would be incredibly original to implement and fund it decently — not on cheap PR "model" basis but citywide, for boys as well as girls. One of the many ironies in the teenage situation is that there's almost nothing for teens who haven't become a social problem — yet. The few community-based projects for adolescents who aren't addicted to drugs or pregnant — e.g., Youth Action Program, the LOFT (Leadership Organization For Teens), the Door, the Institute for the Protection of Lesbian & Gay Youth operate on shoestrings so ragged they wouldn't hold on a Reebok. In a city with educational fiscal practices that would make Dickens' Wackford Squeers blanch, it's hard to imagine much public money for programs like those. But how about cutting a deal with population and family planning interests on school health clinics: Make them match every clinic dollar with one for community youth work and counseling. If they care as much about teenage girls and boys as they claim, let them put their money where their mouths are.

Adoption

♦

A MARKET FOR BABIES
J. Robert S. Prichard

INTRODUCTION

The market is perhaps the most commonly used mechanism for allocating scarce resources. As an allocative mechanism it has many attractive features which permit it to predominate over other systems such as bureaucracies, regulatory agencies, lotteries, juries, queues, and the like. But despite its predominance, the market is far from universal in its use. As a result, an important aspect of economic analysis is to examine the characteristics of situations in which the market is not used as the primary allocative device in order to illuminate the limits and implications of the market as an allocative mechanism.

From J. Robert S. Prichard, "A Market for Babies," *University of Toronto L.J.* 34 (1984), pp. 341–57 (edited).

This essay addresses that task in the context of family law. In particular, I examine the reasons why we are reluctant to use a market mechanism in place of existing bureaucratic procedures for the adoption of newborn babies. The purpose of the essay is to understand the limits of the market rather than to promote its use. However, I pursue the topic by first detailing the affirmative case for a market in babies and then examining its deficiencies. My intention is to use the specific case as a vehicle for a more general understanding of the limits of market mechanisms and concepts in family law and related areas, thus contributing perspective to this symposium issue on the economic analysis of family law.

In proceeding in this way I run the risk of being misunderstood as advocating a market mechanism for allocating newborn babies. The opposite is true. My primary motivation in writing this essay has been a desire to reconcile my intuitive opposition to such a system (opposition which I assume is widely, if not universally, shared) with the analytical methods of economic analysis of law. Indeed, the purpose runs deeper, extending to the vitality of economic analysis of law. For if economic analysis is to remain a vital and creative role within legal scholarship, its limits must be explored as vigorously as its strengths.

The results of the existing regulatory system governing the allocation and adoption of newborn children are in many respects tragic. At present in Canada and the United States many people unable to have children naturally want to adopt, but there are far too few newborn children to meet the demand, leaving many couples deprived of the privileges and joys of childrearing. In addition, the existing regulatory procedures allocating these scarce newborns subject childless couples to very substantial costs.

The evidence of the tragedy is ubiquitous. Local, national, and international observations confirm the point. For example, in at last one region in southern Ontario the local Children's Aid Society has simply closed its intake desk because there is already such a backlog of approved applicant couples that it would be useless to process any further applications. In metropolitan Toronto, there is an enormous disparity between the number of couples seeking to adopt a child and the available supply. The current situation in Toronto involves a minimum wait of one and a half to two years for a childless couple after they first contact the Children's Aid Society. Furthermore, although some couples do receive a child within two years, many wait much longer. In other parts of the province, the wait is now approximately ten years. Similarly, in 1980 in Vancouver there were thirty newborn children available for adoption, while one thousand couples were approved and ready to receive an adopted child.

The evidence of the tragedy can also be found in increasing evidence of black market activity in the sale of babies. News reports from Vancouver, Toronto, and the United States are unanimous in reporting increasing black market activity characterized by very high prices for newborns (as much as $40,000) but continued interest on the part of childless couples. However, these reports also suggest that most of the economic rewards derived from these transactions are being gathered by the physicians and the lawyers involved in arranging them and not by the mothers who bear the children.

The reasons for the shortage are simple. The supply of newborns has decreased dramatically primarily as a result of the increased availability of contraceptive devices and legal abortions. A statistic indicative of the change in availability of newborns can be found in metropolitan Toronto. In 1969, the Protestant Children's Aid Society placed approximately 1,000 children, while in 1979 it placed only 179 children of which only 71 were less than one year old.

The consequences of this very substantial undersupply of adoptable babies are varied. The primary effect is that many couples who desire children are left childless. While accurate statistical information is not available, it has been estimated that up to six percent of couples who desire children are unable to have them naturally. Given the existing short supply of babies, the magnitude of the social tragedy from the perspective of childless couples is readily apparent. The other consequences are somewhat less obvious. Childless couples are tempted to use fertility drugs and other fertility increasing treatments which necessarily increase the risk of children being born with various kinds of infirmities. Couples are also tempted to have children naturally even in circumstances where genetic counseling indicates they should not, since the alternative of adoption is so unavailable. On the supply side, there is no incentive for mothers to give up their newborns since at present those who do so are not remunerated in any way for their children. As a result the decision that the child is unwanted is often delayed for a year or two until the opportunities for and desirability of adoption are substantially decreased. Furthermore, the pregnant woman who plans to give up her child is under no economic incentive to care for her child while it is *in utero* since no reward is paid for producing a well cared for child. Thus, injury-reducing abstinence such as foregoing smoking and

drinking is not economically encouraged by the present system.

In Ontario the present scheme of regulation is created by the Child Welfare Act. This statute creates a virtual monopoly in the adoption business for certain licensed agencies, although it does permit individually licensed adoptions under restrictive conditions. Under the statute, the Children's Aid Societies which are the primary agencies charged with adoption regulation must screen and approve prospective adopting couples. Once a couple is approved, they join a queue formed at a central registry in each geographic district in the province. When a newborn becomes available, three couples who might be appropriate parents for the child are selected administratively. Then the socialworker assigned to each couple engages in an advocacy process within the agency to determine which of the three couples should succeed. As a general rule, there is an attempt to match the educational backgrounds and economic circumstances of the couples and the natural mother. In addition, subject to the best interests of the child, an attempt is made to respect the desires of the natural mother as to the type of home environment she wishes for her child.

One's ability to qualify or even be screened by a Children's Aid Society is determined by the geographic location of one's residence. Thus, in order to qualify for metropolitan Toronto's Children's Aid Society, a couple must maintain a residence in metropolitan Toronto. Since some districts in Ontario have considerably shorter waiting lists than others, an incentive is created to maintain a second residence in a district with a shorter list merely to qualify for an adoption. It has thus been reported that couples from districts outside Toronto where the intakes are closed or very limited maintain apartments for a period of years in Toronto in order to qualify for Metro's Children's Aid Society.

In addition to creating this regulatory scheme, section 67 of the Child Welfare Act provides that "no person, whether before or after the birth of a child, shall make, give or receive or agree to make, give or receive a payment or reward for or in consideration of or in relation to" an adoption or a proposed adoption. As a result, market transactions in babies are strictly prohibited.

Similar administrative and regulatory schemes are in place across Canada. Their details vary substantially but their essential characteristic — administrative allocation — remains constant. A clear alternative would be a market-oriented system in which babies would be allocated to couples based on the prices the couples were prepared to pay. In the section which follows, the possible advantages of such a mechanism are set out.

At first blush the market mechanism might seem to be considerably more attractive than the existing regulatory scheme in that it appears to be able to make most people better off. The reasons are numerous.

First, one would anticipate an increase in the quantity of babies supplied in order to meet the demand, thus eliminating the present queue and satisfying the desires of virtually all the childless couples left unsatisfied by the present system and shortage. Women would engage in the production of children for adoption, responding to the financial incentives of the marketplace.

Second, one would anticipate that the market would lead to the realization of comparative productive advantages in that the supply of newborns would be undertaken by those best able to produce, satisfying the needs of those unable to have children and providing a realistic alternative for those for whom childbirth is possible but genetically unwise. Furthermore, one might anticipate some substitution of producers with relatively low opportunity costs for those with high opportunity costs. That is, persons for whom pregnancy comes only at the cost of substantial disruption of their other activities (for example, employment) might well decline to carry a child, opting to purchase a baby from a substitute carrier whose opportunity costs would be lower. This effect would be limited, of course, by the extent to which mothers derived positive utility (and paid maternity leave) from carrying their own children and by the extent to which parents preferred natural to purchased children.

Third, one would anticipate that the market would generate information about the pedigrees of newborns which would permit the matching of couples' desires and the newborns' attributes. One would anticipate that there would be an incentive to disclose the quality of the newborns and that information certification procedures and agencies would develop to enhance the information market.

Fourth, one would expect the newborns to be of a higher quality than the existing newborns available for adoption. The promise of remuneration for prospective mothers would lead to an incentive for the appropriate care of children *in utero* since a warranty of such behavior would attract a positive reward in the marketplace. In addition, one would anticipate that prospective mothers would exercise greater care in the selection of their sexual mates since the quality of the mate would also influence the price to be obtained upon birth.

Fifth, one would expect an extremely competitive market structure. There would be extremely low entry barriers, a very large number of producers, both actual and potential, slight economies of scale, and enormous difficulties in cartelization. While there might be some brand name identification over time, one would not anticipate that this would lead to significant barriers to entry.

Sixth, the market process would provide an incentive for parents to correct errors in judgment and shortcomings in contraceptives devices since they would be in a position to sell the child for a positive reward rather than simply give it away. This should reduce the number of foster children since the market for newborns would create an incentive to make the disposal at the time of birth. At the same time, however, reducing the cost of errors in judgment and inadequate contraceptive techniques and devices might lead to a corresponding decrease in the care exercised by sexually active friends and couples.

Seventh, one would expect the market to produce the children at a relatively low cost and certainly a cost much below the existing black market prices. The market would be free from the costs of hiding transactions from law enforcement officials, from substantial legal penalties, and from fraudulent practices and the like, which at present permeate the black market. Furthermore, one would anticipate that the suppliers of the children would get a substantial portion of the economic return and that lawyers and physicians would be in a less strong position to take advantage of their clients and patients. With respect to price, one would anticipate that it would approximate the opportunity cost of a woman's time during pregnancy. It should be stressed that this need not by any means equal the amount of compensation that a person would earn in other market activities for the full nine months since pregnancy is far from totally disabling. Therefore, it would not be surprising if a price as low as $3,000 to $5,000 per child were common in some segments of the market.

Eighth, the market could develop various efficiency enhancing mechanisms. In particular, one might anticipate that a futures market would develop in which children *in utero* could be traded, permitting the reallocation of the risks inherent in childbirth so as to better reflect the various tastes for risks of different participants in the market. Furthermore, one might imagine that market intermediaries might form so as to hold portfolios of children *in utero,* thus diversifying and reducing the non-systematic risk.

Ninth, on the distributive side, the market would be likely to display qualities considerably more attractive than the existing system. One would expect that the producers would be persons with relatively low opportunity costs who at present have very limited opportunities for income earning activities. This would present a new source of productive activity at a reasonable level of reward. Furthermore, one could anticipate that this would result in some shift of wealth away from the purchasers of babies to the producers, who would presumably be from less advantaged circumstances. In addition, the distributive effects of devoting some of the economic returns to the mothers and taking it away from those at present able to exploit the illegality of the black market would surely be attractive.

In sum, quite a robust case for the market can be made. It would appear to work well. It would satisfy a lot of unsatisfied people, have attractive distributive results, and increase the degree of individual freedom and choice in the adoption process as the monopolistic regulatory powers at present enjoyed by the Children's Aid Societies would be eliminated.

Despite these attractions, and despite the inadequacies of the present system, most would find the prospect of a market for babies to be grotesque. Indeed, the mere description has a ring of parody to it as the incongruity of market notions and babies jars the reader. Somewhere within most of us there is at least an intuitive reaction that there is something indecent about the prospect of a market for babies. The prospect of prices, contracts, advertising, credit, discounts, specials, and all the other attributes of consumer transactions seems disquieting. But when asked for an explanation for this reaction, can one do better than simply assert its unacceptability? In what follows, I consider a number of possible objections.

There are three categories of objections to relying on a market mechanism. The first might be termed market failure concerns. Here the argument meets the proposal on its own terms, not objecting to the market in principle but stressing that the market would not work well in this particular context. The second category of objections concedes that the market would work essentially as I have suggested, but that, as a market mechanism, is would possess one or more objectionable characteristics which cause us to reject the mechanism as a whole. The third category of objections attacks the entire proposal, not just its market aspects, arguing that it fails in its essential conception.

The first line of reaction to the proposal for a baby market it to meet it on its own terms. That is, a critic might ask whether or not this is a situation in which the market would in fact produce optimal results even if the other categories of objections canvassed below are found unpersuasive. A number of doubts might be raised.

First, there is the problem that "good" babies may drive out the "bad." At present, given the shortage of babies, childless couples are prepared to adopt children who are available although, in the eyes of the adopting parents, less than perfect. If the market proposal were adopted, the supply of children with highly desired characteristics would increase and the demand for other children would diminish. This would presumably increase the number of unadopted children suffering from retardation, birth defects, and other undesired characteristics who would subsequently become foster children. This would presumably reduce the level of welfare of both these children and society in general and must be counted as a substantial negative effect of the market proposal.

Second, there may be some significant information imperfections in the proposed market. While the market mechanism would encourage the disclosure of information concerning the newborns, there would, of course, be an incentive for mothers to disclose the good information and withhold the bad. To the extent that lies and inadequate disclosure cannot be discovered until after the transaction has taken place, a "market for lemons" problem may arise. In some ways this is analogous to concerns about the commercialization of blood donations. It is alleged that a market mechanism for blood donation increases the percentage of donors carrying hepatitis since the donors have a positive incentive to conceal their knowledge that they have had the disease, an incentive not present in a system of collection based on gifts. However, it must be recognized that the continued existence of this phenomenon depends on the absence of a relatively low cost means of screening potential donors for hepatitis. Similarly, the extent to which the "lemon" phenomenon would infect the baby market depends on the possibility and cost of tests designed to verify pedigree information proffered by the mother. Furthermore, since the purchase of a baby is a much more substantial purchase than the purchase of a pint of blood, the costs that a prospective purchaser would rationally be prepared to bear in screening the donor would be proportionately increased. Thus, while there is undoubtedly a potential problem of information deficiency, its magnitude may not be overwhelming and may diminish with further scientific and technological advances.

A third concern with the market solution may be that it would generate a higher total population since one would anticipate there would be some increase in the supply of newborns. It might be argued that this population increase is an externality which the individual market decisions would fail to recognize, leading to what in social terms may be an oversupply of babies. While it is certainly true that the population should increase with the adoption of this proposal, it is enormously difficult to make any judgment as to whether this is a good or bad thing, and even if it is a bad thing whether or not that is cause to reject the proposal. If there is a concern with the total level of baby production, there is a wide range of existing social policies which create financial incentives and disincentives for the production of children. It would seem more appropriate to control the overall level of population through these mechanisms rather than through depriving some small segment of the community of the ability to experience the joys of raising a family. If society must bear a burden with respect to the control of population, it would seem only just that this burden be spread relatively equally across the population.

The fourth concern relates to the possibility that this scheme might permit or indeed encourage genetic breeding in that people would be able to "order" the baby they desire as opposed to merely relying on the genetic lottery that natural parents face. While hypothetically plausible, it does not seem probable in reality that there would be serious breeding effects. While some couples may favor blue-eyed, blond-haired boys and others dark-haired girls, no one set of tastes is likely to dominate, for the same reason that no particular color or make of car seems to capture universal approval. One would anticipate a full range of tastes with respect to children's characteristics as with other commodities, and so while there should be a better matching of couples' preferences with the children they would actually receive through the market, the total distribution of children by type should remain relatively unchanged.

A fifth concern expressed by some critics is that permitting a market in newborns might also encourage a market in "used" children as people would be tempted to "trade in" unsatisfactory children and 'trade up' by purchasing a newborn. If the state did not regulate parental obligations with regard to child support, this concern would no doubt be realized. However, under the market for babies proposal, once a couple has purchased a child they could be required to assume the same obligations, liabilities, and responsibilities that accrue to couples who now adopt children or have children naturally. To the extent there is a trade-in phenomenon at present, it would be continued, but it seems unlikely that it would be substantially increased. Indeed, one might deny entry to the market to any couple who traded in their child if this were thought to be a serious social problem so as to eliminate that couple's access to the market for a second purchase.

A common critique of market oriented solutions relates to their distributive consequences. That is, the typical critic will concede that the market would be efficient, but then stress that its impact on the distribution of wealth would be so unacceptable that the efficiency advantages should fade into insignificance. In essence, the distributive consequences are said to be so strong as to dominate any possible efficiency gains. Is that concern well founded with respect to a proposal for a market for babies? Some might argue that the effect of such a market would be that some people would be so impoverished by having paid for their baby that they would be unable to provide sufficiently high quality care for the child. This seems implausible. It would appear to assume an extremely high price for children, an assumption which would ignore the realities of the low opportunity cost of likely mothers. Furthermore, it ignores the costs incurred by persons attempting to manipulate the existing regulatory system, whether by maintaining a second residence or by spending money to impress socialworkers as to their ability to provide a comfortable home environment for the child. In addition, it ignores the cost of childbirth most natural parents go through. The opportunity costs incurred by most natural parents would not be substantially less than the market price I would anticipate for a child under the market system. In sum, this concern built around the cost of the child seems unpersuasive.

An alternative formulation of the distributive concern is that the rich would get all the "good" babies. In response it should first be noticed that the objection seems to assume that this does not happen already, thus ignoring the reality that one's income and wealth are generally thought by adoption agencies to be important variables in determining one's suitability for parenthood. The objection also seems to ignore the prospect of an increased supply of "good" babies which one would anticipate under the market system. That is, if supply were held fixed, the concern might be persuasive in that the rich would presumably be better able to pay in order to satisfy their desires for children with characteristics found most desirable by adopting parents. However, under the market system the supply of such children would presumably be dramatically increased, leaving the rich with what they want but also leaving many others fully satisfied. Again, the objection seems unpersuasive.

Any arguments as to distributive effects of the proposal must also be counterbalanced by the distributive effect identified earlier of a shift in rents to the suppliers of children, that is, mothers, who would be drawn from a generally poorer class and away from the crooks, shady lawyers, shady physicians, and others who at present trade on the tragedy of the existing regulatory failure and the fears of pregnant women.

One way of testing whether the issue of the distributive impact of the market proposal goes to the core of one's objection to it is to ask whether one would feel better about the proposal if the market were made wealth neutral as opposed to wealth sensitive. If not, then distributive arguments are probably not the central source of one's intuitive opposition to the proposal.

COST OF COSTING

Another principled objection to the market focuses on one of its inevitable aspects: the creation of prices. The concern is that a market for babies would generate negative secondary consequences as a result of the fact that a market mechanism by definition generates explicit prices. In particular, the pricing of babies might violate two principles, each of which we hold dear. The first is that life is infinitely valuable — "a pearl beyond price." With prices of $3,000 per baby, the reality of the limited price of life (at least at the point of creation) and the ideal of the infinitely valuable would contrast starkly. The second principle is that all lives are equally valuable. With higher prices for white than non-white children, and higher prices for healthy than sick children, and other similar forms of price differentials, the reality and the ideal would again clash.

The concern here is real but difficult to evaluate. It is but one example of a much more general problem of public policy. Whenever life is at stake the difficulties of pricing and of costing must be faced. Thus, whether it is the standard of care in tort law, the design of a Pinto, highway design, or medical research one cannot avoid implicitly or explicitly dealing with the price of life. Perhaps it is the degree of explicitness that would be inherent in this scheme that gives rise to the vigor of the opposition. It may also be that the differences in prices would correspond with differences which we strive particularly hard to overcome by means of other social policies. That is, to the extent that differences in price fell along racial grounds, to adopt a policy of a market for babies would be directly contradictory to the wide range of social policies designed to minimize discrimination on racial grounds.

COMMODIFICATION

While related to the previous concern regarding the costs of costing, the concern here is that trading in certain commodities degrades the commodities themselves. That is, certain things should be above the hustle and bustle of the marketplace so as to preserve their dignity, leading to the conclusion that trading in such commodities is inherently bad. That is, by creating a market one would commodify something — life — which should not be treated as a commodity. Put even more strongly, the concern is that the special value we attribute to children depends in part on the fact they cannot be traded. Thus, trafficking in lives becomes presumptively bad. There is a dynamic dimension to this concern as well, since trading activity would alter our view regarding the nature of the commodity at stake, reducing over time our aversion to engaging in this form of trade.

Again, the difficulty in evaluating this concern is that it is hard to know which goods fall within this category of goods that should not be commodified. Trading in babies is not directly analogous to slavery. Is it more closely analogous to long-term contracts for services? If so, why do we not have the same sense of concern about the multiyear contracts of professional athletes as we do about a market for babies?

In addition, in the midst of whatever reactions one has along this line or some of the earlier lines of objection, it is important that they not be treated in isolation from some of the compensating effects of the market proposal. That is, unless these concerns are made absolutes they must be considered in the context of a probable substantial reduction in the number of abortions performed and of the very substantial increase in happiness for previously childless couples. How these compensating effects should be weighted in the balance is unclear, but absent the most extreme forms of rejection of the utilitarian calculus some consideration must be given to them.

OPPRESSION

Put bluntly, the proposal for a market for babies smacks of slavery. More broadly, the concern is that such a scheme would oppressively and involuntarily relegate poor women to an occupation which we do not wish to promote (or be seen to promote) and which would deprive the participants of their dignity. This concern may be similar to concerns about prostitution, wet nurses, and markets for blood. However, it is not entirely clear what makes this matter oppressive when other lines of poorly paid work are seen to be less so. If the concern is simply that wages will be low, regulatory intervention is possible. If the concern is that this type of production takes advantage of women's low opportunity cost, the response must be to recognize the truth of that proposition but to ask how this differs from any other situation of employing someone with a low opportunity cost. If it is a concern for the nature of the work, what is it about childbearing that makes it somehow dishonorable when done for money but most honorable when done for other reasons? Why does paying for childbirth or engaging in childbearing for the sake of money convert a dignified activity into a despised one? The answer must lie in one of the other concerns, for example, commodification rather than in oppression per se. That is, we may object to the commodification of sex (prostitution), blood donation, or mothers' milk production (wet nurses) not only because of the low opportunity cost, but because of the combining of low opportunity cost with an opportunity to engage in market activity in an area where commodification itself is objectionable.

At the same time it is not entirely clear exactly what the focus of the concern is in this respect. Some would argue that it is women who are being oppressed, but others might argue that it is the newborns who are being oppressed. One way to test this proposition might be to ask whether the concern would be the same if the market were in test-tube babies, so as to relieve any concern about a class of women being oppressed. If the concern remains, it seems that it must be broader than merely the oppression of women.

JONATHAN SWIFT'S MODEST PROPOSAL

Swift's satirical solution to the problem of starvation in Ireland may be thought to be analogous to the market for babies proposal. One need not do more than read Swift's proposal in order to be confident of its unacceptability; it is a classic satire. Thus, if the analogy is compelling, one must dismiss a market for babies with similar dispatch. However, to draw the analogy between the two proposals one must find the essence of each to be the *marketing* of babies, thus giving less weight to the distinction between killing and giving life to babies. To me this is not an entirely satisfactory characterization of the two proposals. It fails to distinguish between the giving of life and the taking of life. That is, the Swift proposal depends on terminating a life after its successful creation. That would appear to be so fundamentally in contradiction with the right to life, which is accepted by essentially everyone to be above any utilitarian calculus, that any set of potential benefits becomes irrelevant to the merits of the proposal. However, in the case of a market for babies there is no deprivation of life but rather the creation of new life, and it is only possible objections to this creation of new life that must be offset against the obvious benefits of the scheme. At this point it is more difficult to identify any absolute right equivalent to that of preserving life that would be violated by creating more life.

I end where I started, focusing on the limits of markets by asking whether these objections to a market for babies are persuasive. To the extent that they are, they may help define the limits of markets in other situations requiring an allocative device.

◆

WHERE DO BLACK CHILDREN BELONG?
THE POLITICS OF RACE-MATCHING IN ADOPTION
Elizabeth Bartholet

EARLY FRAGMENTS FROM ONE TRANS-RACIAL ADOPTION STORY[1]

When I first walked into the world of adoption, I was stunned by the dominant role that race played in it. I had thought I understood something about the meaning of race in our society: my life's work as a lawyer had largely involved dealing with issues of racial discrimination. But I discovered that race plays a unique role in the adoption world. It is central to many people's thinking about parenting and a key organizing principle for the agencies authorized to construct adoptive families.

As a single parent of a child from an early marriage, I had decided that I wanted more children, and that I wanted to adopt. My journey took me through the process of considering adoption in this country and abroad. I decided to adopt a child from South America. At one point I was planning to adopt from Brazil, but the Brazilian program closed down just as I reached the top of the list. I had long considered adopting from Peru, sparked by stories from a childhood friend of visits to the "lost city of the Incas." But I had been discouraged by the difficulties of a Peruvian adoption. Nevertheless, when Brazil fell through I picked up the telephone and called a lawyer in Lima, Peru. "Come," she said, "I have the baby for you." A week later I flew to Lima, and that same day met Christopher, my first adopted child. Two and a half years later I returned to adopt Michael.

Early in the process of exploring how I might adopt, I discovered that the first order of business for the agencies responsible for matching children and parents is

---

1. This article is based upon a review of the relevant literature and case law, my own experience as a consultant on adoption issues and as an adoptive parent, and a series of interviews — some by telephone, some in person — with dozens of adoption professionals, students of the adoption system, and related experts (including both critics and supporters of current racial matching policies). For a version of this article that contains specific references to my sources, see "Where Do Black Children Belong?", *University of Pennsylvania Law Review* 139, p. 1163, 1991. Another version of this article will appear in my forthcoming book, tentatively titled *Children By Choice* (Houghton Mifflin), which deals with adoption, reproductive technology, and surrogacy.

From Elizabeth Bartholet, "Where Do Black Children Belong? The Politics Of Race-Matching," in *Adoption,* vol. 1, no. 4, *Reconstruction,* 51, 1992.

to sort and allocate by race. The public and most of the traditional private adoption agencies would not consider assigning a waiting minority child to me, a white person, except as a last resort, and perhaps not even then. The organizations and individual entrepreneurs that arrange independent adoptions, while more willing to place across racial lines, also sorted children by race. In this part of the adoption world, minority children might actually be easier for the white prospective parent to find than a white child, and they were often available for a lesser fee.

I also discovered how dominant race was in the thinking of many prospective adoptive parents. The large majority of people actively looking to adopt in this country are white, and for the most part they want white children, at least initially.

The familiar refrain that there are no children available for adoption is a reflection of the racial policies of many adoption agencies and the racial preferences of many adoptive parents. The reality is that there are very few *white* children compared to the large pool of would-be white adopters. But there are many *non-white* children available to this pool, both through independent adoption in this country and through international adoption. And there are many non-white children waiting in foster care who are unavailable solely because of adoption agency insistence that they not be placed trans-racially.

Racial thinking dominates the world of international adoption as well. When I began to explore the possibility of adopting from South America, I was intrigued by my agency's Brazilian adoption program. Brazil allowed singles to adopt and allowed people my age to adopt infants. Babies were available for placement immediately upon birth. I would only have to spend a week to ten days there to complete

the legal procedures and could then return to the United States with my baby. And there was no waiting list. I could expect to have my baby within a few months of completing the adoption agency "home study" that is required for an international adoption. Given the difficulties that a forty-five-year-old single person faces in other countries, this all seemed unbelievable. The explanation was, of course, race. Much of Brazil's population is of African descent. The children available for adoption from this Brazilian program were part black. This put the program low on the desirability list for many prospective parents despite all its attractive features. Chile, by contrast, is considered a highly desirable country because its population is mainly white. There are sufficiently few dark-skinned minorities that even the children of the poor — the children most likely to be available for adoption — tend to be white. The Latin American countries with significant Indian or mestizo but limited black populations generally fall between Chile and Brazil on the scale of desirability because the adoption market rates Indian as lower than white but higher than black.

I discovered during my two adoption trips to Peru how children may be rated in racial terms in their own country as well as here. Most of the children available for adoption in Peru are of mixed Indian and Spanish heritage. But there is tremendous variety in ethnic features and skin color. For my second adoption, I was offered by the government adoption agency an unusually white, one-month-old baby. My initial reaction upon meeting him was disappointment that he did not look like my first child from Peru. Christopher's brown-skinned face with its Indian features had become the quintessence of what a child — my child — should look like. But I decided that it was foolish to look for another baby-Christopher, as I had decided years earlier that it would be foolish to look for a clone of my biological son. I took this baby home and named him Michael. Within twenty-four hours I found myself tearing through the streets in a taxi, mopping his feverish body with a wet cloth. As I saw his eyes lose contact with mine and begin to stare off into the middle distance, I became terrified that he would die in my arms before we got to the hospital emergency room. At the hospital he was wrapped in a wet towel and his feet were placed in a pan of ice water. I watched the puzzled but surprisingly cheerful little face that peered out from the monkish hood the towel formed about his head while we waited for two hours as his temperature slowly cooled. Sometime during that taxi ride, or in that hospital room, I became hopelessly attached.

Several weeks later I sat with a blanketed Michael in my arms in the office of one of Lima's fanciest pediatricians. Michael had recovered from the fever but had been suffering from nausea and diarrhea almost every since. He had been living on a water and mineral mixture for a large part of this time. Although it protected him from dehydration, it provided no nutrition. He had kept no milk down for five days. I had been to three different doctors in three weeks; none seemed to have any idea what to do. I told the pediatrician the story of Michael's troubles, trying with my words and tone to convey my sense of desperation. The doctor sat impassively, interrupting me only when my three-year-old Christopher wandered over to the bookshelves. Pointing with apparent disgust, as if some small and dirty animal had invaded his office, the doctor asked, "What is he?" I thought the question truly peculiar and the answer rather obvious, but explained that this was my son. At the end

of my story, the doctor, who had still made no move to look at Michael, proceeded to tell me that he could get me another child in a way that would avoid all the troublesome procedures of a Peruvian adoption. Women were giving birth in his hospital all the time who would not keep their babies. He could have the birth certificate for one of these babies made out showing me as the mother and the baby would be mine.

When I finally realized that this hospital baby was being suggested as a substitute for the one on my lap, I said in what I hoped was a polite but firm tone that I planned to keep this child and that I was here because I was afraid the child was seriously ill. I asked if the doctor could please now examine the child. He then shrugged his shoulders and showed me into the examining room.

I put Michael on the table and started to undress him, and for the first time the doctor looked at him. "Oh. I see. I understand. What an extraordinary child." He gave me what was meant to be a knowing look and kept exclaiming his surprise as he continued Michael's physical. "Entirely white," he said. "Not even any Mongolian spots..." (the spots that nonwhite children often have on their backsides in early life). It was overwhelmingly clear that Michael's value had been transformed in the doctor's eyes by his whiteness. Whiteness made it comprehensible that someone would want to cure and keep this child rather than discard him.

Michael got well (although with no help from this particular doctor), and turned out to have nothing more serious than an allergy to cow's milk. But his whiteness proved troubling for the rest of our stay in Lima. I was told by advisers wise in the ways of Peruvian adoptions that his unusual whiteness made him so desirable that I would have to guard against losing him to other adoptive parents or to lawyers hungry for the high fees that he would bring. I was advised to keep him hidden in my apartment so that his whiteness would not become widely known. Thus, when required to take him to the various police and medical examinations and court appearances that are part of the adoption process in Lima, I kept his face covered with a blanket at all times. When dealing with people who had seen him, or might know what he looked like, I talked constantly of how frail and ill he had been since birth, hoping thereby to discount the value of his whiteness.

Through the process of creating my adoptive family, I learned more about my own feelings about race. Adoption compels this kind of learning. You don't just get at the end of one general child line when you're doing adoption. There are several lines, each identified by the race, disability, or age of the children available, together with the length of wait and the difficulty and cost of adoption. In choosing which line to join, I had to think about race on a level that was new to me. I had to try to confront without distortion the reality of parenting someone of another race because the child and I would have to live that reality. I had to decide whether or not I wanted a child who was a racial look-alike. And I had to think about whether it would be racist to look for a same-race child or racist to look for a child of another race, as I was learning that a black socialworkers' organization opposed trans-racial adoption, calling it a form of racial genocide. When I decided on an international adoption, I had to choose which country's line to stand in, and a part of that choice was thinking whether I had particularly positive — or negative — feelings about the prospect of parenting a child of any given racial or ethnic group and musing about whether it was offensive or entirely all right to be engaged in this kind of thinking.

When I finally did adopt, I began life anew as part of a Peruvian-American family, part of a brown-skin/white-skin, Indian-Caucasian mix of a family.

Returning with Christopher from my first Peruvian adoption, we emerge from the airplane in New York City to make our way through customs and immigration. There are signs directing United States citizens to one line and aliens to another. I start toward the line for citizens conscious of finally being back in the land where I belong. I then realize that since the child I am carrying is a legal alien, he and I must join that other line, the one for those who don't belong.

After a few weeks back in the States, I find myself startled on a trip to the supermarket by a stranger's question — "Where did he come from?" I'm genuinely puzzled as to why this person would think that Christopher came from some place other than me — as to why adoption would be immediately assumed. It's as if I have to be educated to see how blatant are the physical differences that others see — his brown skin, black eyes, and straight thick black hair, and my fair skin, blue eyes, and frizzy blond-brown hair. As I push Christopher through the streets in his stroller, I am struck by the appearance of other people's children — they are pale, anemic-looking creatures, with strangely bald heads. The brown-skinned beauty who splashes in my bathtub every night has become, for me, the norm.

As the months go by I begin to hear troubling comments. "Oh, he's from Peru. I didn't know they came that dark there.... But he really seems to be doing very nicely." I realize that I need to develop responses for the things people will say to and about him. I worry about the preponderance of blue-eyed, white skinned children at his child care center and wonder what I can do about it. I listen with new ears to a familiar discussion of affirmative action, this one by members of the child care center's parent body. I hear proponents of "affirmative action" argue that there should be at least one minority child in each class, talking of how the other children will benefit from the minority child's presence, and I am angered by their blindness to the minority child's needs and by their condescending tone. I attend minority-parent support group meetings and learn something of the problems that children of color face as they advance into the grades at the school that my biological child attended and to which I plan to send Christopher.

And then one day, when Christopher is three and a half, he says to me across the dinner table, "I wish you looked like me." I respond, wanting not to understand him, "What do you mean?" And he says, "I wish you were the same color." I try to reassure him, telling him that it makes no difference to me that he and I look different — in fact I like it that way. But my comments seem not to convince him. He repeats that he wishes I looked like him, and his voice and eyes reveal his pain.

I am left to puzzle at the meaning of this pain. Is it one of a thousand pains that a child will experience as he discovers differences between himself and others — in this case a difference between himself and his friends who have same-race parents? Is it, as the opponents of trans-racial adoption would have us believe, the first manifestation of a permanent anguish stemming from the sense that he does not truly belong in the place where he should most surely belong — his family? Or

should I simply take it as a signal that living as part of a multiracial, multiethnic, multicultural family will force us to confront the meaning of racial and other differences on a regular basis?

This child is as inside my skin as any child could be. It feels entirely right that he should be there. Yet the powers that be in today's adoption world proclaim with near unanimity that race-mixing in the context of adoption should be avoided if at all possible, at least where black or brown-skinned American children are involved.

This article looks at the phenomenon of racial matching in adoption. First, I trace the historical development of today's matching policies, from the laws and practices of our segregationist past that systematically prohibited trans-racial adoption, through the period in the integrationist sixties when the barriers to such adoptions were lowered, to the attack on trans-racial adoption made by black socialworkers during the heyday of the black nationalist movement. Second, I examine the nature of today's matching policies, discussing the written and unwritten rules that require minority children to be held in foster care for an appropriate same-race family rather than placed immediately for adoption with waiting white families. I also describe the ways in which subsidiaries, recruitment, and the parental screening process are used to promote same-race placements and prevent trans-racial placements. Third, I examine the evidence relating to the impact of these policies on children. I note that large numbers of minority children who could be placed for adoption with waiting white families spend months or years waiting in foster care for a same-race placement. Some will "wait" for their entire childhoods. Fourth, I examine the empirical evidence regarding the alleged risks created by trans-racial placement. I show that, contrary to many claims, existing studies indicate that those children who have been placed trans-racially are flourishing. Fifth, I examine the law on racial discrimination, and question how current racial- matching policies in the adoption context can be squared with the legal norms that govern elsewhere in our social lives. I conclude that these policies are illegal and unconstitutional. Finally, I address the issue of what our policies should be in the future. I contend that the legal system should not permit racial matching; children in need of homes should be placed with foster and adoptive parents without regard to race.

Throughout the article I explore the meaning of racial-matching policies — why they seem to have made so much sense to so many people over the years; why blacks and whites, conservatives and liberals and radicals, judges and legislators and socialworkers have found common cause in preventing the mixing of the races in the adoption context. My conclusion is that current racial-matching policies represent a coming together of powerful and related ideologies — old-fashioned white racism, modern-day black nationalism, and what I will call "biologism," the idea that what is natural in the context of the biological family is what is normal and desirable in the context of adoption. The laws and policies that govern adoption in this country have generally structured adoption to imitate biology; giving the adopted child a new birth certificate as if the child had been born to the adoptive parents; sealing off the birth parents as if they had never existed; and attempting to match adoptive parents and children with respect to looks, intellect, and religion. The implicit goal has been to create an adoptive family which will resemble as much as possible

"the real thing" — the "natural" or biological family that it is not. These policies reflect widespread and powerful feelings that parent-child relationships can only work, or at least will work best, between biologically similar people, and that parents will be unable truly to love and nurture children that are biologically different. These fears have much in common with fears among both blacks and whites about the dangers of crossing racial boundaries. It is therefore understandable that there would be so much support for racial matching in the adoptive context.

But the question is whether we *should* be so reluctant to cross boundaries of racial otherness in the context of adoption — whether today's powerful racial-matching policies make sense from the viewpoint of either the minority children involved or the larger society. It is a question of growing practical importance. Minority children are pouring, in increasing numbers, into the already overburdened foster care system, and current policies stand in the way of placing these children with available adoptive families. In addition, how we deal with the issue of racial matching will affect how we deal with the related issues of matching parents and children on the basis of ethnic, religious, and national background. It will, for example, affect our thinking about the growing phenomenon of international adoption, which increasingly involves the adoption by whites in this country of dark-skinned children from foreign countries and cultures. Racial-matching policies also pose a question of powerful symbolic importance. What does the way we deal with race in the intimate context of the family say about how we think about the deal with race in every other aspect of our social lives?

THE HISTORY

Until the middle of this century there were near-absolute social, legal, and practical barriers to trans-racial adoption. One of the most important was the practice of matching parents with children who resembled as closely as possible the biological children they might have produced. This was thought to maximize the chances for a successful bonding of parent and child. The underlying assumption was that the parent-child relationship would be threatened by differences. Race, of course, was accepted without question as one of the features to be matched.

The 1960s represented a period of relative openness to trans-racial adoption. This change was brought about by a variety of pressures, the most important of which was the Civil Rights Movement. The Movement brought attention to the plight of minority children who had languished in foster care systems. Moreover, its integrationist ideology made trans-racial adoption an attractive option to many adoption workers and prospective parents. Trans-racial adoption also served the needs of both white would-be parents (for whom there were not enough color-matched children) and adoption agencies who wanted to reduce the foster care population. Agencies began to place waiting black children with white parents when there were no black parents apparently available. The reported number of trans-racial placements rose gradually to 733 in 1968, and it more than tripled in the next three years to reach a peak of 2,574 in 1971.

Trans-racial adoption, however, remained suspect in the eyes of many adoption professionals. As Stewart and Jacqueline Macauley have noted, socialworkers "continued to warn that trans-racial adoption was risky and called

for the utmost caution." They accepted and justified trans-racial adoption only on the ground that it was a better alternative for the children involved than life without any permanent family. At its peak in 1971, trans-racial adoption involved the placement of only a tiny fraction of the black children waiting for adoptive homes and roughly half the black children placed in black homes.

In 1972 this brief era of relative openness to trans-racial adoption came to an abrupt end. That year the National Association of Black Social Workers (NABSW) issued a policy statement opposing trans-racial adoption, arguing that:

> Black children should be placed only with black families whether in foster care or for adoption. Black children belong, physically, psychologically and culturally in black families in order that they receive the total sense of themselves and develop a sound projection of their future. Human beings are products of their environment and develop their sense of values, attitudes and self-concept within their family structures. Black children in white homes are cut off from the healthy development of themselves as black people.

Committing themselves "to go back to our communities and work to end this particular form of genocide," leaders of the NABSW pledged to put a stop to trans-racial adoption.

In the wake of this attack, trans-racial adoptions fell from 2,574 in 1971 to 1,569 in 1972, to 1,091 in 1973. By 1975, the last year in which such statistics were systematically generated, the number was 831. The influential Child Welfare League, which had in 1968 changed its *Standards for Adoption Service* to encourage consideration of trans-racial adoption, revised its standards again in 1973 to re-emphasize the advantages of same-race placements. Adoption agency bureaucrats moved swiftly to accommodate the position taken by the NABSW. A study of this phenomenon gives a persuasive explanation of the dynamics that were involved:

> When the black social work community turned professional attitudes around, it seemed prudent to do such things as turn responsibility for all black children over to black social workers and agencies. The trans-racial adoptive parent organizations might be unhappy, but they were less of a threat than black power exercised directly or through the workers' professional peers.

CURRENT RACIAL-MATCHING POLICIES

A Picture of the Matching Process at Work

Today there is widespread agreement among adoption agency policymakers that children should be placed with parents of the same race if possible, and trans-racially only as a last resort. The standard procedure in most adoption agencies is to separate children and prospective parents into racial classifications and sub-classifications. Children in need of homes are typically separated into black and white pools. The children in the black pool are then classified by skin tone — light, medium, dark — and sometimes by nationality, ethnicity, or other cultural characteristics. The prospective parent pool is similarly divided and classified. The goal is to assign the light skinned black child to light-skinned parents, the

Haitian child to Haitian parents, and so on. The white children are matched with white prospective parents.

The main problem with this system is that there are many more black children in need of adoption than there are black families looking to adopt. For example, the 1991 figures from The National Adoption Center, which maintains a register of "hard-to-place" children waiting for homes, show that sixty-seven percent of the listed children are black, and twenty-six percent are white. By contrast, of the waiting families, thirty-one percent are black and sixty-seven percent are white. These figures only hint at the extent of the numbers mismatch.

Current matching policies place a high priority on expanding the pool of prospective black adoptive parents so that placements can be made without utilizing the waiting white pool. Programs have been created to recruit black parents, subsidies have been provided to encourage them to adopt, and traditional parental screening criteria have been revised to accommodate their circumstances. Nonetheless, the disparities remain. In recent years, the number of children in foster care and the proportion that is black have both been growing.

Despite this reality, today's matching policies generally forbid the immediate placement of black children with waiting white families, requiring instead that they be held for a black family.

The matching process surfaces, to a degree, in written rules and documented cases. But it is the unwritten and generally invisible rules that are central to understanding the nature of current policies. Virtually everyone in the system agrees that, all things being equal, the minority child should go to minority parents. Thus, by the universal rules of the official game, race matching must be taken into account in the placement process. But this vastly understates the power of racial matching. The fact is that the entire system has been designed and redesigned with a view toward promoting same-race placements and avoiding trans-racial placements. The rules make race not simply a factor, but an overwhelmingly important factor in the placement process.

The Proverbial Tip of the Iceberg — of Written Rules and Documented Cases

In recent years, several states have enacted statutes requiring that agencies exercise a same-race preference when placing children in adoptive families. Minnesota and Arkansas, for instance, specify a preference for placing a child with a family of the same racial or ethnic background. If a same-race placement is not feasible, the preference shifts to a family "which is knowledgeable and appreciative of the child's racial or ethnic heritage." California law similarly mandates a same-race placement preference; it also prohibits placement across racial or ethnic lines for a period of ninety days after a child has been freed for adoption. The law further prohibits trans-racial or trans-ethnic adoption after the ninety-day period "unless it can be documented that a diligent search" for a same-race family has been made, using all appropriate recruitment resources and devices. Only on the basis of such documentation can a child be placed across racial or ethnic lines with a family "where there is evidence of sensitivity to the child's race, ethnicity, and culture."

The Child Welfare League's current *Standards For Adoption Service,* designed to establish standards for adoption agencies throughout the country, provides: "Children in need of adoption have a right to be placed in a family that reflects their ethnicity or race." The current policy position of the National Committee For Adoption states: "Usually, placment of the child should be with a family of a similar racial or ethnic background."

The power of the matching ideology is. also revealed in numerous cases that have surfaced in the media, in congressional hearings, and in litigation. These cases involve the removal of black children from white foster families with whom they have lived for long periods. Often removal is triggered by the white family's expression of interest in adopting their foster child. The white parents have poignant stories to tell. Often they have been given a child in very poor physical or psychological shape, or with serious disabilities, and have nursed the child through hard times. The child has thrived under their care and feels a close attachment. They feel a similar attachment and want to make the child a permanent part of their lives. The agency can offer nothing but a shift to a new foster family as an alternative. Experts testify to the destructive impact that disruption will have on the only stable relationship the child has known. Adoption agencies may or may not be forced to back down, whether by public pressure or by court order. But either way, these cases reveal something of the power of the racial-matching policies operating in the adoption agencies, since there is widespread agreement among child welfare professionals that stable parent-child relationships should not be disrupted and that appropriate foster families should be given priority consideration for the adoption of children with whom they have formed such relationships.

Key Features of the Matching System

Holding Policies   If no black parents are available, agencies typically hold black children in foster or institutional care rather than place them with available white families. Sometimes policies specify a definite time period — three, six, twelve, or eighteen months — before a trans-racial adoption may be considered, or after which it must be considered. But the actual holding periods are likely to be much longer. Adoption workers will often refrain from beginning the process of freeing a child for adoption so that the time period cannot start to run until and unless there is a same-race family available. Moreover, many policies require that children be held until active efforts to locate same-race families have proved fruitless. Under these non-time-specific policies, black children are likely to be held for even longer periods.

Rules that mandate only a limited same-race preference often function in a more absolute way. Rules requiring socialworkers to provide documentation of their minority family recruitment efforts before trans-racial placements are permitted force the socialworker contemplating making such a placement to do additional work and bear the other costs associated with making an exception to the general rule. The socialworker also risks incurring the wrath of the NABSW and other vocal critics of trans-racial adoption. The overburdened and underpaid adoption worker have every incentive to avoid the multiple difficulties of transracial placement.

The extreme nature of current policies is revealed by the stories of some of the trans-racial adoptions that are allowed to take place. One director of an adoption program for minority children in New York State told me that ninety percent of his agency's placements were same-race adoptions. He then described one of the few trans-racial placements he had facilitated. The child had been in the foster care system for eleven years and free for adoption for eight. He was finally placed transracially at the age of thirteen only because of concern that, as a result of accumulated bitterness, he would be likely to exercise the option — granted at age 14 — to refuse to accept an offer of adoption. The director, a strong advocate of racial matching, felt that an exception was warranted in these unusual circumstances, but noted that, even so, he had had to do battle with forces within the state and agency bureaucracies in order to implement this trans-racial placement.

The director of another program with a specific focus on recruiting minority parents told me of one trans-racial adoption she had arranged. It involved John, a victim of Fetal Alcohol Syndrome, who was mentally retarded. The director had held John for three years while she looked for a minority family. When a white coupled volunteered their interest in adopting John, the director hesitated, but finally agreed to see them. She eventually placed the child with them, finding herself very impressed by their parenting credentials and the fact that they already had children from a variety of ethnic backgrounds. Another director told me of a transracial placement she had made in a case involving hard-to-place minority siblings. The only available minority family was interested in adopting one child but not the other. Since the director felt separation would be disastrous for the children, she placed them with a white couple. As a result she was subject to intense criticism and pressure from the local chapter of the NABSW.

Recruitment There is general agreement among adoption workers that black families should be actively recruited to increase the pool available to black children. There have been some notable efforts to form organizations and adoption agencies under black leadership and to involve black churches and the media in recruitment campaign. These efforts have had some success in encouraging black families to consider adoption and to complete the adoption process. State, regional, and national exchanges of black and other "hard-to-place" children waiting for adoption have been created both as a means of making their availability more generally known and as a way of recruiting more parents.

There is, of course, no systematic recruitment of white families for waiting black children, since matching policies preclude trans-racial placement except as a last resort. Nor is there much of an effort to recruit white families, even for children for whom there seems little prospect of ever finding black adoptive families. Older black children with very serious mental or physical disabilities constitute a hardcore hard-to-place group. One leader in the world of special needs placement told me that she had recently come to believe that it would be appropriate to recruit white as well as black parents in the interest of finding homes for some of these children, but that she had run into nothing but opposition from her colleagues.

Race-conscious recruitment takes many forms. Agencies target their appeals to minority-oriented media outlets and community organizations. Adoption exchanges often specify that they are seeking black families to adopt the black children listed, "Sunday's Child" or "Wednesday's Child" advertisements in newspapers and on television describing particular children often contain similar specifications.

Subsidies Subsidies are widely available to minority couples and singles to enable and encourage them to adopt minority children. All states make some provision for subsidies to persons adopting certain special-needs children. The federal government encourages such subsidies by providing states with federal funds to match state subsidies. Under federal laws, minority status alone puts children in the special-needs category, making them eligible for subsidies so long as certain other conditions are met, including state eligibility requirements. Though limited in amount, these subsidies are thought to have made a significant difference in encouraging large numbers of minority families to adopt.

Although white families are technically eligible for these subsidies, the fact that whites are rarely allowed to adopt minority children means that the subsidies operate primarily to facilitate same-race adoption.

Differential Criteria for Assessing Parental Fitness In order to increase the prospects for in-race placement, agencies apply significantly different parental-screening criteria to prospective black adoptive parents than to prospective white adoptive parents. To increase the number of black prospective parents, agencies reach out to include the kinds of people traditionally excluded from the white parent pool, or placed at the bottom of the waiting lists for children: singles, older people in their fifties and sixties, and people living on welfare or social security.

As a result, the pool of black adoptive parents looks very different in socio-economic terms from the pool of white parents. Black adoptive parents are significantly older, poorer, and more likely to be single than their white counterparts. A study published in 1986 gives some indication of the differences. Fifty percent of minority adoptive families had incomes below $20,000 per year, and twenty percent had income below $10,000 per year. By contrast, only fourteen percent of non-minority families had incomes below $20,000, and only two percent had incomes below $10,000. Forty-five percent of the fathers in the minority families were age forty-five or older, with fourteen percent age sixty-one or older. Only nineteen percent of the non-minority adoptive fathers were age forty-five or older and only two percent were age sixty-one or older. One study involving a small sample of adoptions reported that one-half of the black single parents involved earned less than $10,000. The former director of one of New York State's major adoption agencies told me that agency policies in New York required that "just about anyone" of minority racial status be considered eligible as an adoptive parent for minority children.

It is important to note than in altering screening criteria for black adoptive families, adoption workers have by no means repudiated these criteria as irrelevant to determining parental fitness. Black and white parent candidates are still assessed and ranked by these criteria, with singles, older people, and economically marginal candidates placed at the bottom of the prospective parent lists. In trying to expand an all-too-short black prospective parent list, adoption workers have sought out the kinds of people they would normally exclude altogether from white parent lists. Because of the importance attributed to the racial factor, those at the bottom of the black list are generally pre-ferred over all those on the white list for any waiting black child.

THE IMPACT OF CURRENT POLICIES

Do racial-matching policies result, on a widespread basis, in delaying or denying permanent placement for minority children? The causal connection has not been proven definitively, but strong evidence suggests that a causal connection does exist. Minority children are disproportionately represented in the population of children waiting for adoptive homes; they spend longer waiting than white children; and they are less likely to be eventually placed. Estimates indicate that of the population of children waiting for homes, children of color make up roughly one-half, and black children alone make up over one-third. A recent study found that minority children waited for an average of two years — twice as long as the average for non-minorities. Minority placement rates were twenty percent lower than non-minority placement rates. The minority children were comparable in age with the non-minorities and had other characteristics which, had race not been an issue, should have made it easier to find adoptive placements (i.e., they had fewer disabilities and fewer previous placements in foster care). The data indicated that racial status was a more powerful determinant of placement rate than any other factor examined.

The most adamant critics of trans-racial adoption argue that even if minority children are disproportionately subject to delays and denial in placement, the solution is to devote more resources to the preservation and the reunification of black biological families, and to the recruitment of minority families for those children who must be removed from their homes. They argue that with such efforts, black homes could be found for all waiting children. They argue further that whites are not willing to adopt the minority children who wait, noting that most of the children in foster care are older and that they suffer from a variety of physical and emotional problems.

But the fact is that the resources devoted to the goal of preserving black biological families and to making same-race adoption work have been limited and are likely to be limited in the foreseeable future. There are, and almost certainly will be for some period of time, too few black families available for the waiting black children. By contract, there are many white families eagerly awaiting the opportunity to adopt. Although white adopters, like black adopters, tend to prefer healthy infants, recruitment efforts in recent years have demonstrated that whites as well as blacks are often willing to adopt older children and children with disabilities. Current racial-matching policies stand in the way of tapping this ready resource of homes for minority children. Moreover, the reason that so many of the waiting black children *are* older is in part because matching policies have kept them on hold.

Although it seems clear that racial-matching policies delay and often deny placement of minority children, it is harder to get a sense for how common and how lengthy the delays are and how frequently minority children are permanently denied adoptive homes. The consensus among adoption professionals seems to be that black homes can be found for healthy young black infants; most children falling into this category are being placed. However, their placement may still require a recruitment process of many months. If the agency is not engaged in active recruiting of minority families, years may go by while the agency waits for a same-race family. For young black children who must be freed for adoption by court proceedings terminating parental rights, there will often be additional years of delay. As they get older and accumulate what are often damaging experiences in foster care, the children are pushed deeper into the hard-to-place category. Delay thus puts the child at risk of yet more delay and, ultimately, the denial of placement altogether.

For children with severe disabilities and for older children the risks of lengthy delay and permanent denial of placement are even greater. Although generally agencies are somewhat more willing to consider trans-racial adoption for these children, it is still likely to be treated as at best a last resort. Accordingly, white adoptive parents are actively discouraged from finding out about or expressing interest in minority special-needs children by the race-specific recruitment devices described above. Moreover, white parents' requests for specific minority children are often rebuffed. The National Coalition to End Racism in America's Child Care System has filed a number of complaints with the United States Department of Health and Human Services charging unlawful discrimination on the basis of race, citing agency rejections of white applicants' requests to adopt hard-to-place children. One such complaint involved a charge that the New York Department of Social Services refused, solely on the basis of race, to consider a white couple as adoptive parents for a 10-year-old mixed-race child listed in a national exchange for hard-to-place children. Although the couple repeatedly expressed their interest in adoption they found the child still listed over two years later.

THE EMPIRICAL STUDIES

A number of research studies have attempted to assess how well trans-racial adoptive families have fared. The studies reflect a bias on the part of those responsible for funding, sponsoring, and conducting research. The general emphasis is on the potential negatives in trans-racial adoption, rather than on the net effects, including potential positives. Moreover, the studies avoid any systematic look at the potentially negative aspects of current matching policies. None attempts to measure the degree to which racial-matching policies result in delay and denial of adoptive placement, or to compare the experience of children placed immediately with waiting white families to the experience of children held for same-race placement.

Despite this bias, the studies provide an overwhelming endorsement of trans-racial adoption. Conducted by a diverse group of researchers that included blacks and whites, critics and supporters of trans-racial adoption, their research indicates, with astounding uniformity, that trans-racial adoption works for the children and adoptive families involved.

These studies constitute the only evidence we have as to what actually happens when children are placed trans-racially. They are often cited by critics of trans-racial placement, by legislators, by the media, and by courts as suggesting problems that arise from such placement. Yet, the studies provide *no basis* for concluding that placement of black children with white rather than black families has any negative impact on the children's welfare. The studies may not *definitively* prove anything: studies seeking to measure human happiness rarely do. But in a world of limited infor-

mation, they provide persuasive evidence that trans-racial adoption serves the interest of children.

The Evidence As to General Adjustment

A number of studies have examined trans-racial adoptees and their families, considering factors such as self-esteem, educational achievement, levels of satisfaction expressed by family members, behavioral problems, and adoption disruption. They consistently show trans-racial adoptees doing well according to the measures of successful adjustment chosen by the researchers. In many of these studies the trans-racial adoptees are compared to control groups of black same-race adoptees; in others they are compared to black children raised in their biological families or to white children raised in white adoptive or biological families. Other studies focus on samples that include same-race as well as trans-racial adoptees and analyze the correlation between racial matching and adoptive success. All of these comparative studies show trans-racial adoptees doing generally as well as the other groups of children in terms of various traditional measures of social adjustment.

Despite the positive findings, there is often a cautious and negative tone to the researchers' characterizations. Many of the studies emphasize that although the evidence looks positive so far, problems may well show up as the trans-racial adoptees reach some later stage of development. The early studies focused on adolescence as the period during which the anticipated problems might manifest themselves. But successive studies have followed the children through adolescence and into early adulthood, and they have found that the children continue to feel good about themselves, to enjoy good relationships with their families, and to do well in the outside world.

Three of the most significant of these studies were conducted by Ruth McRoy and colleagues, by Joan Shireman and colleagues (in conjunction with the Chicago Child Care Society), and by Rita Simon and Howard Altstein.

The McRoy study compared a group of black adolescents adopted by white families to a group of black adolescents adopted by black families. There was rough comparability between the two groups in terms of age at placement and socio-economic level, with some differences in parents' education and employment levels. The study focused initially on the development of self-esteem, in part because the critics of trans-racial adoption had argued that the adoptees would experience problems in this area. The researchers concluded:

> This exploratory study indicated that there were no differences in overall self-esteem between the sampled trans-racially and in-racially adopted children. Furthermore, the level of self-esteem of the adoptees was as high as that reported among individuals in the general population. This suggests that positive self-esteem can be generated as effectively among black children in white adoptive families as in black adoptive families.

This Chicago Child Care Society study deals with a small cohort of black adoptees, comparing those placed trans-racially with those placed in-racially as well as with black children raised in their biological families. The most recent of several follow-up reports, published in 1988, looks at the children in their teen years and concludes that the trans-racial adoptees are generally doing as well as both the other adoptees and the non-adopted children.

Simon and Altstein have conducted the most comprehensive longitudinal study of trans-racial adoptees, reporting the results in three different books, the most recent of which was published in 1987. They followed a group of white families who had adopted black and other minority children, looking at both the minority adoptees and their white adopted and non-adopted siblings. The latest report finds the children in adolescence, with most in their last two years of high school. It confirms all the previous research findings indicating that trans-racial adoptees are flourishing in their families and communities. They write that the portrait that emerges of the great majority of trans-racial adoptive families

> is a positive, warm, integrated picture that shows parents and children who feel good about themselves and about their relationships with each other. On the issue of trans-racial adoption, almost all of the parents would do it again and would recommend it to other families. They believe that they and the children born to them have benefited from their experiences. Their birth children have developed insight, sensitivity, and a tolerance that they could not have acquired in the ordinary course of life. Their trans-racial adoptees may have been spared years in foster homes or institutions. They have had the comfort and security of loving parents and siblings who have provided them with a good home, education and cultural opportunities, and the belief that they are wanted.

Simon and Altstein note that, far from being alienated by parents of a different race, the children seem, if anything, even more committed to their adoptive parents than their parents do to them.

The Evidence As to
Racial Attitudes

The evidence shows that trans-racial adoptees develop a strong sense of black identity. Questions on this issue were raised by some of the earlier research that relied on anecdotal descriptions of trans-racial adoptees who allegedly over-identified with their white families. But more sophisticated comparative research indicates that trans-racial adoptees have essentially as strong a sense of black identity and racial pride as other minority children. Indeed, some of the evidence indicates that trans-racial adoption may even have a positive impact in terms of black children's sense of comfort with their racial identity.

Research does uncover some significant differences between black children raised in-racially and trans-racially concerning attitudes about race and race relations. Trans-racial adoptees appear more positive than blacks raised in-racially about relationships with whites, more comfortable in those relationships, and more interested in a racially integrated life style. There is also evidence that they think race is not the most important factor in defining who they are or who their friends should be. Studies have found some trans-racial adoptees describing themselves as biracial or American or human, rather than black. Most of them are, incidentally, genetically biracial and relatively light-skinned, because these are the kind of black children that have generally been placed trans-racially. These findings are taken as evidence of *inappro-*

priate racial attitudes by the critics of trans-racial adoption. But whether this evidence is positive or negative in its implications for trans-racial adoption depends entirely on one's political perspective. Simon and Altstein, for example, voice what they see as the positive implications of this evidence. They described the trans-racial adoptees as perceiving their world as essentially pluralistic and multicolored. They conclude:

> [T]he trans-racially adopted children... represent a different and special cohort, one socialized in two worlds and therefore perhaps better prepared to operate in both. The hope is that having had this unique racial experience, they will have gained a greater sense of security about who they are and will be better able to negotiate in the worlds of both their biological inheritance and their socialization.

The latest report from the Chicago Child Care Society finds similar implications in the evidence:

> As far as we can tell with our measures, there has developed a positive black self-image, combined with a mixed black-white pattern of social interaction. It seems to us that this pattern may be one which will allow these young people to move with equal comfort in both black and white worlds, allowing them to cull what they wish from each culture, and perhaps creating bridges which will be of use to an even wider world.

From the perspective of one who believes that blacks and whites should be learning to live compatibly in one world, with respect and concern for each other, with appreciation for their racial and cultural differences as well as their common humanity, this evidence is positively heartwarming.

But this evidence is understandably problematic from a black separatist or nationalist perspective. Blacks who believe their group interests will be advanced by building a cohesive black community are likely to find cause for concern in the evidence that black children raised in white families are growing up to feel comfortable in the white community. As the president of NABSW wrote in the association's spring 1988 newsletter:

> The lateral transfer of our children to white families is not in our best interest. Having white families raise our children to be white is at least a hostile gesture toward us as a people and at best the ultimate gesture of disrespect for our heritage as African people.... It is their aim to raise black children with white minds.... We are on the right side of the trans-racial adoption issue. Our children are our future.

The studies indicate that white families vary significantly in the degree to which they engage in deliberate socialization efforts to make their black children feel part of a black cultural community and proud of a black heritage. Such efforts do seem to have an effect in producing a greater sense of interest and pride in their race. But there is no evidence that black parents do a better job than white parents of raising black children with a sense of pride in their racial culture and heritage. Nor is there any evidence that such differences as may exist in racial attitudes have any negative effect on the well-being of those raised trans-racially.

The Evidence As to Advantages for Children of Trans-racial Placement

As noted above, the great body of research on trans-racial adoption has been structured to look for its negative rather than positive potential. But there is every reason to think that there are *advantages* for children in growing up in a trans-racial, multicultural family setting.

An admittedly limited and informal study of the children of interracial marriage conducted by Dr. Alvin Poussaint of the Harvard Medical School is illuminating. Dr. Poussaint interviewed a number of people who had grown up in families with one black and one white parent, inquiring specifically about their views on the positive and negative aspects of their biracial upbringing. He found that they tended to emphasize the positive. Among the advantages cited were the following: they felt that they had access to two cultures and that being bicultural was a plus; that they could move easily in both worlds and have different kinds of friends; that they were less intimidated in the white world than other black children; and that they had developed an unusually broad outlook and were more tolerant of differences. When asked if they would consider interracial marriage themselves and if they would feel comfortable raising a biracial child, they all answered yes. Although the situation of trans-racial adoptees differs from that of these children in important respects, it seems likely that trans-racial adoptees, if asked, would have their own list of advantages to discuss.

Critics of trans-racial adoption have claimed that only blacks can teach black children the coping skills needed for life in a racist society. But there seems at least as good an argument for the proposition that whites are in the best position to teach black children how to maneuver in the white worlds of power and privilege. Indeed, it seems clear that for black children growing up in a white-dominated world, there would be a range of material advantages associated with having white parents and living in the largely white and relatively privileged world that such parents tend to frequent.

Moreover, trans-racial adoption may give rise to other benefits similar to those found by Dr. Poussaint. For example, it could be an advantage to enjoy the kind of comfort in both black and white worlds that the studies discussed above indicate trans-racial adoptees feel. It could also be an advantage for an adoptee to grow up in a family that has not been fashioned to imitate the biological model. Studies indicate that trans-racial adoptive parents are more open in discussing adoption with their children and that the children are more likely to identify themselves as adopted. These findings raise the interesting possibility that, in trans-racial adoptive families, the inescapable difference of race may encourage a healthier acceptance of the fact that the family is in various other ways not the same as a biological family.

The Evidence As to Costs for Children of Current Same-Race Placement Preferences

There is considerable evidence — and a strong consensus — on the costs to children of delays in adoptive placement and in permanent denial of an adoptive home. Child welfare professionals agree with virtual unanimity that children need the continuity of a permanent home to flourish. There is a significant body of research demonstrating that children do better in adoption than in foster care, and that age

at placement in an adoptive family is a central factor in determining just how well adoptees will do in terms of various measures of adjustment. Moreover, to the degree that research studies have attempted to determine whether delay in placement or racial match is a more significant factor in adoptive adjustment, they have found delay to be the key factor. William Feigelman and Arnold Silverman specifically addressed whether race difference and racial isolation in an alien community constitute more potent determinants for a child's adjustment than the discontinuities and hazards associated with delayed placement. In a study involving both black and white children placed with white parents, they found age at time of placement by far the most significant factor in explaining variations in adjustment measures. This and the other available evidence provides a firm basis for believing that the delays in placement and denials of permanent adoptive homes that result from current same-race placement policies are seriously harmful to children.

In the context of a society struggling to deal with racial difference, the studies of trans-racial adoptive families are extraordinarily interesting. They do not simply show that black children do well in white adoptive homes. They do not simply show that we put black children at risk by delaying or denying placement while we await black homes. The studies show that black children raised in white homes are comfortable with their blackness and also uniquely comfortable in dealing with whites. In addition, the studies show that trans-racial adoption has an interesting impact on the racial attitudes of the *white* members of these families. The parents tend to describe their lives as significantly changed and enriched by the experience of becoming an interracial family. They describe themselves as having developed a new awareness of racial issues. The white children in trans-racial adoptive families are described as committed to and protective of their black brothers and sisters. The white as well as the black children are described as unusually free of racial bias, and unusually committed to the vision of a pluralistic world in which one's humanity is more important than one's race.

The studies show parents and children, brothers and sisters, relating to each other in these trans-racial families as if race was no barrier to love and commitment. They show the black adopted children and the white birth children growing up with the sense that race should not be a barrier to their relationships with other people. In a society torn by racial conflict, these studies show human beings transcending racial difference.

THE LAW

Current racial-matching policies are in conflict with the basic law of the land concerning racial discrimination. They are an anomaly. In no other area do state and state-licensed decision makers use race so systematically as the basis for action. In no other area do they promote the use of race so openly. Indeed, in most areas of our community life, race is an absolutely impermissible basis for classification.

The Constitution, state constitutions, and a mass of federal, state, and local laws, prohibit discrimination on the basis of race by public entities. Private entities with significant power over our lives are also generally bound by laws prohibiting discrimination on the basis of race. Over the past twenty-five years this body of law has grown to the point where today there are guarantees against race discrimination not only in housing, employment, and public accommodation, but in virtually every area of our community life.

It is true that the imperative of anti-discrimination has been tempered by the need to respect privacy and free association. But the state is not permitted to *insist* that race count as a factor in the ordering of people's most private lives. Thus, in *Loving* v. *Virginia* the Supreme Court held it unconstitutional for the state to prohibit interracial marriage, and in *Palmore* v. *Sidoti* the Court held it unconstitutional for the state to use race as the basis for deciding which of two biological parents should have custody of a child. *Palmore* involved the issue of whether a white child could be removed from the custody of its biological mother on the basis of the mother's relationship with a black man. The Court unanimously held that in this context reliance on race as a decision-making factor violated the equal protection clause of the Fourteenth Amendment. The Court rejected arguments that removal of the child from a racially mixed household was justified by the state's goal of making custody decisions on the basis of the best interests of the child. Conceding that there was a risk that a child living with a stepparent of a different race may be subject to a variety of pressures and stresses not present if the child were living with parents of the same racial or ethnic origin, the Court nonetheless had no problem concluding that these were constitutionally impermissible considerations.

The anti-discrimination principle has been interpreted to outlaw almost all race-conscious action by the state and by the agencies which control our community lives; there need be no indication that the action is designed to harm or that it results in harm. Race-conscious action has been allowed *only* where it can be justified because of compelling necessity, or where it is designed to benefit racial minority groups, either by preventing discrimination or by remedying its effects (i.e., affirmative action). These exceptions have been narrowly defined.

The adoption world is an anomaly in this legal universe, where race-conscious action is deemed highly suspect and generally illegal. In agency adoptions, as we have seen, race-conscious action is one of the major rules of the child-allocation game. The fact that race is a recognizable factor in decision-making is enough under our general anti-discrimination norm to make out a case of intentional discrimination. Adoption agency policies make race not merely a factor, by the overwhelmingly significant factor in the placement process.

The public adoption agencies, as well as many of the private agencies, are governed by legislative and constitutional provisions forbidding racial discrimination. The Constitution's equal protection clause, and the related limit on legitimate affirmative action, apply to all state and local governmental entities. Title VI of the Civil Rights Act of 1964 bans discrimination by adoption agencies, public and private, that receive federal funds. Many states have constitutional, statutory, and regulatory provisions that broadly prohibit discrimination by public and private agencies.

But for some reason the anti-discrimination principle is thought to mean something quite different in the adoption area than it means elsewhere. The federal policy guidelines that interpret Title VI's meaning in the context of adoption and foster care are symptomatic of how differently the anti-discrimination norm is applied in the adoption field. The guidelines specify that race *can* be used as a basis for decision-making in foster and adoptive placement so long as it is not used in any absolute or categorical way to prohibit consideration of trans-racial adoption altogether:

> Generally, under Title VI, race, color, or national origin may not be used as a basis for providing benefits or services. However, in placing a child in an adoptive or foster home it may be appropriate to consider race, color, or national origin as one of several factors.

The guidelines go on to emphasize that this exception applies *only* in these contexts:

> This policy is based on unique aspects of the relationship between a child and his or her adoptive or foster parents. It should not be construed as applicable to any other situation in child welfare or human services area covered by Title VI.

The racial-matching policies fit none of the recognized exceptions to the anti-discrimination norm. There is no compelling necessity for racial matching. The black community within this nation is not threatened with extinction. The number of black children available for adoption is very small compared to the size of the black community; placing more of those available for adoption trans-racially poses no realistic threat to the existence of that community or the preservation of its culture. It is hard to see trans-racial adoption as more threatening to these interests than racial intermarriage or racial integration in public education. Official efforts to prevent intermarriage or to prevent black children from attending school with white children or being taught by white teachers have been held unconstitutional and would be regarded as intolerable by blacks and whites alike in today's society.

Nor can racial-matching policies be rationalized as a form of affirmative action designed to eliminate or to remedy the effects of prior discrimination. It is easy to argue that there has been such discrimination. Traditional agency screening procedures and criteria can be criticized as having discriminated against prospective black parents, depriving them of an equal opportunity to adopt. Trans-racial adoption, which has operated to place black children but not white children across racial lines, can be criticized as having discriminated against black children, depriving them of an equal opportunity to the benefits of a same-race upbringing. And trans-racial adoption can be seen as part of a continuing pattern of discrimination against the black community. A vast array of social policies going back to the institution of slavery are surely in large part responsible for the fact that it is black families whose children are disproportionately available for adoption and white families who are disproportionately in a position to adopt. Taking all these perspectives together, trans-racial adoption can be characterized, and indeed has been by the NABSW, as one of the ultimate forms of exploitation by whites of the black community and the black family.

The problem is that racial-matching policies are not the kinds of remedial affirmative action programs that the courts have accepted as legitimate. The courts have generally insisted that affirmative action programs be limited in duration and designed to help move society to a point where race can be eliminated as a decision-making factor. By contrast, racial matching policies have no apparent limit in time. Moreover, they are not designed to eliminate the role of race in agency decision-making in the future, but rather to perpetuate its importance.

Racial-matching policies are fundamentally inconsistent with traditional affirmative action rationales in another way as well: racial matching promotes racial separatism rather than racial integration. By contrast, both anti-discrimination law and affirmative action programs have been designed to break down segregatory barriers and to promote integration.

Race-conscious action that has any level of principled support relies on arguments that it *benefits* racial minorities. Even those courts and Supreme Court Justices most sympathetic to affirmative action have argued that allegedly benign racial classifications should be scrutinized carefully to ensure that they are truly benign in impact and do not serve to disadvantage their intended beneficiaries. But there is no obvious answer to the question of whether racial-matching policies are likely to benefit or burden the black community, advance or impede black group interests. It is certainly questionable whether imposing on the black community an obligation to take care of "its own," while providing limited resources for the job, does much to help that community. Black adopters are limited by race-matching policies to children of their race and skin tone. Black birth mothers are often prevented by these policies from obtaining what they most want — immediate placement of their children in permanent homes.

In addition, there is no reason to believe that blacks as a group support race-matching policies. These policies have been developed and promoted by the leaders of one black socialworkers' organization in the absence of any evidence of general backing in the black community and with limited vocal support from any other organization. Reported surveys of attitudes in the black community indicate substantial support for trans-racial adoption and very limited support for the NABSW position or for the powerful matching principles embodies in today's adoption policies. The underlying motivation for these policies includes a complex mix of attitudes, with white opposition to race mixing in the context of the family undoubtedly playing a part.

What *does* seem clear is that current policies are *harmful* to the group of black children in need of homes. Affirmative action is not supposed to do concrete harm to one group of blacks in the interest of promoting what are at best hypothetical benefits to another. And adoption is not supposed to be about adult or community rights and interests, but rather about serving the best interests of children. Adoption laws throughout this country direct agencies to make children's interests paramount in placement decisions.

Advocates for racial matching argue that growing up with same-race parents is a benefit of overriding importance to black children. But the claim that a black person, by virtue of his or her race, will necessarily be more capable than a white of parenting a black child is the kind of claim that courts have generally refused to allow as justification for race-conscious action. The near-absolute presumption under our anti-discrimination laws is that race is irrelevant to qualifications. Moreover, the available evidence does not support the claim that same-race placement is beneficial to black children, much less that it outweighs the harm of delayed placement. Ultimately, the argument that racial-matching policies are beneficial rather than harmful to the children immediately affected rests on the unsupported assumption that black children will be significantly better off with "their own kind." This is not the kind of assumption that has been permitted under our nation's anti-discrimination laws. More importantly, it

is not an assumption that *should* be permitted in a situation where there is evidence that by insisting on a racial match we are doing serious injury to black children.

Although matching policies are inconsistent with the law of the land, many courts have responded to them with either indifference or sympathy. Although courts have generally agreed that race cannot be used by agencies as the sole factor in making placement decisions, a number of judges have ruled that race can be used as a significant and even determinative factor. Some courts actually require that race be considered.

A major problem with the factual analysis in adoption cases is that courts tend to ignore or distort the systemic role race plays in agency decision-making. The cases portray a world in which the general practice is consistent with the courts' current legal doctrine that race shall not function in an absolute or automatic way in placement decisions. Many judges seem to be either unaware or unwilling to acknowledge that, in reality, adoption agencies throughout the country operate under rules that regularly make race a central and determinative factor in placement decisions.

A major problem with current legal doctrine in adoption cases is that it is inconsistent with the way courts define the nature of unlawful discrimination in areas other than adoption. In other areas the anti-discrimination norm forbids decision-makers from giving race *any* role in their decision-making processes. If a party is able to show that race has played a part in arriving at a decision, then that decision is presumptively unlawful.

Judges have come up with little justification for treating the racial issue so differently in the adoption context. Some have relied on unsubstantiated claims that the evidence from the adoption world indicates that black children will necessarily risk serious identity and other problems if they are raised by whites. Some have relied on their own assumptions regarding such problems. Others have expressed what seems to be at the heart of much judicial thinking in this area — the sense that mixing the races in the context of the family is simply not "natural." In one leading case, the majority opinion states: "It is a natural thing for children to be raised by parents of their same ethnic background." The opinion speaks approvingly of traditional matching policies as designed to duplicate the "natural biological environment" so that a child can develop a "normal family relationship."

The sense that same-race relationships are "natural" and "normal" in the intimate context of family is at the heart of the law on trans-racial adoption. But in *Loving* v. *Virginia*, the Supreme Court rejected similar thinking in striking down Virginia's miscegenation statute. The trial court had reasoned as follows:

> Almighty God created the races white, black, yellow, malay and red, and he placed them on separate continents. And but for the interference with his arrangement there would be no cause for such marriages. The fact that he separated the races shows that he did not intend for the races to mix.

The Supreme Court reversed, holding racial classifications embodied in Virginia's "Racial Integrity Act" unconstitutional, "even assuming an even-handed state purpose to protect the 'integrity' of all races."

Legislatures and policymakers in the executive branch, like the courts, have turned a blind eye toward race-based adoption policies, though they have not affirmatively intervened to mandate or permit the use of race as a criterion in adoption placement. One reason for this tolerance of racial-matching policies may be that they have a direct impact on a relatively small and powerless group consisting of minority children without homes and the whites interested in parenting them. When white employees are denied seniority rights or job promotions in favor of minorities this is perceived as a threat to the economic interests of a larger organized portion of the population. The sight of older and disabled black children being held in foster care rather than placed with whites, or taken from whites to be placed with blacks, simply does not trigger the same kind of concern in the larger white community. This helps explain why the powerful, mainstream organizations have not stepped forward to join ranks with white prospective parents to mount a campaign against the racial-matching policies. Moreover, for the black and liberal white organizations that have traditionally focused on the welfare of children, racial-matching policies pose complicated political issues. After all, it is black adoption workers who have most vocally promoted the policies and who have condemned trans-racial adoption as a form of white racism.

Another reason for tolerance of racial-matching policies is the widely held view that black children should be raised by black parents if this is at all possible. Professionals involved in adoption issues agree with near-unanimity on this proposition. Even those most active in criticizing what they see as the excesses of current racial-matching policies tend to concede that trans-racial adoption should be considered only if same-race placement is impracticable. Almost no one advocates the elimination of any preference whatsoever for same-race placement — that is, the creation of the kind of race-blind regime typically considered the ideal in other areas of social life.

DIRECTIONS FOR
THE FUTURE

Racial matching should not be seen as an issue on which black interests are pitted against white interests, with blacks fighting for the rights of "their children" and whites desiring children for their own selfish benefit. There is no evidence of significant black support for current racial-matching policies. There is reason to think moreover, that if fully informed about the nature of these policies and their impact on black children many blacks would oppose them. Clearly they are harmful to those blacks most affected — the children in need of homes.

White support and tolerance for racial-matching policies should not been seen as necessarily benign. It may well be that liberal white guilt helps explain why white adoption workers joined ranks with the NABSW to end the practice of trans-racial adoption that flourished from 1968 to 1971. But something else is going on here as well. One would expect good liberals to worry more about the need for black children waiting in foster care to be placed in the best possible homes at the soonest possible time. If these white socialworkers were reserving for blacks jobs or other benefits prized by the white community, they would clearly meet a great deal of resistance. That they are encountering so little resistance indicates that the white community does not place a high value on the opportunity to parent these black children. Nor does the white community appear to care that much about the fate of black children who wait for homes. Indeed, the notion that the black community has a right to hold onto "its own" is likely to strike a sympathetic chord among whites who would feel uncomfortable at the idea of a white child being raised in a black or biracial family.

The issues at the heart of current racial-matching policies are the significance of racial difference and the role of racial separatism in dealing with difference. Historically, these policies represent the coming together of white segregationists with black nationalists and the merger of their racial separatist ideologies with "biologism." Adoption professionals have idealized the biological family and structured the adoptive family in its image. They have argued that biological sameness helps to make families work and have therefore promoted the goal of matching adoptive parents with their biological look-alikes. Although adoption professionals surrendered various aspects of their matching philosophy as they struggled to keep up with the realities of the adoption world, they held onto the core idea that racial look-alikes should be placed together. The NABSW's attack on trans-racial adoption met with relatively ready acceptance from white as well as black socialworkers, not just because of liberal white guilt, but because it fit with the traditional assumptions of their professional world. The adoption world is part of a larger social context in which there has always been a strong sense that racial differences matter deeply, and a related suspicion about crossing racial lines. Both black nationalists and white segregationists promote separatism, especially in the context of the family, as a way of promoting the power and cultural integrity of their own group. Even those blacks and whites generally committed to integration often see the family as the place to draw the line.

One can recognize the importance of racial and cultural difference without subscribing to separatism. One can celebrate a child's racial identity without insisting that a child born with a particular racial makeup must live within a prescribed racial community. One can understand that there are an endless variety of ways for members of racial groups to define their identities and to define themselves in relationship to various groups. One can believe that people are capable of loving those who are not biological and racial likes, but are "other," and that it is important that more learn to do so. One can see the elimination of racial hostilities as more important than the promotion of cultural difference.

From this perspective, which is one I share, trans-racial adoptive families constitute an interesting model of how we might better learn to live with one another in this society. These families can work only if there is both appreciation of racial difference and love that transcends such difference. And the evidence indicates that these families *do* work. Accordingly, I believe that current racial-matching policies should be abandoned not simply because they violate the law but because they do serious injury to black children in the interest of promoting an unproductive separatist agenda.

Assuming that the powerful matching policies of today were abandoned or outlawed, the question would remain: What role, if any, should race play in the agency placement process? Most critics of today's policies focus their criticism on the degree to which race-matching principles dominate the placement process, rather than on the fact that race is allowed to play any role at all. They tend to argue for a rule that would allow race to be used as a factor but not an exclusive factor in decision-making, and for limits on the delay to which a child can be subjected while a same-race family is sought.

In my view, adoption agencies should clearly be prohibited from exercising *any significant preference* for same-race families. *No delays* in placement — whether for six months or one month — should be tolerated in the interest of ensuring a racial match. Delay harms children because, at the very least, it will cause discontinuity and disruption. And any delay risks further delay.

Accordingly, any preference for same-race placement that involves delay or that otherwise threatens the interest of children in receiving good homes should be viewed as unlawful racial discrimination, inconsistent not simply with traditional limits on affirmative action, but with *any* legitimate concept of affirmative action. The courts and administrators responsible for interpreting and enforcing the law should apply established legal principles of the equal protection clause of the Constitution, Title VI of The Civil Rights Act of 1964, and other applicable anti-discrimination mandates.

The only real question, then, is whether agencies should be allowed to exercise a genuinely mild preference. A mild preference would mean that if any agency had qualified black and white families waiting to adopt, it could take race into account in deciding how to allocate the children waiting for homes. The agency could operate on the principle that all things being essentially equal, it would be better to assign black children to black parents and white children to white parents.

There are some valid arguments in support of a mild preference. There is some reason to think that, all things being equal, same-race placements could serve children's interests. There is, for example, reason to fear that white parents might harbor racial attitudes, on a conscious or subconscious level, which would interfere with their ability to appreciate and celebrate their black child's racial self. One has only to step into the world of adoption to realize how widespread and powerful are the feelings among prospective adopters that race matters as they think about what child they will want to adopt. The adoption world is largely peopled by prospective white parents in search of *white* children. The urgency of their race-conscious quest seems to explain much about that world. But reality is complicated. There is tremendous variation among adoptive parents in their racial attitudes. And their attitudes are shaped and conditioned by messages they receive from adoption workers and the broader society, as well as by the adoption process. Some white adopters look to adopt black American or dark-skinned foreign children as their preferred option. Others begin their adoption quest with the thought of a white child and later turn to trans-racial adoption after considering their options. For them trans-racial adoption may appear to be a "second choice." But the fact is that, for a very large number of adoptive parents, adoption itself is a second choice or "last resort." Many adoptive parents are infertile, and they turn to adoption only after discovering they cannot reproduce themselves biologically. It is understandable in this context that their first instinct would be to look for a racial look-alike. They are, of course, conditioned by current racial matching policies to think that they *should* do this. They are simultaneously conditioned by a variety of forces in our society to think of biological parenting as preferable to adoptive parenting. All adoptions require parents to transcend this kind of conditioning. The evidence indicates that adoptive parents are able to do so and that adoptive relationships work. The evidence similarly suggests that when whites arrive at the point of consciously choosing trans-racial parenthood and enter into parenting relationships with black children, the relationships work, and indeed appear to work as well as biological parenting relationships.

There is nonetheless some reason for concern that trans-racial adoption might add in a problematic way to the adopted child's sense of difference. It is difficult for children to be different from those they see as being in their group or world. All adopted children have to deal with the difference of having lost their biological parents. Many adoption professionals feel that this difference puts adoptees at risk of feeling that they do not really belong. We must ask ourselves whether we want to add to the sense of difference by placing black adoptees with white parents in what are likely to be significantly white communities. We may believe that these children should feel they truly belong; research studies provide some evidence that they do. But it still seems likely that many children would find it more comfortable, all things being truly equal, to be raised by same-race parents.

A mild preference for same-race placement might also seem to serve the interests of black adults who want to parent, as well as the kind of black community interests discussed above. It would counter, at least to some degree, the tendency of trans-racial adoption to work only in one racial direction, with black children placed in white families but practically no white children placed in black families. This tendency has been, understandably, a piece of what critics of trans-racial adoption have found most offensive.

But there would be real dangers in a rule involving even a mild preference. On a symbolic level, it is problematic for the state to mandate or even tolerate a regime in which social agencies, rather than private individuals, decide what shall be the appropriate racial composition of families. It is similarly problematic for the state to decide what the appropriate racial identity for a child is and how it is best nurtured. The Supreme Court decided some time ago that the state should not be in the business of deciding whether interracial marriages are wise. Indeed, we would not want to live in a regime in which social agencies prevented such marriages, or prevented interracial couples from producing children. Trans-racial adoption is, of course, different from interracial marriage in that it involves minor children, many of whom are unable to express their own desires with respect to the kind of family they would like. But it seems dangerous for the state or its agencies to assert that children should not or would not choose to ignore race if they could exercise choice in the formation of their families, and to conclude that it is presumptively in children's best interest to have a same-race upbringing.

The existence of trans-racial adoptive families in which black and whites live in a state of mutual love and commitment, and struggle in this context to understand issues of racial and cultural difference, seems a blessing to be celebrated. The state should not be in the business of discouraging the creation of such families.

On a pragmatic level, there is a real question as to whether it is *possible* to create a genuinely mild preference for same-race placement — a real danger that if any racial preference is allowed, enormous weight will in fact be given to race no matter what the formal rule of law. After all, current adoption law, as reflected in court rulings and the administrative guidelines interpreting Title VI, is that race *should not* be used in the absolute and determinative way that we know it systematically *is* used. Given the extraordinary level of commitment by adoption professionals to same-race placement and the amount of discretion they have traditionally enjoyed in making placement decisions, it may well be that the only determinative role that it plays today is to prohibit its use as a factor altogether.

On balance then, even a mild preference seems unwise. The generally applicable legal rule forbidding the use of race as a factor in social decision-making should be applied to the adoption area as well. Black and white prospective parents should be free to adopt children without regard to any adoption agency's views on which children would make an appropriate racial match. Agencies should use subsidies and other recruitment devices to encourage prospective parents of all races to offer homes to children. Agencies should also revise traditional criteria for white as well as black prospective parents, with the goal of creating a large enough pool of people interested in and capable of providing good homes to accommodate all the children in need.

CONCLUSION

Both common sense and the available evidence from empirical studies indicate that racial-matching policies are doing serious harm to black children. They therefore violate the principle at the core of our nation's adoption laws, namely, that the best interest of the child should govern the placement process. They also violate the anti-discrimination norm contained in applicable statutes and the United States Constitution.

The evidence from empirical studies indicates uniformly that trans-racial adoptees do as well on measures of psychological and social adjustment as black children raised in-racially in relatively similar socio-economic circumstances. The evidence also indicates that trans-racial adoptees develop comparably strong senses of black identity. They see themselves as black and they think well of blackness. The difference is that they feel more comfortable with the white community than blacks raised in-racially. This evidence provides no basis for concluding that, for the children involved, there are any problems inherent in trans-racial placement.

By contrast, the evidence from the empirical studies, together with professional opinion and our common sense, indicate that the placement delays of months and years that result from our current policies impose very serious costs on children. Children need permanency in their primary parenting relationships. They may be destroyed by delays when these involve, as they so often do, abuse or neglect in inadequate foster care or institutional settings. They will likely be hurt by delays in even the best of foster care situations, whether they develop relationships that must be disrupted, or whether they live their early years without experiencing the kind of bonding that is generally thought crucial to healthy development.

Current policies also significantly increase the risk that minority children who are older and who suffer serious disabilities will never become part of a permanent family. Advocates of these policies claim that prospective white parents do not want these children anyway. But the last two decades have demonstrated that efforts to educate and recruit adults of all races are successful in changing attitudes and making people aware of the satisfactions involved in parenting children with special needs. Current policies mean that, now, virtually no such education and recruitment is going on in the white community with respect to the waiting minority children. These are the children who wait and wait. They represent a significant piece of the foster care problem. It defies reason to claim that we would not open up many homes to these children if agencies were willing to look for such homes in the white community.

It is true that more could be done to find black families. More substantial subsidies could be provided and more resources could be devoted to recruitment. But it is extremely unlikely that our society will any time soon devote more than lip service and limited resources to putting blacks in a social and economic position where they are capable of providing good homes for all the waiting black children. It will always be far easier to get white society to agree on the goal of placing black children in black homes than to get an allocation of financial resources that will make that goal workable. The danger in using black children as hostages to pry the money loose is that white society will not see these lives as warranting much in the way of ransom. Moreover, in a desperately overburdened and under-financed welfare system, those who care about children should take children's many needs into account as they make decisions about allocating any new funds that might be available. Money is desperately needed to provide services that will enable biological families to function so that children are not unnecessarily removed from parents who could provide them with good parenting were it not for adverse circumstances. Money is desperately need for services that will protect children from abuse and neglect. It is desperately needed to improve the adoption process so that children who should be permanently removed from their families are freed for adoption and placed as promptly as possible with permanent adoptive families. Money is needed in these and other areas to assure the availability of very basic protections for children. These claims should take priority over the essentially adult agenda of promoting racial separation.

◆

COMMENT ON "WHERE DO BLACK CHILDREN BELONG?"

Rita J. Simon

I assume that when Professor Bartholet writes that "empirical studies indicate that racial-matching policies are doing serious harm to black children" she means that policies requiring a child and a potential adoptive parent to be of the same race prevent thousands of black children from being adopted. I know of no evidence that suggests that adoptions of black children by black families are not as successful as adoptions of black children by white families. The problem is that even though black families have traditionally adopted at a higher rate than white families, there are still somewhere between 30,000 and 60,000 black children available for adoption, and insufficient numbers of black families able to adopt them. At the same time, there are thousands of white families who are able and willing to adopt those parentless black children.

The data on trans-racial adoptions are as Professor Bartholet describes in her piece. Drawing upon the findings of our own twenty-year study of trans-racial adoptees and their families (Simon and Altstein, *Trans-racial Adoption*, (1977); *Trans-racial Adoption: A Followup* (1981); *Trans-racial Adoptees and Their Families* (1987); *The Case for Trans-racial Adoption* (forthcoming), Howard Simon and I have found that black adopted children have as high self-esteem, feel as integrated into their families, and have similar aspirations to go to col-leges and universities as their white birth siblings. The black adoptees have a strong sense of their racial identity and a knowl-edge of black history and culture. More than two-thirds of them believe that they can and will live in an integrated commu-nity in which they will have black and white neighbors and friends. Three-quar-ters of their white birth siblings believe that as well. Some of the specific results we found are that the children, even dur-ing adolescence, and even in families in which relationships were rocky, accusa-tive, and angry, were committed to their adoptive parents. The children (teenag-ers) emphasized that they are part of a family and that their parents are the only parents they have and want. The black adoptees answered the same way as the white birth children to true-or-false ques-tions such as: "My parents know what I am really like as a person," "People in my family trust one another," "I enjoy family life," "If I am in trouble, I know my par-ents will stick by me." Seventy-two per-cent of the black adoptees said they were proud of their racial backgrounds, eleven percent said they would prefer to be white. Among the white children born into the families, eighty-four percent said they were proud to be white and seven percent said they would prefer to be black. The parents in our study empha-sized that twenty years ago, when they decided to adopt their first child, they did

From Rita J. Simon, "Comment On Where Do Black Children Belong?," *Reconstruction,* vol. 1, no. 4, 1992, p. 51.

so because they wanted a child and they were prepared to love and care for it regardless of the child's racial or personal background. Each time we asked them what advice they would give to families who were considering adopting a child of a different race, their response was: "adopt if you love and want children. Do not adopt for political motives; do not do it as part of a crusade, nor to wave a banner, nor out of white liberal guilt." Over ninety percent said they would do it again and eighty-five percent would advise other families like their own to adopt trans-racially.

The findings of our longitudinal study unequivocally destroy the myth that black children adopted in white homes must have psychological problems, must be confused and troubled by their racial identity, and must be ignorant of the history and culture of their community. We found that trans-racial adoptions cause no specific problems and, in fact, produce black, white and Asian adults with special interpersonal talents and skills at bridging cultures. I am not saying that everything went smoothly and that there were not emotional and other psychological costs involved among the adoptions in our study (which consisted of 200 families with 157 trans-racial adoptees and 209 birth children). What I believe is important to emphasize is that our data show that the trans-racial aspect did not involve special problems, traumas, or heartbreak.

How if at all does my position differ from that of Professor Bartholet? The data from our study clearly makes me an advocate for trans-racial adoption. I know it works in the best interest of the child. I also know that adoption is a better placement for a child that institutional life or foster care. Adoption is a permanent placement. It gives a child the love, security, and stability of a family and a home without the fear of disruption and removal. Nevertheless, the data do not lead me to advocate trans-racial adoption over placing children in families of the same racial background. When there are black families available for black children, they should be placed in black homes. My interpretation of the phrase "best interests of the child" leads me to the position that trans-racial adoptions should be actively and enthusiastically pursued when no appropriate permanent same-race placements are available. Thus, Professor Bartholet and I differ. She, I believe, advocates trans-racial placement without canvassing the community for appropriate black families. We agree that trans-racial adoptions have been successful; they clearly comply with the "best interests of the child" standard. Given the realistic alternatives for the thousands of homeless black children and those in foster care, no impediment should be put in the way of trans-racial adoption. The position of the National Association of Black Social Workers (NABSW) that the "placement of black children in white homes is a hostile act against our community" and a "blatant form of racial and cultural genocide" is clearly anti-children and certainly inconsistent with the "best interests of the child" standard. The NABSW does not understand and is unwilling to believe that families can and do transcend racial barriers.

New Reproductive Technologies

♦

DO NEW REPRODUCTIVE TECHNIQUES THREATEN THE FAMILY?

Martha Field

It is sometimes difficult to identify exactly what it is about surrogate motherhood that disturbs people. Fears about commercialization of childbearing and childrearing obviously play a role, as do fears of exploitation of women and of the poor. But equally important is a fear that surrogacy involves an attack on our concept of the family.

The picture of a mother handing over her child and getting paid for it does not fit easily with current values or with conventional notions of family. Surrogacy is also destructive to families in more tangible ways. For example, it must inevitably harm the older children whom most surrogates have. How can a mother explain to her children that she is giving away or selling their newborn sister? How can she make them believe that they do not also have a price tag? If the infant is "a clone" of one of her other children, as Whitehead said Baby M was, will that not have a powerful effect? Often the surrogate's parents and even her in-laws are also very upset that their grandchild is being given away or sold, and the conflict can cause a permanent rift in the family. When Lisa Walters, a Wisconsin housewife, performed as a surrogate, her in-laws threatened a court action to remove her other two children on grounds of unfitness.

Beyond such harms to family life, surrogacy poses threats to the family as we know it. Other new reproductive techniques are like surrogacy in this respect, and they also tend to undermine our concept of the family. Moreover, they can be used in connection with surrogacy and can increase its impact by making surrogacy useful to more people. Some would prohibit or regulate surrogacy as part of a general prohibition or regulation of new reproductive techniques, rather than devising rules for surrogacy as a distinct category. The following paragraphs describe some of the new techniques and the issues they pose and then examine their potential impact upon our concepts of ourselves and our families.

For all of its social complications, surrogacy is technologically the simplest of the various alternative reproductive techniques in use today. In fact when it relies upon natural sexual intercourse between the surrogate-to-be and the man who desires a child, it uses no technology at all. Usually, however, surrogacy arrangements use artificial insemination as the means of impregnating the surrogate.

Artificial insemination, the oldest and simplest of reproductive techniques other than sexual intercourse, has been in use for more than a century. The procedure, which involves depositing ejaculated sperm in a woman's uterus with a needleless syringe, is usually performed by a

From Martha Field, "Do New Reproductive Techniques Threaten The Family?," in *Surrogate Motherhood: The Legal and Human Issues* (Cambridge, Mass.:Harvard University Press, 1988), pp. 33–45.

doctor, but it is sufficiently simple that individuals can perform it by themselves; some individuals in surrogacy cases have performed artificial insemination privately. Artificial insemination has most commonly been used apart from surrogacy, primarily by married couples. A woman may be inseminated with her husband's sperm (AIH) in order to improve her chances of conceiving, or with sperm from a third-party donor (AID) when the husband is sterile or does not wish to pass on his genes. Single women who want children also use AID. Usually when a doctor performs AID, the donor and the woman who is inseminated remain anonymous to each other. Some private inseminations also preserve the parties' anonymity; for example, a go-between can retrieve sperm from the donor without revealing the source to the donee or the donee's identity to the donor. But often when the insemination is privately accomplished, the parties are known to each other.

Some raise moral objections to artificial insemination: "to beget, without the possibility of a continuing father-child relationship, would be to withdraw biological potential from personal potential — to reverse the long process of evolution by which biological capacities have been humanized. In a defined sense, therefore, the donor's action, made possible by human science, is anti-human." But artificial insemination is generally accepted as legally permissible; there is substantially more regulation of it than of other alternative reproduction techniques, and the rules are comparatively clear.

Certain difficult questions are common to artificial insemination and other modern reproductive techniques — for example, whether artificial insemination should be available to facilitate parenthood for anyone other than married couples. Many doctors today refuse to inseminate unmarried women, and in some areas of the United States, it is still difficult for single women to find doctors who will inseminate them. But even where regulations or medical practices concerning artificial insemination are highly restrictive, they cannot easily mold social policy because artificial insemination is so easy to accomplish privately. In that way it is analogous to conventional sexual intercourse: State policy historically has been to limit to married couples sexual intercourse and the childbearing that results from it, but anti-fornication laws have limited effectiveness.

Newer, more controversial reproductive techniques raise social issues similar to those raised by surrogacy and also can be used in combination with surrogacy. So used, they make even more staggering the prospects for change.

A decade ago the first "test-tube baby" was born, and *in vitro fertilization* (IVF) showed its potential to revolutionize our view of our families and ourselves. The term *in vitro fertilization* usually refers to the process by which a doctor stimulates a woman's ovaries, removes several eggs in a procedure called a laparoscopy, and fertilize them in a Petri dish. After the fertilization, there are several options. Two or there days later, when each egg has divided a few times — usually into four-, six-, or eight-cell masses — the doctor can transfer the eggs to the uterus of the woman providing the eggs, with the hope of producing a "test-tube baby" nine months later. Although thousands of babies have by now been born by use of this procedure, the success rate is low; as of 1986, of "over 120 IVF programs... in the United States... most programs have not yet had a pregnancy and even the best programs have less than a twenty-percent success rate per laparoscopy cycle."

A different use of the IVF procedure is to transfer the fertilized ova to the uterus of a woman other than the egg donor. Doctors have recently become capable of accomplishing such a transfer. "Ovum donation," as it is sometimes called, can be accomplished either by *in vitro* fertilization or instead by fertilizing the ovum in the donor, allowing it to develop a short time, and then washing it out and transferring it to the uterus of the gestational mother. This procedure has a greater success rate than *in vitro* fertilization. The first baby so conceived was born in January 1984. Neither *in vitro* fertilization nor ovum donation has been regulated to date.

Either of these procedures, in which a baby is conceived with the sperm and egg of husband and wife and carried to term by another woman, raises questions about the meaning of the genetic tie that are even more pressing than in the classic case of surrogate motherhood. When the egg is donated by one woman and incubated in another, the intention might be either that the gestational mother would act as mother to the child, or that the egg donor, perhaps unable to bear the child herself, would be the child's mother. Indeed the term *surrogate mother* is more appropriate in this latter situation than in the context in which it is typically used; when the parties intend the egg donor to act as the mother, the gestational mother is more of a "surrogate." And the resultant child, though carried to term by the surrogate mother, inherits the genes of both the mother and the father of the couple intending to act as parents after birth.

On October 1, 1987, a gestational surrogate in South Africa gave birth to her own grandchildren. Their story illustrates the complications that surrogacy can bring to traditional family structure, and it also shows the family values that surrogacy can serve. Pat Anthony bore triplets from ova supplied by her daughter Karen and fertilized *in vitro* by Karen's husband's sperm. Mrs. Anthony is recognized as the legal mother in South Africa, even though she has a weaker case for motherhood than the surrogate who provides the egg as well as the incubation. Karen, the egg donor, legally has three new siblings. But all plan for Karen and her husband to adopt the children, so she will become their mother instead of their sister and Mrs. Anthony will change from mother to grandmother. And in a cartoon welcoming their birth, one triplet claims to be the others' uncle.

Why not welcome these new developments? They are being used to *create* families for couples who could not procreate without them. Why, then, should they be seen as undermining our family structure? The Roman Catholic church, which objects to separating sex from procreation, says it threatens the sanctity of the traditional family unit for a third party to have "any role in donating or in gestating the child." From this perspective surrogacy is objectionable because one of the genetic parents will not be part of the child's family unit. But this objection does to explain *why* it is important that the childrearing function not be separated from the genetic tie. The reasons for the church's objections to creating babies without sex are less evident than its reasons for condemning sex without babies. And the practice of adoption, which the Catholic church supports, similarly involves separation of childbearing and childrearing. (A response, of course, is that adoption is laudatory but is not analogous to surrogacy or other methods of creating children because it addresses the needs of children already in existence. Adoption therefore raises very different issues from the questions of what arrangements society should sanction for the creation of children and whether society should strive to keep the biologically related family as the norm.)

Modern reproductive technology is now being used to serve the desires of childless couples to achieve a nuclear family, but potentially it can make the traditional nuclear family even less of a norm than it now is. The threat to the nuclear family is a sufficient reason to many religious groups, political movements, and individuals for opposing surrogate motherhood. Others, conscious of the injustices and inequities the traditional family structure has wrought, would laud the change in social structure that new reproductive approaches would entail. Whether preservation or destruction of the traditional family is the preferable goal, it is important at least to isolate exactly what the objections to modern reproductive technology are.

The problems modern technology entails are various and profound. They challenge not only what remains of the traditional nuclear family as a norm, but even our ways of thinking about ourselves and our families. One set of problems concerns how to regulate the embryo conceived *in vitro* or the newly conceived embryo that has been flushed out of the egg donor. What limits should society place upon how long an embryo developing in a Petri dish can be kept alive outside the womb? If there are no limits, then if and when scientists develop the technological capability they will be able to create people in this way — a development that would fundamentally alter our conception of human life.

Today we lack the technology fully to develop a baby outside the womb. A basic issue that we face today is whether there is a moral obligation — and whether there should be a legal obligation — to transfer all fertilized ova to a receptive uterus. The case for transfer is that each of the fertilized ova represents "life" in some sense; if they can survive only through transfer to a woman's body, those who oppose abortion on "right-to-life" grounds would predictably also oppose death for any of these embryos, arguing that they should not be created in the first place unless transfer is assured. Some programs accordingly require transfer of all fertilized ova — at least all that are developing normally. That policy is not difficult for a program to follow as long as care is taken not to fertilize too many eggs, perhaps not even all that have been removed. Arguably, however, it is not necessary to regard the newly fertilized extracorporeal ovum as "life." The chances that any particular such ovum will actually develop to term are slight, even if the ovum is transferred to uterus; indeed its chances of survival and development are much lower than those of an equally long-lived embryo conceived and carried inside its mother.

In vitro fertilization also raises abortion issues in a much more direct way. The birth on January 12, 1988, of the first American quintuplets conceived through IVF opened up a different debate. The quintuplets — four girls and a boy — were born to Michele L'Esperance and her husband, Raymond, in Royal Oak, Michigan. All babies seemed healthy, despite having been delivered by caesarean section two months prematurely. Mrs. L'Esperance had needed *in vitro* fertilization because her fallopian tubes had been removed. Fifteen eggs had been taken from her ovaries; seven fertilized ova, selected on the basis of healthiness, were transferred to her uterus; and five had developed fully. This was an unusually high survival ratio.

Although Mrs. L'Esperance was permitted to carry to term, doctors generally consider it risky for a woman to bear more than three or four babies at one time, and when they have transferred more than that number of fertilized ova to the mother and all ova seem to be surviving, many of those doctors will abort "the excess." Some doctors want to avoid such selective abortions, fearing they will produce controversy and cause IVF to be regulated. But on moral grounds they believe these selective abortions are unassailable, because their purpose is to preserve life — to enable the remaining fetuses to survive.

It would be possible to avoid both this abortion debate and the ethical problems raised by the destruction of fertilized ova by not fertilizing more than four eggs at a time and then transferring them all. One cost would be that fewer women would produce a child in any particular cycle — even fewer women than do now. And even though programs can adapt to a mandatory transfer policy, there are difficulties in having such a rule. Inevitably, on rare occasions a woman who has given the eggs with the intention of having them implanted in her uterus will change her mind, or become ill, or even die. But the real problem with having a mandatory transfer policy is that it will severely restrict possibilities for research and experimentation.

Should we allow these embryos to be the subjects of experimentation and research? Research involving artificially conceived embryos can contribute to medical advances in genetic disease, infertility, cancer, birth defects, and other areas. Brain tissue transplants from aborted fetuses have recently contributed dramatically to the treatment of Parkinson's disease, for example. Brain tissue transplants from aborted fetuses could create personal and commercial motives for women to conceive and abort; fetuses would become "organ farms." And if it is legitimate to perform research on embryos that exist outside a woman's body, it is important to decide also what limits should be placed on how an extracorporeal embryo may be treated, and how long researchers should be entitled to keep the embryos alive.

Positions vary concerning the legitimacy of embryo research. The Vatican condemns it. Many groups that have considered the issues — including Britain's Warnock Committee, the American Fertility Society's Ethics Advisory Committee, and the authors of the Waller Report in Australia — have decide that it should be permitted but should be subject to prior review and should continue for only fourteen days after conception. Research is proceeding on this basis in the United Kingdom, but it has been effectively halted in this country by denying federal funding despite the favorable reports. Similarly, research — and even tissue and organ transplants — using aborted fetuses is legal here in the United States, but federal funding requires prior review, and there is currently a moratorium on funding experiments transplanting fetal tissue.

The rationale for the fourteen-day line is that it normally takes about that long for a fertilized egg to implant naturally in the uterine wall. Before implantation, there is a reduced likelihood of an egg's survival; in addition, other physiological and neurological facts about this stage of development can justify allowing research before implantation but not afterward. Moreover, the fourteen-day limit has the advantage of allowing a period for research but not too long a period. Some, however, suggest a later cut-off time for research, such as the time when the fetus begins to be sentient and capable of experiencing pain.

Discussion of research on embryos produced *in vitro* usually assumes that there is no requirement that all fertilized eggs be transferred to a woman's body for development; research can obviously be more adventuresome if there is no worry about deleterious effects upon an embryo that might develop into a child. Advocates of such research assume that the duty that is owed an embryo that will be transferred to a woman's uterus is not present when there is no intention to effect a transfer; in the latter situation, research can proceed unchecked — at least for a fourteen-day period.

There are some situations, however, in which doctors and scientists might want to perform research and experimentation upon an ovum and attempt to develop it to term — and those possibilities raise yet another ethical dilemma and another potential legal problem. One consequence of removing the embryo from the woman's body is the possibility for broad genetic experimentation and manipulation. At a minimum, it is foreseeable that parents may want the opportunity to decide, after genetic analysis of the various fertilized ova, which of the eggs should be transferred. It is already the practice even in mandatory transfer programs not to transfer "defective" eggs, even though treating newborn "defective" offspring less favorably than healthy offspring is constitutionally questionable. It is a small step from this practice to diagnosing for hereditary disease before implantation, or even to allowing the parents to select the gender of their offspring.

If society is to allow research at all, it must also decide for what purposes it will allow embryos to be created. Today the usual purpose of IVF is to enhance the opportunity for pregnancy of the woman from whom the eggs have been removed. When using the procedure for this purpose, is it permissible to super-ovulate — to produce and retrieve more eggs than predictably will be used on the particular occasion? One reason to do so might be to avoid a subsequent laparoscopy if initial attempts at conception or implantation were unsuccessful. An additional purpose might be to produce extra ova and extra embryos for purposes of research. Indeed, apart from super-ovulating women who are undergoing laparoscopy anyway, is it permissible to arrange for egg donation from women who are not seeking pregnancy, when the principal aims are experimentation or research? Although current research on extracorporeal embryos is limited, the possibilities for mass production on Petri-dish embryos for a large scale program of research and experimentation exist, once the legal and ethical concerns are resolved. That development could possibly create a profitable occupation for women willing to sell their eggs.

Finally, is it permissible to store and preserve a fertilized ovum, either for future implantation or for future research? Modern medicine is capable of freezing a fertilized egg indefinitely, without any known harm to the embryo eventually transferred. It would be difficult to combine this practice with a mandatory transfer policy, since the contingencies that might make donors unavailable or cause them to change their mind about producing offspring are much more likely to occur over a period of years than during the forty-eight to seventy-two-hour period usually involved between IVF and transfer. But with or without mandatory transfer, the freezing and storing of fertilized ova raise a multitude of unprecedented legal questions and entanglements and could undoubtedly cause fundamental social changes. The time may come, for example, when there is a commercial market for frozen embryos created from the genes of celebrities.

One of the more obvious possibilities that embryo storage creates is transfer of the embryo after the parents have died. (The same possibility exists, of course, with frozen sperms, which can be used after the father has died. In 1984 Corrine Paipalaix, a twenty-two-year-old secretary from Marseilles, asked a sperm bank to turn over to her sperm deposited by her husband before his death from cancer in 1983. The issue was controversial, but a French court approved her request.) Indeed, many years might elapse between the death of both the egg and sperm donors and the transfer of the embryo to the uterus of another woman. Issues about whether an embryo transfer after the donors' deaths is permissible, or even required, received much public attention a few years ago in the case of the frozen Rios embryos. In 1981 Mario and Elsa Rios of Los Angeles had gone to Melbourne, Australia, for *in vitro* fertilization. Three of Mrs. Rios' eggs were fertilized; one was transferred to her and resulted in a miscarriage; the others were frozen. Two years later, both Mr. and Mrs. Rios were killed in a Chilean plane crash, and they had left no instructions for disposition of the fertilized eggs. Is transfer mandatory, is it prohibited, or is it optional — and, if optional, who is to make the decision?

Is the frozen embryo a person who can inherit when her genetics parents die, so that if later transferred and carried to term she will be heir? It is difficult to imagine how the law of estates could adjust to the resulting long-term uncertainties about whether or not heirs would be produced. This is but one example; long-term storage has innumerable possibilities for jarring relationships; this seems inevitable when a person born may have been par-

ented by person who lived many years before. One way to reduce the difficulties considerably, if freezing and storing are accepted, would be to consider the gestational mother the sole legal parent in the event of transfer, since she alone will necessarily be present at the time of birth. If it seems important to locate rights in one person — in order to have a clear rule, rather than deciding custody on a case-by-case basis — that person should be the gestational mother. Whether or not that suggestion is accepted, the new biological techniques will compel society to consider — as both a philosophical and a legal question — the degree of importance to attach to genetic ties.

Embryo storage, experimentation, and research also dramatically increases the possibilities of altering the embryos' genetic characteristics. The need to formulate policies permitting, prohibiting, or otherwise regulating genetic experimentation becomes imperative.

Even apart from genetic manipulation, this combination of new biological possibilities has staggering implications for our social structure. Many of the problems posed by surrogate motherhood assume much larger proportions if IVF and embryo storage are also available. Most important, the ability to use women simply as gestational mothers dramatically increase the appeal of surrogacy. Parents entirely capable of producing their own biological child by themselves could acquire the option of producing a child who is genetically linked to both parents without the necessity of undergoing pregnancy or childbirth. If this possibility leads to a sharp increase in demand for surrogates, including gestational surrogates, the exploitation not only of the domestic poor but also of third-world women is likely to mushroom; it does not seem farfetched to imagine that there will one day be a thriving business of sending frozen sperm and frozen embryos around the world to be transferred to childbearers for the production of children for contracting couples.

Many people who have no objections to the current use of modern reproductive techniques to bring happiness to childless couples would nonetheless be alarmed by some of the possibilities that the new technology offers. Current ethical objections to surrogacy reflect a reasonable prediction that the means we are now using to make the traditional family possible for those who cannot otherwise achieve it carry with them the seeds of destruction of the concept of family as we know it. Of course our views will undoubtedly change as practices change, and future generations will see these issues very differently. It is reasonable to expect that such fundamental views as the merits of genetic manipulation, our notions concerning family, and even what it means to be human will develop and change. It seems inevitable that without regulation modern technology will take this course, and that if we leave technology and individual initiative unchecked, it will be difficult to contain the revolution that will follow.

This prognosis has led to a perceived need to develop rules to contain or at least to regulate modern reproductive techniques, including surrogacy. Rules are needed both for the short term and the long term, and the choices that are made may have profound implications for how society will develop. But the unusual and difficult aspect of devising regulations for these subjects is that society is largely ignorant of the subjects to be regulated. Eliminating the new technology choices, even if that could be accomplished, would cut off our knowledge and prevent society

from learning what technologies may weight the balance in favor of state rather than nationwide regulation. As with surrogacy, in the absence of federal regulation modern reproductive practices are governed by the varying rules of different states — or by the states' failure to formulate any rules.

Jurisdictions cannot decline to have any policy, because a choice of no regulation also has consequences. If the law remains silent, the resulting uncertainty may slow down modern reproductive techniques; on that theory, proponents of surrogacy have supported explicit legalization and regulation. But the absence of regulation also allows all reproductive techniques to develop unchecked.

With or without regulation, modern reproductive technology may sharply transform our future. Once technology has developed the capability of doing something that will add to the happiness of some people, it is likely that the new technological arts will be pursued. Even if we as a society tried to prevent the transformation that the new technology is bringing, we might not be able ultimately to stave it off. As long as some governments permit surrogacy or reproductive technologies, some people can travel to where they are available. Moreover, they can use the technologies from afar by simply transporting their sperm, egg, or embryo. Accordingly, it is likely that in time the new technology will bring the opportunity to many more people to become a biological parent. And for fertile women, conventional childbearing will become only one choice available out of many. Singles and couples will be able to choose whether to parent, whether to donate the genetic material for the child, and whether to undergo pregnancy, and those options will exist independently of one another. For Professor Marjorie Schultz, this transformation from a time when parenting is determined by fate and chance to a time when it will be determined by decision making is a positive development. Accordingly, she suggests that contracts — mutually binding contracts — are an appropriate medium for decision-making concerning childbearing and childrearing.

Conceivably, at some future time people will have very different attitudes toward childbearing than we do today, and they will consider it suitable for the law to recognize a contract that binds all parties at the outset to a custody determination that they, represented by counsel, have agreed to in advance. But even if this future is inevitable, there is no need to hasten it by enforcing surrogacy contracts today. Regulating and even limiting the new reproductive possibilities may mold the form they take and perhaps even substantially slow down the transformation they will bring.

◆

INSIDE THE SURROGATE INDUSTRY

Susan Ince

This article offers a firsthand account of a woman's experience in applying to become a surrogate mother. It exposes the lack of medical and psychological safeguards, the insensitivity to both surrogates and women with infertility, the surrogate's precarious legal and financial position, and the extensive controls over her life by the company. The essay provides a radical feminist analysis of this male-controlled "growth industry."

> This is not a nine-to-five job. It demands enormous commitment and understanding. It requires your total thought and consciousness, full-time, twenty-four hours a day.[*]

The job was for the key position in one of the "growth industries" of the 1980s, and involved rigid application processes, including thorough medical examination, intelligence testing, psychological evaluation, and even genetic screening if indicated. I had just applied to become a surrogate mother.

From first reading the glowing newspaper reports and seeing the self-satisfied lawyers on television, I had been uneasy about the idea of a surrogate industry. I had played out lively and humorous "what if" scenarios with friends, but had no substantive answers to the questions of proponents: What's wrong with it, if that's what the women want to do? Are you against them making money? Are you saying the industry should be regulated by the state? The questions were naggingly familiar, the same ones asked by apologists of the sex-buying industries, prostitution and pornography.

In order to get a firsthand look, I answered an advertisement placed in a local newspaper by a surrogate company con-

---

[*]   From the first telephone inquiry made by the author to the surrogate company [editor's note].

From Susan Ince, "Inside the Surrogate Industry," in *Test-tube Women: What Future for Motherhood,* Rita Arditti, Renate Duelli Klein, and Shelley Minden, eds. (London:Pandora, 1984), pp. 99–116.

sidered reputable and established. Two weeks later, I met with the program's director and psychologist in their basement office on a street filled with small businesses and discount shops. The office looked newly occupied, and the director struggled with the unfamiliar typewriter and telephone system. Decorations included pictures of Victorian children; plump, white, and rosy-cheeked. Missing from sight were file cabinets, desks with drawers, and other standard office paraphernalia.

The director did most of the talking. I was touched by her stories of infertile couples — the woman who displayed the scars of multiple unsuccessful surgeries creating a tire-track pattern across her abdomen; the couple, now infertile, whose only biological child was killed by a drunk driver; the couples who tried in good faith to adopt an infant, and were kept on waiting lists until they passed the upper age limit and were disqualified. Stories like these, said the director, inspired her to offer a complete surrogate mother service to combine all the administrative, legal, and medical aspects of this modern reproductive alternative.

The screening and administrative procedures were outlined by the director as simple and proven successful. As a potential surrogate, I had to pass an interview with the director and psychologist, history and physical examination, and finally meet with a lawyer who would explain the contract before I signed to officially enter the program. Parents desiring surrogate services also had to pass screening by the director and psychologist, and pay $25,000 at contract signing. Surrogate and purchasers never meet, although information about them is described so that both parties can determine if the match is acceptable. Complete anonymity is stressed as a benefit of going to this company in-stead of making private arrangements through a lawyer.

While pregnant, the surrogate receives approximately $200 to purchase maternity clothing, and is reimbursed 15 cents/mile for transportation costs. It is her responsibility to enter the program with medical insurance that includes maternity benefits. The company will pay her medical and life insurance premiums and non-covered medical costs while she is in the program. After delivery of the baby to the father, the surrogate receives her $10,000 fee.

I tried to ask my many questions about the procedure in a curious and enthusiastic manner befitting a surrogate. The answers were not reassuring.

What happens if you don't become pregnant? Artificial insemination is tried twice a month for six months. If the surrogate has not conceived, she is then removed from the program and the father begins again with a different surrogate.

And she receives no money for her participation?" No. Look at it this way. We pay all the fees and medical expenses. What has it cost you? Unless you start putting a value on your time."

What if she has a miscarriage? Again, no money is paid to the surrogate. The father decides if he will take a chance again with her. Then if the surrogate also wants to try again, there is a second attempt.

What if the baby is born dead, or something is wrong with it and the father doesn't want it? In this case, the surrogate has fulfilled her contract and is paid $10,000. 'We are not in the business of paying for a perfect baby. We are paying for a service rendered. Possible fine-line distinctions between a late miscarriage (no fee to surrogate) and a stillborn premature baby (full fee paid) are made by the primary physician provided by and paid for by the company.

What qualities are you looking for in a surrogate? Ideally, they would like her to be married and to already have children. A healthy child provides "a track record. It's as simple as that." And the husband is a "built-in support system." They hastened to assure me, however, that there were exceptions (I am single with no children). "Why, we just entered a single woman who had never been pregnant before. And the next couple that came in *demanded* a single donor. Things just always match up. It's a miracle!"

The director chatted on about the enthusiasm and good spirit of the "girls" in the program so far. Many of them, it seemed, had added to the program by inventing creative ways to include the fathers more in the pregnancy and birth process. The women with infertility, who provide the basis for the industry's foundation, and who will become the adoptive mothers, are notably absent from consideration. It is expected that surrogates will "write a nice note" to the father after conception, and many plan to follow this with a tape recording of the baby's heartbeat. One "girl" even invited the father to be in the delivery room, and this was applauded as an altruistic gesture beyond anyone's expectations. "But wait," I asked wide-eyed. "I thought everything was completely anonymous." She looked at me as if I were a simple-minded child. "Well, he's not going to be looking at her face! He's just there to see his baby come out."

I was nervous two weeks later when I went to meet the psychologist who I thought would administer IQ tests and probe into my motivations to judge whether I was an acceptable surrogate. My plan was to offer no unsolicited information, but to tell the truth about all questions asked (except for my intention to become a surrogate). When I arrived, the psychologist was borrowing

Kleenex from the tailor next door. I made a small wisecrack, "What's a psychologist without Kleenex, right?," and he acted as if this was unusually clever. "Boy, that's funny," he said, continuing to chuckle as he returned to the office. "You are really sharp." Either he was attempting to put me at ease, or this was going to be easier than I thought.

We settled down for the actual interview. I was asked my name, address, phone number, eye color, hair color, whether I had any birth defects (no), whether I had children (no), whether I had a boyfriend (male friends, yes), whether I expected to someday marry, settle down, have babies and live happily ever after (no). He inquired as to my religious upbringing (Protestant) and began reminiscing about a college sweetheart ("Oh, I used to be so in love with a Protestant girl...."). Ten minutes later, we got back on track and I was surprised to find he had no more questions. "I just needed to be sure you're still positive 100 percent. You are, aren't you?" Without a nod or a word from me, he continued, "You seem like it to me."

Because I was "obviously bright," there would be no IQ testing. I was never asked whether I had been pregnant before, whether I was under medical or psychiatric treatment, or how I would feel about giving up the baby. To lower costs and save time, the medical exam would take place after I had signed the contract, while a match was being made. The psychologist pronounced me "wonderful" and "perfect," and I awaited my next call.

Soon the phone rang and the director solemnly said she had two serious questions to ask me. "It's not easy but I think it's important for us to lay our cards on the table...." I gulped, thinking she was suspicious. "I just want to ask you this straight up, right now, yes or no, are you going to have any trouble making appointments?" (I had rescheduled the last visit because of car trouble.) When I assured her that there would be no problem, she asked her second question. "What are you going to do with the money?" This, I later heard her say, was asked of each surrogate to weed out those women who had frivolous motivations, such as "buying designer jeans." My answer was deemed acceptable, and screening was complete.

Although I was repeatedly assured that there had never been a problem with legal and financial arrangements made through the company, it was acknowledged by all concerned that this was a largely uncharted and confusing legal area. The contract itself repeated three times that a surrogate might seek her own legal counsel, fee to be paid by the program, to further her understanding of the concept, rules and regulations, rights and liabilities involved. After I was deemed ready to "enter the fold," I inquired about the independent legal consultation. There had been problems with that, the director said. Some of the "girls" had submitted bills up to $500 for legal fees, which program members thought was exorbitant. Of even greater concern, surrogates had come back from their consultation with new doubts and questions. Because of this, I was strongly encouraged to see a nearby lawyer "not associated" with the program, but already familiar with the contract, and selected and paid by the company to provide 'independent' consultations to all of the surrogates. When I said that I had my own lawyer in mind, she reiterated strenuously that she advised against it. As an example, she said, one girl had come back to her from an outside lawyer, saying "He's asking me all these questions and he's really driving me crazy." The director said, "and after I

sent her to see our lawyer, and he explained it our way, she felt much better and thanked me."

I decided to hear how this independent company lawyer would explain the contract and our meeting was arranged. Before then, the director called to say she was eager for me to sign the contract on the same day as my consultation. A couple had been found who, after she had taken the liberty of describing me, said that they were very interested in me as a surrogate. More hesitant than I had ever heard her, she cautioned that we needed to discuss "certain issues" which might be a problem. The father, she explained, was very bright, but Oriental, and would that be a problem? His wife was Caucasian. I said I couldn't see any problem, since the wife would to be the one I was matching. She said that was *exactly right,* and that the couple could have easily adopted an Oriental child, but they wanted a half-Caucasian. We would talk more at our next meeting.

To my surprise, the independent consultation was held within earshot of the director, who was called on by the lawyer to interpret various clauses of the contract, and who kept a record of questions I asked. The interview was held at the new corporate office, on a block filled with elegant fur and clothing-shops in one of the richest counties in the United States. The move was explained as necessary for the convenience of the buying parents.

The director took me first into her office for a private chat before meeting the lawyer. A new couple was described — in the petroleum business, very wealthy, and building a new house in anticipation of my baby. She explained that this was a very common and positive sign, the parents "inevitably building, remodeling, adding wings, buying new houses, not because they don't live in perfectly lovely homes, but because they want to be doing something for the baby during the pregnancy." I asked if she had any plans to write a book including some of her interesting observations about the surrogate process. She nodded enthusiastically,

> Oh yes, we are collecting data right now — if for nothing else than to dispel the misconceptions people have about surrogates. I'm very sorry to say it, but they don't think our surrogates are nice girls like you. When people think surrogate, they think tight black satin slacks. I don't know why, but they do.

By this time, the lawyer had arrived and we settled down with the contract. Three areas were of greatest concern to me: the extensive behavioral controls over the surrogate, her precarious legal/financial position should something go wrong, and the ill-defined responsibilities of the company itself. Each of these was broached during this interview with what I hoped were sincere and non-threatened requests for clarification. Briefly, the rules governing surrogates' behavior are as follows (quotation marks indicate exact language of contract):

Sex: The surrogate must abstain from sexual intercourse from two weeks before insemination until a conception is confirmed.

The surrogate must not engage in "sexual promiscuity."

Drug use: The surrogate must not "smoke nor drink any alcohol [sic] beverage from the time of initial insemination until delivery."

The surrogate must not use illegal drugs.

Medical: The surrogate must keep all scheduled administrative, medical, psychological, counseling, or legal appointments arranged for her. These may be "set by the physician in accordance with his schedule and, therefore, may not always be convenient for the surrogate mother."

The surrogate must use the services (medical, psychological, etc.) which are chosen and provided by the program. The surrogate must submit to all standard medical procedures and "any additional medical precautions and/or instructions outlined by the treating physician."

"The surrogate must furnish medical and psychological records to the company and the parents."

In general, any action that "can be deemed to be dangerous to the well-being of the unborn child" constitutes breach of contract which means the surrogate will forfeit her fee, and be subjected to legal action from the buyers.

The company lawyer responded to my questions about these restrictions by denying their importance and reiterating the goodwill of all concerned. On alcohol — "You're on the honor system. No one is going to care if you have a glass of wine now and then." On sexual promiscuity — "Who cares? I don't know what that means. I don't know why that's in here." When asked if there was a legal definition, he said, "They just want to be sure who the father is. Intercourse doesn't hurt the baby, does it? Don't worry about it."

I was worrying a lot, mostly about the company's complete control over the surrogate. There was no limit to the number of appointments that could be scheduled requiring the surrogate's participation. If she should become uncooperative, they could simply schedule more psychological visits. If they didn't want to pay her, they could schedule so many that she couldn't possibly keep them. The medical controls seemed particularly ominous: all standard procedure PLUS ANY OTHER precautions or instructions. This could include bed rest, giving up a job, etc. A medical acknowledgment attached to the main body of the contract advised that "there are certain medical risks inherent in any pregnancy. Some of these may be surgical complications, such as, but not limited to, appendix and gall bladder." Of course, these surgical complications would most likely arise from a cesarean delivery, major surgery which is not mentioned at all in conversation or contract. If the doctor should request one, the surrogate would have no contractual right to object.

Complications could also arise after birth. I learned that names of both surrogate and father would appear on the birth certificate, compromising promised anonymity, and that the certificate would only be destroyed several weeks, months, or years later when the child was adopted by "the potential stepmother" (in the same way a new spouse can adopt a child if the former spouse wishes to relinquish her/his rights and responsibilities). "Why not right away?" I asked. The lawyer recommended a reasonable waiting period because an immediate adoption "could be construed, by someone who wanted to construe it that way, as baby-selling."

In fact, he elaborated, the baby-selling argument could also be used by a court to declare the entire contract illegal and void. It is acknowledged in the contract itself that its *"rights and liabilities may or may not be honored in a Court of Law should a breach arise."* The document further states that, in a lawsuit, it could be used to assist "a court of competent jurisdiction in ascertaining the intention" of surrogates and parents.

If the surrogate breaches her contract, by abortion, by violation of rules, or by refusal to relinquish the child, the father may sue her for the $25,000 he paid into the program, plus additional costs. If the parents breach by refusal to accept delivery of the child or failure to pay medical expenses, the surrogate may sue them for her $10,000 fee, plus the expense of child support or placing the child up for adoption. "What about the company?" I asked. "If something went wrong and I had to sue the parents, would they help me or pay my legal expenses?" "No," he replied. "When the shit hits the fan you're on your own." Indeed, each party is required to sign a "hold harmless" clause which says that no matter what happens the company is not responsible. The lawyer explained this clause away as meaningless — everyone would, of course, sue everyone else if there should be a problem.

As we perused the contract, the lawyer discovered a new clause had appeared since his last consultation, the "Amniocentesis Addendum" which stated that, should the treating physician request, the surrogate would submit to amniocentesis for prenatal diagnosis. If results were abnormal, she would consent to abortion at the parents' request. To my surprise, this clause out of the entire contract was worrisome to the lawyer. Why, he asked, should the surrogate abort at 20-24 weeks gestation and receive no fee, when she could carry the pregnancy to term and fulfill her contract regardless of the infant's condition? I was more concerned about what might be considered an abnormality sufficient to request abortion. What about a sex chromosome abnormality? What about just the "wrong" sex? I was also concerned that this again allowed for the total discretion of the treating physician. Why was it left ambiguous in the contract when there is no legitimate indication for amniocentesis that couldn't be known before the pregnancy started? My suspicion was that it would always be requested, as an unacknowledged "quality control" measure.

The lawyer called the director into the room, and asked about this clause's financial disadvantage to the surrogate. Any woman, she stated flatly, who would knowingly carry a defective fetus to term to cheat the parents out of $10,000 would not be acceptable to the program. Nevertheless, the lawyer suggested that I not sign until he spoke with the author of the contract, to suggest that a small fee be paid to the surrogate if there was such an unfortunate occurrence. My one request before signing was to see a copy of the parents' contract, to compare responsibilities, and to "make sure they hadn't been promised something I couldn't fulfill." The request was never honored.

The lawyer called the next day to say the Amniocentesis Addendum must remain as written. He paraphrased the company officials: "The program works because it works the way it is. We cannot make big changes for the surrogate or the parents." We arranged to meet a week later, after I had received the parents' contract, for final signing.

Before then, however, I was called by the director who had become concerned while listening in on my legal consultation. She admonished me for asking too many questions:

> The program works because it is set up to work for the couple. You have to weigh why you are participating in the program. For the money only, or to do the service of providing the couple with a baby. To be very frank, we are looking for girls with both those motivations. I felt after the last visit that this is a gal looking for every possible way to earn that money, and that concerns me.... We are playing with peoples' lives, with people who are desperately looking for a child. They have made an emotional investment... emotionally and in every other way that baby is not yours.... No contract is perfect for anyone, for anything.

She urged me to take an extra week before signing, and if I was still interested to arrange to be reevaluated by the psychologist.

When I called to schedule the interview, I was informed it would not be with the original psychologist (who thought I was perfect) but with a new "more convenient" one. I was very apprehensive about the visit, and when I knocked on the psychologist's door, about five minutes late, I expected to be confronted about my tardiness as yet another sign of my "bad" behavior. No one answered my knock, but I could hear someone coming down the hallway. A woman approached and let me in the unlocked door. I stood in the waiting room a few moments and the doctor arrived. As we shook hands, he said, "I hear you've been knocking at my door."

"Yes,"

"And I you didn't even think to open it." This was not a question but a statement: I felt my every move was open for analysis.

The doctor was in charge for the next one-and-a-half hours. It seemed he pried into every aspect of my family background. He was extremely interested in my romantic life, and my intention not to marry was considered unusual and an indication of not planning for the future. He also wondered how, with no man in town, I managed to "feel loved and affirm my femininity." ("By having this baby, of course!," I didn't say.) As the session went on, I felt violated and bullied by this man, and too intimidated not to tell the truth. Only two of his inquiries obviously concerned becoming a surrogate mother: "How will you feel if you aren't accepted for the program?" and "Are you the kind of person who can start a task and complete it, or do you lose interest in the middle and abort the project?" ("Great choice of words, doctor.") He concluded the encounter with a short analysis of my psyche, explaining that he felt that I deserved this as payment for putting time and thought into the session. Again, I had gone through a psychological evaluation with no questions about whether I was under psychiatric care, whether I used medications or drugs, or how I would feel about carrying an anonymous man's child and giving it up after birth. He also seemed uninterested in my friends, emotional supports, living or employment situations. Only my relationships to men were probed.

About two weeks later, I received the verdict from the director: I was acceptable to the program and could start as soon as possible. I was embarrassed to find myself pleased to have "passed" my analysis. I decided I could find out nothing further without signing the contract. Using a possible job transfer as an excuse, I asked to have my file put on hold a few months.

A few days following my last psychological evaluation, the director and lawyer for the company appeared on a holiday talk show, smiling and discussing at length the "blessing" of this reproductive alternative. They were treated with deference by the host as they told the identical infertility stories, and outlined the tried and true professional process. At the time of my interviews, the "tried and true" process had yet to result in even one pregnancy, so all hospital, contractual, emotional, and financial arrangements were untested.

The careful screening process was a myth. I encountered no evidence of real medical or psychological safeguards; just enough hurdles to test whether I would be obedient. The minimal questioning I did was labeled as selfish, dangerous, and unique in their experience. My impression was that there was a serious shortage of available surrogates and that any appropriate (white and compliant) woman would be rushed into contract signing and immediately told her perfectly matched couple had been located.

Anonymity was also a myth, since the father would know the city where I lived, my name from the birth certificate, and my physical characteristics from required baby pictures, from company files, and medical and psychological reports. He would have visitation rights to the hospital nursery, and perhaps to the delivery room. Company files were said to be confidential, but it was acknowledged that they would be opened upon court order.

It is a myth that women are easily making large sums of money as surrogates. The director of this program acknowledges that the woman who goes through a lengthy insemination process may end up being paid less than $1.00 an hour for her participation. To earn this sum, she is completely "on-call" for the company. She may be required to undergo invasive diagnostic procedures, forfeit her job, and perhaps undergo major surgery with its attendant morbidity and mortality risks. Of course, should there be a miscarriage or failure to conceive, the surrogate receives no compensation at all.

The flow of money is also interesting. I was told that the surrogate's $10,000 fee would be held in an escrow account until delivery, but this was not confirmed by the lawyer or contract. If the parents breach the contract, why must the surrogate sue them for her fee, which the company already holds? And is she breaches the contract, shouldn't the couple be entitled to a refund from the company without taking the surrogate to court? The company holds all of the funds, makes the profit, and attempts to take a minimum of the financial/legal risks.

Control by contract is a crucial element of this surrogate program, with power clearly in the hands of the company officials. Besides the explicit demands in the contract, an additional clause yielding staggering control to the company was brought to my attention by an unaffiliated lawyer later consulted. She pointed out Item Nine in a list of rules for surrogates which reads: "Surrogate mother and her husband must sign all documents provided by the (company) including but not limited to the surrogate mother agreement and contract," plus addendums listed. In essence, at any time I could be handed any new document and be obligated to sign it, no matter what its effect on my well-being or best interests.

It came as no surprise, then, when I later read in the newspaper that the first surrogate to become pregnant was to have none other that the program director as her childbirth coach. I could imagine a surrealistic scene with the director by the woman's side, the father at the foot of the bed to see "his baby come out," perhaps even a bag over the surrogate's head to preserve someone's anonymity. In the interest of delivering a perfect child, all birth technologies would be employed, and at the first sign of fetal distress or maternal

complaint the coach could encourage or insist on a cesarean delivery.

Who is this baby for? It is clear from contract and practice that the purchasing father is the key figure of the industry. From the first phone contact, I was told "the child is the child of the natural parents. That means the father." The contract requires delivery of the child to the father, and every effort is made to include him in the procedures. This is in sharp contrast to the invisible woman who will become the adoptive mother of the child. She is referred to only rarely, as the "wife" of the father, and the "potential stepmother." There were no plans mentioned to try and include her in the process, although it would seem she might have a greater need for company sensitivity and an active role.

The fathers, as described by the industry representatives, are largely upper middle class and well-educated. As the director explained it, "to be able to come up with $25,000 cash, they *have* to be well-educated." They have a desire to biologically father an infant; some have tried adoption and turn in desperation to the surrogate alternative to begin a family; others are already rearing children from their wives' previous marriages, but want a child of their own. The need to continue patriarchal lineage, to make certain the child has the sperm and name of the buyer, is primary.

The public image of the surrogate mother is important to the reputation of the companies who must distinguish their "reproductive service" from both sexual prostitution and baby-selling. The new surrogate image is bright, altruistic, and feminine. She is a very special girl next door, a plucky pioneer in a new industry, a girl who loves being pregnant and is able to give a man what his wife can't. While company spokespersons promote the surrogate as on a par with the buyers, able to provide good genes and a clean prenatal environment, there is also an attempt to place her in a slightly different moral class from the prospective parents. They state the logical economic and convenience incentives to becoming a surrogate, then readily disclose that many have had previous abortions or have given up children for adoption. These surrogates, approximately one-third of applicants according to a Michigan psychologist, may participate in order to atone for their previous abortions. Such public announcements, although seemingly in contrast to the desired altruistic image, and based on spurious research citing a statistic no different than general population estimates, may have at least two positive results for the companies:

1. It may ease the conscience of liberal prospective buyers, who can more easily accept the financial misuse of the surrogate if they believe she is receiving invisible psychological/moral gains.

2. It may lure some prospective surrogates who have unresolved abortion experiences, perhaps exacerbated by new anti-abortion propaganda.

In general, surrogates may be deterred from demanding better treatment, if convinced that giving up this child is part of a moral punishment or therapeutic process.

There is a need for feminists to pay attention to the surrogate industry and to structure debate in feminist terms. There have, of course, been outspoken critics of the surrogate companies, but they have primarily questioned the industry's effect on traditional business dealings and family structure. For example, the only ethical issue raised in a lengthy *Wall Street Journal* article was whether participants might be taking unfair advantage of insurance companies offering maternity benefits. Robert Francoeur, in his 1974 book *Utopian Motherhood* (p. 102), envisioned a gloomy world in which so-called "mercenary mothers" would jeopardize the traditional "monogamous family structure."

The metaphors of description and criticism are fascinating: Is the surrogate mother a prostitute, or is she instead a modern extension of the wet nurse? Is the surrogate arrangement like donating sperm, simply giving women the right to sell their reproductive capacity as men have done for years? Or is the arrangement more like building a house, where the father furnishes half the blueprint and materials and the labor is contracted out? Is it baby-selling? Or is it organ-selling, morally equivalent to allowing the needy to sell their kidneys to rich patients? Each metaphor frames political/ethical discourse in different terms. Even the use of the term "surrogate mothering," or the more recently popular euphemism "surrogate parenting," begins by labeling the biological mother as artificial. Allowing the debate to be structured by the industry has slowed criticism from the feminist community. In California, after an educational session from an industry representative, a NOW chapter passed a resolution supporting efforts to have the surrogate contracts recognize and enforceable under California law.

Our recognition of the problems of infertile women may also be delaying a strong feminist opposition to the surrogate industry. We must not only offer support to women in the painful emotional situation of being involuntarily childless, but we must examine its broader historical basis. The infertility was largely brought to us from the manufacturers of other types of reproductive control, birth control pills, and IUDs. The same laws which make it difficult for many infertile women to adopt children will make the surrogate alternative equally unavailable unless she is part of a wealthy married heterosexual couple. Older children, children of color, and those with special needs will remain unadoptable, and the traditional patriarchal family system will remain intact.

In *Right-Wing Women* (1983), Andrea Dworkin has placed surrogate motherhood in the center of her elegant model of the systematic exploitation of women. In it, she describes the brothel model and the farming model. Simply stated, in the brothel model women are used efficiently and specifically for sex by groups of men. In the farming model, women are used by individual men, not so efficiently, for reproduction. The surrogate industry provides a frightening synthesis of both which

> enables women to sell their wombs within the terms of the brothel model. Motherhood is becoming a new branch of female prostitution with the help of scientists who want access to the womb for experimentation and for power. A doctor can be the agent of fertilization; he can dominate and control conception and reproduction. Women can sell reproduction capacities the same way old-time prostitutes sold sexual ones but without the stigma of whoring because there is no penile intrusion (pp. 181-82).

This system will become increasingly efficient with the refinement of other reproductive technologies such as embryo transplanting. As Genoveffa Corea points out (forthcoming), we are not far from being able to use a combination of artificial insemination and embryo transplant to allow third-world women to become the prenatal carriers of completely white children (at the same time that Depo-Provera and other exports are compromising these women's ability to conceive their own children).

The language and process encountered in my experience within a surrogate company is consistent with the reproductive prostitution model described by Dworkin. The surrogate is paid for "giving the man what his wife can't." She "loves being pregnant," and is valued solely and temporarily for her reproductive capacity. After she "enters the fold" she is removed from standard legal protections and is subject to a variety of abuses. She is generally considered to be mercenary, collecting large unearned fees for her services, but the terms of the system are in reality such that she may lose more permanent opportunities for employment, and may end up injured or dead with no compensation at all. Even the glowing descriptions of the surrogates sound remarkably like a happy hooker with a heart of gold.

The issue of prostitution has been a difficult one for feminists; so ancient and entrenched a part of the patriarchal system that it seems almost impossible to confront. We must not now participate in a quiet liberal complicity with the new reproductive prostitution. It is our challenge to pay attention to our feminist visionaries, and to expose the surrogate industry during its formation.

Foster Care

♦

WHY SHOULD I GIVE MY BABY BACK?
Jane Doe

As work on a corporate project wound down, I made the call. I was ready to take home a "boarder baby."

Boarder babies are primarily victims of the crack epidemic, born in New York City hospitals of mothers who test positive for cocaine and cannot take care of them. They are taken by private agencies operating under the supervision of the city's Department of Social Services and given to foster parents temporarily, until they can be placed with relatives. Unless people open their homes to them, the babies languish in institutions, unloved, untouched, apathetic, cast off.

I had requested a boy. Having raised daughters of my own, I wanted the experience of a son. Next to "race" on my application I wrote "no preference," which meant he would most likely be black. My only other request was that he be healthy, as crack babies go. I didn't have the courage my first time out to deal with the effects of extreme damage.

"Who do we have today?" the cheerful voice on the telephone cried out to someone in his office. "Any newborn boys?" Moments later he was back on the line with news of an available four-week-old boy with "positive tox" from crack cocaine weighing considerably more than his birth weight of six and a half pounds and ready to leave the hospital.

Two days later he was delivered to my apartment by a young man who had been commandeered as a messenger for the trip from Brooklyn to Manhattan by an overworked socialworker friend. He put the infant in my arms and laid his worldly possessions down next to us: two small bottles of formula, one gray cotton sweater, one nightgown, three Pampers and the bright and pretty comforter he was wrapped in, made lovingly by some volunteer from some charity group.

In addition, there was a paper with his name, his mother's name, the hospital he was born in, date of birth and the information that he was on a three-hour feeding schedule. Then the messenger left. I don't remember if I signed a receipt. I think I did.

There we sat, this little being and I. How did I, after years of husband, children and the very mixed blessing of domesticity, end up with another baby in my arms? If I had called yesterday or tomorrow, who would have been my baby then? What was I doing with a newborn infant I had never seen before?

Despite the oft-voiced concerns of my loved ones and friends, I felt perfectly capable of giving him up when the time came, knowing that I had saved him from living death. I'm a big girl, I said. I can handle it. Not without some paid and loss, of course, but I can always take another child and do it again. I'm not about to bring up a child to maturity. Not at my age. I've done that already. Besides, deep down I believed some loving grandmother would come look-

From Jane Doe, "Why Should I Give My Baby Back?," *New York Times*, Dec. 22, 1990, p. 27, col. 2.

ing for him, eager to return him to the welcoming arms of his family.

Well, my son has celebrated his first birthday. He's a real hunk with "thunder thighs" and a smile and a squeal that set my heart afire. His early, uncontrollable muscular tremors are gone and he is filled with the boundless excitement of discovery that all children feel when they are loved. I have gone back to the gym to be able to keep up with him.

No grandma has come to fetch him. No aunts, no uncles, no cousins. No mother. No one has even come to see him. Teams of socialworkers do tireless outreach work, and every few months I am told that they have found someone who "wants him." Translation: They have contacted some overburdened relative who is tempted by the monthly payments to take yet another unwanted child. But these families never request a visit, and each is ultimately rejected as unsuitable.

In my boy's case they seem to have run out of relatives, and the focus now is on his mother. No one is supposed to tell me much. Strict confidentiality, and all that. But I was recently warned that she had entered drug rehab and wanted her baby back. I was told to bring him to the agency for a visit with her, and to be prepared for her taking him on weekends until she was well enough to keep him for good.

"Keep him up all night, make him crabby so she won't see that irresistible smile." "Don't feed him too much." "Dress him in throw-up clothes and pray that he cries for the entire visit." Such was the friendly advice from family and friends — people he had regularly reduced to blithering, ga-ga blobs of ecstasy.

But we showed up for the visit with him sweet-smelling, smiling and full of trust, and me a teary, anxious mess. She never showed up. Neither did her socialworker. We made another appoint-

ment for two weeks later. Again, she didn't show. Neither did her socialworker.

The pain of these episodes is indescribable. To be a mother, to have that ferocious instinct of protectiveness and to be rendered impotent is truly hell. Rather than surrender to my helplessness, I spent days on the telephone seeking the best advice I could find on my rights. Here is what I learned: I was as helpless as I felt.

The sanctity of the family rules supreme. Before the agency can go to court and move to have the mother's rights terminated, they first have to exhaust every effort the law requires. Until he was with me for a year, I had no rights whatsoever. I was a paid baby-sitter for New York City, bonding or no bonding.

I understand that these laws were created for another time, another world, when mothers with emotional or financial problems deserved every opportunity to get their beloved children back, when grandmothers did come to fetch their precious babies if the mothers couldn't get it together. But that was another time, before crack. The grandmothers are getting all used up, and statistics on getting clean and staying that way are hardly encouraging.

My heart goes out to this community of devastation and despair, one that we must look at long and hard and not turn away from. However, the beautiful child who so magically entered my life is my first priority.

Now that he has been with me a year, I have engaged a lawyer and am seeking to terminate the mother's rights. I will do anything I can within my power and possibly beyond to ensure him a life where he will be valued and appreciated for the pure love and joy that he is.

Jane Doe requested anonymity for fear of reprisals in her efforts to adopt a boarder baby.

◆

FOSTER CARE AND THE POLITICS OF COMPASSION
Nanette Schorr

In 1910, a single mother wrote a poignant appeal to the *Bintel Brief* (letters) section of the *Jewish Daily Forward*. The social supports in her community had failed her, and she had nowhere else to turn.

"My husband deserted me and our three small children, leaving us in desperate need.... I am young and healthy, I am able and willing to work in order to support my children, but unfortunately I am tied down because my baby is only six months old. I looked for an institution which would take care of my baby but my friends advise against it. The local Jewish Welfare Agencies are allowing me and my children to die of hunger.... It breaks my heart but I have come to the conclusion that in order to save my innocent children from hunger and cold I have to give them away...."

The dilemma this woman faced is hardly different from that of many working mothers today. But the editor for the *Forward*, in response to the letter, looked beyond the responsibility of the Jewish social welfare agencies to that of the larger social order that forced parents to consider such desperate measures. The *Forward* editor replied: "What kind of society are we living in that there is no other way out than to sell her three children for a piece of bread? Isn't this enough to kindle a hellish fire of hatred in every human heart for such a system?"

The *Forward*'s passionate and righteous anger is unequivocal; the enemy is the capitalist system.

At a time when class-based analyses had greater currency, it was easy to arouse the public's indignation at a skewed division of resources. The moral fault lines were clear — hungry children, innocent parents, guilty social order. But in the course of the twentieth century, denunciation of the social order has been diluted by the need of a large middle class to define social relations in ways that assuage its conscience and shore up its economic position. As a result, contemporary social policy rationalizes unfair distribution of resources without implicating society's fundamental decency. Instead of finding fault in the failure of the current economic system to meet *all* its members' needs, modern social theorists assure us that those who have not achieved a measure of material security are inherently flawed. And as social-service providers, journalists, educators, academics, and others lose faith in a more equitable and meaningful social vision, this view becomes more seductive and powerful.

It is therefore not surprising that "blaming the victim" has become a cornerstone of the way the state provides child-protective services. Partly as a result of the growing sensitivity about oppression within families (an awareness fostered by feminist critiques and the growth of the "children's-rights" movement), but partly as a result of society's unwillingness to acknowledge the social forces that

From Nanette Schorr, "Foster Care and the Politics Of Compassion," in TIKKUN, May/June 1992, pp. 12–22, 80–83.

put stress on families, the state's child-protective bureaucracy fosters the notion that we are dealing simply with "good children" and "bad parents." By defining the parent as a personal failure and abstracting that failure from the social reality within which parenting occurs, the state manages to perform a necessary function — protecting the child from extreme forms of abuse — and at the same time denies the existence of the social conditions that often account for bad parenting. Once having identified the primary problem as bad parenting, the state is free to intervene without restraint in its clients' daily lives by removing children from their parents with minimal investigation and little respect for legal procedures — before exploring avenues for keeping the family together.

These interventions rarely touch the sexual abuse, physical violence, or simple neglect that occurs in middle- and upper-middle-class facilities. This abuse typically comes to light much later in life — in therapy, or in consciousness-raising groups — but not because the state has become involved. Often communities that have already been defined as pathological because they haven't made it in the competitive market economy — third-world people, those on welfare, or the working poor — become the targets of an overzealous bureaucracy.

The case of L. H. is striking in its ordinariness. A mother living in the Bronx in 1987, L. H. was in a position not unlike the mother who wrote to the *Bintel Brief*. She had recently separated from a husband who had abused her and was now alone with three young children, without money or job skills, in a house with broken windows. She sought help from child-welfare authorities — money to fix her windows and someone to watch over her children while she looked for work — but they re-sponded by charging her with neglect for leaving her younger children in the care of her older ones and for causing them emotional distress by arguing with her husband in front of them. As a result, the child-protective system removed L. H.'s children from her care and insisted her problems could be solved with psychology. The institutional foster care providers ignored L. H.'s concerns for the safety of her boys, whom they deemed "fragile," and placed them in separate group homes as a way of treating "parentification" syndrome (older siblings protecting younger ones). L. H. found no justice in the family courts, either. Her court-appointed counsel was inaccessible and unresponsive, and the court itself did not have time to hear her case. L. H. was finally reunited with her children, but only after taking extraordinary legal action. The wounds of the utterly unnecessary separation have yet to fully heal.

I work as a lawyer representing parents who are trying to regain or maintain custody of their children and I see cases like L. H.'s all the time. Most of the time parents don't fight back because they had already come to believe that the system is so rigged against them, and are so steeped in the belief that they are unworthy simply because they are poor, that any serious struggle seems futile. Moreover, the degradation they have suffered — which the child-protective system only compounds by its treatment of poor families — makes some parents doubt their own ability to care for their children.

Of course horrendous things do happen to children in some families. But defining the problem this way provides everyone with an excuse to avoid confronting the way the child-protective system works. It's analogous to questions that similar professionals raised about women who acted irrationally in the days before the women's movement. On the one hand, it was certainly true that some women acted in ways that could be described as irrational — and so one could understand why, given the level of social understanding at the time, mental health workers would typically prescribe doses of therapy, or even institutionalization. On the other hand, as early feminists pointed out, much of the behavior deemed irrational or hysterical was simply a natural expression of women's frustration and rage at an oppressive system of male domination. Similarly, the child-protective system makes things worse by interviewing in ways that focus on rescuing good children from bad parents, without acknowledging the adverse conditions in which families function and the debilitating frustrations that lead parents to abuse or neglect their children.

The good child/bad parent definition works very well for those socialworkers, therapists, and others whose job is to keep the system working smoothly and who long ago have given up any hope of changing the larger society. But the system's very effectiveness is often a disaster for the children and parents caught in its vise. Families are torn apart and children suffer in the process. Children may be separated from their brothers and sisters, moved precipitously from foster home to foster home, or — worst of all for children in such a vulnerable position — abused or neglected in foster care. Their parents are not much better off. As overwhelmed and undertrained caseworkers make arbitrary or impossible demands on them, parents lose hope of being reunited with their children. They complete a drug treatment program only to be told they must find a job. They receive a certificate from a parental skills class, only to be told that they can get their children back only when a thera-

pist determines they are ready. They are told they must find an apartment, but there are no apartments to be rented for what they can afford to pay. Frightened and bewildered, they go to family court hoping to find justice, but instead they are shuffled from one court appearance to the next. Months, sometimes years, pass as cases are repeatedly adjourned and professionals who sit behind closed doors determine the fate of their families.

Children in protective care, meanwhile, are forming bonds with their foster parents and foster parents are becoming attached to their foster children. The longer children live in foster care, the more the state recognizes the bond that is built between foster parent and child — a bond that will be sustained by the state against the aspirations of parents who seek to reunite the natural family. The courts are full of custody battles between foster parents and natural parents, battles in which the state throws its substantial power behind foster parents. Ask yourself to whom a child's affections will naturally turn: the foster parent who daily provides that child's needs (as well as many things above and beyond those needs), or the parent who earns a paltry income or lives on public assistance and is permitted to visit for only an hour once every other week. Social engineering, not child protection, is the net result in this system, as children are taken from poor families and placed in middle-class families that can give them a "better" life. Such interference overextends the role of the state. It is not for the state to decide what constitutes an enlightened upbringing, but rather to establish threshold criteria for the care of children above which its intervention is not required. There are many types of harm from which the state is unable to protect children, such as the emotional harm they experience when their parents argue or divorce, the internalized pain and loss of self-esteem they suffer when discipline is imposed in an arbitrary manner, or the damage they live with when they are punished corporally in ways the state does not deem "excessive." Were every kind of harm subject to state intervention, all children would at some time have been removed from their parents' homes.

Over its century of existence, the child-protective movement has tended to reflect the country's broader political and social context — in the 1940s and 1950s, for example, it adopted the then-burgeoning middle class's rigid definitions of healthy families and began to put growing emphasis on psychiatric labeling. Yet in some sense, the field of child protection has evolved independently of the national discourse, continuities in practice have overshadowed the changes in theory. In the 1900s as in the 1990s, the focus of casework has remained the treatment of individual weaknesses. As a result, caseworkers make little practical distinction between "neglect" and "abuse" — despite the dramatic differences between the two. A neglected child is legally defined as a child whose physical, mental, or emotional condition is impaired or is in imminent danger of impairment because his or her parent fails to supply him or her with adequate food, clothing, shelter, education, supervision, or guardianship. The law defines an abused child as a child whose parent inflicts or allows to be inflicted physical injury, by other than accidental means, that causes or creates a substantial risk of death or serious or protracted disfigurement. Yet whether the case be one of "neglect" or "abuse," the child-protective system treats parents in much the same way.

Until the nineteenth century, when the term "child abuse" entered the national discourse, most Americans saw the suffering of children pragmatically, as part of the human condition. The contemporary child-protective movement reflects internationally recognized human-rights protocols that define children as separate beings of inherent value. But while the discourse of human rights has helped to transcend cultural distinctions and placed the field of "children's rights" squarely within its purview, state intervention has gone far beyond safeguarding the right of children to be protected from harm and provided with basic nurturance. Since child protection became a social institution, compulsory separation of children from their parents has remained the primary form of state intervention in family life. In the nineteenth century, "orphan trains" carried the children of immigrants westward to be loaned out as indentured servants. Now, foster parents and foster-care administrators have an economic incentive to perpetuate the institutionalized practice of child removal and placement. None of this is to say that abuse and neglect do not exist, that parents are not responsible for what happens to their children, or that child protection is merely a capitalist conspiracy to make money by stealing the children of the poor. But one cannot ignore the images evoked by the vocabulary that predicates intervention: Reductive characterizations of parents as "crack mothers," for example, justify dehumanizing social policies and underwrite the state's recourse to criminal sanctions instead of remedial therapies.

Most parents who qualify for therapeutic rehabilitation find that it is administered in a compartmentalized, ineffectual, and ultimately alienating way. Beating your children? Let's talk about learning acceptable outlets for anger — not about what you're really angry about. Leaving your children alone? Go to a parental skills class. No need to consider that what you really need is some day-care assistance, or someone to watch the little ones while you take the older children out to the store or the doctor or simply for a walk. You've sexually abused your child? Go to a sex-offenders clinic, where you will get behavioral modification therapy. No need to explore the physical or emotional violence you experienced as a child or your own lack of self-esteem and sense of alienation. Abusing alcohol? Have your urine tested regularly and exercise greater self-discipline. No need to say that you feel narcotics may be the best thing going, given the conditions under which you're living. This does to mean that these behaviors should not be controlled; indeed, they must be. But in the absence of a real commitment to addressing the isolation and degradation from which abuse and neglect follow, they will only continue.

In the early days of the child-protective movement, the most common approach to "treating" the neglect of children was to preach to parents about morality. Sometimes that morality had a feminist message, as in the Prohibition era, when the battle against domestic violence focused on alcoholism. However, moralizing did little to address the root causes of bad parenting. Gradually moralizing grave way to psychological labeling, and parents who were seen as shiftless and morally lax were redefined as manifesting psychopathology. Now the focus of scrutiny has turned to single parents, many of them women. When these parents criticize a social order that gives their parenting efforts little material or emotional support, social welfare experts term this an "externalization of blame." Instead of treating the crisis in meaning — the despair and

emptiness born of lifelong experiences of physical or emotional violence, unemployment or meaningless work, broken families, inadequate education, loneliness, lack of stable long-term relationships, dangerous, dirty, and violence-ridden neighborhoods, decrepit housing, and lack of community — the symptoms of crisis are treated in isolation from their causes. When one is afraid to leave home for longer than necessary or to let the children go out and play because of the drug dealers in the neighborhood, a sense of social isolation closely follows and, if unrelieved, may very well lead to neglect or abuse.

If you were designing a program to assist troubled families, what are some of the elements you would intuitively include? Instead of instructing parents on how to build ideal family units, you might teach them how to reach out to neighbors and community leaders who are familiar with local resources and address the problems that led to the neglect of their children. You might assist parents in building the kind of mutual support societies that sustained many immigrant communities, giving them financial assistance, emotional sustenance, and connection to their heritage. You might help them locate their own experiences in a historical understanding of the social and economic organization of American life and teach them how to use that knowledge to empower other parents as well. The focus must not be on individual change — ideally that follows of its own accord — but on helping people build new social institutions that can address their needs for support, community, and meaning.

This approach does not easily fall into any ideological camp. There are those on both the left and right sides of the political spectrum who address these issues in analogous terms; however, this is more a linkage of interest than a confluence of values. For the Right, constraining the child-protective system is appealing because they wish to inhibit extensions of the long arm of the state into the sphere of private life — sometimes because such interferences challenge patriarchal organizations of family life that they wish to protect. Others fear that state intervention will destroy the unique fabric of people's intimate lives. But neither the protection nor the destruction of patriarchal structures provides sufficient justification for state intervention where a child's life, health, or safety are not at risk.

The question then becomes: When should children be taken from their parents? Quite simply, when their parents are abusing or neglecting them, when there is imminent risk of harm to their lives or health, or when "reasonable efforts" have been made to ameliorate the problem. While abuse cases may require long-term removal, in the majority of neglect cases a family's needs may be met by limited remedial intervention such as that provided by the homebuilders' program or the "family preservation" models that are being developed around the country. The cost and pain of family separation should be — but aren't — considered before a child is placed in foster care. One client voluntarily placed her children in foster care a number of years ago at a time when she was unable to meet their needs. She could have maintained a parent-child relationship with them, however, had she not been limited to brief biweekly visits. Another client is being threatened with the removal of her grandson because she does not consent to his being treated with psychotropic medication or placed in a residential treatment center — even though protective agencies have made no effort to assess whether a school in her

community could meet his needs. In March of this year, the Supreme Court eviscerated parental recourse to legal remedies for such egregious abuses of power. The Court ruled that parents could no longer use federal law to sue state agencies for failing to make "reasonable efforts" to reunite families. It is now in the hands of Congress to enact legislation that would supersede this ruling.

We shrink from the difficult decisions we cannot avoid: That fear of drawing the line too narrowly leads us to draw it too broadly. When we focus on the neglectful and abusive behavior of individual parents, we allow ourselves to avoid recognizing how their failure reflects larger social failures for which we are all ultimately accountable, since the state — in whose operation we are all implicated — is the most neglectful parent of all. The degree of intervention into parent-child relationships must be tailored to fit (and not exceed or fall short of) the needs and circumstances of each individual family. When the state uses untempered intervention as a blunt instrument, and describes all parental failures of children as "child abuse" — provoking the uniform response of removing all the children from the home — we needlessly destroy otherwise viable families.

What might a profamily politics look like? Can "family" be redefined in ways that support nontraditional alignments based on feminist, gay, and cross-cultural critiques of the nuclear family and recognize extended networks of social relationships based on ties of kinship or affection? How can we support the institution of the family — for all intents and purposes the only social institution based exclusively on loving commitment — without compromising our intolerance of domestic violence and abuse? In part, the answer lies in the emergence of new kinds of households that can renew family life — but only if they are given the social acceptance and nurturance they need in order to flourish. Thus family support policies must be designed in ways that allow such households to be economically viable and create supportive communities in which they can function.

A number of factors have compromised the goals of the child-protective movement. Cynicism born of ineffectual efforts to combat domestic violence, combined with the loss of the sense of community that lent hope to the movements of the 1960s and 1970s, has led us to believe that we need to save who we can (in this case children), since we can't change the larger social and economic environment. Furthermore, the policy of massively applying state intervention to change the balance of power in families where women and children are physically and emotionally abused has often left liberals aligned against people in inner-city and poor communities, who view themselves in an adversarial relationship to an oppressive system that is destroying their neighborhoods and their culture. The source of this problem lies in the failure of liberal policymakers to address the deeper social meaning of the issue by bringing a historical perspective to the problem and by understanding and addressing the reasons for such anger.

An analysis of the child-protective system in the United States requires (for example) understanding the brutalization of African-Americans, starting with the systematic breakup of their families in slavery, and continuing with the racism and class oppression that span from the Reconstruction period to the present time — a history that is distinctly different from that of other oppressed minorities in our country. Like the War on Poverty,

which gave services and money to poor communities without supporting their efforts at leadership and independence, the child-protective system respects neither its clients' cultural heritage nor their humanity. Caseworkers classify angry parents as "noncooperative" clients and treat noncooperation as a reason to keep children in foster care. Professionals need to support the efforts of parents to reassert their dignity, even if that assertion challenges the child-protective system itself.

Neglect cases too often have resulted in unnecessary removal of children, often without prior notice to parents — even when the child faces no imminent danger. The state often removes children with little attention to legal process; and the judges and attorneys in the family court system rarely question the state's actions. The net effect is to ratify the caseworkers' decisions, thereby rendering child-protective intervention arbitrary and unjust.

The courts must respect the rights of parents by ensuring that caseworkers are making "reasonable efforts," both before and after they remove children. The courts can neither rectify the unequal scrutiny given to poor families nor change the social conditions that give rise to neglect. But they can make better efforts to keep families together by ordering and supplying necessary services, even if those services cost money.

The consequences of the liberal approach to child protection are disturbing. The good child/bad parent dichotomy gives credibility to conservative policies that hold parents accountable for their children's criminal acts — for example, the punitive eviction of parents from public housing when their children are found possessing drugs. Such policies mete out equal punishment to parents who have abandoned the effort to influence their children's behavior and parents who simply need support in dealing with their children's rage and hopelessness. Furthermore, such responses show little understanding of the ways in which parental failures represent the defeat of parents' own deepest hopes for the future, just as they symbolically represent the defeated aspirations of the working class. As the ranks of the middle class diminish in the face of unrelieved economic recession, the American Dream is increasingly inaccessible to poor and working parents, who struggle on a daily basis against the drugs, crime, and violence that are claiming their children.

Despite the child-protective bureaucracy's heavy investment in the good child/bad parent dichotomy, the struggles of parents in impoverished communities have moved into the foreground of public consciousness. Movies such as *Boyz N the Hood* reflect a growing humanization of parents' and childrens' struggles to survive and even flourish amid daunting conditions. Ongoing news coverage of issues such as steadily diminishing public support for single mothers and the fears of parents whose children have been involved in violent incidents in the schools has educated the public about the often tragic limitations of liberal approaches to family policy — and helped clear the way to a compassionate, morally consistent response.

The Left urgently needs to address the pain of poor and working parents, and we can begin to do this only by recognizing that the issues are not merely economic, although they often stem from economic privations. Liberal child-welfare experts ignore this pain at their peril since the Right will continue to fill the resulting vacuum by claiming this issue as its own. We cannot allow the language of empow-

erment to be co-opted by the Right, which uses it to justify a hands-off approach to state involvement in employment, education, and welfare in order to "liberate the forces of individual initiative" in the inner city. Properly defined, empowerment of parents means helping them confront racism, condescension, and inequality.

The complexity and immediacy of the issue requires use to respond quickly and decisively. Many of the clients in the child-protective system do need help. The question is, what kind of help? Rather than focusing on child removal as a remedy, that help could take the form of funding "family preservation" programs that assist families before their children are removed and maintain the parent-child bond during foster care with frequent visits. "Family preservation" should be broadly defined to include support for poor and working parents in the form of publicly funded day care and health insurance. In addition to providing services, government should support community organizations and mutual assistance societies such as those formed by many ethnic groups that share day care, provide seed money for new endeavors, and run parenting groups and advocacy efforts.

Recognizing the pain of parental struggle does not mean that all parents are good. It does require recognizing that real support for families must be linked with efforts to change the world of work and reorganize the economy. The social significance of child neglect extends beyond its current impact. Its human implication is also profound because it shapes the lens through which future generations will filter their memories, and, in turn, their hopes and dreams. A compassionate response to children must include an equally compassionate response to their parents.

Mothering vs. Fathering

◆

NIGHT PIECES: FOR A CHILD
Adrienne Rich

1. The Crib

You sleep I bend to cover.
Your eyelids work. I see
your dream, cloudy as a negative,
swimming underneath.
You blurt a cry. Your eyes
spring open, still filmed in dream.
Wider, they fix me —
— death's head, sphinx, medusa?
You scream.
Tears lick my cheeks, my knees
droop at your fear.
Mother I no more am,
but woman, and nightmare.

2. Her Waking

Tonight I jerk astart in a dark
hourless as Hiroshima,

almost hearing you breathe
in a cot three doors away.
You still breathe, yes —

and my dream with its gift of knives,
its murderous hider and seeker,
ebbs away, recoils

back into the egg of dreams,
the vanishing point of mind.
All gone.

But you and I —
swaddled in a dumb dark
old as sickheartedness,
modern as pure annihilation —

we drift in ignorance.
If I could hear you now
mutter some gentle animal sound!
If milk flowed from my breast again....

From Adrienne Rich, "Night Pieces: for a Child", in *Poems, Selected and New, 1950-1974* (New York:Norton, 1979), pp. 81-82.

◆

JUSTICE, GENDER, AND THE FAMILY
Susan Moller Okin

An equal sharing between the sexes of family responsibilities, especially child care, is "the great revolution that has not happened." Women, including mothers of young children, are, of course, working outside the household far more than their mothers did. And the small proportion of women who reach high-level positions in politics, business, and the professions command a vastly disproportionate amount of space in the media, compared with the millions of women who work at low-paying, dead-end jobs, the millions who do part-time work with its lack of benefits, and the millions of

From Susan Moller Okin, *Justice, Gender, and the Family*, vol. 4, 1989, pp. 175–184.

others who stay home performing for no pay what is frequently not even acknowledged as work. Certainly, the fact that women are doing more paid work does not imply that they are more equal. It is often said that we are living in a post feminist era. This claim, due in part to the distorted emphasis on women who have "made it," is false, no matter which of its meanings is intended. It is certainly not true that feminism has been vanquished, and equally untrue that it is no longer needed because its aims have been fulfilled. Until there is justice within the family, women will not be able to gain equality in politics, at work, or in any other sphere.

I think we would arrive at a basic model that would absolutely minimize gender. I shall first give an account of some of what this would consist in. We would also, however, build in carefully protective institutions for those who wished to follow gender-structured modes of life. These too I shall try to spell out in some detail.

MOVING AWAY FROM GENDER

First, public policies and laws should generally assume no social differentiation of the sexes. Shared parental responsibility for child care would be both assumed and facilitated. Few people outside of feminist circles seem willing to acknowledge that society does not have to choose between a system of female parenting that renders women and children seriously vulnerable and a system of total reliance on day care provided outside the home. While high-quality day care, subsidized so as to be equally available to all children, certainly constitutes an important part of the response that society should make in order to provide justice for women and children, it is only one part. If we start out with the reasonable assumption that women and

men are equally parents of their children, and have equal responsibility for both the unpaid effort that goes into caring for them and their economic support, then we must rethink the demands of work life throughout the period in which a worker of either sex is a parent of a small child. We can no longer cling to the by now largely mythical assumption that every worker has "someone else" at home to raise "his" children.

The facilitation and encouragement of equally shared parenting would require substantial changes. It would mean major changes in the workplace, all of which could be provided on an entirely (and not falsely) gender-neutral basis. Employers must be required by law not only to completely eradicate sex discrimination, including sexual harassment, they should also be required to make positive provision for the fact that most workers, for differing lengths of time in their working lives, are also parents, and are sometimes required to nurture other family members, such as their own aging parents. Because children are borne by women but can (and, I contend, should) be raised by both parents equally, policies relating to pregnancy and birth should be quite distinct from those relating to parenting. Pregnancy and childbirth, to whatever varying extent they require leave from work, should be regarded as temporarily disabling conditions like any others, and employers should be mandated to provide leave for all such conditions. Of course, pregnancy and childbirth are far *more* than simply "disabling conditions," but they should be treated as such for leave purposes, in part because their disabling effects vary from one woman to another. It seems unfair to mandate, say, eight or more weeks of leave for a condition that disables many women for less time and some for much longer, while *not* mandating leave for illnesses or other disabling conditions. Surely a society as rich as ours can afford to do both.

Parental leave during the postbirth months must be available to mothers and fathers on the same terms, to facilitate shared parenting; they might take sequential leaves or each might take half-time leave. All workers should have the right, without prejudice to their jobs, seniority, benefits, and so on, to work less than full-time during the first year of a child's life, and to work flexible or somewhat reduced hours at least until the child reaches the age of seven. Correspondingly greater flexibility of hours must be provided for the parents of a child with any health problem or disabling condition. The professions whose greatest demands (such as tenure in academia or the partnership hurdle in law) coincide with the peak period of childrearing must restructure their demands or provide considerable flexibility for those of their workers who are also participating parents. Large-scale employers should also be required to provide high-quality, on-site day care for children from infancy up to school age. And to ensure equal quality of day care for all young children, *direct government subsidies* (not tax credits, which benefit the better-off) should make up the difference between the cost of high-quality day care and what less well paid parents could reasonably be expected to pay.

There are a number of things that schools, too, must do to promote the minimization of gender. As Amy Gutmann has recently noted, in their present authority structures (eighty-four percent of elementary school teachers are female, while ninety-nine percent of school superintendents are male), "schools do not simply reflect, they perpetuate the social reality of gender preferences when they educate children in a system in which men rule women and women rule children." She argues that, since such sex stereotyping is "a formidable

obstacle" to children's rational deliberation about the lives they wish to lead, sex should be regarded as a relevant qualification in the hiring of both teachers and administrators, until these proportions have become much more equal.

An equally important role of our schools must be to ensure in the course of children's education that they become fully aware of the politics of gender. This does not only mean ensuring that women's experience and women's writing are included in the curriculum, although this in itself is undoubtedly important. Its political significance has become obvious from the amount of protest that it has provoked. Children need also to be taught about the present inequalities, ambiguities, and uncertainties of marriage, the facts of workplace discrimination and segregation, and the likely consequences of making life choices based on assumptions about gender. They should be discouraged from thinking about their futures as *determined* by the sex to which they happen to belong. For many children, of course, personal experience has already "brought home" the devastating effects of the traditional division of labor between the sexes. But they do not necessarily come away from this experience with positive ideas about how to structure their own future family lives differently. As Anita Shreve has recently suggested, "the old home economics courses that used to teach girls how to cook and sew might give way to the new home economics: teaching girls *and boys* how to combine working and parenting." Finally, schools should be required to provide high-quality, after-school programs, where children can play safely, do their homework, or participate in creative activities.

The implementation of all these policies would significantly help parents to share the earnings and the domestic responsibilities of their families, and children to grow up prepared for a future in which the significance of sex difference is greatly diminished. Men could participate equally in the nurturance of their children, from infancy and throughout childhood, with predictably great effects on themselves, their wives or partners, and their children. And women need not become vulnerable through economic dependence. In addition, such arrangements would alleviate the qualms many people have about the long hours that some children spend in day care. If one parent of a preschooler worked, for example, from eight to four o'clock and the other from ten to six o'clock, a preschool child would be at day care for only six hours (including nap time), and with each one or both of her or his parents the rest of the day. If each parent were able to work a six-hour day, or a four-day week, still less day care would be needed. Moreover, on-site provision of day care would enable mothers to continue to nurse, if they chose, beyond the time of their parental leave.

The situation of single parents and their children is more complicated, but it seems that it too, for a number of reasons, would be much improved in a society in which sex difference was accorded an absolute minimum of social significance. Let us begin by looking at the situation of never-married mothers and their children. First, the occurrence of pregnancy among single teenagers, which is almost entirely unintended, would presumably be reduced if girls grew up more assertive and self-protective, and with less tendency to perceive their futures primarily in terms of motherhood. It could also be significantly reduced by the wide availability of sex education and contraception. Second, the added weight of responsibility given to fatherhood in a gender-free society would surely give young men more incentive than they now have not to incur the results of careless sexual behavior until they were ready to take on the responsibilities of being parents. David Ellwood has outlined a policy for establishing the paternity of all

children of single mothers at the time of birth, and for enforcing the requirement that their fathers contribute to their support throughout childhood, with provision for governmental backup support in cases where the father is unable to pay. These proposals seem eminently fair and sensible, although the minimum levels of support suggested ($1,500 to $2,000 per year) are inadequate, especially since the mother is presumed to be either taking care of the child herself or paying for day care (which often costs far more than this) while she works.

Third, never-married mothers would benefit greatly from a work structure that took parenthood seriously into account, as well as from the subsidization of high-quality day care. Women who grew up with the expectation that their work lives would be as important a part of their futures as the work lives of men would be less likely to enter dead-end, low-skilled occupations, and would be better able to cope economically with parenthood without marriage.

Most single parenthood results, however, not from single mothers giving birth, but from marital separation and divorce. And this too would be significantly altered in a society not structured along the lines of gender. Even if rates of divorce were to remain unchanged (which is impossible to predict), it seems inconceivable that separated and divorced fathers who had shared equally in the nurturance of their children from the outset would be as likely to neglect them, by not seeing them or not contributing to their support, as many do today. It seems reasonable to expect that children after divorce would still have two actively involved parents, and two working adults economically responsible for them. Because these parents had shared equally the paid work and the family work, their incomes would be much more equal than those of most divorcing parents today. Even if they were quite equal, however, the parent without physical custody should be required to contribute to the child's support, *to the point where the standards of living of the two households were the same*. This would be very different from the situation of many children of divorced parents today, dependent for both their nurturance and their economic support solely on mothers whose wage work has been interrupted by primary parenting.

It is impossible to predict all the effects of moving toward a society without gender. Major current injustices to women and children would end. Men would experience both the joys and the responsibilities of far closer and more sustained contact with their children than many have today. Many immensely influential spheres of life — notably politics and the professional occupations — would for the first time be populated more or less equally by men and women, most of whom were also actively participating parents. This would be in great contrast to today, when most of those who rise to influential positions are either men who, if fathers, have minimal contact with their children, or women who have either forgone motherhood altogether or hired others as full-time caretakers for their children because of the demands of their careers. These are the people who make policy at the highest levels — policies not only *about* families and their welfare and about the education of children, but about the foreign policies, the wars and the weapons that will determine the future or the lack of future for all these families and children. Yet they are almost all people who gain the influence they do in part by never having had the day-to-day experience of nurturing a child. This is probably the most significant aspect of our gendered division of labor, though the least possible to grasp. The effects of changing it could be momentous.

◆

PREGNANCY LEAVE DISCRIMINATES AGAINST MEN!
Dan Wasserman

From *The Boston Globe*, Jan. 27, 1987, p. 14.

◆

THE NEW FATHER
Letty Cottin Pogrebin

Have you ever wondered why there are so many men in the "right-to life" movement and so few in child care? Or why a man who testifies so passionately about "unborn babies" is usually mute about babies already born and living in sickness and poverty? I attribute these contradictions to the fact that on public issues men act as men and not as fathers. They are protecting their power, not expressing their love of children.

It's as if masculinist thinking divides life into dualities — power/love, work/housework — so that men can take the half that suits them. In the case of children, men have divided them into the concept and the reality. Men are in charge of the concept of the child (they decide when life begins, or which child is "legitimate"), while women are in charge of the reality (three meals a day, fevers, snowsuits, baths, and diapers). As men become more familiar with the reality — through deeper forms of fatherhood — they tend to discover that many of their concepts were wrong. The fully involved and sensitized father comes to see all children as fresh and fragile little lives needing daily care, rather than as symbols of patriarchal survival.

How much of each man's essential identity is based on the fact of his being a father? When was the last time you read a profile of a male leader or business mogul that included a paragraph about how he manages to be both a father and a mogul? Or when have you ever heard a male expert introduced to an audience as a "husband and father"? Probably never. Yet time and again, family credentials follow women's names in the newspaper, or precede female speakers to the lectern. "And here she is," I am introduced, "editor, writer, and wife and mother of three..." Are those words simply part of my relevant biography or are they added like a disclaimer on the label of a dangerous drug? Would the audience be less likely to tolerate a dose of feminist opinion without the palliative of a family connection — do they imagine my motherhood *tames* me.

I often think, on the contrary, how much motherhood has radicalized me, how it has grounded me in the gritty earth of human needs. Similarly, I wish that groups of men (and women) cared as much about each man's fathering and considered it as crucial a measure of his character and his humanity as motherhood is for a woman. The trouble is, for most men, the father part of their sense and sensibility shuts down the minute they leave the house. Our duality-ridden culture has let them believe that children are irrelevant to life in a "man's world."

One of my lecture experiences cast a new light on my thinking about fathers and the love/power dichotomy. As a faculty member was introducing me to a college audience, the hushed hall was pierced by the screech of a child imitating a fire engine siren. All heads turned toward the back of the hall where a man was trying to silence a small child, who responded to each "Shhhhhh!" with a shrill "Wrrroooeeee." When I approached the

From Letty Cottin Pogrebin, "The New Father," in *Family Politics* (New York:McGraw-Hill, 1983), pp. 192–211.

microphone, the audience's giggles now punctuating each shriek, the father — unable to quiet his child — nervously hustled toward the exit, babe in arms.

"Please stay," I called after him. "If the baby continues squealing, I'll just speak louder and the audience will listen harder. We've learned to work, think, speak, and listen over the noise of male technology — the air conditioners, phones, jet planes, stock tickers, photocopiers, and word processors — surely we can tolerate the sound of one baby." Motherhood had taught me that babies tire of making noise eventually. Experience reminded me how often, though *mothers* exempt themselves from public events for fear their children will disturb. I told that father he reminded me of all the world's mothers driven from halls of learning because they care for children, and I told the audience, "We must help parents remain in our midst. We will ask father and baby to stay." The crowd roared its approval. The father returned to his seat. I began my speech and in minutes the baby was asleep.

A few days later, my husband and I attended a concert in Manhattan. When a baby started mewing in the balcony, the mother carried it from the concert hall but the father stayed put. When more fathers are caregivers and more mothers are in control of the podium, perhaps family needs will be accommodated in public life.

The trouble is, most people don't even notice. The separate spheres permit men to ignore what happens to children, knowing there is always a mother to care. As I've noted before, the limitations of traditional fatherhood have come to seem so utterly "normal" that we don't hear them in the very words we use and how we use them. For example, "to father" a child refers to the momentary act of impregnation; "to mother" a child means to succor and sacrifice. It means leaving the concert hall, it

means giving up power over your own freedom. Describing nurturant males as men who "mother" is a modern turn of speech that proves the emotional emptiness of the word "father." Somehow, when we watch a man intensively care for a child, we cannot say "look at how he fathers that child" without feeling as though we have misrepresented the scene. Needing to say "he mothers" is like needing to say "the sisters showed real brotherhood." With the growth of a new sisterhood among women and a new fatherhood among men, those words may enter common usage with a refreshed meaning.

Social scientists say that a child who grows up without a mother is suffering maternal "deprivation" (which the dictionary defines as loss, dispossession, bereavement). Life without father, however, is merely called father "absence" (a state of being away). The difference between *deprivation* and *absence* has allowed men to walk out on their families and be bad guys at worst, while women who do so are monsters. As Juliet Mitchell put it, "present or absent, 'The Father' always has his place." It will take a new generation of fathers to give that place real meaning and see father absence as children's deprivation.

When a man is the "head of household," our society calls the family "traditional," but when a women is the "head of household," the family is called "matriarchal" (as in the Moynihan Report on what's "wrong" with black families in America). In America, patriarchy means "power of *men*." Matriarchy has come to mean "power of *mothers*." Patriarchy is the name of an entire social system in which men rule over women. Matriarchy is the name of a house without a man presided over by a mother acting like a father.

What we are really saying with common language usage is that men who care for children are imitation mothers, and women who have the power to take care of families are imitation fathers. Family politics has so poisoned the cultural well that parents cannot overtly love their children or overtly use their power for their children without running the risk of compromising their gender identity.

CAREGIVING AND CARETAKING: A MATTER OF CONTROL

Item: Two little girls are playing house. Karen is the mother, Kathy is the grandmother. "An' who can be the father?" asks Karen. "No one," answers Kathy. "You don't need a father."

If fathers sometimes seem expendable, it is because so many of them make themselves extraneous to family life. Children come to associate men with the world of work, offices, uniforms, money, cars — and only incidentally with the home — and they associate women (employed or not) with family roles, child care, feelings, housework, and cooking. Thus, they learn the double standard of care: Mothers *give* care; fathers *take* care... They take the care that mothers give. Studies show, for instance, blue-collar men get not only household services but far more emotional support from their wives than the wives get from the men — and when all is said and done, the wives are the more depressed.

At the same time as women have always taken care of men, writes Harvard psychologist Carol Gilligan, "men in their theories of psychological development, as in the economic arrangements, have tended to devalue that care. Contrary to the popular belief that women have the greater dependency needs, men's (non-economic) dependency needs are far more insatiable. It's just that they are masked by the "normalcy" of women's caring for men and providing emotional support in the process of fulfilling the feminine role. During childhood, both boys and girls get this care and support from their mothers, but girls lose mothercare when they live with men, while men keep getting maternal support from their wives or girlfriends.

It is considered so "natural" that women give care and men and children take it, that women seem "unnatural" when they want some for themselves. In addition to devaluing women's care, and depriving women of emotional support from men, the imbalance is disguised by another linguistic trick: We turn reality on its head and say that *men* "take care of" women and children. Man's financial support is thus posed as an equalization of women's *caring behavior*, although the felt experience and rewards are completely different.

Rather than result in a simple division of labor, sex specialization in caring atrophies men's capacity to give comfort, thereby eliminating a major source from which women and children can *get* comfort. Furthermore, sex specialization in caring is not fair to children. Men trade support for women's caregiving (although it is far from an even trade), but children lose in the bargain. Women may excuse men's uncaring because they are "taken care of," but children should not have to have only one parent caring for them if they have two living parents. Sex-specialized caring imperils children because it is contingent on parents' sex role choreography rather than children's needs.

This is especially true for children of divorce, who tend to spend most of their time with their mothers. (Joint custody is acceptable in half the states but is still very much the exception.) Their fathers are not just routinely undemonstrative men, they often become little more than weekend visitors and signatures on the child support check. Or else, sad to say, they are "obstinately" delinquent on their payments (of those fathers ordered to pay child support, fifty-one percent pay little or nothing at all). As if refusing to underwrite mother-power, they force their ex-wives to go on welfare at the expense of their children. Having lost the day-to-day control over their children and the caregiving services of their wives, the men cut off their "caretaking."

Although most parents try to assure children the divorce was not their fault, kids believe otherwise. One boy said, "Look, I know the real reason (for the divorce) is that I broke my nose twice and Daddy didn't want to pay any more medical bills, so he left." Feelings of father abandonment are aggravated if the child's mother has a series of relationships with men to whom the child becomes attached, only to lose them when the romance fades. For such children, *a man who cares* becomes a more and more elusive grail.

Kramer vs. *Kramer* mined the truth about the long-neglected theme of single parenthood but reversed the statistically reality of who leaves whom: Hollywood found the one story that made the mother the "heavy."

Nevertheless, the emotional residue the film leaves behind is lasting and radical; *Kramer* vs. *Kramer* subversively taught us what real fatherhood feels like, and what happens to a man who feels it. It showed us that a father who is deeply involved in his child's everyday life, a father who is forced to be the buck-stops-here parent, to give routine and constant care, to *be* there, to witness the heart-stopping injuries, not just hear about them later — that kind of father is unable to let his child go. (It is my hunch

that such a father would not be so quick to send his child to war either.)

Film critic Molly Haskel points out that "Hollywood has habitually developed a lump in its collectively throat at the spectacle of macho man dwindling into a puddle of compassion over a child." But in its recent releases — *Kramer* vs. *Kramer*, *Ordinary People*, *Carbon Copy*, *Paternity*, *On Golden Pond*, and *Missing* — the child in question is always a boy, another version of the male-bonding films of the Seventies, notes Haskel. "The man-to-manness of the bond certifies the virility of the new parenting."

The observation is well taken. But in *Kramer* vs. *Kramer* Dustin Hoffman did not fight for his son just to win a buddy, or to keep the boy from Meryl Streep. He fought because *he could not imagine life without his child*. He could not go back to fathering the way he used to, the way most men are fathers, and certainly not the way most men with visitation rights are fathers. Fathers who have spent a great deal of time with their children cannot let go of them any easier than mothers can.

CHILD CUSTODY

If all fathers were as caring, time-involved and nurturant as Mr. Kramer, I would be totally enthusiastic about the notion of full or shared custody for fathers. After all, it does seem unfair that about ninety percent of the children of divorce are in their mothers' custody, and judges seem to continue to favor women in these cases. However, this is not necessarily *prima facie* proof of discrimination against men. As Nancy D. Polikoff points out in her penetrating critique:

> If a father wants custody of his children and fights for them, the picture

is very different from that which both popular belief and fathers' rights movement ideology would suggest. [In 1968, 20 percent of fathers requested sole or joint custody; by 1977, that percentage was down to 7.8 — and 63 percent of the fathers who wanted physical custody got it.]... The power to decide child custody often lies with the father, not the mother.... By not wanting custody, men, and not judges, are responsible for the 90-percent figure.

Polikoff goes on to question why the fathers' rights movement focuses on getting the child during divorce rather than improving co-parenting during marriage, or helping father-child relationships become closer, of fighting for social and workplace change that would make it easier to be an involved father. This, it seems to me, is the difference between old-style fathers who are hooked on ownership and power, and new fathers whose focus is care and love.

Unfortunately, most men's efforts have centered on defeating the ex-wife regardless of the truth about which parent did or can do most of the caregiving, and regardless of the mother-child bond or the best interests of the child. Here are some of the problems that make me, at times, perceive father's rights as father's coercion:

- If both parents have been employed, it is often the father's claim that both have been equally involved in child-rearing. (As we've noted, in the typical family this is far from the case.)
- If the mother has been a full-time housewife but goes to work to support herself after the separation, the father says that she will have less time and interest in the child than he does —

although he has always been working full-time. Writes Polikoff, "There is an undercurrent of punitiveness throughout custody decisions involving employed women, who, after all, comprise the majority of divorced and separated mothers."

- Rigid ideas about sex role identification (boys need fathers, girls need mothers, both need a man to establish the meaning of authority) allow father to argue on their behalf as *men*, not necessarily as *parents*.
- The popular belief that mother-headed households are inferior and create problem children often leads judges to favor the father without reference to his parenting ability.
- When financial ability is the criterion for custody, fathers almost always win. The idea is to keep women untrained, inexperienced and underpaid in the marketplace and then claim that they don't have the job security or income to support their children. Sometimes a man makes a custody claim against his ex-wife because she is a welfare mother when the reason she is on welfare is because he cut off his court-ordered child support.
- Because of the cultural preference for two-parent families, judges often give custody to the father, who is more often remarried, since a man — whatever his age — is more likely to find a new mate than is a woman if she is middle-aged. Many judges think all women are equally adept at childrearing by virtue of being female. Therefore, the father's new wife, or even his hired housekeeper, seem family enough (and better than the now poor single mother).
- Judges tend to "overrate small paternal contributions to parenting because

they are still so noticeable," writes Polikoff. "In other words, the emphasis in evaluating mothers is on what they do not do, because they are expected to do everything. By this standard, men will always look good for doing more than nothing, and women will always look bad for doing less than everything."

TIME STUDIES

Yet, in terms of time alone, the typical American father has a long way to go to achieve equal parenthood. One famous study found that the average father interacts with his baby for less than 38 seconds a day. In 38 seconds, you cannot change a diaper or sing three verses of "The Farmer in the Dell." The *most* time any father in this sample devoted to his infant in one day was 10 minutes, 26 seconds — barely enough time for a bottle and a burp. Other fathers studied have averaged 26 minutes a day interacting with a child under age five, and 16 minutes with children between the ages of six and seventeen. Still others have logged up to 15 minutes a day feeding their babies, compared to one and one-half hours daily for mothers, almost half these fathers said they had *never* changed the baby's diapers, and three out of four had no regular caregiving responsibilities whatsoever.

Although some researchers make the point that "when the amount of time available to spend with children is considered; the father's involvement with his children is equal to that of the mother's" they fail to examine the willingness to *make* time available or to differentiate the *content* of the time each parent spends with children. When playtime is measured, fathers may well equal or even surpass mothers; but when caring time is measured, fathers are again largely absent. Moreover, it is not enough to excuse men on the basis of their having less "available" time without questioning whether they have made themselves as available as possible or whether they have used masculine role imperatives to justify being *un*available.

Although no one is quite sure how to measure father-involvement with older children who require no feeding and diapering, we have only to look at children's survey responses to learn that what exists is not enough.

- In one study, half the preschool children questioned preferred the TV to their father.
- In another study, one child in ten (aged seven to eleven) said the person they fear most is their father;
- Half the children wished their fathers would spend more time with them; and
- Among children of divorce, only one-third said they see their fathers regularly.

When children were asked how TV fathers are different from real fathers, the TV fathers came out better in two areas: They don't yell as much as real fathers, said the kids, and they spend more time with their children than real fathers. A second-grader commented: "They're always there when the kids need them." "They care for children," added a fifth-grader, "talk to children, show them they love them. Hug them."

Most experts reassure harassed working mothers that what counts isn't the quantity but the quality of the time they spend with their children. For today's father, the challenge is to increase both quality *and* quantity. At this moment in history, caregiving fathering is still the exception; a choice — something a man can decide to do or not to do, and suffer no consequences if he doesn't. This may be changing, though, now that the experts are discovering fatherhood and legitimizing the "new" father.

Dr. Spock, for example. After twenty-seven years and book sales in the tens of millions, Benjamin Spock rewrote portions of his baby bible to make important nonsexist improvements, including this advice to fathers (which I highlighted in *Growing Up Free*):

> *Original:* A man can be a warm father and a real man at the same time.... Of course I don't mean that the father has to give just as many bottles or change just as many diapers as the mother. But it's fine for him to do these things occasionally. He might make the formula on Sunday.
>
> *Revision*: I think that a father with a full-time job — even where a mother is staying home — will do best by his children, his wife and himself if he takes on half or more of the management of the children (and also participates in the housework when he gets home from work and on weekends).

Dr. Spock also helped present and future fathers by retracting his advice about "sex-appropriate" toys. In his revised edition, he wrote:

> I think it is normal for little boys to want to play with dolls and for little girls to want to play with toy cars, and it's quite all right to let them have them. A boy's desire to play with dolls is parental rather than effeminate, and it should help him to be a good father.

The fear of effeminacy causes parents to raise boys under severe sex role pressure to achieve something called "manhood" — which boys must earn and re-earn by establishing the many ways they are different from women. Primary in this proof-of-manhood-by-contrast is the relationship each sex is "supposed" to have with babies and children. And that relationships begins with doll play.

OF DOLLS AND MEN

The notion that doll play makes boys into "sissies" is a homophobic equation that clouds men's minds, obscuring the simple truth that when a boy plays with a doll, he is just modeling the parent-child relationship that he has known himself: He is pretending to be his own father. Presumably, in most cases, his own father is heterosexual. Thus, doll play is a boy's homage to the husband-father role, and one would expect it to be actively encouraged by those who believe heterosexual marriage and fatherhood are desirable for all males. But homophobia turns the culture against doll play for boys on the assumption that it turns boys into *mothers*. Somehow, heterosexist logic cannot imagine turning boys into fathers.

The crazy part is, by making doll play off-limits to boys and squelching their interest in "playing house" or caring for small children, *our culture creates an aversion to the very activities that make a man a good father*. In other words, boys are faced with two contradictory paradigms — the "real man" and the "good father" — and the latter is too often sacrificed for the former. The way to resolve this no-win situation is to reconcile the two masculine archetypes so that both embody the *same* human traits, not contradictory traits. Although a "real man" need not become a father, a man who *is* a father must be able to feel his manhood *confirmed* by active, caring fatherhood, rather than threatened by it.

The route to this state of mind is really quite simple. "Don't be the man you think you should be," I tell the men in my lecture audiences, "be the father you wish you'd had." And I think it is starting to happen — everywhere. In 1980, '81 and '82, I made the rounds of some thirty-five cities doing interviews on shows that take listeners' phone calls. To my surprise, the question that came up most often and aroused the most passion was how can men be better fathers?

- "My father never knew me," said an intense male voice over a Grand Rapids phone-in show. "I don't want to make the same mistakes with my own kids. I'm trying to learn how to father them while I still have time."
- "I'll never forget what happened when I was ten years old, recalled a seventy-year-old San Francisco man. "My mother had just died and my sister and I were standing beside the casket bawling. When my father saw my tears, he grabbed me and said, 'We're *men*; we're not going to cry. We're going to be strong.' I've swallowed my tears for sixty years and all I've got to show for it is a lifelong lump in my throat and mean memories of my father."
- An Indianapolis man said he had made a vow to learn how to take care of his kids after he heard about a local man who killed his entire family because his wife left him and he didn't know how to raise his four children.
- A New York City cab driver told me: "Being a father is more important to me than being a Baptist, being black, or being a man."
- A Washington, D.C. woman reported: "When our son said he'd be home from college on the day of my husband's office Christmas party, my husband asked him to come straight to the office. The boy bounded in, saw his father across the roomful of people, ran and threw his arms around my husband's neck and hugged and kissed him. At first I was embarrassed for my husband, but then I heard one man after another come up to him and say, "I'd give the world if my son would do that with me.'"

It's a young phenomenon but the change is unmistakable. Fathering is becoming a new kind of verb — an active verb — that describes an enlarging role and new behaviors. Children are discovering their "other parent" and men are discovering their "other selves." Fathers are ripping off the stiff patriarchal collars of *their* fathers; men are writing about the old kind of father who couldn't tell his children his love or his fears, who "kept still and died in silence." The American Psychoanalytic Association took up the subject of fatherhood at its 1982 conference, where scholars presented a paper on the rarely acknowledged traditional father, the father of the colonial period and the early years of this republic, who turns out to have had more in common with "the more nurturing" modern father that with the Victorian paterfamilias so sacred to "pro-family" conservatives.

Everywhere, everyone, not just scholars, seems to be thinking and writing about the fathers they have or the fathers they are, and fatherhood is being redefined, reinvented, and redeemed. Men are taking more time away from the offices and factories where they have spent their lives being paid more *the more they stayed away from their families*. Old-style fathers, like Robert Townsend, the top Avis executive who wrote *Up the Organization*, have realized that the price paid for career supremacy was too dear: it cost him his family.

> I cheated them, worked like crazy — seven days a week, long hours. My children were an interruption. Today I don't know the oldest three at all. When I retired from business they were gone and it was too late. I'm sorry... because I've had more fun with the two youngest kids than I had in all those years of work.

One economist claims that it is the "fear of uselessness" that keeps men out of the family circle and oriented toward the outside world. Because the disciplinarian-breadwinner had little to do around the house, he never got fully woven into the tapestry of family life. To compensate for that uselessness, for the emptiness of the old father role, men have concocted jobs, politics, sporting events, war, religion, and other "diversionary activities" that help them pretend to be important.

The new father does not have to pretend. A man in Albuquerque, for example, loves being a father so much that he wanted to share his enthusiasm with a father-to-be. He gave his best pal a baby shower at which men friends gathered to toast the forthcoming baby with goodwill, good food, and a rap session about father feelings. All over the country, men are materializing in childbirth courses, child-care centers, and early childhood education; they are staying home to care for their own children, braving the quizzical stares of cops and mothers as they push a baby carriage or watch their children in the playground; asking for joint custody; de-

manding paternity leave; and taking baby-care classes to prepare to be more skillful, better prepared fathers.

New research has given substance to the father role and its meaning to men and to children. At Yale, studies have shown that babies with stay-home fathers develop social and problem-solving skills at a precocious rate, not because men are better at childrearing but because these babies are getting love and attention from *both* parents. (Unlike many working fathers, working mothers form these attachments to their infants even when they are not the full-time parent.) Other studies reveal that men deeply share the highs and lows of childbearing: They get morning sickness, food cravings, and postpartum blues; fathers seem as adept as mothers at reading clues about what babies need; single fathers have been found to give "as much nurturance and warmth" as single mothers if they choose to, and giving it is as good for the father as it is for the child; and this newly acknowledged "fathering instinct" among human males has been corroborated in many other species.

Suddenly, magazines have discovered "Father Love," "A New Kind of Life with Father," and a "fathering boom." Newspapers seem to be running more pictures of male sports stars and politicians holding or playing with their kids. The media made much of Senator Edward M. Kennedy's dropping out of the 1984 presidential race because of concern for his children. He claimed the pressures of a political campaign would be too hard on them so soon after the pain of their parents' divorce. "I believe that my first and overriding obligation now is to Patrick and Kara and Teddy," he said, and though cynics may have raised a suspicious eyebrow, the fact is he made the announcement without apologies, with his children at his side, and with the confidence that his political future would survive it. In 1972, Edward Muskie ruined his career by showing "unmanly" emotion; ten years later; Teddy Kennedy could sacrifice power for love and still be a man.

At last, books and newsletters have been published by, for, and about the new father that do not address him as a glorified "mother's helper" but as a full participant in childrearing — whether his fathering fervor begins during the pregnancy, at birth, or at some midpoint in his children's lives, whether he is a co-parent or single parent. Meanwhile, observing and evaluating these developments is the Fatherhood Project at the Bank Street College of Education, which will eventually issue a national report on men's actual involvement in parenthood, trends in child custody agreements, father education courses, and company policy on paternity leaves.

New fathers, understandably, spawn new mothers, mothers willing to give up their preeminence in the nursery, mothers who never enjoyed being emotional surrogates for the too-busy Dad. Many women have began to understand that nothing — no law or career breakthrough — will alter women's place more profoundly than men's increased fathercare. We are learning to relinquish whatever home-based power women exercise as monopolists of child development because that loss is more than offset by an increase in our personal freedom and the pleasures of shared parenthood. We too must give up power for love if we want more from our children's fathers than most of us got from our own.

As I write this, it is three weeks since my father died at the age of eighty-two. I have been stunned to discover that I remember every single thing he and I did together. There were so few. One visit to the zoo, one Sunday ice-skating, a horseback-riding adventure, a night at a street carnival, a few times at the circus, one — just one — family vacation, at the Top o' the World Lodge somewhere in the mountains, and my father's teaching me to drive. The rest is just a blur or his comings and goings — off to work, home for dinner, off to meetings, conventions, the synagogue. My father was parent to a dozen religious and charitable organizations; to me, he was judge and teacher, critic and goad. I remember bringing him an A-minus and being asked for an A. I remember trying to impress him, to charm him into wanting to be with me and my mothers, trying to be smart for him, dressing to please him, but nothing I did could compete with his other world: the law, the war veterans, the bond drive, political campaigns, fund-raising events, the Talmud, the Men's Club, his minions.

I know that some people have rich memories of fathers who were there when needed and I'm glad there is a growing literature about the very large ways fathers contribute to child development. I've heard my women friends talk about watershed moments when their fathers helped them define who they were as women, what they would demand of life, how much they might expect from men. One grown woman, facing the first Father's Day after the death of her father, composed a testimonial that describes the father many of us wish we'd had:

> As far as he was concerned, a child and parent should exchange love and respect every day, not save appreciation and recognition for special occasions.... I depended on him to be there, to catch me when I fell and put me back on my feet. I know that just being able to talk to my father, or to see him... was reassurance enough that, as Browning said, "All's right with the world."

My father instilled confidence in me and my abilities, never doubting that I would succeed. His faith was so unswerving — and so unconditional.... Now I wonder if I'll ever stop aching over the loss of that tender, non-judgmental mirror that always reflected the me I so longed to be.

The good news is long overdue. The truth-telling is cleansing. The reports of caregiving fathers are encouraging. But what makes me feel especially optimistic about the permanence of this phenomenon are three developments that could significantly letigimate the new father.

First, we are breaking the absurd linkage of Father with breadwinner, understanding that the role is not dependent on the other and that neither role determines "masculinity." This is happening both because of the necessity for working mothers to share in the breadwinning, and because of the increased number of unemployed men in America. If that many men are out of work, all of them cannot be exhibiting a failure of "masculinity" or a lack of male role responsibility. Clearly, the fault is a larger failure, the economic and political failure of a system that has been allowed to blame the victim. Initially, the unemployed father feels guilty, inadequate, "unmanned." And then, judging by the men who speak out on TV talk shows and in press interviews, they begin to analyze what has happened and why they feel as they do.

Tom Wayne: When your kid comes home and asks for a couple of dollars... what do you tell them when you ain't got it?... I mean when they're used to saying, "Dad, give me a couple of bucks," and you're used to pulling out your wallet and giving it to them. Now

it's "sorry, son or daughter, I ain't got it."

Phil Donahue: Do you feel like a failure?

Tom Wayne: In a way, yes.

Terry Perna: Well, he said he feels like a failure; maybe he shouldn't. I don't know how you can get yourself from not feeling like a failure but it's not really his fault or anybody else's fault that they're not working.

The cruel equation of Father with Breadwinner (money equals power, power equals manhood) results in nonworking fathers' feeling like non-men in their wives' and children's eyes, while Big Breadwinner fathers "earn" their manhood with a paycheck but sometimes lose their children in the process. Ironically, the misfortune of unemployment has had a positive side effect: It has introduced men to their children. Said a Detroit man about his layoff: "I've got to spend a whole lot more time with my kids. When I worked nights in the tire shop, I would never see them. Yeah. That's about the only good thing that's come out of it."

And an unemployed executive with a graduate school degree confessed on the *Donahue* show:

...there are a lot of positives about this, too... and one of them is seeing my children walk for the first time and being there when they're in their bright and alert and awake hours rather than at the end of the day and the very beginning when they're just getting up or they're just ready to go to bed. That part has been an incredible joy to me and will be irreplaceable as long as I live.

The second reason for my optimism is the dramatic change in the advertising images of men. Major advertisers are showing men diapering babies, giving middle-of-the-night bottles, helping kids brush their teeth, baking cookies — engaging in a three-dimensional fatherhood that far exceeds the old cardboard image of Dad carving the Thanksgiving turkey or driving the family car. If American business has begun to sell its products with the positive force of such fathering images, than that force must be formidable indeed.

Finally, I am optimistic because of the recent proliferation of child-care training courses for young *boys*. It started with an elective course for fifth-grade boys offered at a Manhattan private school, was given national visibility in a book called *Oh, Boy! Babies!*, spread to other schools, and was further publicized by a made-for-TV movie based on the book. As with all social change, the old ideas about fathering cannot be permanently replaced until new ideas reach back and alter the *source* of our misconceptions. Childhood is that source; it is where our ideology of fatherhood takes root through experience with our own fathers, images of other fathers, and our own sex-role socialization. *Child-*

hood is where fatherhood must be changed. Thus, the baby-care class for boys, with its curriculum of care-giving skills development and its reinforcement of male nurturance, could forever eclipse the caricature of the formal or blundering father and replace it with a new father who wants to be involved, knows what to do and is proud he can do it.

Mike Clary is such a father. He spent two years as a full-time parent to his daughter Annie. He says that his kind of fatherhood taught him as much as moving to Walden Pond taught Thoreau:

> Annie makes me vulnerable — to longing, to daydreams, to fears, to pain. She has also made me capable of a love that seems boundless. That lack of constraint sometimes scares me. I feel responsible for that love, and wary of its energy, but I have grown comfortable with its weight. Annie has, finally, by making me a father, made me more of a man.

This, then, is the new father. We've been waiting for him for a long, long time.

Who May Marry?

First religious and then secular laws have specified who may marry, although the content of these laws has changed over time. The history of American slavery included prohibitions on marriage between slaves, although Texas and Georgia applied the evidentiary bar based on spousal testimony to slaves whose very marriages they refused to acknowledge. The states were permitted to outlaw interracial marriage until 1967 when the Supreme Court decided the landmark, and fittingly named, case of *Loving* v.

Virginia, 338 U.S. 1, (1967). Religious and secular rules prohibiting incest have denied marriage to close relatives, and yet the definition of incest has varied across states and over time. Under bigamy statutes, the U.S. Supreme Court permitted criminal prosecutions of Mormons engaged in polygamy, despite constitutionally based claims of a free exercise of religion. Yet studies estimate that a larger portion of American men and women have more than one spouse during their lifetimes than do adults in most polygamous societies — it is just that Americans do it serially rather than simultaneously. No state currently permits legal recognition of marriages by gay or lesbian couples, although such restrictions have received many challenges, and increasing numbers of gay and lesbian couples have found it possible to participate in religious ceremonies recognizing their unions.

But is marriage, as a legal institution, desirable? Used by the state and employers to distribute benefits, marriage may be an important means to other ends. Laden with a legacy of male authority and racist application, marriage may be precisely the institutional form some people hope to avoid in framing their relationships of love and intimacy. Instead, some people may prefer to register as domestic partners under the growing number of jurisdictions recognizing this status. Others may prefer to avoid any entanglement with officials regarding the status of their intimate ties. Still others may welcome legal and community reinforcement for the emotional and financial support of an intimate relationship. Changes in marriage rules are entirely foreseeable, and questions about this institution are especially timely.

◆

AN IMPOSSIBLE MARRIAGE: SLAVE LAW AND FAMILY LAW

Margaret Burnham

INTRODUCTION

The perversion of the human soul wrought by American slavery have been well told. Fictive and historical modes, songs and sonnets, have carried over the centuries the bitter seeds of the awful deeds. In lengthy tracts, scholars have retraced the crimes of the trade and the plantation, while slaves themselves have borne witness in searing personal narratives. We all know something of the horrific legacy of the peculiar institution: a warped national personality and a twisted color consciousness which has invaded every facet of our lives.

Recent studies of slavery have begun to turn to the law which undergirded the institution in an effort to understand this legacy more fully. The questions posed by those of us who study slave law are of two types: we seek to comprehend the manner in which legal principles were molded and manipulated to serve the institution's interests, and we employ the law to help fill

From Margaret Burnham, "An Impossible Marriage: Slave Law and Family Law," *Journal of Law and Inequality*, vol. 5, no. 198, 1987, (edited).

out the historian's understanding of slavery's social reality. In this sense, the law becomes another tool of historical reconstruction.

During the nineteenth century, the law sought to give new definition to family life — prescribing the roles of husband and wife, setting the parameters of marriage and divorce, and adjusting ancient rules and taboos about sex and procreation outside of marriage. The body of law that emerged recognized the family as an organic, autonomous legal entity, and established the framework for the public governance of private life still remaining to this day.

The slave family, however, was constructed outside of legal developments governing family relationships. The notion of legal autonomy within the private sphere had no meaning for the slave family, whose members could lawfully be spread to the four corners of the slave south. Notwithstanding blood ties and romantic love, the slave family could not be an organic unit of permanently linked, interdependent persons. In the eyes of the law, each slave stood as an individual unit of property, and never as a submerged partner in a marriage or family. The most universal life events — marriage, procreation, childrearing — were manipulated to meet the demands of the commercial enterprise. Although slaves did marry, procreate, and form families, in some cases even under the compulsion of the master, they did so without the sanction of southern law.

In the nineteenth century, the denial of legal protection to slave family formation created an impossible tension in the law. The tenets of family law held that marriage and family were natural, sacred, and morally compelled. The family — husband, wife and child — was an earthly

representation of the holy trinity. Thus the law was deemed to be based both on God's plan and command, and on natural law which is but itself a reflection of divine law. That slaves, who were admittedly human creatures of God, were excluded from these sacred rules presented a profound challenge for a purportedly rationally based, consistent legal system.

This article argues that the courts wrote slaves out of family law by declaring them to be a different kind of human being — innately and immutably immoral (therefore not legally marriageable), too dumb and childish to themselves parent (therefore incapable of childrearing) and sexually licentious (therefore unsuited to marriage and family bonds). The legal gyrations required to accomplish this feat infected family law into the twentieth century. Further, this legal endorsement of the idea that the slave family was inherently "different" has been reflected in the reality of black family life for decades.

The Slave As Member of the Plantation Family

In the mid-nineteenth century, with increasing pride in their peculiar institution, southerners came to employ the description "domestic slavery" (the relationship between the colonists and England) and "civil slavery" (suffered by free blacks denied civil rights) from the perpetual nature of African slavery in the South.

The term signified more than merely the lowest level of political and civil deprivation. By "domestic," slaveholders and their apologists meant to imply two dimensions of slavery. First, in their estimation, the slavery of their day had been tamed, or domesticated. They boasted that conditions of life and work for the slave were far milder than had been the case in earlier generations. Second, by "domestic," these observers meant that slavery had placed master and slave within the same domestic sphere. Each lived more or less in close proximity. The nature of the domestic domain of the slave was determined by the master, and the slave's fate was buffeted by both the economic and the domestic fortunes of the master. It is this second point that is addressed here.

Often referring to all of the inhabitants of the plantation as "my people," the master considered it his reign and responsibility to govern the social and work lives of his slaves as well as that of his nuclear family. The image cultivated was that of the beneficent patriarch, master of both his slaves and his own household. One North Carolina slaveholder expressed in his will this view of the extended plantation family: "I lend the whole of my property... to my beloved wife... for the purpose of raising, clothing and educating my children, and also raising the young negroes that are, or may hereafter, be born in my family."

There were three social configurations over which the slaveholder exercised primary control. Yet, it was the master who held the ultimate right to control his wife, any property she brought into the marriage, and the couple's children. In the quarters, slave husbands exercised circumscribed authority over their wives and children, but the right to control the shape and integrity of the slave family rested with the master.

This "one big happy family" image celebrated by slavery's adherents portrayed social and economic relationships on the plantation, among slaves and freemen alike, as organically interconnecting ones. This portrayal echoed the idealized nineteenth century view of the family as a refuge and safe haven, where flourished man's purest and most selfless instinct.

The southern environment was much acclaimed as a natural setting for the family, and it became a tableau upon which images depicting pastoral simplicity and the wholesome virtues of rural life were painted. According to the ideal, the arms of the extended plantation family shielded the white mistress and her children as it did the black slave and her children.

This "plantation as extended family" rubric also provided multiple layers of moral defenses for the slaveholder, defenses which were much needed as antislavery forces increased in number and strength. The family was deemed to be the spiritual and moral hub of the society; it was a morally superior place.

Slavery's advocates argued that the plantation-extended family was the best suited institution to transmit moral imperatives to an otherwise heathen population of African slaves. The family constellation — man, woman, and children — and the superior position of the husband in the family was believed to be commanded by both nature and God. Similarly, the subjugation of slaves to the will of the master, head of the plantation-extended family, was deemed natural and divinely ordained. Sanctified and sacred relations characterized the plantation-extended family, both within the planter's blood family and between him and his slaves. As one South Carolina court stated, "unless there be something very perverse in the disposition of the master or the slave, in every instance where a slave has been reared in a family there exists a mutual attachment.... The tie of master and slave is one of the most intimate relations of society."

Slaves were the moral inferiors of white men. White women were white men's moral superiors, but their physical and intellectual inferiors. Therefore, both slaves and white women, whether morally weak or physically fragile, required the protection of the master, which was best provided in the context of the plantation-extended family.

Moreover, slavocracy's claim that the plantation provided the slave with a family experience was the answer to those who charged that the trade was the very antithesis of family. When, as frequently happened, the partners lived on different plantations, each master had to grant consent. In these cases, called "broad-marriages," the family was united only on weekends and holidays when the husband traveled to the wife's plantation.

The marriage ceremony itself was performed by the master, or officiated by a black preacher, or, sometimes, a white one. The Christian ceremony mimicked that afforded whites, except with respect to the promise of permanence. It was also a practice for couples to set up housekeeping with the master's consent, but without a ceremony.

Procreative and Sexual Control of Slave Women

The slaveholder had two principal interests in promoting slave unions, both of which were tied to the plantation economy. First, he was in the business of producing crops and of reproducing capital in the form of slaves. Second, family ties were believed to promote slave stability and docility.

The economic value of the mater's slave holdings depended in part on the proven reproductive capacities of his bondwomen. As her "increase" was his property, the female slave was priced for both her labor-producing and reproducing ability. Fertile women brought a higher price on the market, but sterile women were often sold. One master, in his will,

proffered freedom as the incentive for a high yield: "If Jeany brings ten live children... she shall be at her... liberty ...."

Since economic interest was found in both her productive and reproductive labor, the slaveholder asserted rights of ownership over his female slaves' sexuality. The slave woman was deemed sexual property not just as an instrument of reproduction, but along the full range of her sexuality. She was owned as both a procreative and a sexual object. Thus, she was available to be raped and sexually abused with impunity by the slaveholder, his sons, the overseer, or any other white man. And here, racist and sexist ideology combined to justify the wrong.

For its procreative potential, the bondwoman's union in marriage was promoted, and sometimes demanded, by the master. If she was separated from her husband, or widowed, the master could require her to take another husband. On the slave block, she was sometimes randomly coupled with a male slave so as to "play on the sentiments of prospective buyers who would purchase a pair rather than separate them." In some cases, she was explicitly worked as a breeder.

The master also employed socio-sexual control in the quarters in order to contain resistance and enhance his power. Due to the female slave's status as the master's lifetime captive, family ties placed her in a cruel double-bind: the slave's yearning for freedom was whetted by her love for her family, and in particular, for her children, whom, above all, she wished to see delivered from the tyranny she had known. But, it was that very love, the desperate desire to be *with* her family, that also tied her down. Family life at once emboldened and dampened the slave's quest for freedom.

This dynamic was appreciated by the slavemaster, who saw the family as an important support for the slave system. Marriage was considered to have a quieting effect on restive slaves. Men were "given" wives in order to keep them sexually satisfied.

The interior family life of the slave was also subject to governance and interference by the master. He could foment dissent, encourage reconciliation, or simply specify the allocation of domestic responsibilities. In regard to the master or his designees, slaves had no right to personal privacy in their quarters; and had only a derivative privacy right *vis à vis* other persons. The developing law of personal privacy held that "[t]he house of the slaves is the house of the owner; and the fact that it is used by the former as his "dwelling does not change its character...."

Even if the master paid no attention to home life in the quarters, slaves fully realized that he could intervene at any time. The master played a role in the termination, as well as the initiation of marriage. As he saw fit, he would permit or deny mismatched couples to divorce and remarry. He, himself, sometimes brought about a separation which he determined to be in the best interest of the couple. It was argued by one contemporary legal scholar that the slaveowner had to have the power to separate couples, for

> to fasten upon a master of a female slave, a vicious, corrupting negro, sowing discord, and dissatisfaction among all his slaves, or else a thief, or a cut-throat, and to provide no relief against such a nuisance, would be to make the holding of slaves a curse to the master.

Slave couples sometimes violently resisted the actions of a master who sought to keep them apart. A Tennessee court upheld a death sentence imposed upon a slave for a "cruel murder inflicted on a feeble old man, who had always been kind to [him], and for no other reason than that [the old man] would not consent that [he] should gratify the unlawful desire, to abandon [his] wife and take another."

The master's primary weapon of discipline and social control was, of course, the threat of separation, which hung like a dark cloud over every slave couple family. That a commitment to marriage and family life endured despite this emotional devastation is one of the small miracles of African-American culture. Although it was surely one of the worst features of slavery, the courts often turned a blind eye to the cruelty of family separation. In one such case, the sale of an entire family consisting of parents and ten children in "one lot" was challenged by the heirs of an Alabama estate, since family groups sold for less than individuals. The court noted that "although it would doubtless be proper to sell husband and wife, or parent and small children together, it could not be tolerated that twelve slaves, most of whom were grown, should be sold in one lot...."

The nature of the economic relationships was such that the slave marital bond was exposed even when the master himself eschewed family separation. As property, the slave could be seized at any moment and sold to pay off a living owner's debts, or be transferred following the owner's death during the settlement of his estate. A kindly master was no assurance of family security.

The Slave Parenting Experience

The threat of sale and separation that so pained romantic ties was an equally awful tool of terror for the slave mother and father. The slave father was considered all but irrelevant. He was expected to procreate, but he had neither a moral nor a legal right to parent. As succinctly expressed by a Kentucky court, "the father of a slave is unknown to our law..." While the slave mother performed a critical reproductive function, as a parent, she too, was unknown to the law. The law treated the birth of a slave child not as a social, but as a commercial event.

Typically, slave children lived their early years with one or both of their parents in the quarters. About four weeks after birth, the mother was sent back to work in the fields or the big house. The mother was allowed to nurse her baby, who might be under the care of an elderly plantation nurse. As soon as the child was able, usually around five or six, the child would be put to work. On the larger plantations the initial tasks were with the "trash gang," composed of youngsters who tended the grounds, fetched water, and the like. As a young girl matured, she would be assigned tasks requiring ever greater strength and skill until she could take her place as a full hand in the fields or a servant in the main house. Anytime after age ten, the child was subject to being permanently separated from her family. Eventually, sometimes as early as the mid-teen years, she would leave her parents' house, either to set up with a husband and children of her own, or to be hired out or sold. Motherhood sometimes came very early, as evidenced by one case concerning a dispute over the price paid for "a woman, aged 17 years, and her three female children — one of the age of six years; another, four; and the youngest, about one."

After bringing her baby into the world, a slave mother had little control over her child's existence. Mother and father could and did exercise some discipline and provide guidance and all-important survival skills, but the child soon learned it was the master who really held the whip and the reins. He, or his overseer, prescribed the daily regimen. It was he, not the parent, who had the right to tell the child when to rise, how long to work, what to eat and wear, when and how to recreate, and when to go to bed. It was he who could as readily discipline the parent or the child. And, it was he who determined whether the child and parents could have any relationship beyond the biological one at all.

In the eyes of the master and of the law, good childrearing was not essential; good slave-rearing was. As one traveler noted, slave children had "[n]o education — no God — their whole life — food and play, to strengthen their muscles and fit them for the work of a slave." Although the system discouraged parents from forming strong bonds, the slave mother was nevertheless constantly accused of neglecting her children, and the father of brutality. Indeed, slaves were cursed as both immoral and incompetent parents.

But, even though the institution squelched parental love, the literature is replete with material demonstrating deep parental devotion. One Louisiana case, in which the plaintiff sought return of the price paid for a slave, sets forth the story of a mother gone mad with grief at having been separated from her children.

> [After the sale and separation] she refused, from religious scruples, to eat or take medicines on Fridays ... saying that God had appeared to her and forbidden it. This, and the fact of her having on one occasion burnt her clothes ... induced the belief ... that the girl labored under an aberration [sic] of mind, which they ascribed to religious enthusiasm and grief at being separated from her children.

Parents in name only; the slave mother and father could not shape their child's existence, nor could they exercise control over their child's fate — either immediate or long-term. Such control is the essential feature of the parenting relationship, marking the parent as different from other adults with whom the child might interact. But the slave child was the equal of the parent at birth. What slave parents did transmit was critical to the child's formative years, but the nature of the parenting relationship wholly depended upon the grace of another, in whose hands the child's future actually lay.

THE CONTRADICTIONS IN SLAVE LAW AND FAMILY LAW

Conjugal Rights and Slave Law

There was one primary reason advanced to justify the denial of the right of civil marriage to slaves. Marriage was described as a civil contract, and, since slaves could not contract, they therefore could not marry. Further, the contact-like incidents of the marital relationship were deemed unenforceable with respect to slaves. Fathers could not be held financially responsible for the support of their wives and children because they had no legal right to be paid for their labor. Slaves also could not be imprisoned for adultery or bigamy since they were the mere property of their masters. As slaves were deemed morally inferior, it was considered to be unduly and unnecessarily harsh to hold them to the legal standards of monogamous marriage. But, the real reason to deny legal marriage to slaves was expediency: the sexual exclusivity and permanence implicit in marriage were inconsistent with the master's right to sexually control and to alienate his slave property.

Chief Justice Thomas Ruffin of the North Carolina Supreme Court, an exceptionally capable jurist who had provided leadership to the entire South in the development of the law of slavery, explained why the law could deny slaves marital rights in the case of *State* v. *Samuel*.

It was a lover's triangle that gave rise to the prosecution. Samuel, a slave, had killed his estranged wife's new lover. He appealed his murder conviction to the state high court, claiming as error the trial judge's evidentiary ruling permitting the State to call his wife as a witness against him. The defendant sought to establish that his wife's testimony was barred by the marital privilege. The facts at trial showed he had been married to the witness for ten successive years; the couple had five children; they had separated; and, subsequent to the separation, the wife had then, with her master's permission, taken the victim, now deceased, as her new husband.

The Chief Justice did not pause to ponder the evidentiary wrinkle presented by the separation and purported remarriage. He went right to the core of the case: "The question of evidence made in this case, is not without difficulty; but, after the best reflection the court could bestow on it, that difficulty seems to arise rather from moral considerations than to be founded on legal principles." After quickly identifying the moral dilemma, however, Judge Ruffin perceived that the law offered no option: he had to wiggle out of it. He first analyzed the reason for the common law evidentiary rule of marital privilege:

> No code could justly, by one of its edicts, pronounce that an union between two persons once formed, should by no means be severed, and yet, by another of its edicts, coerce them to acts necessarily productive of dissensions, that would deprive

their union of all cordiality, separate them in feeling, and make their connexion intolerable.

He then asserted that, as the privilege is grounded on the legal requirement of marital permanence, it ought not be held to apply where no contract exists to require such permanence:

> This privilege... owe[s] its origin to the duration of the legal obligation of the contract of marriage. It cannot be yielded to any persons but such as have entered into that contract: in that rightful and formal method which is recognized in law as binding the parties throughout life, absolutely, and independent of the continuing inclinations of one or both of them, or the continuing license of any third person. Hence a marriage *de facto* will not, but only a marriage *de jure*, will exclude one of the partners from giving evidence for or against the other.

The "continuing license of any third person," namely the master's license to separate one spouse from the other, in part prevented the execution of a "contract" of permanent marriage. Here Judge Ruffin faced an intractable collision between three inviolable, sacred tenets he felt a legal duty to protect: marriage, the right to contract, and the right to hold slaves as private property.

In Judge Ruffin's jurisprudential time, each of these "rights" was deemed in some sense secured by natural law, the axiomatic law of first principles. The problem had yet another dimension, giving it even greater density. Marriage was sacred both because it was the command of natural law, and because it was considered to be a contract, which was sacrosanct in its own right.

But, the very *sine qua non* of marriage — its intended permanence — made marriage unlike a commercial contractual relation which could easily be terminated at the will of both parties. Moreover, the terms of the marital relation were not the subject of bargaining by the spouses, but were prescribed by the law. Marriage was only a contract in the sense that the parties agreed to become married to one another. In this sense, slave marriages were no different from any others. Slaves could agree, or contract, to "have and to hold," and they could promise to do so until parted by death, but that promise was unenforceable.

Properly viewed, the hard problem the court faced was not that slaves could not cross the marital threshold in a "contractual" sense; it rather was that, because they had no civil existence, they could not assume the civil benefits and burdens of husband and wife.

Judge Ruffin acknowledged the weakness of the "inability to contract" argument. He noted that, because,

> slaves are human beings, with passions and senses impelling them to [marry], and with a natural capacity to contract it, which no municipal regulation can annul .... It has been urged that the essence of this, as of other contracts, consists in the consent of the parties; which ... renders the contract obligatory by the law of nature and of reason, and it was thence inferred, that it is necessarily binding in our law, in the absence of positive provisions to the contrary.

But, Judge Ruffin insisted on his vicious circle: only legal marriage is legal, and an individual who cannot legally marry cannot agree to *be* married:

> [I]t has been constantly required as an essential requisite of a legal mar-

riage, that it should either be celebrated by some person in a sacred officer, or be entered into before some one [sic] in a public station and judicial trust....

...How can that be deemed to any purpose a legal marriage, which does not, in any respect, conform to the only legal regulations upon the subject of marriage?

Finally, recognizing that slave ownership was simply incompatible with slave marriage, Judge Ruffin conceded that the courts had no solution:

[It] may unfortunately be the law [that slaves cannot legally marry]; and may have been intended by the legislature to be the law, upon the general ground of the incapacity of a slave to enter into this, as into other contracts, upon the presumption of the want of free consent, and upon the further ground of the difficulty of giving legal validity to the marriage, in respect to its most important legal incidents, without essentially curtailing the rights and powers of the matters. If it be so, it may be a fit subject for legislative interposition, to avert this melancholy addition to the misfortunes and legal disabilities of this depressed race.

Having thrown the ball to the legislature, Judge Ruffin did not then make a graceful exit from what one of his contemporaries termed a "question of exceeding nicety and difficulty." Rather, casting yet another eye on the "difficulty...aris[ing] ...from moral considerations," he laid blame at the feet of the slaves themselves, for whom, he suggested, marriage would impose too great a moral burden. His argument was that, were the court to recog-

nize slave marriage for the purpose of the evidentiary rule in question, it would, in logic, effectively be grafting all of the incidents of civil marriage onto the slave relationship, including exposure to prosecution for bigamy:

[T]he court is not prepared, without a mandate from a higher authority than our own, to apply to this class of our population a rule, which would in innumerable instances, either subject them to legal criminality of a high grade, or deprive them almost entirely of their greatest solace — that of having families of their own, frail as may be the right, and temporary the enjoyment, dependent, as they are, upon the caprice of the parties themselves, and yet more upon the necessities or caprice of their owners.

Thus, "after the best reflection the court could bestow on it," the argument reduced to two simple, related, syllogisms: slave marriages are not legally valid because slaves cannot be legally married, and the moral commands of marriage are not held to apply to slaves because slaves are immoral. This then, was the answer to Judge Ruffin's conundrum: the law of marriage required adherence to the moral norm, but slave morality was, by nature, different from the norm. Therefore, the law did not violate the moral norm in excluding slaves from the rules governing marriage.

Employing the rationale that there was an innate difference in the races, an entirely different set of moral standards could therefore be applied to blacks without offending natural law. This double moral standard provided the underpinning for the criminal law governing sexual interactions as well as the law of marriage.

Procreative and Parenting Rights and Slave Law

Like the denial of martial rights, the denial of parental rights to slaves flew in the face of ideological trends and their legal echoes. This was the era of the cult of motherhood and domesticity. Indeed, the identification of womanhood with motherhood was near complete. Mother was now on her infamous pedestal, and ironically, her singular and unique importance as mother served as a threshold to greater legal rights for women. The judicially created "tender years" doctrine enlarged women's guardianship and custodial rights while diminishing the legal hold of patriarchy.

At the same time, the state, employing the doctrine of *parens patriae*, was grasping a greater role for itself in childrearing. The young child was increasingly being viewed as an individual and an incipient citizen, whose proper upbringing had become the state's interest. State intervention to protect the parenting relationship, or to sever it in cases of abuse or neglect was regarded as appropriate to advance the "best interests of the child."

In light of these developments, how could the law close its eyes to the erasure of the slave parent? How could it sanction the divorce of the birthing function from the mother function, childbearing from childrearing? And how could it withhold its *parens patriae* oversight in the case of the slave child, who was subject to the greatest abuses and the harshest conditions?

In contradistinction to the common law, the slaveholding states all adopted the civil rule, partus sequitur ventrem — the issue and descendants of slaves follow the status of the mother. The justification for the rule was the same as that offered by its Roman originators: "From the principles of justice, the offspring, the increase of the womb, belongs to the master of the womb."

In providing that the fruits of the bondwoman's womb were the "property" of her master, slave law echoed early non-slave domestic law. The master was deemed to "own" his wife and her children, just as he "owned" the slave woman and her children. Thus, the genesis of the rule involved two entangled proprietary relations: the master's marriage (a property relation) produced property for him (children), and his slave property also produced more property (slave children).

The slave husband, however, had no marital ownership interest in his wife, and therefore he had no ownership interest in his children. This effected a double diminution of the slave father's legal and social status: He could not claim ownership of his children, as could free men, nor could he, through his progeny, enrich his master, as could slave women. He had only his own labor to "give" his master, not that of his wife or his children.

In the mid-nineteenth century, changing views of white women and children had begun to challenge the principle of male ownership of the "increase of the womb." No longer were women seen as vessels whose exclusive vocation was to produce heirs. Property concepts were increasingly viewed as inappropriate in the law of family relations. But since property was the sine qua non of the slave-master relation, the rule persisted, reducing slave women to machines of reproduction and slave men to social irrelevancy.

This use of a commercial principle to vitiate a social relationship led to a confusing legal situation. The courts responded prodigiously to the many legal wrinkles produced without ever really questioning the underlying premise or its social meaning. Courts were, for example, perplexed by questions having to do with the legal status of the children of an enslaved but soon to be emancipated mother, and the fate of children born to a fugitive or momentarily free mother.

In addition to the question whether a slave's child was born free or not, another highly litigated issue was who owned the child. The courts debated whether in determining ownership disputes, slave children could be treated like the offspring of farm animals. At common law, animal offspring were "natural fruits" which were deemed the property of the mother animal's owner. Yet, since the judges were dealing with the relationship between mother and child, a relationship which the culture deemed sacred and fundamental, the commercial analogy to farm animals was not altogether satisfying. As one court put it, "the law... treats [slaves] as human beings, deprived, doubtless for wise purposes, of their freedom... and in our opinion the rule which applies to [the disposition of animals' issue] has no application to them."

The legal controversy typically arose in the interpretation of a slave owner's bequest of a slave mother to one legatee for life with a remainder interest in another legatee. The question became which legatee owned the children she bore during the life estate. If, as was the case in Delaware and Maryland, the children born during the life estate became the property of the life tenant, then, upon the death of the life tenant, the slave mother would be, by operation of law, separated from her children, who became part of the life tenant's estate.

One Tennessee case presents an especially chilling example of how the slave mother and her children could get caught in the vise of the potentially conflicting interests of the life tenant and the remainderman. The bequest was of the slave woman, Sally, to the testator's widow for life with the remainder interest in Sally to go to his children. The rule in Tennessee was that the offspring of the slave born during the life tenancy went to the remaindermen. The life tenant, the widow, petitioned the court to sell Sally because of "her bad temper, violent passions, immoral habits, and refusal to submit...." But Sally, having given birth to several children, had shown herself to be fecund, and it was therefore in the interest of the remaindermen to hold onto her. The Tennessee court refused to sanction the sale, noting that the "sale of the slave, so peculiarly valuable for her physical capacity of childbearing, so far from being for the benefit of the owners of the remainder-interest, was an enormous sacrifice, though it may have been otherwise, as to the life-owner."

Other questions as to the ownership of a slave mother's issue were equally fraught with difficulty. Where there was a lawsuit over ownership of a slave woman, there was a question as to who owned the children she bore during the pendency of the suit. Another problem arose upon the master's divorce: Were slave children to be deemed community property, or were they the separate property of the spouse who owned their mother at the commencement of the marriage? The courts ended up on both sides of these questions, without ever a query as to the role of the slave father or the best interests of the slave child.

Indeed, just as the slave mother and father had no recognized legal relations with the child, the slave child could claim nothing from its parents. The lot of slave children was more damned and unfortunate than that of illegitimate children, although slave children were not strictly considered bastards. The slave child inherited its mother's status but was not assured of its parentage, whereas the bastard was its mother's child in every sense. A slave child could not claim membership in a household, or the right to maintenance, nurturing, or custody from its birth parents.

One case illustrating the perversity of this situation involved the claim of a black, free father of a slave child to recover support payments of his child. The father sued the estate of his son's owner, arguing that his support of the boy when he was too young to work inured to the benefit of the master, who by right should have borne the cost. The reviewing court reversed a jury verdict in the father's favor, holding that the father "had no just claim whatever on the administrator for taking care of his own child."

Family Law, Sexual Morality, and the Law/Morality Dichotomy

As the cases discussed above demonstrate, the courts took varying avenues to resolve the vexatious law/morality split presented by the contradiction between the legal constructs of the family and slavery. Few of the judges had the perspicacity of North Carolina's Chief Justice Ruffin, but all of them confronted the dilemma which inhered in the very nature of the two institutions. The dimensions of the problem were hardly unique to issues of the family, but rather traversed the entire law of slavery.

That slaves had to be, by virtue of their "nature," exempt from laws embodying moral commands was the underlying principle in a Mississippi case which considered whether a slave could be charged with intra-racial rape. The defendant was indicted under the statute making it a crime to have sex with a child under the age of ten. The victim, in this case, was also a slave. The reviewing court reversed the conviction and dismissed the indictment for the reason that the statute did not explicitly include slaves, and the common law did not cover slave crime.

The slave, George, was not just a lucky defendant who fell through a legal loophole. The lawyer for the accused argued that black rape was different from white rape:

> The crime of rape does not exist in this State between African slaves. Our laws recognize no marital rights as between slaves; their sexual intercourse is left to be regulated by their owners. The regulations of law, as to the white race, on the subject of sexual intercourse, do not and cannot, for obvious reasons, apply to slaves; their intercourse is promiscuous, and the violation of a female slave by a male slave would be a mere assault and battery.

The court, noting that "[m]asters and slaves cannot be governed by the same common system of laws: so different are their positions, rights, and duties," apparently concurred.

Indeed, because of the "difference" between black and white rape, a similar statutory lapse produced a wholly different result in a case where the alleged rape victim was white. In the North Carolina case of *State* v. *Peter*, the slave, Peter, appealed his rape conviction, pointing out that the slave code only prohibited attempted rape, and that since the code covering rape referred to "persons" committing the crime, it did not cover the slave. The court held, however, that the failure of the relevant rape statute to explicitly bring slaves within its ambit was not cause to reverse the conviction. It found a presumption that slaves were meant to be covered by the statute "unless from the nature of the subject matter and the punishment imposed, it appears not to have been the intention to embrace slaves."

The existence of the loophole through which the defendant in *State* v. *Peter* sought to escape was unusual, for in contrast to the plight of the black woman, who was much more likely to be victimized by rape, the rape of a white woman by a slave (or a black freeman) was a capital offense in virtually every jurisdiction. One Georgia court reflected the pervasive hysteria about this most unspeakable offense: "The crime, from the very nature of it, is calculated to excite indignation in every heart; and when perpetrated on a free white female of immature mind and body, that indignation becomes greater, and is more difficult to repress."

Moreover, even though a Mississippi court held, in *George* v. *State*, that a black girl under ten could not be legally raped, in the slave rape case of *State* v. *Sam*, a North Carolina court queried whether perhaps the common law age of incapacity ought to be reduced from fourteen so as to allow the prosecution of black boys charged with rape:

> A large portion of our population is of races from more Southern latitudes than that from which our common law comes. We have indeed an element of great importance from the torrid zone of Africa. It is unquestionable that climate, food, clothing and the like, have a great influence in hastening physical development. Whether it may not be advisable to move down to an earlier age than 14, the period of puberty, for a portion, of not all of the elements in our population, may be a proper inquiry for the statesman.

Since, in theory, the "nature" of the black man was not affected by the race of his victim, taken together, *George* v. *State* and *State* v. *Sam* stand for the proposition that, while it was in the black man's "nature" to rape, it was not within the black woman's "nature" to *be* raped.

Indeed, for some time, the law did not recognize the rape of the black woman by *any* man, either black or white. In questioning the wisdom of this legal void, the Georgia legal scholar, Thomas Cobb, first inquired "whether the offense of rape, committed upon a female slave, should not be indictable; and whether, when committed by the master, there should not be superadded the sale of the slave to some other master." He went on, however, to note that a change in the law would be only for the sake of appearance, for "[t]he occurrence of such an offence is almost unheard of; and the known lasciviousness of the negro, renders the possibility of its occurrence very remote."

The "lasciviousness" of which he spoke was laid at the feet of black women. For, to the nineteenth-century mind, sexual morality property resided in the souls of women; men could not, by nature, be expected to keep its commands. Thus, while the black race as a whole was bereft of moral values, it was black women who bore the brunt of the accusation of lasciviousness.

Thus, the courts reasoned that, by nature, black men and women were incapable of adhering to a code of sexual morality, and that they were therefore exempt from the natural moral strictures of marriage and family. But this double standard worked both for the system of slavery and against it. For while the system wished to exclude slaves from marriage laws, including adultery and bigamy, it also wanted to impose harsher penalties for black man/white woman sex crimes than for all-white sex crimes.

The argument that race created different "natural" propensities which the law should account for was problematic, for in some instances, it was crucial to recognize the common humanity of all to whom the law spoke, slave and non-slave alike. In exempting slaves from certain moral edicts, these commands lost their universality. This challenged the idea that the laws were divinely derived, diminishing their binding force for whites.

These conflicting goals made it impossible for the courts to achieve doctrinal consistency. The core of the problem here, as in all of slave law, was the slave's dual status as person and chattel. Moreover, southern jurists were operating within a legal framework whose moorings were embedded in bourgeois ideology. Slave law and bourgeois law were at odds — one idealized personal will; the other denied its relevance to the law. To define slavery itself was to define the legal contradiction: the master owned the slave, and yet could not own the person of the slave.

The courts traveled many avenues in search of a rational solution to this contradiction. In some respects, the courts sought to limit their own purview to the regulation of matters pertaining to the slave's commercial character, leaving to the slaveholder the regulation of his bondman's social character. The jurists sought to circumvent their dilemma by taking slave law out of the reach of the common law, intervening only upon explicit statutory authority, or where the analogy with areas of tort or contract law was clear, and keeping strictly within the bounds of precedent.

It was impossible, however, to keep this line between the social and commercial sides of the system sharp, because — as with the case of black man/white woman rape — the slave's social interactions often fell outside plantation justice

and brought the law "on the books" into play. Therefore, in order to maintain white supremacy, the courts were compelled to regulate relations between whites and blacks. In order to hold slaves answerable for crimes they committed, they had to be recognized in law as morally and socially responsible persons. The reverse was also true, for, as exemplified by the rule, *partus sequitur ventrem*, commercial rules inevitably invaded the slave's social existence. Thus, the slave was, from a legal perspective, at once a person and a thing.

The implications of the slave's dual status for the law of the family were difficult to untangle, for there was an analogous duality in family law itself. Marriage, for example, legally changed both social and property relations. Parenting created new social and property relations. The law favored and protected family relationships and sought to regulate these social relations using, among other legal tools, criminal sanctions. Therefore, if the criminal law was properly an instrument of social control for both slave and non-slave alike, how could its inapplicability to slave sexual morality be explained?

The hybrid nature of family relationships such as marriage was the source of the problem. As the slave was a moral and social being, the strictures of legal marriage logically should have been applied to him or her. But the slave was a chattel, and, therefore, as legal marriage altered property relations for the new husband and wife, the law of marriage had no meaning for the slave.

Similarly, parenting should have brought for the slave mother and father mutual social ties and financial responsibilities. As the slave mother was merely an instrumentality of reproduction, however, the laws of bastardy, custody and the like — which served to legally define the parent-child relation — were dysfunctional as applied to her. As the slave father could not be paid for his labor, he also could assume no legal responsibility for his children.

CONCLUSION

As Harriet Beecher Stowe set the scene at the beginning of *Uncle Tom's Cabin*, she described the handsome and talented young slave, George, relating a tale of woe to his beautiful wife, Eliza. Eliza, who is owned by the Shelbys, and George live on neighboring plantations and George, who has recently been tormented to the breaking point by a mean and jealous master, is visiting to deliver his wife the news that the marriage might be short-lived. This is their conversation:

> **George:** I wish I could be good; but my heart burns, and can't be reconciled, anyhow. You couldn't in my place — you can't now, if I tell you all I've got to say. You don't know the whole yet.
>
> **Eliza:** What can be coming now?
>
> **George:** Well, lately Mas'r has been saying that he was a fool to let me marry off the place; that he hates Mr. Shelby and all his tribe... and he says he won't let me come here any more, and that I shall take a wife and settle down on his place. At first he only scolded and grumbled these things; but yesterday he told me that I should take Mina for a wife; and settle down in a cabin with her, or he would sell me down river.
>
> **Eliza:** Why — but you were married to *me*, by the minister, as much as if you'd been a white man!
>
> **George:** Don't you know a slave can't be married? There is no law in this country for that; I can't hold you for my wife, if he chooses to part us.

George spoke the bitter truth. The law had a lot to say about marriage, but for him and Eliza it boiled down to this: a slave could not be married if his or her master opposed.

This article has attempted to demonstrate how slave law perverted George and Eliza's marriage vows and how it tortuously twisted relations between slave parents and their children at a historical moment when marriage was a moral imperative and the family a divine institution. At a time when the church, the law, popular culture — indeed, all voices — placed the traditional family on a pedestal, where it was sacred and revered, the slave could only experience a cruelly mediated and debased version.

The needs of slavery have corroded both our legal legacy and our collective family experience. A careful analysis of the contribution of the slave experience to the current vicissitudes of the African-American family must take account of the failure of the courts to exercise moral and legal authority and the consequent quasi-lawmaking role of the slavemaster.

After emancipation, as African-Americans removed their chains to take a new place on the social and political landscape, the theme of black immorality that had served the antebellum judges so well persisted. With the end of slavery, its functional place in the law was transformed. The idea that blacks were immoral by nature became a foundational stone, *not* for slave property, but for social segregation and Jim Crow. The story of this link between racial ideology and sexual morality in our antebellum legal inheritance is one of tremendous contemporary significance, for it can provide the historical antecedents and assist in decoding the hidden messages in much of family and sexual law today.

◆

SOME COMPLICATING THOUGHTS ON SAME-SEX MARRIAGE

Nitya Duclos

In this essay, I will briefly describe some of the salient features of anti-essentialism as it has been articulated in the context of feminist theory. I will then sketch out what an anti-essentialist approach to same-sex marriage might look like. My (anti-essentialist) objective is not to conclude by determining that same-sex marriage is, on the whole, a good or bad thing, but to complicate the question to the point where it is clear that good/bad is not a sufficient range of answers. Many able writers have presented strong arguments in favor of recognition of a right to marry for lesbian and gay couples. In this process, however, less has been written about possible negative aspects of the institution of marriage for some lesbian and gay people. By adopting an anti-essentialist perspective in this paper, I want to explore this latter set of considerations, not to conclude that same-sex marriage is a bad idea, but to show that an anti-essentialist approach can offer lesbian and gay communities debating the "marriage question" a fuller appreciation of the complexities of the issue.

ANTI-ESSENTIALISM IN FEMINIST THINKING

Feminist anti-essentialist thinking developed out of feminist theories that exposed relations between women and men as relationships of oppression in which men exercised dominance over women. These theories revealed men's power over women as a hierarchy of gender dominance so deeply and pervasively entrenched in social institutions, including the legal system, that it seems natural and inevitable. Within this system, men are the norm; women sometimes conform to the norm and sometimes they diverge from it. Divergence is always measured in terms of distance from the norm; the centrality of the norm itself is unquestioned.

These feminist insights exposed hitherto universal social and legal norms as reflections of male power and perspective, opening seemingly objective rules to feminist allegations that the institutions of society are designed by and for men in ways that preserve the privileges and power that attach to their gender simply by appearing neutral. This led feminist thinkers to the conclusion that it is the exclusion of women as social norm generators that makes it impossible to achieve equality for women: Men possess the power to make society from their perspective, to substitute what is male for what is human. Women are stuck with trying to be the same or different; they never get to make the rules.

While some feminist academics were developing a theory of gender oppression as the product of male essentialism (that is, the assumption that men are the essence of the human), other feminists began to turn these anti-essentialist insights inward, examining

From Nitya Duclos, "Some Complicating Thoughts on Same-Sex Marriage," *Law & Sexuality,* vol. 1, 1991, pp. 31–61 (edited).

and exposing the existence of intra-gender oppression. Just as men have been the dominant gender group in society, white, middle-class women have been the dominant group within feminism. Just as men exercise power over women on the basis of their position within the socially constructed hierarchy of gender, women exercise power over women on the basis of other, equally fundamental and hierarchical, differentiating characteristics such as race, class, culture, sexual identity, disability, and age. The experience of gender oppression has not sensitized otherwise privileged women to oppression in these forms. Instead, these women have entrenched themselves as the feminist norm, constructing around themselves a model of gender oppression that is actually gender oppression coupled with race, class, and other privilege.

Privileged women's feminism has excluded and oppressed women who do not fit this mainstream mold both in its theory and in its practice. Feminist theory as it has been practiced by privileged feminists fails to perceive that differences between women affect their experiences of gender oppression, taking for granted that the pressing concerns of privileged women are as central to the lives of less privileged women and assuming gender to be the primary (if not the sole) site of oppression in all women's lives. The feminist practice that emerges from this essentialist foundation is similarly limited and incomplete. Not only are some of the "victories" celebrated by the Canadian women's movement of little relevance to women who do not conform to the dominant feminist norm, but these supposedly feminist gains may have actually hurt nonconforming women.

With the unpleasant realization that privileged feminism suffers from the same sort of entrenched dominance that feminists have criticized in men came the suspicion that *any* attempt to generalize hides similarly exclusive and oppressive norms. Instead, anti-essentialist feminist theorists argue, we must begin to carry on feminist practice and theory in new ways that avoid the perils of simplistic universals and unquestioned norms. The problem is to figure out how to do this. What would an anti-essentialist feminist theory look like? How do you theorize without generalizations and abstractions? How can a theory or a political strategy take account of all of our many differences and all of the ways they affect our experiences of any particular issue without becoming paralyzed by particularity? Ironically, it is easier to describe an anti-essentialist perspective in general, theoretical terms than it is to specify what such an approach requires in concrete and useful ways. In general, then, the "essence" of anti-essentialism is that differences really matter:

> [T]he way to begin to resolve issues of difference without oppressing those who are labeled different is to notice them. The challenge is not to see our own reflections in their eyes, or to imagine what we would want if we were they, but actually to pay attention to what they are saying about who they are. If this is to be done, quests for essences and identity, for simple, universal rules... grounded in a fixed and finite... set of ideals must be relinquished.

Respect for the many differences between us means that there are no easy answers. Yet an anti-essentialist approach is neither nihilistic nor solipsistic. Giving difference its due does not mean that we cannot generalize or speak for others — empathy and imagination are important but they are not everything. It does mean curbing our great fondness for comprehensive theories, conceptual simplicity, and grand finales, and settling for more modest, partial solutions. It also means that those of us who have the privilege to speak and to be heard must do so responsibly, focusing not so much on our power as a license to speak *for* others, but as imposing a duty to speak *with* them — a process that can lead to tentative conclusions about common concerns. Conclusions, of course, must be tested by returning with them to our diverse communities not only in theory but in practice. Anti-essentialism requires us to question our perspectives and our norms, to move away from assumptions and to find out what is really going on. A much more useful understanding of the possibilities of anti-essentialism can be gained, however, by seeing it in action. In the remainder of this essay, I will explore the potential of applying an anti-essentialist framework to a consideration of same-sex marriage.

ANTI-ESSENTIALIST EXPLORATIONS OF SAME-SEX MARRIAGE

My anti-essentialist approach proceeds in three stages. First, I think it is important to shift perspective, to formulate the issue itself in a way that exposes and questions the dominant perspective from the standpoint of the group (or groups) with which the inquirer is concerned. In this way, the framework within which the inquiry is conducted is made a part of it and becomes just as subject to challenge. Next, it is important to engage in a process analogous to the intra-gender critique of feminism. That is, the many differences within the groups whose perspective has been adopted need to be explored, particularly as they may bear on group members' experience of the

issue. The issue itself needs to be deconstructed and analyzed from many angles, especially in relation to the various ways in which it affects different people. In this stage, the goal is to embrace the issue in all its complexity, which entails acceptance of its contradictory effects on different people. The urge to simplify must be resisted here. The final stage is the least determinate. It consists of trying to identify some common concerns of different groups that emerge from their many differences and to direct reform efforts in those directions. If no consensus can be found, an anti-essentialist approach would suggest that, in making the inevitable decisions about what to do in concrete situations, the potential consequences for lots of different people (instead of only a few) be fully appreciated. Anti-essentialism does not (and cannot) promise universally beneficial solutions to any particular problem; it does try to ensure that hard decisions are made responsibly, with everyone in mind.

Throughout this process, the inquirer cannot hide behind a cloak of authorial omnipotence. One of the first lessons of anti-essentialism (and modern physics) is that there is no such thing as an outside observer. It is important to reflect upon your own location in relation to the issue and the people under discussion, because your perspective necessarily affects the way you perceive and the way you are perceived by others. This may or may not involve "coming out" to your audience, something that is necessarily more or less voluntary in different contexts. Inserting a footnote in a paper (or writing it into the text) about your race, class, gender, and sexual orientation is one way to acknowledge your location in relation to your subject. On balance, I am not sure that this is always a good thing. The reader can gain important information with which to assess the work by knowing something about the writer. When one reads an article written by a friend, the writing is interpreted in light of a sophisticated understanding of the person, as a member of certain groups and as a particular individual. Relevant personal experience rightly adds weight to an author's opinions. However, a brief categorical summary of personal characteristics can also be very misleading. Each "standard" category (race, gender, *etc.*) contains a series of embedded assumptions about that category as well as others. For example, if I describe myself as "straight," readers would tend to assume that I have never been in a same-sex relationship and have no interest in such a relationship in the future. Perhaps other inferences about my sexual and marital history would be made. It would also likely be assumed, in the absence of further clarification, that I am white, male (if my name is ambiguous), middle class, able-bodied, and so on. *All* of these inferences become the lens through which the writing is read. While it is natural and probably inevitable that readers construct a picture of the author from his or her work, I worry about encouraging prejudgment of the work because of known or assumed characteristics of the author. To what extent our thoughts are the product of our biographies is a difficult and perhaps unresolvable question. Particularly when the biography is going to be incomplete and inaccurate, the decision about what to reveal in one's writing is important and should be undertaken with care.

I think that it is most important for an author to try to indicate to the reader, either directly or indirectly, what experiences or perspectives she or he feels are especially important to the particular piece of writing. I bring to this essay my experiences of teaching, writing, and thinking about marriage and divorce in my capacity as a legal academic, which have been shaped by my general and personal experiences with marriage and divorce as a heterosexual, first-generation, East Indian woman raised primarily in Canada. I wish to contribute to the debates about same-sex marriage within and outside lesbian and gay communities by locating myself as an outsider from a lesbian or gay perspective, but as an insider from a marriage perspective.

Shifting Perspectives

The greater part of the answer to a question is found in the way that the question itself is phrased. Questions tend to get phrased in conformity with dominant ideology, in ways that take for granted the existing social order and its institutions. All of us unconsciously assume the existence of the norms into which we have been socialized. However, to the extent we belong to groups that have been ill-treated by the dominant group in a society, we are not likely to be understood from dominant perspectives nor are our needs likely to be met by institutions that were not designed for us. We should therefore resist our socialized tendencies to pose questions in ways that accept the dominant framework as natural and inevitable.

Too often when writing or talking about same-sex marriage, the basic question seems to be something like, "Should homosexuals be allowed to enter a legal marriage?" The hidden subject of this sentence is the state; it gets to give or withhold permission. Lesbians and gay men get lumped together into "homosexuals," an abstract and over-simplified sexualized label. Marriage is reified; it assumes a shape fixed by ideological and legal norms that "homosexuals" may or may not fit; the complexity and dynamism of this longstanding legal relationship is collapsed into the point of entry (marrying). The question is posed from the dominant perspective; the yes/no answer it commands presupposes a singularity (or essence) in the categories "homosexual" and "marriage" that does not actually exist.

This is not to say that the question does not need to be posed from the dominant perspective. Clearly, framing the issue in those terms is important, because the dominant perspective constitutes the framework within which the answers to questions acquire the force of law. And, in my view, the answer to the dominant perspective question is obviously "yes." It is a glaring injustice to preclude lesbian women and gay men from marrying their partners. But to take this answer as the whole answer is to accept the dominant perspective as the only perspective. Given that a same-sex marriage bar is a bad thing for the state to impose, lesbians and gay men still need to ask whether marriage is a good thing for them to seek.

Shifting perspectives means changing the subject of the sentence and opening up the field of responses. We could ask something like, "Will lesbians and gay men or some of them benefit from legal recognition and regulation of their relationships through the marriage system?" This puts lesbian and gay men front and center as people with whom and for whom we are concerned. It specifies that legal recognition is one form of recognition and that the issue involves the *regulation* of those relationships by law. It expressly removes from consideration any doubt that lesbians and gay men *have* relationships — something that earlier question left open. And it asserts that marriage is a system of legal and social rules, not elemental but socially constructed and open to change.

Embracing Complexity

The shift from "homosexual" to "lesbians and gay men" is a first step. Expanding from one category to two is hardly sufficient, however. Neither "the" lesbian community nor "the" gay community exist any more than "the" homosexual community or "the" family. These are not homogeneous groups, and being a lesbian or a gay man does not automatically confer representative authority for the whole group of lesbians and/or gay men. Responsibility to these communities requires appreciation of the great diversity *within* lesbian and gay communities. We need to call to mind as many of the complex ways in which lesbians and gay men differ as possible, since these differences affect not only their views and expectations but also their likely experiences of marriage and its corollary, divorce.

Paying attention to only relatively standard categories of difference, namely, race, class, and gender, creates a small wealth of differences. Differences such as sexual identity, culture, religion, age, and disability substantially increase the degree of diversity, as do education and political affiliations. There are also other differentiating characteristics that, although less universally recognized as such, are especially important in the context of this issue. Consider, for example:

- Is the person single or involved in a relationship? If in a relationship, what kind of relationship is it and how does the person feel about it (about to break up? just beginning?)?
- Is the person a parent, including genetic parents, gestational parents, and functional parents? If a parent, does the person live alone with his or her child(ren) or with a co-parent? Does the parent have legal custody of or

access to the child(ren)? What is the age(s) and sex(es) of the child(ren)? What kind of relationship does the parent have with the child(ren)? ,

- Is or has the person been legally married? If married, has he or she ever gone through a legal divorce? How does the person feel about these experiences?
- In what kind of community does the person live? What are his or her relationships with parents, siblings, and other family members? What kind of support network does the person have?

Obviously, the list could go on and on. Facing this multiplicity of differences is difficult for it is clearly impossible to ascertain each constituency's views on the issue or to analyze the likely impact of legal recognition of their relationship(s). The purpose is not to paralyze reform or to defeat activist efforts, but to stimulate a greater awareness of the need to think about and talk to (some) others and, when mapping out legal and political strategies or making predictions, to *test* them with many different people in mind.

A second component of embracing the complexity of the issue involves deconstructing marriage. Specifying the components of marriage is a crucial step toward identifying *what* it is about marriage that is desired or will benefit various constituencies within lesbian and gay communities. Marriage is not a monolith, although we are socialized to think of it as such. It is an extremely complex social, economic, legal, and religious institution, with deep emotional (but certainly not the same) significance to most individuals. It is closely tied to concepts of family and sexuality, both of which generate a strongly held set of social taboos in contemporary Canadian and American societies.

Marriage includes a state licensing procedure at the point of entry that permits the state to control who can and cannot marry and to raise money from marriage license fees. It also includes divorce, a process that permits the state to control exit from the institution and to raise more money. A complex series of economic benefits and burdens flow from the status of being married, both in the public sphere and in the private sphere. For example, some people who are married get tax breaks, but marital or "family" status also disentitles some people from access to benefits provided through the social welfare system. In the classic "private" context, being married leads to extended employment benefits but it may also hurt a spouse's ability to obtain credit. Marriage confers social legitimacy on relationships, it expresses a conformity with social norms that is good or bad in different communities and at different times, and it provides some people with psychological and emotional security within their relationships. The marriage system also includes the whole set of social, economic, legal, and emotional consequences of divorce. Legal systems governing marital property, spousal and child support, custody, and access all confer a host of benefits and burdens upon those who have been married.

All of these features, and others, constitute the institution of marriage as it presently exists in our society. When lesbian women, gay men, and others argue in favor of recognition of same-sex marriage, however, they do not always have the whole marriage system or the whole group of lesbians and gay men in mind. Asking an anti-essentialist question about same-sex marriage requires identifying what kinds of things lesbians and gay men want out of marriage, and then working through how the institution is likely to respond to those needs, considering the many different people within lesbian and gay communities. Only after this kind of analysis, it seems to me, should conclusions be drawn about whether struggling for the right to a marriage license (as compared to other kinds of reform) is a good strategy and for whom.

Those who advocate recognition of same-sex relationships through the legal system of marriage frequently assert roughly four distinct yet inter-related objectives that lesbian and gay people seek in marriage. Two of these are more abstract and two are more concrete. First, some people advocate marriage for primarily altruistic, political reasons, arguing that legal recognition of lesbian and gay relationships as marriages will revolutionize marriage and force society to confront and rethink its collective views of sex and sexuality. Second, some people argue that public validation and legitimation of same-sex relationships as equally worthy of respect can be realized through recognition of a legal right to marry. Third, some people see in marriage a range of socioeconomic benefits that could make a big difference in the lives of lesbian and gay families. Fourth, some people see in marriage a way of legitimating their relationships in the eyes of courts so that it is easier for them to keep their children.

Political Reform   The argument that legally recognizing same-sex relationships as marriages will force our society to confront its deeply rooted sexist, heterosexist, and repressed beliefs about human sexuality and stimulate a complete rethinking of sexual relations is, I think, a brave but ultimately misdirected political strategy. It is courageous because it conceives of lesbian and gay couples who seek to marry as catalysts for and possibly the victims of radical social change —

victims, since fundamental social changes are never accomplished without human cost. However, I worry whether the existence of a group of married lesbians and gay men can really revolutionize the institution of marriage. My concern arises from the fact that this argument is precisely the same as that used by reactionary groups *against* legal recognition of same-sex relationships as marriages. Perhaps the lesbian or gay activist's confidence in the radicalizing potential of same-sex marriage reflects an unconscious acceptance of homophobic rhetoric, which assumes the inevitability of marriage, distracting attention from more radical projects of social reorganization. After all, marrying is on its face an assimilationist move, and, although society is not universal in its responses to change, it is likely to be regarded as such by most people. Without a compelling strategy that maps out *how* acquiring a right to legally marry will trigger desired social changes, I find it more probable that current views of sex and sexuality will persist and that the public will continue to marry and divorce, noting only with passing interest that lesbians and gay men can now do the same.

Finally, legal recognition of same-sex relationships as marriages or as equivalent to marriages may not simply prove ineffective to attain the political goal of sexual liberation, it may also prove harmful to this effort. In particular, the creation of fixed alternative categories of legal matrimonial relationships may contribute to the entrenchment of mutually exclusive and immutable categories of sexual orientation. In the process, less "mainstream" sexual identities may suffer further marginalization.

Public Legitimation   The second argument in favor of legal recognition of same-sex relationships as marriages, that allowing same-sex marriage will publicly legitimate lesbian and gay relationships, is expressly assimilationist. That is, its advocates do not seek the transformation of the institution of marriage so much as its extension to same-sex couples, in the name of equality. While it is obvious that the current marriage system flagrantly discriminates against lesbians and gay men and should be condemned for this, as I have argued earlier, it does not automatically follow that acquiring the right to marry is a sufficient solution for lesbians and gay men. What is undeniably conceptually offensive to liberal ideology should not be conflated with what is actually harmful to people: it is important to know who is hurt by not being able to marry and divorce, and how, and whether getting married and divorced will actually address these harms.

The assumption in the "public legitimation" argument that marriage is a good thing should be questioned. Historically, the experience of marriage has been generally destructively for half of those who have married: women. Marriage has condoned and sustained class and racial segregation within a sexist context, it has stripped propertied women of their possessions, and it continues to play a significant role in the feminization of poverty. Marriage has also sheltered and legitimized violence against women and children. It is true that all of this damage has occurred while marriage has been restricted to opposite-sex couples and that individuals in same-sex relationships do not suffer gendered economic inequality relative to each other. However, this does not mean that lesbian and gay couples will be able to avoid these ills of marriage any more easily than straight couples. We have all been socialized into the mores of our sexist, racist, classist, and heterosexist society and a lesbian or gay male identity

is not a reliable shield against them. Although same-sex relationships are not the same as opposite-sex relationships, they nonetheless still exist within the context of powerful social ideologies that ingrain gendered, classed, and racial patterns of exploitation. Lesbian or gay male partners may differ from each other on the basis of class, race, age, education, and other differentiating characteristics, which, because of their position in the social hierarchy, also tend to alter the balance of power within relationships. Battery is not unknown in lesbian and gay relationships. Some same-sex couples divide household responsibilities along lines that reflect traditional gender patterns — and it is hard not to do so in a system that makes this division of labor economically advantageous whenever there are young children in the household. Marriage strengthens the force of dominant ideologies both in its symbolic and social influences, and in more concrete ways. For example, pressure to conform to traditional gendered roles increases when judges rely so heavily on these ideologies in arbitrating the consequences of termination of marital or marriage-like relationships.

The process of seeking such legal reform can also be damaging. Cases in which lesbians and gay men seek recognition of their family or spousal status have been based on trying to establish that lesbian and gay relationships conform to prevailing legal ideologies of family and marriage. The effort of making out a case of "sameness" has costs both for those who try to fit the mold and for those who clearly cannot. Even if some lesbian and gay marriages will not reproduce the pattern of subordination and domination that characterizes heterosexual marriages, struggling for a right to marry legitimates and entrenches the institution — which has adverse consequences for heterosexually identified women.

Another assumption underlying the "public legitimation" argument for legal recognition of same-sex marriage is that marriage is voluntary. The equality that is sought is the right to *choose* to marry so that acquiring the right simply increases the field of options for lesbian and gay couples. But the premise of choice in this formulation is misleading. One of the major trends in family law in Canada in recent years has been the assimilation of more and more *unmarried* heterosexual couples into the legal marriage system. That is, it is increasingly difficult for individuals living within heterosexual relationships to avoid being considered "married" by the state with respect to support obligations, pension and other employment benefits, and so on. If lesbians and gay men who wish to marry gain the "right" to choose to marry, cohabiting lesbians and gay men who wish to choose otherwise may find this increasingly difficult.

The goals of lesbians and gay men who seek to marry for this reason are equality and public validation of their relationships. Both are undeniably important goals that touch on the deep structure of the injustice that society has inflicted on lesbians and gay men. The community approval of a loving relationship as one deserving of public recognition and respect that the marriage ceremony signifies would likely ameliorate the social inequality and stigmatization felt by lesbians and gay men to some extent. But it is important not to overestimate the magnitude of the consequences flowing from the issuance of a marriage license. The very necessary struggle for formal equality does not guarantee any degree of substantive equality. There is still lots of room for *de facto* double standards, and lesbian and gay marriages could easily come to occupy one of the lower tiers of an already hierarchical social marriage system. Possession of a marriage license may not be sufficient for lesbian and gay couples to marry within particular religions, and a legal change of status may not be a persuasive means of gaining family acceptance and support for the relationship. Moreover, for some lesbians and gay men, gaining legal recognition of their relationships will not address the most significant reasons for their experiences of inequality and oppression. The problem is that a claim for a "right" to marry is at best an argument for legal *toleration* of same-sex relationships, but such tolerance falls short of social *respect*.

Socioeconomic Benefits   The next two rationales for seeking legal recognition of same-sex relationships leave the realm of ideals and come down to earth. They are pragmatic, not theoretical, and they seek in marriage material benefits from which same-sex couples are currently excluded.

Clearly there are some socioeconomic benefits to marriage, and it is unjust to exclude same-sex couples from them. However, the socioeconomic benefits sought by advocates of same-sex marriages do not apply equally to everyone nor do they all flow automatically from marriage. In addition, marital status carries with it certain economic burdens that disproportionately affect some people. Just what these various benefits and burdens are and how they affect different people should be calculated before concluding that marriage will improve the economic position of lesbian and gay couples. In conducting this analysis, whether the benefit or burden applies to married couples exclusively or also to unmarried cohabitants in heterosexual relationships, as well as whether it applies to "spouses" or to "families" must also be considered. Finally, the benefits and burdens that flow from the termination of marriage should not be omitted. To give a sense of the complexity of this enterprise, here is a list of some of the socioeconomic benefits and burdens that marriage brings:

Benefits

- public pensions
- immigration preferences for family members, married spouses, and engaged persons
- municipal benefits such as "family" zoning ordinances
- dependent married spouse tax deduction
- health insurance (lower "family" rates)
- eligibility for prisoner "family" and conjugal visiting programs
- adoption (administrative policies favoring married couples)
- intestate succession laws favoring "spouses"
- testator's "family" maintenance legislation (when the deceased has not adequately provided for his or her "family")
- right to sue for the wrongful death of a "spouse"
- no criminal liability for married spouses who would otherwise be considered accessories after the fact
- compensation for "families" of deceased crime victims
- interspousal transfer of property by will or trust
- protection against eviction upon death of a tenant for "spouses" or "family" members
- right to receive worker's compensation payments upon death of worker "spouse"
- "spousal" and "family" employment benefits in collective agreements, legislation, or private employers' benefit packages (*e.g.*, bereavement leave for death of a "spouse's" relative)

- power to make medical decisions for an incapacitated "spouse" or "family" member
- "family" discounts for clubs and other recreational activities

Burdens

- "spouse in the house" rules for state welfare assistance (counting as claimant's income any income received by opposite-sex cohabitant)
- prohibition against income-splitting for tax purposes
- disentitlement from state benefits on the basis of availability of financial claims against former married or unmarried cohabitant
- termination of state benefits upon marriage
- income tax income attribution rules for interspousal transfers loss of "status" upon marriage for First Nations women in Canada
- criminal liability for failure to provide "dependents" with the necessities of life
- disentitlement from government student loans on the basis of "spouse's" income
- conflict of interest legislation
- anti-nepotism rules in employment
- "spouse's" credit history taken into account in credit rating
- discounting of a "spouse's" income in bank's mortgage calculations on the assumption that she is likely to leave the workforce to care for children

With respect to economic benefits if the relationship ends, there is widespread acknowledgment that the current system of legal regulation of the economic consequences of divorce and separation is inequitable both in cases of direct legal intervention and in the approximately ninety percent of cases that are settled out of court. The people the system works worst for (in economic terms) are women with children; however, most people who encounter it feel it is unjust. In this context, it is hard to know whether legal provisions governing the economic aspects of marital termination are a benefit or a burden. For example, spousal support payments may seem to be a burden to the payor and a benefit to the payee. However, the payor's burden is significantly offset by being able to deduct support payments for income tax purposes; extremely high default rates and very low enforcement rates may mean that a spouse or former spouse is worse off than a non-spouse who may receive less from the state but can rely on getting it. Finally, it should be remembered that acquiring marital status will not end all socioeconomic discrimination on the basis of sexual orientation.

It is beyond the scope of this paper to calculate how these various benefits and burdens will likely affect different same-sex couples. What should be clear from this discussion, however, is that statements that lesbians and gay men benefit socioeconomically from being able to marry will likely have only some lesbians or gay men — and some benefits or burdens — in mind. On the basis of this brief catalogue of socioeconomic consequences of marriage, I would guess that those individuals who most benefit from the socioeconomic advantages of marriage are members of the middle class. Those who rely for most of their income on state benefits are more likely to be economically penalized for marrying. Given that class relations are interpenetrated by gender and race relations, I suspect that, for example, white gay men as a group will likely benefit more from marriage than will black lesbian women, in purely socioeconomic terms.

Children   Marriage has sometimes been advocated as a way for lesbian or gay parents to keep their children, particularly when the challenge to custody is made by a heterosexual individual or couple, or in situations in which a genetically related parent denies the parental claims of a former lesbian partner. Marriage might also be seen as a way of safeguarding one's children from the state on the assumption that children living with unmarried lesbian or gay parents are more likely to be found by the state to be children in need of protection under the standard tests in child protection legislation.

This argument rests on the assumption that possession of a marriage certificate will legitimize the sexual relationship between the adults in the household in the eyes of the court so that the judge will not consider the lesbian or gay relationship to be a threat to the "best interests of the children" (the governing principle in all child custody cases). But is the absence of a marriage certificate really the problem? The history of judicial treatment of same-sex relationships in the custody context constitutes such appalling evidence of deep-seated and visceral anti-lesbian and anti-gay feeling in the judiciary that it seems naive to think such attitudes can be wiped out by a marriage certificate. In fact, the enormous social significance vested in a marriage certificate may provoke greater hostility on the part of homophobic judges toward married lesbians and gay men. Even when the judge is not overtly homophobic, heterosexist bias may well manifest itself in matters, such as assessment of credibility, that are critical to success in a contested custody case. It is also important to remember that alongside the catalogue of anti-lesbian and anti-gay rulings, judicial titillation and inappropriate inquiry into sexual relationships, and offensive moral pronouncements about the lives of litigants in custody cases involving lesbians and gay men, lies a similarly reprehensible list of judicial actions in cases involving heterosexually identified married women attempting to retain custody of their children.

In fact, the excessive judicial scrutiny, moral pronouncements, and serious constraints on behavior that characterize custody cases regardless of how the litigants' sexual orientation is described to the court may be more reflective of the defects in our system of custody dispute resolution in general than of the importance of a marriage certificate. Custody disputes arise in a wide variety of contexts — for example, a lesbian may be seeking custody of children against their biological father, or she may be opposing his relatives, or she may be litigating against a former lesbian partner with whom she has had children (and she may or may not be the biological mother), or she may be opposing her lover's relatives — and they are always agonizingly painful, stressful, and expensive. In the vast majority of cases, both parties clearly meet the minimum standards of parenting ability required by law, and the judge is required to select between people who desperately want custody of the child(ren) on the basis of the child(ren)'s "best interests." No one knows what that means. In the face of this vast discretionary power to do what is "best" for the child(ren) and overwhelming pressure to decide cases as quickly as possible, judges rely on "common sense," conventional morality, and a whole host of considerations that reflect the prejudices of privileged groups in our society to which virtually all judges belong. Thus, while not being married may well be a mark against some parents (whether gay, lesbian, or heterosexually identified), being a lesbian or a gay man will likely also be a negative factor — as will being a working mother, belonging to a nontraditional religion, and so on. As long as the custody dispute resolution system remains unchanged, there will be an informal hierarchy of preferred parents, reflecting judges' assumptions about who is a good

parent. Married lesbians and gay men will simply take their place in the ranks (likely above unmarried lesbians and gay men and below heterosexual parents). Trying to conform to the evolving judicial standard of "good lesbian mother" may acquire a further gloss if it becomes possible to be a married lesbian mother, but the stereotype will remain and may even gain strength if same-sex partners can (and so can be expected to) marry.

Given the serious inadequacies of the custody dispute resolution system, it may be wise to pause before seeking a reform that would inevitably bring lesbian and gay parents into greater contact with it. Although it is true that custody disputes often arise outside the context of marriage, the termination of a marriage necessarily involves the intervention of a court to scrutinize and resolve custody arrangements. And the adversarial nature of the system exerts a powerful influence at a time when individuals, regardless of their sexual identities, are terribly vulnerable to feelings of antagonism against their former partners. Contact with the marriage dissolution system, especially when young children are involved, heightens conflict, exacerbates emotional strain, and costs a lost of money, to the detriment of everyone. Adding a new and growing category of custody disputes between divorcing same-sex couples may well increase the magnitude of the problem rather than ameliorate the injustices already experienced by lesbian and gay parents.

It is true that lesbian and gay parents are currently at greater risk in custody litigation, both against heterosexually identified persons and biological parents; it is shocking that an absentee genetic father has more legal rights to his genetic offspring than does the lesbian co-parent who lives with, cares for, and loves the child along with its genetic mother. Similarly, it is manifestly unfair that a lesbian parent who is not genetically related to her child has no legal rights as against a former partner who is a genetic parent. The injustice and psychological harms in these situations should galvanize reformers to action. But turning to custody law and the courts in the absence of substantial legislative reform, with only a marriage certificate in hand, may not make a very big difference.

I do not believe that it is coincidental that those whom marriage is most likely to benefit are those who are already fairly high up in the hierarchy of privilege that pervades society at large. Thus, another possible consequence of legal recognition of same-sex marriage is that differences of power and privilege within lesbian and gay communities might be exacerbated.

When to seek a "right" to marry and how to do it, if at all, are complicated questions that do not admit of easy answers. In this essay, I have attempted to show just how complicated these questions are. By pausing to consider the many different situations of lesbian and gay people and by carefully dissecting the various elements of the institution of marriage, genuinely progressive reform is possible. While the legal institution of marriage is one of society's most basic institutions and one from which lesbians and gay men should never have been barred, I think the message of this paper is that we should all be wary of package deals.

◆

MOST LIKE AN ARCH THIS MARRIAGE
John Ciardi

Most like an arch — an
    entrance which upholds
and shores the stone-crush up
    the air like lace.
Mass made idea, and idea held
    in place.
A lock in time. Inside
    half-heaven unfolds.

Most like an arch — two
    weaknesses that lean
into a strength. Two fallings
    become firm.
Two joined abeyances become
    a term
naming the fact that teaches
    fact to mean.

Not quite that? Not much less.
    World as it is,
what's strong and separate
    falters. All I do
at piling stone on stone apart
    from you
is roofless around nothing. Till
    we kiss

I am no more than upright and
    unset.
It is by falling in and in we
    make
the all-bearing point, for one
    another's sake,
in faultless failing, raised by
    our own weight.

From John Ciardi, "Most Like an Arch This Marriage," in *John Ciardi, Selected Poems* (Fayetteville:University of Arkansas Press, 1984), pp. 30–31.

Cohabiting Without Marriage

If an adult couple cohabits without marriage, should the individuals involved be entitled to any of the legal or social benefits of marriage? This question is particularly pronounced if the couple splits up or if one of the individuals dies without leaving a will that benefits the other one. Images of relationships held by others may affect legal treatment of these questions. What does it take to change those images? It may be a matter of time, confrontation, or, as one of these readings suggests, snowstorms.

◆

DECONSTRUCTING CONTRACT DOCTRINE
Clare Dalton

THE CASES

State courts have increasingly confronted cases involving various aspects of the cohabitation relationship, and their decisions have attracted a fair amount of scholarly attention. I focus on two such decisions: that of the California Supreme Court in *Marvin* v. *Marvin*, and that of the Illinois Supreme Court in *Hewitt* v. *Hewitt*.

In *Marvin*, Justice Tobriner addressed the question of whether plaintiff Michelle Triola, who had lived with the defendant, Lee Marvin, for seven years, could recover support payments and half the property acquired in Lee Marvin's name over the course of the relationship. The court found that the plaintiff, in alleging an oral contract, had stated a cause of action in

express contract, and further found that additional equitable theories of recovery might be applicable. On remand, the trial court found that there existed neither an express contract nor unjust enrichment, but awarded the plaintiff equitable relief in the nature of rehabilitative alimony. The court of appeals then struck this award on the theory that relief could be granted only on the basis of express contract or quasi-contract.

The alleged oral agreement provided that plaintiff and defendant would, while they lived together, combine their efforts and earnings and share equally any property accumulated. They agreed to present themselves publicly as husband and wife. Triola also undertook to serve as the defendant's companion, homemaker, housekeeper, and cook. A later alleged

From Clare Dalton, "Deconstructing Contract Doctrine," *Yale Law Journal*, vol. 94, no. 997, 1985, pp. 1096–1113 (edited).

modification to the contract provided that Triola would give up her own career in order to provide these services; in return, Marvin promised to support Triola for the rest of her life. The relationship ended when Marvin threw Triola out.

The plaintiff in *Hewitt* was in many respects a more sympathetic figure than Michele Triola. When she and Mr. Hewitt were both college students, she became pregnant. He then proposed that they live together as man and wife, presenting themselves as such to their families and friends, and that he thereafter share his life, future earnings, and property with her. She borrowed money from her family to put him through professional school, worked with him to establish his practice, bore him three children and raised them, and otherwise fulfilled the role of a traditional wife. After over fifteen years he left her. She sought an equal division of property acquired during the relationship and held either in joint tenancy or in the defendant's name.

The appeals court ruled that she could have an equitable share of the property if she were able to prove her allegation of an express oral contract, although it did not preclude the possibility of alternative equitable theories of recovery in appropriate circumstances. The Supreme Court of Illinois reversed, basing its decision principally on considerations of public policy.

EXPRESS AND IMPLIED AGREEMENT

The opinions in the cohabitation cases indicate that the distinction between the intention-based express contract and the public institution of quasi-contract may be central to the question of whether to grant relief. As I have earlier argued, however, techniques for interpreting the express contract are indistinguishable from techniques used to determine the presence of a quasi-contractual relationship. If the interpretive techniques employed highlight factors external to the parties and their actual intentions, even express contracts seem very public. If, in contrast, the techniques used have as their stated goal the determination of the parties' intentions, then quasi-contracts appear no less private or consensual than express contracts. The cohabitation opinions employ both public-sounding and private-sounding arguments to reach a variety of conclusions. In some cases courts determine that the parties are bound by *both* real and quasi-contract obligations, in others that they are bound by neither, in yet others that they are bound by one but not the other. The arguments do not determine these outcomes — they only legitimate them.

In these cases, as in the earlier-discussed *Hertzog*, there is a common presumption that agreements between intimates are not contractual. While this model of association was developed in husband-wife and parent-child cases, nonmarital cohabitations are assumed, for these purposes, to have the same kind of relationship. As in *Hertzog*, express words are taken to be words of commitment but not of contract; conduct that in other circumstances would give rise to an implied-in-fact contract is instead attributed to the relationship. These cases also reach a conclusion only intimated in *Hertzog*: They find no unjust enrichment where one party benefits the other.

One possible explanation for this presumption against finding contracts is that it accords with the parties' intentions. It can be argued that cohabitants generally neither want their agreements to have legal consequences, nor desire to be obligated to one another when they have stopped cohabiting. It can further be presented as a matter of fact that their services are freely given and taken within the context of an intimate relationship. If this is so, then a subsequent claim of unjust enrichment is simply unfounded.

This intention-based explanation, however, coexists in the opinions — indeed sometimes coexists within a single opinion — with two other, more overtly public, explanations that rest on diametrically opposed public policies. The first suggests that the arena of intimate relationships is too private for court intervention through contract enforcement to be appropriate. In *Hewitt*, for example, the Illinois Supreme Court suggests that "the situation alleged here was not the kind of arm's length bargain envisioned by traditional contract principles, but an intimate arrangement of a fundamentally different kind."

While it has some intuitive appeal, the argument that intimate relationships are too private for court enforcement is at odds with the more general argument that all contractual relationships are private and that contract enforcement merely facilitates the private relationship described by contract. To overcome this apparent inconsistency, we must imagine a scale of privateness on which business arrangements, while mostly private, are still not as private as intimate arrangements. But then the rescue attempt runs headlong into the other prevailing policy argument, which separates out intimate arrangements because of their peculiarly public and regulated status. Under this view, it is the business relationship that by and large remains more quintessentially private.

According to this second argument, the area of non-marital agreements is too public for judicial intervention. The legislature is the appropriate body to regulate such arrangements; courts may not help create private alternatives to the public scheme. In *Hewitt*, the supreme court directly follows its appeal to the intimate nature of the relationship with an acknowledgement of the regulated, and hence public, character of marriage-like relations. With respect to intimate relations conceived as public, the judiciary can then present itself as either passive or active. The argument for passivity is that judges should "stay out" of an arena already covered by public law. The argument for activity is that judges should reinforce public policy by deterring the formation of deviant relationships, either because they fall outside the legislative schemes organizing familial entitlements and property distribution, or because they offend public morality.

Neither the private nor the public arguments for the absence of contract in this setting are conclusive. Both private and public counterarguments are readily available. If the absence of contract is presented as flowing from party intention, competing interpretations of intention can be used to argue the presence of contract. If, within a more public framework, the court categorizes the concerns implicated by the relationship as private, then an argument can be made that within the boundaries expressly established by legislation, the parties should be free to vary the terms of their relationship without interference by the state. If the focus is the place of cohabitation agreements within the publicly-regulated sphere of intimate relationships, then an argument can be made that certain kinds of enforcement in fact extend and implement public policy rather then derogate from it.

Judges' differing interpretations of virtually identical agreements seem to depend quite openly on either their views of what policy should prevail or their own moral sense. Rarely does a judge even appear to make a thorough attempt to understand and enforce what the parties had in mind. For Justice Underwood in *Hewitt*, for example, nothing but "naivete" could explain the assertion that "there are involved in these relationships contracts separate and independent from the sexual activity, and the assumption that those contracts would have been entered into or would continue without that activity.

Justice Tobriner in *Marvin*, on the other hand, rejects the idea that the sexual relationship between parties to a cohabitation contract renders the contract as a whole invalid. He explicitly uses the divide between objective and subjective, form and substance, to carve out a much larger space for enforceable agreements than that envisaged by Underwood. Tobriner's test has two components: Contracts between non-marital partners are enforceable unless they *explicitly* rest "upon the immoral and illicit consideration of meretricious sexual services." Furthermore, such contracts are unenforceable only "*to the extent*" that they rest on this meretricious consideration.

Tobriner is not so naive as to suppose that the Triola-Marvin agreement did not contemplate a sexual relationship. But he feels that the "subjective contemplation of the parties" is too "uncertain and unworkable" a standard. He relies instead on formal criteria of intent — on the manifestations of agreement alleged by Triola — to determine if his two-part test of enforceability has been met. For the purposes of this analysis Tobriner describes the agreement as follows: "[T]he parties agreed to pool their earnings,... they contracted to share equally in all property acquired, and... defendant agreed to support plaintiff." None of this strikes Tobriner as necessitating a conclusion that sex invalidates the agreement.

Of course the formal criteria are themselves empty of significance until given meaning by judicial analysis. The very same language construed by Tobriner had been given very different effect in an earlier decision. In *Updeck* v. *Samuel*, a California District Court of Appeal considered the statement that the woman would make a permanent home for the man and be his companion as indicating precisely the sexual character of the relationship. Unwilling or unable to disapprove *Updeck*, Tobriner is forced to distinguish this case in a fashion that directly undercuts the legitimacy of his stated reliance on form or manifestation. He argues that the *Updeck* agreement was found invalid because the court "[v]iew[ed] the contract as calling for adultery." But the very act of "viewing" the contract, or interpreting its terms, involves an explanation of substance. The court in *Updeck* supplied sexual substance, while Tobriner supplies economic substance. *Jones* v. *Daly*, a case subsequent to *Marvin*, provides another striking illustration of the manipulability of form. In *Jones*, which involved a homosexual partnership, a California Court of Appeal denied relief on the ground that an agreement, in other respects almost identical to the *Marvin* agreement, contained the word "lover."

[As] the courts wrestle with these interpretive questions, we see them apparently infusing a public element, external to the parties' own view of their situation, into their assessment of cohabitation agreements. We also can see how this is a necessary result of the tension between manifestation and intent, of the way in which intent requires embodiment in manifested forms, even while the forms require an infusion of substance before they can yield meaning. Indeed, to accuse judges of moving from the private to the public sphere is only to accuse them of the inevitable. If there is force behind the accusation, it is not *that* they have made the transition from private to public, but that they have made the transition *unselfconsciously*, and that the particular values, norms, and understandings they incorporate are different from the ones we would have favored, or different from the ones we think would correspond with those of one or both of the parties to the agreement.

CONSIDERATION: ITS SUBSTANCE

Consideration doctrine offers yet other opportunities for the conflation of public and private, and the introduction of competing values, norms, and understandings into the resolution of these cohabitation cases. Just as in the area of interpretation, the crucial additions are judicial conceptions of sexuality, and of woman's role in her relationship with man. Two aspects of consideration doctrine recur in the cases. Each illustrates the proposition that formal consideration doctrine cannot be implemented without recourse to substance. Substance, here as elsewhere, can be provided by assessments of objective value or by investigations into subjective intent. It is with respect to these substantive inquiries that ideas about sexuality and relationship come to play so potentially important a part.

The first use of consideration doctrine in this context shows up in the disinclination of courts to enforce contracts based on "meretricious" consideration. Courts frequently search beyond the express language of the agreement in order to "find" that sex is at the heart of the deal — specifically that the woman is providing sexual services in return for the economic security promised by the man. Insofar as this investigation depends on divining what the parties had in mind, consideration turns on subjective intent. For these purposes, it matters not at all that "intent" has been derived from the judge's own feelings about such relationships, even when the express language of the parties would appear to point in an opposite direction.

The treatment of meretricious consideration also illustrates how consideration may depend on a finding of objective value. When courts refuse to enforce contracts based on the exchange of sexual services for money, they are, for long-standing policy reasons, declining to recognize sexual services as having the *kind* of value that they will honor. This decision, based on an objective measure of value, is no different from the decision that "nominal" consideration will not support a contract. There, too, courts disregard intention in the name of a policy that depends upon societal recognition of certain sorts of values and delegitimation of others.

The second aspect of consideration doctrine of interest in this context is the traditional conclusion that the woman's domestic services cannot provide consideration for the promises made to her by the man. This is usually linked to the idea that the relationship itself is not one the parties see as having a legal aspect. The standard explanation is that the woman did not act in expectation of gain, but rather out of affection, or that she intended her action as a gift.

Tobriner in the *Marvin* decision rejects this conclusion by recasting the issue as one properly belonging in the selfish world of business. Unless homemaking services are considered lawful and adequate consideration for a promise to pay wages, the entire domestic service industry will founder. Just as plainly, such services can provide the consideration for an agreement concerning property distribution. Tobriner thus appeals to the substance of objective value: There is a market in which domestic services receive a price; when intimates arrange that one will deliver those same services to the other, that promise is therefore capable of supporting a return promise.

Even as Tobriner uses ideas of objective value, however, his reasoning reveals that the ultimate rationale for this aspect of consideration doctrine depends upon arguments of subjective intent. Like the promise in the *Michigan* case, the services could constitute consideration if they were offered with the intention of bargain or exchange. It is only the altruistic context, revealing the beneficent intention, which invalidates them.

Thus, while one route of access into this issue threatens to expose the public determination of what values the law will and will not recognize, that route is apparently closed off by the reminder that it is private intention, not public power, that assigns value. But then the very public role abjured in the context of objective value is placed out instead through the "finding" of intent according to criteria that are essentially and inevitably public rather than private.

THE QUESTION OF POWER

Under duress and unconscionability doctrines, policing the "fair" exchange is tied irretrievably to asking whether each party entered into the contract freely, whether each was able to bargain in equally unconstrained ways, and whether the deal was a fair one. I suppose that any of us would find these questions even harder to answer in the context of intimate relationships than in other contexts — harder in that we would require a much more detailed account of the particulars before we could hazard an opinion, and harder in that even this wealth of detail would be likely to yield contradictory interpretations. Yet we acknowledge the importance of these questions in the area of intimate relations; we do not imagine either that most couples wind up with a fair exchange, or that most couples have equal bargaining power vis-à-vis one another.

The doctrinal treatment of cohabitation agreements, however, like the treatment of contracts in general, usually pays little attention to questions of power and fairness. Duress and unconscionability are the exceptions that prove the rule. Those doctrines identify the only recognized deviations from the supposedly standard case of equal contracting partners. Intimate partners are conceived of as fitting the standard model. One consequence of this conception is that courts can justify the failure to enforce cohabitation arrangements as mere nonintervention, overlooking the fact that the superior position in which nonaction tends to leave the male partner is at least in part a product of the legal system. Another is that courts can idealize the private world in which their "nonintervention" leaves the parties, disregarding the ways in which that world is characterized by inequality and the exercise of private power. Yet another is that courts can talk blithely about the intentions of "the parties" in a fashion that ignores the possibility that one party's intentions are being respected at the expense of the other's.

Not all of the cohabitation contract opinions ignore the issues of fairness and power. They are more likely to receive explicit attention when a judge frankly invokes "public policy" instead of relying exclusively on contract doctrine. They appear, for example, when the Illinois appeals court in *Hewitt* explains why enforcement of such agreements promotes rather than undermines the institution of marriage. When a judge casts his opinion in traditional doctrinal terms, using intention, for example, or consideration, then any sensitivity he has to questions of power and fairness must be translated — translated, for example, into a willingness to assume that the parties did intend to enter a relationship of reciprocal obligation or that the woman has provided services that require compensation. Frequently this involves construing the male partner's intentions *as if* he were the concerned and equal partner the law assumes him to be. Again, these devices parallel those used by courts across the range of contract decisions. But only when judges move outside the framework of traditional contract doctrine will they be in a position to grapple with the full range of problems posed by these disputes.

There are several ways to begin a richer examination of the cohabitation cases. First, we can learn from the truths underlying contract doctrine while rejecting the idea that doctrine alone can lead us to correct answers. The dichotomies of public and private, manifestation and intent, form and substance, do touch on troubling questions that are central to our understanding of intimate relationships and the role of the state in undermining or supporting them. The problem with doctrinal rhetoric is twofold. First, it recasts our concerns in a way that distances us from our lived experience of them. Second, the resolution of the cases that the application of doctrine purports to secure offers us a false assurance that our concerns can be met — that public can be reconciled with private, manifestation with intent, form with substance.

Once we realize that doctrinal "resolutions" are achieved only by sleight of hand, consideration of the identified dichotomies helps us to explore more fully the cohabitation agreement. What is the nature of this relationship, or what range of cohabitation arrangements precludes us from making general statements about the nature of the relationship? To what extent do these relationships need protection from authority, and to what extent do they require nurturing by authority? To what extent do they reflect the shared expectations of their participants, and to what extent the imposition of terms by one party on another? How can we harbor intimacy within institutions that offer the flexibility to accommodate individual need, while at the same time providing a measure of predictability and stability? What stake does the society have in limiting the forms of association it will recognize? Given our dependence on our social and cultural context, what freedom does any of us have to reimagine the terms of human association?

Study of the play between public and private, objective and subjective, shows us that these same dichotomies organize not only the strictly doctrinal territory of contract interpretation or consideration, but also the broader "policy" issues that are folded into the cases. Questions of judicial competence, for example, turn out to involve precisely the question of whether a private sphere can be marked off from the public sphere. Similarly, whether enforcement of cohabitation agreements is a pro-marriage or an anti-marriage position turns out to depend on questions of intention and power. Even as this analysis illuminates the policy dimension of the cases, it refutes the claim that the addition of policy considerations can cure doctrinal indeterminacy.

If neither doctrine nor the addition of policy can determine how decision-makers-choose outcomes in particular cases, the next question is whether the opinions contain other material that illuminates the decision-making process. The dimension of these co-habitation cases that cries out for investigation is the images they contain of women, and of relationship. And since images of women and of relationship are the central concern of feminist theory, I have used that theory as the basis for my inquiry. This does not, of course, foreclose the possibility that other inquiries, in this or other settings, might prove equally possible and promising once doctrine is opened up to make room for them.

I am not claiming that judges decide cohabitation cases on the basis of deeply held notions about women and relationship in the sense that these notions provide a determinate basis for decision. For this to be true, attitudes toward women and relationship would have to be free from contradiction in a way that doctrine and policy are not. I believe instead that these notions involve the same perceived divide between self and other that characterizes doctrine, and are as internally contradictory as any doctrine studied in this article. My claim, therefore, is only that notions of women and relationship are another source of influence, and are therefore as deserving of attention as any other dimension of the opinions. These notions influence how judges frame rule-talk and policy-talk; in a world of indeterminacy they provide one more set of variables that may persuade a judge to decide a case one way or another, albeit in ways we cannot predict with any certainty.

One introductory caveat is in order. To say that "the opinions" convey images of woman and relationship is to miss the distinction between images that appear to inhere in the doctrine as it has developed, and images woven into the texture of opinions seemingly at the initiative of a particular judge. I think this distinction is worth

noting, even though in practice it cannot always be made. It becomes clearest, perhaps, when a judge struggles against images he sees embedded in the doctrine, and offers new images that in turn provide him with new doctrinal choices.

One powerful pair of contradictory images of woman paints the female cohabitant as either an angel or a whore. As angel, she ministers to her male partner out of noble emotions of love and self-sacrifice, with no thought of personal gain. It would demean both their services and the spirit in which they were offered to imagine that she expected a return — it would make her a servant. As whore, she lures the man into extravagant promises with the bait of her sexuality — and is appropriately punished for her immorality when the court declines to hold her partner to his agreement.

Although the image of the whore is of a woman who at one level is seeking to satiate her own lust, sex — in these cases — is traditionally presented as something women give to men. This is consistent both with the view of woman as angel, and with the different image of the whore as someone who trades sex for money. In either event, woman is a provider, not a partner in enjoyment. When a judge invokes this image, he supports the view that sex contaminates the entire agreement, and that the desire for sex is the only reason for the male partner's promises of economic support. If sex were viewed as a mutually satisfying element of the arrangement, it could be readily separated out from the rest of the agreement. In most cases, the woman's career sacrifices and childrearing and homemaking responsibilities would then provide the consideration for the economic support proffered by the man.

Marriage is often presented in the cases as the only way in which men and women can express a continuing commitment to one another. This suggests that when men do not marry women, they intend to avoid all responsibility for them. Women therefore bear the burden of protecting themselves by declining the irregular relationship. At the same time, the institution of marriage as an expression of caring is portrayed as so fragile that only the most unwavering support by the state will guarantee its survival. This could mean that other expressions of caring would entirely supplant marriage without vigilant enforcement of the socially endorsed forms of relationship, although that would be inconsistent with the portrayal of marriage as the only expression of commitment. Alternatively, it could mean that men and women would not choose to enter relationships of caring without pressure from the state.

These nightmarish images have much in common with what other disciplines tell us men think about women and relationship. The conception of women as either angels or whores is identified by Freud, and supported by feminist accounts. The evil power of female sexuality is a recurrent subject of myth and history. The contrast of men fearing relationship as entrapping, and women fearing isolation, is the subject of Carol Gilligan's work in the psychology of moral development; others have explored the origins of that difference in the context of psychoanalytic theory. Raising these images to the level of consciousness and inquiry therefore seems to me an important aspect of understanding this particular set of cases. It is also a way of stepping beyond the confines of current doctrine and beginning to think about other ways of handling the reciprocal claims cohabitants may make of one another.

◆

INTO THE BADLANDS

Robin Becker

When Helen Levine came to live with my daughter, I wasn't exactly pleased; in fact, I was against it. They met at the university in Minneapolis where a lot of these odd combinations come about, and they've been here since which is almost two years. Carol got a job teaching math at the Indian school near Turtle Mountain, so they came out here after graduation. I've worked with Indian women from the reservation most of my life at the factory.

Helen grew up in Minneapolis. I don't think South Dakota was what she had in mind; tourist photos of the Badlands, dust storms, endless blank highways. As far as I know, she's the only Jew around except for Ephriam Epstein from Russia who was the first president of the university.

I work for the Bulova Watch Company. During my breaks, I sit with the Chippewa women whose husbands work in the Morell meat-packing plant in Sioux Falls. They see each other on weekends, since the men commute clear across the state. On Monday mornings they gather downtown and climb into pick-ups for the drive. My husband died when Carol was fourteen. He was a quiet man, but when he talked, he had something to say.

From Robin Becker, "Into the Badlands," in *The Things That Divide Us: Stories by Women* (Seattle:Seal Press, 1985), pp. 15–26.

They drove down from Brookings on 81 and headed west on 90.

"Mom, this is Carol," she said on the phone. "We blew a tire, but we'll be home tomorrow."

Every sentence had a "we" in it somewhere. We'll be home by such-and-such, or we're looking forward to going house-hunting with you. I'd raised one daughter and I didn't like the idea of getting another. Still, I was luckier than most, whose kids light out for Sioux Falls or Rapid City and never come back except for two days at Christmas.

First thing, Helen wanted to see the Badlands.

"Mrs. Stokes," she said softly, "would you like to come? We'd be happy to have you." She was standing in my kitchen, her dark hair pulled back in a red bandanna. She was trying to be kind, but I wouldn't be a party to it.

"No, you girls go. I've been to the National Park more times than I care to remember. I know that place as well as I know anything." I've walked in the gummy Badlands, ruined shoes, stared at fossils while someone read from a guide-book. All alligator bones and sixty-million-year-old imprints. I watched ferrets whipping past, and now they say they're almost gone.

"Extinct Is Forever," read her bumper sticker and "Save the Ferret." She was trying to save the world; I just wished she'd forget about my daughter. The post-card she sent me said, "It's so stark — the buttes and knolls. I've never seen such brick-red soil. The mesas have an eerie glow at dusk" She sounded like a brochure from the Chamber of Commerce.

By the middle of August, they'd rented a place that looked like a pioneer shack. That must have been Helen's idea of country life, because Carol knows better. They rented it for the barn, they said.

"If we're gonna live out here, Mom, we might as well have horses," Carol said one Friday evening. She'd started picking me up after work on Fridays. Sometimes I fed her dinner.

"Look," I said, taking some chops from the oven, "if you want to live like cowboys on a cattle ranch, that's your business."

She put her arm around my shoulder. "Oh, Mother, I know it's hard for you." She looked me in the eye. "With Helen and everything, but you could try to get along with her and..."

"Aren't I trying? Do I laugh when she asks me what I know about Calamity Jane?" Carol turned her palms up to the sky.

"It's her way of trying to make conversation," she muttered. "You know what I mean."

"Listen, honey, your friend Helen won't be happy until I re-enact the Battle of Little Bighorn here in the kitchen."

"That's not fair," Carol shouted.

"I'll tell you what's fair." I squeezed the kitchen table with both hands. "She wants to see me dressed in a buckskin suit with a prairie rose between my teeth." I strode across the linoleum floor. "Every day it's 'Mrs. Stokes, what do you remember about the thirties?' or 'Mrs. Stokes, were you ever in a duststorm?' or 'Mrs. Stokes, what do you think about the Path-finder Power Plant?'"

Carol was slumped in a chair. She looked long and lean and athletic.

"What is she, an F.B.I. agent? A sociologist?" I was disgusted. "One question after another. It's not polite."

They got settled in their broken-down farmhouse, and two weeks later, they started looking at horses. They picked me up one Saturday morning in September, and we headed north to Sturgis where I knew an Indian family with horses to sell.

"I'm so glad you could come with us, Mrs. Stokes," Helen said. Carol drove their banged-up blue Toyota, and Helen sat in the back. She kept leaning forward in the space between the bucket seats, making me nervous.

We left the plains for the Black Hills. Occasionally, we saw a gas station or a gift shop. I always found the mountains a relief after that unbroken expanse.

"I'll tell you what kind of horse I'm looking for," Helen began. I turned to look at her, and our noses almost collided. "Well, first," I said, "I'd better tell you what's available." Carol glanced at me. I knew she was thinking I should take a nicer tone with Helen, but I couldn't. "Appaloosas, pintos, palominos. Don't expect any Eastern horses."

"What kind of horses did you ride, Mrs. Stokes?"

"Anything we could get." Carol glared. "I lived on a farm, you know."

"That must have been something," said Helen emphatically.

"That was something a person was happy to leave! Those winters... ah, well, what's the use..." I paused. "Someday Carol, tell Helen some stories."

"Why don't you tell us one now?" Carol asked.

"No," I said.

"Ma, please. Go on."

"For weeks on end, blizzards had us housebound. My father would go out to feed the livestock, but that was all. The farms were far apart, so we hardly saw our friends during the long winters. School was often shut down. When I go visit the Waters on their farm, I wonder how I stood it for so long. We used to cover the windows with burlap bags, on top of every other type of insulation people used back then." I had forgotten about Helen for a second, just remembering and seeing

again that farmhouse, those fields, the animals. Coming back gave me a start.

"Carol and Helen?"

"Yes, Mom?

"Mrs. Stokes?"

"The Pino family are friends of mine; I've known them for years." I wasn't sure how to continue. "I just want you to know that I care what they think of me."

Juana was in the yard when we arrived at their place.

"Hello, Emma!" she called and rushed toward the car. She looked fine — round and tan and healthy.

Juana reached for Carol to give her a hug. "It's been a long time." She wore a flowered-print skirt and a black cotton shirt which pulled at the buttons. I saw the muscles in her arms.

"This is my friend Helen, from Minneapolis," Carol said.

Helen put out her hand and Juana took it in both of hers.

"I'm happy to meet a friend of Carol's," she said.

"Here comes Decklin," I said.

"Well, look who's here," Decklin said softly, putting his hands on my shoulders. I had always loved this boy, my friend's middle son and the sweetest of the three. Now, at twenty-three, he was tall, handsome, strong. His skin was the color of the leaves of the cottonwood tree. This was a joke with us, for as a boy, Decklin was always climbing them.

"Where's Decklin?" someone would ask.

"In a tree," someone else would answer, and we would all laugh. That was when we lived near Edgemont, when Carol's father was mining.

"I hear you want to buy a horse," Decklin said to Carol.

"Well, it's really for Helen. We figured we'd try one and see how it worked out. Then, maybe, we'd try for a second."

"That's how Decklin started," Juana said, "and look what we have now."

Helen asked, "How many horses do you have, Decklin?"

He smiled and said, "Oh, eighteen."

Juana had made a barbecue lunch; we all sat around a table in the yard. Helen wasn't her usual self, which meant she wasn't asking a million questions. I watched Decklin and Carol. Once, a few years back, I'd hoped they might get together. They went out a couple of times, but nothing came of it. Now, they acted like old friends, like children who had grown up together and, as adults, took one another for granted.

"Remember the Crawfords who lived in Custer?" Juana asked reaching for a family-size bottle of cola. "Well, they moved to Sundance." Juana shook her head. "They'll never find a prettier spot than the one they had here."

"Things change," Decklin said wistfully, looking off to the hills. "They'll be back to visit."

"Once it gets cold, no one's visiting anybody," Juana said. She turned to me. "Emma's one of my closest friends, and how often do we see each other? The cold keeps everyone at home."

"We were just talking about the winter storms Mother remembers. She was telling us about her father's farm."

Right then, something in me wanted to be mean to Helen. I wanted to shock her or shake her or make her see that she was not one of us; she was an outsider, and she would always be.

"Once our dog and her litter of puppies froze in a storm," I said. "They were all dead by the time I found them." I watched Helen's face. Her lips puckered, and when our eyes met, she looked down.

"Iced coffee?" Juana asked.

"There are always accidents on a farm," Decklin said. "Especially in this climate."

I was wondering what Helen was thinking.

"Drink your iced coffee, now," Juana said. "We have to go see the horse Decklin chose for you all."

I was feeling low, like I'd ruined everybody's lunch, especially my own. But I was grateful to see that Juana and Decklin carried on as if nothing had happened. Only Helen was subdued.

Decklin's stables were small and cramped. I'd seen poor farms; I knew the hardship, the sacrifices you had to make to keep a stable of horses, keep them fed, sell them, buy them, breed them.

Decklin unlatched a stall door and put out his hand.

"Hello, Kadoka," he said to the horse. Holding on to his halter, Decklin led him down the corridor toward the door.

Out in the yard, I could see that Kadoka was a beauty. He was big for an Appaloosa, but fine-boned with a handsome head. I was surprised to see that Decklin brought an English saddle from the tack room. Juana and I had always ridden western.

"English saddle for the lady," Decklin said winking at Carol. I wondered for a moment if he knew that they were more than friends.

We all walked over to the ring, a dusty fenced-in area where horses had worn a path in the dirt. Helen took the reins from Decklin. He gave her a leg-up, and, before she had settled into the saddle, Kadoka walked to the gate. I was feeling kind of excited in a nervous sort of way.

"Looks like he knows where he's going," Carol said trying to ease things.

Decklin paused at the gate. Helen bent to adjust the stirrups. For a moment, I felt a thrill, like someone watching a disaster, and I realized that I was hoping Helen would show her true self — make a mistake, make a mess — for everyone to see.

She sat straight in the saddle, hands low, legs motionless. When she trotted close to where I was standing, I could hear her making strange clucking noises; she was talking to the horse.

"He can go English or western," Decklin said leaning on the fence. "Look how smooth he is."

I was ashamed at my desire. I stood there waiting, hoping to see Helen do something foolish or inept.

She began to trot, posting up and down in the saddle. Her knees didn't flap and her body didn't wriggle. She rode like she knew what she was doing.

"He looks like a nice horse to me," Carol said. "What do you think, Mom?"

"Can't tell yet, but he looks all right," I said.

Juana was silent. She stayed out of Decklin's affairs.

I saw Helen lean forward and gather up the reins. The horse, collected, broke into a lope. He had been well trained, I could see.

They went around several time, and then Helen switched directions.

"She's a good rider," Decklin said to Carol. "She has a nice touch."

I could see that Decklin was taken in by Helen, too. Neither Juana nor her son could see that she was unnatural, that she was having a bad influence on Carol.

Helen pulled up in front of us. Sweat trickled down the side of her face.

"I like him," she said to Carol. "Would you ride him and see what you think?"

"Sure."

Helen got off and patted the horse's neck as Carol raised the stirrups. Then, Helen came and stood beside me along the fence. Didn't she know that we were enemies? How could she be so casual?

Carol was a sloppy rider — more confident, more slouchy. She'd ridden English in Minneapolis, but had grown up in western saddles and was used to neck-reining.

"Look!" she called.

She was holding the reins in one hand imitating a cowboy.

Decklin and Juana laughed as she galloped by. Why was I sad? Why did I feel so distant, so separate from my friends and my daughter? Somehow, their pleasure seemed far away, remote as my memories of Carol riding our old buckskin named Buffalo.

Not long after they bought Kadoka, Carol and I started fighting over Helen.

"Take it up with her!" Carol would yell.

"I don't need to take it up with her, because she's not my child, and her life is not my concern," I would reply.

"Then don't come to me with your complaints."

"It was you who brought her here."

Carol's eyes narrowed. "Don't say things like that, Ma." She walked toward me shaking her head. "You don't want to go saying things like that."

"I know what I mean to say, dammit." I'd go off to another room and feel bad for hurting Carol, but I was the one with the honest hurt.

There were times when I wanted to talk about Carol and Helen with my friends, but I just couldn't bring myself to say the truth. I'd tell myself that no one else could say things I hadn't already thought of. That things were going to be hard for them. But things weren't hard for them. Carol liked her job teaching math. They liked their falling-down farmhouse and their horse and the new friends they made in Rapid City. They weren't lonely for friendship. I kept wondering when Helen was going to get a job. By September, when Carol started teaching, she hadn't found anything. She kept coming up with projects to work on, all for no pay. First, she volunteered at the community center, answering phones, helping with the after-school program. Then she decided to teach a course, Women in Literature, but only four people showed up, including Carol. Next, she decided to write for the local paper; an article called "Rereading Hamlin Garland" and a piece on the girl's track team came out of that.

In November, when Carol couldn't pick me up after work one Friday, Helen came instead. It was desolate and cold. I remember seeing a book called *The Woman Warrior* on the dash.

"Where's Carol?" I said as soon as I got into the car. "Is she all right?"

"She's fine, Mrs. Stokes. She was tired, so I offered to pick you up."

It was snowing by the time we go to my house. "Tell Carol I said she should get some rest this weekend," I said gathering up my things.

"I just want you to know something, Mrs. Stokes. I love Carol very much." She sounded as though she might cry. I heard my voice come out cold and steady.

"I haven't got anything against you personally, Helen. I just wanted something else for my daughter." It was a lie of course, I didn't like Helen and she knew it. She was just trying to anger me with her little confidences.

I stepped out of the car. For a second, I thought we were both thinking the same thing: Carol chose this life; no one forced it upon her. She chose Helen of her own free will.

The following Friday, Helen came again.

"I think it's the flu or something." Helen said. I slammed the door.

"Have you called a doctor?"

"She wouldn't let me."

"Oh, for God's sake."

"I tried, but she said I was an alarmist."

"That girl."

"Mrs. Stokes, where would you like to go?" It was snowing and the wind was blowing. I couldn't tell if Helen was worried about Carol or the weather.

"I'd appreciate it if you could take me home," I said. I huddled in my coat.

"You're welcome to come home with me. I'm sure Carol wouldn't mind." Cars moved slowly down the street. I knew Helen had to get going if she wanted to make it home before the roads froze.

"Looks like we're in for a big one," I said. "I'd better go home."

Helen bit her lip. "Do you mind," she asked, "if we stop at the market on the way?" She turned the key in the ignition. "I think I'd better stock up on a few things, especially if Carol's sick."

"Go ahead. I'll pick up some things, too."

The market was crowded with people. Their boots made the floor slick; twice I had to reach for the cart to keep from falling. Helen knew her mind and steered up the aisles, checking items off her list. I carried a basket which quickly filled.

"Just put your things in with ours, Mrs. Stokes, and we'll figure out the money later."

It was almost six by the time we got out of the market.

"Why don't you just come home with me? We can set you up in the spare room," Helen said zipping up her parka.

Snow fell in thick, wet flakes.

"Think I'll take you up on your offer," I said before I had a chance to stop myself.

"Fine!" said Helen, a big smile spreading across her face. "I'll take you back first thing tomorrow morning."

Carol was in bed when we got there. When we took her temperature, we found that she had a fever of 102 degrees.

"What's all the fuss?" she asked. "Can't a person get sick without everyone making a federal case about it?"

There was a pot of chicken stock on the stove. Helen made some toast and took it along with a bowl of soup into the sick room.

"Sit up, honey," I heard her say softly. I stood in the hall.

"Want some hot tea?" I asked poking my head into the room.

"No thanks, Mom. Maybe later."

The house had a nice feeling to it. Helen and Carol had fixed it up with paintings and things from their friends in Minneapolis. There was a wood stove in the center of the big room which made that part of the house cozy. They had throw rugs and rocking chairs and lots of books and magazines. Everything was used, but there was a warmth.

About eight o'clock, Helen came out to where I was sitting with our dinner. We had soup and chicken and green beans and salad sitting right there by the stove. In her room, Carol dozed.

"There are some young girls like you," I began, "in my factory, who have been trying to start a union." Helen looked up. "Everyone was afraid of them at first, but now — there are two of them — the rest of the women have started to like them."

"Are they from around here?"

"Nope. Chicago."

"What are they doing out here?"

"Organizing," I said. Helen raised her eyebrows.

"And what do you think of them, Mrs. Stokes?"

"I'm not sure," I said.

That night I slept in the spare room. When I woke, I found snow falling and drifts three feet high against the house.

"Good morning," Helen called. A door slammed. "Wow! What a storm." I shivered in my borrowed robe and slippers.

She stood with a red face, her felt-lined boots covered with snow. She dropped her mittens and blew on her hands.

"How's Carol?" I asked.

"The same," Helen said pulling off her boots.

I walked down the hall and knocked on her door.

"Come in," Carol called.

She looked pale against the white sheets. When I felt her forehead, I thought I could detect a fever.

"How do you feel?"

"OK," she said. "I'm achey."

"How about a ginger ale?"

All day, Helen and I took turns checking on Carol. We kept the stoves going, kept a steady pot of soup cooking, exchanged a few sentences when our paths crossed. I picked up a copy of *Main-Traveled Roads* and read a few stories. Helen fed Kadoka and let him out in their tiny ring for a few minutes. Straining to see him from the window, I could hardly make out his shape in the driving snow. It was dark by three-thirty.

"Can I get you some tea?" I asked when she came in.

She lowered her eyes. "Sure. That would be nice."

I brought two cups of tea and two biscuits which I'd found in the breadbox.

"It was like this when I was a child," I said. "Weeks and weeks like this."

"We could get out if we *had* to," Helen said sipping her tea. "If we had to get Carol to a doctor or something, we could drive to town."

"Snowbound," I said, unable to give any shape to my feelings. I wanted to tell her something, but what? Something to show her I thought she was a real trooper, but I said nothing.

That night we watched a movie called *Missing* on the television. Helen said she'd seen it before, but that it was good and I'd like it. The movie was about an American boy who goes to South America and disappears. His father gets involved in the search to discover what has happened to him.

"I guess the movie means something special if you're a parent," Helen said softly. "It's hard to imagine being in the father's position."

"Not so hard," I said. "It was a good movie, Helen. I'm glad you recommended it." How could I tell her that children disappear in many ways?

"Does your mother work?" I asked.

"Yes. At a museum in Minneapolis."

I was carrying our teacups into the kitchen. "Does she know about you and Carol?" We both stopped, surprised at my question.

"She does know, Mrs. Stokes, and she's trying to accept it." Helen smiled a sad smile. "She has her problems with me."

We turned off the lights in the kitchen. "Let's check on Carol," I said feeling a sudden tenderness for Helen and her mother.

Carol was asleep. We left the door slightly ajar and said goodnight.

By the following morning, the snow had stopped.

"I'm feeling better," Carol announced during breakfast in bed. "I think I'll go shovel snow and take a ride on Kadoka."

Helen and I looked at each other and laughed.

"What have you two been talking about while I've been dead to the world?"

"Oh," I said, "Things."

I helped Helen shovel a path to the car, while Carol got out of bed for the first time in three days. We left her sitting by the stove drinking hot chocolate and reading.

I kissed her on the forehead like I used to do when she was a child.

Although the roads had been plowed, some power lines were down. We passed cars completely buried in drifts, shops with "closed" signs in the windows.

I felt a stab of melancholy when we parted. Something had changed in the last two days. There was nothing to say or, more truthfully, I am a person who does not say such things.

"We'll call you soon," Helen said, and "I'm glad you were with us."

For Christmas, I bought Kadoka a winter blanket and I got the girls a green glass antique lamp. Helen still troubles me at times, but she is someone real to me — though I have no words for what she means.

THREE

Violence and Neglect

There may be no greater betrayal of human trust than violence committed within the family. And yet mounting reports reveal alarming rates of parents striking, beating, or burning their children. Adults assault their lovers or their spouses; usually it is men who batter women, but sometimes women batter men, and sometimes assaults occur within same-sex relationships. Sometimes, adult children abuse or neglect their elderly parents. Sexual abuses of children and rape within marriage or intimate adult relationships can damage people long after physical wounds heal. What should the law — the police, the courts, the legislatures — do in the face of growing public recognition of these dangers usually committed behind closed doors? In many ways, the Temperance Movement of the last century that ultimately yielded Prohibition expressed outrage at the violence and neglect committed when people, especially men, drink alcohol. Ultimately repealed by Constitutional amendment, even during its heyday Prohibition stood as one of the most poorly enforced legal initiatives in American history.

Campaigns to protect children from abuse produced child welfare agencies and juvenile courts over the past century; law reform efforts have more recently initiated civil actions for domestic violence that allow the victims to evict the abuser; mandatory arrest laws in some jurisdictions also trigger criminal action. Each of these initiatives treat failures of action by government officials as violations of individual rights to be protected against family violence. The state, then, will either help or stand complicit. Failures to act become culpable neglect.

Yet there are risks that state involvement itself may produce injuries. If done crudely, state efforts to protect children from their parents can disrupt or destroy their relationships. Foster care may expose children to new dangers of abuse while depriving them of the basic connection with anyone committed to them over the long term. Experts employed by the state may simply substitute their biases for those of parents about how to rear children. Some suggest that the socialworker, employed by a state child protection agency, faces an inevitable and insuperable conflict between offering genuine assistance to the family and serving as an investigator obliged to report violations and empowered to trigger the removal of the child from the parents' home. Should these two roles be separated? Does their combination imply that the legal system is not serious about providing help but instead uses that avowed purpose to accomplish techniques of social control?

Even if socialworkers were entirely devoted to helping families or victims of family violence or neglect, they may be constrained by an emphasis on the psychological problems of the abusive or neglectful individuals. This emphasis could deflect attention from the social and economic structures and pressures on the entire family, or replicate patterns of racism, sexism, and class prejudices already embedded in society. Public portrayals and regulation of private abuse may subvert more profound social criticism or produce solutions as problematic as the underlying abuses. Law enforcement may even accelerate or exacerbate violence; a batterer may escalate after an initial encounter with the law. Judges may fail to perceive the dangers and resist full compliance or enthusiastic enforcement. The violence, then, may be public as well as private; neglect may be private as well as public. What, then, should be done? Should there be changes in legal rules or the legal institutions and the roles they create?

Violence in Families, Neglect by the State

Workers in shelters and family lawyers report that many women do not identify themselves as "battered women," even though they report incidents that would place them in that category. Finding language to describe the experience may be difficult when the experience leaves one speechless, when the available words carry stigma, or when the ways of talking allow observers to feel remote from other people's problems. Neither vivid, unique stories nor dry, statistical generalities disturb this public sense of distance from family violence for long. Instead, these forms of expression may contribute to cycles of brief attention followed by extended passivity. Perhaps a combination of statistical explorations, personal narratives, exploration of sensational cases, and analysis of legal responses can prompt richer understandings of violence within families and neglect by the state.

♦

INTIMATE VIOLENCE
Richard J. Gelles and Murray A. Strauss

PEOPLE HIT FAMILY MEMBERS BECAUSE THEY CAN

One of the first abusers we met was a middle-aged man who had been beating his wife on and off for most of their twenty-year marriage. Normally he was a mild-mannered person whose outward demeanor was a far cry from that of the stereotypical wife beater. Chet was not brawny, not macho, not visibly short-tem-pered. Yet, he freely admitted that he often lost his temper with his wife and that he beat her when this happened. Chet said that he became especially enraged when his wife, Margorie, did a poor job keeping the house neat. Margorie, also mild-mannered and conservatively middle class, had sought help because she wanted Chet to stop beating her. Yet, as Chet calmly explained the times when he lost his temper and hit Margorie, she nodded sadly and

From Richard J. Gelles and Murray A. Strauss, *Intimate Violence* (Newbury Park:Sage Publications, 1988), pp. 20–25.

agreed that Chet had indeed been angry and this led directly to the beatings. "What can I do," she asked, "to keep him from getting angry and hitting me?"

We met David and Marie in the emergency room of a children's hospital. Their three-year-old son, Peter, was on his way to be X-rayed for a possible skull fracture. Peter, it seems, had accidently knocked over David's new television set and the picture tube had shattered. David had saved for the set for more than a year, and had explained to little Peter that he should not touch the new TV. Peter, a typically curious toddler, had touched the screen and played with the dials. Each time, he had been slapped or spanked by David. Amid the shattered glass of the picture tube, David simply "lost it" and had slapped Peter harder than ever. Peter fell onto the coffee table, striking his head. The X-ray would tell how much damage had been done. When we met David and Marie, the chief of the hospital child abuse team was explaining the state child abuse law and why she had to file a report to the state department of social services. David nodded that he understood. He was clearly distraught about the incident and repeated over and over that he wished he had not got so angry with little Peter.

The common thread that appears to run through both homes is that anger with a wife or a child led to loss of control and violence. This is not, however, an adequate explanation. Let us change the scenarios and see why.

Imagine that Chet is the manager of a medium-size office. The office employs a janitor who comes in the evenings to empty ashtrays, dust, vacuum, and clean the office. David runs an automobile agency. In the waiting room of the agency is a new television. One day, Chet comes to work and finds that although the janitor has been in, there is barely a sign that anything has been cleaned. That same day, a three-year-old overturns

David's television. What is the outcome? Does Chet, finding his office a mess, pounce on his janitor and begin to pummel him? Unlikely. Does David slap, spank, or even beat the wayward three-year-old? Absurd. How is it that the very same situations at home can produce anger strong enough to lead to abusive violence? Why can Chet and David control their anger outside of the home, yet lose it with family members?

The answer is rather obvious. Let's suppose Chet grabs his janitor and begins to punch him. What could happen? Well, the janitor could hit back and beat up Chet. The janitor might not be able to do so, but he most surely would report the outburst to Chet's boss and perhaps call the police. Chet would stand a fairly good chance of being punished or even fired by his boss. The police would most certainly arrive on the scene quickly and probably arrest Chest for assault and battery. David would have major trouble on his hands. The three-year-old's parents would take a dim view of seeing their son hit by an auto salesperson. David could safely assume that the boy's parents would buy a car somewhere else, which would be the least of his problems. The little boy's father might attack David. Or, he could call the police. The police would soon arrive, and David, like Chet, would be subjected to arrest for assault and battery.

The unconscious knowledge that all these potential costs and punishments would await them if they struck strangers or fellow workers would constrain Chet's and David's anger. Anger that led to violence would surely result in significant costs for the violent perpetrators. The rewards would be slim. The best Chet could hope for would be that his janitor would clean better or quit. David would have little to gain by striking a three-year-old.

The anger and violence these two men exhibited in the home led to few costs. Margorie called the police the first couple of times Chet hit her. The police were slow to come to the house. When they did finally arrive they counseled Margorie to "kiss and make up" with Chet. Once they took Chet out and had him walk around the block a few times to "cool off." Margorie thought about divorcing Chet, but she said that she loved him and besides, "the black and blues go away, and he hasn't hit me in a couple of months." David and Marie spent an anxious hour in the emergency room waiting for Peter's X-rays to be taken and read. Peter had a bad cut, and a bruise, but no fractures. The child abuse report was filed. A few days later, David and Marie were visited by a socialworker who talked with them, looked over the house, and left. The socialworker's report described David and Marie as a nice professional couple, who lived in a neat and attractive home. Both worked, neither had a drinking problem, and the incident appeared to be an aberration. Given that the department of social services had more than thirty cases of maltreatment per socialworker, it did not appear that anything had to be done with David and Marie. They seemed to care genuinely for Peter. The case was closed with no recommendation for services or follow-up.

The proposition that people hit family members because they can is based on the principles of social exchange theory, which assumes that human interaction is guided by the pursuit of rewards and the avoidance of punishments and costs. When an individual provides services to another, he obliges the other to fulfill the obligation to reward him. When a reciprocal exchange of services and rewards occurs, the interaction will continue. If there is no reciprocity, the interaction will be broken off, since the costs of the exchange for the first person exceed the rewards. All take and no give is not a formula for happy

or continued social interaction, unless one of the participants is a masochist.

Family behavior adds an important dimension to the normal assumptions of social exchange theory. Simply stated, it is not so easy to break off interaction with a family member, regardless of whether there is a reciprocal exchange of rewards or services. One can separate from or divorce a spouse, but almost always decisions about property, living space, and perhaps children are required. One can, with effort and typically with legal counsel, achieve the status of ex-wife or ex-husband. To become an ex-parent is typically impossible. Give-and-take with children is another dimension of exchange theory. Unable to break off inequitable social relations easily, individuals can become frustrated, angry, and resentful. Conflict is a common result. The principles of exchange theory suggest that people would only use violence toward family members when there are rewards for violent behavior and when the cost of violence do not outweigh the rewards. When we discussed the cases of Chet and David, we mentioned that there are relatively standard costs for being violent in our society, which are rarely paid by those violent in the home.

What about the police and the criminal justice system? Violence in the home, after all, is assault, and all fifty states have laws prohibiting child abuse. The simple fact is that the police tend to respond slower to a domestic disturbance call than to a public disturbance. There are a variety of reasons for the less than timely responses. First, and perhaps foremost, dealing with domestic disturbances can be dangerous work. The National Institute of Justice reports that between 1972 and 1984 there were sixty-nine officers killed in domestic disturbances — thus accounting for six percent of all officers killed in the line of duty. This number is less than the 210 officers who died answering robbery calls, and less than the figure of twenty-three percent that has been quoted by numerous students of domestic violence. Yet, even this number is high when one considers the assumption that the streets pose much greater danger than homes. A second explanation for the reluctance of police officers to answer domestic disturbance calls is that this kind of police work is generally considered low prestige. Few police officers are rewarded or promoted for being especially effective in dealing with domestic assault. Arresting a battering husband or parent is considered less prestigious and less indicative of good police work than arresting a robber or drug dealer. The culture of the modern American police department simply does not place high esteem on one's ability to handle domestic calls.

What happens when the police do arrive? As we saw with Chet arrest is not a common response in instances of wife abuse. Unless a victim of parental violence has been brutally tortured or slain, violence toward children almost always is treated as a child welfare and not a criminal justice matter. At present in the United States, the chances that a person will be arrested for hitting his partner or children are relatively slim. Our most recent national survey of family violence found that fewer than one in ten police interventions ended in the arrest of the offender. Thus, the cost of arrest, which is very real for public violence, is nearly nonexistent in cases of intimate violence and abuse.

In the rare case when a violent family member is arrested, what are the chances that there will be further costs paid? Again, the answer is slim. The criminal justice system is loath to break up families. Wives who press charges against their husbands are frequently advised to drop the charges. "After all," the prosecutor or judge may argue, "if he goes to jail, he will lose his job and you will have to go on welfare." The same line of reasoning is presented when a man batters his children. If the offender is a mother, the courts are even more reluctant to send women to jail, for fear of further harming the children. A second argument against jailing offenders is that the courts may fear that this will only further provoke or anger the violent individual. Battered wives are often told to go home and "kiss and make up." "You don't want to really make him mad, do you?" they are warned. Only the poorest offenders, those with inadequate legal counsel, or those who have committed the most outrageous crimes against partners and children are sentenced to jail.

The criminal justice system holds very little threat of cost for the average violent family member. Worse still, the very lack of real costs may actually encourage further violence. We spoke with a thirty-five-year-old woman who felt it was a drastic mistake to call the police. She had been the victim of gradually increasing violence over the first five years of her marriage. Finally, unable to bear more hitting, she called the police. She recounted the results:

> He threatened to beat me again, and I told him that if he tried I would call the cops. I forget what actually happened that night — I think the pizza was cold or something like that. Anyway, he threw a fork at me and started to chase me. I told him that I would call the cops if he didn't stop. Well, he didn't, so I called. The cops came pretty quick. Turns out that they knew Dan [her husband]. He had gotten into a couple of fights at Spencer's [a local bar]. They took him aside and told him he should try to calm down. The told him he had

better go for a walk, and they took him outside. One police officer told me that if I had trouble again to call. Well, Dan was back in about forty-five minutes. He had calmed down, but he had a kind of a mean look on his face. When he came in he said, "Well, you played your ace — see what happened — nothing! Now you know who's out there to help you." Christ, calling the cops made it worse. Now he figured he could really beat the shit out of me and no one would do a thing.

Other battered women have sought restraining orders and all too frequently found that such orders offered little resistance to a violent man.

There are other possible costs. Using violence could lead to a loss of status, or to economic costs. Both Chet and David could lose their jobs for hitting a fellow worker or client. But, with few exceptions, there are practically no instances where a violent family member was fired because it became known he beat his wife or children.

SOCIAL ATTITUDES, PRIVACY, INEQUALITY, AND VIOLENCE

We can expand our first proposition that people hit family members because they can into three basic propositions:

1. Family members are more likely to use violence in the home when they expect the costs of being violent to be less than the rewards.

2. The absence of effective social controls (e.g., police intervention) over family relations decreases the costs of one family member being violent toward another.

3. Certain social and family structures reduce social controls in family relations and, therefore, reduce the costs and increase the rewards of being violent.

The social and family structures that are most important in reducing the costs of intimate violence and, to some degree, increasing the rewards are: (1) the social attitudes concerning violence and, more specifically, family violence; (2) the private nature of the modern household; and (3) the structural inequality that exists in the modern family.

Social Attitudes: The Marriage License As a Hitting License

Violence, the commentators tell us, is as American as apple pie. Violence is considered a socially appropriate means of solving interpersonal problems. Duels and fistfights have long been considered the manly way of resolving differences between gentlemen. Such a duel ended the life of the first treasurer of the United States, Alexander Hamilton (killed by the former vice president of the United States, Aaron Burr, in 1904). When fifty-two Americans were taken hostage in Iran in November 1979, one of the public reactions was that the United States should "bomb Iran back into the Stone Age" in order to obtain the release of the hostages. Force was also considered as a means of obtaining the release of Americans held hostage by Lebanese terrorists in a hijacked TWA airliner in the summer of 1985. More than 65 percent of Americans polled support the use of the death penalty as a legitimate means of punishing capital crimes. There are countless other signs of public support for violence. The legitimization of violence can be seen on Saturday morning cartoon shows, as when the wily coyote is regularly pummeled and crushed by the road runner. Culture heroes John Wayne, Clint Eastwood, and Charles Bronson all share the ability to be quick with their fists to right a wrong or defend the helpless.

Early in our research, we concluded that the level of violence in historical and contemporary families was sufficiently great to justify our calling the marriage license a hitting license. Numerous surveys have discovered that a large number of people believe that under certain circumstances, it is perfectly appropriate for a husband to hit his wife. Approval of using violence to raise and train children is practically universal.

The U.S. Commission on Causes and Prevention of Violence conducted a national survey on violence in the United States during the late 1960s. The survey focused not just on public violence, but on attitudes toward private violence. Among the findings of the commission were that:

- One quarter of adult men and one in six adult women said they could think of circumstances in which it would be all right for a husband to hit his wife or the wife to hit her husband.
- Eight-six percent of those polled said that young people needed "strong" discipline.
- Seven out of ten thought it was important for a boy to have a few fistfights while he was growing up.

Fifteen years after the U.S. Commission on the Causes and Prevention of Violence conducted their survey, we conducted our fist national survey of violence in the home. We asked our national sample of more than two thousand subjects two questions that focused on their attitudes about violence between intimates. About one in four wives and about a third of the husbands we talked to thought that a couple slapping one another was at least somewhat necessary, normal, and good. More than 70 percent of those surveyed thought that slapping a twelve-year-old child was either necessary, normal, or good.

Parent-to-child violence is so common and so widely approved that one needs few case studies to make the point. In general, the large majority of Americans believes that good parenting requires some physical punishment. Over and over again, when we interview parents about hitting their children, we are told that kids "deserve to be hit" or "need to be hit." Among the thousands of people we have interviewed, it was *absence* of physical punishment that was thought to be deviant, not the hitting of children.

Even if violence is considered inappropriate by an individual, a group, or even by the society, the fact that violence is between family members means that most people will not want to intervene. One of our first research projects involved interviewing violent couples and their neighbors. Quite by chance we learned that the neighbors knew about the violence occurring next door. While neighbors might call the police, they almost never tried to get involved personally. Some feared for their own safety, but most simply said, "That's a family matter." Police officers, prosecutors, and judges have been known to say the same thing when confronted with domestic violence. When it comes to violence toward children, very few people try to intervene when a parent spanks or slaps a child in a supermarket or department store. While again, people might be hesitant because of fear for their own safety, by and large, even if one detests seeing a child hit, one tends to view it as the parent's own business.

Television also plays a role in perpetuating the support of private violence. Millions laughed (and still laugh) when Jackie Gleason rants, "Alice, you're going to the moon!" or, "One of these days, pow, right in the kisser!" while shaking his fist at his television wife on the popular program, "The Honeymooners."

For those who think that it is just television that portrays and supports family violence, a quick examination of fairy tales, folklore, and nursery rhymes will graphically illustrate that a variety of media has for many years supported intimate violence, abuse, and neglect. Mother Goose's "Old Woman Who Lived in a Shoe" beat her children soundly when she sent them to bed. "Humpty Dumpty" is a thinly disguised metaphor of the fragility of children, and "Rock-a-Bye, Baby" is not even thinly disguised, with the baby and cradle falling from the tree. Wicked stepmothers abound in children's fairy tales. Snow White's stepmother had Snow White taken out into the woods to be beheaded by the huntsman. Hansel and Gretel's parents left them to starve in the woods because money was scarce.

A final means of making the marriage license a hitting license is to deny that the behavior is violent. Parents who hit children are not considered violent; they are thought to be properly disciplining their children. We have countless euphemisms such as "family matter" or "domestic disturbance" to serve as smokescreens for behaviors that would be considered assaults if committed by strangers. Denial also occurs when we create stereotyped images of what so-called "real violence" is. Stereotypical violence tortures, maims, or kills. For wife abuse, this has been labeled "burning bed" violence after the case of Francine Hughes, the Michigan housewife who endured years of violence before finally killing her husband by set-

ting his bed on fire. In the case of child abuse, the stereotypical abuse is the 220-pound father punching his defenseless five-month-old son. There is little public support for these acts. Defining them as acts of "real violence" hides the more common forms of intimate violence, such as slaps, pushes, shoves, and occasional punches, behind doors.

Privacy

A number of years ago we attended a conference where the family and social change were being discussed. One of the aspects of social change that was on the program was our own presentation on child abuse and family violence. There was a general discussion of whether violence in the home was a new phenomenon or if we had simply not attended to a problem that had long existed in the family. The anthropologists in attendance were asked about their own observations of other cultures and societies. Beatrice Whiting, the eminent cultural anthropologist, observed that among the societies she had studied, violence between family members did not occur when families lived in communal residence. She concluded that, "when the walls [of separate houses] went up, the hitting started."

The social historian Barbara Laslett has studied the evolution of the modern family. A major distinction between the family in the twentieth century and earlier families is the private nature of the modern family and the public nature of the historical household. These differences can be observed in terms of family size, residents in the home, and the use of household space.

One major historical change is that today's mother gives birth to fewer children than mothers two hundred years ago. Laslett notes that privacy of the home is increased when there are fewer children to serve as members of the family audience. A second change is the reduction in the number of non-kin group residents in the home. In the distant past, as well as the nineteenth century, the household contained numerous categories of non-kin residents. Obviously, the presence of a boarder, servant, or apprentice greatly reduced the amount of privacy that existed in the home. The growth of a smokestack economy and the factory system eliminated the apprentice from the home. So, too, the development of a service society reduced the need (and the cost-effectiveness) of live-in servants. Urbanization and the explosive growth of apartment-type housing removed boarders and lodgers from the modern family. As the adult audience dwindled, privacy increased.

Architecture and space usage further changed as the family evolved. The medieval household was but one room. When dinner was over, the dining table was moved away and the beds or mats set out for sleeping. Anyone who has shared a motel room with children can attest to the amount of privacy provided by a single room. The historian John Demos described the typical colonial house in the Plymouth Colony as a few rooms, with limited sources of heat.

The single-family detached house with which we are so familiar did not evolve until the beginning of the nineteenth century. Increasing modernization — central heating, indoor plumbing, air-conditioning, radio, and television — further influenced the space utilization of the modern home.

In short, industrialization, urbanization, and modernization had a consistent impact on the family, changing it from a public institution with large and diverse audiences, to a private institution with the regular audience limited to husband, wife, and one or two children. Laslett explains that as the family became private, so too did it become more insulated from social control. Although children are not significant agents of social control, they do exert some — as anyone who has delayed an argument with a spouse until the children have gone to bed can attest to. Non-kin residents were also possible agents of control — implicitly by just "being around," and explicitly by their ability to intervene in family conflict. The less observable family behavior is, the less opportunity exists for formal or informal social control.

What are the consequences of increased family privacy and decreased social control? The private nature of intimate violence shelters offenders and victims from an audience, public eyes, and social control. The multiroom architecture of the modern home means that partners can fight away from the eyes (and supposedly ears) of children. Sexual and physical abuse of children can be committed by one parent in a separate room from the nonabusive parent. While it is a bit naive to believe that the nonabusing parent is ignorant of the actions, it is not unrealistic to assume that separate rooms gives the nonabusing parent a justification for noninvolvement and not exercising social control. Quite inadvertently, the family has evolved over the years into a perfectly shielded setting for private violence.

Inequality

Social attitudes set the stage for violence as an acceptable means of solving problems and self-expression, and privacy shields the family from social control in circumstances when the violence may not be considered normative. The socially structured inequality of the family further reduces the costs to violent partners, parents, and even children. Sexual and generational inequality take on many forms. First and most obvious, are the physical size differences. Husbands are typically larger and stronger than their wives. Parents are almost always bigger and stronger than their young children. Such physical size difference are important. We learned in one of our early analyses of mothers' use of violence toward their children, that mothers of teenage children are less likely to hit their children than are mothers of younger children. When we talked to the mothers we learned that the reason for this was not that there were less conflicts between mothers and teenagers than between mothers and preadolescents; actually there are more. Rather, the mothers said they were afraid that their teenagers would hit back. These sentiments were expressed by a forty-seven-year-old mother of a teenaged son and daughter:

> I used to spank my two kids until they got to be about fourteen or fifteen. . . I still wanted to hit them but, you see, they got to be so big that I just was too afraid to hit them anymore. Why, if they even pushed me now they could really hurt me.

There is more to inequality than size. Men typically enjoy more social and economic status than do women. Because of their economic and social power, men can hit their wives without fear that their wives can extract a social or economic cost. By the same token, parents control the social and economic resources of their children.

Over and over again, the victims of family violence whom we have come to know say the same thing: The black and blue marks go away, the violence is only occasional, and they are willing to accept pain against the costs of trying to survive

outside of the home with little money, credit, or experience.

The inequality we describe is part of a centuries-old legacy in which women are men's property and children are the property of their parents. The sociologist Lenore Weitzman finds that our traditional and still widely accepted conceptions about marriage can be traced back to tenth- and eleventh-century Anglo-American family law. One characteristic of traditional marriage was the husband being viewed as the head of the family with the wife and children subordinate. According to Weitzman, this hierarchy derived from the common-law doctrine of coverture, under which a husband and wife took a single legal identity at marriage — the identity of the husband. Although coverture was repealed in the nineteenth century, the assumption of a man as head remains embodied in statutory and case law in the Untied States.

The sociologists Russell and Rebecca Dobash have noted that there are very few historical references to women as important, powerful, and meaningful contributors to the lives and times of societies. There are, on the other hand, abundant legal, historical, literary and religious writings that describe the subordinate and propertied status of women. Saint Augustine wrote that in marriage, "women ought to serve their husbands as unto God." The Roman father decided whether his newborn children would live or die, selected marital partners for his children, and could put an adulterous wife to death.

The legacy of women and children as property was carried forth with laws that allowed, under certain circumstances, the chastisement and physical punishment of women and children. The expression "rule of thumb" is said to come from old English common law which stated that a husband could beat his wife with a rod no thicker than his thumb. Colonial "stubborn child laws" gave Puritan parents the right to put unruly children to death, although there is little historical evidence that such a drastic punishment was ever meted out.

The sociologist Dair Gillespie points out that before the Civil War, American wives had many duties and few rights. Wives were not permitted to own property, even if they had inherited it. Husbands could collect and use their wives' wages, choose the education and religion of their children, and punish their wives if they displeased them. Husbands could even will children (born or unborn) to other guardians. If a divorce was granted, it was the husband who would decide who would have custody of the children. Husbands, according to Gillespie were their wives' companions, superiors, and masters.

The victims of violence in the home are disproportionately the smaller, the weaker, and the less powerful. Part of their weakness comes from hundreds of years of subordination and being treated as property. Part of the weakness is due to the current social organization of society which offers few places to which victims can flee and live life safely with adequate social resources. The stigma of being a runaway child or a single parent serves to imprison many victims of violence in their homes. In few, perhaps no other, social settings are the cards so stacked against victims of personal violence. Few victims of public violence have to think about trading off the rewards of a home, hearth, and relationship against the costs of being physically assaulted. If you patronize a bar where you get beat up every fourth time you go there, you can freely stop going or change bars. Such options are not typically available to victims of intimate violence.

THE REWARDS OF INTIMATE VIOLENCE

We have said that people hit family members because they can, and we have argued that they can because the costs of being a violent family member are so low. There is another side to the equation. There are also rewards for being violent. James Q. Wilson and Richard J. Herrnstein, in their book *Crime and Human Nature,* make the point that there are a number of rewards for crime and criminal violence: working off momentary anger, money, and having fun. Most importantly, these rewards are felt quite soon after the behavior. In the case of intimate violence, the rewards of working off momentary anger are immediate. Nowhere is this quite as obvious as in the use of force and violence against children. Childrearing can be an immensely frustrating task. Over and over again, parents explain the frustration of raising children and trying to enforce discipline. While many parents try diligently to use a reasoned and rational approach to training children, as often as not parents report that they resort to hitting because "hitting works." When we ask how they know the hitting works, they say, "because he, or she, or they stopped what they were doing." For example:

> My daughter is two and she gets into everything. Sometimes I try to explain to her that she could get hurt or break something that is valuable. But she is so little that she really doesn't understand. So I slap her wrist or hit her bottom. That she understands and she stops touching the stuff right away.

or,

> I know I shouldn't lose my temper and hit them [her children]. But I get so frustrated I just lose control.

Besides, they do stop the things that got me mad in the first place.

It does little good to try to explain to parents that force and violence are not really effective ways of training and disciplining children.

It would do no good to explain to husbands that hitting their wives is not an effective means of encouraging conversation or debate. The reason for this is the rather immediate gratification the violent individual gets from hitting. For example, a husband described why he hit his wife: "She just nags and nags. I can't get her to stop and listen to me. So, I slap her in the face — that sure gets her attention and then she listens to me."

Violent parents or partners see immediately the reactions to the violence. If the force is sufficient to hurt a child or a spouse, they will most certainly stop whatever they were doing. Clearly, the immediate rewards of using violence to work off anger or frustration are quite valuable to some individuals who would rather not wait to see the longer-term benefits of more reasoned and rational discipline and conversation with their children or partners.

Power, control, and self-esteem are other rewards of family violence. The sociologist William Goode has stated that force or its threat is a fundamental part of all social systems, because all social systems are, to one degree or another, power systems. Force, or violence, Goode explains, is one of four major sets of resources by which people can move others to serve their ends. The four sets are: (1) economic factors (giving or withholding economic rewards or services); (2) prestige or respect; (3) likability, attractiveness, friendship, or love; and, (4) force and its threat. One can exert influence on people using any of these systems. One can give money, offer respect, provide love or friendship, or threaten to do bodily injury. All of these factors are in operation in the family and all are used because they can effectively control the behaviors of loved ones.

You can hardly walk in a public place where there are parents and children without overhearing what has become the virtual motto of American parents: "You better watch out or you're going to get it!" Force is threatened because parents want to control the behavior of their children. Hardly anyone would intervene if they saw a parent spank a child who had just run out into the street. Here, force is considered a perfectly legitimate means of controlling the child's behavior and teaching the child a valuable lesson.

The consequences of intimate violence further increase the rewards for individual who desires to control another. Repeated violence tends to beat down victims to the point where they will do anything, or say anything, to please their batterers and avoid violence. Betty, a thirty-five-year-old schoolteacher, said that after two years of violence she went to any length to please her husband.

> I would do anything. I would try to anticipate his moods. Cook his favorite dish. Dress the way he like. I would have the kids washed and in bed when he got home from work so there wouldn't be any stress at home. I gave up my first job so I could be home, but then he got too worried about money, so I got another job as a teacher. I think I spent twenty-four hours a day either doing things to please him or thinking ahead to prevent his getting mad.

For the person doing the controlling, the reward is not just control or power, but also self-esteem. Being in control, being master (or apparent master) of a situation, increases one's sense of self-worth. For men or parents whose sense of self-esteem may have been damaged or devalued by experiences outside of the home (losing a job, being humiliated by a boss or fellow worker, etc.), control at home is even more important. Over and over again we heard from men who first discussed how hard a time they had outside of the home and how they "had" to use hitting to keep their wives or kids in line. Obviously, the hitting served to make these men feel that they could control something in their lives.

One pattern of family violence we observed underscored the use of violence to control and increase self-esteem. It is not unusual to find a pattern of violence in a home where the husband hits his wife, the wife in turn uses violence toward her children, the older children use violence on the younger children, and the youngest child takes out his or her frustration on the family pet. One explanation for this pattern is that at each level the most powerful person is seeking to control the next least powerful person, and that this control is satisfying because it raises the hitter's feelings of self-worth.

A last reward for those who hit is revenge. "Revenge can be sweet," and one of the earliest patterns we identified in our study of intimate violence was that those who hit tended to do so after they felt that their self-worth had been attacked or threatened. Partners and parents are experts when it comes to understanding other family members' vulnerabilities. Conflict between intimates can quickly escalate because each person knows the other's most vulnerable points. If the conflict escalates the one partner goes for the other's jugular, violence may

be the only way the partner can defend himself or herself. Wives often hit husbands and children strike their parents to extract some kind of revenge for a psychological or physical assault.

Our society and our families are organized to not only allow but often encourage violence between intimates. The combination of social attitudes (that sometimes encourage but often just simply allow violence), with the private nature of the modern family, and the socially structured inequality that is part of every household, makes for a tinderbox of emotions and possible violent outbursts.

If people are violent because they can be, and if the modern family and system of social control is organized in such a way as to provide minimal social control over family behavior, does this mean that all families are violent? The answer is yes and no. Yes, there probably is some hitting in almost every household at some time. Almost all children are hit by their parents. Virtually all brothers and sisters hit each other. Perhaps half of all husbands and wives will physically fight at some point in their marriage. And many children, young and old, strike their parents, young and old. The answer is no if one confines the definition of violence to the outrageous acts of abuse that we hear about in the news each day. Abuse is not a common act, probably because enough social control is exerted over most individuals and most households to keep minor hitting from escalating into major abuse. Where abuse occurs, more often than not it is because a combination of factors exist — low social control, perhaps due to social isolation, high stress and frustration, and attitudes that hitting and even violence that causes injury are appropriate ways to raise children and control wives.

◆

VIOLENCE IN INTIMATE RELATIONSHIPS
bell hooks

We were on the freeway, going home from San Francisco. He was driving. We were arguing. He had told me repeatedly to shut up. I kept talking. He took his hand from the steering wheel and threw it back, hitting my mouth — my open mouth, blood gushed, and I felt an intense pain. I was no longer able to say any words, only to make whimpering, sobbing sounds as the blood dripped on my hands, on the handkerchief I held to tightly. He did not stop the car. He drove home. I watched him pack his suitcase. It was a holiday. He was going away to have fun. When he left I washed my mouth. My jaw was swollen and it was difficult for me to open it.

I called the dentist the next day and made an appointment. When the female voice asked what I needed to see the doctor about, I told her I had been hit in the mouth. Conscious of race, sex, and class issues, I wondered how I would be treated in this white doctor's office. My face was no longer swollen so there was nothing to identify me as a woman who had been hit, as a black woman with a bruised and swollen jaw. When the dentist asked me what had happened to my mouth, I described it calmly and succinctly. He made little jokes about, "How we can't have someone doing this to us now, can we?" I said nothing. The damage was repaired. Through it all, he talked to me as if I were a child, someone he had to handle gingerly or otherwise I might become hysterical.

This is one way women who are hit by men and seek medical care are seen. People within patriarchal society imagine that women are hit because we are hysterical, because we are beyond reason. It is most often the person who is hitting that is beyond reason, who is hysterical, who has lost complete control over responses and actions.

Growing up, I had always thought that I would never allow any man to hit me and live. I would kill him. I had seen my father hit my mother once and I wanted to kill him. My mother said to me then, "You are too young to know, too young to understand." Being a mother in a culture that supports and promotes domination, a patriarchal, white-supremacist culture, she did not discuss how she felt or what she meant. Perhaps it would have been too difficult for her to speak about the confusion of being hit by someone you are intimate with, someone you love. In my case, I was hit by my companion at a time in life when a number of forces in the world outside our home had already "hit" me, so to speak, made me painfully aware of my powerlessness, my marginality. It seemed then that I was confronting being black and female and without money in the worst possible ways. My world was spinning. I had already lost a sense of grounding and security. The memory of this experience has stayed with me as I have grown as a feminist, as I have thought deeply and read much on male violence against women, on adult violence against children.

From bell hooks, "Violence in Intimate Relationships," in *Talking Back: Thinking Feminist / Thinking Black* (Boston: South End Press, 1989), pp. 84–91.

In this essay, I do not intend to concentrate attention solely on male physical abuse of females. It is crucial that feminists call attention to physical abuse in all its forms. In particular, I want to discuss being physically abused in singular incidents by someone you love. Few people who are hit once by someone they love respond in the way they might to a singular physical assault by a stranger. Many children raised in households where hitting has been a normal response by primary caretakers react ambivalently to physical assaults as adults, especially if they are being hit by someone who cares for them and whom they care for. Often female parents use physical abuse as a means of control. There is continued need for feminist research that examines such violence. Alice Miller has done insightful work on the impact of hitting even though she is at times anti-feminist in her perspective. (Often in her work, mothers are blamed, as if their responsibility in parenting is greater than that of fathers.) Feminist discussions of violence against women should be expanded to include a recognition of the ways in which women use abusive physical force toward children not only to challenge the assumptions that women are likely to be nonviolent, but also to add to our understanding of why children who were hit growing up are often hit as adults or hit others.

Recently, I began a conversation with a group of black adults about hitting children. They all agreed that hitting was sometimes necessary. A professional black male in a southern family setting with two children commented on the way he punished his daughter. Sitting them down, he would first interrogate them about the situation or circumstance for which they were being punished. He said with great pride, "I want them to be able to understand fully why they are being punished." I responded by saying that

"they will likely become women whom a lover will attack using the same procedure you who have loved them so well used and they will not know how to respond." He resisted the idea that his behavior would have any impact on their responses to violence as adult women. I pointed to case after case of women in intimate relationships with men (and sometimes women) who are subject to the same form of interrogation and punishment they experienced as children, who accept their lover assuming an abusive, authoritarian role. Children who are the victims of physical abuse — whether one beating or repeated beatings, one violent push or several — whose wounds are inflicted by a loved one, experience an extreme sense of dislocation. The world one has most intimately known, in which one felt relatively safe and secure, has collapsed. Another world has come into being, one filled with terrors, where it is difficult to distinguish between a safe situation and a dangerous one, a gesture of love and a violent uncaring gesture. There is a feeling of vulnerability, exposure, that never goes away, that lurks beneath the surface. I know. I was one of those children. Adults hit by loved ones usually experience similar sensations of dislocation, of loss, of new found terrors.

Many children who are hit have never known what it feels like to be cared for, loved without physical aggression or abusive pain. Hitting is such a widespread practice that any of us are lucky if we can go through life without having this experience. One undiscussed aspect of the reality of children who are hit finding themselves as adults in similar circumstances is that we often share with friends and lovers the framework of our childhood pains and this may determine how they respond to us in difficult situations. We share the ways we are wounded and expose vulnerable areas. Often, these revelations provide a detailed model for anyone who wishes to wound or hurt us. While the literature about physical abuse often points to the fact that children who are abused are likely to become abusers or be abused, there is no attention given to sharing woundedness in such a way that we let intimate others know exactly what can be done to hurt us, to make us feel as though we are caught in the destructive patterns we have struggled to break. When partners create scenarios of abuse similar, if not exactly the same, to those we have experienced in childhood, the wounded person is hurt not only by the physical pain but by the feeling of calculated betrayal. Betrayal. When we are physically hurt by loved ones, we feel betrayed. We can no longer trust that care can be sustained. We are wounded, damaged — hurt to our hearts.

Feminist work calling attention to male violence against women has helped create a climate where the issues of physical abuse by loved ones can be freely addressed, especially sexual abuse within families. Exploration of male violence against women by feminists and non-feminists shows a connection between childhood experience of being hit by loved ones and the later occurrence of violence in adult relationships. While there is much material available discussing physical abuse of women by men, usually extreme physical abuse, there is not much discussion of the impact that one incident of hitting may have on a person in an intimate relationship, or how the person who is hit recovers from that experience. Increasingly, in discussion with women about physical abuse in relationships, irrespective of sexual preference, I find that most of us have had the experience of being violently hit at least once. There is little discussion of how we are damaged by such experiences (especially if we have been hit as children), of the ways we cope

and recover from this wounding. This is an important area for feminist research precisely because many cases of extreme abuse begin with an isolated incident of hitting. Attention must be given to understanding and stopping these isolated incidents if we are to eliminate the possibility that women will be at risk in intimate relationships.

Critically thinking about issues of physical abuse has led me to question the way our culture, the way we as feminist advocates focus on the issue of violence and physical abuse by loved ones. The focus has been on male violence against women and, in particular, male sexual abuse of children. Given the nature of patriarchy, it has been necessary for feminists to focus on extreme cases to make people confront the issue, and acknowledge it to be serious and relevant. Unfortunately, an exclusive focus on extreme cases can and does lead us to ignore the more frequent, more common, yet less extreme case of occasional hitting. Women are also less likely to acknowledge occasional hitting for fear that they will then be seen as someone who is in a bad relationship or someone whose life is out of control. Currently, the literature about male violence against women identifies the physically abused woman as a "battered woman." While is has been important to have an accessible terminology to draw attention to the issue of male violence against women, the terms used reflect biases because they call attention to only one type of violence in intimate relationships. The term "battered women" is problematical. It is not a term that emerged from feminist work on male violence against women; it was already used by psychologists and sociologists in the literature on domestic violence. This label "battered woman" places primary emphasis on physical assaults that are continuous, repeated, and unrelenting. The focus in on extreme violence, with little effort to link these cases with the everyday acceptance within intimate relationships of physical abuse that is not extreme, that may not be repeated. Yet these lesser forms of physical abuse damage individuals psychologically and, if not properly addressed and recovered from, can set the stage for more extreme incidents.

Most importantly, the term "battered woman" is used as though it constitutes a separate and unique category of womanness, as though it is an identity, a mark that sets one apart rather than being simply a descriptive term. It is as though the experience of being repeatedly violently hit is the sole defining characteristic of a woman's identity and all other aspects of who she is and what her experience has been are submerged. When I was hit, I too used the popular phrases "batterer," "battered woman," "battering" even though I did not feel that these words adequately described being hit once. However, these were the terms that people would listen to, would see as important, significant (as if it is not really significant for an individual, and more importantly for a woman, to be hit once). My partner was angry to be labeled a batterer by me. He was reluctant to talk about the experience of hitting me precisely because he did not want to be labeled a batterer. I had hit him once (not as badly as he had hit me) and I did not think of myself as a batterer. For both of us, these terms were inadequate. Rather than enabling us to cope effectively and positively with a negative situation, they were part of all the mechanisms of denial; they made us want to avoid confronting what had happened. This is the case for many people who are hit and those who hit.

Women who are hit once by men in their lives, and women who are hit repeat-edly do not want to be placed in the category of "battered woman" because it is a label that appears to strip us of dignity, to deny that there has been any integrity in the relationships we are in. A person physically assaulted by a stranger or a casual friend with whom they are not intimate may be hit once or repeatedly but they do not have to be placed into a category before doctors, lawyers, family, counselors, etc., take their problem seriously. Again, it must be stated that establishing categories and terminology has been part of the effort to draw public attention to the seriousness of male violence against women in intimate relationships. Even though the use of convenient labels and categories has made it easier to identify problems of physical abuse, it does not mean the terminology should not be critiqued from a feminist perspective and changed if necessary.

Recently, I had an experience assisting a woman who had been brutally attacked by her husband (she never commented on whether this was the first incident or not), which caused me to reflect anew on the use of the term "battered woman." This young woman was not engaged in feminist thinking or aware that "battered woman" was a category. Her husband had tried to choke her to death. She managed to escape from him with only the clothes she was wearing. After she recovered from the trauma, she considered going back to this relationship. As a church-going woman, she believed that her marriage vows were sacred and that she should try to make the relationship work. In an effort to share my feeling that this could place her at great risk, I brought her Lenore Walker's *The Battered Woman* because it seemed to me that there was much that she was not revealing, that she felt alone, and that the experiences she would read about in the book would give her a sense that other women had experienced what she was going through. I hoped reading the book would give her the courage to confront the reality of her situation. Yet I found it difficult to share because I could see that her self-esteem had already been greatly attacked, that she had lost a sense of her worth and value, and that possibly this categorizing of her identity would add to the feeling that she should just forget, be silent (and certainly returning to a situation where one is likely to be abused is one way to mask the severity of the problem). Still I had to try. When I first gave her the book, it disappeared. An unidentified family member had thrown it away. They felt that she would be making a serious mistake if she began to see herself as an absolute victim which they felt the label "battered woman" implied. I stressed that she should ignore the labels and read the content. I believed the experience shared in this book helped give her the courage to be critical of her situation, to take constructive action.

Her response to the label "battered woman," as well as the responses of other women who have been victims of violence in intimate relationships, compelled me to critically explore further the use of this term. In conversation with many women, I found that it was seen as a stigmatizing label, one which victimized women seeking help felt themselves in no condition to critique. As in, "who cares what anybody is calling it — I just want to stop this pain." Within patriarchal society, women who are victimized by male violence have had to pay a price for breaking the silence and naming the problem. They have had to be seen as fallen women, who have failed in their "feminine" role to sensitize and civilize the beast in the man. A category like "battered woman" risks reinforcing this notion that the hurt woman, not only the rape victim, becomes a social

pariah, set apart, marked forever by this experience.

A distinction must be made between having a terminology that enables women, and all victims of violent acts, to name the problem and categories of labeling that may inhibit the naming. When individuals are wounded, we are indeed often scarred, often damaged in ways that do set us apart from those who have not experience a similar wounding, but an essential aspect of the recovery process is the healing of the wound, the removal of the scar. This is an empowering process that should not be diminished by labels that imply this wounding experience is the most significant aspect of identity.

As I have already stated, overemphasis on extreme cases of violent abuse may lead us to ignore the problem of occasional hitting, and it may make it difficult for women to talk about this problem. A critical issue that is not fully examined and written about in great detail by researchers who study and work with victims is the recovery process. There is a dearth of material discussing the recovery process of individuals who have been physically abused. In those cases where an individual is hit only once in an intimate relationship, however violently, there may be no recognition at all of the negative impact of this experience. There may be no conscious attempt by the victimized person to work at restoring her or his well-being, even if the person seeks therapeutic help, because the one incident may not be seen as serious or damaging. Alone and in isolation, the person who has been hit must struggle to regain broken trust — to forge some strategy of recovery. Individuals are often able to process an experience of being hit mentally that may not be processed emotionally. Many women I talked with felt that even after the incident was long forgotten, their bodies remain troubled. Instinctively, the person who has been hit may respond fearfully to any body movement on the part of a loved one that is similar to the posture used when pain was inflicted.

Being hit once by a partner can forever diminish sexual relationships if there has been no recovery process. Again there is little written about ways folks recover physically in their sexualities as loved ones who continue to be sexual with those who have hurt them. In most cases, sexual relationships are dramatically altered when hitting has occurred. The sexual realm may be the one space where the person who has been hit experiences again the sense of vulnerability, which may also arouse fear. This can lead either to an attempt to avoid sex or to unacknowledged sexual withdrawal wherein the person participates but is passive. I talked with women who had been hit by lovers who described sex as an ordeal, the one space where they confront their inability to trust a partner who has broken trust. One woman emphasized that to her, being hit was a "violation of her body space" and that she felt from then on she had to protect that space. This response, though a survival strategy, does not lead to healthy recovery.

Often, women who are hit in intimate relationships with male or female lovers feel as though we have lost an innocence that cannot be regained. Yet this very notion of innocence is connected to passive acceptance of concepts of romantic love under patriarchy which have served to mask problematic realities in relationships. The process of recovery must include a critique of this notion of innocence which is often linked to an unrealistic and fantastic vision of love and romance. It is only in letting go of the perfect, no-work, happily-ever-after union idea, that we can rid our psyches of the sense that we have failed in some way by not having such relationships. Those of us who never focused on the negative impact of being hit as children find it necessary to reexamine the past in a therapeutic manner as part of our recovery process. Strategies that helped us survive as children may be detrimental for us to use in adult relationships.

Talking about being hit by loved ones with other women, both as children and as adults, I found that many of us had never really thought very much about our own relationship to violence. Many of us took pride in never feeling violent, never hitting. We had not thought deeply about our relationship to inflicting physical pain. Some of us expressed terror and awe when confronted with physical strength on the part of others. For us, the healing process included the need to learn how to use physical force constructively, to remove the terror — the dread. Despite the research that suggests children who are hit may become adults who hit — women hitting children, men hitting women and children — most of the women I talked with not only did not hit but were compulsive about not using physical force.

Overall the process by which women recover from the experience of being hit by loved ones is a complicated and multifaceted one, an area where there must be much more feminist study and research. To many of us, feminists calling attention to the reality of violence in intimate relationships has not in and of itself compelled most people to take the issue seriously, and such violence seems to be daily on the increase. In this essay, I have raised issues that are not commonly talked about, even among folks who are particularly concerned about violence against women. I hope it will serve as a catalyst for further thought, that it will strengthen our efforts as feminist activists to create a world where domination and coercive abuse are never aspects of intimate relationships.

♦

SOCIAL POLICY AND ELDER ABUSE

Stephen Crystal

Elder abuse has recently taken on a new visibility and has become a subject of public concern. It has received considerable attention from elected officials and the press, as well as from the social welfare community. This interest in the problem, and the concomitant pressure to "do something about it," has considerably outpaced research that would permit us to ascertain the extent of elder abuse, its relative severity, and the most appropriate means of addressing it.

As a particularly dramatic social problem elder abuse captures the imagination in a way that other, more routine problems do not. Even though the available research is plagued with definitional and data problems, the public has been persuaded of the importance of the problem: seventy-nine percent of the public believe elder abuse is a serious issue in the country, according to a Harris poll, and seventy-two percent believe it should be a "major responsibility" assumed by government.

In seeking to respond to the public interest surrounding this "new" problem, categorical responses have frequently been proposed and often implemented. Such responses are aimed at establishing specific social service or law enforcement measures to address the problem of elder abuse. Elder abuse reporting laws, for example, are paradigmatic of such measures. These statutes have been widely enacted during the last several years, as attention has come to be focused on elder abuse. In 1980 they existed in seventeen states; by 1983, such statutes had become law in thirty-three states.

CATEGORICAL APPROACHES

There are several problems with such categorical responses to the elder abuse problem. First, the nature and extent of the problem has not yet been clearly established, and there is no consensus or reliable knowledge base on the effectiveness of alternative approaches to resolving elder abuse when it occurs. Second, many of the responses that have been proposed or implemented in legislation are based on a false analogy to the child abuse problem. Third, categorical approaches by their nature tend to define the abuse element as the central problem to be addressed in what often turn out to be very complicated situations. Fourth, programs, policies, and legislation defined in terms of elder abuse establish a separate set of public responses, based on age, to problems that are shared with those of many nonelderly people.

These concerns, and other discussed below, center on the question of whether elder abuse is best responded to categorically, through legislative and programmatic solutions focused directly on the abuse issue, or whether it is best seen as a problem to be addressed mainly within more generic social service approaches and structures. The answers to these and related questions need to be based on as

From Stephen Crystal, "Social Policy and Elder Abuse," in *Elder Abuse: Conflict in the Family,* Karl A. Pillemer and Rosalie S. Wolf, eds. (Dover: Auburn Publishing Company, 1986), pp. 331–40.

complete an understanding as we can muster of the incidence and nature of abuse.

A central question is whether abuse typically exists as a relatively self-contained problem that can be successfully addressed frontally and in its own terms, or whether it is typically a single dimension of a much more complex set of problems. Although the available research is limited, there appears to be good reason to believe that the latter of these situations is considerably more typical than the former.

CASE CHARACTERISTICS: THE SCOPE OF THE PROBLEM

An important issue that tends to confuse policy discussions on elder abuse is imprecision of definitions. The term "abuse" clearly connotes to the nonspecialist some type of direct physical harm or exploitation, and this is what is visualized in the public concern over the issue. Psychological abuse is a more elusive and subjective category than physical abuse but one that is at least a meaningful extension of the notion of a victim being actively abused. The inclusion of neglect as a type of elder abuse, however, although a frequent practice, considerably distorts common sense semantics, particularly since care of a parent, as opposed to care of a minor child, is in general not a legal obligation. Even less helpful and confusing is the somewhat oxymoronic use of the term "self-neglect" as a form of abuse, which is often referred to in the literature and which has even appeared in statutory definitions of abuse.

In statistics generated from studies or programs using such broad definitions, the more peripheral types of cases such as passive neglect are usually predominant. Such statistics generally reflect cases of a type very different from those envisioned by typical consumers of statistics. Widely cited estimates, such as one million elder abuse cases per year (derived from Block and Sinnott and used *inter alia* by the Senate Special Committee on Aging), are based on very broad definitions. The impression conveyed to the public and to policymakers — that a million elderly people are beaten up by their children or other caretakers each year — is palpably wrong. Carefully read, these studies typically reflect much lower rates of actual direct abuse; indeed, one of the problems in the research has been the difficulty in identifying sufficient numbers of truly abused victims to study.

This is not to suggest that elder abuse is not a real problem, but that the responses to it need to be proportionate to its actual scope and its importance relative to other problems of the frail aged (e.g., lack of a caretaker as opposed to presence of an abusive caretaker).... [P]ublic perceptions and the perceptions of social service workers serving frail elderly populations seem to diverge in the importance assigned to abuse in comparison with other typical problems of the frail elderly. Since many of the types of intervention contemplated by legislative approaches to elder abuse, such as mandated central reporting and investigation, carry a risk of inappropriate intrusion and violation of elders' privacy and autonomy, it is all the more important that these risks be balanced accurately against the scope of the problem. In the discussion below, the term "abuse" is generally used to refer to some form of active harm.

Abuse is one of a number of forms of harm or endangerment that may call for protective intervention. While dramatic, it is not even necessarily the most severe or emergent, particularly when broadly defined. Experience with a broad range of programs organized to respond to harm and endangerment — adult protective services programs in particular — suggests that abuse is only one of a variety of problems encountered by impaired adults (those under sixty-five as well as the elderly); that is not necessarily the most common or most severe form of harm or endangerment requiring protective intervention; and that where abuse does appear to be manifest, it is usually encountered as part of a complex set of problems, often revolving around an unmet or poorly met care need and/or an abuser who is himself or herself functionally compromised.

THE CHILD ABUSE ANALOGY

Elder abuse statutes such as mandated reporting have frequently borrowed from the child abuse field. Despite the obvious lack of parallels between child abuse and elder abuse, many of the recently enacted statutes borrow directly from child abuse models, as does much of the literature on policy responses to elder abuse. Kerness, in proposing a model statute drawn mainly from child abuse statutes, is typical: "Experience under child protective reporting laws in the states as well as a growing body of professional literature argues in favor of a strong statutory reporting system as a powerful tool to protect vulnerable individuals against abuse and neglect."

Yet the differences between the situations are fundamental. A minor child is assumed to require a guardian with custodial authority, while an adult is assumed to be competent to make basic life decisions on his or her own. Parents have both the responsibility to care for a child and the authority to make decisions for that child, in investigating the possibility of child abuse or neglect, the state acts in *parens patriae*, exercising its traditional responsibilities to look after the welfare of legal incompetents such as minors.

In overruling the professional confidentiality privilege of a physician or other professional, mandatory reporting statutes place the state in the position of substitute parent. The appropriateness of this in many cases of suspected elder abuse or neglect is dubious. The responsibility of an adult protective services worker or other worker dealing with possible elder abuse, unless and until the client's competency comes into serious question, should normally be to help the client make his or her own choices — not to make decisions on the client's behalf.

The parent of a minor child has the legal obligation to support and care for the child and the legal authority to have physical custody of the child. Where neglect or abuse is substantiated and counseling or casework assistance cannot ensure the child's safety, a central and crucial tool is temporary or longer-term foster care placement: substitution of the state's custodial authority for that of the parent and physical removal of the child. Child abuse investigation and enforcement revolves around custodial decisions; the difference between this situation and adult abuse is fundamental, both at a philosophical/legal level and at a practical service delivery level. At the former level, mandatory reporting and investigation of child abuse reflects society's *parens patriae* responsibility and authority toward individuals who by their age are *ipso facto* legally incompetent, and reflects the fact that the child can be assumed in virtually all cases to be both legally (as a ward) and factually incapable of dealing with the abuse. At the practical level, a large-scale system for reporting and investigation of child abuse makes sense in part because tools such as foster care placement exist as feasible remedies in many of the cases encountered. Neither assumption is necessarily valid for adults.

The child protective services system is backed up by an extensive array of services linked specifically to it; foster care placements made as a result of child abuse and neglect investigations represent billions of dollars annually in expenditures in the United States. There is no real analogy for foster care placement in the adult abuse situation; removal of an adult from his or her own home purely as a solution to abuse would seldom be appropriate, and, in fact, this possibility is of real concern as a possible outcome of elder abuse investigations.

Reporting and increased case finding and investigation alone will not improve matters (in fact, such measures may well not even succeed in identifying any significant numbers of previously hidden cases). Why, given the problems discussed above, are mandatory reporting statutes, in and of themselves, so popular? The political dynamic is familiar: Legislators and governors are anxious to find a way to "do something" about a highly visible problem without the need to spend substantial sums on new services. Hence, an approach that appears to address a problem with high visibility and a touch of the exotic through existing service programs has considerable appeal. The need to develop a comprehensive set of services to address a range of forms of endangerment, not merely elder abuse, lacks appeal by comparison. Topics such as the need for financial management, adequate adult protective services staffing, and guardianship services are complicated and lack popular appeal, while the problems of those who simply lack a caretaker (a much larger group than those abused by caretakers) are old hat and seem uncomfortable and costly to address, possibly creating an open-ended demand for services. Perhaps, then, in addition to the problems of effectiveness and appropriateness discussed above, the real problem with legislative approaches that center on mandated reporting is that they create an illusory sense of progress on these complex and difficult problems.

♦

WORDS AND THE DOOR TO THE LAND OF CHANGE: LAW, LANGUAGE, AND FAMILY VIOLENCE
(Part One)

Martha Minow

In February 1989 the Supreme Court of the United States rejected the claim by Joshua DeShaney and his mother that the Winnebago County Department of Social Services violated his constitutional rights when it failed to protect him from the violence of his father. Joshua's father's violence put Joshua into a coma and left him paralyzed and without the functioning of half of his brain. The doctors found pools of rotted blood inside his brain as the result of months of bleeding from repeated assault. Joshua was just two weeks short of his fourth birthday. He is now in an institution for persons with profound mental retardation.

The technical legal question raised in the case was whether the due process clause of

From Martha Minow, "Words and the Door to the Land of Change: Law, Language, and Family Violence," *Vanderbilt Law Rev.* vol. 43, no. 179, 1990, pp. 1666–77 (edited).

the federal constitution should be interpreted to provide a basis for financial recovery after a government, its agencies, and employees failed to protect a child known to be at risk of severe physical abuse by his custodial parent. Many difficult issues are implicated in this question. Do precedents in the field of due process and other elements of legal analysis offer guidance? Would financial liability for failures to act lead to more effective or less effective social services programs to respond to family violence? Alternatively, instead of seeking to deter bad conduct through the threat of financial liability, should lawmakers articulate duties of socialworkers or seek changes in social services programs in order to produce greater responsiveness to situations like that of Joshua DeShaney? Are there standards of professional judgment that can be articulated to permit judicial evaluation of the role of the social services department in this case? Can those standards guard against both the risks of state over-intrusion into families and the risks of state failure to intervene? Or is the very use of law misguided, and do more promising alternatives lie in efforts to increase the funding and enhance the training of social services personnel? Can non-legal resources such as cultural mediums and religious and communal activities help shape conditions that will provide better education for the next generation of parents and reduce social isolation and offer more sustenance and protection for children at risk of violence at the hands of their caretakers?

Beyond these important and difficult questions are the attitudes about family violence embedded in the language of the Supreme Court's opinions. The bottom line in the *DeShaney* case is judicial inaction — the Court's refusal to act in response to a claim for redressing child abuse. That is too simple a statement, however, of the judicial attitude toward

family violence. Such a headline report does not communicate the nuance and complexity that the Justices themselves tried to convey to the watching community.

The case prompted three opinions from the Supreme Court. Chief Justice William Rehnquist wrote for the majority; Justices William Brennan and Harry Blackmum wrote the dissents. The opinions offer varied rationales and approaches to the relationship between law and family violence. According to Chief Justice Rehnquist's opinion, for example, the major reason why Joshua and his mother lost their suit is that the state has no obligation under the Constitution to provide affirmative governmental aid. The due process clause of the Constitution guarantees only against governmental acts that interfere with an individual's life, liberty, or prosperity. There is no entitlement to governmental aid that may be needed by individuals to realize the advantages of freedom. Judicial decisions mandating care for individuals who are institutionalized by the government in prisons and hospitals are exceptions because under those circumstances, the government has deprived the individuals of liberty.

Chief Justice Rehnquist reasoned also that the state acquired no duty to provide adequate protection for Joshua even though the agency had multiple reports of the risk to Joshua. To Chief Justice Rehnquist's majority, it did not matter that the state had taken Joshua into temporary custody before deciding to return him to his father's custody. The state court or state legislature might decide to impose such a duty, but the federal court, under the federal constitution, should not.

Two significant assumptions are at work here. The first is that violence is private and that the distinction between public and private actions makes violence, on occasions like this one, beyond public control. The second is that the government has to act in order to invade someone's rights; failing to act is not an invasion. For both assumptions, conceptual distinctions between categories, expressed through words remote from the facts of the case, do the work of judgment. The Justices in the majority point to words like "private" and mere "failure to act" as the basis for the judgment denying Joshua's recovery. Such words work as talismans to ward off the facts of the case.

Justice Brennan's dissent probed beneath these talismans. To do so, he chose different words. He dealt powerfully with the second assumption. Justice Brennan explained that the case was one of governmental inaction only in the sense that the agency failed to take steps to protect Joshua. In another sense, the government actually did act. It acted when it established a system of public social services and directed all other actors — neighbors, school teachers, and medical personnel at hospital emergency rooms — to direct any suspicions of abuse to the public agency and to rely on the agency to proceed from there. Thus, when a police department or sheriff's office receives a report of suspected child abuse, it refers the report to the local social services department for action. Justice Brennan observed that "[i]n this way, Wisconsin law invites — indeed, directs — citizens and other governmental entities to depend on local departments of social services such as [this one] to protect children from abuse." In the case of Joshua DeShaney, the state's invitation was accepted when relatives, emergency room personnel, and neighbors all reported to the agency that they suspected Joshua was being abused.

The government also acted when its employee socialworker duly compiled her observations from nearly twenty home visits. The department did not do nothing: it obtained extensive information about Joshua through outside sources and through its own staff. It removed Joshua temporarily from his father's care, but then returned him to his father. The department conveyed to others that it was monitoring the situation. All the information gathered on Joshua produced no efforts to protect him from his father, but this was not inaction. The Department acted when it decided not to take steps to protect the child. In his separate dissent, Justice Blackmun concluded that "the facts here involve not mere passivity, but active state intervention in the life of Joshua DeShaney — intervention that triggered a fundamental duty to aid the boy once the State learned of the severe danger to which he was exposed."

Justice Brennan and Justice Blackmun also challenged the distinction between action and inaction. Their opinions are dissenting views in this case and in law generally. The distinction between acting and failing to act could be used by judges to stymie efforts to prod police departments to respond to the battery of women and children. In the *DeShaney* case Justice Brennan wrote that "inaction can be every bit as abusive of power as action, [and] that oppression can result when a State undertakes a vital duty and then ignores it." Thus he explains how action and inaction are intertwined, and that inaction by one who takes on a responsibility is different from inaction by one who does not.

Justice Brennan himself paid deliberate attention to the way in which the Court's own conduct mirrored that of the Winnebago Department of Social Services: conduct that could be called simply inaction instead should be called action — affirmative choices not to act, not to respond. Justice Brennan concluded his opinion this way: "Because I cannot agree that our Constitution is indifferent to such indifference, I respectfully dissent."

Justice Blackmun also evoked analogies between judicial behavior and the behavior of the social services department that could be described as inaction, but might be described better (though these are my words) as violations through complicity. Justice Blackmun drew an analogy to the conduct of judges before the Civil War who opposed slavery but who, nonetheless, felt bound by formalistic legal analysis. They felt bound by something like the distinction between action and inaction and, therefore, concluded that they could not do otherwise but adhere to that distinction — even if that meant enforcing fugitive slave laws and returning runaway slaves to their masters. Justice Blackmun reasoned that "[l]ike the antebellum judges who denied relief to fugitive slaves, the Court today claims that its decision, however harsh, is compelled by existing legal doctrine. On the contrary, the question presented by this case is an open one" that leaves choices for the Justices.

These, dissenting Justices are on the brink of considering that violence itself is public as well as private — that law is part of the violence and that law itself can be violent. But again, these are dissenting views. The usual legal rhetoric about violence often makes the law's violence and the law's part in violence harder to see.

What usually remains unseen? The violence encountered by people within their families has roots and consequences not confined to those families. When clerks in a local court harass a woman who applies for a restraining order against the violence in her home, they are part of the violence. Society is organized to permit violence in the home; it is organized through images in mass media and through broadly based social attitudes that

condone violence. Society permits such violence to go unchallenged through the isolation of families and the failures of police to respond. Public, rather than private, patterns of conduct and morals are implicated. Some police officers refuse to respond to domestic violence; some officers themselves abuse their spouses. It is a societal decision to permit such police practices. Some clerks and judges think domestic violence matters do not belong in court. These failures to respond to domestic violence are public, not private, actions.

The language distinguishing public from private separates law from violence. Yet judicial inaction, as well as action, can be violent. Law is part of the violence when a court leaves in place a foster-care system in which child abuse is rampant, or when a judge refuses a restraining order requested by a woman claiming she fears battery by her boyfriend. Law itself is violent in its forms and methods. Official power effectuates itself in physical force, threatened or carried out. Judges and top-level bureaucrats, however, are not forced to witness violence. Their jobs are structured so that violence happens well down the chain of command, and they often have no point of reference for acknowledging the violence they hear others describe.

Judges and court personnel frequently blame the victim, trivialize the cases, or deny the victim's experiences. These attitudes reflect the failures by public servants to understand and reveal problems deeper than their own lack of contact and more profound that their clumsy language. Redefining as unacceptable that which previously has been acceptable will remain difficult unless society can acquire a different language, a language that reflects the experiences of those abused by domestic violence. In one recent Massachusetts case, for example, the judge turned to a man accused of choking and beating his wife and said: "You want to gnaw on her and she on you, fine, but let's not do it at the taxpayers' expense." In another case, a judge commented on the allegations that two children were physically abused: "Well, maybe they've been hit. I was hit when I was young, too." The same judge in the same case responded to allegations that the father also had abused his wife: "He may have abused her, but that doesn't necessarily make him a bad father." A judge may ask a complainant: "How often does he hit you," or "How did the child come to have a hematoma?" Compare these statements with the phrase, "a pool of blood rotted in the brain." Judges more often use the former language — like that of a remote clinical examination. In the *DeShaney* case Chief Justice Rehnquist talked of "abuse," "multiple bruises and abrasions," "suspicious injuries," "injuries... believed to be caused by child abuse," and a "series of hemorrhages caused by traumatic injuries to the head."

How can any of us talk about the pain and grotesqueries of violence that people inflict on one another, especially those whom they know? Elaine Scarry has written a remarkable book called *The Body in Pain*. She suggests that pain does "not simply resist language but actively destroys it, bringing about an immediate reversion to a state anterior to language, to the sounds and cries a human being makes before language is learned." Yet she also tells of the use of language by torturers that can become part of the pain and the ritual unleashing pain. When the unspeakable becomes spoken, its significance may seem lessened, the horror brought down to the scale of other words in the sentence, staidly positioned between commas or parentheses. At the same time, further injury and helplessness arise when we lack words to give meaning to our experiences.

Silence and words for those victimized by violence must differ from the silence and words of those who observe violence. Observers at least have a chance to assert some distance from pain and terror. But perhaps a fear of proximity to the unutterable experience of victimization prompts silence or remoteness by observers such as judges. Perhaps judges believe they would be unable to do their jobs if they spoke truly of violence, if they acknowledged the emotions they may feel about what they hear and see. The Supreme Court Justices in *DeShaney* certain knew the emotions and passions evoked by the facts of the case. Their responses to the emotion and passion are especially telling.

The *DeShaney* majority, represented by Chief Justice Rehnquist, explicitly declared that the Court has to restrain itself against emotion. The body of the opinion begins, "The facts of this case are undeniably tragic." These Justices seem to be saying that even we cannot deny our response to the facts here, even we who are Justices sequestered in this splendid marble courtroom, even we who will reject the plea of Joshua and his mother. This statement, of course, simply could be a ritualistic nod to the emotional, the passionate, as well as an indication that the complaining parties will lose. After the opening statement, the opinion is strikingly devoid of emotional color and expression; it is as if the initial acknowledgment called for tucking in and hiding away the reactions that the Justices as individual persons may have had to the case — until, that is, the end of the majority opinion. There, as if to serve as the other bookend, or the doorway at the end of the corridor of passionlessness introduced by the majority opinion, Chief Justice Rehnquist closed by stating: "Judges and lawyers, like other humans, are moved by natural sympathy in a case like this to find a way for Joshua and his mother to receive adequate compensation for the grievous harm inflicted upon them." Judges and lawyers, like other humans — but this sentence, too, is the opening to another stern demand for self-restraint, another "but."

Indeed, the next sentence begins, "But before yielding to that impulse...." Stop before yielding, cautions the phrase. Do not yield to that impulse — an impulse to act with sympathy, to act against reason. Impulse, of course, is the word long used by judges as a key factor in the test for the insanity defense: irresistible impulse. Impulse is thoughtless, irrational, crazy. Before yielding to impulse, the Chief Justice admonishes, "it is well to remember once again that the harm was inflicted not by the State of Wisconsin, but by Joshua's father." The tragedy is a private one; the sin is not the state's. Emotion should not obscure these "facts," although as the previous discussion of act and omission, of public and private, suggests, these are not facts, but rather choices about how to read the world. It is as if Chief Justice Rehnquist directs judges to use a wooden distinction between reason and emotion even if to do so restrains understanding and response. He acknowledges the possibility of responsiveness but argues against it; he recognizes the possibility of feelings but cautions against them.

What does it mean to hear someone say, "I'd better not feel?" The majority of the Supreme Court may be afraid of feeling, may be afraid of feeling overwhelmed by the pain the Justices hear about and by the sense of how much remains to be done. It is with this feeling that the Justices collectively don their hair shirts and summon self-restraint with statements of their own pain. This is not freedom from emotion and passion; this is a choice to submerge sympathy under fear, a choice to seek and

then cling to totemic concepts — acts and omissions, public and private — to avoid confronting our mutual implication in one another's lives. Justice Felix Frankfurter also urged judges to adopt a stance of disinterest, yet his own passion in so urging disclosed something quite the contrary.

The dissenters in *DeShaney* are more willing to describe the violence in vivid terms and more willing to draw from emotions and passions. Justice Brennan writes of reports of Joshua's father "beating or otherwise abusing Joshua," "the blows that destroyed Joshua's life," and his "last and most devastating injuries." Justice Blackmun writes of "the severe danger to which [Joshua] was exposed" and describes him as a "[v]ictim of repeated attacks by an irresponsible, bullying, cowardly, and intemperate father."

Justice Blackmun explicitly embraces a " 'sympathetic' reading" of the relevant constitutional principles, one which "recognizes that compassion need not be exiled from the province of judging." He begins his final paragraph with just this: "Poor Joshua!" He uses an exclamation point — not the punctuation mark of choice in Supreme Court opinions. He uses the dissenting judicial opinion, which otherwise wields no power, to perform the act of expressing compassion and care even though the Court's majority denied Joshua a legal remedy. Justice Blackmun describes the Court's treatment of the case as "a sad commentary upon American life." He also quotes with obvious approval and urgency this statement by Dr. Alan Stone, a psychiatrist who teaches at Harvard Law School:

> We will make mistakes if we go forward, but doing nothing can be the worst mistake. What is required of us is moral ambition. Until our compos-

ite sketch becomes a true portrait of humanity we must live with our uncertainty; we will grope, we will struggle, and our compassion may be our only guide and comfort.

Justice Brennan argues that Wisconsin's system of child protection "invites — indeed, directs — citizens and other governmental entities to depend on local departments of social services... to protect children from abuse." He notes the "almost eerie" detail with which the socialworker recorded her growing perceptions of Joshua's abuse, "almost eerie in light of her failure to act upon it," and her comment upon hearing of his devastating injuries: " 'I just knew the phone would ring some day and Joshua would be dead.' " This is an opinion written with drama and anger. The words are not typical for a law reporter: "[o]ppression can result when a State undertakes a vital duty and then ignores it."

These are dissenting views. Nonetheless, one week after the Court's decision in *DeShaney*, a majority of the Court reached a decision strikingly similar to the *DeShaney* dissent. In *City of Canton v. Harris* the Court held that a city could be found liable under the Constitution for failing to train its employees to recognize and respond to health problems of individuals arrested by its police. In *Harris*, Geraldine Harris was arrested by the city police and slumped to the floor of the patrol wagon, seemingly unable to respond to questions. After being taken to the police station, she twice slid to the floor and still did not respond to questions. The police department sought no medical attention and released Harris after an hour in custody. Her family then had her transported to a hospital where she was diagnosed with severe emotional difficulties. Harris required one week of

hospital care and a year of outpatient care. In the subsequent lawsuit, Harris claimed a violation of her due process rights because the police department failed to provide necessary medical attention while she was in police custody. The Supreme Court agreed with her.

By contrasting this case with *DeShaney*, I do not mean to suggest that Geraldine Harris was not entitled to recover money damages for the police department's failure to act. To the contrary, it is the Supreme Court's very willingness to impose liability when a public body failed to recognize someone in need — the grant of a grievance against the state for its failure to train police officers to seek medical care for someone held in custody for just one hour — that makes me wonder why the Court found it could do so little for Joshua DeShaney.

The Court treated Geraldine Harris as an adult. Perhaps this explains why the Court conceived of her time in state custody as sufficient to establish a duty of care, but viewed the state's temporary custody of Joshua DeShaney, a child, so differently. Nonetheless, *Harris* shows that a different result in *DeShaney* would not have required innovative legal categories: the Court simply could have viewed the Department as having taken on a special relationship with Joshua when it monitored his care. The choice to adopt this view was within the hands of the Justices.

Gloria Anzaldúa, a poet, wrote: "I can't reconcile the sight of a battered child with the belief that we choose what happens to us, that we create our own world." Neither can I. A close look at how law deals with violence, however, provides some clues. When those with power create and employ concepts to make themselves feel constrained from acting, they give a clue to the relationship between law and violence.

Neglect by Families, Violence by the State

Legal responses to abuses within families may be critical to the health and safety of individual family members. Although parents are legally presumed competent to act as parents, they may breach that presumption and trigger civil or criminal prosecution by the state. Yet sometimes those state responses compound the problem, or create new difficulties. Especially when state officials justify intervention in families on the basis of neglect, conflicts over values and cultural practices may be at stake rather than protection of health and safety. Sometimes, the alternatives offered by the state cause new injuries or mirror larger social dilemmas, such as racism or tendencies to blame victims. In light of these issues, explored by the readings, is it possible to articulate a legal standard to signal what is appropriate or justifiable state involvement in families? What tools can law deploy to protect individuals from abuse by both families and the state?

◆

I STAND HERE IRONING
Tillie Olsen

I stand here ironing, and what you asked me moves tormented back and forth with the iron.

"I wish you would manage the time to come in and talk with me about your daughter. I'm sure you can help me understand her. She's a youngster who needs help and whom I'm deeply interested in helping."

"Who needs help."... Even if I came, what good would it do? You think because I am her mother I have a key? She has lived for nineteen years. There is all that life that has happened outside of me, beyond me.

And when is there time to remember, to sift, to weigh, to estimate, to total? I will start and there will be an interruption and I will have to gather it all together again. Or I will become engulfed with all I did or did not do, with what should have been and what cannot be helped.

She was a beautiful baby. The first and only one of our five that was beautiful at birth. You do not guess how new and uneasy her tenancy in her now-loveliness. You did not know her all those years she was thought homely, or see her poring over her baby pictures, making me tell her over and over how beautiful she had been — and would be, I would tell her — and was now, to the seeing eye. But the seeing eyes were few or non-existenct. Including mine.

I nursed her. They feel that's important nowadays. I nursed all the children, but with her, with all the fierce rigidity of first motherhood, I did like the books then said. Though her cries battered me to trembling

From Tillie Olsen, "I Stand Here Ironing," in *Tell Me a Riddle* (New York, Dell, 1981), pp. 9–21.

and my breasts ached with swollenness, I waited till the clock decreed.

Why do I put that first? I do not even know if it matters, or if it explains anything.

She was a beautiful baby. She blew shining bubbles of sound. She loved motion, loved light, loved color and music and textures. She would lie on the floor in her blue overalls patting the surface so hard in ecstasy her hands and feet would blur. She was a miracle to me, but when she was eight months old I had to leave her daytimes with the woman downstairs to whom she was no miracle at all, for I worked or looked for work and for Emily's father, who "could no longer endure" (he wrote in his good-bye note) "sharing want with us."

I was nineteen. It was the pre-relief, pre-WPA world of the depression. I would start running as soon as I got off the streetcar, running up the stairs, the place smelling sour, and awake or asleep to startle awake, when she saw me she would break into a clogged weeping that could not be comforted, a weeping I can hear yet.

After a while I found a job hashing at night so I could be with her days, and it was better. But it came to where I had to bring her to his family and leave her.

It took a long time to raise the money for her fare back. Then she got the chicken pox and I had to wait longer. When she finally came, I hardly knew her, walking quick and nervous like her father, looking like her father, thin, and dressed in a shoddy red that yellowed her skin and glared at the pockmarks. All the baby loveliness gone.

She was two. Old enough for nursery school they said, and I did not know then what I know now — the fatigue of the long day, and the lacerations of group life in the kinds of nurseries that are only parking places for children.

Except that it would have made no difference if I had known. It was the only place there was. It was the only way we could be together, the only way I could hold a job.

And even without knowing, I knew. I knew the teacher that was evil because all these years it has curdled into my memory, the little boy hunched in the corner, her rasp, "why aren't you outside, because Alvin hits you? that's no reason, go out, scaredy." I knew Emily hated it even if she did not clutch and implore "don't go Mommy" like the other children, mornings.

She always had a reason why we should stay home. Momma, you look sick, Momma. I feel sick. Momma, the teachers aren't there today, they're sick. Momma, we can't go, there was a fire there last night. Momma, it's a holiday today, no school, they told me.

But never a direct protest, never rebellion. I think of our others in their three-, four-year-oldness — the explosions, the tempers, the denunciations, the demands — and I feel suddenly ill. I put the iron down. What in me demanded that goodness in her? And what was the cost, the cost to her of such goodness?

The old man living in the back once said in his gentle way: "You should smile at Emily more when you look at her." What *was* in my face when I looked at her? I loved her. There were all the acts of love.

It was only with the others I remembered what he said, and it was the face of joy, and not of care or tightness or worry I turned to them — too late for Emily. She does not smile easily, let alone almost always as her brothers and sisters do. Her face is closed and somber, but when she wants, how fluid. You must have seen it in her pantomimes, you spoke of her rare gift for comedy on the stage that rouses a laughter out of the audience so dear they applaud and applaud and do not want to let her go.

Where does it come from, that comedy? There was none of it in her when she came back to me that second time, after I had had to send her away again. She had a new daddy now to learn to love, and I think perhaps it was a better time.

Except when we left her alone nights, telling ourselves she was old enough.

"Can't you go some other time, Mommy, like tomorrow?" she would ask. "Will it be just a little while you'll be gone? Do you promise?"

The time we came back, the front door open, the clock on the floor in the hall. She rigid awake. "It wasn't just a little while. I didn't cry. Three times I called you, just three times, and then I ran downstairs to open the door so you could come faster. The clock talked loud. I threw it away, it scared me what it talked."

She said the clock talked loud again that night I went to the hospital to have Susan. She was delirious with the fever that comes before red measles, but she was fully conscious all the week I was gone and the week after we were home when she could not come near the new baby or me.

She did not get well. She stayed skeleton thin, not wanting to eat, and night after night she had nightmares. She would call for me, and I would rouse from exhaustion to sleepily call back: "You're all right, darling, go to sleep, it's just a dream," and if she still called, in a sterner voice, "now go to sleep, Emily, there's nothing to hurt you." Twice, only twice, when I had to get up for Susan anyhow, I went in to sit with her.

Now when it is too late (as if she would let me hold and comfort her like I do the others) I get up and go to her at once at her moan or restless stirring. "Are you awake, Emily? Can I get you something?" And the answer is always the same: "No, I'm all right, go back to sleep, Mother."

They persuaded me at the clinic to send her away to a convalescent home in the country where "she can have the kind of food and care you can't manage for her, and you'll be free to concentrate on the new baby." They still send children to that place. I see pictures on the society page of sleek young women planning affairs to raise money for it, or dancing at the affairs, or decorating Easter eggs or filing Christmas stockings for the children.

They never have a picture of the children so I do not know if the girls still wear those gigantic red bows and the ravaged looks on the every other Sunday when parents can come to visit "unless otherwise notified" — as we were notified the first six weeks.

Oh it is a handsome place, green lawns and tall trees and fluted flower beds. High up on the balconies of each cottage the children stand, the girls in their red bows and white dresses, the boys in white suits and giant red ties. The parents stand below shrieking up to be heard and the children shriek down to be heard, and between them the invisible wall "Not To Be Contaminated by Parental Germs or Physical Affection."

There was a tiny girl who always stood hand in hand with Emily. Her parents never came. One visit she was gone. "They moved her to Rose Cottage" Emily shouted in explanation. "They don't like you to love anybody here."

She wrote once a week, the labored writing of a seven-year-old. "I am fine. How is the baby. If I write my leter nicly I will have a star. Love." There never was a star. We wrote every other day, letters she could never hold or keep but only hear read — once. "We simply do not have room for children to keep any personal possessions," they patiently explained when we pieced one Sunday's shrieking together to plead how much it would mean to Emily, who loved so to keep things, to be allowed to keep her letters and cards.

Each visit she looked frailer. "She isn't eating," they told us.

(They had runny eggs for breakfast or mush with lumps, Emily said later, I'd hold it in my mouth and not swallow. Nothing ever tasted good, just when they had chicken.)

It took us eight months to get her released home, and only the fact that she gained back so little of her seven lost pounds convinced the socialworker.

I used to try to hold and love her after she came back, but her body would stay stiff, and after a while she'd push away. She ate little. Food sickened her, and I think much of life too. Oh she had physical lightness and brightness, twinkling by on skates, bouncing like a ball up and down up and down over the jump rope, skimming over the hill; but these were momentary.

She fretted about her appearance, thin and dark and foreign-looking at a time when every little girl was supposed to look or thought she should look a chubby blonde replica of Shirley Temple. The doorbell sometimes rang for her, but no one seemed to come and play in the house or be a best friend. Maybe because we moved so much.

There was a boy she loved painfully through two school semesters. Months later she told me how she had taken pennies from my purse to buy him candy. "Licorice was his favorite and I brought him some every day, but he still liked Jennifer better'n me. Why, Mommy?" The kind of question for which there is no answer.

School was a worry to her. She was not glib or quick in a world where glibness and quickness were easily confused with ability to learn. To her overworked and exasperated teachers she was an overconscientious "slow learner" who kept trying to catch up and was absent entirely too often.

I let her be absent, though sometimes the illness was imaginary. How different from my now-strictness about attendance with the others. I wasn't working. We had a new baby, I was home anyhow. Some-times, after Susan grew old enough, I would keep her home from school, too, to have them all together.

Mostly Emily has asthma, and her breathing, harsh and labored, would fill the house with a curiously tranquil sound. I would bring the two old dresser mirrors and her boxes of collections to her bed. She would select beads and single earrings, bottle tops and shells, dried flowers and pebbles, old postcards and scraps, all sorts of oddments; then she and Susan would play Kingdom, setting up landscapes and furniture, peopling them with action.

Those were the only times of peaceful companionship between her and Susan. I have edged away from it, that poisonous feeling between them, that terrible balancing of hurts and needs I had to do between the two, and did so badly, those earlier years.

Oh there are conflicts between the others too, each one human, needing, demanding, hurting, taking — but only between Emily and Susan, no, Emily toward Susan that corroding resentment. It seems so obvious on the surface, yet is it not obvious. Susan, the second child, Susan, golden- and curly-haired and chubby, quick and articulate and assured, everything in appearance and manner Emily was not; Susan, not able to resist Emily's precious things, losing or sometimes clumsily breaking them; Susan telling jokes and riddles to company for applause while Emily sat silent (to say to me later: that was my riddle, Mother, I told it to Susan); Susan, who for all the five years' difference in age was just a year behind Emily in developing physically.

I am glad for that slow physical development that widened the difference between her and her contemporaries, though she suffered over it. She was too vulnerable for that terrible world of youthful competition, of preening and parading, of constant measuring of yourself against every other, of envy,

"If I had that copper hair," "If I had that skin..." She tormented herself enough about not looking like the others, there was enough of the unsureness, the having to be conscious of words before you speak, the constant caring — what are they thinking of me? without having it all magnified by the merciless physical drives.

Ronnie is calling. He is wet and I change him. It is rare there is such a cry now. That time of motherhood is almost behind me when the ear is not one's own but must always be racked and listening for the child cry, the child call. We sit for a while and I hold him, looking out over the city spread in charcoal with its soft aisles of light. "*Shoogily*," he breathes and curls closer. I carry him back to bed, asleep. *Shoogily*. A funny word, a family word, inherited from Emily, invented by her to say: *comfort*.

In this and other ways she leaves her seal, I say aloud. And startle at my saying it. What do I mean? What did I start to gather together, to try and make coherent? I was at the terrible, growing years. War years. I do not remember them well. I was working, there were four smaller ones now, there was not time for her. She had to help be a mother, and housekeeper, and shopper. She had to set her seal. Mornings of crisis and near hysteria trying to get lunches packed, hair combed, coats and shoes found, everyone to school or Child Care on time, the baby ready for transportation. And always the paper scribbled on by a smaller one, the book looked at by Susan then mislaid, the homework not done. Running out to that huge school where she was one, she was lost, she was a drop; suffering over the unpreparedness, stammering and unsure in her classes.

There was so little time left at night after the kids were bedded down. She would struggle over books, always eating (it was in those years she developed her enormous appetite that is legendary in our family) and I would be ironing, or preparing food for the next day, or writing V-mail to Bill, or tending the baby. Sometimes, to make me laugh, or out of her despair, she would imitate happenings or types at school.

I think I said once: "Why don't you do something like this in the school amateur show?" One morning she phoned me at work, hardly understandable through the weeping: "Mother, I did it. I won, I won; they gave me first prize; they clapped and clapped and wouldn't let me go."

Now suddenly she was Somebody, and as imprisoned in her difference as she had been in anonymity.

She began to be asked to perform at other high schools, even in colleges, then at city and statewide affairs. The first one we went to, I only recognized her that first moment when thin, shy, she almost drowned herself into the curtains. Then: Was this Emily? The control, the command, the convulsing and deadly clowning, the spell, then the rearing, stamping audience, unwilling to let this rare and precious laughter out of their lives.

Afterwards: You ought to do something about her with a gift like that — but without money or knowing how, what does one do? We have left it all to her, and the gift has as often eddied inside, clogged and clotted, as been used and growing.

She is coming. She runs up the stairs two at a time with her light graceful step, and I know she is happy tonight. Whatever it was that occasioned your call did not happen today.

"Aren't you ever going to finish the ironing, Mother? Whistler painted his mother in a rocker. I'd have to paint mine standing over an ironing board." This is one of her communicative nights and she tells me everything and nothing as she fixes herself a plate of food out of the icebox.

She is so lovely. Why did you want me to come in at all? Why were you concerned? She will find her way.

She starts up the stairs to bed. "Don't get me up with the rest in the morning." "But I thought you were having midterms." "Oh, those," she comes back in, kisses me, and says quite lightly, "in a couple of years when we'll all be atom-dead they won't matter a bit."

She has said it before. She *believes* it. But because I have been dredging the past, and all that compounds a human being is so heavy and meaningful in me, I cannot endure it tonight.

I will never total it all. I will never come in to say: She was a child seldom smiled at. Her father left me before she was a year old. I had to work her first six years when there was work, or I sent her home and to his relatives. There were years she had care she hated. She was dark and thin and foreign-looking in a world where the prestige went to blondeness and curly hair and dimples, she was slow where glibness was prized. She was a child of anxious, not proud, love. We were poor and could not afford for her the soil of easy growth. I was a young mother, I was a distracted mother. There were the other children pushing up, demanding. Her younger sister seemed all that she was not. There were years she did not want me to touch her. She kept too much in herself, her life was such she had to keep too much in herself. My wisdom came too late. She has much to her and probably little will come of it. She is a child of her age, of depression, of war, of fear.

Let her be. So all that is in her will not bloom — but in how many does it? There is still enough left to live by. Only help her to know — help make it so there is cause for her to know — that she is more than this dress on the ironing board, helpless before the iron.

1953-1954

♦

HAVEN IN A HEARTLESS WORLD: THE FAMILY BESIEGED

Christopher Lasch

Thus the family struggles to conform to an ideal of the family imposed from without. The experts agree that parents should neither tyrannize over their children nor burden them with "oversolicitous" attentions. They agree, moreover, that every action is the product of a long causal chain and that moral judgments have no place in childrearing. This proposition, central to the mental health ethic, absolves the child from moral responsibility while leaving that of his parents undiminished. Under these conditions, it is not surprising that many parents seek to escape the exercise of this responsibility by avoiding confrontations with the child and by retreating from the work of discipline and character formation. Permissive ideologies rationalized this retreat. When parents cannot altogether avoid disciplinary decisions, they seek to delegate them to other authorities. The father cites the de-

Christopher Lasch, *Haven in a Heartless World: The Family Besieged* (New York: Basic Books, 1979), pp. 172–74.

mands of his work as an excuse for assigning daily discipline to his wife. She in turn avoids the most painful encounters by invoking the ultimate authority of the father, threatening children with a fearful reckoning when he finally returns to the scene. Both parents shift much of the responsibility for the child's development to his peers — against whom, in the absence of firm standards of their own, they also measure the child's academic, athletic, and psychological progress. Seeley and his associates found that upper-middle-class parents in "Crestwood Heights" hesitated to impose their own tastes on the child and left the formation of taste to the child's peers. "Crestwood parents who would deem it morally wrong and psychologically destructive to regulate the expression of their children's tastes, after self-examination realized and stated that they were able to afford these views because... in these areas the peer group performed a satisfactory policing function for them." Permissiveness thus rests, in part, on peer-group control.

The peer group not only regulates taste, it puts forward its own version of ideal family life. It circulates information about parental regulations currently in force, about the regulations that are violated with impunity, about what the world upholds as the norm of parenthood. The child's mastery of this information gives him an important tactical advantage in negotiations with his parents. If he can show that they have departed from established norms, he further weakens their self-confidence. Having made it clear that their own actions are to be submitted to the same standards of justice to which the child himself is expected to conform, parents find it difficult to specify those standards. In theory, justice derives from reason, but community practice turns out to be the only reliable guide. The child

knows more about this ambiguous and constantly shifting practice than his parents do, and he skillfully exploits their uneasiness. Parental training has collapsed not because of the inevitable supersession of parent's technical knowledge but because organized interest groups, such as the health and welfare professions and the adolescent peer group, have a stake in promoting their own conceptions of the world, which compete with those of the family. Like the health industry, the peer group spreads information that parents cannot hope to master in its complexity but on which they nevertheless depend in their unsuccessful struggles to discipline their children and at the same time to retain their devotion.

Relations within the family have come to resemble relations in the rest of society. Parents refrain from arbitrarily imposing their wishes on the child, thereby making it clear that authority deserves to be regarded as valid only insofar as it conforms to reason. Yet in the family as elsewhere, "universalistic" standards prove on examination to be illusory. In American society, most rules exist only to be broken, in the words of a popular axiom. Custom has reestablished itself as in many ways the superior of reason. The administration of justice gives way, in a therapeutic society, to a complicated process of negotiation. Just as prices in the neocapitalist economy, allegedly determined by the impersonal laws of supply and demand, are really fixed by negotiations among corporations, unions, and government (with the corporations taking the leading role), so justice is fixed by means of similar bargains among interested parties. In learning to live by the law, therefore, the child actually learns how to get around the law, in the first place by getting around his parents.

◆

NO NAME MADDOX: CASE HISTORY OF CHARLES MANSON

Kenneth Wooden

My home town is jail house
   city,
Police took me from my
   mama's titty.
I got no thought and got no
   pity.
Your society treated me
   mighty shitty.
       — *Charles M. Manson*

Charles Manson was thirty-five years old when he stood trial for the Sharon Tate-LaBianca murders. The macabre multi-murders and the trial that convicted Manson commanded national media attention. So absorbing was the story that even Richard Nixon, President of the United States, found time in August of 1970 to say, "Here is a man who was guilty, directly or indirectly, of eight murders. Yet here is a man who, as far as the coverage is concerned, appeared to be a glamorous figure."

Today, Manson sits in a maximum security cell in San Quentin Prison in northern California. What was called one of the most baffling and horrifying murder cases of this century is now well-known history. What is not well known is the early childhood of Charles Manson and the effect of some twenty-two years spent in more than a dozen penal institutions.

Manson was born to sixteen-year-old Kathleen Maddox on November 12, 1934, in Cincinnati. His mother was allegedly violated by a Colonel Scott, so Charlie's birth certificate read: "No Name Maddox." Two years later Kathleen Maddox filed a bastard suit in Boyd County, Kentucky, and the father agreed to a judgment of twenty-five dollars and a five-dollar-a-month support for the child. She later married a William Manson, and gave his name to the illegitimate boy — Charles Milles Manson.

During the first few years of his life, Charlie was bounced between the care of his grandmother and maternal aunt because his mother, leaving the baby with neighbors "for an hour," would disappear for days and weeks at a time. In 1939, Kathleen and her brother were arrested for armed robbery when they knocked a service station attendant unconscious with a Coke bottle. She was sentenced to five years in the West Virginia State Penitentiary. Manson also went to West Virginia, to live with an aunt and uncle, who, he later told prison authorities, had a "difficult marriage until they found religion... and became very extreme." During this time, he started school.

Charlie was eight years old when his mother was released from prison. The youngster then began to live with a long line of "uncles," who, like his mother, drank heavily. Home was an assortment of run-down hotel rooms, where many times Charlie was forced to stay alone all day. He ran away, but returned.

From Kenneth Wooden, "No Name Maddox: Case History of Charles Manson," in *Weeping in the Playtime of Others* (New York: McGraw Hill, 1976), pp. 47–57.

Manson was next placed with foster parents for about a year — perhaps the best situation of his young life. But it was short-lived. His mother moved to Indianapolis with a salesman and sent for her son. A later report would state: "Manson received little attention from his mother and from the many men who were reputed to have lived with her."

In 1947 his mother tried to place him in another foster home, but there was none available. So Charlie became a ward of the county, who sent the unwanted boy to his first of many institutions, the Gibault Home for Boys in Terre Haute, Indiana. His record there revealed: "Poor institutional adjustment... his attitude toward school was at best only fair... during the short lapses when Charles was pleasant and feeling happy, he presented a likable boy... a tendency toward moodiness and a persecution complex." (Mrs. Angles McMoney, a volunteer at his second institution in Plainfield who tried to help Manson, told me: "He was very quiet, very shy, didn't want anything to do with anyone else." Teachers said, "He professed no trust in anyone.")

After ten months at Gibault, Manson ran away to his mother, who again rejected him. (This "return-rejection" pattern was to persist right up to the time of the Tate-LaBianca murders.)

Manson now drifted toward a life of crime. From the take of burglarizing a grocery store, he was able to rent a room. Later, however, he was caught stealing a bike and sent to the Juvenile Center in Indianapolis. He escaped but was apprehended and sent to Father Flanagan's Boys Town. Four days into that institution, he and another boy stole an old Plymouth and made it to a ditch in Johnsonville, Iowa. Along the way, they committed two armed robberies — a gambling casino and

a grocery store. They hitched the rest of the way to the other boy's uncle — a World War II disabled veteran, who tutored them in "slipping through skylights." Their first take was $1,500; the second time they were arrested. Manson was still only thirteen.

He was incarcerated at the Indiana Boys School at Plainfield. He stayed three years and attempted to run away eighteen times. On his nineteenth try, with two other youths, Charles Manson finally made good his escape from the thousand-acre youth jail with its own cemetery of over 135 graves. Stealing cars and burglarizing gas stations for transportation and support, they headed for California but were stopped near Beaver, Utah, at a roadblock set up for another robbery suspect. Crossing state lines with a stolen car is a federal offense (Dyer Act). Sixteen-year-old Manson was now under federal jurisdiction and was sent to the National Training School for Boys in Washington, D.C., to which he was sentenced to stay until he reached twenty-one.

In the late fall of 1974 I visited the Gibault Home in Terre Haute. The Catholic brothers there declined to discuss Manson and were embarrassed that he had ever been under their care. They told me it would take approval by the board of trustees for me to review his record. I was, however, given the opportunity to tour the facilities and see some of the buildings and grounds where Manson, the neglected child of thirteen, had been forced to live. I was struck by the old dormitories where the boys slept. Eight beds lined the walls and in the middle of one end of the room was a toilet within a windowed structure resembling a telephone booth. I also learned that discipline was meted out via the rod. I don't know how severe the beatings were. No one was talking.

When the Manson murder story broke, the Indiana Boys School in Plainfield refused anyone in the media permission to see his file in its entirety. So again, very little is known about Manson's treatment during a critical time of his young life. An enterprising New Yorker offered superintendent Al Bennett a good price if he would review and reveal the records, but Bennett declined. However, when I visited the Indiana school, Bennett did tell me that when Manson or any inmates ran, they were beaten, then thrown into solitary. He showed me the leather straps that were used. They were 26 inches long, 3 inches wide and 1/2 inch thick. The handles were stained from sweat, the ends worn thin by those who administered the beatings. The youngsters who were to be disciplined were placed on wooden racks at an appointed time (4 P.M.) "with their ass up in the air." The big debate was "should they beat the boys with their trousers on or off." When the leather strap had no effect, the guards would "take them out in the cornfield and beat the piss out of them."

According to the superintendent, records hidden from press and public reveal that on several occasions Manson was beaten so severely that he received treatment at a local hospital. Many years too late, in January 1974, the United States Court of Appeals for the Seventh Circuit ruled on the Indiana Boys School:

> In beating the juvenile, a "fraternity paddle" between 1/3" to 2" thick, 12" long, with a narrow handle was used. There is testimony that juveniles weighing about 160 lbs. were struck five blows on the clothed buttocks, often by a staff member weighing 285 lbs.... It is...constitutionally cruel and unusual punishment.

It was also at Plainfield that Charles Manson was first homosexually attacked and raped. Thereafter he too engaged in homosexuality.

From Manson's records at the National Training School for Boys, Washington, D.C., a profile emerged: Though he had had four years of schooling, he was illiterate, with an IQ of 109. His first caseworker found him a "sixteen-year-old boy who has had an unfavorable family life, if it can be called a family life at all" and "aggressively antisocial." Three months later: "It appears that this boy is a very emotionally upset youth who is definitely in need of some psychiatric orientation."

Still, during the early years in the training school, a psychiatrist noted that though Charles Manson had a number of strikes against him, he hadn't quite given up on the world: "Because of a marked degree of rejection, instability, and psychic trauma — because his sense of inferiority in relationship to his mother was so pronounced, he constantly felt it necessary to suppress any thoughts about her. However, because of his diminutive stature, his illegitimacy, and the lack of parental love, he is constantly striving for status with the other boys... has developed certain facile techniques for dealing with people, those for the most part consist of a good sense of humor and an ability to ingratiate himself.... This could add up to a fairly slick institutionalized youth, but one is left with the feeling that behind all this lies an extremely sensitive boy who has not yet given up in terms of securing some kind of love and affection from the world."

In a special progress report during Charlie's stay at the National Training School, the following entry was made in his file:

He got along fairly satisfactory at the school although it was felt that he might be a custody risk unless something could be done to work out his feelings of depression and moodiness. He had a fairly good attitude and was cooperative when not in a depressed mood.

Shortly thereafter, officials at the National Training School decided that the Natural Bridge Honor Camp, a minimum security institution, would be the best possible place for the youth. Three weeks later he turned seventeen and was visited by his aunt, Mrs. W. L. Thomas of McMechen, West Virginia, who promised him a home and employment if he was released to her supervision. Manson was due for a parole hearing three months later, and with his aunt's offer his chances for release were very good. However, one month before the hearing, he pressed a razor blade against a fellow inmate's throat and sodomized him.

For that offense Manson was transferred to the federal reformatory at Petersburg, Virginia, and classified as dangerous. He became more and more involved in homosexual acts and unceasingly entered into institutional mayhem. He served time in solitary confinement for "stealing food from the kitchen, shirking his assigned duties in the kitchen, fighting with another inmate, etc." During this time he had no visits from anyone and received only a few letters from his aunt and mother.

Finally officials felt that for the protection of Manson as well as others, it would be best to transfer him to a more secure prison, the federal reformatory at Chillicothe, Ohio. He arrived on September 23, 1952, and by now it was written: "in spite of his age, he is criminally sophis-

ticated." And later: He "... has no foresight for the future, is thoroughly institutionalized and doesn't appear to be the type that will take advantage of the opportunities afforded him." The report concluded: "He has been a neglected child all his life."

Manson's conduct improved at Chillicothe, however, and he was granted parole on May 8, 1954. He was nineteen. He went to live with his aunt in McMechen, where he married seventeen-year-old Rosalie Jean Willis in early 1955. He worked at a number of odd jobs, from busboy to parking-lot attendant. During this time he saw his mother briefly.

He began to hustle cars, two of which he took across state lines, and was arrested again for violation of the Dyer Act. He pleaded guilty in a federal court and requested medical assistance by telling a judge: "I was released from the Federal Penitentiary in Chillicothe, Ohio, in 1954 and having been confined for nine years, I was badly in need of psychiatric treatment. I was mentally confused and stole a car as a means of mental release from the confused state of mind that I was in."

The judge had Dr. Edwin McNeil examine Manson on October 26, 1955, in the Los Angeles county jail. The psychiatrist commented on both Manson's early family life and his years of incarceration: "It is evidence that he has an unstable personality and that his environmental influences throughout most of his life have not been good.... This boy is a poor risk for probation; on the other hand, he has spent nine years in institutions with apparently little benefit except to take him out of circulation."

Manson told the psychiatrist he had spent so much time in institutions that he never really learned much of what real life on the outside was all about. Commenting on his wife, Charlie said: "She is the best wife a guy could want. I didn't realize how good she was until I got in here. I beat her at times. She writes to me all the time. She is going to have a baby." He opined that since he was about to become a father, it was important for him to be with his wife on the outside. "She is the only one I have ever cared about in my life." Perhaps it was Rosalie Jean Willis who touched Manson when he wrote the following lines to the presiding judge:

> Only walls of your prisons
> Is all I've ever seen
> I run away from your cities
> My brothers who are so mean.
>
> Once I did see the sun
> Where the eagle flies
> I look at the agony of my world
> And all the love that dies.

The judge placed Manson on probation for five years.

But Manson still had another charge to face — auto theft in Florida. A hearing was set, but he skipped town. A warrant was issued; he was arrested and sentenced to three years at Terminal Island, San Pedro, California. The new father held his baby son in the courtroom just before he left for prison.

At Terminal Island, a caseworker observed: "We have here a young man who comes from a very unfavorable background, has no worthwhile family ties and has been subjected to institutional treatment since early childhood. He is an almost classic textbook case of the correctional institution inmate.... His is a very difficult case and it is impossible to predict his future adjustment with any degree of accuracy."

In April 1957: "the only one I have ever cared about in my life" ceased to visit Manson. His mother brought the news that

his wife was living with another man. Charlie attempted to escape from the minimal custody unit to which he had been transferred. A parole committee commented: "This episode, however, is in keeping with the pattern he has exhibited from early childhood of attempting to evade his responsibilities by running away" and refused parole. Rosalie then filed for divorce, which was granted in 1958. She was given custody of their child. Manson has never seen either of them again.

Now, because his institutional conduct and behavior became intolerable to prison officials — he would not dress properly and "contraband[ed] food" — the man was placed in "punitive segregation on a restricted diet for indefinite periods of time." His medical and psychiatric record revealed that he had now become totally dependent on institutional life and had anxiety over leaving the security of confinement. Bill Casey, an official at Terminal Island, told me during an interview that he felt Manson was a "real introvert, a loner and a quiet type — like a cat ... strictly an institutionalized person who didn't want to leave prison." Casey said he was a little surprised at the violent behavior of Charlie Manson, but "when they grow up in institutions, they have a tendency toward violence. It gives them an identity and makes them somewhat of a hero, a leader, something they never were."

When released from prison, Manson quickly returned to the routine of stealing cars. He then started to pimp and he was arrested for trying to cash a stolen government check for $37.50. After a series of such episodes, Manson, at twenty-six, was back in jail, this time the United States penitentiary on McNeil Island, Washington. Staff evaluation summarized a neglected childhood and years of incarceration:

The product of an emotionally disruptive formative period,

> Manson has never really reconciled the overt rejecting aspects of his maternal relationship and has functioned primarily in a dependent manner, hiding his loneliness, resentment, and hostility behind a façade of superficial ingratiation. In many respects, he has a childish need for acceptance without knowing how to go about securing such acceptance in an adult manner. He has commented that institutions have become his way of life and that he receives security in institutions which is not available to him in the outside world.

During his last five years of imprisonment before the Tate-LaBianca murders, total institutionalization was effected. A second marriage, just prior to incarceration, to Leona Musser (1959) failed and terminated in divorce. It was now that Manson struck up a friendship with the last survivor of Ma Barker's gang, Alvin Karpis, who taught him to play the guitar, opening a whole new world to Charlie. He also developed a keen interest in scientology and, accordingly to the annual progress reports of the penitentiary, that interest "has led him to make a semi-professional evaluation of his personality which strangely enough, is quite consistent with the evaluations made by previous social studies." Another year, the report read: "Even these attempts and his cries for help represent a desire for attention, with only superficial meaning.... In view of his deepseated personality problems... conti-

nuation of institutional treatment is recommended."

Finally, in June 1966, Charles Manson was transferred back to Terminal Island Prison in California for release. His last report read: "Manson is about to complete his ten-year term. He has a pattern of criminal behavior and confinement that dates to his teen years. This pattern is one of instability whether in free society or a structured institution community. Little can be expected in the way of change in his attitude, behavior or mode of conduct.... He has come to worship his guitar and music ... has no plans for release as he says he has nowhere to go."

On the morning of his release from prison, Charles Manson begged his jailers to allow him to remain: "Prison has become my home"; he doubted he could "adjust to the world outside." His request was denied. On March 21, 1967, Manson hit the free world and drifted into the Haight-Ashbury section of San Francisco. There the Manson family, which was to terrorize and take the lives of forty-odd people, was born.

Manson did not choose his own pathway to oblivion and crime. It was charted for him, first by parental abandonment, and then, in a far greater sense, by the massive failure of the correctional system, particularly those in charge of juvenile offenders. Manson was the product of too many impersonal institutions, too many endless days in solitary confinement, too many sexual assaults by older boys and far too many beatings by guardians and institutional personnel. The U.S. Court of Appeals, which ruled the use of wooden paddles cruel and unusual punishment, also documented the destructiveness of beatings: "... the practice does not serve as useful punishment or as treatment, and it actually breeds counter-hostility, resulting in greater aggression by a child."

A review of all Manson's prison records reveal some interesting facts: Of twenty-two years in prison, seventeen were spent in federal facilities for crimes that, under state jurisdiction, would carry sentences totaling less than five years. There was never once a serious treatment program for young Manson. At the federal reformatory at Petersburg, Virginia, his rehabilitation program consisted of helping in the kitchen; he bitterly opposed being enrolled in elementary school, so he never showed up after the first class. Also he was always physically "fit for regular duty," and reports consistently recommended that he "continue on the same program." But what was the program?

The Chillicothe federal reformatory listed his treatment as follows:

Medical:	Fit for regular duty
Athletics:	No restrictions
Psychiatric:	Not indicated at this time
Employment:	Foundry
Education:	Voluntary enrollment
Religion:	Routine contact
REMARKS:	"Because of this man's history of vicious homosexual assaults, he was given Close Custody and assigned to Cell House #1."

Although Manson had held a razor blade against the throat of an inmate and sodomized him, no psychiatric help was "indicated." Treatment for Charles was "close custody" and "continue on same program."

Manson and the countless thousands of children locked away from society during the late forties and fifties became part of the bitter harvest of crime this country reaped in the late sixties and early seventies. What of future children? According to the FBI's annual report, more than 80,000 children under ten were arrested in 1972. Charges were placed against 585,000 children between eleven and fourteen years of age. Without proper treatment, without proper care and education, how many future Charles Mansons will emerge from these statistics? How many, in a new harvest of failure, will echo the words Charles Manson spoke just before being convicted of murder?

... I haven't decided yet what I am or who I am. I was given a name and a number and I was put in a cell and I have lived in a cell with a name and a number.... I never went to school, so I never growed up in the respect to learn, to read and write too good. So I stayed in that jail and I have stayed stupid, and I have stayed a child while I have watched your world grow up.... I have ate out of your garbage cans to stay out of jail. I have wore your second-hand clothes. I have done my best to get along in your world and now you want to kill me.... Ha! I'm already dead, have been dead all my life. I've lived in your tomb that you built. I did seven years for a $37.50 check. I did 12 years because I didn't have any parents.... When you were out riding your bicycle, I was sitting in your cell looking out the window and looking at pictures in magazines and wishing I could go to high school and go to the proms, wishing I could go to the things you could do, but oh so glad, oh so glad, brothers and sisters, that I am what I am.

◆

RACE, GENDER, AND VIOLENCE AGAINST WOMEN: CONVERGENCES, DIVERGENCES AND OTHER BLACK FEMINIST CONUNDRUMS

Kimberlé Crenshaw

I observed the dynamics of structural intersectionality during a brief field study of battered women's shelters on Los Angeles. The physical assault that leads many women to the shelter is often only the tip of the iceberg. Many women who seek protection at shelters are unemployed or underemployed. A good many of them are poor. Shelters dealing with these women cannot afford simply to address the violence inflicted by the batterer apart from the social and economic context in which the battering occurred. Instead, they must also confront the multilayered and more mediated forms of violence that often visit these women's lives. The burdens of illiteracy, child care responsibilities, poverty, and lack of job skills, along with the pervasiveness of discrimination make it much more difficult for women so burdened to establish independence. Securing the most basic necessity of housing is beyond the reach of many of the women. This is not uncommon among the population of women in the shelters given that women with resources are more likely to seek private shelter. Yet even women who have sufficient economic resources often face housing problems because they often encounter severe discrimination on the basis of race, gender, class and family status. This is especially true for African-American women. Similar problems are apparent in employment as well. One worker reported that nearly 85 percent of her clients returned to the battering situation largely because of

difficulties in finding employment and housing. Higher rates of community unemployment also contribute to the problem because battered women may be unable to lean on friends and relatives for temporary shelter. The result for many women is homelessness — nearly 50 percent of homeless women and children are fleeing violence in the home.

These dilemmas illustrate how structures of subordination intersect; battering is only part of the problem. That is, the immediate gender issue intersects with race and class disadvantage in a manner that shapes and often limits the opportunities for effective intervention. In battering, the economic and the cultural contexts exacerbate the general difficulties that abused women face complicating efforts to deal effectively with the violence that awaits them in their homes.

Illustrations of structural intersectionality are apparent in the experiences of immigrant women as well. One way in which immigrant women were made particularly vulnerable to double jeopardy was created by the Marriage Fraud Amendments of the 1986 Immigration Act. This provision required women who immigrate to the United States to marry an American citizen or a permanent resident to wait two years before they receive permanent resident status. Applications for this permanent residence status were to be filed by both spouses. Due to the constraints of the Marriage Fraud

Kimberlé Crenshaw, "Race, Gender, and Violence Against Women: Convergences, Divergences and Other Black Feminist Conundrums" (*forthcoming*), *Stan. L. Rev.* (edited).

Amendments, immigrant women residing in the United States under this conditional status were reluctant to flee from the violence they faced in their homes. When faced with what they believed to be a choice between securing protection from their batterers and protection against deportation, many not unsuprisingly, chose the latter. Women who were deemed by the Act to be conditional residents were thus made especially vulnerable to abuse. Reports of the tragic consequences of this conditional status led to efforts to amend the immigration act to provide an explicit exemption for hardship caused by domestic violence.

In November 1990, Congress amended the Immigration Act to provide a waiver from the requirements for establishing permanent residence to women who were battered or exposed to extreme cruelty by the spouse during their conditional status. Yet, despite the passage of the Act, interventions in violence against immigrant women will continue to be shaped by their immigrant status — if not legally, then socially. First, the very terms upon which the waiver is to be granted may be difficult for many women to satisfy. The evidence required to support a battering or cruelty waiver "can include, but is not limited to, reports and affidavits from police, medical personnel, psychologists, school officials, and social service agencies." Since immigrant women generally have more limited access to these resources, they might be precluded from obtaining a waiver under this section. Moreover community activists, many of whom laud the new Immigration Act of 1990, nonetheless stress that cultural barriers may still bar women from escaping battering situations. Tina Shum, a family counselor at a social service agency, points out that even though "[t]his law sounds easy to apply, there are cultural complications in the Asian community that make even these requirements difficult... Just to find the opportunity

and courage to call us is an accomplishment for many." The typical immigrant spouse, Tina Shum suggests, may live "[i]n an extended family where several generations live together, there may be no privacy on the telephone, no opportunity to leave the house and no understanding of public phones." Moreover, many immigrant women are wholly dependent on their husbands as the link to the world outside their homes. Language barriers, for example, are often critical in limiting opportunities for intervention. Not only do language barriers limit access to information about shelters, they also limit access to the security shelters provide since many shelters turn non-English speaking women away for lack of bilingual resources.

Even immigrant women who do speak English are still vulnerable to their spouse's violence because many depend on their husbands for information regarding their legal status. Many women who are now permanent residents continue to take abuse under the threat that their husbands can have them deported even if they cannot. Finally, although the Marriage Fraud Amendments focus on women whose husbands are permanent residents, one cannot overlook the countless number of women married to undocumented workers who suffer in silence for fear that the security of their entire family will be jeopardized should they seek help or otherwise bring attention to their family.

These illustrations of structural intersectionality suggest that although violence is a common issue among women, such violence usually occurs within a specific context that often varies considerably depending on the race, class, and other social characteristics of the woman. I do not mean to imply that other women are not constrained in numerous ways from seeking some end to the cycle of violence they experience. Rather, my point is that these constraints can be better understood and addressed through a framework that links them to broader structures of subordination which intersect, sometimes in fairly predict-able ways. These intersections limit the util-ity of interventions that are not constructed with them in mind.

♦

MAKING AN ISSUE OF CHILD ABUSE
Barbara Nelson

The date was March 26, 1973. The weather in Washington, D.C., was rainy and mild. On this typical early spring day a very atypical event was under way. Senator Walter F. Mondale (D., Minn.), an erstwhile presidential candidate, was holding the first day of hearings on his Child Abuse Prevention Act. Never before had Congress demonstrated so great a con-cern for child abuse. These hearings were proof to all who were interested that child abuse was firmly established on the con-gressional agenda. The hearings began at 9:30 A.M. in the wood-paneled offices of the Dirksen Building. Second among the witnesses, and the most riveting, was "Jolly K.," founder of Parents Anony-mous. Mondale asked her if she had abused her child:

> "Yes, I did, to the point of almost causing death several times.... It was extreme serious physical abuse.... Once I threw a rather large kitchen knife at her and another time I stran-gled her because she lied to me.... This was up to when she was 6–½ years old.... It was ongoing. It was continuous.
> "I had gone to ten county and State facilities. Out of those, all but one were very realistic places to turn to. Six of

them were social services, protective service units.... Even the most ignorant listeners could have picked up what I was saying, that I was abusing [my daughter], and that I was directly ask-ing for mental health services.... I wanted to keep my child. I wanted to get rid of my problem. She wasn't the problem. She was the recipient of my behavior."

Senator Jennings Randolph (D., W. Va.) turned the questioning to Jolly K.'s experience with Parents Anonymous, the self-help group for abusive parents styled after Alcoholics Anonymous (AA). Like AA, Parents Anonymous encourages abu-sive parents to talk about their fears and frustrations with childrearing, and their guilt and anguish over the harm members have caused their children. Randolph went straight to the political heart of the matter, asking how successful Parents Anony-mous was in eliminating further abuse and keeping children at home. Happily, Randolph learned of the program's success:

> "Most of them have the children in the home. Most of them have the symptomatic behavior of abuse now removed...."

Barbara Nelson, *Making an Issue of Child Abuse* (Chicago: University of Chicago Press, 1984), pp. 1–18.

"We encourage parents to utilize us until they feel comfortable enough to go out and utilize other existing services.... where they can work more deeply with internal problems.

Jolly K. was the perfect witness, cutting through academic pieties to convince the assembled senators, witnesses, and journalists of the gravity of the problem. She was, figuratively, a sinner who had repented and been saved by her own hard work and the loving counsel of her friends. But more importantly, she embodied the American conception of a social problem: individually rooted, described as an illness, and solvable by occasional doses of therapeutic conversation.

Senator Mondale encouraged this conventional understanding of the problem. Any more elaborate view, especially one which focused on injustice as a source of social problems, threatened to scuttle his efforts to move this small piece of categorical legislation through Congress. With able maneuvering, Mondale's approach prevailed, and on January 31, 1974, President Richard M. Nixon signed the Child Abuse Prevention and Treatment Act (CAPTA) into law. The legislation authorized $86 million to be spent over the next three and a half years, mostly on research and demonstration projects, though some funds were earmarked for discretionary social service grants to the states.

Eighty-six million dollars for child abuse, a problem which did not even warrant an entry in the *Readers' Guide to Periodical Literature* until 1968! How did this happen? Or, asked more elaborately, how did child abuse, a small, private-sector charity concern, become a multimillion-dollar public social welfare issue? This book tries to provide an answer. It is a study of the politics of child abuse and

neglect, a history and analysis of political issue creation and agenda setting.

The book has three broad aims. *The first aim is, of course, to recount the history of child abuse policy-making over the last three decades.* The story begins in 1955 with the renewed efforts of the American Humane Association (AHA), a charitable organization engaged in research on child and animal maltreatment, to ascertain the extent of physical child abuse and the adequacy of governmental response. The AHA shared its findings with the U.S. Children's Bureau, which in 1963 proposed a model statute to encourage reporting of physical child abuse. Other organizations as diverse as the American Academy of Pediatrics and the Council of State Legislatures proposed different model reporting laws. Bombarded with model statutes and facing no opposition, state legislatures passed child abuse reporting laws with dizzying speed. The demand for services, or at least the demand for workable service models, encouraged Mondale to sponsor federal legislation in 1973; legislation which was successful despite opposition from the Nixon administration. That legislation appeared to be untouchable until President Ronald Reagan was elected and stripped social programs bare in an attempt to balance the budget and shift the initiative for solving social problems to the private sector.

But the history of child abuse policy-making is also a vehicle for the discussion of political agenda setting more generally, this book's second aim. E.E. Schattschneider, the dean of agenda-setting studies by virtue of his classic work *The Semi-Sovereign People*, asserted that the most important decisions made in any polity were those determining which issues would become part of public discourse. "Some issues are organized into politics while others are organized out," Schattschneider said with the economy.

This book tries to elaborate the process by which issues get "organized into politics." It is an attempt to advance our understanding of the first step of the policy process, the step where those issues which *will* receive governmental attention are chosen from among those issues which *could* receive governmental attention.

The third aim of the book is to discuss what I call "the public way of private deviance." My interest here is to link child abuse with other issues dealing with violence and personal autonomy (e.g., rape, domestic violence, incest, sexual abuse, and attacks on the elderly) which have recently become part of the governmental agenda. Like child abuse, each of these issues was accepted as a proper concern of government in part because it was represented as deviance improperly protected by the privacy of the family. But the focus on deviance — and medical deviance at that — turned policymakers away from considering the social-structural and social-psychological underpinnings of abuse and neglect. The advantages and limitations of the deviance approach, which are essentially the advantages and limitations of liberal reform, constitute the third theme.

The book focuses on decision-making in governmental organizations. I am most interested in the process whereby public officials learn about new problems, decide to give them their personal attention, and mobilize their organizations to respond to them. Of course, this process is influenced by the type of problems considered and the organizational and political milieu in which officials work. Thus the book will give particular attention to the fact that during the agenda-setting process child abuse was vigorously portrayed as a noncontroversial issue. Disagreements about how best to respond to abuse were suppressed, along with the great debate over the extent to which government ought properly to intervene in family matters. These conflicts became much more apparent as the political climate grew more conservative in the late 1970s and early 1980s. Indeed, government's attention to child abuse in the post World War II period must be understood as part of a larger concern with equity and social justice. So too the movement away from governmental responsibility for child protection should be viewed as part of a larger concern with governmental efficiency and traditional patterns of family authority.

The book is organized chronologically, presenting three case studies of agenda setting in governmental institutions, and an analysis of the role of the mass and professional media. Chapter 2 discusses the theoretical approaches to agenda setting, expanding and linking the organizational, interest group, and economic literature. Chapter 3 shows how the first contemporary governmental interest in child abuse arose through communication between the American Humane Association and the U.S. Children's Bureau. Chapter 4 makes the connection between governmental response to child abuse and popular awareness of the problem, and illuminates the varying roles played by the professional and mass media in making the public aware of child abuse. Chapter 5 presents the states' response to child abuse. Here we shall discuss the rapid adoption of child abuse reporting laws — all fifty states passed legislation in only five years — as well as present a case study of the passage of New Jersey's first reporting law. Chapter 6 considers how Congress became aware of popular and professional interest in abuse and chose to do something about it. Chapter 7, the last chapter, reviews the findings about agenda setting and concludes with an assessment of the future of the public use of private deviance. The remainder of this chapter sets the stage by defining social problems, discussing the invention of child abuse as a social problem, presenting the difficulties in defining and measuring abuse, and elaborating on the theme of the public use of private deviance.

THE INVENTION OF CHILD ABUSE

Defining Social Problems

Examples of the brutal or neglectful treatment of children are found as far back as records have been kept. But the mere existence of a condition like cruelty to children does not mean that every society which witnessed abuse condemned it, although some individuals may have. A social problem goes beyond what a few, or even many, individuals feel privately: a social problem is a social construct. Its "creation" requires not only that a number of individuals feel a conflict of value over what is and what ought to be, but also that individuals organize to change the condition, and achieve at least a modicum of recognition for their efforts from the wider public.

The social problem we know as child abuse is a product of America's Gilded era. Until the 1870s maltreatment of white children was not a part of public debate. Extreme brutality was handled by the court on a case-by-case basis. Less severe cases may have upset the neighbors, but childrearing decisions were considered the prerogative of parents, particularly fathers.

What happened, then, to make the public think of abuse as a social problem? The answer rests in part with the "Mary Ellen" case, a rather grisly instance of abuse which received widespread publicity in New York in 1874. A "friendly visitor" discovered that the girl had regularly been bound and beaten by her stepmother. Outrage over the incident precipitated the forming of the New York Society for the Prevention of Cruelty to Children, the first child protection association in the country.

A single incident, however momentous, does not guarantee that concerned individuals will view the event as an example of a larger problem, and organize to solve it. To bring a problem to light requires leadership to create the groups necessary to act, and a cultural willingness to accept the problem as defined. Sociologist Neil Smelser calls this latter requirement "structural readiness for change." The requirement of structural readiness does not mean, of course, that if certain conditions are not defined as problems the time is simply not right for recognition. Repression keeps certain conditions from being defined as problems. Nonetheless, the creation of a social problem does require some public receptivity.

The idea of a "protected childhood" provided the cultural backdrop necessary for the acceptance of abuse as a social problem. Cruelty to children, especially by parents, appeared much more troublesome when contrasted with the "modern" image of childhood as a safe and sheltered period of life. Scholars have offered a number of rather different explanations for the creation of the modern family and its reverence for childhood. Phillipe Ariès suggests that the transformation of formal education under the Scholastics, the idea of privacy, and the rise of a partly urban, commercial society, conjoined to initiate the affective family and attention to childhood as a separate time of life deserving of protection. Lawrence Stone proposes another explanation. The rise of "affective individualism" in the West produced a bourgeois family based on friendship and sentiment.

Both Ariès and Stone locate the origins of the modern family in the bourgeoisie. In contrast, Edward Shorter locates the origin of the modern family in changes in village culture. Technological innovations which allowed capital surplus freed villagers from patriarchal village mores and permitted the development of "familiar empathy."

Though they disagree on many points, these explanations all concur with the idea that in the modern family, normal, correct childrearing excludes excessive violence or gross inattention. In America, belief in a protected childhood was the product of three forces — natural rights ideology, commitment to civic education, and the increasing number of bourgeois families — which converged in the post-Civil War period. During Radical Reconstruction natural rights ideology, with its commitment to equality, drew a growing number of supporters. Its rhetoric frequently extended natural rights to animals and children. Elbridge T. Gerry, one of the founders of the New York Society for the Prevention of Cruelty to Children, was an advocate of this position. In 1882 he wrote that "at the present day in this country, children have *some* rights, which even parents are bound to respect," sentiments much less evident a century earlier.

Those who might not fully support the notion of the natural rights of children could still see the wisdom of educating children for citizenship. Indeed, America's experiment in republican government produced a long-standing commitment to civic education. But after the Civil War the support for civic education in part superceded older, more traditional educational concerns. Childhood was no longer seen only as the time to form a moral adult, but also the time to forge a separate citizen of the republic. Historian Stanley N. Katz nicely summarizes this transformation:

> Philip Greven has graphically described how evangelical and even moderate colonial Americans self-consciously set out to subdue their children's independence and to make them conform to the dictates of divine law and parental wisdom. So long as salvation was generally perceived as dependent upon conversion, it was obviously the parents' highest duty so to treat their children. For the Rousseauian modern parent, however, precisely the opposite was indicated. For them the child was a fragile flower to be cultivated, nourished and appreciated so that its finest qualities could realize their potential. The discovery of childhood and an optimistic view of child psychology thus transformed child-parent relations.

The increasing number of bourgeois families, where the wife and children did not work for wages, gave substance to this view. A protected childhood became a standard by which well-to-do families could measure the social adequacy and integration of less fortunate families. Well-to-do activists, who could afford to provide such protection for their children, organized child protective societies beginning in the 1870s. But as we shall see later, they were immediately confronted by the unsettling observation that economic conditions constrained many parents from providing such protection for their children.

The Mary Ellen Case

The first child protection society was formed in 1874, in response to the notorious Mary Ellen Wilson case. Mary Ellen's plight was crushingly Victorian. She lived in the home of Francis and Mary Connolly, but she was not the blood relative of either, being the illegitimate daughter of Mrs. Connolly's first husband, Thomas McCormack, and Fanny Wilson. A neighbor noticed that Mrs. Connolly treated the child brutally, beating her with a leather thong and allowing her to go ill-clothed in bad weather. The neighbor told Mrs. Etta Angell Wheeler, a "friendly visitor," who then went to Henry Bergh, the founder of the American Society for the Prevention of Cruelty to Animals (ASPCA) to ask if the ASPCA could help the child.

The popular version of Bergh's response reports that Bergh successfully argued in court that Mary Ellen ought to be removed from her cruel guardians because she, as a member of the animal kingdom, deserved the same protection as abused animals. Actually, the case was argued by Bergh's friend and counsel, Elbridge T. Gerry, who had Mary Ellen removed from her unwholesome surroundings by a petition for a writ *de homine replegando*, an old English writ for removing a person from the custody of another. The case was a staple in New York newspapers for months, no doubt aided by the fact that Mrs. Wheeler's husband was a journalist. In December 1874 the New York Society for the Prevention of Cruelty to Children (New York SPCC) was formed, with Gerry, who had successfully removed Mary Ellen from her home and won a prison sentence for her stepmother, as the moving force.

Gerry and his friends had a ready model for action when the Mary Ellen case came to their attention: the British and American animal protection societies. Animal protection societies were first formed in England in 1824. Henry Bergh, who founded the American SPCA in 1866, explicitly used the Royal British SPCA as his guide. When not ignored, both the English and American SPCAs were objects of laughter and scorn. Only the meat-packing industry, whose unsanitary and cruel practices were often attacked, ever paid them much attention. Indeed, the important role of the animal protective societies in promoting sanitary meat and milk processing has largely been forgotten today, when we remember the SPCAs only as the perfect example of frivolous Victorian do-gooding.

In 1870, at Bergh's invitation, Gerry became counsel for the ASPCA. Though fourteen years separated them, Bergh and Gerry had similar careers. Both came from prominent Protestant families which provided them with private incomes, both attended Columbia University, both practiced law, and both were devoted to a vision of rational Christian social improvement. Their friends and acquaintances included the political and social leaders of New York City and State. It is no wonder, then, that when Mary Ellen's plight became known to them, one of their responses was to call a meeting.

The Rise of Protective Societies

The objective of the New York SPCC was to rescue children from situations which imperiled their morals, safety, health, or welfare — pretty much in that order. The New York Society's emphasis was on child rescue rather than family rehabilitation. It created for itself a police and placement function whereby it identified and prosecuted abusers, referring the children it "saved" to large child-minded institutions. It is often assumed that the New York SPCC usurped the policelike powers it wielded, but this is completely untrue. Rather, the cruelty and neglect statute passed by the New York legislature in 1881 at the Society's request made it a misdemeanor to interfere with the work of designated child protection agents. As a consequence the Society had enormous power over the poor families it monitored, even if it did help many children out of dangerous situations.

The New York SPCC's emphasis on controlling the poor is perhaps best portrayed by the engravings (and later photographs) depicting children "before" and "after" the Society's intervention. The *Annual Report* of 1876 shows two engravings of Ellen Conners. In the "before" picture, the child is portrayed as wild, ragged, badly cut about the face, and rather suspiciously scratching her genitals. In the "after" picture, Ellen is sweetly dressed in layer upon layer of fashionable clothes, and her hands, far from being anywhere near her crotch, are decorously hidden in a rabbit-fur muff. The emphasis on personal control in the engraving reflects the social goals of the organization: "These little waifs of society were destined to become the fathers and mothers of this Republic. If they were neglected the permanent interest of the Republic would be neglected."

Not all SPCCs ran on the child rescue model favored by the New York Society. The Philadelphia and Illinois (Chicago) SPCCs responded more to problems of drunkenness, desertion, or neglect than to physical abuse of children. These SPCCs (as well as the New York Society) ran temporary shelters where women and children could find a brief respite from violence or economic distress. The Massachusetts (Boston) SPCC was among the first of the protective societies to em-

phasize "family rehabilitation." Its members worked to bring about the social, political, and economic changes necessary to relieve "destitution." The child rescue and family rehabilitation approaches were at war for almost forty years. The old-line Scientific Charity advocates favored child rescue, which often separated parents and children. The Progressives, on the other hand, promoted the family rehabilitation view, which kept the child at home or in a homelike setting.

The Decline of Protective Societies

The family rehabilitation approach ultimately won. Many reasons are offered for its victory, most centering on the philosophical tenets of the Progressives. The Progressives, with their commitment to childhood as a stage of physical and civic development, felt that normal childhood was childhood in a home and thus the breakup of the family was not favored. To implement their beliefs, the Progressives encouraged the creation of a familylike setting in the juvenile courts and argued that the state had a positive duty to protect women and children. Progressives dismantled the poorhouse, fought against child labor, and encouraged mothers' pensions.

The power of the family centered response to child welfare was best demonstrated at the first White House Conference on Dependent Children in 1909, whose report stated unequivocally that

> home life is the highest and finest product of civilization. It is the great molding force of mind and of character. Children should not be deprived of it except for urgent and compelling reasons. Children of parents of worthy character, suffering

from temporary misfortune and children of reasonably efficient and deserving mothers who are without the support of the normal breadwinner, should, as a rule, be kept with their parents, such aid being given as may be necessary to maintain suitable homes for the rearing of the children.

The Conference also supported the establishment of a federal Children's Bureau, a proposal first introduced in Congress in 1906. The Progressives further urged that child protection become a responsibility of public child welfare departments, and in this they were often supported by socially minded SPCCs like the Massachusetts Society. In 1923, C.C. Carstens, once the secretary of the Massachusetts SPCC and later director of the Child Welfare League of America, wrote that only half of the more than 800 humane societies formed since 1874 had survived, and many of them were only limping along.

But the decline of SPCCs and the eclipse of cruelty as a separate problem of child welfare can be explained by the operation of large institutions as much as by the philosophical beliefs of the Progressives. These organizational reasons have gone largely unnoticed until now. The child rescue approach was made possible by the previous existence of large, asylumlike institutions which would accept the rescued child. But in the 1870s and 1880s the "placing out" system (i.e., foster care), which assigned children to willing and interested families, began competing with orphanages.

The increasing popularity of the "placing out" method had enormous consequences for the SPCCs, whose special function originally had been to identify and refer children. When one more child was added to an orphanage, the personality or characteristics of that child were not terribly important to the functioning of the institution. To say the least, institutional care in the late nineteenth century did not promote individualism among children. But when a child was referred for placing out, the characteristics of the child were very important. The family which took the child had to deal with him or her as an individual. "Placing out" agencies thus wanted desperately to control the composition of their clientele.

As public agencies began taking over such functions, they too wanted to do their own casefinding. Programmatic success required that public child welfare agencies pick which clients they would serve. In this light the reasons for the decline of SPCCs become clearer. For organizational as well as philosophical reasons, other agencies were opposed to the SPCCs' avowed function of casefinding. Only in place like New York City, with its firmly entrenched child-minding institutions, did the traditional SPCCs survive. Elsewhere their work was incorporated into public child welfare agencies.

The longevity of the New York SPCC was also aided by a well-established contract system which dispensed public money to private institutions for the care of poor, abused, neglected, or wayward children. Homer Folks estimated that in 1890 the New York SPCC "practically controlled the lives of an average number of about fifteen thousand children, and an average annual expenditure for their support of more than one and one half million dollars. Its influence has done more to strengthen and perpetuate the subsidy or contract system, as it existed prior to 1894, than any other one factor." The large institutions and the New York SPCC formed a partnership wherein the SPCC found children, the orphanages provided the care, and the state supplied a constant stream of funds. Opposition to this arrangement came from the fact that it encouraged institutional care, not that it lacked accountability for the spending of public monies. The potential exploitation of a per capita billing system went largely unrecognized. The main management problem, as seen by Josephine Shaw Lowell, was access by the State Board of Charities for inspection of the institutions for health code violations.

The experience of the New York SPCC was unusual, however, and even its power declined with the Great Depression. By World War II, the SPCC movement was completely enervated nationwide. The pressing needs of children displaced by war drove protective work even further into the social services backwater.

The Rediscovery of Child Abuse

By the 1950s, public interest in abuse and neglect was practically nonexistent, and even socialworkers did not rate it highly as a professional concern. How were these issues rediscovered and ultimately adopted as problems which government should help to solve? The specific answers to these questions need to be understood in their historical context.

The rediscovery of child abuse occurred in an era when issues of equity and social responsibility dominated public discourse. A long period of concern with a variety of equity issues began with the civil rights movement in the mid and late 1950s. The 1962 amendments to the Social Security Act urging child welfare services in every county demonstrated that the interests of children were part of the equity cycle. The child welfare amendments were followed by the "War on Poverty," which emphasized the importance of services to children as a method of

eliminating poverty. In 1967 the equity cycle was given tremendous impetus by the Supreme Court's *In Re Gault* opinion, which extended Bill of Rights protection to children. Later, the months spent crafting the Comprehensive Child Development Act (ultimately vetoed by President Nixon) educated members of Congress to the centrality (and difficulty) of providing adequately for the needs of all children.

Not unimportantly, this equity cycle coincided with years of great economic prosperity. Real GNP doubled between 1950 and 1970. Consequently, the material gains of one group did not appear to threaten the gains of others. It was a time when politics seemed to exist without trade-offs.

The concern for children was not limited to government. Pediatricians, the most prestigious group dealing with youngsters, enjoyed two decades of notable success in conquering deadly childhood diseases. With the ability to cure or prevent many children's diseases, pediatricians had the status, skills, and the slack resources to invest in research on problems which were at least party behavioral in origin.

But it was the work of radiologists like John Caffey, P.V. Woolley, and W.A. Evans which alerted pediatricians to the specific problem of abuse. In 1946 Caffey first reported a number of cases in which infants had multiple long bone fractures and subdural hematomas. He did not, however, speculate on the causes of trauma. In 1953, Woolley and Evans suggested that similar injuries might be caused by the children's caretakers. In 1957, Caffey reexamined his original data and concluded that the trauma might well have been willfully perpetrated by parents. It took almost a decade for physicians to conclude that some parents were violently assaulting their children, a delay caused by professional cautiousness and a profound psychological resistance to recognizing that some parental behavior departed so radically from the ideal.

This research, as well as the early work done by socialworkers, was well known to pediatricians like C. Henry Kempe and his colleagues, who were investigating the causes as well as the appropriate responses to physical abuse. In 1962 they published their famous article "The Battered-Child Syndrome" in the prestigious *Journal of American Medical Association.* Within weeks of its publication, stories on child abuse were featured in popular magazines like *Time* and the *Saturday Evening Post.* The publication of the Kempe article is often used to date the rediscovery of child abuse as a social problem. But in point of fact, the popular articles based on Kempe's research were equally important in creating the sense of an urgent national problem.

DEFINING AND MEASURING CHILD ABUSE AND NEGLECT

Problems of Definition

The first people to identify a problem often shape how others will perceive it. Nowhere is this truer than with the issue of child abuse. In "The Battered-Child Syndrome" Kempe and his associates define the problem as "a clinical condition in young children who received serious physical abuse, generally from a parent or foster parent." Based on a survey of the literature and an examination of 302 cases reported in 71 hospitals, the authors suggested that abusers had serious psychological problems but were not psychopaths:

> Psychiatric factors are probably of prime importance in the pathogene-

sis of the disorder, but our knowledge of these factors is limited. Parents who inflict abuse on their children do not necessarily have psychopathic or sociopathic personalities or come from borderline socioeconomic groups, although most published cases have been in these categories. *In most cases some defect of character structure is probably present; often parents may be repeating the type of child care practiced on them.*

The individually centered psychological construction of the problem made it seem very self-contained. Governmental response to a self-contained, serious, but noncontroversial issue ought to be easy to obtain. And easy it was. Once alerted to the problem, the U.S. Children's Bureau and other organizations drafted model child abuse reporting laws which were rapidly passed by all state legislatures. The speed of adoption rested largely on this narrow construction of the problem. The early California reporting statute reflected this view. Child abuse was defined as "physical injuries or injury which appear to have been inflicted upon [the child] by other than accidental means."

Almost as quickly as this narrow view took substance in the law, it was replaced by a more comprehensive construction of the problem. As scholars in a number of fields examined the problem, the socioeconomic considerations of child abuse — its connection to joblessness, inadequate housing, and other chronic social ills — became evident and popular. (Interestingly, gender and power considerations were absent from most of this analysis.) In 1974, the federal Child Abuse Prevention and Treatment Act (CAPTA) incorporated a fairly comprehensive definition of the problem.

CAPTA defines child abuse and neglect together:

> "Child Abuse and Neglect" means the physical or mental injury, sexual abuse, negligent treatment, or maltreatment of any child under the age of eighteen by a person who is responsible for the child's welfare under circumstances which indicate the child's health or welfare is harmed or threatened thereby.

The definition of child abuse found in CAPTA provides a more comprehensive statement of the problem than one might expect after reading the transcripts of the legislative hearings. In the public debate over the congressional legislation, comprehensive definitions were actively suppressed in order to enhance the noncontroversial nature of the issue.

In fact, at each point when child abuse achieved a governmental agenda, the narrow definition was emphasized. The narrow definition predominated during agenda setting for three related reasons. First, agenda setting by the Children's Bureau and state legislatures occurred while the narrow definition was still quite popular. Second, physicians preferred the narrow definition because it best fit their experiences in hospital emergency rooms, and physicians, by virtue of their high status, had easy and early access to officials. Third and most important, a narrow definition of abuse reduced conflict, particularly from right-wing critics. The use of a narrow definition thwarted a potential conservative challenge to what might be seen as governmental action against normal parental discipline.

Favoring the narrow definition during agenda setting had important, long-lasting effects on the shape of child abuse policy. By ignoring neglect, the connection between poverty and maltreatment was purposely blurred. In fact, strenuous efforts were made to popularize abuse as a problem knowing no barriers of class, race, or culture. For some politicians, particularly Mondale, this was part of a conscious strategy to dissociate efforts against abuse from unpopular poverty programs. The purpose was to describe abuse as an all-American affliction, not one found solely among low-income people. While acknowledging that abuse and neglect were found in all strata of society, a number of scholars severely criticized this approach and maintained that the larger number of cases found among the poor was not only a function of reporting biases, but was present because poor people actually abused or neglected their children more. The message of the research was not that poor people were bad people or bad parents, but that the deprivations of poverty were real and encouraged abuse. These findings were very unpopular, however, and the "myth of classlessness" promoted during agenda setting was very difficult to counter.

Measuring Child Abuse

No one actually knows the extent of child abuse and neglect, or whether their incidence is increasing or decreasing. At the National Conference for Family Violence Researchers, Professor Richard Gelles summed up the difficulties in measuring abuse and neglect: "We don't know a *damn* thing about whether child abuse is increasing, decreasing or staying the same." It is not merely the lack of a commonly agreed-upon definition which hinders counting but also problems of methodology — of criteria, applications, and evidence — which make the task so difficult. Not surprisingly, the numbers vary widely. One of the lowest estimates comes from a *Pediatric News* (1975) report suggesting that one child dies of abuse every day, yielding a yearly incidence of 365 deaths. Using national survey data, David Gil (1970) offers a much higher figure, but for a different phenomenon. Gil suggests that for the year ending in October 1965, between 2.53 and 4.07 million American adults *knew* of physically abusive families which Richard Light (1974) statistically adjusted to reach his estimate of approximately 500,000 cases of physical abuse during the year under study.

From a public policy perspective, two estimates have been more important than all the others: one "guess" in an early medical article and the official reporting statistics gathered over the last several years. In fact, this early medical "guess" did not even mention statistics. Instead child abuse was described as possibly more life-threatening than a host of well-known and feared childhood diseases. The story of the nonnumerical estimate bears telling because it shows how powerful a credible source can be in defining the extent of a social problem, even when that source offers no figures whatsoever.

In 1962, Dr. C. Henry Kempe and his associates published their famous article "The Battered-Child Syndrome" in the *Journal of the American Medical Association*. In an accompanying editorial, the country's most powerful arbiters of medical knowledge wrote that "it is likely that [the battered child syndrome] will be found to be a more frequent cause of death than such well recognized and thoroughly studied diseases as leukemia, cystic fibrosis, and muscular dystrophy." The editors were merely speculating about the extent of abuse and qualified all their comparisons. Politicians and journalists were not always as careful. Official after official and article after article repeated the comparison as though it were fact.

The consistency with which the AMA *Journal's* editorial was cited was probably more important that its accuracy. Gilbert Y. Steiner suggests that where estimates of problem size differ substantially, it is difficult to establish the legitimacy of the problem. He noted that the differing estimates of the size of the problem of domestic violence (ranging from 7.5 million to 526,000 episodes a year) allowed detractors to chip away at congressional support. Modest and consistent estimates seem to inspire the most confidence, especially in cases of the public response to private deviance. Deviance can only exist as such if there is not too much of it.

The official reporting statistics, the second important measure of child abuse, do not indicate a modest problem at all. In 1979, the Child Protection Division of the American Human Association compiled all the official abuse and neglect reports made in the fifty states and the territories. Nationwide there were 711,142 official reports of maltreatment, but the type of maltreatment could only be discerned in 234,000 of the reports. Of these, 25.1 percent were designated solely as abuse. Of course, there is a certain amount of comparing apples and oranges in the compilation of these figures. No uniform legal definition exists, and case-counting procedures differ markedly from state to state. Nonetheless, these figures give us some sense of the magnitude of the problem as understood by officials, regardless of how many or what kind of cases are not reported.

These official figures have been used to promote and maintain interest in the problem. Similar figures were paraded during the first CAPTA reauthorization hearings in 1977 and again in 1981 to show the magnitude of the problem. These numbers are susceptible to political manipulation in an era of social service cutbacks. If reporting is lax and service positions go unstaffed, the number of cases will eventually fall off as concerned individuals concede the futility of reporting. If the numbers decline, then the problem can be described as waning, perhaps even as disappearing because of the application of a measured dose of governmental intervention. Lower numbers, in turn, can be used to justify lower expenditures, in a widening circle of verbal deceit and programmatic despair.

THE PUBLIC USE OF PRIVATE DEVIANCE

Neglect and abuse are so common that it ought to be hard to maintain the image that they are rare, deviant behaviors. But the construction of this problem as one of medical deviance has proven extraordinarily durable. Because physicians played such a large role in setting governmental and media agendas, the first public presentation of the problem was as a social illness. The considerations of power politics are rarely added to the discussion, perhaps because "power" is a public word and "child abuse" is understood to be a private problem.

Many behaviors with significantly aggressive or violent components have been similarly "medicalized." In addition to child abuse, examples include alcoholism, drug abuse, hyperkinesis, and to a lesser degree rape and domestic violence. Earlier in this century alcoholism was variously considered a sin, a crime, or a labor discipline problem, but now it is most often described as a disease. Similar transformations have overtaken drug abuse and hyperkinesis. Rape and domestic violence have been more resistant to this reconstruction, however. Their obvious power connotations limit the applicability of medical metaphors, and thus limit the likelihood of government's adopting the is-

sues. This is not to say that governmental action is necessarily the best way to respond to rape and domestic violence. Instead, the point is that government more readily adopts issues which are constructed as social illness than issues which confront long-established power arrangements.

There are two explanations of the trend toward constructing social problems concerning aggression and violence in terms of medical deviance. The first reason — little discussed in the social policy literature — is that one model of conventional illnesses is constructed on statistical deviation from population norms. In describing this approach to illness David Mechanic writes:

> Doctors frequently can recognize disease because it becomes apparent that in various ways the patient deviates from "normal values." In many cases the range of normal values has been established through observations of community populations over a period of time and thus marked deviations can easily be determined.

In the case of behaviors rather than physical functioning, it is quite easy to assert that particular actions diverge from the measured — or even assumed — norm. With the rise of the concept of mental illness in this century, practically any disvalued behavior can be defined as medical deviance. In fact, merely by its being statistically rare a behavior can become disvalued and subject to medical response.

The second reason for constructing some problems in terms of medical deviance is that medicine offers solutions to these problems, solutions which in the short run appear to be — and often are — humane and caring. Medicine professes to have solutions — ranging from psychotropic drugs, to therapy, to the mental hospital — which are supposed to treat rather than punish the sick person. Medical solutions both maintain and promote the power of medicine and medical professionals while simultaneously reassuring us that we live in a humanitarian rather than a punitive or repressive society.

The political advantages of the construction of social problems as medical deviance are easy to see. Medicine views illness as individual in location if not cause, so a medical construction is consonant with the American individualistic approach to solving problems. By defining problems in terms of medical deviance, the status quo is maintained, at least in the short run.

The political limitations of the medical deviance approach are also obvious. Individualizing problems turns policymakers away from considering their structural causes. Policies which "treat" medical deviance no doubt help thousands of people, but they do so at the cost of expanding state intervention without increasing the state's ability to redress the fundamental inequities which underlie, say, abuse and neglect. Conservative critics then bemoan the loss of family autonomy and liberal critics bemoan the band-aid quality of public efforts, particularly the fact that public monies are not targeted where the problem is most severe and pressing. So-

cialist critics add that individually centered responses to social problems are designed to maintain existing power relations.

The people who promoted governmental interest in child abuse were mostly social welfare liberals, although the construction of the problem encouraged support across the political spectrum. They saw child abuse as a public health matter, with implications much like those of venereal disease. The case for state action was made on the grounds that child abuse was a social illness which had been improperly protected by the private status of the family. The government used the notion of medical deviance as the rationale for intervening in the family — hence the phrase "the public use of private deviance." At the same time government reaffirmed the essential split between the public and private spheres. Theorists like Zillah Eisenstein suggest that such actions eventually destabilize the liberal state and work to break down the public-private distinction which such policies intend to uphold. The bureaucrats and legislators who promoted an interest in child abuse did not take such a long-sighted view, however. They believed that governmental action would aid the afflicted even if only modestly. They gave child abuse their professional attention, and then went about their jobs.

Responding to Violence and Neglect

A range of responses to family violence and neglect includes private shelters, legal theories about learned helplessness, and legal claims enforceable by judges who themselves need training to understand and respond to family violence. Each of the responses has triggered a round of criticisms and reforms of the reforms. When a new issue hits the public agenda, issues such as drug and alcohol exposure to infants prior to birth, how should the law respond? Should existing legal rules authorizing state officials to charge a parent with abuse or neglect be deployed — or should new programs or responses be crafted?

♦

FOR SHELTER AND BEYOND
Massachusetts Coalition of Battered Women Service Groups

LETTER FROM A
BATTERED WOMAN

The following is a letter from a battered woman who attended a presentation on battering:

You will never be able to realize how it felt to sit there looking like a well-dressed, middle-class woman knowing that you were talking about me. It was the very first time I have ever heard anyone say that I wasn't for being beaten!

You asked help from any woman who is subjected to this horrible form of physical abuse. You asked for anonymous case histories given to someone by the battered wife. I have no one to give a history to, as there isn't anyone who knows about the situation well enough to be confided in.

I will give you my own experiences at first hand and hope that it will be useful to you.

I am presently married to the man who beats me so I will have to remain unidentified.

There is so much to say. Most has never been said before. It is very difficult.

I am in my thirties and so is my husband. I have a high school education and am presently attending a local college trying to find the education I need for support. My husband is a college graduate and a professional in his field. We are both attractive people and for the most part respected and well-liked. We have three children and live in a middle-class home with all the comforts one could possibly want.

I have everything, except life without fear.

For the most part of married life I have been periodically beaten by my husband. What do I mean by "beaten"? I mean those times when parts of my body have been hit violently and repeatedly causing painful bruises, swellings, bleeding wounds, unconsciousness, and any combination of those things.

Beating should be distinguished from being hit and shoved around, which I define as all other physical abuse which does not result in a beating.

And let me clarify what I mean when I refer to threats of abuse. I am not talking about a man warning me that he may lose control. I'm talking specifically about a fist shaking against my face or nose, a punching-bag jab at my shoulder, or any gesture which threatens me with the possibility of a beating.

Massachusetts Coalition of Battered Women Service Groups, *For Shelter and Beyond, An Educational Manual for Working with Women Who Are Battered* (excerpts).

I have had glasses thrown at me. I have been kicked in the abdomen when I was visibly pregnant. I have been kicked off the bed and hit while laying on the floor — while I was pregnant. I have been whipped, kicked and thrown, picked up and thrown down again. I have been punched and kicked in the head, face and abdomen on numerous occasions.

I have been slapped for saying something about politics, having a different view about religion, for swearing, for crying, for wanting to have intercourse.

I have been threatened when I wouldn't do something I was told to do. I have been threatened when he's had a bad day — when he's had a good day.

I have been beaten, slapped and threatened when I have stated bitterly that I didn't like what he was doing with another woman.

Each time my husband has left the house and remained gone for days.

Few people have ever seen my black and blue face or swollen lips because I have always stayed indoors feeling ashamed.

I was never able to drive after one of these beatings, so I could not get myself to a hospital for care. I could never have left my young children alone and I certainly could not have left them alone even when I could have driven.

Hysteria sets in after a beating. This hysteria — the shaking and crying and mumbling — is not accepted by anyone so there has never been anyone to call.

My husband on a few occasions did call a day or so later to provide me with an excuse which I could use for returning to work, the grocery store, the dentist appointment, and so on. I used the excuses — a car accident, oral surgery, things like that.

Now the first response which I myself think of is, "Why didn't you seek help?"

I did. I went early in our marriage to a clergyman who after a few visits told me that my husband meant no real harm, he was just confused and felt insecure. I was to be more tolerant and understanding. Most important I was to forgive him the beatings just as Christ had forgiven me from the cross. I did.

Things continued. I turned this time to a doctor. I was given little pills to relax me and told to take things a little easier. I was "just too nervous."

I turned to a friend and when her husband found out he accused me of either making things up or exaggerating the situation. She was told to stay away from me. (She didn't but she could no longer help.)

I turned to a professional family guidance agency, was told there that he needed help and I should find a way to control the incidents. I couldn't control the beating — that was his decision. I was asked to defend myself against the suspicion that I wanted to be hit, invited a beating. Good God! Did the Jews invite themselves to be slaughtered in Germany?

I did go to doctors on two occasions. One asked me what I had done to provoke him and the other asked if we had made up yet.

I called the police one time. They not only didn't respond to the call, they called several hours later to ask if things had "settled down." I could have been dead by then!

I have nowhere to go if it happens again. No one wants a woman with three children. Even if someone is kind enough, they wouldn't want to become involved in what is commonly referred to as a "domestic situation."

Everyone I have gone to for help has somehow wanted to blame me and vindicate my husband. I can see it there between the words and at the end of sentences. The clergyman, the doctors, the counsel, the police — every one of them has found a way to vindicate my husband.

No one has to "provoke" a wife beater. He'll hit when he's ready and for whatever reason he wishes.

I may be his excuse but I have never been the reason. I know that I do not want to be hit. I know, too, that I will be beaten again unless I can find a way out for myself and my children. I am terrified for them also.

As a married woman I have no recourse but to remain in the situation which is causing me to be painfully abused.

I have suffered physical and emotional battering and spiritual rape all because the social structure of my world says I cannot do anything about a man who wants to beat me. Society says that I must be committed to a man without any opportunity for an education and earning capacity. That my children must be subjected to the emotional battering caused when they see their mother's beaten face or hear my screams in the middle of the night.

I know that I have to get out but when you have nowhere to go you know that you go on your own and with no support. I have to be ready for that. I have to be ready to completely support myself and the children and provide a decent environment.

I pray that I can do that before I am murdered in my own home.

I've learned that no one believed me and I have only the hope that I can get away before it is too late.

I've learned also that the doctors, the police, the clergy and friends will excuse my husband for distorting my face but won't forgive me for looking bruised and broken.

The greatest tragedy is that I am still praying and there is no human person to listen. Being beaten is a terrible thing but more terrible if you are not equipped to fight back.

I recall an occasion on which I tried to defend myself. I actually tore a pair of pajamas. He produced them to a relative as proof that I had done something terribly wrong. The fact that I was sitting with several raised spots on my head hidden by hair, a swollen lip that was bleeding, and a severely damaged cheek with a blood clot which caused a dimple didn't even matter. The only thing that mattered was that I tore his pajamas. It didn't matter that I tore them in self-defense.

This is such an earthly position for a woman to find herself in. I would guess that it is incomprehensible for anyone who has not experienced a like situation. I find it difficult to believe myself.

Another point is that while a husband can beat, slap and threaten his wife, there are "good days" and this is what causes most people to wonder, why does she stay.

The good days tend to wear away the effect of the beating. They tend to cause the wife to put aside the trauma and look to the good. First, because there is nothing else to do. Second, because there is nowhere to go, and no one else to turn to. Third, because the defeat is the beating and the hope is that it will not happen again.

A loving woman like myself hopes that it will not happen again. When it does, she simply hopes again, until it becomes obvious after a third beating that there is no hope.

The third beating may be too late. Several of the times that I have been abused, I have been bewildered that I remained alive. Imagine that I have been thrown to a very hard slate floor several times, kicked in the abdomen, the head, and the chest and still remained alive.

What determines who is lucky and who isn't? I could have been dead a long time ago, had I been hit the wrong way. My baby would have been dead, aborted or deformed had I been kicked the wrong way. What has saved me?

I don't know. I know that it has happened and that each night I dread what may be the final strike which will kill me and leave my children motherless.

I believe that is why I am telling someone all that I have to relate. There is more, much more, and I have tried to keep it short but I know your program will be a strong and a much needed contribution to the community.

In conclusion, I sincerely hope that the emotion which I have revealed is not a detriment to your purpose. I have tried several times to hand compose this letter but it wouldn't come properly. The writing was shaky. The typing is not very good either, although I am a good typist.

The truth is that I am emotional about what has happened to me because it is so much more real than I can ever describe.

I have tried to give you a little of both the physical and mental abuse which comes out of a man who has not the self-orientation to combat the presence of a woman in his life.

I would like to do more but that would take a book — and there is no market because there are no ears.

Thank you,
Jane Doe

SUPPORTING THIRD-WORLD WOMEN

For the past few years I've been involved with a shelter, Casa Myrna Vazquez, which serves primarily (but not exclusively) Hispanic and black women and their children. This group of women faces many barriers and obstacles because of their cultural upbringing/conditioning. Also, their race and economic status often means poor housing, health and general living conditions for them and their families. Shelter workers and volunteers need more awareness and sensitivity to these issues to "help these women help themselves." I would like to explore a number of these issues and the challenge they present to those in the role of counselors, supporters, and advocates.

Coming to a shelter is a radical step for most women. For Hispanic women it may mean even greater change in a period of tremendous upheaval and transition. They are dealing not only with the emotional trauma of leaving their husbands, but also with the stress of adjusting to a new environment, especially if they have recently moved from Puerto Rico or another Latin American country to the United States. For many it is the first time they have stepped outside the closed and isolated circle of their homes. Simultaneously they may have to adjust to an urban U.S. setting and a totally different life style, with differing expectations for women.

Second, facing the decision to leave usually presents more intense personal conflict for a Hispanic woman due to the very strong cultural tradition of "a woman's place is in the home." Having resisted the pressures of church and relatives to keep the family together at all costs, in making a decision to leave she often feels tremendous guilt and betrayal toward her children.

Third, the personal resources in education, skills and confidence to make decisions and take action are limited for many third-world and low-income women. Since many started having children as teenagers and/or married young, they often have little formal education, contributing to their sense of low self-esteem, and financial and emotional dependency. Hispanic women, particularly, have had little familiarity in dealing with social service and housing agencies outside their homes or the family circle, having relied on husbands/boyfriends to make decisions and relate to such agencies. Additionally, many women are confined by their inability to speak English. Learning English is difficult since it involves a process of acculturation which many resist because it can be a threat to their cultural support systems. Handicapped by language and poor self-image, they are fearful of tackling bureaucracies whose assistance they may need to survive.

Fourth, the economic realities of life in the U.S. have far-reaching effects on Hispanic and black family relationships; on power relationships within the family and the woman's sense of self-worth. When the husband can't find a job or becomes unemployed, the shift of husband as breadwinner to wife as holder of the purse strings via welfare can start or escalate family violence. A woman often overlooks or excuses her husband's beatings out of feelings of guilt for a situation not of her own making and because she still cares for the man.

It is crucial for staff to understand the interplay of cultural imperatives and racial/economic pressures on third-world women's feelings, sense of personal value and service needs in order to build supportive relationships. These women need encouragement without pressure, direction and guidance in identifying options, and advocacy without substitution of another kind of dependency.

At Casa Myrna the racial/ethnic composition of the house often changes overnight, and with these changes comes a new set of problems and possibilities. At one moment the house might have a few or one English-speaking woman, then shift to an equal balance of the three ethnic groups. Whether the women remain isolated, segregate themselves, or freely intermingle depends on several factors: (1) how many women are bilingual; (2) women's prior exposure and experience with other ethnic groups; (3)

how strongly racial/ethnic prejudices and feelings are held and acted on. Food preferences, childrearing practices and housekeeping habits are three areas which serves as focal points for the women to vent their unconscious or conscious racist feelings and attitudes. The shelter can become a "tempest in the teapot" simmering with racial/ethnic tensions and hatred, camouflaging the fear, tensions and sufferings common to all the women.

We feel that the interpersonal dynamics of sharing multiracial/multicultural living space offers shelter workers and volunteers a unique opportunity to address the racist attitudes and beliefs of everyone's upbringing. In any and all cases, staff can help maintain harmonious relations.

EMPOWERMENT

A self-help model leads to empowerment. As a result of our oppression, we have been made to feel powerless: that we can't control our own lives, don't have control over our bodies and can't change things that hurt us. Battered women, in particular, have been told that they are worthless, stupid, incapable, and responsible for the pain they feel. Therefore, our program must contradict these lies and help women gain a sense of personal power and capabilities. By empowerment, we mean women beginning to direct their own lives, to control their own bodies, to decide what they want and to try to get it. This also means taking responsibility for their own actions while recognizing that they are not to blame for the violence done to them.

In particular terms, empowerment within a shelter is residents having control over the children's care, the meals, cleaning and general operation of the house, as well as having input into anything which affects them such as site visits and new house policies. It means gaining knowledge from each other and from staff, and then being able to share that with other women.

There are obviously limits to any one woman's power, especially in our society: she may well not have the power (financial) to get an interesting, well-paying job, or the power to stop her violent man from being violent, and she won't have total power over the service group either. She can't have control over institutions around her and doesn't have power over other people. However, in gaining knowledge and confidence in herself, she can go a long way toward developing her personal power and her ability to get what she needs from those around her.

Language

We need to look at our language to see what philosophy and attitudes it represents. Words like "client" connote unequal relations: the professional has knowledge, answers and power, and the client seeks help and feels powerless. "Counseling" often connotes such a power difference as well, because the roles are seen as static: the counselor always in the helper position, the client needing help.

Other seemingly harmless words can also have a negative impact. For example, calling a shelter, crisis line or support group an "agency" may, in a battered woman's mind, equate the group with the welfare department and other bureaucratic agencies. Similarly, constantly referring to a battered woman as "the victim" suggests that that is *all* she is; she will always be without any control or decision-making power over her life. The knowledge that she has been a victim of the batterer and the society which allows battering can help to free a woman from the guilt and shame of violence; but if we identify a woman as "victim" we only box her in and lock her into a passive role. She can and should move away from that role by taking control in her own time.

When feminists first brought battering to the public awareness, it was called woman abuse or wife-beating, noting who was getting battered. Now, many funding agencies, social services, even feminist groups refer to the problem as domestic violence or spouse abuse. This language change reflect an attempt to mask the real issue — the battering of women, an act committed by individual men, as a part of women's systematic oppression. We need to look at how language affects us and the women for whom we provide services. Our language should acknowledge women's growth and power. Staffing in a shelter, crisis line or support group is a constant learning experience, and we have to share our ideas and experiences with other staffers and residents. Information and learning have their own special kind of power; by sharing these with each other, we help to empower all women.

What Staffers Should Do

- Help women think about their situations, to realize they're not alone, that other women have had similar experiences.
- Help women figure out what they want (a novel question for most women because we've never been thought to think in those terms).
- Identify feelings (such as fear, helplessness, powerlessness, hopelessness) which may be preventing women from making decisions.
- Be honest, be for real: our lives are not perfect either; offer your own experiences if relevant. We can't say what to do, but we can offer ideas from our

own lives and from what options we see open for women.

- Give women the help they need to do things for themselves — even if it means saying no to requests sometimes; that can be the best thing to do.
- Offer resources: who, what, when, where.
- Help women gain a sense of self-confidence and the ability to take care of themselves.
- Be challenging, even if you're afraid of not being "nice" or not being liked. Being supportive does not mean allowing women to take advantage of us or our organizations.
- Be open to women's choices: each woman has control over her life and needs to make her own decisions; we can't be too invested in what decision she makes.
- Hear what women have to say; don't assume that you know the answers or even the questions.
- While realizing and building on the commonality of women's experiences, recognize the differences and diversity of women as well. Equality is not sameness; women of different races and cultures experience many things differently.

Answering the Hotline

As a staffer, you may be nervous when you first answer the hotline. It is okay to make mistakes. Be sure to ask for help or support from other staffers if you need it. Remember that your role is to offer support, safety, information, and an opportunity to share feelings with someone who understands. You may be the first person to whom a woman has spoken about her situation.

Much has been written which gives labels to skills that most of us already possess. Here are a few basic suggestions

which might help you best utilize your natural skills when answering the hotline.

- Make sure the woman on the other end of the phone knows that you are there, that you are listening. Sometimes, a woman will be too upset to absorb a lot of practical information, but she will be able to absorb your caring.
- Be yourself. You have feelings about what the caller is saying and it is okay to express them in your personal style.
- Remember that although a woman may not be able to make certain decisions now, the information and support you give now may be a catalyst for change at a later date.
- Make sure she knows that it's fine to call back any time.
- Talk about difficult calls with other staffers to share ideas about how to handle them.

— Gail Sullivan and Jane Weiss

SUPPORTING LESBIANS WHO ARE BATTERED

Lesbians who have been abused may need our shelters and support services. Some lesbians are being abused by ex-husbands or boyfriends, some are still living with abusive men while involved in lesbian relationships, and others are being battered by their women lovers. We need to be prepared to offer effective and supportive services to lesbians, acknowledging the similarities and differences that exist between lesbian and non-lesbian women and their situations.

In working on a hotline, we need to keep in our minds that the woman calling might be a lesbian. Some lesbians are not "out" about who they are; a lesbian might say that she is with a man (even when she is not) in order to feel safe enough to make the call. All hotline workers should be prepared to sensitively handle a call from a lesbian, while knowing that she could prefer to talk to a lesbian volunteer or staff person.

In doing advocacy, a staffer should be aware that the society does not acknowledge lesbian relationships and that the attitudes a lesbian faces and the subsequent services she receives could be very different than those for heterosexual women.

Lesbians who batter other lesbians are not men, though the violence in some instances can be of the same intensity. We need to be careful not to equate all violence, taking the focus away from the system of male dominance which condones and perpetuates violence against women. Although violence in any form is inexcusable, some lesbians have had no other model for dealing with conflicts than what they have learned from male-female relations in this society. However, women on either side of the battering relationship do not have the social, political, economic or personal power of men. A lesbian brought into a courtroom for battery will face much different treatment than a male batterer would. She will be judged for the "crime" of being a lesbian as well as for the acts that she committed.

A lesbian coming to the shelter needs to know that it is OK for her to be there and that there will be support for her. If she is coming from a battering situation with a man, she needs to be able to talk about all aspects of her feelings about her relationships with her batterer, her lover and her children (if she has any). Staffers and other residents should be careful not to jump to the conclusion that a woman has become a lesbian as a result of having been battered by a man. If possible, we should be prepared to refer the woman to other lesbian resources in the community if she doesn't want to stay in a shelter with all non-lesbian women, or if the shelter is not a supportive place for her. We need to make sure that she is not left alone to deal with homophobia in the shelter, whether or not it is directed at her.

Most women have the potential to be allies and to be supportive of each other in all kinds of situations. As part of our work of empowering all women, we need to be aware of and actively combat all of the ways that women have been divided from each other. Homophobia is one of these ways. By providing good, conscious services to a lesbian, we are not only helping this one woman, we are continuing to build strength and alliances between all women.

— *M. Smith*

LEGAL ADVOCACY

Introduction to the Legal System

The legal system is broken into two general categories: civil and criminal. The civil category usually concerns two or more persons who are involved in some matter that has caused harm to one or more of them. For example, if two people are in a car accident, one might sue the other for money, claiming that the other person was at fault. The Commonwealth of Massachusetts doesn't have any interest in this private dispute because it doesn't "affect the stability of the state" or the health, welfare and safety of Massachusetts residents generally. On the other hand, a criminal action (e.g., one person presses assault and battery charges against another), by definition affects these things because the law has been violated. The state issues a complaint against the offender and asks the court to punish (or reform) the offender supposedly to protect the state's interest in preserving the peace and safeguarding its citizens. In a civil action the woman chooses whether or not to file and follow through with the case; in a criminal action, the state decides whether or not to take the case and how to handle it.

This can get very confusing when one court can handle both civil and criminal cases; for example, the district courts handle criminal complaints like assault and battery and civil cases like abuse prevention. The court you're in, therefore, does not automatically determine whether the legal action is civil or criminal. As advocates the two courts that you will regularly use are the district court and the probate court. District courts handle civil and criminal matters; probate courts handle only civil matters. Both district and probate courts handle abuse prevention cases which are civil in nature.

The criminal courts have traditionally ignored criminal cases involving spouses or household members. Most such cases never make it to trial because the woman is intimidated by the abuser or the court into dropping the case. Many cases are dismissed or continued without a finding; of the few that go to trial with sufficient (overwhelming) evidence of guilt, most end in suspended sentences and/or probation. The man is then back on the street — or in the woman's home — in no time at all. The following overview therefore does not deal with the criminal system but rather uses examples from abuse prevention cases which are civil. The generalizations regarding attitudes toward women — particularly battered women and women of color, whether battered or not — apply equally to civil and criminal court personnel.

Going to Court

Always keep in mind that not every woman needs to go to court; it depends on the circumstances and on what she wants. Many battered women want to go to court because they think that the legal system exists to protect them. Laws, however, were made by and for white, middle-class men, and most people working in the legal system have conservative/traditional ideas about men and women and their respective roles in society — particularly within the family. They accept the view that a man is the head of the household and that family matters are private and confidential. Because they have a vested interest in keeping families together and preserving the status quo, they will often downplay or ignore outright the danger that "staying together" will create for the woman by discouraging her from taking legal action against the abuser.

In district courts many judges and clerks consider abuse cases family matters that do not belong in their courts. Some make abusive comments about the woman living with someone to whom she is not married, or suggest that she's only going to make things worse for herself by taking him to court, or misinform her about the law and her rights. It is not unusual, for instance, for a married woman to be told that she must go to probate court and file for divorce, or for a single woman to be told that she must go to district court, or even that she is not entitled to orders because she is single. The law, in fact, gives both married and single women the right to file and to request protective orders in either the district, probate or superior court. The choice is hers, not the court's.

She must often face the judge in a public courtroom after waiting hours for her case to be called. Even if she has visible bruises and other evidence of battering, she may be asked a number of questions about the battering, and a number of irrelevant questions such as who pays the rent on her apartment, or what did she say or do to anger the abuser. In some cases a clerk or judge may accuse her of exaggerating or even lying about the violence. Some judges are more concerned with protecting a man's due process rights than with preserving a woman's physical safety. She may have come all this way fighting fear, embarrassment, lack of knowledge about the law, and perhaps a difficult clerk, only to be denied orders by the judge. If she gets her orders, she must then try to get the police to enforce them.

Because the legal system is intended primarily to protect the interests of white men of property, women of color often have an even more difficult time getting protective orders. Racist clerks and judges often assume that people of color are more violent than white people, and that some violence in the family should therefore be tolerated. (Similar assumptions are made about working-class people.) Third-world women thus have to deal with the racism of an almost-all-white environment at the courthouse, and then face blatant, overtly racist treatment by clerks and judges. Furthermore, if a woman comes away from that experience with protective orders, she must then deal with the police who are infamous for their hostility and racism toward all people of color.

Dealing With the Police

Although having protective orders makes things a little safer, women usually expect the orders to have a much greater impact on the abuser and the police than they generally have. The abuser may ignore the orders and continue to harass the woman; the police may not enforce the orders.

Despite the fact that the Massachusetts Abuse Prevention Act established certain basic responsibilities for the police, many officers have refused to meet them. For instance, the police now have the power to arrest a man who has violated protective orders as long as they have reasonable cause to believe that he violated them (whether or not they witnessed the violation). In most cases however, the police have outrightly refused to arrest even when they've actually witnessed a violation of orders. Similarly, when the police respond to a "domestic disturbance" call they have to inform a victim of abuse of her rights with a simple rights card in English and Spanish which details her legal rights and the officer's responsibilities. Many officers ignore this responsibility by simply telling the woman that they can't do anything and that she has to go to court, without any further information, explanation or support.

Back to Court

When the police refuse to enforce her protective orders, the woman may decide to press criminal charges against the abuser for violation of orders. In some very serious cases a police officer may arrest the abuser and press charges against him. In most cases, however, the woman will have to press charges against the abuser on her own in the district court for the place in which the violation occurred. Women trying to press criminal charges for violation of orders are often shuffled back and form between probate and district court, each telling her that she must go to the other or between the district court for the area in which the violation occurred. Even if her case is taken seriously and the abuser is prosecuted, the most she can hope for is that he will be put on probation in the majority of abuse cases.

LEGAL ADVOCATES: WHERE DO WE FIT IN?

Legal advocates have often been able to make the system work somewhat better for battered women. They usually are better able to persuade or argue with difficult clerks, fill out court forms, etc., because they are less emotionally involved in the process. An advocate can often make the difference between a woman getting or not getting protective orders by stepping in when she is having difficulty explaining what has happened or what she needs.

The danger of this is that the advocate will take over for the woman and deny her the opportunity to be in control of the situation, or that the advocate will buy the myth that only "professional" or "semi-professional" people can effectively use the legal system. Many clerks and judges avoid dealing directly with battered women because they are elitist and want to deal with "professionals"; from their perspective, an advocate is the next best thing to a lawyer. Don't exclude the woman you're supporting form the process that is much more important to her than to you or the judge.

This is particularly destructive if the woman you're with is a woman of color and you are white. Judges and clerks are particularly disrespectful and contemptuous toward third-world women, and will use any means to exclude them from the process. Be sure that you're not reinforcing that behavior by appearing to be "providing social services" for this "unfortunate" woman who needs the help of white people to "straighten out" her life!

Before agreeing to go to court with a woman, make sure that that is what she wants to do and that she is aware of her options, both legal and non-legal. Explain the law to her and discuss what protective orders are available and what they can do and what they cannot do to help her, so that she can make an informed decision about whether or not to use the law.

If she chooses to go to court, you should discuss the facts with her ahead of time; in telling you about what happened (what the abuser did), the woman will get used to telling the story and be a little less embarrassed/intimidated once she's in court. You can also help the woman to write her affidavit (a written statement of facts signed under the penalties of perjury), if one is required by the court you are using. Explain the basic court procedures involved — where she'll stand, who she should talk to, what the judge or clerk might ask her, etc.

Part of our work is giving emotional support through the very difficult and emotionally draining experience of trying to use the legal system. A little pressure — or even a lot of indifference — could prevent a woman from demanding her legal rights. An advocate can prevent this from happening by supporting her in explaining her situation and intervening for her when the clerk is being pushy and/or giving her the wrong information (an all-too-frequent occurrence).

Dealing With Clerks And Judges As an Advocate

Be friendly and polite; dress well. It can get the woman's case called at a reasonable time, make the interview with the clerk less painful and get respect for you. Seeing you treated with respect can make things easier for the woman.

While it's important to act friendly and respectful to court personnel, it is also important to strike a balance between getting along with them and advocating for the woman. Don't be afraid to point out a mistake or misinformation by the clerk;

don't hesitate to demand to see the judge if the clerk is refusing to deal with you. Like police, clerks will sometimes change their behavior toward you when you ask for their name or to see their superior. Gauge your behavior to theirs. When friendly persuasion doesn't work, don't be afraid to demand what the woman is entitled to by law or to express dissatisfaction.

When you get before the judge, explain who you are and that you are there to give the woman emotional support. If the judge excludes you from the process, there's nothing you can do; so if you're not sure what will happen till you actually speak to the judge, warn the woman that she may have to face the judge on her own. Judges are not necessarily any more sensitive or cooperative than clerks, but you and the woman should be aware that they have the power to hold you in contempt of court depending on your behavior.

If the woman gets her orders, make sure that she has a copy of them before you leave the courthouse that day, and that she understands them and knows when to come back to court for the second hearing. Remember that she may need your support even more during the second hearing if the abuser shows up at that time.

Finally, remember that your control of the situation is limited; there are some judges and clerks who will never be reformed. We can't expect to change a whole system and some of its most invested (and corrupted) members in a short time. Do as much as you can to help the woman through the process, but don't be afraid to suggest (remind her of) other options open to her. And even after a rash of courtroom successes, try not to forget that while we can make a difference in individual cases which affect women's lives, we cannot completely reform a system that is constantly reinforcing and perpetuating itself in patriarchal, racist and classist ideas and practices. Laws were established and are maintained by and for white, middle-class men, and it's going to take a long time to change that.

— *Chris Butler*

◆

WELCOME AND RULES
Waltham Battered Women Support Committee

Welcome to the Waltham Battered Women Support Committee, Inc., shelter. We are a temporary shelter for women and their children who have decided to leave battering situations. We hope that during your short stay you will find the support and peace of mind that will enable you to start to rebuild your life and the lives of your children.

Our philosophy is one of self-help and self-reliance. We are mostly a volunteer organization. You will be on your own most of the time, although we will help in whatever way we can.

Since so many women are in need of refuge, we hope our turnover rate will be great enough to constantly accommodate new women. You are expected to find new

Welcome and Rules, Waltham Battered Women Support Committee, Inc. (Massachusetts).

housing as quickly as possible. Hopefully, when your stay comes to an end, you will take an on-going interest in our organization.

Women who have been to court, to welfare, or apartment hunting can be of great assistance to you. When you have gone through some of this, please help new women who come to the WBWSC house. For most women the support and the feeling that people really do care is the most important part of their stay. The shared experiences of other women can provide a valuable tool in understanding and dealing with your circumstance.

The WBWSC house hopes to provide a protective and supportive environment for all who stay with us. To ensure this, we have rules which must be followed by all. YOU AND YOUR FAMILY ARE GUESTS IN OUR HOME. IT IS EXPECTED THAT YOU WILL COOPERATE WITH STAFF AND OTHER HOUSE GUESTS. IF, IN THE JUDGMENT OF THE STAFF, YOU OR YOUR CHILDREN ARE NOT BEHAVING IN A COOPERATIVE MANNER, YOU WILL BE ASKED TO LEAVE.

Violence

Violence by word, deed or instrument (including toy guns) is not permitted at the house.

Mothers (or other women) may not hit their children.

Security

CONFIDENTIALITY OF THE HOUSE IS ESSENTIAL. To ensure your safety and the safety of the other women, the address and phone number of the house must not be given out.

Given your mailing address as P.O. Box 24, Waltham, MA 92254.

No visitors are permitted in the house at anytime for any reason.

When meeting family or friends ask staff to help you determine a safe meeting point.

Secrecy in the neighborhood is also important. Neighbors should not know the name, telephone number, or purpose of the house. Contact with people in the neighborhood should be avoided.

Drugs and Alcohol

Have you ever had a drug or alcohol problem? *(Please circle the appropriate answer and sign your name on the line below)*

yes   no

Name of house guest

_____

If you have had a drug or alcohol problem, what steps are you currently taking to deal with this?

_____
_____
_____

I understand that no drugs or alcohol are permitted in the shelter and that I may not use drugs or alcohol outside of the shelter while a guest is at the house.

Signature of house guest

_____

Women with severe emotional, alcohol or drug problems will be referred to other sources of help. We simply are not equipped to help people with problems that need professional counseling.

Because they are dangerous to children staying at the shelter, all over-the-counter and prescription drugs must be left with the staff and locked in the office. It is your responsibility to get your medications while a staffer is here so that you can take your medication as prescribed, especially overnight and on weekends.

Getting Along With Other Guests

During your stay you will be asked to share a room with other women and children. We expect that you will make the best of this necessity.

Our shelter is open to all women regardless of color, culture, origin, or religious background. You are expected to try to get along with everyone and to treat everyone respectfully.

Length of Stay

Women with children may stay six weeks. Women without children may stay four weeks.

If you come back a second time your stay will be shorter.

You will be unable to return a third time.

For security reasons, it is necessary to find other accommodations for teenage boys (boys over 12). Relatives, friends or other agencies may provide temporary housing.

Contact With the Batterer

During your stay at the shelter you will not be permitted to contact your batterer for any reason.

Support Groups and House Meetings

All women staying at the shelter are required to attend support group meetings and house meetings.

Support groups are held on Friday from 1 P.M. to 3 P.M. and are not held at the house. You are expected to arrange your schedule to be there. Women who work during the day will be required to attend evening groups.

House meetings are held daily from 10 A.M. to 11:15 A.M. This is the time for you to talk with staff about your plans and problems. It is also the time when arrangements are made for collective child care. You should be up, dressed and ready for the 10 A.M. meeting.

Food Preparation and Household Chores

Unfortunately, WBWSC, Inc., is not able to provide food. You are responsible for getting your own food. We will help you apply for food stamps if necessary.

Shopping and food preparations are a collective effort among residents.

Women staying at the shelter are required to sign a duty roster each week to help with chores. Each woman must share in household duties.

Each woman is responsible for making certain her children are fed and that food is confined to the kitchen.

Your living space must be kept neat.

Trash pick-up is on Monday. Women staying at the shelter are responsible for putting trash at the curb on Sunday night.

Clean linens will be supplied by the Support Committee, but it will be your responsibility to see to it that they are laundered before you return them to us.

Children

You will be entirely responsible for the care of your children at all times.

Children are not permitted in the office.

Children must be in their rooms by 9 P.M. so mothers may have time to themselves.

Children are not permitted on the top floor of the shelter. The quiet room and the library are for adults only.

For safety reasons as well as security reasons, children are not allowed in the front yard.

Children must be supervised BY AN ADULT AT ALL TIMES when outside.

Parenting Skills Groups

Parenting skills groups are held periodically, usually on Monday evenings. When they are held, all women staying at the shelter who have children are required to attend. Child care is provided during parenting skills groups.

Going Out

If you plan to go out and return in the evening please be considerate of others. Tell staff and other guests when you are going out and when you expect to return.

The curfew is 10 P.M.

You may not stay out with friends and relatives overnight. We believe that if you could find a place to stay, you would not need shelter.

Phone Calls

The Hot Line may not be used to make personal out-going calls under any circumstances.

There is a telephone located in the kitchen that you may use for local calls. If you make long-distance calls, you must pay for them. You will be expected to keep track of how much time you spend on the phone and pay for calls accordingly. Staff will explain the procedure to you once you are at the house.

Calls out of state are not permitted except with special permission and supervision of staff.

No one is permitted to use the phone between 9:55 P.M. and 10:15 P.M. each night. This is to allow staff to get through.

Smoking

Because of the danger of fire, smoking is permitted in the kitchen and quiet room only. Only one person at a time may smoke in the quiet room.

If you do not understand the reasons for all these rules, please ask a staff person to discuss them with you.

Please read and sign the following statement to indicate that you have read and understand the above rules:

I AGREE TO FOLLOW ALL THE ABOVE RULES AND REGULATIONS AND TO COOPERATE WITH STAFF AND OTHER HOUSE GUESTS. I UNDERSTAND THAT I AM A GUEST IN THIS HOUSE AND MAY BE ASKED TO LEAVE AT ANY TIME.

Signature of house guest

_____

I understand that the Waltham Battered Women Support Committee, Inc., a non-profit organization, will provide me and my children with lodging and cooking facilities. The organization will also provide referral to medical, legal, social, child care, and other services.

In the event that I or my children should suffer injury, accident or illness while a resident at the Waltham Battered Women Support Committee, Inc., shelter, I hereby agree to waive any and all possible claims which I may possess against the Waltham Battered Women Support Committee, Inc., as a result of any damage resulting from such occurrence.

This agreement is made in consideration of the services which the Waltham

Battered Women Support Committee shall provide to me and my children.

I understand that I am responsible for any personal belongings that I or my children bring to the Waltham Battered Women Support Committee, Inc., shelter and that the Waltham Battered Women Support Committee, Inc., shall not be liable for any theft of such belongings which may occur while I am a resident.

♦

WOMEN'S EXPERIENCE AND THE PROBLEM OF TRANSITION

Christine Littleton

THE LAW'S PICTURE OF BATTERED WOMEN

It was late evening when 23-year-old Josephine Smith returned to her apartment in Atlanta. She was met outside by her live-in boyfriend David Jones. David lived at Jo's place "most of the time," leaving for days or weeks at a time to take care of business, hang out with his buddies or just get a little distance. Jo and David had had two children together, both of whom are spoken of as "her children," and only one of whom carries David's last name.

Jo finished the laundry while David hung around, then went upstairs to go to bed. Feeling amorous, David began to rub himself against Jo, who asked him to stop because she was tired. (By this time it was 1 or 2 A.M.) David grabbed Jo and shook her, saying, "You don't tell me when to touch you." Afraid, upset or just disgusted, Jo got out of bed, pulled on some street clothes and started to leave the bedroom. David held up a balled fist and told her she "wasn't going anywhere." Sighing, Jo sat down on the foot of the bed and started rolling her hair. David kicked her in the back. Jo placed her hair pick between her back and David's foot, and, as a result, his second kick gave him a flash of pain. He responded by hitting Jo in the head with his fist, grabbing her by the throat and choking her. Then he threw her against the door.

Jo ran to the bureau, grabbed her gun and ran downstairs. She tried to call her mother, but David had already taken the upstairs phone off the hook, and now took the receiver out of Jo's hand. Jo tried to run back to the bedroom, but David caught her. She tried to run out the door, but David slammed the door on her foot. Remembering the gun in her hand, Jo fired three times with her eyes closed, turned and ran. She begged a neighbor to let her in and used the telephone to call the police. When the police arrived, David was dead. Jo was arrested and charged with voluntary manslaughter.

Jo is not a typical battered woman. Most obviously, she had a gun and she used it. Over a million and a half women are beaten each year by the men they love, but only a few hundred kill. By contrast, several thousand women are killed each year by the men who supposedly love them. She may also be unusual in another respect — she was not married to the man who beat her. Apparently many wife-beat-

From Christine Littleton, "Women's Experience and the Problem of Transition," *U. Chi. Legal Forum,* vol. 23, 1989, pp. 33–47, 52–56.

ers do not engage in premarital battering. Those who do tend to increase the frequency and severity of such abuse after marriage. Nevertheless, Jo's case offers an opportunity to examine how the law distorts women's accounts, as well as to question why it does so.

At trial, Jo asserted that because she had acted in fear of her life, and thus in self-defense, she should be acquitted. In furtherance of this defense, she testified that:

> [David] hit her in the eye with his fist about a month after they met, that he had beaten her periodically, particularly when she dated so she quit seeing other men, that she was scared to quit seeing the victim because he threatened her, that the beatings increased in frequency when she moved from her mother's house to the apartment, that after he beat her he would apologize and say he loved her, that she didn't call the police or tell her friends because she believed him when he said he wouldn't do it anymore, and that earlier on the day of the shooting the victim threatened her and she gave him ten dollars after asking him not to do that in the presence of her sister. She testified that on the night of the shooting victim said he was going to do something to her and call her mother to come to get her, that she was scared he was going to hurt her more than before, and that she shot the victim in fear of her life.

The jury found Jo guilty of voluntary manslaughter, and she was sentenced to fifteen years. Jo appealed her conviction on the grounds that the trial court had excluded expert psychological testimony during both the trial and the sentencing hearing. The court of appeals affirmed on the basis that such expert testimony would have invaded the province of the jury (that is, deciding whether Jo had acted out of fear for her life). The Georgia Supreme Court reversed, however, holding that "[e]xpert opinion testimony on issues to be decided by the jury, even the ultimate issue, is admissible where the conclusion of the expert is one which jurors would not be ordinarily be able to draw for themselves; i.e., the conclusion is beyond the ken of the average layman." The "average layman," the court reasoned, might think that the " 'logical reaction' of a battered woman would be to call the police or leave her husband (boyfriend.)" Only through use of expert testimony on the "battered woman syndrome" could a jury learn that "typically victims of battered woman syndrome believe that their husbands are capable of killing them, that there is no escape, and that if they leave they will be found and hurt even more." Without such expert testimony, a jury probably would not suspect that battered women believe "that they themselves are somehow responsible for their husbands' violent behavior, and that they are low in self-esteem and feel powerless." Nor would they know that the primary emotion of a battered woman is fear.

Jo's conviction was reversed, and the opinion in her case opens the door to other women in Georgia (and potentially elsewhere) who seek to bolster their self-defense claims with expert testimony. Yet the sub-text of the opinion is deeply troubling.

First, battered women were viewed by the *Smith* court as alien, their reasoning and actions "beyond the ken of the average layman." This view is indeed plausible: Not only battered women, but all women, may appear alien from a male perspective. In this sense, the court's characterization may be even truer than the court itself imagined. Second, whether accurate or not, the truth of an expert's assertion that the battered woman's "primary emotion is fear" is largely irrelevant. Unless she can convince the jury that she was afraid in a way they understand, she will go to jail. *That* is a powerful truth. Third, battered women are said to believe that there is no escape. This statement seems consistent with women's accounts, but it is also incomplete in a particularly insidious way. That is, not only is the objective accuracy of the belief deemed irrelevant, but so is its very reasonableness. It is precisely because the belief appears so incredible that expert testimony is introduced.

Whether or not Jo's belief that she could safely escape the relationship with David was accurate is, of course, not the point. Whether her belief was *reasonable,* however, was precisely the point of feminist theorists and litigators who worked so hard to gain acceptance of expert testimony on behalf of battered women claiming self-defense. There are, in fact, very strong empirical grounds for believing that escape is sometimes impossible, or at least as dangerous as staying. Every battered women's shelter has stories to tell of the men who follow "their" women, hammer at the door, and try to force their way through. Restraining orders do not prevent men from returning to threaten us again; moving only delays the day that they find us; even jails sentences do not assure safety. It is no coincidence that a book subtitled "Violence Against Women and Children" has as its primary title, "NO SAFE PLACE." The statistical incidence of "recapture" — men finding women and beating again — makes a mockery of the standard self- defense analysis regarding "duty to retreat." It also makes battered women's belief that there is no safe escape rational. That rationality, however, is truly "beyond the ken of the average layman."

What difference does it make whether the belief that escape is impossible is rational, or an aspect of women's abnormal psychology? In either event, the belief will, when allowed into evidence, provide some way to educate a jury, some way to let women use the self-defense doctrine that has always been available to men.

The characterization of the belief makes a difference in four interrelated ways. The first is that, paradoxically, the focus on the personal, interior, subjective nature of the belief without considering its class-wide, external, statistical rationality, denies the defense to those individual women who have not yet been beaten "enough." For example, in giving Jo Smith the benefit of expert testimony, the Georgia Supreme Court distinguished an Idaho case upholding the exclusion of psychiatric opinion "as to whether or not the defendant was in a state of fear at the time of shooting her husband." That case was seen as different because there "the defendant testified as to *only one* prior occasion of physical abuse."

A second consequence of focusing on subjective belief rather than social reality is that it allows society, and encourages women, to deny the extent of male violence and the threat of such violence to our lives. Thus, women who are battered are viewed by many other women as deviant, unusual, perhaps even rare. Such denial and lack of identification undermine the unity of women necessary to bring about political and legal change, as well as cutting off battered women from potential sources of support and nurturance.

The third consequences is even more subtle. In bypassing the question of *statistical frequency,* the law's imagery and categorization allows, perhaps even encourages, a notion of the *natural inevitability* of violence against women. In *Dothard* v. *Rawlinson,* for example, the

United States Supreme Court decided that a female prison guard's "very womanhood" and the resultant likelihood of sexual assault would undermine her ability to maintain control over male prisoners. By failing to identity the problem as one of male violence or as one of conditions that make male violence a real possibility, the Court made it impossible to see that changing the prison conditions was a viable alternative to excluding women from the job. In similar fashion, identifying the problem in battering by focusing on a woman's psychological reaction rather than on the battering itself makes it harder for the legal system to craft solutions that will stop the violence, and easier to blame the woman for not fleeing.

Finally, this notion of natural inevitability causes the jury immediately to accept the dead husband or boyfriend as "the victim." To gain acquittal, the battered woman's only option is to make herself even more of a victim. If she is successful, she will gain the sympathy of a jury, but not necessarily its respect. Rather, a successful showing of victimization will lead the jury to characterize her as incompetent rather than as reasonable. Labeling those women who finally and desperately resist the imposition of male power as unreasonable, incompetent, suffering from psychological impairment or just plain crazy supports, rather than undermines, the assumption that male power over women is natural and unalterable.

Beyond characterizing the battered woman as unreasonable, however, the law in its present cast is also able to maintain an absolute focus on whether the battered woman "chose" correctly between the risk of leaving and the risk of staying, and away from whether men should be able to impose *either* set of risks on us. This fact, above all others, leads me to think that the problem is much more than various

judges' and juries' tendency to hold onto sex stereotypes. Translating women's victimization into a problem *with women* masks the pervasiveness and extent of men's ability to oppress, harm and threaten us. It protects the legal system from having to confront the central problems of battering — male violence, male power, and gender hierarchy.

FEAR, RATIONALITY AND "LEARNED HELPLESSNESS"

In order to claim self-defense, a defendant must demonstrate that she acted "in fear of her life." But fear can mean many things. It can be rational or irrational. It can be incapacitating and dehumanizing, but it can also be the necessary precondition of bravery (to be brave is to act in spite of fear, not in its absence) and the trigger for effective action. The law's tendency to characterize women's fear as irrational is understandable if viewed as stemming from a desire (whether consciously experienced or not) to avoid seeing the extent of male violence against women. As feminists, we frequently underestimate this desire, and fail to protect ourselves against the consequences of "dropping our guard."

Consider the extent to which Lenore Walker's brave attempt to articulate women's experience with battering has been used and abused to blame the victim. In *The Battered Woman,* Walker stated her feminist assumptions: "I believe it will only be through listening to what battered women say that we will be able to understand what happens to a battered woman, how she is victimized, and how we can help a society change so that this horrible crime can no longer be perpetrated upon women. Yet she, like all of us, in underestimating the extent to which a phallocentric system could use even feminist impulses against women, failed to exercise the extreme care necessary to prevent such misuse.

The core of Walker's first book, or at least the core of what has been accepted legally, is the "psychological theory of learned helplessness." She first described the origins of the theory in animal experiments:

> Experimental psychologist Martin Seligman hypothesized that dogs subjected to noncontingent negative reinforcement could learn that their voluntary behavior had no effect on controlling what happened to them. If such an aversive stimulus was repeated, the dog's motivation to respond would be lessened.
>
> Seligman and his researchers placed dogs in cages and administered electrical shocks at random and varied intervals. These dogs quickly learned that no matter what response they make, they could not control the shock. At first, the dogs attempted to escape through various voluntary movements. When nothing they did stopped the shocks, the dogs ceased further voluntary activity and became compliant, passive, and submissive. When the researchers attempted to change this procedure and teach the dogs that they could escape by crossing to the other side of the cage, the dogs still would not respond. In fact, even when the door was left open and the dogs were shown the way out, they remained passive, refused to leave, and did not avoid the shock. It took repeated dragging of the dogs to the exit to teach them how to respond voluntarily again. The earlier in life that the

dogs received such treatment, the longer it took to overcome the effects of this so-called learned helplessness. However, once they did learn that they could make the voluntary response, their helplessness disappeared.

The movement from animal to human behavior is quite sudden, occurring within a paragraph:

> The learned helplessness theory has three basic components: information about what will happen; thinking or cognitive representation abut what will happen (learning, expectation, belief, perception); and behavior toward what does happen., It is the second or cognitive representation component where the *faulty expectation* that response and outcome are independent occurs. . . .It is important to realize that the expectation may or may not be accurate. Thus, if the person does have control over response-outcome variables but believes she/he doesn't, the person responds with the learned helplessness phenomenon.

Application of the theory to battered women follows without hesitation:

> Once we believe we cannot control what happens to us, it is difficult to believe we can ever influence it, even if later we experience a favorable outcome. This concept is important for understanding why battered women do not attempt to free themselves from a battering relationship. Once the women are operating from a belief of helplessness, the perception becomes reality and they become passive, submissive, "helpless."

Walker concludes that the expectation that response and outcome are independent is indeed "faulty," and a problem *with the women*:

> When one listens to descriptions of battering incidents from battered women, it often seems as if these women were not actually as helpless as they perceived themselves to be. However, their behavior was determined by their negative cognitive set, or their perceptions of what they could or could not do, not by what actually existed. The battered women's behavior appears similar to Seligman's dogs, rats, and people.

The picture of battered women offered here is more complex than it often appears in judicial opinions. While describing battered women's behavior as "similar to Seligman's dogs, rats, and people," and characterizing them as passive and submissive, Walker also places "helplessness" in quotes and juxtaposes it against the general perception that they "were not actually as helpless as they perceived themselves to be." However, even given this distinction between psychological state and behavior, the concept of learned helplessness, as used in law, is markedly inconsistent with Walker's own description of a "common behavior" among the battered women she studies. Walker reported that many of these "helpless" women attempted

> to control other people and events in the environment to keep the batterer from losing his temper. The woman believes that if she can control all the factors in his life, she can keep him from becoming angry. She makes herself responsible for creating a safe environment for everyone. One

woman interviewed spent an enormous amount of time talking about her efforts to control her mother, his mother, and their children so that none of them would upset her husband. She found that if she kept all these people in check through some interesting manipulations, life was pleasant in their home. The moment someone got out of line, her man began his beating.

As the subtlety of the relationship between psychological state and behavior has been lost in translation, so has Walker's cautionary note in he second book *The Battered Woman Syndrome* that "[t]he issue of the woman's response to violent attacks by the man who loves her has been further clouded by the mythology that she behaves in a manner which is either extremely passive or mutually aggressive. Rather these data suggest that battered women develop survival or coping skills that keep them alive with minimal injuries."

If we take women's own statements about their situation seriously, a picture emerges of women in positions of extreme danger and uncertainty performing literally amazing, and often successful, stunts to keep going, to stay alive. Along with "interesting manipulations" of other people who might affect the batterer's precarious balance come even more interesting manipulations of self-consciousness that allow battered women to continue taking care of pragmatic necessities:

> Two days after he broke the glass in the door, it was the middle of a hot summer afternoon. My son was asleep in his crib in my room, my daughter was taking a nap in hers. I was lying in bed reading. Suddenly, I heard a popping noise, and glass

started crashing to the floor. Someone was shooting through the windows. There were no bullets flying around — I remember wondering if it was an air rifle. The windows kept shattering, and I didn't know what would happen if anything hit the baby. I grabbed him out of the crib, got down toward the floor, and half-crawled out of the room. I took him downstairs. Or course, he was only three months old, when he woke up he had to nurse. Then I had to change his diaper. Then my daughter started crying — she had waked up from her nap. Then I had to change her diaper. The she was hungry. Then I had to change his diaper again. By then he had to nurse again. . . . .At 5:30 when I took them upstairs for their baths, I noticed the glass all over the floor. That was when I remembered what had happened.

This woman does not sound helpless to me.

In Walker's account of learned helplessness, the *cause* (random, uncontrollable violence inflicted by men) is at least part of the "syndrome." In the case law, the cause disappears while the "syndrome" remains. In neither case, however, is the focus explicitly and continuously placed where it belongs — on the intolerable conditions under which women live.

BEYOND LEARNED HELPLESSNESS

Is there some way to reconcile the conflicting images of women who report that they "cannot leave" and yet seem capable of heroic efforts on behalf of themselves, their children and other family members?

There may be several plausible explanatory theories. In this section I will try to use the methodology of feminism to construct at least one. What I describe as "feminist method" is the process of constructing theories of explanation, critique and reconstruction from the perspective of the experience of women. In *Feminism Unmodified,* Catharine MacKinnon suggests that feminism's "methodological secret, is that feminism is built on believing women's accounts of sexual use and abuse by men." While this formulation of feminist method is cryptic in the extreme, its first step is both clear and illuminating. Let us start by believing women's own accounts, rather than by asking them to fit into pre-existing legal categories, and see what develops.

As described above, battered women engage in a variety of active strategies consciously directed either at reducing the frequency and severity of violence against themselves and their children or at taking care of themselves and their children despite the violence. Many of these women nevertheless describe themselves as unable to leave. Walker characterizes the latter account as "inaccurate," reflecting the psychosocial phenomenon of "learned helplessness" rather than objective, or even unconditioned subjective, reality. What if it is not "inaccurate," but only lacking in the articulation of a tacit predicate? In other words, these women may simply be saying "I cannot leave *without giving up something important,*" perhaps even "*without giving up something I cannot give up*":

The witness testified further that the history she took from [Jo Smith] revealed a four-year relationship with her boyfriend in which abuse began very early and escalated over the course of that relationship, that [Jo] continued the relationship for three basic reasons — *she loved him, she believe him each time he said that he loved her* and *that he was never going to repeat the abuse,* and she was afraid that if she tried to leave she would be endangering her life.

Jo gave three reasons for staying — love, faith, and fear. The law only had a category — self-defense — for the last, and so it heard only fear. If the person reporting these emotions or attributes — love, faith and fear — had been male, would the law have heard only one of them?

In 1979, Walker suggested that battered women were likely to have a "traditional orientation...evident in [their] view of the woman's role in marriage." In 1984, however, without cross-referencing the earlier statement, she stated that "[b]attered women held attitudes toward women's roles that were more liberal than most of the population. They reported that *batterers* were very traditional in their attitudes toward women."

This change in characterization may stem from increasing attention to what battered women themselves say about their experience *and* the conditions under which they live. In other words, battered women may stay in relationships that are physically dangerous to them because they value connection, yet the connection they seek may have little or nothing to do with the traditional, patriarchal image of family. Walker's later work categorizes these women as "more liberal" than most because they value their work outside the home, believe in shared responsibility in the home and try to engage in co-parenting. The fact that in 1979 Walker could only see these women as "traditionalists" even while she wondered over the fact that they often wielded great influence and demonstrated marked self-esteem in the workplace, says far more about the strength of traditional images of family than it says about battered woman's commitment to those images.

■ ■ ■

The phenomenon of some battered women choosing to remain in the relationship despite "objective" judgments that they would be safer if they left can be explained in several different ways — all of which have been, or could be, described as "feminist." One explanation accepts the accuracy of the outsider's judgment and ascribes the battered woman's behavior to some dysfunction in character, broadly described as "learned helplessness." A second view has stressed the *un*safety of leaving, pointing out the lack of equal pay in female jobs, the practical problems of finding alternative housing and the difficulty of raising children alone. Few, if any, commentators have suggested that women are doing anything other than misperceiving the danger to themselves, or settling for the lesser of two evils. A third explanation, however, is that those women who stay in battering relationships accurately perceive the risks of remaining, accurately perceive the risks of leaving, and choose to stay either because the risks of leaving outweigh the risks of staying *or* because they are trying to rescue something beyond themselves.

Broad-based acceptance by the legal system of the first explanation has already been explored. Focusing on women's reactions to what men do to them is an all too common strategy of male jurisprudence. The failure of the second explanation to gain similar acceptance in law could concomitantly be related to the law's reluctance to acknowledge the extent of male violence against, and oppression of, women outside the home. It is also plausible that, despite the dangers of leaving, women are indeed marginally safer in leaving a demonstrably violent relationship. But if women value connection enough to keep trying despite marginally greater risks of harm, both problems of evaluating women's accounts and problems of transition arise.

For most men to whom I have spoken about this issue, it seems literally incomprehensible that a battered woman is not lying — at least to herself if not to others — when she says that one reason she has not left yet is that she loves this man and believes that he will stop beating her. Love and pain are mutually exclusive, they say, at least outside of masochism. It does not seem that men fail to value relationships per se, but rather that they value them for the *pleasure* they can give. That's what relationships are *for*, they seem to say.

I often wish it were that easy; I wish I could explain Jo's statements ("She continued the relationship for three basic reasons — she loved him, she believed him each time he said that he loved her and that he was never going to repeat the abuse, and she was afraid that if she tried to leave she would be endangering her life") as only one reason (fear), mixed with a large dose of false consciousness. Jo's love and hope made her intensely vulnerable to David's violence, and to the fear such violence engenders. Jo's love and hope led to tragedy. To ask society — and especially to ask the law — to take that love and hope seriously is to run headlong into the problem of transition. How could we possibly take seriously women's accounts of love and hope without undermining the little protection from male violence women have been able to wrest from the legal system, without indeed increasing our already overwhelming vulnerability?

TOWARD A SAFE CONNECTION

If battered women seek to maintain connection in the face of enormous danger, perhaps the key to accessing the legal system on their behalf lies in taking seriously *both* the connection they seek *and* the danger they face in that quest. What would legal doctrine and practice look like if it took seriously a mandate to make women safer *in* relationships, instead of offering separation as the *only* remedy for violence against women? This is a complex question, and I offer only a tentative agenda for research and programmatic development. Nevertheless, one thing already seems clear: We cannot afford to accept the terms of debate set by male jurisprudence. Moral theories of self-defense and excuse distract us from political theories of change. We cannot afford to treat our goal as the limited, albeit important one of gaining acquittal for battered women who kill; our goal must be the far more difficult one of stopping the violence. "No woman is free until all women are free" is not merely a slogan. If a simple prescription is needed, here it is: Fewer law review pages devoted to the "problem' of battered women" and more to "stopping male violence."

The agenda, at least initially, seems to lead in several directions. First, change the batterer so that he fits within female models of community, rather than insisting that women fit within male norms of self-sufficiency and independence. This option takes seriously the equal status of female and male norms. Second, decrease the cost of rupture to women, so that both sexes face roughly similar disadvantages from the potential break-up. This option takes seriously the double-bind that women face in that even attempts to conform to male standards are currently very expensive for women. It also allows for the possibility that men also value connection, at least when it is threatened. Battered women themselves report that the single most effective strategy to stopping particular incidents of violence is a *credible* threat to leave the batterer. Third, increase the perceived costs of battering behavior. This option places responsibility for battering where it belongs — on the batterer. Fourth, expand the options for community so that women might validate desires for connection without running the 50–50 risk battering male partners impose. This option takes most seriously the relational values expressed by women. None of these directions is exclusive of the others, and I would suggest that if we are serious about stopping battering we consider moving in all four.

Change the Batterer

If women choose, or are compelled, to remain in heterosexual marriages or marriage-like relationships, why should they have to take the batterer as they find him? Evidence indicates that therapy can overcome even long-ingrained patterns of violent behavior — but *only* if the therapy is completed. Many of the programs that require therapy for the batterer make his agreement to *enter* therapy a reason for diversion from the criminal system, rather than making *completion* a condition of probation or parole. "Few would disagree that the concept of diversion, when it works, works well." When it works is when the batterer remains in therapy; when it does not work is when he walks into court agreeing to enter therapy and, on that basis, has the case against him dropped. He then never shows up to another therapy session, and a cycle of battering begins again.

Effective behavioral change on the part of those who make connection dangerous to women might be accomplished

through other means as well. Social disapproval — especially from other men — could be effective in some cases. Such disapproval might be mobilized through educational programs designed to rebut the mythology that wives are "appropriate" targets of violence.

Decrease the Cost of Rupture to Women

As noted earlier, Lenore Walker suggests that the battered women's threat to leave is the most effective means to stop any particular incident of battering. If the law really cares about stopping the violence against women, then it should use every means possible to make that threat credible. Instead, over and over, it has constructed means to make the threat seem empty.

First of all, the law assumes that the woman must leave the battering relationship. Why should the woman leave? It's her home too — in fact, often it's her home, period. Evicting a batterer from home, even if it is *his* home, is not unthinkable, and would reduce the costs of the rupture both to the battered woman and to the children who are usually additional victims of violence.

Indeed, the need to care for the couple's children often acts to keep women in violent relationships, at least until they too are threatened with violence. Women have good reason to fear that when they leave they may lose their children, as custody is awarded to fathers in approximately sixty percent of cases in which custody is contested.

Not only do men typically have access to greater economic resources to provide for the children, but they often know how to manipulate women's fear of losing them. Recently, a women I had met once asked me for a referral. She had woken up one night to find the husband against whom she had obtained a restraining order standing in her bedroom busily slashing her clothes and shoes. When she ran out of the house to get away from him and the knife he was wielding, he walked down to the corner booth, called juvenile services and told them that she had "abandoned" her children. She is still trying to get the kids back.

Battered women usually do work outside the home, but — like all women — they work for significantly less pay than men. Continued legal indifference to comparable worth claims has the indirect effect of keeping women in relationships they would like to leave, but can't afford to. If women cannot afford to leave, they can't make credible threats to stop male violence. Paradoxically, if women are going to be able to maintain community, it may only be through the ability to make that community optional and not mandatory for women. So long as discontinuing the relationship is costly to women but not to men, women lack the power to make credible threats to leave, and thus lack the power to use the single most effective (and non-violent) weapon in their arsenal.

Increase the Costs of Battering — to the Batterer

Feminists have make some gains in getting the criminal law to take battering seriously. Police intervene more often; batterers are more likely to be arrested; meaningful sentences, although still characterized as "unusual," are at least not unheard of. But these gains are still too little, and, besides, have been made by increasing separation at the expense of connection. Even recognizing a complete defense for those women who finally turn and kill, while no doubt increasing the perceived costs of battering, does so only via the most extreme form of separation.

Perhaps this trade-off is unavoidable. It does seem that the general failure to date of restraining orders in keeping battering men away from the women who obtain such orders bodes ill for any attempt to use restraining order to battering women while sharing the same space. Yet greater legal and social sanctions may discourage some men from engaging in the rupturing activity of battering in the first place, thus eventually leading to increased safe connections.

Expand the Options for Community

Currently no state sanctions lesbian marriage. Given the statistics on battering, the legal definition of marriage as a relationship between a man and a woman subjects most women to a 50-50 chance of violence within the *only* type of relationship sanctioned by law. As Gloria Steinem once opined, the reason why there are so few female compulsive gamblers is that women use up all their gambling impulses on the biggest gamble of all — marriage. While lesbian partnering does not guarantee the absence of battering, it does significantly reduce the odds. For women who are lesbian in orientation, the law's absolute preference for heterosexual relationships imposes significant costs on statements of personhood and connection. For women who *could* find happiness with a female partner, that same absolute preference channels them away safer relationships and into much riskier ones.

Similarly, commitedly heterosexual women are not equally free to choose between singlehood and marriage. Jennifer Jaff has recently explored the myriad ways in which the legal system disadvantages unmarried people and the concomitant legal pressure to marry. In addition to the social pressure to "couple," the law piles on disadvantages in health care, social security benefits, parenting rights and inheritance. Single women in partnership with each other (whether in dyads or larger communities), or in relation to their children, provide alternative models of community that need not be so expensive compared to legal partnership with a man.

Women who work in shelters for homeless or battered women often report that such women are reluctant to leave the shelter for the single apartments currently presumed to be their ultimate goal. Perhaps we should consider ways to expand the shelter movement from the perspective of providing potential long-term community rather than only short-term emergency housing.

The possibilities of alternative forms of connection are numerous. Why should the law be permitted to pressure women into the most dangerous form of social union? Making alternatives less costly and more available will help at least some women achieve connection without risking their lives and health.

◆

WORDS AND THE DOOR TO THE LAND OF CHANGE: LAW, LANGUAGE, AND FAMILY VIOLENCE
(Part Two)
Martha Minow

The turn toward narrative by legal scholars may help illuminate the difficulties of speaking about domestic violence against children and against women. Literary accounts and narratives of experience can offer new language to challenge conventional legal understandings, or misunderstandings, of domestic violence. Narratives with evocative, rich details about subjective experiences can be used to persuade people — like judges — who have sufficient power to make a difference actually to do so for people — like children and women — who face persistent risks of violence at the hands of intimate fellow householders.

At least, this is the hope. But does the hope carry any promise for practices beyond the pages of law reviews? Does the turn to storytelling and literature offer any chance that words may halt the violence, or at least strengthen those in a position to punish and deter the violence? Toward this end, I have joined others in a project of continuing education for judges in which we create settings to discuss family violence by using works of fiction. The project began as a response to a problem named in the trade as "judicial burnout." For one day, fifteen to twenty judges come to the campus of Brandeis University to discuss several works of literature.

From Martha Minow, "Words and the Door to the Land of Change: Law, Language, and Family Violence," vol. 43, 1990, *Vand. L. Rev.*, pp. 1665, 1688–1695, 1699.

We begin each session by noting that we have two sets of texts before us — the assigned literature and our own lives — and both will engage us in interpretation for the whole day. I call the judges by their first names. Some of them know one another. Some of them talk with a kind of reserve that may come from not talking often with strangers who call them by their first names.

Sometimes there are moments of empathy engendered by the readings; a character seems quite appealing, or a difficult situation seems recognizable. Sometimes the judges express their irritation with litigants, the press, and society. Sometimes there are surprising insights into texts or intense arguments about the literature and about what judges should do. In one session, several judges begin by criticizing women who come to court seeking temporary restraining orders to halt the physical abuse by their husbands or boyfriends. Two judges spoke: "These women come for the order, and then they never follow up with the hearing and final disposition," and questioned, "Are they serious or not?"

I suggest that we turn to Mary Gordon's short story, *Violation*. The story begins with this statement by an unnamed narrator: "I suppose that in a forty-five-year life, I should feel grateful to have experienced only two instances of sexual violation." I ask the judges, "What do you think is her tone of voice as she says or thinks this?" A judge responds, "I don't know, I found her baffling." Another says, "I think she is passionless. There is no emotion when she says it." We talk some more. How could she feel lucky? Is this an ironic statement, or is it a sober response to the world she has known?

We examine two incidents the narrator describes. In the first one, she recounts her post-college trip to Europe, a conversation with a sailor in a bar, the walk she took with him, and the way he raped her. "She should have known better," says one judge. "She wouldn't have talked with a sailor in a bar at home; it's only that she felt free and adventuresome during her travels," says another. A woman judge, one of the few present, recalls her own experiences traveling and says quietly, "Why should she have to watch what she does, why should she be blamed for what happened?" An intense discussion follows: the judges talk of their daughters, themselves, of the cities they know, of dangers outside.

We turn to the other incident described in the story. An uncle visiting the family comes to the narrator's bed; he is drunk and he makes a sexual overture. After experiencing an inner paralysis, she resists him with humor and then struggles with the knowledge that telling anyone would seem a betrayal of the whole family. One judge comments, "She handled it perfectly." Another says, "I don't understand what is the big deal here." Another responds sharply, "So, it's okay if it happens in the family?" After a series of exchanges, I return to the opening sentence of the story. What do we know, now, about this person; why would she describe herself as lucky? One judge says he feels sad for her because she seems repressed, she seems to have cut off feeling in response to the events in her life. Another disagrees, but says, "I still don't understand why she never told anyone."

We return to the first incident. After the rape, the narrator has missed her travel connection and checks into a hotel. She describes how she gladly paid extra for a private bath because she could not bear the idea of sharing a bathtub. "It wasn't for myself I minded; I cared for the other people. I knew myself to be defiled, and I didn't want the other innocent, now sleeping guests, exposed to my contamination." We talk about what she felt and why she could not tell anyone. After we converse, one judge volunteers, "I guess it's hard for anyone to come to court after something like this happens." I do not know exactly what prompts the thought, but I am glad for it.

We break for coffee. A judge who has said little or nothing all morning talks to me alone about a very difficult case, one in which the state removed a child from a family partly because the socialworkers thought the mother was mentally incompetent. They later found out that the mother only spoke a particular East Asian dialect. Meanwhile, the child has been with a foster family for eight months and has developed ties to them. Should the court correct the original injustice, or would this inflict a new injustice from the child's perspective?

After returning from the break, we discuss a story by William Faulkner. It is called *Barn Burning* and the story begins with a hearing before a justice of the peace in which a boy's father is accused of burning down a man's barn. The complainant mentions that the boy knows what happened. The justice of the peace calls on the boy and Faulkner lets us hear the boy think about how his father wants him to lie and how he would have to do so. The justice asks the complainant, "Do you want me to question this boy?" After a pause, the complainant explosively answers "no." Why does he not want the boy questioned? "Because he knows the boy will lie," says one judge. "Because he knows it will be excruciating for the boy to testify, whether he lies or tells the truth," responds another. "Because the father will beat the child, if he doesn't lie," says another judge.

A few pages later in the story, the father beats the child anyway. He "struck him with the flat of his hand on the side of the head, hard but without heat, exactly as he had struck the two mules at the store."

We talk about the father and about the boy: who are they, what do they think, what is their world like? The judges are deeply sympathetic with the boy. They despise the father. They give him psychiatric labels. We try to examine his social and economic position. As a "poor white," he is angered by his dependency as a sharecropper. He despises blacks, treats his family members like property, and moves constantly to elude the repercussions of his vengeful acts, like the barn burning. It is hard to elicit any respect or understanding for him, although I try. We look at why he seems so humiliated by other people's expectations. We debate his motives and his capacity for self-reflection or self-control.

I then ask, "Does the boy ever strike anyone?" "No," says one judge. "Oh yes, he does," says another, pointing to the fist fight the boy started after another boy called his father "Barn burner!" We trace the son's course through the story and our own course with him — how he comes to warn a landowner that his barn is about to be burned down by the father; how he comes to run away; whether this is strength or weakness of character; what we think about his abandonment of his mother and sisters; whether we should admire him; how much the boy knew at the time he ran away; and whether we have access to anything but what he thought years later about these events. What did Faulkner think about it all?

During these discussions, I sometimes sense a shift in the room. I sense a shift in loyalties. I hear imaginations exercised. Sometimes nothing like this happens. I often wonder whether we, the conveners, merely are providing a break from the routine of too many cases for these judges, or worse, a salve before sending the soldiers back to the war. My thoughts wander back and forth. Are they on our side? Am I on theirs? Who is "we," anyway?

After lunch, where I sit at a table with judges who complain about the lack of funding for court personnel and retell war stories about problems with the media, we read and discuss a story called *A Jury of Her Peers*. In this story by Susan Glaspell, a feminist writing in 1917, a farmer has died and his wife is the chief suspect. The story depicts the inquiries made by the prosecutor and the sheriff, both men, who unsuccessfully look for clues to the motive behind the murder. The story presents the contrasting inquiry undertaken by the sheriff's wife and her woman friend when they visit the farm kitchen to gather items for the imprisoned widow. Seeing her world and imagining the details of her life, these women glimpse the widow's relentlessly desperate loneliness and the signs of abuse by her husband. The women find clues indicating an altercation between the husband and wife; they figure out that he had crushed her songbird. They conclude that she had felt her husband crushing the life out of her, and that she had responded by strangling him in his sleep. The women decide to share neither the clues nor their conclusions with the men.

I ask the judges, "Did the women forgive the farmer's wife and protect her for that reason? Or did they feel they could not judge her because they themselves were partly to blame for her isolation? Did they believe that the formal legal system, with no women judges, lawyers, or jurors, never could yield understanding and fair judgment about what happened here?"

No one responds at first. As in all the sessions, the judges are mostly men. There usually is tension in the room, often defensiveness, and sometimes suppressed anger. The judges seem distrustful even before we start. One responds that he is dismayed that a woman could excuse another woman despite concluding that she indeed did commit a murder. Another crit-

icizes the story for suggesting that women see the world differently from men, observe clues that men miss, and judge those clues differently. Another judge objects to the men being portrayed as stick figures. (So were the women, notes a woman judge.) One judge trumpets a temporal difference: we are now enlightened; we now recognize a defense for battered women who attack their batterers. Another objects that this case does not fit our standard for the battered woman's syndrome defense. I intervene. Let's not talk about what the law says; let's talk about the story. A judge explains that the story made him think about his difficulties judging immigrant families who use extensive corporal punishment with their children. "They are in our country now, they must obey our laws," he says. He then wonders aloud about a man who killed his wife and then received a light sentence after explaining to the judge how his culture viewed her adultery.

I worry about these discussions. Am I simply sponsoring cultural relativism and undermining a commitment to disapprove of family violence? The judges reassure me, and themselves, that their commitment is to enforce the law, regardless of individual or cultural differences. But should we not learn to distinguish minimum norms — such as a right to be protected against physical harm — that warrant legal intervention no matter what competing demands we may endorse concerning tolerance for cultural differences? Then the business of understanding is not inconsistent with the business of judging, and cultivating empathy would not conflict with strengthening judgments about the unacceptability of some acts, especially violent acts. Understanding the complex reasons why people abuse others does not mean condoning that abuse. Perhaps understanding reasons for violence strengthens a commitment to draw violent actors into the human community and subject them to its judgments. I worry still about those who remain silent, even in this room of judges — those whose point of view remains unspoken because it would not be popular. I wonder if anyone in the room has been a participant in family violence but does not speak about it.

I enjoy these sessions, yet I worry about them, too. I relish the thirst the judges show for probing conversation. I delight when I see them scour the texts for meaning. When I hear them talk with intensity, and sometimes humility, I learn about their frustrations. I sometimes see the literature illuminated by their lives, and their lives by the literature. I fear disserving the texts, however, by my sometimes crude readings or by those offered by the students. I fear my fear of this. Do I betray an elitist academic sensibility toward "right" or "sensitive" readings of texts and toward the meaning of doing "justice" to a text? I genuinely hope that engagement with literature can enlarge our understandings and our sympathies. Reading literature can provide occasions for the moral act of taking the perspectives of others. I still worry, however, that in our pride in this enterprise we may neglect the possibility that we do not understand — that silenced discomfort over who is "we" is itself a serious stumbling block to understanding. I see a difference between readings that lead to sage nodding because "we" claim to share an understanding of the text, and readings that lead to struggle and disagreement because I did not see it the way you did, or because you catch a glimpse of a character you know and I do not, or because she reads against the text for what it does not say, or because he believes we are kidding ourselves about

what we really would do under similar circumstances.

Perhaps in these struggles, we make a way to talk about violence. Perhaps. If so, we may come closest in those moments of silence in which we — individually and together — realize some of that which we do not know how to say.

Cornelia Spelman, a psychotherapist, recently wrote:

> The stuffed clown flies across my office and hits me in the head. "Use *words*," I say to my six-year-old patient, a little girl. "Use words to tell me if you're mad; don't throw the clown."

Spelman explains that a psychotherapist tries to help patients learn the power of words:

> Using words to teach and comfort, listening, I am witness and midwife to the slow, painful rebirth of people whom language failed. For them, words had been used by others only to wound and destroy.

A week later the six-year-old was carefully cutting paper. "This," she announced, pointing to a hole she had made in a piece of paper, "is a Door to the Land of Change."

For survivors of family violence, words may be doors to the land of change. Words may provide these survivors with something to hold on to and thus something to aid recovery, something to grasp for a modicum of control and recollection of self. What words can open doors for those not yet victimized and for those who have been standing by?

Debates Over "State Intervention"

However difficult it may be to devise legal rules to produce appropriate state responses to violence and abuse within families, the very notion of "state intervention" prompts debate among scholars. Some suggest that the idea is incoherent because the state is always intervening — whether through action or inaction — or through the very definition of what counts as a family. Others suggests that deep social structures regulate families by using ideologies about gender, class, reproductive, and even love. Law is one of many structures, and perhaps a relatively powerless one, in this process of regulation. Do these or other views assist evaluations of ambiguous facts in a particular case that comes to court? How should a judge respond, for example, to the efforts by an unmarried father to claim a child the mother has surrendered to the state? What theory or set of themes can help evaluate the court's own response to such a case? These readings provide theories in hopes of illumination.

◆

THE MYTH OF STATE INTERVENTION IN THE FAMILY
Frances Olsen

Most people concede that there are times when state officials should intervene in the private family. Doctrines of family privacy are no longer thought to justify societal neglect of beaten wives or abused children. Yet society continues to use the ideal of the private family to orient policy. It seems important therefore to examine the concept of state intervention in the private family. In this essay, I argue that the private family is an incoherent ideal and that the rhetoric of nonintervention is more harmful than helpful.

Although most people accept in general the assertion that the state should not intervene in the family, they qualify the assertion with the caveat that the state should sometimes intervene in order to correct inequality or prevent abuse. I refer to this widely accepted caveat as the "pro-tective intervention argument" against nonintervention in the family.

This essay presents a different argument against the policy of nonintervention in the family. It suggests that the terms "intervention" and "nonintervention" are largely meaningless. The terms do not accurately describe any set of policies, and as general principles, "intervention" and "nonintervention" are indeterminate. I refer to this argument as the "incoherence argument."

A useful comparison can be drawn between arguments against a policy of nonintervention in the private family and arguments against a policy of noninter-vention in the free market. The policy of nonintervention in the free market, often referred to as laissez-faire, was pursued by many American courts in the nineteenth

From Frances Olsen, "The Myth of State Intervention in the Family," *University of Michigan Journal of Law Reform*, vol. 18, no. 835, 1985 (edited).

and early twentieth centuries. The group of scholars known as legal realists played an important role in discrediting the legal theories that supported laissez-faire. Their arguments form a useful contrast and resource for the arguments I present in this essay.

The protective intervention argument applies in a similar manner to both laissez-faire and nonintervention in the family: whenever either the market or the family misfunctions, the state should intervene to correct inequality and protect the defenseless. The most common and easily accepted argument against laissez-faire is that the free market sometimes breaks down or works to the serious disadvantage of particular individuals or groups; state intervention is then necessary to protect the interests of the weaker economic actors and of society in general. This parallels the protective intervention argument regarding the family. Sometimes the family misfunctions; instead of being a haven that protects and nurtures family members, the family may become a center of oppression and exploitation. When this happens the state should step in to prevent abuse and to protect the rights of the individual family members. Both the market version and the family version of this protective intervention argument presuppose that it would be possible for the state to remain neutral, but present reasons that the state should not do so.

The incoherence argument against nonintervention in the family parallels the legal realists' argument against laissez-faire. Both laissez-faire and nonintervention in the family are false ideals. As long as a state exists and enforces any laws at all, it makes political choices. The state cannot be neutral or remain uninvolved, nor would anyone want the state to do so. The staunchest supporters of laissez-faire always insisted that the state protect their

property interests and that courts enforce contracts and adjudicate torts. They took this state action for granted and chose not to consider such protection a form of state intervention. Yet the so-called "free market" does not function except for such laws; the free market could not exist independently of the state. The enforcement of property, tort, and contract law requires constant political choices that may benefit one economic actor, usually at the expense of another. As Robert Hale pointed out more than a half century ago, these legal decisions "are bound to affect the distribution of income and the direction of economic activities." Any choice the courts make will affect the market, and there is seldom any meaningful way to label one choice intervention and the other laissez-faire. When the state enforces any of these laws it must make political decisions that affect society.

Similarly, the staunchest opponents of state intervention in the family will insist that the state reinforce parents' authority over their children. Familiar examples of this reinforcement include state officials returning runaway children and courts ordering incorrigible children to obey their parents or face incarceration in juvenile facilities. These state actions are not only widely supported, they are generally not considered state intervention in the family. Another category of state policies is even less likely to be thought of as intervention. Supporters of nonintervention insist that the state protect families from third-party interference. Imagine their reaction if the state stood idly by while doctors performed non-emergency surgery without the knowledge or permission of a ten-year-old patient's parents, or if neighbors prepared to take the child on their vacation against the wishes of the parents, or if the child decided to go live with his fourth grade teacher. Once the state undertakes to prevent such third-party action, the state must make numerous policy choices, such as what human grouping constitutes a family and what happens if parents disagree. These choices are bound to affect the decisions people make about forming families, the distribution of power within the family, and the assignment of tasks and roles among family members. The state is responsible for the background rules that affect people's domestic behaviors. Because the state is deeply implicated in the formation and functioning of families, it is nonsense to talk about whether the state does or does not intervene in the family. Neither "intervention" nor "nonintervention" is an accurate description of any particular set of policies, and the terms obscure rather than clarify the policy choices that society makes.

THE EXPERIENCE OF STATE INTERVENTION

The assertion I have made — that the concepts of state intervention and nonintervention in the family are essentially meaningless — might ring hollow to an impoverished mother struggling to keep the state from taking her children away from her. More tragically, my assertion could sound absurd or seem totally meaningless to many innocent children who live in fear of the juvenile authorities. Hundreds of youngsters, the quality of whose lives has already been diminished by poverty and neglect, have been forced into silence and concealment. The specter of state intervention in the family denies to many of them even the partial relief they might get from sharing their pain and humiliation with a friendly neighbor or sympathetic teacher. Many such children

exist, and to them state intervention can seem real and frightening.

There are many other examples of situations in which people experience themselves to be victims of state intervention. In the 1960s a husband and wife in Connecticut were denied legal access to contraceptives until they sued and appealed their case to the United States Supreme Court. Earlier in the century, Lillie and O.B. Williams were prosecuted for bigamous cohabitation and sentenced to jail terms when state officials in North Carolina decided to challenge the Nevada divorces they had obtained from their previous spouses. They too took their case to the United States Supreme Court and won, only to lose on a retrial and second appeal. To both these couples state intervention would seem to be a very real concern.

State intervention may also have considerable meaning to the lover who, upon the death of his beloved, finds himself with no status, their jointly shared property snatched away by the beloved's long-estranged parents. The lover has no say about funeral arrangements and cannot even attend services without the permission of the parents. Even if the couple drew up wills, the beloved's testament would once have been routinely set aside for presumed undue influence.

The parents, however, might well consider their family intruded upon if the state were to limit their rights for the sake of their child's lover. Lillie and O.B. William's first spouses may have resented the courts of Nevada intervening in their family affairs by granting divorces against them when, under their own state law, they had committed no wrong and would expect to have a right to remain married.

The experience of state intervention in the family can involve either affirmative coercive behavior by state officials, such as physically forcing a child away from his or her parent, or a refusal by state officials to come to the aid of one claiming a family right, such as the state's failure to order foster parents to relinquish a child to her natural parent. From the child's perspective, the transfer of custody to natural parents the child barely knows would seem to be as serious intervention as it would be to take her away from a natural parent.

The experience of intervention depends upon having some expectation disappointed or some sense of entitlement violated. Disappointment and violation are very real experiences. Unfortunately, they cannot be avoided by a simple policy of nonintervention in the family. Moreover, disappointment and violation of hopes and dreams may be as distressing as the disappointment and violation of expectations and entitlements. It is not clear, in the example above, that the state should sacrifice the interests of a lover for the sake of the beloved's parents, just because the parents, under present law, have more settled expectations and entitlements.

Because the notion of state intervention depends upon a conception of proper family roles and these roles are open to dispute, almost any policy may be experienced by someone as state intervention. In many situations, someone's expectations will be disappointed or sense of entitlement violated no matter what actions the state takes or refuses to take. One can often argue that in a particular case nonintervention really means whatever one wants the state to do; any policy one dislikes might be labeled intervention.

For example, from one perspective, the state intervenes in the family when it provides contraceptives to minors. The "squeal rule" proposed by the Reagan administration, although not preventing the distribution of contraceptives, would have required that parents be notified that contraceptives had been given to their children. This was supposed to reduce state intervention in the family and to enable parents to counsel their children about the problems of adolescent sex. Opponents feared it would deter the youngsters from obtaining contraceptives (but not from engaging in sex), and argued that this particular intervention in the family was justified.

From another perspective, the "squeal rule" does not reduce state intervention (whether for good or ill), but is itself a crude, abusive form of intervention. The state achieves a virtual monopoly on effective birth control by impoverishing young women and forbidding inexpensive over-the-counter sale of prescription contraceptives. It then proposes to use this monopoly to intrude into the parent-child relationship and pass along information to the parents that the parents have neglected to obtain the old-fashioned way — by talking with their children. The state thus rewards neglectful parents and removes from them an incentive to maintain supportive communication with their children. It encourages parents to neglect their child's sex education and to ignore the pressures put upon their child until after the child has become sexually active and the state so notifies them.

Nonintervention arguments can be leveled against laws and regulations that refuse to treat unmarried couples enough like a family or against laws that treat them too much like a family. Nonintervention arguments can be used to keep children from being put into foster care, to remove them from foster care, or to keep them from being removed from foster care. Nonintervention arguments can even be leveled against a policy of enforcing contracts between unwed couples. While one can sympathize with anyone who is disappointed by a state policy, it is hard to see that anything is actually gained by characterizing the cause of that disappointment as state intervention.

WHY IT MATTERS

The protective intervention argument, that the state should intervene in the family when necessary, has gained so much acceptance — just as the protective intervention argument against laissez-faire has gained widespread acceptance — that one might wonder why we need the incoherence argument, that intervention and nonintervention are meaningless concepts. First, it is not the case that the exception has swallowed the rule. Under the protective intervention argument, the state is treated as having a policy function — to detect and correct those rare circumstances that disturb and disrupt the family, without questioning any of the basic individualistic foundations of society. The assertion that the state can and should avoid "intervention" in the family plays an important but generally unrecognized ideological role. Further, focusing on "nonintervention" tends to mush and confuse the ethical and political choices we make. It directs our attention to a false issue and obscures genuine issues of ethics and policy. Finally, both laissez-faire and nonintervention in the family have sprung up in modern versions — law-and-economics in place of laissez-faire and the individual right to privacy in place of nonintervention in the family. These new forms, one labeled conservative, the other liberal, are flawed in the same way the originals — laissez-faire and nonintervention — are flawed. The standard liberal criticism of law-and-economics and the standard conservative criticism of the right to privacy are both versions of the protective intervention argument. In each

instance, I believe the incoherence argument presents a more important critique.

CONCLUSION

State intervention in the family is an ideological, not an analytic concept. The incoherence argument demonstrates that neither intervention nor nonintervention has a coherent meaning. The protective intervention argument, that the state should intervene in the family whenever necessary to defend the interests of society or of individual oppressed family members, does not go far enough. First, it presupposes that nonintervention is a possible choice; and second, it usually accepts nonintervention as a norm or as an ideal.

The protective intervention argument misperceives the problems caused by unfortunate social policies. For example, the problem with state officials taking children away from poor parents is not really a problem of state "intervention," but a problem of the substance of that state behavior. What the state does is sometimes *so bad* that people would rather it did nothing — which of course is not possible. The effort to get the state to do nothing, even if it were possible, misfocuses attention. It is misguided to treat freedom as the polar opposite of state "intervention" or of government regulation. As Morris Cohen noted in another context, real freedom depends upon opportunities supplied by institutions that involve legal regulation. The attempt to criticize state "intervention" instead of criticizing the particular policies pursued may be especially limiting for poor people, who often have to rely on various government programs and are thus less likely to benefit from any political strategy based on the myth of nonintervention.

Sexual abuse of children provides an example of the inadequacy of the rhetoric of nonintervention. It also illustrates problems with the state giving adults so much authority and power over children. A child's failure to report sexual abuse may often be her best response to a bad situation. Incest deprives a child of autonomy and corrupts the protection the abusing parent offers the child. And when abuse is discovered, instead of empowering the child and making it possible for him or her to resist the adult, state officials tend to move in and take over — sometimes making matters worse. After revealing sexual abuse the child is all too likely to have even less autonomy and fewer options for dealing with his or her vulnerability and hurt. The child may be summarily denied the opportunity to maintain any relationship with the abusing adult, even if the child wants desperately to maintain a relationship. In cases of child abuse, including sexual abuse, state policy should end the abuse or empower the child to end it, not force the child to leave home.

If we think in terms of intervention versus nonintervention, and consider our options to be thus limited, we are less likely to devise effective alternatives. As we become less preoccupied with the myth of state intervention, perhaps we can focus proper attention on the realities of people's lives.

Medical Treatment Decisions

A basic common law rule assigns to each person the power and authority to consent — or to withhold consent — regarding medical treatment of his or her person. Treatment in the absence of consent amounts to the tort of battery, unless special circumstances, such as an emergency, can be demonstrated. What happens, and what should happen, to this basic rule when the patient is a child, or a person so disabled as to lack the ability to make judgments about medical treatment? Is "the family" the next best decision-maker? Who in the family should be authorized to give or withhold consent? What role should the state play? These questions pose classic philosophic problems about who can know the interests of another and about how public and private control should be allocated. These questions also pose practical dilemmas within a legal system that assigns different responsibilities to legislatures and courts, and to federal and state governments. When medical treatment becomes an occasion for potential disagreements, should new institutions be crafted, such as hospital review boards, to safeguard the interests of those who cannot speak for themselves?

Medical technologies increasingly turn tragic circumstances into occasions for decision. Should the severely disabled newborn receive all the technical assistance modern medicine can offer, or merely nutrition and hydration? Should the aged individual who slips into a coma be resuscitated or left alone, put on life support or removed from the ventilator? Should the child with Downs' Syndrome be given a life-saving operation or denied one on the theory that his life is not worth living, or on another theory that his parents worry he will outlive them and their ability to provide for him? These choices again reveal the prior question about who should make the choice. Should the parents or the lover of the patient make the medical treatment decisions? Should parents or hospital staff make a medical treatment decision? Should parents or friends who volunteer to serve as foster parents make the choice?

More basically, is it so clear that we know which individuals are capable of making medical treatment decisions for themselves and which are not? How do stereotypes about persons with disabilities, about gender, or other prejudices affect who the law treats as self-determining or as worthy of treatment? Should cost considerations ever enter into these judgments?

When framed as the fundamental choice about who should decide, medical treatment decisions become intense legal moments. They can be moments of insight or violence, moments of suspended animation or peremptory judgments, moments of error corrected by later action or moments reminding everyone involved that the presence of choice does not mean human control, but instead, occasions to learn humility. Issues of violence and neglect by families and by governments resurface here; what legal ground rules or presumptions should determine who decides disputed issues of medical treatment?

♦

A RECKONING
May Sarton

Laura did not relish having to see Dr. Goodwin, but his secretary had insisted on the telephone that there were things he felt it necessary to discuss. "There will be time enough for doctors later on," Laura thought, "but of course he has me over a barrel because he knows so much that I don't know." Suddenly she remembered her father's saying in his dry way, "Of course, when you see a doctor, you take your life into your hands." But the awful thing was that one simply *had* to trust. Doubting Jim Goodwin would be like walking into quicksand. There had to be somebody to care for her crumbling body.

She was tense, when she sat down opposite Jim Goodwin and saw that he was looking at a sheet of X-rays.

"Well?" she asked, "what's all this about?" She couldn't keep the hostility out of her voice.

Jim coughed. "I want you to arrange for someone to be in the house. It's not a good idea to wait till you are feeling too weak to cope."

"Will that be soon? I feel remarkably well. Only, when I lie down, there is a sensation of stifling, but quite bearable so far. I hate the idea of a stranger hovering about."

"The alternative is the hospital, Mrs. Spelman."

Laura swallowed.

"I'm sorry to be brutal about this, but you must understand that I am your physician."

May Sarton, *A Reckoning* (New York: Norton, 1981).

"Meaning that I have given my life into your power — what is left of it."

"Meaning," he said gently, "that I have some experience about such things. I want to help you all I can."

"Very well, I'll try to find a house-keeper."

"We may be able to help. Miss Albright has a list of possible people — of course they may all be employed at the moment. What you need is a practical nurse. Then, I would be glad if you would agree to a few days in the hospital. I would like to have a consultation with a surgeon, to be quite sure, frankly, that surgery is impossible, as I believe it to be from the X-rays."

"No," Laura said quietly. "I don't want to be interrupted."

"Interrupted?"

"Well," she sat up straight, "I'm living just now. I'm learning in a queer way how to live, what is important, and what isn't. I don't want to be interrupted."

"You're just like your mother," Jim Goodwin said with a smile.

"God forbid!"

"She was a great woman, a great personality."

"Yes, she was." For the first time Laura was close to tears. "I'm not a personality. I'm just trying to be human."

"Mrs. Spelman, would you like me to have a talk with your son Brooks?"

Laura was startled. "Why Brooks?"

"Someone in the family has to be alerted."

"Oh, not yet, please! I must have a little time. You're making it all seem so near, so close — I'm not ready!" She was unashamedly weeping now. "All right, tell him, if you must." She got up and blew her nose. "Tell him I want to die at home." But then she sat down again and recovered herself. "On second thought, don't tell Brooks. Aunt Minna knows. I went over there just after you told me what was what

last week. You'll be glad to hear that she too insisted I get someone to be with me in the house."

"Very well — but there will be decisions —"

"I'll tell Brooks myself when I feel the time has come when..." there was a pause. Then she smiled. "You see, I don't want to abdicate until I have to. If you tell Brooks, it's as though..."

"It would have been only to spare you."

"I realize that. Thank you. But the real thing is this sense I have that I need a little time just to live, as long as I am able, not to be impinged on by other people's feelings. Yes," she said, looking him straight in the eye, "that's it. That's the point — to be free of other people's sense of doom, *their* fears, if you will."

"Very well, I won't insist. There's one other thing, however. Your lungs are filling up, and the time will come fairly soon, I fear, when we shall have to drain out the fluid, at regular intervals, so you can breathe more easily."

"Oh," Laura said in a dull voice.

"I'll be glad to come and do it for you — after all, I live nearby."

"That's awfully kind of you."

For the second time Laura's eye filled with tears.

"I'll do everything I can, Mrs. Spelman."

"There's really no hope, is there?"

"There's always hope," he said, leaning back in his chair. "There are remissions, very mysterious because we really don't know why. There are sometimes remissions of a month or more, although with a malignancy in the lung — in your case in both lungs — well, as I say, it would be foolish to be too sure of anything. I'll tell you something. It's surprising that you feel as well as you say that you do, so, you see, one never knows."

Before Laura left the office Miss Albright called several possible practical nurses. One was willing to come in ten days. Laura had begged for that interval so passionately that Jim Goodwin had agreed to it. Mary O'Brien was to come and see her in Concord the next day, and they would talk things over.

"She's a very sweet woman," Miss Albright said, "a widow whose children are grown up. I'm sure you'll like her."

Laura sighed, then said, "I'll do my best." She hurried away then, compelled by some inner need so urgent that she hardly took time to button her coat.

◆

AS FAMILY PROTESTS, HOSPITAL SEEKS AN END TO WOMAN'S LIFE SUPPORT
Lisa Belkin

In a case that medical ethicists and legal experts say is apparently a first, a Minneapolis hospital plans to go to court for permission to turn off a patient's life support system against her family's wishes.

For eight months, 87-year-old Helga Wanglie has lain in Hennepin County Medical Center in a world created by modern medicine: dependent on a ventilator for oxygen and a feeding tube for nutrition, unaware of and unresponsive to her surroundings. Her doctors say she will never recover and they do not want to give medical care that they describe as futile.

ANY LIFE OVER DEATH

But Mrs. Wanglie's husband and two children describe her as an extremely religious woman who would prefer even this life to death.

"This is the opposite of Cruzan," said Arthur Caplan, director of the Center for Biomedical Ethics at the University of Minnesota, referring to Nancy Cruzan, the Missouri woman whose family fought for years to remove her from the feeding tube that was keeping her alive. Over the objections of the state hospital where Miss Cruzan lived in a vegetative coma, the tube was removed and she died last month.

"We've all worked long and hard for the patient's right to say stop," said Susan M. Wolf, an associate for law at the Hastings Center, a research center for biomedical ethics in Briarcliff, N.Y. "That leaves the lurking question of whether it's a symmetrical issue and they also have the right to say do everything indefinitely, even when the doctors believe it's futile."

It is a rare termination-of-care case of any kind that reaches the courtroom. Decisions to withdraw medical technology are made daily around the country. The American Hospital Association estimates that seventy percent of hospital deaths are preceded by a decision to stop some form of care. Yet Dr. Caplan said he knew of no more than forty state court opinions about the termination of care.

Lisa Belkin, "As Family Protests, Hospital Seeks an End to Woman's Life Support," *New York Times*, Jan. 10, 1991, p. A1.

It is even rarer that a dispute finds the doctors arguing for withdrawal of life support against the wishes of the patient's family. "None of those forty address that situation," he said. "If there is such a case, it's the exception."

Ms. Wolf agreed. "Maybe one other case has been reported where this kind of role reversal took place," she said, but she added that she was not familiar with one.

The reason there are few court cases of this type, experts say, is because doctors are reluctant to publicly advocate the death of a patient.

Dr. Eugene Boisaubin, an emergency room doctor who is head of the biomedical ethics consultation service at the Methodist Hospital in Houston, said circumstances similar to those of the Wanglie family arise regularly.

He estimates that ninety-five percent of the disagreements can be resolved with talking and time. In the other five percent of cases, he said, "we do what the family wants, even though it goes against our medical judgment. We do know that the patient will die, but not until weeks or months later. Until this, no one had the guts to go to court."

He has heard of hospitals that have chosen to override the family and disconnect life support without a court order, he said, but said that his hospital has never chosen to do so.

IT BEGAN WITH A FRACTURED HIP

The case that Hennepin County Medical Center plans to take to court began on December 14, 1989, when Mrs. Wanglie tripped on a scatter rug in her hallway and fractured her right hip. She was taken to a private hospital near her home where she underwent surgery.

The next month she developed breathing problems and was transferred to the Hennepin County Medical Center were she was placed on a respirator. She stayed there for five months, fully conscious and alert, writing notes to her doctors and her husband, Oliver, since the breathing tube down her throat prevented her from speaking.

In May she was weaned from her respirator and transferred to a long-term care institution across the river in St. Paul. She had been in the institution for less than a week when her heartbeat and breathing stopped suddenly. By the time she could be resuscitated she had suffered severe brain damage and was transferred back to Hennepin County Medical Center in a persistent vegetative state.

"She doesn't know anybody or anything," said Mr. Wanglie, eighty-six, a retired Minneapolis lawyer. He and his children, Ruth, forty-eight and David, forty-five, visit two or three times a week, he said. They stay about a half an hour and talk to the nurses about Mrs. Wanglie's condition, but they do not talk to his wife, he said because "she wouldn't even know we were there."

HUSBAND OBJECTED FROM START

Mr. Wanglie said the doctors caring for his wife first raised the question of turning off her ventilator in late May. At a meeting in a hospital conference room, he said, the family vehemently objected. He told the doctors that his wife of fifty-three years would have wanted to live.

Mrs. Wanglie, a retired schoolteacher, is the daughter of a Lutheran minister "and she has strong religious convictions," her husband said in an interview. "We talked about this a year ago. If anything happened to her, she said, she wants everything done.

"She told me, Only He who gave life has the right to take life," Mr. Wanglie said of a discussion he had with his wife before her fall. He said she had never put those thoughts into writing.

"It seems to me they're trying to play God," Mr. Wanglie said. "Who are they to determine who's to die and who's to live? I take the position that as long as her heart is beating there's life there."

Dr. Michael B. Belzer, medical director of Hennepin County Medical Center, said that he sympathized with the Wanglies. But a heartbeat no longer signifies life, he said in an interview. Modern machinery can keep a patient's heart beating long after there is any hope of recovery, he said, adding, "We don't feel that physicians are obliged to provide inappropriate medical treatment that is not in the patient's medical interest."

The case of Mrs. Wanglie illustrates a broader debate over when medical care becomes futile.

The broadest interpretation is that care is futile if it will not cure the underlying condition or make the patient more comfortable. Dr. Stanley J. Reiser, director of the Program on Humanities and Technology in Health Care at the University of Texas Medical School in Houston, uses the analogy of a patient who has cancer and whose family demands that he be given antibiotics or have his appendix removed.

If that would not cure him, he said, the doctors would not accede to the family's wishes. Similarly, he said, if the cancer patient were being given a certain type of drug that was not fulfilling expectations, that drug would be stopped even if the family asked that it be continued.

"Those things create no benefit in the underlying condition," Dr. Reiser said. "That is the definition of futile medical care."

Other ethicists agree with the analogy but not the broad definition of futility. Ms. Wolf and the Hastings Center have de-fined futile medical care as care that does not accomplish its immediate purpose. If a respirator keeps a patient breathing, she said, it cannot be defined as futile.

"Once you broaden the definition and say something is futile because it's just not worth it, you're on shaky ground," she said. "A patient or a family should have the right to decide whether something is worth it, but should the doctor?"

Mrs. Wanglie's case is unusual because her family's health insurance covers her hospitalization almost entirely.

"This is a pure ethics case," Dr. Caplan said. "It's not about money but futility and what we mean by futility. We've talked around that concept in recent years, using the smokescreen of 'Can we afford to do this?' There's been a harder question buried under that layer of blather about money, namely, 'What's the point of medical care?'"

Dr. Belzer said his hospital hopes to raise that question publicly by asking the County District Court to allow the removal of Mrs. Wanglie's life support system. He said it was a step they decided to take after other options failed.

In recent months, he said, the hospital staff has met with the Wanglie family and asked them to have Mrs. Wanglie transferred to another hospital or to file for an injunction against Hennepin County Medical Center forcing it to continue care. That would have brought a legal ruling without having the hospital appear to aggressively advocate a patient's death.

Mr. Wanglie and his children refused to do either. "I want her to stay where she is," Mr. Wanglie said. "And I don't think I need a court order to ask a hospital to provide medical care."

Hennepin County Medical Center is a public hospital whose governing body is the elected County Board of Commissioners. Before the hospital could petition the court to appoint a conservator or a guardian for Mrs. Wanglie, who in fact would seek to have her life-support system removed, it needed the board's permission.

The board members approved the hospital's action, 4 to 3, with the tie-breaking vote being cast by a commissioner who has known the Wanglie family for thirty years. He announced his decision today after more than a month of deliberation.

That commissioner, Randy Johnson, said in an interview that he decided to allow the hospital to bring its request to court because "I don't think this is a decision to be made by a board of elected commissioners who happen to be trustees of the hospital.

"These are issues that we're going to be confronted with more and more often as medical machinery becomes more and more able to keep people alive," he said. "These issues are not going to go away just because a commissioner in Hennepin County Minnesota didn't want to deal with them."

[Editor's note:

Hennepin County Probate Judge Susan Bownes decided the case in favor of Oliver Wanglie in a written opinion issued on July 1st, 1991. Judge Bownes found that Wanglie is in the best position to act upon his wife's religious and moral beliefs even though Helga Wanglie had never specifically discussed her desire about medical treatment with her family. The judge found Oliver Wanglie understood his wife's condition and was more qualified than a stranger to be his wife's guardian. The hospital said in a statement that it would not appeal the ruling.

On July 4th, 1991, three days after the court's ruling, Helga Wanglie died. The hospital said the primary cause of death was multiple organ failure caused by infection which was aggravated by an earlier brain injury. In a statement issued after her death, Oliver Wanglie said, "We felt that when she was ready to go that the good Lord would call her, and I would say that's what happened."

See "Brain-Damaged Woman at Center of Lawsuit Over Life-Support Dies," *New York Times,* July 6, 1991, p. 8, col. 1.]

◆

GUARDIANSHIP OF PHILLIP BECKER
Superior Court of Santa Clara County

Phillip Becker is a Down's Syndrome afflicted child who has by parental decision been denied a life prolonging operation and who has parentally been consigned from birth to board and care facilities for his basic needs and for childrearing. Our unique case presents a clear conflict between two legal doctrines. On the one hand the historically venerated "parental rights" doctrine, and on the other hand the more recently emerging doctrine of "best interests of the child."

Who speaks for the child? In our case we have two contending sets of parents who claim the right to speak. They are the biological or *de jure* parents, the Beckers, and the claimed psychological or *de facto* parents, the Heaths. We have discussed biological parental rights, what are the

Guardianship of Phillip Becker, Superior Court of Santa Clara County, California , 1981, No. 101981.

legally recognized rights of psychological parents? In the analysis of the rights of the Heaths, as psychological parents this court must come to some factual conclusions.

Both sides agree that the seminal case regarding psychological parenting rights is found in the California Supreme Court decision of, *In re B.G.* the High court relied in its formulation on the concept of authors Goldstein, Freud, and Solnit who defined a psychological parent as a "parent ... who, on a continuing, day to day basis, through interaction, companionship, interplay, and mutuality, fulfills the child's psychological needs for a parent, as well as the child's physical needs ... (it is the person to whom the child turns to for affection and care)." California courts have found psychological parents to be foster parents, aunts, and grandparents. This court knows of no case whether in California or elsewhere which has determined that overnight home visiting and weekly visiting of a child in a board and care facility by adults such as the Heaths have done with Phillip constitutes psychological parenting. A review of the decided cases indicates that psychological parenting has only been accorded judicial standing if the claimed psychological parents have had ongoing and continuous care of the child for a considerable period of time.

However, the facts in our case are unique. Phillip Becker is a Downs child who from the age of birth has been in the care of caretakers. He has never received nurturing by his biological parents; he has never received that constancy of affection and love from his biological parents so necessary toward the maturation of a child into happy healthy adulthood; he has never had the opportunity to develop that basic trust and confidence in his biological parents so essential to good parent-child relationships. Each of these elements are the *sine qua non* of parenting, and each of

these elements are found by this court to be lacking in the relationship between Phillip and Mr. and Mrs. Becker. It is quite evident from the facts at trial that this mentally retarded and emotionally deprived child was ripe for affection and love from any appropriate stranger who bestowed it upon him.

The expert and lay evidence at trial makes clear that a psychological parenting relationship has developed between Phillip and the Heaths. We test the evidence of this by asking and answering the following three questions: (1) Is there a continuity of the relationship between child and adult in terms of proximity and duration? (2) Is there love of the adult for the child? (3) Is there affection and trust of the child toward the adult?

The continuity of the relationship is shown by the visiting and association with Phillip by the Heaths since he was five years old. Their love for him is unquestioned, their testimony in court was charged with their emotional attachment to the child; they offer love and home care, tutoring, and all that Phillip may need in terms of educational, vocational, and basic skills training. Their magnanimity is astonishing and consistent with anyone's ultimate views of good parenting. That Phillip loves them is evidenced by the testimony of witnesses who have described his attachment to the Heaths. These witnesses have also described the adverse psychological effects visited on Phillip by the termination of custodial type visitation of Phillip with the Heaths by the Beckers. The expert testimony has also indicated that Phillip will suffer further psychological damage if his relationship with the Heaths as well as others is terminated. In sum we find that psychological parenting between the Heaths and Phillip exists.

The court has now determined who may speak for the child in these proceedings. Let us examine briefly the procedural framework within which this case arises. It is not an adoption nor a proceeding to terminate all parental rights. It is a proceeding to establish a limited guardianship with the Heaths as guardians of Phillip under supervision of the court and with the parental ties remaining intact. In California, state interference by way of court action can take many forms with California having eight separate proceedings dealing with child custody. At least one California court has approved of guardianship of a child to a non-parent over parental objection without severing the parent-child relationship. Legal commentators have suggested that this hybrid form of parenting, custody in a stranger and the non-severance of parental ties, may actually be in a child's best interests for a child can benefit from two sets of parents. Our case is a test case of this concept. One final note on procedure, whatever of the eight methods a California Court may use to deal with child custody, the California Supreme Court has held that Section 4600 of the Family Law Act governs any of the proceedings along this custody continuum.

With our doctrines decided, our "parents" determined, and the procedural framework outlined, the court will discuss the conclusions that it has drawn from the evidence. These conclusions or findings will be made in narrative fashion. They need to be made in order that the court may come to its ultimate determination of what is in the best interests of the child, and the least detrimental alternative for him in this custody battle. These conclusions are based on what this court considers to be clear and convincing evidence.

Phillip Becker was born on October 16, 1966. The initial news of the birth elated the family, but within hours of birth Mr. Becker, to his devastation, discovered that the second fruit of the Becker union was a "mongoloid, Downs child with simian characteristics." Within six days of birth, the Beckers placed Phillip in a board and care facility operated by Neva Lippard and decided to step back so they could "truly understand the situation."[1] They left the question of permanent placement for Phillip open, but never thought of bringing him home. Mrs. Becker felt inadequate to provide Phillip with his needs and undertook no efforts toward the care of Phillip. Mr. Becker's attitude toward his child was one of puzzlement if not anger at having sired a defect. Visits to Neva Lippards by the Beckers were sporadic and occasional at best. The endings of each visit was the same, they left the nursery numbed by their crushed expectation for Phillip. The Beckers initially and with growing clarity as the days, months, and years passed concluded that Phillip would always be retarded, always be a defect, would always need constant custodial care, and should be institutionalized for life. They decided that he should never be close to anyone, or any families nor develop any special attachments. They concluded that Phillip would be happy so long as his physical needs were met and that he did not need his mother for his daily needs or for nurturing. In their view Phillip would always be a burden and of little appreciable value for the rest of *his* life.

---

1. In deference to the Beckers regarding this initial placement, they have testified that their decision was based on careful consideration and after the securing of advice from various sources. Even though the expert testimony in our case is to the effect that Phillip needs a home placement and environment, the 1966 decision of the Beckers could very easily have been made on the then current thinking, to wit, "a board and care home can best provide for all of Phillip's needs. Leave him in such a facility and raise the rest of your family." Presently, California is making extensive efforts to provide home placement with their families for the development disabled. (*See* Welfare and Institutions Code Section 4685.)

Their basic opinion of Phillip was that he was a permanent mentally retarded low IQ Downs child who would never have a hope of living in society.[2]

Their concern for Phillip has a curious ambivalence to it. While they express love for him, they do not display it. While they speak of having an open mind on the issue of surgery, they have not only refused it but have never taken any steps to initiate the basic testing, examination, and review necessary to make such an important decision. In this regard their actions toward Phillip's health needs, educational needs, and basic skills needs is marked by a puzzling inertia of inaction on their part. Why wasn't Phillip catheterized or tested at age six to see if he might be a good candidate for surgery? Why was he still in diapers at age six? Why did all his teeth rot? Why didn't he have pre-school? Why wasn't he brought home for overnights at the Becker's prior to 1981? Why was it necessary for Rebecca Wells to alert the Beckers of care deficiencies when

Phillip was transferred from Neva Lippard's hands to the Blanks in 1971? Why doesn't Phillip have real motor skills? Why does Phillip test as a High Downs in social skills and is low in certain basic skills? The list of whys can become endless, but they point out one thing clearly, that Phillip was considered so retarded and defective by the Beckers that the only appropriate placement for him was in a warehouse permanently and with no more than basic care afforded to him.

The available psychological evidence, the demeanor evidence of the witnesses at trial, as well as the inferences to be drawn from the testimony is that the necessary bonding between biological parent and child has even occurred.

Phillip Becker refused to be quiescent in his storage places. Soon after his transfer to the We-Care facility in 1972, Phillip, although devoid of most basic social or developmental skills, began to demonstrate that he had value.[3] Staff members at

---

2.   The historic view that mental retardation is permanent and an immutable defect of intelligence is a popular myth. This view has been supplanted by the recognition that a person may be mentally retarded at one age level and not at another. He may change as a result of changes in the level of his intellectual functioning, *or he may move from retarded to non-retarded as a result of a training program which has increased his level of adaptive behavior* to a point where his behavior is no longer of concern to society. (*See* United States President's Panel on Mental Retardation, Report of the Task Force on Law, 1963. (Judge David L. Bazelon, Chairman, Cited in: *Wyatt v. Stickney,* 344 F.Supp. 387, 389, fn.2 (M.D. Ala. 1972). (The expert testimony at trial is also to this effect.) Without doubt the retarded need to be helped to escape their retardation. The Beckers' attitude in this regard was to "wait and see what comes." Again in deference to the Beckers, their low expectations of Phillip may have been based on their own family observations, conversations with friends who had Downs in their family, their reading and study, and so on. Thus, their attitude of once a Downs, always a Downs may have been pre-conditioned by their background and the historical myth.

3.   Whether Phillip had value or lacked value became a central issue in this case. The adversary process highlighted this disagreement as *thesis* v. *antithesis* was evidenced in the dynamic dialectic of this trial. Whenever the Becker side claimed he couldn't do something, the witnesses for Phillip Becker proved the counter. Thus:

Becker Thesis	**Friends of Phillip Becker Anti-Thesis**
Phillip can't talk.	Phillip can talk.
Phillip can't communicate.	Phillip can communicate.
Phillip is a low Downs.	Phillip is a high Downs.
Phillip can't write his name.	Phillip can write his name.
Phillip can't draw.	Phillip can draw.
Phillip can't cook.	Phillip can cook.
Phillip is not educable.	Phillip is educable.
Phillip can't form loving attachments.	Phillip can form loving permanent attachments.
Phillip has few basic skills.	Phillip has many basic skills.

We-Care and volunteer workers were attracted to an engaging Downs child. These helpers of the handicapped sensed Phillip's message of value and began to work with him to develop his basic skills and his social department. It was during the course of these efforts that the Heaths and Phillip became attached to each other.

Unfortunately, Phillip's upward movement toward societal living was abruptly halted by the issue of surgery for an at birth ventrical septal defect of the heart. The Beckers, although warned of the defect to Phillip's heart and the possible need for surgery when Phillip was three or four years old, had refused to take any steps toward providing life prolonging surgery for Phillip. In 1977, they refused Doctor Gary Gathman's entreaty for this heart repair work. In 1978, in a dramatic and highly publicized juvenile court hearing pursuant to Welfare and Institutions Code section 300b, the parental decision of no surgery was upheld and Phillip was rejected as a ward of the Juvenile court.

That hearing must be place in its proper context. For the issue then was not parenting, but rather child neglect for not authorizing life prolonging surgery. It was a hearing which lasted only two days while our hearing has run the course of 12 long court days.

Although the courts have often been quick to order medical care when a child's illness is life threatening, their response has been mixed when the threat to life has not been imminent. Basically if surgery has been refused it is on the grounds that a person is conditionally entitled to be free from a non-consensual invasion of his bodily integrity. Additionally, courts which have refused permission for surgical intervention for a minor have held it may only be performed on an infant if consent is first obtained from the child's natural guardian or of one standing in *loco parentis* to the infant. Such consent is also required when surgery is to be performed upon an incompetent.

Our California courts are peculiarly sensitive in regards to state interference in the parent-child relationship. Our courts take the view that the government through the Superior Court should not run family life. We feel that the law has limited ability to supervise interpersonal relations. In commenting on this legal incapacity, behavioral scientists have postulated the courts' dilemma thus: "Families know their values, priorities and resources better than anyone else. Presumably they, with the doctor, can make the better choices as a private affair. Certainly, they are more than anyone else,must live with the consequences... If they cannot cope adequately with the child and their other responsibilities and survive as a family, they may feel that the death option is a forced choice.... But that is not necessarily bad, and who knows of a better way?" As pointed out by authors Goldstein, Freud, and Solnit: "If parental autonomy is not accorded recognition and if society insists through law that such children (neurologically handicapped or mentally retarded) received medical treatment rejected by their parents, the state must take upon itself the psychological resources essential to making real the value it prefers for the child it saves. The state would have to demonstrate its capacity for making such unwanted children wanted ones. Minimally, it should fully finance their special-care requirements. In the event parents do not wish to remain responsible for their child, the state would have to find — what is rarely available — adopting parents or other caretakers who can meet not only the child's physical needs but also his psychological requirements for affectionate relationship and emotional and intellectual stimulation."

Is it any wonder therefore that the wardship proceedings of Phillip Becker and the request for surgery floundered on the rock of parental rights? The issue in those proceedings was too narrow, that is, the risks of surgery. The basic issue is and always has been the one of parenting. Because even with the surgery ordered by the Juvenile Court, would Phillip Becker ever escape the grip of institutionalized living? The answer is No, but this case through the dynamic of the dialectic has pointed out the future alternative for Phillip. By positing the two parental thesis as found to be true by this court based on the evidence we will readily see what is the least detrimental alternative for Phillip.

The Becker's alternative for Phillip is institutional placement for the rest of his life. No life prolonging surgery. Little if any attention to the development of his basic skills, motor skills or social skills. A denial of visits with people who have affection and love for Phillip. A fierce desire to never let Phillip have any permanent attachments to anyone or to have any home life. Their expectations for Phillip and his future is none.

The Heath's alternative is an abundance of personal affection, love, and care. A placement of Phillip into their home, a situation which the psychological evidence shows Phillip desperately needs. A full-time mother; a constant one to one training relationship; a private tutor. Attention will be paid to development of his basic skills, his motor skills, and his speech. In short they are willing to do everything necessary to make Phillip a better person. Most important of all they promise to give the issue of surgery for Phillip the most careful and searching consideration possible. This done in the best of parenting fashion by gathering that breadth and quantum of evidence and information necessary to make the correct decision.[4] Their expectations for Phillip's future are great, for they believe that he may be employable as a semi-skilled person, and believe that he may be taught to live in and be a part of society. They will always treasure him as if he were their son. They will do everything possible to bring together the two families to the end that Phillip may have a better life by having two sets of parents. All of these promises they make without expectation of financial gain. Their hoped for reward is the love and affection of Phillip and the bestowing upon him of a life worth living.[5] By this succinct recitation of the choices of parenting it must be obvious what is the

---

4.   The commentators on this subject have suggested an appropriate test for the Court to use in deciding any issue of surgery. Thus parental refusal of medical care would be overcome if: (1) the medical profession is in agreement about what non-experimental medical treatment is appropriate for the child; (2) that the denial of the treatment would mean death for the child; and (3) that the expected outcome is what society agrees to be right for any child — a chance for a normal healthy growth or a life worth living.

5.   These are surely an astonishing series of promises. This is the kind of "miracle caretaker" that the commentators who have discussed state intervention in child "risk cases" have despaired of ever finding. Thus the dilemma of any court considering medical intervention, that is, who is responsible for follow-up parenting, is resolved by this magnanimous offer. Mr. Becker has cynically observed that there is gain. I can find none other than the satisfaction that any parent would have with the growth and mature development of a child. One can only marvel that anyone would want to take on the awesome responsibility of trying to raise a near adult child with Downs Syndrome and afflicted with a ventrical septal defect, myopia, hearing loss, some spasticity, suffering from lack of basic skills, and presently showing signs of a mysterious narcolepsy. In view of these difficulties, a cynic might suggest that the Heaths will try to salvage the child and then finding the effort too much, abandon Phillip, leaving the Beckers or the state responsible for Phillip. There are four answers to this: (1) Phillip would be no worse off at that time than he is today; (2) the Heaths have made it unmistakably clear in gripping courtroom testimony that they love Phillip and will care for him; I feel certain that they will not give up on Phillip; (3) this case has re-

least detrimental alternative for Phillip Becker.

Before making that finding required by the Family Law Act, of detriment, let us discuss Phillip's rights. For separate and independent of the rights of *de jure* parents and *de facto* parents, there are the rights of the mentally retarded and gravely disabled. It is said that those who are so afflicted are possessed of an inviolable constitutional right to habilitation. This constitutional right is one in which such persons are given a realistic opportunity to be cured or to improve his or her mental condition. Habilitation for the handicapped is the process by which the handicapped person acquires and maintains life skills which enable him to cope more effectively with the demands of his own person and of his environment and to raise the level of his physical, mental, and social efficiency by programs of formal structure — education and treatment. Succinctly, habilitation means that each handicapped person is given a realistic opportunity to lead a more useful and meaningful life and to return to society.

Recently in California a body of law has been developing aimed at protecting the rights of mentally retarded and gravely disabled minors. Our current view is that minors as well as adults possess constitutional rights. That as to the mentally retarded or gravely disabled minor, the state's interest is that they mature into healthy adults capable of full participation in society. Such a minor is entitled to be free of any injury to his reputation and an interest is not being improperly or unfairly stigmatized as mentally ill or disordered. Thus our high court has held that an erroneous conclusion by a parent that a child is sufficiently mentally ill to be institutionalized may well affect the health or safety of the child or have the potentiality for significant social burdens triggering intervention by the state of the protection of the child.

This court is aware that the above legal principles have so far only been applied by the courts to mentally handicapped or gravely disabled young people in state institutions. However, Phillip Becker being over fourteen years of age and emancipatable; ordinarily having a right to state a preference in a custody proceeding; and having a right in this court's opinion to secure habilitation and avoid the permanent stigmatization of mentally ill or disordered should be allowed to make a choice and thereby state a preference as to whether he wishes to remain warehoused for the rest of his days or to secure the opportunity for a life worth living by placement in the home environment offered to him by the Heaths. I point out that at sometime in Phillip's adult life he has a right to take that choice, why not now.

California does not provide a method by which a mentally retarded child may state a preference. Other states have used a substituted judgment procedure to allow the court to state such a preference for the incompetent. This doctrine requires the court to ascertain as nearly as possible the incompetent person's "actual interests and preferences." The substituted judgment doctrine has been used by the courts in other states do determine a child's preferences and is held to be consistent with the "best interests of the child" doctrine.

In our case the use of the substituted judgment method to arrive at Phillip's preference may best be stated in the form of a platonic dialogue with the court posing the choices to Phillip and Phillip's preference being ascertain from the more logical choice. The dialogue beings:

---

ceived so much publicity that public pressure will ensure a continuing and ongoing effort by the de facto parents to save Phillip; (4) even though the Court deals in a land of broken promises, we must still trust people to keep their word. The Heaths are trustworthy.

The Court: "Phillip I am convinced by the evidence that you have arrived at a cross road in your life. Whatever path you choose you must follow and will be bound to for the rest of your life. Your first choice will lead you to a room in an institution where you will live. You will be fed, housed, and clothed but you will not receive any life prolonging medical care. If you do receive medical care, it will be basic care only. You will not be given an opportunity to add to your basic skills or to your motor skills and in fact will be treated as if you are a permanently mentally retarded person incapable of learning and not fit to enter into society. You will not be allowed to become attached to any person, in fact efforts will be made to prevent any such attachments. Your biological parents will visit you occasionally, but their love and caring for you will be at best ambivalent. In fact they believe that you will be happy so long as your physical needs are taken care of, and that this kind of care may come from other people, your institutional caretakers."

"Your second choice Phillip will lead you to a private home where you will be bathed in the love and affection of your psychological parents. You will be given all of the benefits of a home environment. You will be given private tutoring and one-on-one training. The purpose of this education and training will be to improve your motor skills and your basic skills in order that some day you may enter into society and be a productive member of our community. Your psychological parents believe that you are educable and will do all in their power to help you receive the education you may need to care for yourself and to secure

work when you are an adult. You will have a chance for life prolonging surgery as well as receiving all the medical care that you need. Even if life-prolonging surgery cannot be performed, your psychological parents will always be there to comfort you and care for you in the dark times or your final illness. Best of all, your psychological parents will do all in their power to involve your biological parents in your habilitation and to unite both families together in ensuring for you a life that is worth living."

In my view, the dialogue would end with Phillip choosing to live with the Heaths.

Sad to say the foregoing legal analysis has no precedent in California law. There is no way under our present law for a mentally retarded child like Phillip to say: I want habilitation. I want life prolonging surgery. Those choices belong to his parents or guardians. Phillip's case may pave the way for recognition of a developmentally disabled child's right to choose his fate or destiny by the substituted judgment approach, or by the type of legal proceedings we are presently engaged in.

As to our required finding of detriment. If we define detriment as harm, then Phillip has suffered harm by the parenting of the Beckers. He has suffered severe emotional harm by their severance of all attachments by others to Phillip. He has suffered physical harm by their failure to attend to the basic skills, and motor skills of Phillip. He has suffered medical harm by their refusal from infancy to consider any life prolonging surgery for him, or to take any interest in seeing that his medical needs are taken care of. He has suffered lasting harm by their stigmatization of Phillip as permanently mentally ill and disordered. If we define detriment as lack of benefits, then simply stated, Phillip can never receive any benefit from custody with the Beckers because they have no expectations for him and will therefore do nothing to allow him to win a place in our society. Clearly the Heaths provide for Phillip his best alternative because their expectations for Phillip are in direct opposition to the Becker's point of view, and they offer Phillip the best chance he will ever have of securing a life worth living and the chance to grow and avoid the stigmata of the defective. The court finds that it will be in Phillip's best interest to award his custody to the Heaths.

This has been both a wonderful case and an irrational tragedy.[6] It has been wonderful because so many people have come forward to try to make a little boy's life better. They have braved a storm of parental indignation including scathing cross examination and a multi-million dollar lawsuit. The only observable gain is the love and affection of the child and a personal feeling of doing what is right for children.

This case is tragic, because God and nature may already have determined Phillip's future life course. He may very well be entering the dark time of his existence.[7]

This tragedy is irrational because the contestants are spending thousands of dollars and thousands of hours fighting over rights. That time could be better spent by trying to make the last part of Phillip Becker's life happier than the earlier part. Since the Beckers feel that Phillip can't do and since they have been indifferent to his care, why not give the Heaths a chance to show what Phillip can do to improve his physical condition? With our solution to the problem so obvious, why are there so many sacrifices onto the altar of parental rights? We are stretching important legal doctrines to the utmost in order that a little one's life can be made better. Is there any gain by letting false pride rule our hearts? It seems to me that any victories based on such a shaky premise must indeed by pyrrhic, and any legal defeats must be person-

---

6. This case is also a haunting one. It never leaves the mind during every waking moment of this Court. As we in our private life see young and old enjoying living at a wedding and the reception that follows; as we see people at play in the park; as we see people laughing and gay at the theater. The thoughts are always there of the Beckers, Phillip, the Heaths and of what might have been and of what should be, not only for Phillip but for all of the people who suffer grave mental or physical disability. It seems to me that any society must take a stand as to what they intend and what they will do for their infirm One alternative is that of the Spartans of ancient Greece who cast their defective infants onto Mount Taygetus or into a deep well. Such a solution is unthinkable. Another is to let the weak live but to provide them only warehouseman's care, food, clothing, shelter and very little else. Allowing the retarded and disabled to vegetate and rust away in some institutional setting. The horrors of these places are illustrated by the description of Willowbrook School for the Mentally Retarded set forth in the opinion of Judge Judd in *New York State Assn. for Retarded Children, Inc.* v. *Rockefeller*, 357 F.Supp. 752, 755-757 (E.D.N.Y. 1973). Because of the mayhem that may occur in such minimum level institutions, a cynical pragmatist could easily suggest that the Spartan method is far less cruel and inhuman. The third and best alternative is that we as a society set as our goal habilitation for our ill. That we provide them with a sufficiency of care and of programs that will afford them a real opportunity to enter into the mainstream of life. The gains for us as a people are enormous, for those who are sick will be given the realistic hope of a life worth living, and those who are strong will believe that in their weak time, we as a society will care for them as well Pollyannish perhaps but Christian goal and a goal worth striving for. If we can achieve this end of caring for each other, then the Biblical ideal as mutual trust will arise, and the lion may truly lay down with the lamb.

7. I have read all of Phillip's admissible medical and nursing records. I note with mounting anguish the developing and growing course of his strangling cyanotic illness; and as I read, I weep uncontrollably at the struggles of this wee lad to survive. My soul reaches out to him and to his laboring heart to try to give it ease, and in this time of grief, I think of Tiny Tim and what might have been but for old Marley's ghost.

ally destructive. Let's end the legal struggle now and have two sets of parents working for Phillip's best interest.

Yet despite all our hopes for Phillip his cause may again flounder. It may flounder because the Heath's home may not be suitable for him after our juvenile department inquiry. It may flounder because the court has somehow created legal error, and the parental rights doctrine may be paramount in this area. It may flounder for any number of other reasons, but one thing is clear to me, this court should state that it does not approve of the Becker's lack of parenting, and strongly urge that it is time for them to change.[8]

---

8. A great criticism of the Beckers has been their refusal of life-prolonging surgery for Phillip. This decision of the Beckers was made while Phillip was [a]n infant. The only ostensible reason for their decision was the parental label that the Beckers applied to him at an early age of incurable defect and family burden. How do children ever escape the labeling of their parents? How do they overcome the life and death decisions parents make for them? How does a child in Phillip's situation ever have a voice on the question of his right to surgery to prolong his life? By the time he is an adult, it is too late. I have written earlier of a neighbor child with cerebral palsy, spasticity, presumed to be mentally retarded. She was cared for at home by her mother and given the best of care. She is reasonably normal, healthy, happy and in college. Another parent close to the Court had a son afflicted at birth with an abnormal brain spiking. It took thousands of hours and thousands of dollars and a host of doctors and private schooling to cure him. He is now a normal healthy adult working and living a socially useful life. Another neighbor has a Downs child. She tried in vain to keep her at home and care for her there but to her ever-lasting grief, her efforts did not succeed and the child had to be institutionalized. In every neighborhood in every city in our country, there are stories like these, and in most of these neighborhoods, the heartwarming part of the story is the same: dedicated parents are doing the best possible job for their children. No court of any county could have told them what to do or how to do it for their children. What if some parents fail in their efforts? Should they be faulted by some court or judge and their children taken from them? The answer to that is no. There is no court that can make those tough family decisions I have described, and no court should. It is basically for the family and for good parents to make the decisions for the family. Why then deprive the Beckers of custody of Phillip? Is it because of their inattention to the surgical needs of Phillip? The surgery refusal is only a small part of the reason. The primary reason is found in the soul of the case. Whenever a child with the unique problems of Phillip Becker surfaces into the legal system asking for life prolonging surgery, for habilitation, and a place in society, the court, which is the great moral force of the community and the protector of individual rights and liberty, must make a choice. Do we do as the Spartan Greeks and abandon such infants onto the nearest mountain? Unthinkable. Do we agree with parental decisions to warehouse them and let them rust because mother and father know best, leaving our judicial hands in the waters of parental authority and turning our backs to the developmentally disabled supplicant who is before us like Pontius Pilate? Or do we say that the developmentally disabled are entitled to the same rights as everyone else; that they are entitled to habilitation, entitled to avoid the stigmatization of being mentally ill, entitled to a life worth living, and entitled to a chance at entering into our great society? Mr. Van Smith at the beginning of this trial demanded a closed hearing because if it was open to the public, we would add a circus atmosphere to our proceedings. The inference was that the freaks would frolic, using the trial as a publicity campaign against the Beckers and that the Beckers' rights would be hurt thereby. In summing up his case, Mr. Van Smith said that the Heaths are not here for the cause of Phillip; they and their witnesses are here for the cause of the mentally retarded. "Justice demands," he said, "that the decision of the Beckers against surgery be upheld." I might also add that he inferred that justice also demands that the decision of the Beckers to institutionalize Phillip for life must be upheld by the Court. He posits very succinctly the soul of this case. Does the Court now swallow all of those pompous legal phrases like the right of the mentally ill to habilitation, the right of the handicapped to escape the stigmatization of mental disability, the right of the developmentally disabled to take their place in society, and wash its hands in the waters of parental authority, draw its black toga around it and turn away into its ivory tower, muttering phrases like "no detriment" and "best interests of the child", thus denying Phillip and all those like him a chance of life prolonging surgery and a chance of a life worth living, thereby consigning Phillip and all whom he represents back into their warehouses to rust away? I think not. For Phillip Becker has spoken to us throughout this trial of his rights. He has spoken to us by and through

One final word, this is not a hearing to determine surgery for Phillip. That must await another time and a sound parenting decision. This is a hearing for the purpose of giving Phillip Becker another parenting choice. It is a hearing responsive to Phillip's need for habilitation, and responsive to his desire for a chance to secure a life worth living. *I will give him that chance.*[9]

The petition of the Heaths for an order of guardianship of the person of Phillip Becker is granted. Authorization is given for immediate catheterization to determine the feasibility of surgery for his ventricle septal defect.

DATED: August 7, 1981.

William J. Fernandez

_____

Judge of the Superior Court

---

the voices of his many friends, and Phillip and they have spoken not only to Phillip's rights but of the hopes and the aspirations and the rights of all the developmentally disabled. They through him ask for a chance of life, a chance for habilitation, a chance for life in our society, a chance for a life worth living. This Court has listened and will stand by our promises of habilitation for our deprived ill and for all the Phillip Beckers who come before it seeking the Court's help and assistance in making that long step into the world of the living.

9.   In this most fundamental of family cases involving the most basic and primitive of all human emotions, the love of parent for a child, this Court has tried to remain objective. Any court or other body who reviews this decision must understand that they are only reading words from a transcript. I have had the opportunity to see and judge the demeanor and conduct of the witnesses both on and off the stand. I have seen anguish, despair, sadness, concern, fear, worry, and suffering; I have seen disdain, indifference, cynicism and disbelief. I have seen the full gambit of human emotions as mirrored in the faces and voices of the participants in our trial. However, the cynic might point to footnote [7] and suggest, "Judge, isn't that just a little bit subjective, if not maudlin and trite?" My answer is no. It is the most important single finding on the evidence that I have made. How so? Judges are humans and not machines. From my point of view I believe that we prefer to be judged by a real person with emotions, common sense, and all those other important characteristics of a Homo sapien. A computer somehow does not fit any person's conception of a dispenser of justice. Being human, I am a parent, having raised four great and wonderful sons and having had all of the worries, anxieties and concerns of a parent. I read all ten years of Phillip's medical and nursing history, from 1972 to 1981. I read what the doctors had to say about the progression of a ventricle septal defect, and I was aware of the symptoms of the illness. As I read his file and I could see that this little boy was beginning on his trip towards death, and that he realized it, I was stricken with anguish and parental grief. It is at this point that the Solomon story becomes instructive for the emotions of 3,000 years ago are still true today. When the Israelite King ordered the division of the babe, the true mother with anguish in her voice, her bowels yearning upon her son, said, "Oh, my Lord, give her the living child, and in no wise slay it." The false mother, with indifference, said, "Let it be neither mine nor thine, but divide it." (Holy Bible, 1 Kings, 3 verse 26.) Intuitively, I reason if I a stranger but a parent can be so overcome with grief as I read the symptoms pointing to the slow but inexorable approach of the child's death, what does the real mother feel? I am struck by the indifference towards Phillip's doom displayed by Mr. and Mrs. Becker. I can only come from a failure to associate with the child and see him on a daily basis. No true parent can watch a child's life slowly ebbing and not cry out, "Oh, Lord, let the child live." (See 1 Kings, 3 verse 26.) Mrs. Heath, on the other hand, has anguish and grief exuding from every pore of her body and mirrored in her face and voice. Her wild statements made to the crisis center people are understandable. What does a caged mother do who must watch from the bars her child's life slowly ebbing and be unable to do anything about it? Indifference *vs.* anguish the Solomonic wisdom applies today as it applied yesterday. It may be argued that I used the footnotes too much to philosophize and state some personal views, experiences and anecdotes. My defense is that in a case like ours which is so fundamental and basic to life, people should know how some of their "governors" think and have their opportunity to judge the judgment of the judge. It is with the gratefulness of the community and of the Court that we extend our sincere thanks to Mr. Sterling L. Ross, Jr. for his yeoman service in the cause of Phillip Becker. His generosity is magnanimous. His concern for the child and for the honor of the legal profession accord him the highest commendation. Both sets of parents are ordered to pay one-half each of his expenses and cost.

◆

PACT ON CUSTODY LEADS TO SURGERY
Robert Lindsey

A ten-year-old boy who suffers from Down's syndrome returned to his home here this week after a potentially life-saving heart operation. The surgery followed a six-year legal battle with national implications for the rights of children and the handicapped.

On one side of the dispute were the natural parents of the boy, Phillip Becker, who turned the child over to an institution at birth and denied permission for the operation, which his doctors said was essential if he was to live past the age of thirty. On the other side was a couple who cared for him at the institution, grew affectionate toward him and fought successfully in court to gain his custody and then let the operation take place.

After his natural parents had exhausted all appeals in the case, Mr. Becker entered the University of California Medical Center in San Francisco September 26 for the operation to repair a small hole between the pumping chambers of his heart. He returned to the home of his foster parents Wednesday and was well enough this weekend to walk around and joke with visitors.

STRENGTHENS RIGHTS OF DISABLED

The dispute over the custody of Phillip Becker drew national interest because of issues it raised involving parental rights, the rights of dependent children and what some medical researchers regard as archaic attitudes toward the mentally retarded.

According to lawyers for the winning side, the decision taking custody of Phillip Becker from his natural parents, which was upheld by the California Supreme Court, will strengthen the legal rights of the handicapped, including retarded children.

Among other things, said one of the lawyers, Jay M. Spears, it emphasizes that "institutionalized retarded children, like other children, are entitled to have their basic human needs met, including the need for love and emotional support; the need for educational and developmental guidance to help them enter society; and the need for essential medical care."

But to Warren Becker, the boy's natural father, a patent lawyer who specializes in the electronics industry, the case represented an "outrageous" intervention by the state "in the rights of parents to make decisions concerning their children."

TWO VIEW OF DOWN'S SYNDROME

The long-running legal dispute involved two opposing points of view regarding how society should treat the severely retarded: a belief, long held in this country, that almost all victims of Down's Syndrome, a genetic anomaly often called Mongolism, are so physically and mentally defective that they should be placed in institutions; and a view, increasingly

From Robert Lindsey, "Pact on Custody Leads to Surgery," *New York Times*, Oct. 10, 1983, p. A10.

common in the 1980s, that many, if not most children with Down's syndrome, have the capability, if nurtured, to enjoy a satisfying life at home.

The dispute has also drawn attention to the difference in worth that two sets of parents, both in their 40's, placed on the life of the same human being.

Phillip Becker was born October 16, 1986. According to court testimony, his father referred to the newborn child as "a Mongoloid, Down's child with simian characteristics."

The child was immediately placed in an institution where, according to court records, he was rarely visited by his parents. In 1972, Herbert Heath of San Jose, who worked on the Polaris missile project for Lockbree Aircraft Corporation in nearby Sunnyvale, and his wife, Patricia, met Phillip and liked him.

A CARING LITTLE BOY

"He had curiosity and a sense of humor," Mrs. Heath recalls. "What turned me on," her husband said, "was his laughter and his real understanding of what was going on; he was just a caring little boy."

Tests of Phillip's intelligence taken over the years have rated his I.Q. variously from 36 to 70. State aid has paid for most of his support since he was an infant.

With written permission from the Beckers, who had never met them, the Heaths began taking Phillip to their home on weekends; they toilet-trained him, taught him to use a fork and treated him as a member of their family.

In 1977, according to court records, a physician said he believed it was essential that Phillip have the heart operation or he would face a painful, early death. A year later, after his parents refused to permit the operation, the operator of Phillip's nursing

home complained, and the Beckers were charged with criminal child neglect. They were found not guilty.

After the issues of their alleged negligence was raised, the Beckers refused to allow their son to continue to visit the Heaths. According to trial testimony, this caused a substantial regression in Phillip's development.

In February 1961, after a prominent San Francisco law firm agreed to represent them free of charge, the Heaths filed a suit seeking guardianship of Phillip.

A thirteen-day trial ensued in which the Heaths depicted Phillip as a happy, joyful and personable young man who was capable of learning and leading a productive if limited life, while the Beckers depicted him as imbecile, helpless, immature and as an inevitable burden to others. Mr. and Mrs. Becker said they were prepared to let him die rather than have the operation, because he would forever be a burden to others.

STORY OF SOLOMON EVOLVED

When the trial was over, Judge William Fernandez of the Superior Court here, saying they had become his "psychological parents," granted custody of Phillip to the Heaths in a decision that borrowed from the story of Solomon.

Recalling the biblical dispute over a child between two women who claimed to be his mother, the judge said he was persuaded to let the child go to Mrs. Heath, who said she wanted to let the life-saving operation take place. "No true parent can watch a child's life slowly ebbing," she said and as in the story of Solomon, "not cry out 'Oh, Lord, let the child live.'" It was not until this summer that the Beckers lost their final appeal and the Heaths were allowed to arrange Phillip's operation. An out of court settlement recently ended years of litigation brought by the Beckers against the Heaths and a number of people who had supported them.

Phillip's prognosis is good, his physicians say. Dr. Hanson said that, as with most children who have Down's syndrome, it will be possible for him with help, to lead a productive life in terms of working and "establishing relationships with other people."

Asked why he had resisted the operation so long, Mr. Becker said "it wasn't in his interest. It was risky. What's the point. It might extend his life for a few years, but for what purpose? He's almost seventeen and he's still carrying a teddy bear. Who's going to take care of him when the Heaths are gone?"

Mrs. Heath said that they had established a financial trust to help Phillip survive after their death and that, with training, in time he would be able to live in a "semi-sheltered" environment where he can live and work with other handicapped people.

At that moment, Phillip walked into the kitchen of their home here. He said "hello," smiled and gave Herbert Heath an affectionate punch on the shoulder.

Mrs. Heath said society in past decades has made the mistake of placing all Down's Syndrome children in the same category assuming that none could be helped. "The message I want to get out," she said, "is that you judge Down's people just like anyone else; that child, when he is born, is unknown as any child."

◆

REPRESENTING LESBIANS
Anne B. Goldstein

What is involved in representing a lesbian in law or in literature? The premise of this article is that the work of novelists is enough like the work of lawyers that useful insights can be drawn in at least one direction. That is, lawyers can learn how to represent lesbian clients better by studying books with lesbian characters.

The work of a lawyer is, in some respects, like the work of a novelist. Litigation is a story-telling contest. To win, a lawyer representing any client before a decision-maker must tell a compelling story. This story is not pure fiction; the lawyer is obligated to present the truth, but truth is a conclusion. Every one of us experiences the world differently. From our particular vantage points, we see and

hear what others do not, and we miss some of what they perceive. Six witnesses to the same event will swear to six different versions of it, and none will be lying. The lawyer's job is to take these conflicting accounts and, by selection and emphasis, construct a version that will convince the finder of fact. A litigator is a technician of the truth.

The lawyer needs convincing characters and a strong plot for her story as much as any novelist does. Generally speaking, the lawyer wants to portray her client in the most appealing light possible, in order to show that the client's actions and motivations are justified. Presenting a believable version of any client's character involves imagining it, constructing it, and

From Anne B. Goldstein, "Representing Lesbians," *Tex. J. Women and the Law*, vol. 1, pp. 301–313, 1992 (edited).

presenting it. Usually the hard part begins with construction and presentation, but sometimes — as when representing a self-identified lesbian, or a women who is likely to be perceived as one — the hard part begins earlier. If the client has proclaimed herself a lesbian or is likely to be perceived as one, or if the case itself is somehow intertwined with the idea of lesbianism, the lawyer is unable to rely either on the fact finder's presumption that the client is heterosexual or on the hope that the fact finder will find the client's lesbianism irrelevant. In these cases, the lawyer cannot avoid grappling with perceptions about lesbianism. Any attempt to avoid this issue will only make the client vulnerable to innuendoes she cannot challenge. In order to protect herself, she must confront, understand, and master the stigma.

This is not an easy job. Our culture is rich with mutually inconsistent and generally unfavorable stereotypes of lesbians. Lesbians are predatory, possessive, promiscuous, jealous, sadistic, masochistic, unhealthy, bitter, man-hating, masculine, aggressive, frustrated, over-sexed. Creating a favorable image for a lesbian client requires challenging these stereotypes — certainly not merely selecting from among them.

Fortunately, the lawyer need not struggle alone with this problem. Help is available from the client herself, who, after all, will have had to confront this problem in her daily life. Moreover, the lesbian community can be a rich resource of self-conscious attempts to understand and represent lesbianism in positive ways.

Contemporary lesbian novels have proven to be a valuable source of this community understanding. Ever since Radclyffe Hall invented the genre with *The Well of Loneliness*, lesbian novels have been argumentatively engaged in portraying, explaining, justifying, and apologizing for the lesbian. Read carefully, these books can illuminate the problem of creating a sympathetic lesbian character and help the lawyer solve it. A lawyer can learn the strengths and weaknesses of many possible strategies by studying novels employing these potential techniques.

Alice Walker's novel *The Color Purple*, which certainly has a larger agenda than simply rewriting *The Well of Loneliness*, takes the strategy of disempowering the true lesbian to perhaps its furthest possible extreme. Celie, the novel's heroine, is in some respects a classic true lesbian: the only person she is ever sexually attracted to is another woman, her husband's mistress, Shug Avery, whom she loves even before first sight (when she sees Shug's photograph). Yet Celie is also the most powerless person in the book. She is raped by her stepfather, her babies are taken away from her, and she is married against her will to a man who treats her like a slave, even bringing his sick mistress home for her to nurse. For a long time, Celie passively endures these outrages; even when she begins to act independently, she never becomes particularly bold. It is simply not possible to see Celie as predatory, or even seductive. Yet Shug Avery (who is beautiful, powerful, and primarily attracted to men) comes to love Celie, eventually choosing her over everyone else. Because Shug Avery is clearly just about the best thing that ever happened to Celie, Shug runs no risk of being seen as predatory.

A variation on this strategy is to reimagine the lesbian couple as composed of two true lesbians rather than of one true lesbian and one pseudo-lesbian. *Patience and Sarah* is remarkably successful at this. The novel is set in the early 1800s in

New England. Patience is a middle-class Quaker spinster in her late twenties; Sarah is six years younger, the tallest daughter of a poor farmer who had raised her to do men's work because he had no sons. Neither woman was sexually attracted to men. They met, fell in love, and planned to homestead on the frontier together. When their families intervened, Sarah went away alone, dressed as a boy, to discover the limits of that impersonation and the dangers of the road. Upon her return, Sarah reconciled with Patience and they became lovers. When Patience's sister-in-law interrupted their lovemaking, the two were compelled to leave their community together. Patience's brother bought out her share in the family farm, and she used the money to buy a new farm in a distant community where, as the novel makes clear, she will live out her life with Sarah.

The novel alternates Patience's first-person narration of the story with Sarah's. This technique provides the reader with a window into each character's internal life, showing that each woman is moving autonomously toward the other, that their love is mutual, and that their sexual relationship is equally desired and equally important to them both.

These novelistic strategies can be applied by lawyers to help in solving the problems involved in representing lesbians. The famous case of Sharon Kowalski and Karen Thompson will be used to suggest the lineaments of a literary approach to the problem of understanding how to represent a lesbian client. This case involves a woman, who, with difficulty, successfully recast the meaning of "lesbian lover," so that her relationship with her severely injured lover became a reason for the court to make her the lover's guardian rather than a reason to prevent her from visiting her lover.

Karen Thompson and Sharon Kowalski are perhaps the most famous lesbian couple in the United States. They are famous because, after Sharon was so severely brain-damaged in an automobile collision that she became paraplegic and unable to speak, Karen insisted on the importance, continuity, and permanence of their relationship. They are famous because Karen refused to go away when Sharon's parents asked her to; Karen instead hired a lawyer and fought to become Sharon's guardian. And when she lost that fight, Karen did not give up. She fought for the right to visit Sharon over the objection of the guardian the court had chosen, Sharon's father. When she lost that fight, too, Karen didn't give up; she fought to have Sharon's competence re-examined so that experts could determine whether Sharon was able to decide for herself who she wanted to have visit her and where she wanted to live.

Karen Thompson and Sharon Kowalski are famous because, in order to raise money for the legal battles, Karen named them and their love "lesbian" (something she had not done before her troubles began), and she made their story public in such a tremendously affecting way that, in 1989, on Sharon's thirty-second birthday, National Free Sharon Kowalski Day was celebrated with parades and vigils in twenty-one United States cities. They are famous because two weeks after Sharon was moved from a nursing home to a rehabilitation facility for evaluation and treatment, and more than three years after Karen had last been allowed to visit her, Sharon asked to see Karen. They are famous because finally, eight years after Sharon's accident, the Minnesota Court of Appeals named Karen as Sharon's guardian, ruling that "Sharon... has clearly chosen to return home with [Karen] if possible" and that

"[Karen] Thompson and Sharon [Kowalski] are a family of affinity, which ought to be accorded respect."

Sharon Kowalski and Karen Thompson are famous because their story is so arresting; it makes good copy. So many useful morals can be drawn from it; the importance of committed but unmarried couples exchanging durable powers of attorney; the necessity of legalizing gay marriages; the possibility of women triumphing over adversity; the importance of disabled persons having a voice in their own destinies.

But notice this: the now-dominant version of the story, in which Karen has been steadfastly, faithfully, and courageously keeping the vows she made to Sharon when, in 1979, they secretly exchanged rings and promised to share their lives, was not the only possible interpretation of the evidence. Indeed, the trial judge twice rejected this view in favor of Sharon's father's competing version. According to Donald Kowalski, Sharon was not a lesbian and Karen was not her lover. Karen alone was a lesbian, with a predatory, aggressive, possessive, and unnatural interest in Sharon that exposed his gravely disabled daughter to possible sexual abuse.

Sharon's car crashed in November 1983. After that, once it became clear that Sharon had been gravely injured, both Karen Thompson and Sharon's father, Donald Kowalski, sought to become Sharon's guardian. The judge believed that Sharon and Karen had a significant relationship, and therefore, although he named her father as Sharon's guardian, the judge at first required Donald Kowalski to let Karen visit. Unfortunately, Karen's relationship with Sharon's parents was, in the court's delicate words, "difficult," and it "deteriorated." Karen and the Kowalskis fought repeatedly in court over access to

Sharon's medical and financial records and over Sharon herself. Finally, the judge decided that only one of them could be in control, and, in July 1985, he picked Sharon's father. When he made this choice, the judge surely knew that Donald Kowalski would use his power to move Sharon three hundred miles away from Karen's home and not let Karen visit. When Donald Kowalski barred Karen from seeing Sharon, the judge backed him up. The Minnesota Court of Appeals upheld the trial judge's decision both times.

In fact, although Karen's version of the story is undoubtedly the one that, by helping her raise money for legal expenses, enabled her finally to succeed in court, it has never been entirely the source of that success. The trial judge finally let Karen visit Sharon not because he believed that Karen had a right to visit because she and Sharon were "spouses in every respect except the legal," but instead because he became convinced that Sharon was capable of knowing and expressing her own mind. Similarly, Karen has succeeded in becoming Sharon's guardian at last because the Minnesota Appeals Court, too, has become convinced that Sharon is capable of choosing her own guardian, and now believes that Karen is extremely caring and devoted to Sharon, and because it rejected the competing version that Karen is "possessive, manipulative and domineering."

When Donald Kowalski portrayed Karen as an unhealthy, domineering, masculine woman who had to be prevented from preying upon his naive, innocent, and normal daughter, he was casting Karen as a congenital invert. In certain respects, she fit this stereotype, being a college professor of physical education — that is, both an athlete and an intellectual. Moreover, she was nine years older than Sharon, had been her teacher, and had even encouraged Sharon to coach track and then to teach physical education at the high school level.

Karen Thompson's response to Donald Kowalski's version of the story seems to have gone through two phases. In the first phase, she offered the court a competing version of her relationship with Sharon. In her book, *Why Can't Sharon Kowalski Come Home?*, Karen emphasized that it was Sharon who had pursued her. Sharon sought her out and asked to help coach the track team; Sharon visited her at home, and in Ohio when she went there to finish her degree; Sharon rode a motorcycle. Sharon pushed Karen to declare her love, and, after they exchanged rings, it was Sharon who took the sexual initiative. Without access to transcripts of the court proceedings, it is difficult to tell whether Karen intended to show that only Sharon was the true lesbian... or that, like Patience and Sarah, she and Sharon were mutually attracted lesbians.

Either way, the story did not work for Karen. I offer two possible accounts of this failure. First, Karen's story may not have been believed. Karen's version fit the evidence before the court no better than Donald Kowalski's did. After all, Karen was nine years older than Sharon, had supported her from time to time, and was the sole owner of their house. Moreover, the persuasiveness of *The Price of Salt*, *The Color Purple*, and *Patience and Sarah* all depend upon their presentation of the interior reflections of both members of the couple. For Karen's version to be persuasive, Sharon would have had to be able to second it. At first, she could not. Inevitably, Sharon's present vulnerability was read back into the past, undermining Karen's story.

The second possibility was that Karen's version was believed, but it did not prove enough. In effect, Karen's story was that she was Sharon's spouse, and should therefore be treated by the court as

her natural guardian. But Donald Kowalski, Sharon's father, was an equally natural choice for guardian, as the Minnesota Court of Appeals pointed out in denying Karen's first appeal.

Karen's response to Donald Kowalski's version entered its next phase after she lost her second appeal. Now Karen relied not on her own right to be Sharon's guardian, but on Sharon's right to make her own decisions. Perhaps recognizing that her earlier loss was linked to the court's failure to see Sharon as autonomous, Karen pressed to have Sharon's competence independently and professionally evaluated. If Donald Kowalski had won because he was Sharon's father, then let the court consider the risk of his patriarchal authority unnecessarily infantilizing his daughter.

This second strategy has finally proved successful. Thanks to Karen's efforts, Sharon was moved from the nursing home where Donald Kowalski had been keeping her to a rehabilitation facility. Soon afterwards, she asked to see Karen. Since then, Karen has visited "three or more days per week, actively working with her in therapy and daily care." In December, 1990, Karen again sought to be Sharon's guardian, with the support of all of the medical and allied health professionals who care for Sharon. Although the trial named a "neutral third party" guardian, instead, Karen Thompson won on appeal.

By emphasizing and supporting Sharon's autonomy, individuality, and choice, Karen both undermined the basis for Donald Kowalski's version of her as a predatory, domineering invert and created the conditions for Sharon to speak for herself. Whether or not her lawyers learned it from the book, they seem to have succeeded by adopting the narrative strategy of *Patience and Sarah* to tell Karen's and Sharon's story.

FOUR

Family Break-Up and Reorganization

In some ways, the field of law most similar to family law is corporate law. Both leave most kinds of governance to the discretion of the entities while simultaneously establishing baseline abuses that the state will not tolerate. A central focus for both bodies of law addresses the creation and reorganization of entities. Divorce may resemble bankruptcy not just metaphorically; the legal and emotional task in both instances involves reorganizing the enterprise as much as it does dissolving it. Legal disputes arising between those who were once part of an ongoing enterprise — whether a corporation or a family — raise sticky questions about who can speak for the interests of the enterprise or its offspring (or subsidiaries), and about how to allocate responsibility for ongoing debts and costs.

But of course, families are not corporations. The break-up of a family, and its reorganization, involve complex emotional activity that cannot be ordered by a court. The law may make things easier or harder, but it cannot make people love one another or stop hating each other. Should judges, mediators, and other legal actors take these emotional issues into account, or instead focus on articulating hard-edged obligations that can be enforced when family members decide to end or change their collective lives? Does the very expense and delay of the legal process make things worse?

And how should a family reorganize itself as its members grow older? When, if ever, should adult children be responsible for the needs of their parents, or their siblings? Should the law establish any rules in this area, or leave the matter to private decisions?

Why Should the State Care? Fault and No-Fault in Divorce and Child Abandonment

If marriage is a contract, the economists' notion of "efficient breach" might come into play: breaking the contract then would raise no moral or emotional questions but instead trigger the financial assessment of whether the ongoing agreement is worth less than paying the damages accruing upon breach. Yet even this notion from contracts theory seems thin in a world that associates promises with trust and ongoing relationships with value that cannot be measured in cash. When applied to marriage, this economic analysis may seem especially harsh and neglectful of the moral and psychological dimensions of human intimacy and reliance.

At the same time, on what grounds should government officials have a say about whether a marriage should be terminated? What justifications are there for allowing or requiring courts to review the arrangements private parties devise to reorganize their family affairs? Historically available only rarely — at dispensation of the legislature through private bills — divorce became a remedy for the failures of one of the parties to perform the terms of the marriage. Crucial here were notions of fault. Divorce, once recognized, required proof of a defendant's fault in the marital break-up. The fault could be due to cruelty, adultery, desertion, and in some jurisdictions, drunkenness, drug addiction, nonsupport, vagrancy, infecting the wife with a veneral disease, public defamation of the spouse, lewd behavior of the wife, gross misbehavior or wickedness. Defendants could defend — and prevent divorce — by establishing recrimination (or mutual antipathy), collusion or connivance in the grounds alleged for divorce, or condonation (resumption of marital cohabitation).

In 1956, a Pennsylvania court denied a divorce when it found both parties to blame, and reasoned: "The fact that married people do not get along well together does not justify divorce.... If both are equally at fault, neither can clearly be said to be the innocent and injured spouse, and the law will leave them where they put themselves." *Rankin* v. *Rankin*, 181 Pa., *supra.* 414 (Pa. 1956). This kind of thinking consigned many couples to unhappy relationships, or else simply barred them from remarrying because not even the law could force people to live together.

Pressure to reform the fault-based regime mounted, though, as people manufactured fault grounds, and paradoxically, as people developed higher expectations of happiness in marriage and sought divorce due to disappointment. Today, all states make some form of no-fault divorce available. What does this change in the grounds for divorce do to the meaning of marriage? Why, under a no-fault regime, should courts retain any involvement in divorce? Should fault notions persist in the allocation of support following divorce? Who is helped and who is hurt by no-fault divorce? Some evidence suggests that women and children have been more hurt than helped. Can such problems be remedied with better rules and enforcement practices concerning alimony and child support? Can reformers better anticipate the consequences of law reform? Do the legal rules themselves affect people's decisions to divorce?

Perhaps the rules about divorce should vary depending upon the presence or absence of children. Some people advocate eliminating the role of courts and lawyers altogether and making divorces available through a judicial clerk or even shopping mall outlets if no children or financial support questions are involved. Summary divorce procedures already exist, and Mary Ann Glendon reported that "the symbolic ultimate in summary divorce may already have been reached in California where in 1979 a couple parachuted from a plane, and during their fall, exchanged papers that terminated their sixteen-year marriage."[1] Should the state ever retain an active involvement in divorce — with lawyers and judges — such as when children are involved?

---

1. Mary Ann Glendon, *The New Family and the New Property* (Toronto: Butterworth's & Co., 1981) p. 34.

◆

EPILOGUE: THE PURSUIT OF HAPPINESS
Elaine Tyler May

Mercy and justice to the mismated are creeping into the law. Without doubt marriage is throwing off the shackles of blind intolerance and groping toward a form in which human beings may find sanity and contentment.... Divorce — like medical anesthesia — so lately despised, is beginning to be recognized as the next great step along the way. The way to where? The only answer is happiness.

The pursuit of happiness took on a new direction and urgency in the decades surrounding the turn of the century. Focusing on private life, men and women turned to each other and to the home in a fervent personal quest, dramatically reflected in the rising rate of marriage and the soaring rate of divorce. The hundreds of court cases used in this study provide a rare glimpse into marriage and family life during the years when marital breakdown rose most rapidly, revealing the thoughts and emotions of ordinary individuals facing a major crisis in their lives. Taken together, they reflect a larger historical drama: the emergence of modern American life and the great expectations for personal fulfillment that came with it.

The story unfolds in the 1880s, in a growing city on the western edge of the American frontier. Here we find the heirs of Victorianism forging a new community and establishing religious, political, and cultural institutions. As they took hold of the reins of power, they began the task of building a city in tune with their cultural ideals. The divorce cases filed during this decade indicate the strength of the Victorian world view these settlers brought with them. Compared to later decades, divorce was relatively rare. When it did occur, it was usually among these native Americans themselves, whose marriages did not meet traditional standards. If one spouse flagrantly violated the code of behavior expected within marriage, the other would seek a divorce. We find very little confusion, ambivalence, or contention over these accepted roles.

Women discarded husbands if they failed in the fundamental duty of providing the necessities of life: a comfortable place to live, enough to eat, and adequate means for reasonable well being. If they polluted the domestic environment through overindulgence in vices such as drinking or gambling, they were deemed unworthy. Sexual excess was also beyond the bounds of reasonable behavior. The limits and duties were clearly defined: husbands were to provide the necessities of life, treat their wives with courtesy and protection, and exercise sexual restraint. Men who found that their wives deviated from proper norms of conduct also sought redress. A wife's duty was to maintain a comfortable home, take care of household chores, bear and tend to the children, and set the moral tone for domestic life. She was to remain chaste and modest in her behavior, frugal in matters of household

Elaine Tyler May, "Epilogue: The Pursuit of Happiness," in *Great Expectations* (Chicago: University of Chicago Press, 1980), pp. 156–163.

expenses, and her conduct was never to reflect badly upon her home and her husband's good name. A woman who was not genteel in her demeanor, who acted like (or indeed was) a "whore," or who violated the boundaries — physical as well as moral — of a woman's proper sphere, might be shed in the divorce court. The roles for both husbands and wives, then, were well understood. These norms formed the basic requirements for attaining domestic peace and building solid communities around well-disciplined homes.

As couples whose marriages did not conform to these standards headed for divorce, the vast majority of their contemporaries stayed married and went about the task of building a city that would provide an appropriate setting for their moral homes. They closed vice districts, outlawed prostitution, raised the age of consent, established churches, closed saloons on Sundays, and set up supervised recreational facilities. Yet these efforts were not aimed toward preserving the past; the goal was to build a better future. Ennui had crept into work and public life. Americans were restless and reaching out for new experiences. Faced with the decline of Victorian traditions, they tried to shape their environment in a way that would allow the positive aspects of modern life to flourish, while screening out the negative elements. As a part of this effort they built sprawling suburban homes in protected neighborhoods and created legitimate amusements which would provide constructive and wholesome recreation. As they accumulated more money and more free time in which to spend it, these migrants to Los Angeles, like their contemporaries all over the country, sought to make affluence and leisure both safe and satisfying. In this pursuit, they turned with increased fervor to the private side of life,

perhaps to compensate for a loss of satisfactions elsewhere.

What, then, did these modern urbanites want out of marriage by 1920? Had they buried the remnants of Victorianism, in the quest for a life truly liberated from the past? This study suggests that such was not the case. Men and women in 1920 seemed to want a more satisfying home. But there was a confusion surrounding domestic aspirations that had not been present in the 1880s. "Marital happiness" was not clearly defined; no universal standard held for everyone. Contrary to the assumptions of contemporary observers as well as historians since, most divorcing urbanites were not in the vanguard of a moral revolution. Although they displayed desires for a new excitement and sensuality, most were caught between traditions of the past and visions of the future.

In general, wives in 1920 still preferred care and protection to a job and independence. Like their grandmothers, they wanted husbands to provide for them and respect their delicacy. These modern women were still antagonistic to sexual excesses and inclined toward a peaceful domestic life with children, albeit with greater opportunities for fun, leisure, and affluence than their Victorian predecessors. Men in the sample reflected similar ambivalence. They may have been attracted to youthful and exciting "new women," but they also wanted domestic, frugal, and virtuous wives who would keep house and tend to the children. These expectations held true for couples in New Jersey as well as Los Angeles, with very few variations. There is no reason to assume that significant differences appeared anywhere else in the country.

If most moral attitudes survived the early decades of the twentieth century without radical changes, this is not to imply that aspirations surrounding marriage and family life had not altered. Traditional notions of virtue were enveloped by modern desires, heightening hopes for marital fulfillment. This overlapping of cultural values caused a great deal of upheaval in many marriages, as a number of the cases in this study suggest. Divorces often resulted from myriad problems, rather than one specific issue. The case mentioned at the very beginning of this study illustrates how numerous difficulties might erupt simultaneously. Lorimer Linganfield was attracted to a sensual, exciting young woman, but was chagrined when she refused to settle down into proper wifely behavior. His wife, in turn, was excited by the new life, especially urban amusements, and wanted a man who would provide high-level affluence. Unlike most of her contemporaries, she did not want children. But similar to many Victorians, she was reluctant to have sex with her husband, in spite of her sexy appearance.

The pursuit of happiness took couples like the Linganfields into wedlock, and then out again. Along with marriage, divorce was another step in the quest. But the break itself was rarely a happy one. In fact, it was almost always painful. Rather than a triumph, it often seemed like a personal failure. In the divorce court, unhappily married individuals blamed their spouses. But away from the court, they often blamed themselves. The cases in this study are filled with highly emotional expressions of remorse. As one errant husband wrote to his wife:

> As a man, I should have acted differently, but through all these years my whole system has been poisoned with drink.... Your struggle, working and saving, was the only way... but I, like a fool, couldn't realize that.... I don't believe any other woman would have put up with as

much as you have. You were a neat, good housekeeper who lived for and loved a good home. But already I am suffering from remorse.... I often wish myself dead in order to have an end to it all.... We will go our separate ways — good-bye from Adolph.

Similar was the statement of Henry Northam, a piano salesman and tuner, married to Elizabeth, an "even-tempered, church-going" woman who "worked until she had a breakdown." They lived together for seven years after their marriage in 1905 and had no children. When the case for desertion had been granted, Henry wrote his wife a letter, saying he was not resentful. He claimed that his "illness" had been the "sole cause of our disaster....I was a victim of ignorance and superstition and the penalty is unavoidable." Yet he will cherish what had been "ideal" between them and hopes that she will find someone and make a "happy home for which you are rarely and richly endowed by nature." Another such case was that of Harrison Drinon, whose wife Mary divorced him on the grounds of habitual intemperance. After a twenty-five year marriage beginning in Illinois in 1882, he wrote,

> I am quite well aware that my actions of late precluded the possibility of my returning to the house and very deservedly so.... I seek no sympathy, for I deserve it all. I have been a failure as a husband and father and in every other conceivable way.

Perhaps the most moving and poignant of these cases of remorse is of a woman who defied the very essence of virtue: chastity and marital fidelity. Yet in her misery she indicated what had led to her downfall. Rose and Charles Pearson were married in Cameron, Missouri, in 1910. Their union came to an end when Charles discovered a letter from his wife's lover, a married man who urged that they both divorce and marry each other. Rose's anguished response overflowed with guilt — and yet this ultimate violation of marital vows did not represent any flaunting of wedlock or any rejection of the domestic ideal. In fact, it was the very pursuit of that personalized relationship that led to her adultery:

> I am blind and stunned.... My suffering and sin is greater than I can bear. I deserve all.... Will try to answer questions while I am able to write. The date of first sin was the last day of October. Never on bed, I held that sacred. No, no, not daily, and altogether five times.... I never had any of my clothes off not even my corset. Always dressed. He gave me altogether $75. I fought till I could fight no longer.... He promised me a home a future and a little one...

Here Rose revealed her own marital disappointments, and the promise of fulfillment with her lover. It was not illicit excitement she sought; rather, it was a "home a future and a little one," desires not satisfied by her husband. Yet even in the midst of sexual relations with another man, she did not transgress easily. Indeed, she still held her marriage bed "sacred." Her confession, however, contained several accusations: lack of spending money which her lover apparently supplied, security with the promise of children, and an affectionate man at her side. Communication with her husband broke down, and Rose found solace with another.

> I do not ask you to take me back, I hoped and prayed you would take me into your arms again. Now I have lost last. There is only one thing left. Death. One last favor I ask of you dear Charles do not tell my sisters all

my sin and wrong.... It is torture for me to stay here under this sin.... Charles, I know there were times when I did not speak to you. I needed your love then, that was all that was the matter. I was aching and hungry for love. One loving word then or if you had taken me in your arms would have made me happy again... and that would have drawn us closer together. You never could understand this and you left me alone to suffer in silence.

Rose was left with her wish to die rather than face her shame. The home she so desired now seemed beyond her grasp. Yet she blamed her husband for his lack of responsiveness and reproached him for being totally oblivious to her needs. This woman did not want independence. Her marriage ended because of her unfulfilled desires for affection, security and domesticity. Her husband remained detached, unable to comprehend:

> When I needed your love most you withheld it. Forgive me my husband. Forgive me is the cry in my heart.... Pray for me my husband and if you hear of my death in the next few weeks or month you will know what to say to shield my name from public shame.... I have loved you more than I realized.... I am heartbroken, helpless, and alone and forsaken. My husband, try to forgive, the girl you never seemed to understand what she wanted — *much love*. Your lost Rose.

Rose Pearson felt lost. She failed in her primary role in life. Like many of her contemporaries, her quest for happiness led her away from her disappointing marriage toward the promise of a better one. The desperation of these wives reflects the high stakes placed on marriage. Because most women viewed matrimony as the only place they could truly express themselves, it is misleading to equate the desire for marital dissolution with any widespread urge for freedom from marriage itself. The high rate of remarriage among divorced persons testifies to this fact. Those who divorced once often divorced twice, as our Los Angeles sample from 1920 illustrates. Twenty-six of the women and eleven of the men had been divorced at least once prior to the filing of this action. Out of those whose marital status was known, this represents eighteen percent of the women and eight percent of the men. It is significant that over twice as many women as men were headed for their second divorce, in spite of their younger age. These findings suggest that divorce did not indicate a rejection of marriage; rather, it reflected the increased personal desires that matrimony was expected to satisfy, especially for women.

Although men who sued for divorce were just as likely as women to have petitions granted in their favor, most of the cases were filed by wives. More eager for domestic perfection, women were also more easily disappointed. Realizing this, one judge admonished a dissatisfied young wife without concealing his exasperation. He felt that her hopes for happiness were unrealistically high:

> I think it is another of the cases in which the husband did not treat his wife as he should and she was in a pretty big hurry to get a divorce. So she puts together everything that happened in their domestic history to make out extreme cruelty.... I do not understand why she is in such a hurry.... She will probably get married again and have some more trouble.... It is not going to hurt this woman at all not to have a decree of divorce just now. This is the judg-

ment.... She is hereby denied a decree of divorce.

This judge, no doubt, had heard more than one too many pleas for divorce; his attitude was undeniably callous. Yet he perceived a profound reality: marriage was not likely to sustain the high hopes that all too often were brought to it. When these hopes were shattered, the result was tragedy rather than triumph. One Los Angeles divorcee wanted to let the presiding judge know that her successful decree was purchased at the cost of tremendous emotional suffering:

> I hardly presume you have much personal interest in cases tried before you, but I do want to say a little bit about the case just finished, and to thank you for the decision; and yet, your Honor, that decision did not cause the heart thrill you seemed to anticipate, for I loved my husband up to the time of his desertion, which was a staggering blow to me.... Anyway, I am placed in the position of having to thank you for making of me something I never wanted to be — a divorced woman. Very respectfully, Mayme E. Johnson.

Divorce represents a painful step on the road to personal fulfillment. Scenes of marital failure, admittedly, are not the place to look for happiness. Obviously, broken marriages cannot serve as examples of marriages in general. But were the couples in the divorce samples really deviations from the norm, or were they rather the "tip of the iceberg," representing only a fraction of couples with similar problems who managed to live with their difficulties? I suspect that the problems we have explored here were not unique to failing marriages, but existed to a greater or lesser degree among far more couples than ever reached the divorce court. Indeed, as the twentieth century has progressed, we have seen more and more of the iceberg. Americans are still coupling, uncoupling, and recoupling at an astonishing rate.

Today, broken marriage has lost the stigma it had a century ago. Divorced parents are no longer considered social mishaps or moral deviants. But is divorce really a liberation? Do people discard matrimony in favor of other alternatives — or do they merely move on in a perpetual quest for "the perfect relationship"? Personal life seems to have become a national obsession in twentieth-century America. It is not likely that the domestic domain will ever be able to satisfy completely the great expectations for individual fulfillment brought to it. As long as the American pursuit of happiness continues along this private path, divorce is likely to be with us.

◆

BUT WHERE ARE THE MEN
Ruth Sidel

somebody almost run off wit alla my stuff/& I was standin there/looking at myself/the whole time & it waznt a spirit took my stuff/waz a man whose ego walked round like Rodan's shadow/was a man faster n my innocence/waz a lover/I made too much room for/almost run off wit alla my stuff/& I dint know I'd give it up so quik/& the one running wit it/dont know he got it/& I'm shoutin this is mine/& he dont know he got it/my stuff is the anonymous ripped off treasure of the year.
— *Ntozake Shange*

Over and over as I interviewed women in different parts of the country I heard stories of men walking out on women. Sometimes the couple was young and had been together a short time, other times they were middle-aged and had been together for many years; but almost always, the man was the one who walked out — often with little or no warning — and the woman and children were left to cope as best they could. From the women of Maine to the Native American families of New Mexico, I met mothers and children trying to make it on their own and trying to deal with their pain and anger.

Men are not always the ones who walk out, of course. Sometimes the women leave; sometimes the split is mutual; and sometimes the man was never really there. But whether because of divorce, separation, or not marrying at all, the grouping that remains is mothers with their children, children with their mothers. And where are the men? Some have simply vanished, gone on to other things. Others have started new families. Some feel that they cannot live up to their roles as fathers because they cannot live up to their roles as breadwinners.

Barbara Ehrenreich, in her recent book *The Hearts of Men*, claims that over the past thirty years American men have been

From Ruth Sidel, "But Where Are the Men," in *Women and Children Last* (Penguin: New York, 1986), pp. 101–114.

fleeing from commitment to the family. She points out that in the 1950s "adult masculinity was indistinguishable from the breadwinner role...." Gradually, according to Ehrenreich, the prodding of cultural forces such as *Playboy* — which encouraged, as one sociologist has described it, the "fun morality" — and the health profession's warning that the stress that came from the role as breadwinner could well lead to coronary heart disease encouraged men to drift more and more toward a commitment to self, toward "doing one's own thing," and away from the confines and conflicts of wife, children, mortgage, and the pressures of new shoes for the first day of school. As Ehrenreich states, "The result of divorce, in an overwhelming number of cases, is that men become singles and women become single mothers."

While there is little doubt that much of Ehrenreich's analysis is valid, it is not the whole story. In the first place, her analysis is valid not just for men but for much of American society as a whole. The shift toward concern with self, with individual needs and desires, with personal growth, toward narcissism, has been widespread and is a result, I believe, of fundamental societal developments over the course of the twentieth century — urbanization, the changing nature of work, and the development of a consumer society.

Urbanization has, as is well known, been a major factor in the fragmentation of primary groups. The pressures, variety, and opportunities of the city, together with the anonymity it provides, have made it increasingly possible for individuals to shake off their obligations to others, to walk away without fear of censure from the "group," for there is hardly any group left. If family members are scattered, if there is no defined community, if there are no elders to censure, why not simply walk away from upsetting and restrictive commitments?

While urbanization was disrupting networks of community and kin, specialization was becoming the primary mode of work in twentieth-century America. As French sociologist Emilé Durkheim pointed out nearly a hundred years ago, when societies are small and everyone does much the same kind of work, a "collective consciousness" develops based on similar socialization and shared experiences and values. When, however, each person does just one small piece of an overall task, and this task has little relationship to what others are doing, individualism is fostered. Durkheim predicted that such a division of labor and the resulting growth of individualism would lead to a breakdown in commitment to social norms, the situation Ehrenreich seems to be describing. Add to urbanization and an extreme division of labor the pressures of a consumer society — in which we are systematically taught to believe that we are what we wear, what we own, what we buy; an unrelenting pressure to acquire new goods in order to redefine ourselves continually — and a social milieu develops in which individualism and self-gratification are rewarded, and commitment to others is devalued. That commitment is particularly constraining if it seems to diminish one's own options, one's own pleasures, one's own "personal growth."

And, of course, men are not the only ones who have been affected by these profound changes in American society. Women, and specifically those in the women's movement, have been affected by the emphasis on individualism, by the increasing legitimacy of individual needs and aspirations, of individual happiness. If "We Shall Overcome" was the anthem of the 1960s, perhaps Madonna sings the anthem of the 1980s in her song "Material Girl."

It is striking, however, that while many women are concerned with the quality of their lives, with their own development and careers, with their "material world," they remain, as Ehrenreich correctly points out, the primary caregivers for their children. While many men have abdicated their parental responsibilities, women for the most part have not.

Part of the explanation of women's special relationship to their children lies, clearly, in the special nature of the mothering role, with the bonding that takes place *in utero* and then during the first few weeks and months of an infant's life, and the ongoing intimate relationship women continue to have with children. But another part of the explanation of the male ability to avoid the responsibilities of fatherhood may well lie in the nature of the fathering role in our society. Is the role of father such that it produces a lack of genuine involvement with children, a lack of real connectedness? Are the majority of fathers simply expected to bring home a paycheck and occasionally to throw a baseball around — and is this kind of relationship just too tenuous to bind men to their children? With the increasing erosion of the patriarchal role, we must develop an equally meaningful way for men to relate to their children.

Profound class differences exist in the ways men relate to their families today. The models written up on the women's pages of leading newspapers — of men trying to take paternity leave, of "househusbands," of a recent best-seller in which a father lyrically describes the first year of his daughter's life — are those of relatively few, usually highly educated, upper-middle-class white men. While a fair number of men near Columbia University or in Harvard Square or in Berkeley may lovingly carry their babies in Snugglies, it is hardly a common sight at the entrance to auto plants, in accounting firms, or among men who hang out on the street corners of urban ghettos. Clearly behavior that is encouraged and rewarded in one segment of the upper middle class is considered unacceptable in much of the rest of the country; until the perceptions and values and norms of the larger society change, we cannot rationally expect individual behavior to alter significantly.

The bottom line of the male flight from commitment, of many fathers' lack of involvement with their children and, above, all, of economic factors usually beyond the individual's control, is that the majority of men who are not living with the wives and children are also not supporting them. The issue of child support has received considerable attention over the past few years because of the unprecedented increase in the number of female-headed families during the 1970s. The importance of child support to the economic well-being of mothers and children is underscored by women's low earning ability. According to a Working Paper published by Wellesley College Center for Research on Women, women "with the sole custody of children experience the most severe decline in family income." A spring 1982 Census Bureau survey found that over eight million women are raising at least one child whose father is absent from the home. Of these eight million women, only five million had been awarded child support by the courts. Of the women who were supposed to be receiving payments in 1981, forty-seven percent received the full amount, thirty-seven percent received less than half of what they were supposed to receive, and twenty-eight percent received no payments at all. Ironically, the women most likely to receive court-ordered child support are "educated, employed, divorced women" rather than separated, never married, minority

women. The average annual child-support
payment in 1981 was $2,180 for white
women, $2,070 for Hispanic women, and
$1,640 for black women.

Why don't men pay child support
more regularly? Some men withhold payment in reaction to the bitterness of a divorce, some as a way of protesting what
they feel is an unfair financial settlement,
and some because they want to use their
money to recapture the sense of being
single, of being free.

Betty Levinson, a New York lawyer
who devotes approximately one-third of
her practice to matrimonial law, feels that
in most divorce cases she sees there is
simply not enough money to support two
households. These families, mostly middle and upper middle class, are "premised
on plastic." Often these couples cannot
afford to separate; both husbands and
wives must learn to "trim their expectations in planning for their lives after
divorce."

On the issue of nonsupport Levinson
feels that many men would rather pay for
a lawyer than support their children. She
suggests that one scenario is: "Now that
it's over I can't deal with you anymore.
You represent a failure for me and therefore I don't want to deal with the kids
either because I associate the kids with the
failed marriage and with you." Another
scenario is that the man has remarried and
is supporting his new wife and her children who, in turn, are not being supported
by their father. Part of the message such a
man gives to his former wife is, "When
you took custody you took responsibility."
The fathers who say this, according to
Levinson, are frequently men who do not
see their kids very often, because they live
in another state or for some other reason.

The third scenario involves the father
who sees his kids, but mainly for Sunday
visits. According to Betty Levinson, "It's

incredible the kind of money these fathers
will spend on these weekly visits — theater, ski trips, and so forth — but they
resist giving more in the way of child
support. Often the father's feeling is, 'Yes,
I understand that the child needs this now,
but I have to think of my future.' The
ultimate responsibility for the children,"
she states flatly, "is with the mother. No
matter what happens, the mother takes
care of the children."

Researchers and activists, both those
who work for more stringent child-support
legislation and spokespersons on behalf of
men's groups, agree that the payment of
child support is often tied to the altered
parent-child relationship. Researchers
have found that after divorce fathers often
experience a loss of identity, a loss of
status within the family, and a "particularly poignant sense of loss associated
with the altered father-child relationship.
The divorced father is no longer part of the
day-to-day life of the child, but is abruptly
relegated to a visitor status.... Many fathers cope by distancing themselves from
the parent-child relationship." What better
way to do this than by withholding financial support?

James A. Cook, president of the National Congress for Men, a four-year-old
coordinating group of 125 men's rights
organizations with ten thousand members,
also ties the problem of economic support
to fathers' lack of access to their children.
He asks, "Can we levy responsibility on
these fathers without an equivalent right,
the right of access to the child?" John A.
Rossler of the Equal Rights for Father of
New York State agrees: "Many men have
had to beg for access to their children. The
system of divorce in America often results
in the removing of all father functions save
for one, the monetary obligation. A man is
more than a wallet to his kids." Rossler
and other representatives of men's groups

strongly endorse custody reform: "Whether you call it joint custody, shared custody, liberal visitation or co-parenting, we are talking about actively involving the noncustodial parent in all areas of his child's upbringing."

Betty Levinson, on the other hand, feels that joint custody is a very "trendy" issue; it is thought to be "the thing to do." She claims that men are made to feel that if they do not demand joint custody that they are not the father they should be. But it is, she points out, a very difficult arrangement. The husband and wife must cooperate extremely well for it to work. She goes on to state emphatically:

> Joint custody becomes an economic bludgeon on the wife by the husband. Asking for joint custody or trying to take custody away from the mother is a surefire way to freak out the mother. And after they have freaked her out, the father and his lawyer will often say, "Okay, you take 75 percent of our financial agreement instead of 100 percent and I'll give you full custody." It has become a way of negotiating the money.

On August 16, 1984, a comprehensive bill to enforce payment of child support became federal law. Approved by unanimous roll-call votes in both houses of Congress, the new law required child-support orders issued or modified after October 1, 1985, to permit the withholding of wages if a parent becomes delinquent in payments and enables states to "require that an absent parent give security, post a bond or give some other guarantee'" to ensure final payment of child support in cases where there has been a pattern of delinquency. The law is a significant victory for those groups that have been advocating more stringent regulations and collection methods to improve the rate of payment of child support.

But voluntary nonpayment of child support is clearly only one facet of the problem of the absent father. Many fathers provide little or no support — either in economic or emotional terms — to their children and to the children's mothers because they are unable to play the traditional fathering role, that of breadwinner. In January 1983 approximately twelve million people, over ten percent of the American workforce, were actively looking for jobs and were the officially designated unemployed. While that number has since fallen to 7.2 percent, this stark figure, the highest rate since the Great Depression, has stimulated additional studies on the physiological, psychological, and sociological aspects of unemployment.

First, it must be pointed out that federal unemployment statistics significantly minimize the problem of unemployment. Figures released by the Bureau of Labor Statistics do not include those who reluctantly move from full-time to part-time employment; those who take jobs well below their skill level; those who must move from one temporary, low-paying job to the next; and those who become "permanently discouraged" and stop looking for work altogether. Nor do the statistics, as one researchers has movingly written, "reflect the anxiety, depression, deprivation, lost opportunities, violence, insecurity, and anger people feel when their source of livelihood is severed and they lose control of a significant aspect of their environment." As Paula Rayman, sociologist and director of the New England Unemployment Project, has written, "When an adult has work taken away, the focus of life's daily pattern is removed. Time and space, the sense of self, are radically altered, and what is left is a sense of impotence."

The work of Johns Hopkins sociologist and epidemiologist Harvey Brenner demonstrates the dramatic effect unemployment has on the entire family's health and well-being. Brenner has found, for example, that admissions to psychiatric hospitals, deaths from cardiovascular and alcohol-related illnesses, homicide and suicide rates increase significantly during periods of economic decline. Other researchers have found that male unemployment is associated with high blood pressure, alcoholism, increased smoking, insomnia, anxiety, and higher levels of psychiatric symptoms among men. In addition, "The wives in unemployed families were significantly more depressed, anxious, phobic, and sensitive about their interpersonal relationships" than spouses in families in which there is no unemployment. The longer the period of unemployment, the greater the stress on the family and on family cohesion. In a study of the unemployed in Hartford, Rayman and Ramsey Liem found three times as much marital separation among the unemployed group as among the control group.

Clinical observations of unemployed people who go to social agencies for counseling indicate that they are coping with feelings of loss, anger, and guilt — a "sense of losing a part of the self." Observers have likened these feelings to feelings of bereavement. Studies find that people anticipating or experiencing unemployment "suffer loss of self-esteem, loss of personal identity, worry and uncertainty about the future, loss of a sense of purpose, and depression." With these reactions to unemployment, is it any wonder that family stability is being undermined?

While there has been a limited economic recovery since the height of the 1982-83 recession, many workers' incomes have declined sharply since the late 1970s. For example, the average income of workers laid off by the United States Steel Corporation's South Works in Chicago has fallen in the last five years by fifty percent. Over 2,000 workers were laid off from 1979 to 1981, and another 3,300 were laid off from 1981 to 1983. Many of these workers have had long periods of unemployment; forty-six percent remained unemployed as of October 1984. The laid-off workers, whose annual household income averaged $22,000 in 1979, had a median household income in 1983 of approximately $12,500. According to one worker, "To go from earning $20,000-plus to being at an employer's mercy for $3.35 an hour is devastating." Moreover, unskilled workers and black and Hispanic male workers have extremely limited opportunities for work and suffer from the highest unemployment rates. In a 1983 study of the New York City job market, it was found that the decline in manufacturing and the expansion of the service sector have led to a decrease in job opportunities in the city for workers with few skills and limited education. Of all adults, black and Hispanic men twenty-five to thirty-five years old, "generally do the worst in the job market": They experience extended periods of unemployment, withdraw from the labor force because they become "discouraged," and have a high rate of involuntary part-time work. Moreover, among blacks and Hispanics, the length of unemployment for men is twice what it is for women: for black men, twenty-seven weeks; for black women, twelve weeks; for Hispanic men, twenty-two weeks; for Hispanic women, nine weeks.

Nationally, unemployment among blacks is officially twice the rate for whites, but the statistics tell only part of the story. Researchers at the Center for the Study of Social Policy claim that the true figure is that four million out of nine million working-age black men — forty-six percent — are jobless. For white men the comparable figure is twenty-two percent. Unemployment of this magnitude must have a dramatic impact on family stability and therefore be a major cause of the feminization of poverty. In 1960, according to this method of calculation, approximately three-quarters of all black men were employed; today only fifty-four percent are employed. Since 1960 the number of black families headed by women has more than tripled. There is little question that the unemployment of black men has had a direct impact on the rise of black female-headed families.

Furthermore, unemployment is only one of many severe problems black men must face. The National Urban League recently released a report stating that black men must deal with a "singular series of pressures from birth through adulthood." The report stated, "The gauntlet that black men run takes its toll at every age." In addition to the problems of educational and employment discrimination, Dr. James McGhee, the league's research director, cited higher mortality rates, greater likelihood of being arrested, and the rising incidence of self-destructive behavior such as drug and alcohol abuse. Black men have the highest death rates from accidents and violence of all groups, and their suicide rate has risen far more sharply in recent years than that of white men. In addition, homicide is the leading cause of death for black males ages fifteen to forty-four. Black men represent only five percent of the U.S. population but represent forty-four percent of its homicide victims. Many studies suggest that there is a direct correlation between feelings of frustration, powerlessness, and hopelessness and high rates of violence. According to sociologist and researcher on black families Andrew Billingsley, because of racial discrimination, many black men are distant from "any meaningful engagement with the economy, education, and the social system."

Elliot Liebow, in what has become a classic study of street corner black men in Washington, D.C., points out the close connection between a man's work and his relationships with family and friends: "The way in which the man makes a living and the kind of living he makes have important consequences for how the man sees himself and is seen by others; and these, in turn, importantly shape his relationships with family members, lovers, friends and neighbors." Liebow points out that the unskilled black man has little chance of obtaining a permanent job that would pay enough to support a family. He eventually becomes resigned to being unable to play the traditional father role, and rather than being faced with his own failure day after day, year after year, he often walks away.

Ironically, the children with whom these men are closest are not those they have fathered and therefore have an obligation to support; but rather the children of women they are currently seeing, who have been fathered by someone else. With someone else's children, whatever the men can give in the way of financial or emotional support is more than they need to give, and it therefore represents a positive gesture rather than yet another failure.

What is saddest about these dismal facts is how American ideology, which is apparently accepted by the majority of Americans and has been legitimized by the Reagan administration, blames the poor, rather than racism and the economic system, for their plight. While some of these issues were briefly addressed during the 1960s, the War on Poverty was woefully inadequate to reverse the damage done, particularly to blacks, in our society; and no sooner did it get started that Vietnam, inflation, and the Nixon administration had begun to subvert it. As Michael Harrington has so aptly stated, "The savior that never was became the scapegoat that is."

American policymakers have an uncanny ability to obfuscate and compartmentalize social problems — to recognize on the one hand that the United States has an unacceptably high level of unemployment, particularly among specific groups, and to recognize that we also have an incredibly high number of female-headed families, particularly within the same groups; but to avoid the cause-and-effect relationship between the two phenomena. This unwillingness to recognize the obvious correlation between the lack of economic opportunities for millions of American men — a lack of opportunity that will consign them, in all likelihood, for their entire lifetimes to the bottom of the class structure — and their lack of commitment to and steady participation in family life, is a shocking denial of the obvious impact of social and economic factors on the well-being of the family group.

As Eleanor Holmes Norton, former chairperson of the Equal Employment Opportunity Commission and currently a professor at the Georgetown University Law Center, has stated:

> This permanent, generational joblessness is at the core of the meaning of the American ghetto. The resulting, powerful aberration transforms life in poor black communities and forces everything to adapt to it. The female-headed household is only one consequence. The underground economy, the drug culture, epidemic

crimes and even a highly unusually disparity between the actual number of men and women — all owe their existence to the cumulative effect of chronic joblessness among men.

This avoidance has several advantages for those who seek to maintain the status quo in the United States: It discourages those at the bottom from developing a viable political and economic analysis of the American system, instead promoting a blame-the-victim mentality; a false consciousness of individual unworthiness, of self-blame; a belief that if only the individual worked harder, tried harder, he would "make it" and be the success every American thinks he should be. Not only does the unemployed male blame himself for not getting and keeping a decent job, thereby being unable to provide for his family in the way he would like, but the woman may also blame him. As one woman in *Tally's Corner* says with a bitter smile, "I used to lean on Richard. Like when I was having the baby, I leaned on him but he wasn't there and I fell down.... Now I don't lean on him anymore. I pretend I lean, but I'm not leaning." Or the woman blames herself for not choosing her man more wisely, for not holding the family together despite the odds, for being either too assertive or not assertive enough. And yet virtually no one blames an economic system that deprives millions of workers of jobs and then somehow indicates it is their fault.

Sandra Wittaker, a black woman from California who is raising her two children alone puts it this way:

> Black men are able to cope far less than black women. They are feared more by society and therefore have far fewer opportunities. All the men

I have known, my brothers, my father, my male friends, my husband, have not made it in society. Many of them take to drinking and dope — some kind of escape. Black males are suffering far more than females.

My son has had three role models and none of them were any good. He has not had a mature man to model himself on.... He has nightmares. He's afraid of being a failure and he's already opted out. By the time he was four, my son did not even want to be black. It is terrible to watch your child and know that he is going to be hurt constantly.

If there is a group that has been hit even harder than blacks, it is Native Americans. Unemployment among the 1 million American Indians is said to range between forty-five and fifty-five percent, but it reaches eighty percent in some areas and in some seasons.

Among the Pueblo Indians who live approximately sixty miles southwest of Albuquerque, New Mexico, for example, the unemployment rate is seventy percent. After the nearby uranium mines were closed in 1981-82, there were no other jobs available. According to Jean Eller, a young physician who worked at the Acoma Canonita Laguna Indian Health Hospital in Acoma, New Mexico, people now just "hang around." There is nothing for them to do. And the young people are torn between their desire to find a job in a nearby town or city and pressure from their elders to return to the reservation. The elders are afraid the young people will lose touch with their culture if they move off the reservation, but there are few opportunities there, either.

Tied to the unemployment rate, Dr. Eller believes, is an enormous problem with alcohol and a suicide rate that is the highest of any ethnic group in the country. Alcohol is mainly a male problem; some of the younger women drink, but the older women usually do not. According to Dr. Eller, there are three bars, run by non-Indians, near the reservation. One bar half a mile from the reservation serves "all the beer you can drink" free on Monday nights. These bars serve thirteen-year-olds, fourteen-year-olds and never check their IDs. "Many people hate these places and would like to blow them up!" Dr. Eller states quietly but angrily. She feels the significant amount of wife abuse that exists on these reservations is directly related to the amount of drinking, particularly on the weekends.

According to other medical personnel who work in the area, women are the backbone of the Indian family. Many feel that men have fallen apart more than women and are in a "cycle of destruction." The rates of alcoholism, wife abuse, child neglect, homicide, and suicide are at least three to four times the national rate.

There is also a high rate of teenage pregnancy, particularly among girls fifteen and under. The men rarely support their children, and some women move up and out of the reservation; many are, in fact, ostracized by their communities for doing so. The infant is then often cared for by the grandmother and brought up with the grandmother's own children as siblings. Indian women are clearly not first-class citizens even within Indian culture but they have very little recourse since the tribal councils are largely run by men.

The reservation in Acoma is in the middle of incredibly beautiful terrain. As you approach Acoma, the earth varies from beige to darker shades of brown, sometimes flat, sometimes hilly, with stark red clay rock formations that look almost like amphitheaters. Acoma is famous for handsome pottery, much of it black, white, and clay-reddish brown; several of the potters from this reservation sell to private collectors, some to museums. Mt. Taylor, snowcapped even in late spring, can be seen in the distance. Amid this truly splendid scenery, the reservation seems unbearably barren and depressed. During the day there is hardly a man to be seen. There are only women, children, and dogs — scrawny, hungry-looking dogs who roam near the houses.

Lena Ross is a heavy set woman with a weathered face and dark hair pulled back at the nape of her neck. She has moved within the past few days to a modern adobe-colored house in a settlement of new homes, most of which are still empty. The house has several bedrooms furnished with beds and colorful quilts and blankets, a kitchen with the latest in modern appliances, and a large, empty living room.

Ten of Lena Ross's thirteen children and her two grandchildren live with her. She has no husband. "I take care of the children myself," she tells me. She receives AFDC for the children who are in school, and social security for the grandchildren. While we talk, her one-and-a-half-year-old grandson sits on his grandmother's lap. He is a lively boy with long, dark hair and beautiful dark eyes. He is wearing a good-looking blue-and-white-striped shirt and is playing with a small car. Through the living room window is a picture-postcard view of Mt. Taylor.

While some of these families' material needs are being met, there is an overriding sense of hopelessness, of being caught in a net not of their own making, and from which they cannot get free. For they know, as a CBS news report stated succinctly, "Their destiny is in the hands of strangers." The juxtaposition of the new, modern house and this immovable hopelessness is profoundly disturbing.

Mary Sanchez is a thirty-six-year-old mother of five. Her oldest child is seventeen, her youngest ten. Her seventeen-year-old sister is also living with her; she finished only the eighth grade and has two children, one four and one ten months old. In addition, Mary's oldest daughter has a ten-month-old who also lives there, and one of her brothers lives with her as well. In all, eleven people live in a small wooden house off of a small dirt road; Mary's parents live next door.

Mary and most of the children are on welfare and receive food stamps. The two youngest, the ten-month-old babies, are not on welfare because the welfare worker said she wanted to force the fathers to pay for their upkeep. Mary told the worker to forget it.

Both of the men who fathered her children are dead. The first died of natural causes, but the second, the father of four of her children, died while hitchhiking with another man and two women. "They all must have been drunk," she says simply, "and weaving down the street. A gas truck was coming along and swerved to avoid hitting them. The truck turned over and exploded and all four were burned to death. When relatives went to claim the body, they couldn't tell who it was."

The entire time we talked, a soap opera was on in the background, an intricate melodrama of well-dressed upper-middle-class Anglos lulling these women and their children through the day. The women do not seem despairing but rather fatalistic. When I asked if it was hard for them to manage, they said they managed. When I asked what could be done to make things better, they couldn't think of a thing. It feels as though it takes everything they've got just to get from day to day.

◆

NEW FAMILY CAR
Pamela Painter

A snow day for Emily's high school and my car's transmission problems have marooned us inside, unexpectedly together. Emily and her friends are sprawled on beanbag chairs in the adjacent dining room, which has no dining table, only stereo equipment, an exercycle and books. I can see them — five in all — through the archway across from where I'm stretched out on the couch grading freshman comp papers. Two pizzas are baking in the oven.

I'm still in my bathrobe, no bra, even though it is late afternoon and soon I'll have to turn on a light. A cup of cold tea beside me on the floor makes me want a glass of white wine. The comp papers are weighing flat and heavy on my chest, along with the news that Arnie is moving out. I haven't yet told Emily.

Their voices come to me like a radio at low volume till I hear Zack ask Becka, "So where are your parents?" Since when did kids care where their parents were — except to decide at whose house to throw the all-night party? Now I'm listening in.

"Mom's here. Dad's in L.A.," Becka says. Becka is the new drummer in the band Zack's putting together. Emily says their gigs have increased since she joined up. Zack is Emily's boyfriend.

"No shit! L.A.," he says.

"You can have it," Becka says. "It's mostly Mexicans, hot pavement, cars, and smog."

"Don't you ever go back?" Taj asks ("Taj as in Taj Mahal," Emily said.) Taj is their songwriter and singer — vocalist, they call her. Emily is French-braiding Taj's long blond hair, something she refuses to do for me. I watch the fat braid curve slowly over the crown of Taj's head. "You know," Taj prompts. "Go out to see your dad?"

Becka shakes her mowed head. She has a half-inch growth of auburn hair under an equally short lawn of matte black. Not one of her six earrings matches. She tells them her dad has this two-year-old kid and treats Becka like a babysitter. "As soon as I arrive, he and Fay whip out a list of new restaurants they want to try. One night they came back stoned and he told Fay to drive me home like I was a sitter from the neighborhood. I don't even know how I'm related to the kid — first he married this woman — after divorcing Mom — and they fought all the time. Then they got a divorce. Then they had a kid. They're still divorced, but now they're living together again."

"You got a half sister," Zack says, cradling his guitar. "Thank God my parents are divorced. But Dad still rants and raves about Mom all the time. I agree with him just to shut him up. He says she buys purses like Marcos's wife bought shoes. Once he tried to get me to count them."

"That's really sick," Emily says. She goes over to Zack and kneads her fingers in his curly hair and he reaches up and pulls her in close for a kiss. Please keep it light. I turn my head to watch the snow swirling heavily against the windows, no

Pamela Painter, "New Family Car," in *The Graywolf Annual Eight: the New Family*, Scott Walker ed. (St. Paul: Graywolf, 1991), pp. 241–50.

pattern to its falling. Arnie is probably in his new apartment assembling bookshelves and unpacking his share of dishes pots and pans.

"You gotta shut them down sometimes," Franco says. He's a lanky kid with a black mohawk, the band's leader. "I just hold up my hand and say, 'Hey, Mom, I've heard it before.'" He scratches his mohawk with a pencil — somehow, it resembles Taj's braid. He says his father used to drink straight vodka all day from a brown coffee mug. "I give him credit for going off the booze, but now he's cheating on Karen just like he did on my mom. She's dumb for sticking around. But I'm not about to get involved."

Involved, I think. Franco, my boy, you are involved. I remember saying to a friend that we're traumatizing our kids with all these divorces and recouplings, and he said, No, we're just giving them emotional information.

Becka is talking. She says the problem is you never know how to treat stepparents. "Fay always wants to play serious makeup with me. Mud packs, manicures. Last time there I said what she really needs is a two-tone punk cut like mine. Now she doesn't bug me anymore."

Zack rolls his eyes in sympathy and says his father was living for a while with an old high school girlfriend named Jeanette who'd named her daughters Lynnette and Fayette. "I told her if she had a son they could name him Crockette. She didn't think it was funny. 'Funny' to them is this game they play at dinner." Zack puts down his guitar to demonstrate. "First night I'm there, Fayette burps and suddenly everybody's laughing and pointing at me. I look around the table and they're all sitting with a thumb poking into their foreheads. 'You're last,' Lynnette said. 'That means you have to eat it.'"

Zack burps and I rise upon my elbow to watch him smash his thumb against his forehead. "I *refused* to play," Zack says. "I 'ate it' every time. Dad finally smartened up and moved out."

"Gross." Emily pauses, braiding again, her hands holding the blond strands of Taj's hair like reins. She says she remembers when Arnie moved in. I lie back down and close my eyes, not sure I can take it. She says, "Suddenly there was this stranger in the bathroom trimming his toenails. I could hear it in my bedroom two doors away. His tennis shoes smell like rotten eggs."

She's right. Arnie's tennis shoes reek. He used to count on me to tell him when to buy new ones. I haven't had the nerve to do that for a while. And he hasn't suggested I take off a little weight either. Unexpectedly, tears well up in my eyes and I need to blow my nose, but that would expose my couch-cover. I turn my face into the cushion and sniff softly and fast.

"You think you got it bad," Franco says. "My mom's living in this humongous loft with this painter who's ten years younger. He listens to Philip Glass all day and cooks in an old black wok — everything tastes like fried shrimp. When I sleep over this guy borrows my clothes. I wake up late and there he is, working in my shirt or jeans." He points to black splotches on his Levis.

"At least you don't have to live there full time," Zack says. "Anyway, it probably won't last." I go back to reading an essay on a pet raccoon for the third time.

"Trouble is all those divorces really mess up the photograph albums," Emily says. And here it comes. My pen freezes on the page. "Mom butchered ours. 'There's only about two pictures left of Dad in all twelve albums."

I glance at the albums lined up on the shelf beside the fireplace. I'd always wondered if Emily and Greg noticed — heads missing, hands emerging from uneven borders.

But Emily isn't finished. She goes on to reveal how her father and I had to get married. Uncharacteristically, I'm speechless as she continues, "Dumb, but that's what you did in Mom's day if you got pregnant. They didn't have the pill."

"No wonder they got divorced," Becka says. "Why didn't she have an abortion?"

"It wasn't legal. And anyway, you're talking about my brother, Greg. He's at school," Emily says, giving Taj's head a hard push.

Taj's shoulders shrug. "My father could have arranged it — even back then."

"What's he do?" Becka asks.

"He was a dealer. Dead now," Taj says, her tone matter-of-fact as she describes his sudden heart attack in St. Bart's.

"Tell Becka the rest of it," Zack says. Clearly he's heard this story before because, having ushered it in, he leaves to check on the pizzas.

"When I was six, Dad got me every other weekend. He used to take me on drug deals — said I was good luck." Taj pats down the length of her braid to see how far it's done. Then she describes how she helped him weigh stuff out on special scales —back then it was grass. "We put it in baggies and tied it with those wire things. He died before they invented Ziploc bags," she says. Saturdays were their big days. First they checked in at the zoo to see the bears or lions, or a hallway of snakes — just to give her something to tell her mother. Then they'd have to go make deliveries. I picture a small girl sobbing as she is dragged away from giraffes, elephants, monkeys. There's the song Taj should write.

Emily winds a rubber band around the end of Taj's braid and flips it over her shoulder. Then Emily flops down next to Zack. The beans in the chair crunch and shift. "So who's the guy answering the phone in such a sexy voice?" she asks Taj.

"Mom swears she's not getting married again, but she has guys — one just moved in, and one on the phone. I mean it's not exactly a revolving door or anything. They're OK. The time one came on to me I told Mom and he was gone that same night."

"Pervert," Emily and Becka say in unison.

"Mom's bottom line is they have to have a job. She says it keeps them busy."

"Not busy enough," Emily says. "My dad's had seven jobs in the past three years. Trouble is they don't last longer than two weeks. Now I don't ask," she says. "You meet him and he mentions Yale in the first twenty minutes. Mom says it was all downhill after Yale."

"Emily! Goddamn it, that's enough," I yell, throwing the comp papers on the floor and sitting up. "At least I never told you how low that hill was to begin with."

No one says anything.

I tighten the belt on my old chenille bathrobe, wishing I'd put on underwear and combed my hair. Where did they think I was anyway? Taking a goddamn bubble bath? I search for my flip-flops and stand up. "You ought to be out there shoveling walks, not sitting around here —"

"Mo-om," Emily says. She gives Zack a push and tells him to go check on the pizza. No one looks at me. What would they do if I announced, 'Yea, well, another thing: Arnie and I are splitting up. He's taking his tennis shoes with him; we won't have Arnie's old toenails to step on anymore.' Would Franco shrug and say, 'Hey, these things happen'? I mean, how cool can these kids be?

"Come and get it," Zack calls from the kitchen and slams the oven door. They all exit fast. I marvel at their appetites.

At twelve, the comp papers are finished and I'm in bed with a book, waiting for Emily to get back from Zack's house where they all fled after the pizza. I tried calling Greg at school but he wasn't in, so I missed the chance to rehearse my eleventh-hour news.

Outside, the snow stopped as the temperature fell and now, outlined with lacy frost, the small window panes have become black valentines. Boxes of Arnie's books and papers, three overflowing duffles, and a mountain of shoes tug at my peripheral vision. He's coming early tomorrow to move his things out, say good-bye to Emily. But first I need to tell her myself.

It's close to one when I hear her coming up the stairs. Angry with relief, I pull on my robe and go down the hall to her room. "What are you doing up so late?" she asks. Expertly, she crosses her arms in front of her and pulls the red sweater over her head in one movement. Her long hair swings free.

I sit down on the other twin bed, and my first words surprise me. "Jesus. Did you need to tell them your father and I had to get married?"

"Yeah, you're right," Emily says. "I guess I said too much, huh?" She turns her back to slide her bra around and pulls on a red nightshirt. Then she lifts her quilt and flops into bed. The wool quilt, made by my grandmother, is almost in tatters but she refuses to sleep with anything else. Her eyes are closed as she says, "I'm sorry, Mom." A little too easily. "I really am. They won't remember." And definitely too cool.

"Don't give me that shit," I say, reaching over to yank her pillow hard from under her head the way magicians do with tablecloths and plates.

Emily jerks up onto her elbow and clutches the quilt to her chest. "What are you doing. What the fuck is wrong?"

"I'm trying to talk to you," I say.

"But it's two in the morning. Can't it wait? Where's Arnie?"

I tell her then. In a calmer voice I say that last night Arnie and I agreed to split up — that he'd be coming over tomorrow morning to officially move out. To say good-bye to her.

"Oh, shit," she says, rolling her glistening eyes.

"What do you mean 'oh, shit?'"

"I mean I'll miss him," she says. Tears are running down her cheeks now, darkening her freckles. "I mean he was okay."

"Give me a break," I yell. "First you complain about him and now he's a saint."

"That bad, huh?" she says.

I nod and hug the pillow I swiped from her. "You've probably overheard enough to know what happened."

"Yeah, I guess it's been coming."

My mouth quivers as I say, "But you don't have to make a big deal about it. I mean you don't have to announce it to your friends — 'Hey, guys, no more smelly tennis shoes,' — like you did this afternoon."

Emily points her finger at me. "You were spying on us."

"I was not. I was grading papers in the living room. I was hearing you talk. There's a difference — and I don't like my life paraded around for a bunch of kids."

"You forget. It's my life too," Emily says, lurching up. She grabs her pillow back from me and squashes it to her chest. "You ever think of that? Did you and Dad ever once think of that? Of me and Greg and what we were going through?" She buries her face in her pillow as I move across to sit on her bed. I hug her hard and soon her fingers are pressing and smoothing the soft chenille ridges of my robe where she holds my shoulders.

"Oh, Emmy, of course we thought about it. We stayed married one whole year longer, agonizing over what it would do to you and Greg. And Arnie and I talked about it, too. It isn't like we didn't try — for you." My voice is rising, catching as it soars, but I can't stop "But I know that's not what you and your friends all think, complaining about half sisters, and boyfriends and stepparents. You think you'd have been better off if your father and I had stayed together."

"What's the matter with that?" Emily says, pulling back and glaring at me. Trying not to cry harder.

"Because it wouldn't have been true," I say.

"But that — doesn't help. Don't you see?" she hiccoughs, his chin trembling.

"So why talk about it?" I ask.

"Oh. So that's it," she says. "You're still thinking 'what will people say?' Jesus, Mom. If you're going to listen in, you have to lighten up."

"But it's like — it's like you're playing games."

"Games!" Emily's eyebrows, tiny arcs, rise.

"You're playing — I don't know." I shake my head — somehow it is all so familiar, and then I do know. "You're playing 'My-family's-more-fucked-up-than-your-family.'"

Emily's shoulders shake and suddenly she's laughing hysterically, wiping her face with both hands. "That's funny, Mom. That's really funny."

"It is *not*. It's how we used to one-up friends. Only we did it with the number of

bathrooms we had, or who went on vacations to Niagara Falls — or whose family had a new car. No one ever had two cars."

"So what?" Emily says. "So now it's fucked-up families." Then she grins. "You're lucky we don't flunk out of school, do crack, or join the Hare Krishnas. Besides, some kids can't play. You know, they have dumb happy homes. Their parents have been married for twenty-seven years and they go to church on Sunday and in summer they trot off to family reunions two states away. Like NOT having a new car was for you twenty-five years ago. I mean what are these kids going to say? Nothing. So they can't play." She tugs open the little drawer in her nightstand and fishes around. "Here. You want to see something?" She pulls out a creased envelope and empties it onto the quilt between us. "See. I saved all those pieces of Dad. So that wasn't a big deal either." And there they are, ragged photographs of my first husband — small glossy heads, square torsos, bits of me. She stirs the pieces around with a wet, glistening finger.

"Oh, Emmy, I wish —"

"No. Stop. You're right. It's better this way." She scoops her dad up and dumps him back into the envelope. We're all still in pieces. "Arnie too," she says. "You going to operate on him?"

Our laughs are damp and sniffly. Then I lean over her to smooth her shining eyebrows, kiss her wet cheeks and bangs. She puts her arms up to hold me tightly for a moment, then she lets me go. I tell her I love her. When I turn off the light, her windows sparkle with the same black lacy valentines. They'll be white come morning.

"Hey, Mom," she calls out from the dark, her voice still offering too-small comfort. "So maybe it is a game, so what? At least I didn't win."

◆

CONSIDER THE CONSEQUENCES: REVIEW OF LENORE WEITZMAN'S *THE DIVORCE REVOLUTION*

Martha Minow

We learn too late. And yet we have to keep on going. This book offers both lessons. Professor Lenore Weitzman reveals the often devastating economic consequences of recent divorce reforms for children and women. By studying what California divorce reform has meant financially and socially to the men, women, and children affected by it, Professor Weitzman shows that reform can have disturbing and unanticipated consequences. In so doing, she presses a persuasive case for new reforms — with no guarantee of avoiding new, unanticipated consequences.

Although focused on the California experience, the book offers information that bears relevance to the rest of the country. Most states have followed California's lead in introducing no-fault divorce, divorce without spousal consent, reduction or elimination of financial compensation or retribution, preference for joint child custody, and elimination of gender-based duties and rights. Thus, the California experience seems not an oddity but the leading edge of a trend. If the picture offered by Lenore Weitzman holds any prediction for other places, it is a stark warning about how recent divorce reforms produce unintended but potentially disastrous consequences for women and children.

Using the data and insights gathered in *The Divorce Revolution,*[*] I will summarize those consequences and then ask: Why were they unexpected? What can we learn now to reduce surprise — and dismay — in the next rounds of divorce law reform? Can we learn to anticipate how opposition to reform persists despite official success, and how competing possible meanings for central concepts, like equality and freedom, may yield unexpected consequences?

THE UNEXPECTED CONSEQUENCES

California first introduced no-fault grounds for divorce; the California legislature initiated efforts to reduce or eliminate gender distinctions in family roles, entitlements, and obligations following divorce, and California then led national experiments with joint custody. *The Divorce Revolution* asks, what effects have these reforms had on the economic and social welfare of Californians who go through divorce? The book's

From Martha Minow, "Consider the Consequences: Review of Lenore Weitzman," in *The Divorce Revolution*, *Law Review*, vol. 84, February–April 1986, pp. 900–18 (edited).

---

[*] For criticisms of Weitzman's methodology, *see* Herbert Jacobs, "Faulting No-Fault," *American Bar Research Journal*, vol. 4, no. 773, Fall 1986; Marygold Meli, "Constructing a Social Problem: The Post-Divorce Plight of Women and Children," *American Bar Research Journal*, vol. 4, no. 759, Fall 1986 [editor's note].

stark and at times startling findings deserve the publicity they have been receiving. Based on a rich variety of data sources, Weitzman found that:

— " [O]n the average, divorced women and the minor children in their households experience a seventy-three percent decline in their standard of living in the first year after divorce" (p. xii).

— "Their former husbands, in contrast, experience a forty-two-percent rise in their standard of living" (p. xii).

— Although the new rules for dividing marital property embrace a principle of equality, the courts typically exclude from the division the most valuable assets — "the major wage earner's salary, pension, medical insurance, education, license, the goodwill value of a business or profession, entitlements to company goods and services, and future earning power" (p. xiii).

— " [T]hose displaced homemakers who had been married to *upper-income* men stood a good chance of being awarded the support that the new law [protecting women in long-term marriages] promised them. But those who had been married to *lower-income* men did not" (p. 189).

— " [W]ithin six months of the divorce decree, one out of six men was already in arrears on alimony payments, owing, on the average, over $1,000" (p. 192).

— Judges have interpreted reforms requiring equal division of property assets upon divorce to force the sale of many family homes, effectively dislocating women and children from old neighborhoods, schools, and friends (pp. 358-59).

— Although there is a "steadfast persistence of mother custody awards despite the change" from maternal preference in child custody (p .232), "by 1977, a surprisingly large proportion — close to two-thirds — of the fathers who requested custody were awarded it" (p. 233)

— Despite the legal preference for joint custody, introduced by California in 1980, " [m]ost men — and most women — prefer not to share post-divorce parenting" (p.251).

— "More than half (fifty-three percent) of the millions of women who are due child support do not receive the court-ordered support" (p. 262).

— Using national census data compiled in 1981, "the mean amount of [child] support ordered was $2,460, but the mean amount paid, including those who received nothing, was $1,510" (p. 265).

— " [N]o matter what his income level, a divorced man is rarely ordered to part with more than *one-third* of his net income" — even though "the judges and the attorneys we interviewed often referred to a *one-half* limit: they said there was an informal rule that judges should never require a man to pay more than one-half of his net income in support" (p. 266).

In short, California's divorce reforms, which were supposed to eliminate the trauma — and the gender discrimination consequences — of divorce, have instead, in effect, drastically reduced the financial security previously available to women and children under older divorce rules. In addition, nonenforcement of even the reduced financial benefits under these reforms further contributes to divorce's crushing effects for women and children. The patterns of inequality, unfairness, and constraints for divorced families unearthed by the book are all the more stunning when located within the broader demographic picture of divorce rates: not only will at least half of current American marriages end in divorce (p. xvii), " [t]he total number of children affected by divorce has more than tripled since 1960.... [I]t is now projected that *more than half of all the children in the United States* will experience a parental divorce or dissolution before they reach age eighteen" (p. 215, emphasis in original).

Weitzman offers some useful analysis that helps to explicate the meaning of her findings. For example, she explains that despite the promise that no-fault divorce would replace old gender-based rules with a conception of the equal marital partners, gender inequality after divorce nevertheless emerged because the partner caring for the children has to spread her half of the family resources to cover the children as well as herself. Because the child care is typically managed by one partner, and because that partner statistically is generally the woman, it is women who are the financial victims of divorce.

Further, the division of assets at divorce frequently has yielded too little for the woman and children because the division did not reach the couple's career and educational investments — forms of "new property." It is true that some reforms eliminated rules that seemed to express and reinforce sexists stereotypes — like alimony from a husband to support a woman presumed incapable of supporting herself. But these reforms left completely unprotected many women whose lives actually fit a sexist stereotype (p. 360). Freed of gendered role expectations, the conception of marital partnership seems to dissolve into an ideology and a practice of autonomous individualism (p. 374).

How could major law reform produce such dismal results? Why were these results unexpected? Why did the reformers fail to anticipate these results?

I believe that law reform may yield unexpected consequences for at least two reasons. First, the reforms, although well-conceived, may encounter barriers to implementation due to human and institutional opposition. Failures to confront and overcome these barriers can compound the problem. Second, the reforms may suffer from insensitivity to competing goals and complexity within any given goal.

Pressing behind the search for equality after divorce is the fundamental question of whether families will cease to be the primary social organization that tends to individual needs. Will a decision to marry no longer carry even short-term — much less permanent — economic obligations to the spouse? And what about obligations to children, or elderly parents, or other relatives? The economic devastation faced by so many women and children after divorce expresses the abandonment of the most economically vulnerable to the vicissitudes of a marketplace and governmental system that presume individual economic needs are fulfilled by the family unit, a family unit that includes a wage earning man. Studies like Lenore Weitzman's make this presumption less and less plausible, and expose not just the inequality but also the unacceptable quality of the lives of too many women and children in this society.

CONTESTED MEANINGS OF FREEDOM: ONE PERSON'S FREEDOM IS ANOTHER'S DISASTER

Besides equality, a justification for divorce reform recently — and in the more distant past — has been the promotion and protection of individual freedom. Women and men should be able to free themselves from bickering or hellish marriages. Indeed, it's hard quite to reimagine the world view that condemned two unhappy people to the private misery of a mutually disagreeable marriage. Perhaps the contemporary view emerged when the ideal of the companionate marriage replaced notions of marriage for economic security and raised expectations about satisfactions in the marital union — and thereby inspired more dissatisfactions, and more desires to leave unhappy marriages. Whatever the sources of demands for divorce, those demands helped to push waves of reforms easing legal exit from marriage. By eliminating fault requirements for divorce, and authorizing unilateral actions by one spouse to end a marriage, recent divorce reforms around the country seem to advance individual freedom.

Weitzman notes how these transformations use law to reward individualism rather than partnership in marriage. Celebrating individual independence after marriage, the reforms in property, custody, and support rules also "confer economic advantages on spouses who invest in themselves at the expense of the marital partnership" (p. 374). Weitzman criticizes these developments for several unanticipated consequences: the reforms give no rewards for good behavior, or altruistic behavior in the marriage (p.

29); and the reforms help to dislodge moral condemnation of divorce and thereby undermine the notion of reciprocal obligations in marriage (p. 23). Finally, privileging individual freedom in essence harms the weaker party in the union (pp. 19, 26). Freedom untethered by equality, in this view, unleashes selfishness and exposes the less powerful to the will of the more powerful. In short, one spouse's freedom can be the other spouse's disaster.

While I do not contest these assessments, I suggest that such unanticipated consequences can be traced to complexities in the idea of freedom itself. Despite popular views that freedom is at odds with both equality and dependency, there are other plausible meanings of freedom that actually rely on equality and dependency, submission and limits, dependency and interdependence. Divorce reforms that failed to account for these competing meanings of freedom thus rightly can be criticized in their light. And we should not be surprised by charges that such reforms actually undermine at least some versions of freedom.

Just as a starting point, the notion of "ordered liberty" in the Constitution rests on the recognition that there are societal preconditions for individual liberty. Only if groups agree to respect individual freedoms — and to enforce such respect even at the cost of interfering with other individual's freedoms — can anyone be free, or so goes the general refrain. I can be free only if you are disciplined, and you can be free only if I am disciplined enough to protect your freedom. Yet the paradox could be even more immediate, as put by the dancer who said that only through discipline can the dancer himself be free. This seeming irony at the core of legally enforceable freedoms has occupied much scholarly attention, but also united foes.

When it comes to family relationships, this irony only deepens. For only if people choose to turn their freedom to some mutual goals can they form relationships; the freedom to form relationships would mean little without a willingness to pursue something besides freedom to leave them. And yet even this understates the irony. For only by preserving the possibility of leaving — the possibility of individuality — can anyone survive to connect in relationships. From one angle, then, individual freedom demands submission to societal ground rules; from another, freedom demands submersion of individual whim into binding attachments; from still another, freedom requires limits even upon the limits on freedom. Such contrasting meanings of freedom have been bound up in our culture with views about dependency and independence, and with views about gender roles. The very freedom of the traditional male role — to participate in public life and move in and out of the private family realm — depended upon the traditional female role that maintained continuity in the family realm and provided a person, the wife, who could be subject to the husband's freely exercised power. The sense of freedom in relationships could be sustained by men who had women who made relationships for them; but "[t]he fact that men have always dominated women has obscured the fact that they are mutually dependent ...; in a fundamental sense, men need women as much as women need men."

Despite a language of radical individualism, we exercise our freedom in relationships to others; indeed, "[w]e discover who we are face to face and side by side with others in work, love, and learning."

WHAT TO EXPECT NEXT

Professor Weitzman ends her important study with specific recommendations: Child support should be based on an income-sharing approach likely to equalize the standards of living between custodial and noncustodial households; support awards should have automatic increases based on the cost of living; college-age children should be included within support obligations; special rules recognizing the expectations and foregone opportunities of older or long-married wives should be adopted as "grandmother clauses" for those who played by the traditional rules; and all future reforms should await careful consideration of their economic consequences (pp. 379-83). These proposals look sensible and worth pursuing.

Yet they will not solve the problem of anticipated consequences in the next wave of reform. Some unanticipated consequences will follow from the politics of reform itself. Reform may necessarily focus more on what is wrong presently than with what should be in its stead, and that focus may end up generating so many impossible hopes for a better world that some visions, and some supporters, are bound to be disappointed. Other unanticipated consequences will follow because the politics continue long after the reform-official succeeds. Opposition persists in the form of administrative obstacles, attitudinal barriers, and resistance by parties and publics, and lawyers and judges, to formally adopted changes. And yet the particular expressions of such resistance can never be fully anticipated by reformers.

I have also suggested, though, some especially deep problems that will continue to plague divorce reform, and will continue to surprise or even dismay reformers. The visions of fairness, equality, and freedom that help animate reform depend on contestable terms whose meanings elude consensus and consistency. The meanings that prevail will remain suspect against the meanings that do not yet find form, and nonetheless capture human hopes. And what seems a natural boundary for current reforms may well seem an arbitrary cut-off in retrospect — or a step too far. Perhaps reformers in the last round stopped too far short with issues of equality after divorce when they located the problem within each household facing a break-up, rather than connecting the needs of wives and children with husbands' employment, businesses, and even broader public resources. And perhaps the reformers went too far in pursuing a version of freedom that underestimates the dependence of freedom itself on interpersonal connection. Perhaps if they knew now what Lenore Weitzman has shown, some of the reformers would not have taken the steps they did.

What seems most likely is that we will not know the next set of contested meanings and disappointments until we take further steps, and see what we cannot yet see. A dismal thought? Yet, it could be this very condition of imperfect knowledge that allows us to push toward what others know to be impossible.

CHILD CUSTODY, VISITATION, AND SUPPORT

When marriages or adult relationships break up, people are often strained emotionally and psychologically. Children can be injured by their parents' arguments over divorce and custody matters. Children also face more complicated arrangements for their care and for their contact with both parents. Visitation, joint custody, and potential new relationships with the boyfriends and girlfriends of their parents may enrich children's lives but may also provoke tensions and call for considerable adjustment. Experts offer competing analyses of the effects of divorce and custody arrangements on children both as a general matter and in specific cases. It is especially difficult to know whether remaining in a family without divorce, but with estranged parents, is any better for children than undergoing divorce and its aftermath.

When the adults do decide to divorce, but cannot agree about child custody, what stance should the law take? Should the law prefer the mother? Should the law pursue a gender neutral rule favoring custody for the "primary parent"? Should the law create a presumption favoring joint custody, and induce more parents to work together? Does the custody issue look different when the competing custodians include people other than the biological parents, people such as grandparents, stepparents, or other relatives? Should custody disputes arising from divorce be treated any differently than custody disputes growing from foster care or other child welfare situations?

Some theorists emphasize that the process of legal disputing itself can injure children during custody disagreements. The time period such disputes take is often beyond the comprehension of particularly young children; the sense of uncertainty during the months and even years of disputes can itself be damaging. Although many jurisdictions call for resolving custody disputes in light of the "best interests of the child," a more realistic assessment would direct the attorneys and the judge to try to produce the least worst alternative.

Courts increasingly face new challenges, such as arguments that the noncustodial parent should retain authority over the child's religious upbringing. Some argue that the parent's life style — including sexual activity — after the divorce should be taken into account when the judge determines visitation and custody. Others argue that only demonstrable harm to a child should be considered at this time. How should a court respond to a visitation dispute between a biological mother and her estranged boyfriend who has no biological tie but still loves the child? What about a dispute over visitation raised by an estranged lesbian lover who had jointly planned and cared for the child with the biological mother until the two adults broke off their relationship? Whose values should govern the basic questions about what kinds of custody disputes can even be heard in court, as well as the ultimate decisions to be made there? In a nation of cultural variety and political conflict over life styles, can the law be neutral? Should it even try to be?

Perhaps the most widespread difficulties surround the financial status of children whose adult caretakers do not live together. Whether following divorce or simply birth outside of marriage, children who live in single-parent households are much more likely to be poor than other children. Typically, it is mothers raising children and fathers who fail to provide support. Typically, it is the assumption that women will provide for children that leaves both women and children at economic risk when the fathers do not or cannot provide financial assistance. Why do fathers fail to support their children? What punishments could make a difference? What incentives, such as visitation arrangements, could make a difference? Should even effective measures be used or are there independent moral judgments to consider alongside behavioral effects? When if ever should a parent be able to avoid or reduce an existing child support obligation because he (or she) now has additional children in another family setting? Should support issues solely involve the division of the family's own resources, or also implicate governmental income supports? What governmental policies would meet children's needs when their parents split up — and how can those policies become politically feasible? Can legal officials recognize and support informal kinship ties that can help children when adult relationships end?

◆

THE POLITICS OF FAMILY LAW
Francis Olsen

Family law, like law in general, has two different aspects: an apologetic aspect and a utopian aspect. In its apologetic aspect, family law tends to justify the domination of women by men and the oppression of children by parents. Family law reinforces the most common forms of male domination and parental oppression by characterizing them as legal. Family law tends to pacify family members by concealing from their scrutiny how damaging and restrictive family relationships often are. Furthermore, family law makes our present forms of family life seem "natural," and therefore unlikely to change very much. In this way, family law encourages minor reforms and individual adjustments, while discouraging imaginative speculation or creative changes in family structure. We forget that a radically different form of social life would seem equally natural once we had established it.

In its utopian aspect, family law records successive efforts to make the reality of human association live up to our hopes and aspirations. Legal struggles have resulted in a variety of family reforms and have increased the options available to each individual. Lawyers and judges have introduced notions of fairness into family life; they have created the vocabulary necessary to argue for justice for women and for children. Family law helps to shape our culture and contributes to the development of shared meanings and aspirations regarding family life.

When I say that family law legitimates oppression or that it contributes to our utopian aspirations, I am much more concerned with the kinds of arguments that courts and attorneys frame and accept than with the particular outcomes of legislative battles or with the direct results of court decisions. The arguments presented in these battles and decisions illustrate and support particular patterns of thought and behavior. Family law both reflects and helps create an ideology of the family — a structure of images and understandings of family life. This ideology serves to deny and disguise the ways that families illegitimately dominate people and fail to serve human wants. Embedded within the ideology of the family are notions of (1) the kinds of roles that individual members should serve within the family and what they should get out of these roles, (2) the kinds of bonds that hold families together; (3) the actual and the proper role of families in society; and (4) what the state or law can and should do to encourage desirable family life.

Most family law scholarship focuses on the utopian aspect of law, and ignores law's apologetic, legitimating role. In family law, perhaps more than in any other field of law, the literature tends to rationalize and criticize existing doctrine on a low level of abstraction, and to focus attention primarily upon some proposed reform. Most family law scholars argue in favor of some minor change in the law and analyze previous cases to show that the legal reasoning or the results of the cases support the proposed change. Occasionally, scholars vary this method by presenting the

From Frances Olsen, "The Politics of Family Law," *Jour. of Law and Inequal.*, vol. 2, 1984, pp. 1–19 (edited).

reasoning or results of earlier cases as an abomination, thereby dramatizing the great need for the particular reform they have proposed. Regardless of their intentions, these scholars help perpetuate oppressive family law, they convey the message that family law is basically fair. Because they discourage us from considering more radical change, their work contributes to the apologetic project of legitimating the status quo.

This essay explores the political significance of family law.

LAW AND POLITICS

We can counteract some of the negative effects that often accompany legal victories. The lawyer's characterization of a legal outcome can serve to enhance the positive and diminish the negative ideological effects of using the court system for a partial gain. A particularized evaluation of the actual effects of a lawsuit is important also because the practical benefits may be unexpectedly insignificant or counterbalanced by unanticipated disadvantages. If we anticipate or recognize only negative ideological effects and positive practical effects, our analysis is less accurate than it should be. Almost every legal change has both practical and ideological advantages and disadvantages. It is crucial for us to recognize and analyze each of these effects.

THE LIBERALIZATION OF THE FAMILY

The phenomenon I refer to as the "liberalization of the family" should be understood in the context of these complex effects. The pre-liberal family, which I characterize loosely as the "feudal" family, was a social, economic, and political unit of feudal society. For many years after the disintegration of feudal society, the image of the "feudal" family was a communal hierarchy, based on unequal duties of protection and obedience, and was expected to serve important public functions. The "liberal" family, on the other hand, is thought to be a voluntary collection of individuals held together by bonds of sentiment in an egalitarian structure. Supposedly, it constitutes a private realm, clearly divorced from the "public sphere." Although there are relatively few defined roles in the "liberal" family, the few family obligations that do exist are considered properly enforceable by the state, generally through broad discretionary standards. It is said that standards, unlike rules, permit the state to deal with each situation on the basis of its own particular facts.

The shift from the "feudal to the liberal" family, which has occurred in America during the last three centuries, is often conceptualized as progress: the bad, the old, rigid, patriarchal family was replaced by the modern, all-American egalitarian family. Alternatively, some see this change in negative terms: the feudal, or at least the openly patriarchal family is romanticized as a stable, loving refuge from the world of commerce and industry, in contrast to the modern, "liberal" family, which is considered alienated, isolated, atomistic, and even pathological. Both of these characterizations — the positive and the negative — are severely flawed. We must develop a richer and more detailed description of the liberalization of the family to understand and begin to unravel the structure of thought and the patterns of behavior that affect our present conception of "the family" and its relationship to the state.

The liberalization of the family has entailed significant changes along many different dimensions. This essay explores two of these dimensions: the hierarchy — equality dimension, and the group — individual dimension.

Each of these dimensions describes gradual changes in the substantive behavior and roles expected of family members. The hierarchy — equality dimension involves the shift from an intentional, acknowledged hierarchy, to a supposedly egalitarian family of juridical equals. The group individual dimension involves the shift from the family as a corporate unit to the family as a voluntary association of individuals.

The Hierarchy Dimension

Each of these dimensions can best be conceptualized as a continuum, involving matters of degree rather than an all-or-nothing choice. The hierarchy continuum, however, also involves gradual shifts between four different structures of hierarchy. With some overlap, these four structures have succeeded one another chronologically.

1. *Structures of Hierarchy* In the more feudal, less-liberal family — for example, the family described by Blackstone — the father was the undisputed head of the family, and the wife and children were all subordinate to him. Within this structure, there were differing images of the father as a sovereign head or as the representative of the family, and differing notions of the extent and nature of the subordination of the family to the father. There was, however, basic agreement that the father had the authority and responsibility to act for the family.

Successful political and legal struggles eroded some of the father's power, and the family began to have a new structure. The father was still head of the family and still the hierarchical superior, but the hierarchy itself became more open to question. If the father were removed from the family, the mother would become the new head of the family. Under the first structure, according to Blackstone, the mother was entitled to nothing more than "reverence and respect," under this second structure, in the father's absence, the mother had the same kind of authority enjoyed by the father. Although the father in this second structure still retained considerably more authority than the mother, and although his authority took complete precedence over the mother's, the change was nevertheless important. The second structure treated the mother as a separate person with a juridical personality of her own. If the father died, the mother became entitled to the custody and services of her children, just as the father had been during his life. Also, some courts claimed the authority to find a father unfit, remove him from the hierarchy, and award custody to the mother.

The third and fourth structures embody today's ideologies of legal equality in family life. The third structure represents a significant shift: Here, the mother and the father are juridical equals. Theoretically, both have similar rights over their children, and neither spouse is legally superior to the other. The fourth structure is the least hierarchical: Hence, the child comes into her own as a legal personality, and each person in the family is treated as a juridical equal.

2. *The Legitimation of Hierarchy* Different explanations or rationalizations for the inferior status of women correspond to these different hierarchical structures.

Within each of these four structures, men have offered somewhat different justifications for the subordination of women.

The first two structures involved similar justifications. In the first structure, the subordination of women was so taken for granted that it was almost invisible. The father was the head of the family; fathers had been the heads of families since "time immemorial." In the second structure, women were said to be inferior because God or nature made men superior. Apologists of male supremacy generally did not argue that women implicitly consented to an inferior status when they agreed to marry men, but these apologists explained the hierarchy as natural or as a matter of convenience, if not necessity.

In the third structure, apologists deny the inferior status of women. Women are not subordinate to men; they are just different from men. Men have their sphere, and the women have their separate "but equal" sphere. The apologists hope that no one notices the very real differences between these two spheres — that men keep wealth, power and influence in their sphere, and leave in women's sphere unpaid service and nurturance obligations.

Current justifiers claim that in the fourth structure, everyone is equal. Here, they say, perceived differences among family members are simply private, isolated occurrences. Members of the family are juridically equal, in the same sense that workers and their bosses are juridically equal. This view treats women's subordination as though it occurred by chance. That men happen to earn almost twice as much money as women, and that this affects the social relations between the sexes is, according to this view, not the state's concern. Similarly, that children are economically dependent upon their parents, and that parents sometimes use this dependency to dominate or exploit their children, is likewise not the state's concern. Rather, the mistreatment of wives and children is simply a series of unfortunate individual occurrences.

The Group Dimension

The group-individual dimension places the family as a corporate unit at one end of a continuum, and the family as a collection of individuals at the other end. The more communal or collective direction focuses on the family as a single, undifferentiated unit; the more individual direction focuses not on the family unit itself, but rather on the particular members of the family and on their contractual agreements, implied or express.

Historically, the hierarchy dimension and the group dimension were related — the more hierarchical family was also more communal, and the more egalitarian family was also more individualistic. This was empirically true, but not logically necessary. It could have been different. A communal (or juridically intermingled) family could be non-hierarchical, just as a hierarchical family could be non-communal. Nevertheless, we often forget the contingency of history and unnecessarily limit our conception of the possibilities of human association. Our historical experience with the liberalization of the family makes us assume — often without realizing it — that the only alternatives are patriarchy on one hand, and atomistic individualism on the other. This is similar to the choices available to the nineteenth-century woman: she could join a patriarchal family or be alone. There were almost no other alternatives. Many of today's right-wing women similarly see no alternatives and urge a return to the patriarchal family as the only way to achieve closeness and commitment.

We can understand the group-individual continuum best by considering each of its two poles. The early notion that the legal personality of a married woman merged into her husband's is an extreme illustration of communalism. The ideas of guardianship and wardship of children likewise are classic communal notions. At the opposite end of the continuum, the individualism pole ignores group membership and focuses on the autonomous individual.

The significance of marriage varies across the continuum. In the more communal direction, marriage creates the group; it marks the beginning of a new family. In the more individual direction, marriage alters the individual rights of the two people who marry. As one moves along the continuum from the more communal toward the more individual direction, people's rights cease to change automatically by marriage and begin to change only by the implicit or explicit agreement of the parties. Marriage ceases to create an entity or to be a status; instead, it becomes a contract negotiated between two individuals.

THE TENDER YEARS DOCTRINE

The "tender years doctrine" is actually not a single doctrine, but a collection of various rules that once gave preference to the mother in a custody battle over a child of tender years. It arose in the nineteenth century, flourished early in the twentieth, and was abolished in the latter part of the twentieth century. The rise and the fall of this doctrine were both partial victories and partial defeats for women. To understand why this is so, we must examine the

ideological significance of the tender years doctrine as well as its more immediate, practical effects.

The Rise of the Tender Years Doctrine

Throughout the nineteenth century, there were scattered custody cases in which courts preferred the mother simply because she was the mother, but this practice did not actually become a doctrine until early in the twentieth century. In some jurisdictions the tender years doctrine was a "tie-breaker": if other factors were equal, the court placed a child of tender years in the custody of the mother. In its strongest form, the tender years doctrine mandated that a court award custody of a young child to the mother unless she were proven unfit or a danger to the child.

1. As a Victory for Women

Ideological Victory   The rise of the tender years doctrine was an ideological victory for women insofar as it acknowledged and established that women were capable of heading families. Not only could women head families after their husbands died, but they were also the preferred parent upon the breakup of a marriage. This maternal preference both reflected and reinforced a greater acceptance of female-headed families. The rise of the tender years doctrine marked a clear shift from the second structure of hierarchy toward the third.

Practical Victory   The rise of the tender years doctrine was an important practical victory for women, especially for separated or divorced women who wanted custody of their children. Not only was the doctrine an improvement over the common law rule preferring the father as custodial parent, but it also provided an appealing alternative to the "fault rule" — followed by some courts — that the parent not at fault in the marital breakup should receive custody of the children. During the nineteenth and early part of the twentieth centuries, the law defined "fault" in such a way that a husband could make married life intolerable without giving his wife legal grounds for a separation. Often, the wife's only recourse was to leave the family home. More often, her only weapon against such abuse was to threaten to leave. If a wife exercised her only option, or carried out her threat, her husband could charge that she deserted him and take away her children. For women, the tender years doctrine marked a clear improvement over child custody decisions based on fault.

In addition to enabling more women to leave abusive husbands without losing their children, the tender years doctrine also increased the power of women both during the marriage and in the event of separation or divorce. Men usually had, and continue to have, more economic power and greater earning potential than women. This has given men greater power within their marriages; women generally have had a greater economic incentive to make their marriages successful. The tender years doctrine began to distribute power somewhat in the woman's favor. When fathers stood to lose their children upon separation or divorce, men had a greater emotional incentive to keep their marriages intact.

2. As a Defeat for Women

Ideological Defeat The rise of the tender years doctrine was also an ideological defeat for women. The characteristics attributed to women and said to make them ill-suited for public life were the very same characteristics embraced by the rhet-

oric of the tender years doctrine. The doctrine reinforced the ideology of inequality, which stated that a woman's place is in the home. The doctrine therefore helped keep women in their place — that is, in the home serving others, and not out in public gaining power or making money.

Practical Defeat — The rise of the tender years doctrine was also a practical defeat for women. The doctrine always allowed courts discretion to deny custody to a mother found "unfit," and judges manipulated the concept of unfitness to keep women subservient to their husbands. If a woman was too independent, or did not fit the pedestal image of the tender years doctrine, courts would label her unfit. Thus, a woman might compromise her own happiness within the marriage and make considerable personal sacrifices only to be branded "unfit" and have her children taken away. The tender years doctrine discouraged women from pursuing their own goals and encouraged women to be subservient and obedient.

The Fall of the Tender Years Doctrine

In the late-twentieth century, the tender years doctrine came under increasing criticism. Fathers argued that it discriminated against them irrationally on the basis of their gender, and that courts should decide custody simply on the basis of the child's best interests. Each case, according to these fathers, should be decided on its individual facts, and the gender of the parental contestants should be irrelevant. The majority of courts accepted these arguments and most states have not abolished any custodial preference for the mother. The fall of the tender years doctrine correlates with the shift from the third to the fourth structure of hierarchy.

1. As a Defeat for Women

Practical Defeat One practical effect of the fall of the tender years doctrine is that many more mothers are losing custody of their children. Practicing lawyers complain that almost any father who really tries can now win custody of his children. It is not necessary to know the precise statistics in order to know that for most mothers, the risk of losing their children in a custody battle is considerably greater after the fall of the tender years doctrine than it was before. This risk increases women's fear of divorce and it may well reduce their power within the marriage. The husband still maintains his economic advantage, but the wife has lost the emotional advantage she might have had. Moreover, fathers can extract significant economic concessions from mothers and can generally harass and intimidate women with the threat of a custody battle. The outcome of a custody fight is very unpredictable because custody decisions are now highly individualized determinations made on a case-by-case basis, rarely subject to meaningful appellate review. This creates an anomaly: the more devoted a mother is to her child, the more the mother has to lose in a custody fight. To avoid the risks of a custody battle, many mothers who are clearly the better custodian for their children are nevertheless intimidated into giving up alimony, property settlement and child support money that they and their children need in order to live comfortably. This dynamic contributes to the widespread poverty of women and children.

Ideological Defeat Although the fall of the tender years doctrine is usually considered an ideological victory for women, it is also an ideological defeat. The individualized nature of current custody decisions denies the political significance of women as a group; when women lose custody of their children, the state, and many people, consider the phenomenon to be a private, individual matter. They overlook the fact that custody decisions also reflect and shape society's attitude toward women and motherhood. Within this privatized perspective, women lose their group identity. Women no longer have a political definition as women, and the custody of children ceases to be an issue of gender politics. The fall of the tender years doctrine thus depoliticizes the issue of custody and deprives individual mothers of their children one at a time, mother by mother.

2. As a Victory for Women

Ideological Victory The fall of the tender years doctrine is an ideological victory for women because it is an assertion of sexual equality; it reinforces notions of co-parenting and of fathers sharing responsibility for the emotional development of children. The fall of the tender years doctrine legitimates the desires of those men who wish to nurture children; it also legitimates the wishes of those mothers who do not want custody of their children. An implication of the tender years doctrine, that only unfit mothers do not have custody of their children, loses some of its strength with the fall of the doctrine.

Practical Victory There are practical benefits that result from the fall of the tender years doctrine. In some cases, the absence of the doctrine leads to a better custody decision for the child. Additionally, the courts' focus on the best interests of the child enables some women who do not fit the stereotypical maternal image associated with the tender years doctrine to present a coherent argument and occasionally to obtain custody. Under the tender years doctrine, for example, courts frequently decided that any evidence of non-marital sexual activity proved a mother "unfit." From such a perspective, lesbianism would certainly be the epitome of unfitness. While it is still extremely difficult for lesbians to keep custody of their children, they now have a better chance at custody because of the current focus on the child's needs.

An Alternative to the Tender Years Doctrine

My assertion that there are both good and bad effects to every reform or to every change does not imply that these effects balance out and, therefore, make little difference. Rather, I maintain that we must or should be far more thorough in evaluating any proposed reform or change. An important reason for examining the particular good or bad effects of any proposal is that, by doing so, we can make a more precise and correct evaluation of the actual overall effect of any reform.

A close examination may also help to devise alternatives or a middle ground between the status quo and a proposed change. For example, in the case of child custody, a possible middle ground is a doctrine giving custodial preference not to the mother, but to the child's primary attachment figure, be it the mother or the father. Such a rule, like the abolition of the tender years doctrine, would avoid sexual stereotyping and encourage male responsibility for children. But because the "primary attachment" test is more determinate than the "best interests of the child" test, the suggested rule would reduce the potential intimidation that fathers can now exercise by threatening a custody battle. This change is especially important in the case of an economically dependent mother who has devoted most of her married life to child care. Moreover, a court applying the "primary attachment" test will have greater difficulty, taking custody away from a lesbian mother who proves that she is the child's primary attachment figure.

Although I support the primary attachment doctrine, I recognize that it has disadvantages. The doctrine tends to make child custody decisions dependent upon the "experts" who determine "primary attachment." Many people believe that experts already determine too much of our lives. Furthermore, the doctrine presupposes that a child will be primarily attached to *one* person. Thus, the doctrine reinforces some of the worst aspects of the nuclear family ideology, including the assumption that one person is primarily responsible for child care. Also, the proposal assumes child custody determinations will remain adversarial and create winners and losers in a patriarchal legal system. Finally, the primary attachment doctrine diverts attention from the destructiveness of a society trying to raise children in unstable nuclear families with no significant group support.

CONCLUSION

Legal reforms have ambiguous and contradictory effects. Yet the only way to bring about major changes may be to begin with minor ones. We must make political decisions and act, even though our efforts may sometimes backfire. The more completely and accurately we analyze reforms, the greater the possibility we have to promote those reforms that — sometime in the future — we will recognize to have been the beginnings of a revolution.

♦

CULTURAL PERSPECTIVES ON CHILD WELFARE
Carol Stack

The 1970s saw the emergence of new research and new rhetoric concerning the family structures of people of color. Alongside traditional dogma that the nuclear family is the preferred structure, the viability of the extended family among poor people became accepted doctrine. Research provided new perspectives on the resilience of kinship networks, giving credence to rhetoric which touted the strengths of families and to the argument that policies should support family independence, rather than render families ever more dependent on public programs. However, class and cultural issues remained muddled, new data on kinship networks and psychological parenthood within extended families created new dilemmas for practice, and child welfare advocates were torn between the best interests of children and the integrity of parenthood.

There is a fundamental difference, however, between recognition of family structures and an understanding of family functions. It is far easier to pay rhetorical tribute to extended family groupings than to design policies which respect the functions of kinship networks. Few bureaucrats within the child welfare system understand the functions of kinship in a cultural context.

One cannot argue that current child welfare practice entirely fails to recognize kinship networks. However, it is safe to say that current practice more often than not fails to respect the integrity of the bonds of psychological parenthood that forms between children and nonparent kin. As a result, the system takes children from their families when removal is unwarranted. The Adoption Assistance and Child Welfare Act of 1980 (Act) mandates "permanency planning," which makes it more difficult to remove children from their families and requires that a permanent plan be devised for each child in the system. Yet even under these guidelines, the kin group as a resource is often ignored or discounted. And when removal is warranted, the child welfare system does not often look to the kinship network for foster caretakers.

Indeed, for lack of experience, it is difficult to apply psychological parenting theory, upon which permanency planning is based, in a cross-cultural context. Psychological parenting theory emerged out of a nuclear family model, and the concept of "parental autonomy" has not encompassed significant kin who become psychological parents in an extended family.

Even in the context of a divorce in a middle-class nuclear family, identifying the best interests of children is not an easy task. Some argue that it is best to nourish the continuity of bonds between divorcing biological parents and their children while others place their hope in the custodial household of one parent. In 1973, Goldstein, Freud, and Solnit — a law professor, a psychiatrist, and a psychologist — collaborated to write *Beyond the Best Interests of the Child* and then in 1979, *Be-*

From Carol Stack, "Cultural Perspectives on Child Welfare," *N.Y. Univ. Rev. of Law and Social Change*, vol. 12, 1983–84, pp. 539–547.

fore the Best Interests of the Child. The goal of the first book was to provide content for the best interests standard; in the second book the authors asked when it is appropriate for the state to invade family privacy or violate parental autonomy. Their guidelines and theories of psychological parenting have been applied both to divorce and to child placement issues arising after state intervention.

My argument is not with psychological parenting theory nor with the child welfare system per se, but with the unintended consequences of well-intended policies. Applying psychological theories to diverse cultural and family groupings is difficult, and it becomes impossible when practitioners are overloaded with cases or do not understand cultural variations in the way that families work. Highly complex issues emerge when we ask why a disproportionate number of minority children are placed by the child welfare system in foster homes and institutions, and why so few return to their parents, kin groups, or communities.

This paper attempts to provide a cultural perspective on parenthood and on state intervention in families. My goal is to show how misunderstood and misinterpreted cultural patterns have generated the placement in foster homes and institutions of many minority children who are not abused or neglected, and how the traditional reluctance of the social welfare system to reunify these children with biological parents or kin will remain a problem even under the Act's requirements. I hope to deepen professional wisdom regarding the best interests of children by clarifying the relationship between cultural patterns and child welfare policy.

Anthropologists have long been interested in cross-cultural differences in child socialization, attachments, and parenting.

Children's lives are profoundly affected by their parents, and by other adults who share responsibilities toward them and rights in them. The study of how these rights distribute socially is central to cross-cultural study of families.

I use the phrase "rights in children" to include moral claims, privileges, responsibilities, and rites that grow from customs, rituals and practices. Although anthropologists have long recognized the distinction between biological and psychological parenthood, until recently many experts in child welfare have assumed that within families biological mothers and fathers are unique in their capacity for and commitment to childrearing. This ethnocentric assumption overlooks cultural differences in the meaning that members of ethnic groups in the United States assign to the chain of parent-child, child-kin connections. We need to examine these differences more closely, especially in light of the social implications of our child welfare decisions. In other words, we need to understand who, in addition to biological parents, can be expected to rear children in low-income, minority communities.

In order to understand cultural differences in child socialization, attachments, and the distribution of rights in children, we can examine various cultural patterns of informal fosterage, adoption, and child exchange. In many nonindustrial areas of the world, adopting parents and natural parents are known to one another. In eastern Oceania, for example, children adopted by kin usually maintain ties with their natural parents. In Tahiti, as in other parts of Polynesia, relationships between parents and children are more contingent on choice than on biology; parents have the right to give their children to foster parents and frequently do so. Many Polynesians actually strive to model relationships with their "natural" children after those between adoptive parents and children, rather than vice versa.

Instances in which children actually choose their homes abound in the ethnographic literature. Caribbean children, for example, may ask permission to come and live with close kin or friends. Natural parents are expected to agree to this change of residence, as well as to reciprocate at the request of other children.

In other cases, it is parents who make these requests. It is not unusual for mothers in the Caribbean, in Ghana, or in black America to request or require kin to care for one of their children. Kinfolk create alliances among one another — alliances and obligations that may be called upon in the future.

In the West Indies, most transactions involving children take place outside of the legal system. Socialization of, and responsibility for, children on the island of St. Lucia are shared among relatives. Children are seldom confined to one household either for residence or in their interaction with adults; but, some particular adult is recognized as having primary responsibility for each child. This pattern is even more pronounced among emigrating parents, many of whom go to Great Britain and leave their dependent children on the island. While the rate of informal fosterage for the children of immigrants is higher than for the general population, they are absorbed by extended kin in much the same child-lending patterns that existed previous to migration.

Among the Gonja children of northern Ghana studied by Esther Goody, over one-half of all children over seven or eight years of age live with relatives other than their parents. Parental and maternal kin share equally in caring for their nieces, nephews, and grandchildren. These aunts, uncles, and grandparents are felt to possess certain rights in children. In fact, the Gonja believe that parents may never refuse requests from their own siblings, parents, or lineage heads for the right to raise a child. In response to such requests, parents *must* delegate or share rights in their children. Such fosterage patterns are typical both in rural West Africa and among urban migrants, for whom kin ties and fictive kin relationships are important resources.

Similarly, children in Honduras may be "loaned" by their parents to close kin or to neighbors with whom they share an ongoing, affectionate relationship. The lending or giving of children teaches children patterns of reciprocity. They learn how to establish and maintain exchange relationships.

Returning to the United States, we find examples of multiple parenting in Kathryn Molohon's study of the Pueblo and Navajo, where children are circulated throughout kinship networks along the same lines of distribution as economic and other resources. Based on her observations of Navajos who have migrated to West Coast cities, Molohon observed that urban Indians "regard themselves as emotional, financial, strategic, and geographical continuations of kin on home reservations." Indian children and adolescents move back and forth between the cities and home reservations, and develop strong emotional ties among their dispersed kin.

The black community in the United States also has long-standing cultural traditions of shared parenting responsibility among kin. These traditions enable parents and kin to cope with the difficulties of poverty. My own research in the "Flats" provides examples of circumstances among urban black families requiring kin to take care of one another's children. In the Flats, maternal and paternal kin, not just mothers and fathers, often share responsibilities in caring for nieces, nephews, and grandchildren.

Many children growing up in the Flats move back and forth between the households of close female kin, including women who are close kin to children's fathers. A statistical study of 1,000 children in the Flats revealed that on the average, children lived with their father's kin at least one-third of the time. The woman who temporarily assumes the kinship obligation to care for a child acquires the major cluster of rights and duties traditionally associated with motherhood.

Although the role need not be filled by a single actor, the responsibility of caring for children in the Flats is a kin obligation. Rights in children are delegated to kin who participate in domestic networks of cooperation. Within a network of cooperative kin there may be three or more adult women with whom, by turns, a child resides. Although younger children usually sleep in the same household as their mother, the size of the dwelling, employment, and many other factors determine where older siblings sleep. Patterns of eating, visiting, and child care may bring mothers and their children together for most of the day, but the adult immediately responsible for a child may change with a child's residence.

From the viewpoint of children, there may be a number of women who act as "mothers" toward them, some just slightly older than the children themselves. Likewise, these women regard their own children and their informally adopted children with equal love and concern. A woman who intermittently raises a sister's or niece's or cousin's child regards that child's offspring to be as much her grandchildren as children born to her own sons and daughters. Children may retain ties with their parents and siblings and at the same time establish deep relationships with other kin.

People in the Flats view child-keeping as a part of the flux and elasticity of residence. The constant expansion and contraction of households, and the successive recombinations of kinsmen residing together, require women to care for children residing in their households. (While men, young and old, also participate actively in child care and babysitting, the primary responsibility for parenting remains with women.) As households shift, rights and responsibilities in children also shift.

Uncontrollable economic and legal pressures from outside the community also affect domestic groups. Unemployment, migration, welfare requirements, housing shortages, high rents, or eviction all may necessitate residence changes, as may disasters or calamities such as death, murder, accident, or fire. Such occurrences are commonly related to the need for child care arrangements. A mother may request or require kin to "keep" one of her children, with a variety of implications. It may be that the mother has come upon hard times and desperately wants her close kin temporarily to assume responsibility for her children. Kin rarely refuse such requests. Kin and friends in domestic networks establish mutual ties of obligation; they bestow rights and responsibilities upon one another. As these responsibilities are satisfactorily fulfilled, the depth of the involvement between kin or between friends increases. Females simultaneously acquire reciprocal obligations toward one another's children and rights in them. As responsibilities for specific children evolve, women are ultimately allowed to occupy parental roles which are recognized both by the adults and the children involved.

In many low-income black communities, when one woman begins to take on all of the responsibilities toward a child that are culturally specific to motherhood, members of her kin group assume that she has activated her parental rights toward that child. The undertaking of major responsibilities toward a child — providing love, care, food, clothing, and shelter — constitute criteria by which kin become eligible to assume parental roles. Like professionals in child welfare, members of kin groups in black communities discourage the creation of strong emotional bonds between children and merely transient caretakers. It is only when people fulfill the criteria by which kin are eligible to assume parental roles in the eyes of the community that the role of an informal foster parent becomes that of a psychological parent.

That children in black communities become deeply attached to non-parent kin caretakers is well understood and articulated by community members. However, these patterns are often invisible to the child welfare system, with the result that children are removed from the kin network against their best interests.

The cultural patterns outlined here that create informal adoptions and psychological parenthood in black communities are described in greater depth and detail in Robert Hill's *Informal Adoption Among Black Families* and in *All Our Kin*. These patterns are complex and sometimes baffling to "street-level bureaucrats" — teachers, socialworkers, lawyers, judges, and physicians — who work directly with clients and who have tremendous power and discretion in implementing policy. Professionals, and outsiders in general, often perceive only chaos in ethnic families, but their own biases affect what they see and how they interpret it. At times, these professionals cannot find children in the "right" household or in the "right" beds, and they may react angrily when they find the "wrong" people in the "right" households. Thus cultural differences elicit punitive state action.

Street-level bureaucrats form their own stereotypes about client behavior, which are incorporated into policy decisions. For example, in 1982 I was an expert witness in a child welfare case in the Southeast. The case became a debate between two value systems, between the socialworker's notion of proper psychological parenting and that of the kin group. When the socialworker could no longer contend with constant household changes, in which one young child and an older sibling moved back and forth between their mother's and aunt's household, she recommended removal.

The system grants broad discretion to all of the bureaucrats involved, and the poorer the clients, the more power these outsiders have over them. In addition, federal funds until very recently have been targeted primarily for foster parents and foster homes, not for preventive services or to help biological kin. Sometimes, funds are available for a child only within the context of removal; an approach indicative of the way in which we discount the responsibility and abilities of low-income families.

To date, psychological parenting theory has not been broadly utilized by the child welfare system to protect the attachment of the children to members of the kin group. In fact, many socialworkers find it difficult to identify the psychological parent even if the family and child do not. Although cross-cultural data show that children are capable of forming multiple attachments to psychological parents who are members of their kin groups, attachments of this kind are characteristically ignored by the child welfare system.

Children drift into the foster care system for a variety of reasons. Some are placed voluntarily by parents who need respite care. Others are removed, as reported in a recent North Carolina study, simply because the parents are too poor. Poor children with family problems are more likely than are middle-class children to be brought to the attention of authorities by physicians, schools, and teachers.

Many states have been willing to pay a premium well above welfare stipends to keep a child in foster care, rather than in the child's own home or with close kin.

The Adoption Assistance and Child Welfare Act of 1980 mandated periodic review, a permanent plan for placement, and speedy adoption of children in foster care. My concern is that this relatively enlightened legislation may fail to avoid the pitfalls of custom and tradition inherent in the child welfare system. It is imperative that child welfare workers understand how rights in minority children are distributed within kin groups; that they are able to distinguish well-functioning from poorly functioning kin networks; that preference is not given to placement in the homes of strangers over placement in the homes of members of the kin group; that social workers know how to utilize kinship networks as resources for children; and that informal "adoptive" parents not be forced to pursue legal adoption and terminate the legal rights of biological parents in violation of cultural traditions. Adoption of these principles will help assure that permanency planning is not used

as an unwarranted interference with the rights of kin.

When the rights of children and parents come into conflict, our society has traditionally protected the rights of parents if those parents are affluent or middle class. We respect the privacy and autonomy of middle-class families. In contrast, we have accepted intervention and intrusion in low-income families, and we have discounted the cultural backgrounds and solid parenting skills of low-income parents. To protect poor children, we have created a legal structure that disregards the rights of their parents and the cooperative values of many minority families.

Termination of a biological mother's parental rights is not only a violation of her individual rights as a parent. It may also violate the rights of members of her kin group. There are instances in which the protection of the legal rights of the individual child or parent may be in direct conflict with the cooperative and communal values of minority communities. This cultural oversight has led to a failure to protect the natural rights of children, parents, and the other members of the kin group.

◆

CHILD SUPPORT AND VISITATION: RETHINKING THE CONNECTIONS
Karen Czpanskiy

The complex personal and legal relationships between child support and visitation have led to the development of different sets of rules which "connect" or "disconnect" these two issues to varying degrees. Connecting rules link the two together.

For example, a parent who fails to pay child support can be denied visitation, and vice versa. Conversely, a parent sued for nonpayment of child support could assert denial of visitation as a defense. Some states have developed more restrictive

From Karen Czpanskiy, "Child Support and Visitation: Rethinking the Connections," *Rutgers L.J.* vol. 20, 1989, pp. 619–665 (edited).

connecting rules which permit linkage between child support and visitation only by court order or parental contract. The current trend is toward developing disconnecting rules. Under these rules, one parent's failure to pay child support or permit visitation bears no relationship to the other parent's duty to pay support or permit visitation. That trend, however, is neither universal or unidirectional.

A successful solution to the questions of whether, how and to what degree, child support and visitation should be connected is one which strikes the right balance among three interests: the child's needs for financial support and emotional and physical nurturance from both parents; the parents' need for human association; and the parents' need for personal autonomy. Unfortunately, neither the connecting rules not the disconnecting rules satisfactorily balance these interests.

Both sets of rules fail the child. They permit optional parenthood on the part of the nonresidential parent who is free to decide whether to participate in the upbringing of the child or to ignore the child completely. Connecting rules even further disadvantage the child. The nonresidential parent can withhold support payments whenever she believes visitation is being denied, depriving the child of necessary financial support.

Both connecting and disconnecting rules fail the parents as well. The residential parent's need for personal autonomy goes unsatisfied because neither set of rules requires the nonresidential parent to share in the nurturing tasks. At the same time, under connecting rules, the nonresidential parent can be denied opportunities to be with the child, thus limiting her need for human association. Moreover, gender bias permeates both sets of rules. Under connecting rules, the father's desire for contact with his child is given a preference

over the mother's need for regular financial support for the child. Further, she is subject to indefinite and restrictive standards about facilitating the father's access to the child, while he is subject to no standards about what he must do. Under disconnecting rules, the parental paradigm is a gendered one of distinctly separate mother/father, female/male roles. Nurturing work is associated exclusively with women and mothers and is accorded no recognition. At the same time, the sole legally cognizable paternal contribution is money, no matter what the level of nurturing a particular father may have been giving to his children.

A new and different approach is needed to balance the relationships between child support and visitation — an approach which serves the needs of the children and parents and does so in gender-neutral ways. Under a new approach, priority should be accorded to the needs of the child for security on both the financial and emotional/physical levels. Both parents should be given incentives to be responsible to the child on both levels. At the same time, the needs of both parents for personal autonomy and for human association should be considered and accommodated to the extent possible that is consistent with the child's needs. Finally, both parents' needs should be considered without regard to gender. This type of approach, a dual parent/dual responsibility formula, calls for both parents to provide the child with support of all kinds, whether financial, emotional or physical. It recognizes that the child and both parents are members of a family system, even though they occupy separate households, and that the actions of each one affects the others.

The separation of the roles gave the traditionally female role of caretaker recognition and a status similar to that of the traditionally male economic role. Over time, however, the economic support role has become degenderized; mothers and fathers now share the responsibility of providing economic support of children. At the same time, the caretaking role remains solely with the residential parent — usually the mother. So "equality" has come to mean economic equality solely; the residential parent's additional role as caretaker is being ignored. So far, equalizing the caretaking role along with the economic role has not been considered. The residential mother gets no recognition for her double burden.

Another gender-biased aspect of the disconnecting rules is the sense that it is possible to make separate categories of parental involvement with a child and not have those categories intersect. That is, the rules rest on the notion that whether a parent provides child support has nothing to do with whether the parent should be allowed to visit the child. Thus a parent is allowed to compartmentalize the types of support offered to a child: money is one thing, while caretaking is another.

Compartmentalization is gender-biased in a society which assigns parental roles based on gender stereotypes. The stereotypically good residential parent should act like a mother. No good mother would intentionally compartmentalize types of support which she provides a child and parcel out each type of support in limited degrees. Thus, when a judge approves of a parent doing this kind of compartmentalizing, the judge is not thinking of the usual expectations associated with residential parents. The stereotypically good nonresidential parent should act like a father, a role which is subject to less all-encompassing norms of parenting. Therefore, what a judge may be voicing in approving of compartmental-

ization is a culturally approved male standard for parenting.

An interesting question is why the disconnection of child support and visitation between poor families is more extreme than those whose parents have more resources. Many judges have a candid explanation: the taxpayers should not have to bear the burden of supporting these children if they have a parent who can pay. The more defenses that parent can raise to the child support claim, the less the state can recover. Since denial of visitation is one more defense, it is simply not allowed. The message to both parents it that only money counts; the emotional support a parent might provide or seek to provide a child has no importance at all.

BETTER SOLUTIONS

Given the many deficiencies in existing sets of rules which connect and govern child support and visitation, a completely new approach is needed. Such an approach should require both parents to provide financial and physical/emotional support to the child. Under this "dual parent/dual responsibility formula," child support and visitation would be linked, in an extended and positive way, so that the child would get the benefit of mutual and enlarged parental duties.

The formula would require that financial support be calculated based on the child's needs and the ability of each parent to pay — just as it is today in most states. Parents would fulfill their physical/emotional nurturance responsibilities differently depending on who had custody. The primary residential parent would continue to be responsible for most of the day-to-day care of the child. The nonresidential parent would also be required to provide care on a regular basis, although for a smaller amount of time. On the average, the nonresidential parent would be expected to care for the child about twenty percent of the time. Under this dual parent/dual responsibility formula, the emphasis is not solely on the number of hours a parent spends with a child, but on the regularity and normalcy of the parent's participation in the child's life. Thus, just like the residential parent, the nonresidential parent would be expected to provide the child with care on a regular and predictable basis, whether during weekdays, weekends, vacation periods, or a combination of those times. Further, the nonresidential parent would be expected to do normal parental tasks, such as overnight stays with the child, homework supervision and transporting the child to regular activities. Simply providing entertainment for the child would not be adequate or appropriate.

Defaults by either parent as to either the financial or the physical/emotional nurturing responsibility would be subject to judicial sanction. Thus, if a residential parent denied the nonresidential parent regular and appropriate time to provide nurturing for the child, the contempt procedures already available to enforce visitation rights could be invoked. In addition, the nonresidential parent should be entitled to substitute time with the child. At the same time, if a nonresidential parent failed to provide physical and emotional nurturance to the child, the court could be asked to intervene. Sanctions would be graduated, beginning with an order that the nonresidential parent spend time with the child. If that failed, the nonresidential parent would be required to pay for the supplemental care the residential parent supplies because of the default of the nonresidential parent. If the nonresidential parent still failed to

provide physical/emotional nurturance, the residential parent could be given the additional option of denying future visitation altogether. This would allow the parent and the child to rearrange their lives in light of the decision of the nonresidential parent not to participate in the child's upbringing.

Most states already take into account the ability of both parents to provide support when establishing a child support award, so no change would be necessary. The mechanisms already in place for the collection of child support, while deficient in many ways, would not be improved by using visitation as an incentive to pay.

The basic elements of the dual parent/dual responsibility formula are designed so that the child can have both parents working to meet the child's needs to the greatest extent possible. Within their abilities, both parents will be required to provide both financial support and emotional and physical nurturance. Unlike the present situation, the nonresidential parent will be encouraged to remain involved with the child, rather than be given incentives to avoid the child. The nonresidential parent's interest in personal autonomy should be given less deference than previously. At the same time, his need for human association with the child is respected to a greater degree because substitute visitation would be provided if necessary, and because visitation would not be denied if he fails to pay support. The need of the residential parent for personal autonomy is elevated in importance by the provisions allowing the residential parent to demand that the nonresidential parent share the nurturing of the child. She is also given recognition for the nurturing work provided the child, and at the same time is relieved of sole responsibility for providing emotional and physical support.

The dual parent/dual responsibility formula is gender neutral because the needs of both parents are treated with equivalent respect. Both are required to take part in meeting as many of the child's needs as they are capable of handling, and neither is allowed to impose their burdens on the other. The parenting model is one of interconnection and fulfillment of human possibilities, not distinct gender-typed roles; autonomous activities do not take precedence over connective activities.

Exceptions to the dual parent/dual responsibility formula are appropriate in certain circumstances, such as when a nonresidential parent is violent toward the children. For that parent to be involved with the child may be more harmful than helpful, and the time such a parent can be permitted to spend with the child may be limited or denied altogether. However, that parent's child support duty should not be terminated. A parent should not be rewarded for committing violent acts against a child.

Children who live with one parent may suffer many disabilities, ranging from poverty to deprivation to alienation from the other parent. The current legal rules governing whether and how child support and visitation should be linked have not solved the problems of these children; in some ways they have made them worse. In addition, the rules contain gender-biased assumptions which cannot easily be expunged. This permits gender-biased results which cannot easily be changed. Better approaches are needed to maintain the child's relationship with both parents and both parents' full responsibility to the child. The dual parent/dual responsibility formula proposed here accomplishes this goal by providing for both parents to perform all the services which they are capable of providing for the child. At the same time, the dual parent/dual responsibility formula leaves room to serve both parents' legitimate needs for separateness and autonomy during the child's minority.

◆

JUSTIFYING THE CONTINUED USE OF JAIL
David Chambers

Jerry Neal's mother is seventy-eight. I called and asked her if I could see her sometime and, weeks later, called again and paid a visit. Jerry's father wasn't home. Mrs. Neal was reluctant to talk. She repeated several times that she knew she was going to get into trouble for speaking to me.

We sat at her kitchen table. She pulled at the folds of her dress and talked about her family. Jerry was her baby, the last of her four sons. The other three, like their father, had spent their adult lives to this point working in the local General Motors plants. They had jobs to be proud of. They went to church and stayed married to the same women.

To her, Jerry had many of the good qualities of his brothers. He was "a good hard worker." He came out and fixed the

From David Chambers, "Justifying the Continued Use of Jail," in *Making Fathers Pay* (Chicago: University of Chicago Press, 1979), pp. 241–253 (edited).

cars from time to time. He helped his Dad in other ways. "He'd give the shirt off his back for you."

"Then what made Jerry different?" I asked. After a long pause, she replied, "I don't know. That's the way it goes. I guess." I could hear the same words out of Jerry's mouth.

She said that, when she heard that Jerry had been jailed for nonsupport, she cried and cried. "He hadn't killed anybody or hurt anybody, had he?"

Yet, Mrs. Neal's own life is the visible proof of Jerry's sin. Her man — she always referred to her husband as "my man" — had always taken care of her and brought home his paycheck for his family. They lived on five acres in a small, well-tended farmhouse that he had bought over forty years before. Cared for financially, Mrs. Neal had looked after this house and raised her sons. She had never been on welfare. She had never felt compelled by need to take a job outside the home. Mr. Neal had shared with her the task of raising the sons, had disciplined them when they needed it, had provided an image of reliability for them to emulate.

Throughout her life, Mrs. Neal had been cared for and protected — as Jerry himself as a child had been cared for and protected — in ways that Jerry had failed to provide for Dolores or for his children. Maybe Jerry had not killed anyone, but by Mrs. Neal's moral code it could hardly be said that he had not hurt anyone.

If we share Mrs. Neal's code or even that part of the code that makes parents responsible for their children, Jerry's moral failure alone might appear to justify locking him up in jail. Jail can serve admirably as an instrument of retribution. Many women wish their former husbands some unspeakable torture, and in this country the county jail is about the best we have to offer. Remember Dolores Neal's

smile as she recollected that two of her husbands served time in jail together for failing to pay. Especially if the nonpayer's children are receiving welfare benefits, judges and many members of the public might join Dolores in her chuckle.

So long as states rely on a child support system that depends on divorced parents making payments after earnings are in their pockets, there is probably no sanction other than jail that will work as well: Threatening fines seem pointless given the sort of behavior the government is trying to induce; cutting off fingers or branding foreheads would be rejected as barbaric; other forms of public mortification — such as publishing the names of defaulters — might be tried but such lists have never been a favored form of sanction in this country, and might have little effect on the large numbers of persons who pay little attention to newspapers.

If jail induces high payments and the extra dollars collected outstrip the dollar costs of the jailing policy, can there be any serious objections to its continued use? The measure of jail's justifiability cannot lie alone in its effectiveness in deterring undesired conduct. America keeps a larger portion of its citizens in prisons than any other Western nation. The reason is not merely that we suffer from a high incidence of violent crime; it is also that our judges and legislators prescribe jail easily. If a person is "bad," he belongs in jail. Thus, today, even many liberals who deplore the conditions in our jails advocate the greater use of penal sanctions on men who beat their wives or assault them sexually.

I think jail should be selected as a sanction with greater caution. Except for the death penalty, our society inflicts no more serious sanction than sentences of jail or imprisonment. Sentencing a man to jail involves two steps of greater significance than most of us consider on first reflection: first, there is a determination that the man has engaged in some sort of conduct serious enough that we are willing to place a stamp of social condemnation on him — willing to saddle him with a "criminal record." Though nonsupport proceedings are formally denominated "civil," the public surely makes no such distinction when hearing of a man sentenced to jail for six months or a year. Second, there is a decision to sever the man's ties for some period from the activities in the community that he depends upon — access to friends, the satisfactions of work, heterosexual contacts, religious ceremonies of his own choosing, strolling, chatting, and chewing the fat with friends on his front stoop. We accomplish the severance by locking him in an institution in which he will be subjected to complete loss of privacy, to the substantial likelihood of physical and sexual assault, and to the degradation of placement in a servile relation to guards with power to punish, ignore, or humiliate. We have commented earlier on the conditions of the jail in Genesee County. Most jails in this country are older and in worse condition than Genesee's. Indeed, the county jails that house misdemeanants, nonsupporters, and persons awaiting trial are America's vilest institutions of incarceration — typically far worse than our prisons, for unlike prisons, jails, generally in the middle of cities, offer little opportunity for physical exercise. Most people in jails just sit or sleep.

Over the last few decades, a great deal that is unsettling has been learned about the effects of labeling a person "bad." The label sticks in the man's own head and often reshapes his vision of himself; he is as likely to accept the label as a confirmation of his own sense of worthlessness as

he is to resist the label and resolve to live up to the expectations of society. Moreover, in a seemingly perverse manner, many men become dependent upon the loss of autonomy jail affords. They become "institutionalized," to use the term adopted by students of institutions of confinement.

That we find men staying around Flint who make no payments and are jailed four or five times for long terms surprises no social scientist who has examined the behavior of other men with contact with the criminal justice system. The rate of reimprisonment of previously convicted men remains so high that many social scientists and penologists despair of the utility of either jail or prison to deter, by fear of recommittal, most of those put there or to rehabilitate by programs that instill new attitudes. Given these attributes of jailing and the conditions of jails, does nonsupport still seem an appropriate offense for jail's use, even if it has useful general deterrent effects?

One part of the answer should lie in answering another question: how heinous an act is willful nonsupport? At first blush it seems particularly vicious — the conscious disregard of one of a person's most sacred duties. Nonetheless, two aspects of jailing for nonsupport should give us pause: first, it is a form of jailing for debt; and, second, it arises as an offense between family members.

By any common sense understanding, jailing for arrearage in court-ordered support is indeed a form of jailing for debt. Jailing for debt. The very phrase transports us back to Fielding, Defoe, and Dickens, to eighteenth- and nineteenth- century England when thousands of debtors were jailed each year in the vilest conditions. In the 1750s, three-quarters of the prisoners in London's jails were debtors, committed on the bare assertion of an unpaid bill for owing as little as a sixpence or a shilling. In this country most state constitutions, including Michigan's, bar jailing for debt.

Why do most Americans, even today, recoil from the idea of jailing for debt? If there are good reasons to recoil, can jailing for nonpayment of child support be distinguished from jailing for debt? To many people, failing to pay a commercial debt simply does not seem sinful enough to justify a criminal record and penal incarceration. We do not think in terms of a criminal law as a part of business transactions between consenting persons. Rather we think in terms of commercial remedies — suits in contract, refusal to continue to deal, refusals to extend credit — and consider them adequate. In a commercial context, jailing becomes simply another collection technique of creditors, a powerful supplement to garnishment and default judgments. The debtors who would be subject to jailing today would probably be persons of low income involved with loan companies and with furniture, automobile, and appliance dealers. In these transactions, many would feel that adding to the seller's arsenal the power to secure the buyer's commitment to jail would simply add weight to the stronger side of the transaction. Moreover, tending to consider crimes in terms of victims, many would find it hard to picture a relation between a single person's nonpayment and any significant harm to the creditor. It is indeed typically the case that the loss suffered by the corporate creditor is significant only when there has been default by large number of debtors. Ma Bell is really no one's mother.

In most respects the failure to pay child support seems vastly different from the failure to pay commercial debts. With child-support nonpayment outside the welfare setting, there is for each nonpayer a victim — a child, visible and often hurt-

ing. Moreover, the victim has not been in an overweaning bargaining position with regard to the transactions that led to the debt. Nor can the child victim adequately protect himself for the future by tightening his credit practices or relying on repossession. Perhaps, most compellingly, the welfare of children is simply more important than the welfare of automobile dealers. These differences may explain why Congress has long provided that commercial debts can be discharged in bankruptcy but arrearages in child support obligations cannot. It also explains the underlying reason why state courts have almost uniformly read their constitutional prohibitions against jailing for debt as not including debt arising from court-ordered obligations of support. If analogies to old practices of jailing for debts were the only reason to feel queasy about jailing for nonsupport, we might well decide that nonsupport is justly considered different.

What, however, do we make of the fact that we are dealing with a "family" offense? While the family nature of the child support debt makes nonpayment seem more egregious than nonpayment of commercial debts, there are other aspects of the "family nature" of the child support offense that may make nonpayment seem less appropriate for criminal sanctions. A recent British government committee that studied all aspects of the problems of one-parent families criticized the continued wide use in Britain of jailing for nonpayment of support. Citing the "emotional stress" of the post-divorce period and child support's connection with the "intimate personal relationship," the committee recommended that Parliament eliminate penal sanctions for nonpayment of support.

The stress of the post-divorce period is important to remember. In many cases the nonpaying male who appears to have a callous disregard for the welfare of his family is in fact caught in a much more nearly forgiveable struggle, often the continuation after divorce of patterns of behavior that were a part of the marital relationship: withholding as a form of communication. Divorced men thus often "forget" to pay from quite prosaic human feelings of jealousy or anger, just as divorced women similarly forget that Tuesday is the day the father planned to visit the children. At one hearing, a Genesee man confessed to the judge with some embarrassment that he had withheld support, in an effort he admitted was childish, to make the woman realize her dependency on him and come back. Jailings commonly occur during this period of particular stress. The reader may recall that nearly half of the men in our sample of jailed man had been first jailed for failing to pay within a year of their final judgment of divorce.

To be sure, men who murder their wives may similarly claim that they acted during a moment of "emotional stress," growing out of an "intimate family relationship." If there is a difference between killing and nonpayment, it lies in the seriousness of the act of killing. When an addled man or woman kills his or her spouse, the law recognizes and juries commonly concur that the act deserves punishment, although often not for first-degree murder. Second-degree murder or manslaughter are more common verdicts. With nonsupport within the family, the emotional turmoil may suggest to us that the act simply no longer seems to justify criminal sanctions at all. "Second-degree" nonsupport may not seem an appropriate occasion for jail.

Our exploration of the propriety of jailing for failing to pay support has thus far focused on the nature of the offense. To many persons, what we have examined so far points in opposed directions: the intrafamily nature of the offense makes nonpayment at once more serious and more pardonable, in differing degrees in different cases. Whatever one's judgment to this point, however, the nature of the offense is not the sole basis for doubt about the appropriateness of penal sanctions in this context. The offense itself cannot be separated from the process through which the offender must pass before jailing, and it remains important to ask whether the offense is sufficiently susceptible to evenhanded and fair administration to meet some minimum notions of justice. Our review of the actual administration of the collection of support in Genesee County, a system with many disturbing attributes, is relevant to our inquiry here but not dispositive. Our inquiry is whether, given the limits of human competence, discriminatory or unfair administration inheres in the nature of the offense and whether any system widely relying on jail can meet tolerable standards of fairness. We have suggested in our discussion of Genesee that it is unlikely that such standards can be met, but some points need emphasis and generalization.

The task of assessment is difficult at best. It involves paring away the day-to-day facts of administration that we viewed in Michigan to get down to some core of characteristics nearly certain to be shared by all systems of enforcement — the task of separating the dancer from the dance. And then, once we have divined the core, we must make judgments about fairness in a context in which there is, in this country, no widely agreed upon set of minimal standards for appraising systems of criminal justice. The United States Constitution suggests some important shared values about evenhandedness and just methods of arrest and adjudication, but the divergent views of the current Justices of the Supreme Court mirror the diverse feelings of Americans generally about how much fairness "guilty" people deserve. For all these difficulties, we can identify a few characteristics, almost certain to be present in any system of child support enforcement, that many people, perhaps most, can agree are troubling. The first is that vastly more parents will fail to pay at one time or another than will ever be arrested or jailed, creating countless opportunities for abuses in selecting who shall be punished and who shall be spared. The second is that, even with conscientious efforts at evenhandedness, the task of sorting out those who "deserve" to be arrested from those who do not will involve troubling questions about acceptable excuses and acceptable plans for deferred payments about which there will be much disagreement. The third is that those who will in fact end up in jail — and particularly those who will stay there for any significant period of time — will almost certainly include a large portion of the persons whose "guilt" will seem more dubious.

We have seen that even in Genesee County, over sixty percent of the men ended up in arrears by at least twenty-six weeks' worth of payments at some point, but fewer than a third of this group were ever jailed. Wayne County, a large urban county reasonably well-organized for enforcing, provides even starker figures. During 1974, of over 100,000 men under orders of support in divorce or paternity cases, over half paid less than ten percent of everything due. Of the more than 50,000 defaulters only 914 were sentence to jail. This low rate occurred despite the fact that the identities of all offenders were known to the agency.

Given the experience across Michigan, it seems likely that other states will continue to have large numbers of nonpayers, even if they develop enforcement systems that mirror Michigan's system. The defaults will include men who fail to pay for all sorts of reasons — anger over visitation, unemployment, layoffs, jealousy, competing expenses, distaste for the child, and so on. And, everywhere, as in Michigan, human beings — enforcement officers or police and judges — will have to decide who shall be branded with a penal record.

Statues provide little guidance for sorting out who should and should not be punished. Today, courts can hold someone in contempt only when the violation is willful, but only a few nonpayers are persons utterly unable to make any payments. The vast bulk of nonpayers, including those who are unemployed, are persons who could pay more — a few dollars at the very least — if they placed payment of support above all other uses of their money. Even for the limited number of unemployed men who literally can pay nothing more than they do, statutes invite courts to ask the impossible suppositional question, "Could this man have been employed if he really tried?" Especially in the context of mass administration of justice, that question seems beyond the capacity of judges to answer except by reference to their own skewed experiences in the labor market and their own ill-informed guesses about employment opportunities.

Can legislatures write statutes that would provide better guidance? Even if courts or legislatures recognized a defense for the unemployed as well as for persons with incomes below the single-individual Lower Standard Budget level — both of these are changes I would recommend — there would still be vast numbers of offenders for both enforcing officers and judges to pick among. The problem is not in defining the undesirable conduct but in developing a system of responses that is both equitable and flexible — a nearly impossible task. Nonsupport is hardly unique in this regard. The closely comparable offense of willful failure to pay taxes calls similarly for judgments by enforcers.

What is troublesome, however, about selective enforcement in the area of child support is that there are many inviting subgroups of nonpayers likely to be singled out inappropriately for especially disfavored treatment. Within Michigan, for example, there are counties in which it appears that most of the jailing befalls those whose children receive welfare benefits, despite the fact that no just claim can be made that this group is either more villainous for failing to pay or that it constitutes an especially visible group to scare other potential defaulters. In Dane County, Wisconsin, fathers in welfare cases were similarly singled out, as was another worrisome group; those with criminal records for other offenses. Like other offenses thought easy to prove as a matter of law, nonpayment of support lends itself to use by police or prosecutors as a way of holding men suspected of offenses more difficult to prove. Enforcement is also certain to fall unevenly on those who have difficulty communicating with middle-class persons in authority. To many men, nonpayment involves a series of excuses to fend off prying enforcement persons. As stated by one Friend of the Court we have earlier quoted. "No one gets jailed for failing to pay. They get jailed for failing to cooperate."

Those who do not communicate with the agency after warnings and those who do, but are inept, are the ones whom enforcing officers are most likely to carry through the discretionary screens to arrest. Nearly all the filters before jail lead to an overrepresentation in the jailed population of blue-collar males and an under-representation of white-collar males, just as we found in Genesee County. It is similarly inevitable that those who spend any substantial length of time in jail, unable to come up with lump-sum payments, will be the most down-and-out among these men, those with the fewest resources of their own and those with the fewest relatives warmly disposed to bail them out. It seems quite probable that the high representation of alcoholics in Genesee County among men who serve the longest terms would be repeated under any system. It is ironic that this group should bear so much of the brunt of the enforcement system since there must be more doubts regarding its capacity to pay than there are about almost any other group of nonpaying men.

No matter how we regard the defaulting parents, we should also examine the jailing system from the perspective of the children it is intended to benefit. When we do so, we encounter a bit of a puzzlement.

For some children, the effect of a jailing policy will be an unalloyed gain, for others both a gain and a loss, and for still others solely a loss. We have frequently noted the dollar gains for some children. For some other children, however, there will predictably be a dollar loss. We learned in Genesee County that significant numbers of the jailed men leave town and do not pay again. While it is probably the case that most of these men were determined not to pay, for some others it is probably the case that they could have been cajoled into better payments through less severe measures. Their jailing may have contributed in some small measure to overall collections at the expense of their own children. The same is probably the case for some families of men never jailed: the man, resistant to paying and aware of jail's possibility, leaves town before lesser forms of cajolery can be applied.

The effects on children cannot be measured in dollars alone. A jailing policy will have psychological effects on children that may be similarly unevenly distributed. For those children who receive more money than they would in the absence of jailing, there is not only the fact of more dollars available for food and clothing, there may also be a psychic value in payments: they may make the child feel that she is loved and lovable. Many fathers will never consciously recognize the place of jail in their decision to pay, and the continuity of payments will help sustain a relationship with their children. We have no measures whatever in our study of the extent to which steady payments increase the warmth of relationships between father and child. Even assuming that they do, and it seems plausible that they do, if only by reducing friction between the parents, there is little evidence on the importance in the development of a child of sustaining a close tie to the parent who ceases to live with her or participate regularly in the decisions affecting her life. What speculative literature there is about the relation of a noncustodial parent to a child points in two directions — some of it suggests that the relationship between the child and the custodial parent almost inevitably dominates and that the other relationship become relatively insignificant, some of it suggests that the relationship with the noncustodial parent remains critical to the child's image of herself and to her growth.

But let us accept for the moment what is probably the case: for some children, a jailing policy induces, in subtle ways, higher payments from their fathers, their long-term ties with the fathers are thereby improved, and they (and perhaps their fathers) are happier. The dilemma is that it is no less plausible, and equally beyond this study's capacity to prove, that other children will be harmed by a jailing policy. The children whose fathers flee not only lose the money, they lose a tie with the father and quite possibly with other members of the father's family. For some men who flee, their nonpayment before leaving town will not have been because they did not care. They may have been truly unable to pay but fearful of being jailed anyway. They may also have been fathers of children on welfare who knew that their payments did not affect the income available to the child. While government may wish to combat this latter father's nonpayment, it is still the case that the father's leaving can produce an unfortunate loss for the child.

Even more elusive to measure is a loss that may occur for some children whose fathers do not leave and continue in fact to maintain contact with them. Especially for those children whose fathers are most conscious of jail's possibility, the hovering image in the father's mind of a clanging cell door may alter the tone of the relationship between him and his child. At some level, the relationship may shift from one based solely on affection to one based in significant part on fear. To be sure, simply the entry of a formal court order to support may produce a partial shift in the father's view of his relationship to the child, but it is surely possible that the potential of jail may distort the relationship further. If the child becomes at some level a spectre of jail, one would expect the father to avoid the spectre or to feel uncomfortable in its presence. Moreover, in some cases of men actually jailed, it is possible that some fathers will view the child as the "cause" of their jailing and that the child, in a no less great inversion, will accept the view and feel guilt.

SUMMARY

Stack up all the dubious aspects of jailing for nonsupport: the offense is an intrafamily one with complex emotional roots; jails are debilitating institutions — they exceed rather than fit this crime; jailing in this setting is difficult, nearly impossible, to administer in an evenhanded manner; when widely used, the prospect of jailing may well affect adversely the relationship between children and the parent under an order of support, even when the parent pays with unflagging regularity. On these grounds taken together, I, were I a legislator, would vote to remove the sanction of jailing for contempt from the permissible range of techniques for enforcing support. Many others, however, would hear my complaints about jailing and admit them to be troubling, but at the same time they would also hear another small voice whispering compellingly in the background, "But jail works." It works not merely in the sense of satisfying a public

need for retribution. It works by altering the very behavior toward which it is addressed, an impact so rarely demonstrated for penal sanctions that we may wish to hold on to it for its very rarity — a whooping crane in the criminal justice system.

To my view the effectiveness of jailing is largely irrelevant, if my reasons for deploring jailing are sound. Nonetheless, persons troubled by jailing but strongly moved by its success in extracting dollars should lose much of their enthusiasm for jailing if equitable alternatives exist that permit even more reliable support for children without the unfortunate aspects of jails. And I too would say that if effective alternatives exist — "less restrictive alternatives" than jailing, to borrow a term from constitutional law — it would be immoral for government to continue to rely on jailing. It would be immoral in much the same sense that it would be immoral to use a sledgehammer to swat a mosquito on a friend's back.

◆

FAMILY STRUCTURE, BLACK UNEMPLOYMENT, AND AMERICAN SOCIAL POLICY

Kathryn Neckerman, Robert Aponte, and William Juilus Wilson

Over the past two decades, explanation of the sharp rise in female-headed families among blacks has focused on the incentives that welfare programs provide. Charles Murray is simply the latest and perhaps the most prominent representative of this point of view. But while the welfare hypothesis was plausible in the early

1970s, following the simultaneous sharp increase in proportions of female-headed families and the unprecedented expansion of welfare, it can no longer be sustained. Sophisticated empirical research on the subject shows only modest effects of AFDC on family structure. Welfare benefit levels appear to have their greatest in-

Kathryn Neckerman, Robert Aponte, and William Juilus Wilson, "Family Structure, Black Unemployment, and American Social Policy," in *The Politics in the United States*, M. Weir, A. Orloff, T. Skocpol, eds., 1988, pp. 397, 414–419.

fluence not on the incident of out-of-wed-lock births or on rates of separation and divorce, but on the living arrangements of young single mothers. The experience of the past ten years confirms this research: the proportion of families headed by women has continued to rise even as the real value of welfare benefits has fallen.

As the welfare hypothesis had proven unfruitful, the effect of black male economic status is again receiving attention. In historical and ethnographic studies as well as in multivariate analyses of survey data, male economic status is consistently related to family stability. Recent research indicates that increasing black male joblessness, in combination with the high mortality and incarceration rates of black men, has resulted in dramatic declines over the past twenty-five years in the ratio of employed men to women, or the "male marriageable pool index." Not only are national trends consistent with the hypothesis that male joblessness is related to the rise of female-headed households, but also, when these data are disaggregated by region, they show that in regions where the black MMPI fell the most — the Northeast and Midwest — the proportion of black female-headed families also increased the most. The more modest increase in families headed by women among whites is accompanied by little change in white MMPI values.

Recent economic shifts are likely to be a major factor in the increasing joblessness of black men. Regional differences in the change in MMPI discussed earlier point to the particular importance of industrial transformations occurring in the Northeast and Midwest. The shift from manufacturing to services and the geographic shifts in production activity have altered both the number and the characteristics of jobs available in areas where blacks are concentrated. Most inner-city blacks cannot qualify for high-skilled po-sitions in the finance, real estate, and information-processing sectors; low-skilled service jobs, however, are characterized by low wages, restricted opportunities for advancement, and unstable employment.

Despite the consistent evidence linking male economic status to family stability, until recently most scholars and policymakers have overlooked joblessness in their discussions of changing family structure. Because official unemployment statistics do not take into account discouraged workers, or those who have dropped out of the labor force, they understate the increase in black male joblessness, thus it is possible that the extent of the problem has escaped the notice of social scientists concerned with the black family. A more likely explanation, however, lies in the sensitive and highly politicized nature of the debate over the black family. Although previous historical and ethnographic accounts had often portrayed the lower-class black family as unstable or disorganized, Moynihan's *The Negro Family* generated a tremendous amount of controversy, and this criticism had a chilling effect on research on the black family. Most scholarly writing that addressed the subject at all emphasized the resilience and adaptability of lower-class black families in the face of overwhelming disadvantage. Ironically, this focus had led to a neglect of traditional liberal concerns, such as problems of racial isolation and restricted economic opportunity and the impact of these problems on the family, even as the economic and demographic shifts of the 1970s have made these concerns increasingly timely. Conservative scholars, who were not inhibited by this ideologically tinged criticism, came to dominate the debate with their arguments of welfare dependency and the culture of poverty.

Research agendas on the family must be broadened to take account of macrostructural forces such as employment trends. Although we have evidence that male economic status is related to family stability, much work remains to be done. Still unresolved is the role of factors such as ethnicity, class, and community in mediating the influence of male unemployment on marriage and family relations. Those concerned with contemporary family problems may be able to draw on the insights of a rich and growing literature in history of the family.

Even as this research proceeds, however, we must develop new policy approaches to female-headed families and the related problems of welfare dependency and teenage childbearing. Although the liberal social welfare programs of the 1960s cannot be blamed for the increase in black female-headed families, they also have been helpless to stop it. Further, these Great Society programs have shown only limited success in alleviating the poverty of female-headed families; even when poverty rates are adjusted for receipt of non-cash benefits, one-fourth of all female-headed families are still poor.

One major component of a policy approach to the problems of female-headed families must be a comprehensive economic reform package designed to promote and enhance employment among the disadvantaged — both men and women. Fundamental to this approach are policies that will foster economic growth and create a tight labor market. The logic of supply and demand indicates that policies to create a tight labor market may also raise wages; historically, in addition, other employer concessions such as company-sponsored day care have also been provided when labor is scarce. However, without protectionist legislation or measures such as employer ownership/control, unskilled or semiskilled workers, especially those in production, are vulnerable to the same economic shifts now dev-

astating the older industrial cities. Low-skilled workers who are paid well enough to escape poverty are for that very reason likely to lose their jobs, either to mechanization or to international competition. To address the problem of joblessness, we need macroeconomic and labor market policies sophisticated enough to come to terms with this dilemma.

This problem points as well to the importance of measures such as adult education, on-the-job training, and apprenticeship to raise the skill levels of the disadvantaged. Wide disparities in education and training perpetuate inequality in the American labor force and represent a formidable obstacle to anti-poverty efforts. Lack of skills also leaves workers vulnerable to fluctuations in economic conditions and to future technological change. Improved manpower policies would ensure that the disadvantaged are not permanently trapped on the lowest rungs of the job market.

Employment policies are not typically seen as an answer to the problems of female-headed families. Research shows that a rising tide does not raise all boats equally: Economic growth helps male-headed families more than female-headed families. Our work suggests that these employment policies will address the problems of female-headed families indirectly, by improving the job prospects of men and enhancing the stability of low-income, two-parent families. But even under our current set of social policies, economic growth improves the economic status of women who head families, and it will do so more effectively with policy efforts to improve child care services and child support enforcement. The majority of women heading families are in the labor force, and more can be drawn in by more attractive job prospects and better child care. In addition, in combination with better child support enforcement, economic growth helps custodial parents, mostly women, by raising the earnings of absent parents.

In the foreseeable future, however, employment by itself may not raise a family, whether single-parent or two-parent, out of poverty. Many families will still need income support. Therefore, these economic policies must be supplemented with a program of welfare reform and related measures to address the problems of the current income transfer system: inadequate levels of support, cross-state inequities, work disincentives, and lack of provisions for poor two-parent families. At the very minimum, a national AFDC benefit standard, adjusted each year for inflation, is certainly needed. Income support for single-parent families might take the form of the Child Support Assurance Program, developed by Irwin Garfinkel and currently underway on a demonstration basis in Wisconsin. Under this program, a minimum benefit per child is guaranteed to single-parent families regardless of the income of the custodial parent. The absent parent's earnings are taxed at a fixed rate, and if the resulting payment is less than the minimum benefit, the state contributes the rest out of general revenues. This program provides a more adequate level of income support — less stigmatized, with no work disincentives, but with little or no additional cost to the state.

Some Western European countries provide support through family or child allowances. Moynihan has recently noted that tax expenditures through the Earned Income Tax Credit and standard deductions are a form of child allowance already available to American families — one that has been severely eroded by inflation, but one in place nevertheless. It may be easier to make incremental changes in this arrangement than to institute an entirely new program. Even more important than Moynihan's specific policy recommendations, however, may be this reminder that "no government, however firm might be its wish otherwise, can avoid having policies that profoundly influence family relationships. This is not to be avoided. The only option is whether these will be purposeful, intended policies or whether they will be residual, derivative, in a sense concealed ones."

These policies are likely to enjoy more widespread political support than the set of means-tested programs presently targeted at the poor. "Universal programs," those available to working- and middle-class segments of society as well as the poor, are more likely to attract political support, and therefore more generous and stable funding, because all classes have a stake in them. Means-tested programs, on the other hand, are associated with a low-income and minority constituency, and thus they are not programs that most voters identify with. Economic growth and tight labor market policies, child allowances, and child support enforcement are programs that all segments of society might participate in or benefit from, even though the most disadvantaged groups (such as the ghetto underclass) would reap disproportionate benefits.

An emphasis on universal programs to attack problems in the black community that historically have been related to racial subjugation represents a fundamental shift from the traditional approach of addressing problems associated with race. It is true, as we have tried to show in this paper, that the growth in the proportions of families headed by women, and the related problems of poverty, long-term welfare dependency, and teenage out-of-wedlock childbearing, are for historical reasons concentrated in the black community. And, as we have also noted, failure to address racial differences in family structure will distort the debate over changes in family structure and lead to neglect of the plight of the black urban underclass. However, to stress the prevalence of these problems among blacks does not mean that race-specific policies are the only or the most effective way to address them. Indeed, race-specific policies such as affirmative action traditionally have aided the most advantaged members of the minority population, have difficulty attracting widespread popular support, and have failed to address the fundamental source of recent black family disintegration — the economic shifts have fallen most heavily on the truly disadvantaged segment of the black community. America's future challenge in social policy, therefore, is to improve the life chances of groups such as the ghetto underclass by emphasizing programs to which the more advantaged groups of all races can positively relate.

ACCESS TO LAWYERS, ACCESS TO COURT, ACCESS TO LAW

Where family law involves administrative or judicial action, a specialized knowledge seems necessary to maneuver through the process. Divorce, child protection actions, and adoption each involve technical legal doctrines and local legal cultures that are the ambit of lawyers' expertise. How do lawyers relate to clients in family law settings? How expensive are lawyers and what kinds of clients may be priced out of their markets? Are there alternatives to lawyers for individuals who cannot afford them? The legal profession has guarded its position (and protected clients from mistreatment) through rules forbidding the unauthorized practice of law. Do those rules prevent the provision of legal services to people who cannot afford lawyers — and maybe do not need lawyers? Some access to court or other legal settings can be facilitated through self-help books, paralegals, and efforts by people with similar problems to help one another. Should these routes be promoted or discouraged? Should the legal rules themselves be changed to make access to lawyers less critical to those who seek divorces or other changes in their family status?

♦

NORTHSIDE SECRETARIAL SERVICE: CHARGE OF UNAUTHORIZED PRACTICE
Leila Kern and Frank Sander

The reason for prohibiting the practice of law by those who have not been examined and found qualified to practice is frequently misunderstood. It is not done to aid or protect the members of the legal profession either in creating or maintaining a monopoly or closed shop. It is done

From Harvard Law School Program on the Legal Profession, Northside Secretarial Service: Charge of Unauthorized Practice, 1982, prepared by Leila Kern under the supervision of Frank Sander.

to protect the public from being advised and represented in legal matters by unqualified persons over whom the judicial department can exercise little, if any, control in the matter of infractions of the code of conduct which, in the public interest, lawyers are bound to observe.

State v. *Sperry,* 140 So.2d 587, 595 (Fla. 1962)

According to the ABA's Code of Professional Responsibility, "The prohibition against the practice of law by a layman is grounded in the need of the public for integrity and competence of those who undertake to render legal services." But by 1982, several widely publicized disputes between unlicensed providers of "legal" services and the organized bar had raised many questions as to exactly how much harm resulted from assistance which, according to certain state bar associations, fell under the heading of unauthorized practice. Among the most controversial of these disputes was the lawsuit brought against Rosemary Furman by the Florida Bar Association.

Rosemary Furman, a trained legal secretary with over thirty years of experience at the time, opened the Northside Secretarial Service in Jacksonville, Florida, in 1975. She was the sole proprietor and owner of the service. According to Furman, about twenty to twenty-five percent of the work of the service involved assistance to "self-filers" in obtaining divorces. In Florida, as in all states, a marriage could be dissolved only by the state, and in Florida dissolutions were accomplished through the courts. Florida was a "no-fault" divorce state, so that if a marriage were "irretrievably broken," the court was compelled by law to grant the divorce provided that the petitioner met the six-month residency requirement. Florida law

also specifically provided that individuals, including those seeking divorce, were entitled to represent themselves in civil actions (pro se). Despite the apparent simplicity of the procedure, most people were unable to obtain a divorce in Florida without assistance. Court procedures were generally unfamiliar to lay persons, and many found the process frightening. For many Florida residents, the normal response — hire a lawyer to help — was foreclosed by the cost. Lawyers were charging an average of $350 for an uncontested divorce involving no property or custody issues. Even those eligible for free legal services were often unable to obtain assistance.

> The current funding levels, legal aid programs come nowhere close to meeting demands for divorce or other services by eligible clients. Estimates of legal problems per year among the poor range from 6-132 million.... Even before Reagan cutbacks, Legal Services Corporation Program could handle at most two million matters per year, about 3 percent of which involved divorce and family-related services.

The inability of low-income individuals to proceed pro se, without some kind of assistance, has been frequently commented upon. According to Furman's attorney, "it was to fill this vacuum that Furman... began to assist self-filers...."

After clearly stating to customers filing for divorce that she was not a lawyer, Furman proceeded to question them, and with the information that they gave her, type the necessary documents. In addition, she had given her customers a detailed practical explanation of how to proceed, including where to file their cases, what to do with each copy of the papers, how to pay the court fees, how to set up an appointment for the final hearing, whom to bring to the hearing and even how to address the court. As Furman explained:

> Most of them have never been to the courthouse in their lives. You have to tell them to go to the courthouse. "It's next to the City Hall, one is the tall building and one is the short. You go to the main floor in the courthouse and find Room 103. Take this folder. You have two folders, one folder with your own papers in them and one folder for the court, which has to be kept separate. These are the signed, sealed, notarized originals and these are what you give the court. The other folder is marked Personal Folder. Disregard that for these purposes. You are going down to file. When you go down to file to the courthouse, go through the main entrance and find Room 103 marked Clerk of the Court, S. Morgan Slaughter, with double doors. You enter there and walk straight forward and see a sign that is marked Law Department. You find the counter and put your folder down. The young lady will ask you, 'May I help you?' You say 'Yes, ma'am, I would like to file this action.' The young lady will say, 'That will be $32 cash filing fee, cash, no checks.' You be prepared to pay cash, and she will give you a filing receipt."

In like manner, Furman had given her customers very explicit instructions about all they had to do in the courthouse, and she had even included a diagram of the building. She would instruct her customers to return to her office before going to court for the final hearing so that she could brief them on how to conduct it; "that way, they didn't waste the court's

time." Furman also gave each female customer seeking divorce (ninety percent of her customers were female) a copy of a pamphlet titled "The Legal Status of Homemakers in Florida," by James F. O'Flaherty, Chairman of the Family Law Section of the Florida bar. She additionally gave all customers a copy of Florida Statute Chapter 61 (dealing with divorce) and Florida Statute 454 (dealing with attorneys-at-law and indicating that people had a right to represent themselves in court). She had all of her customers sign an acknowledgment of the fact that she was not an attorney.

Furman described most of her clients as functionally illiterate, and even those who were able to read and write often had difficulty understanding the legal forms, papers and procedures. She observed: "They don't understand the system. They don't understand why they have to go before a judge if they are both in agreement on getting a divorce."

For all of her services Furman charged no more than $50, regardless of the work involved, and she often accepted $25 or even nothing if the client could not afford to pay more. At the time she began helping self-filers, members of the bar were charging $350 for an uncontested divorce, involving no property or custody issues. The Florida bar contended

> [t]he full effect of attorney advertising has yet to be felt in Florida and attorneys' fees for dissolutions may decline to a level lower than that charged by [Furman]. In addition, if customers can "afford" to pay Furman's fee, are they unable to "afford" to pay a licensed attorney $60 or even $100?

However, other commentators disagreed. One *National Law Journal* report noted: "In...states, such as California and Florida, lay competition from pro se secretarial services may be one of the factors accounting for dramatically lower prices." Furman contended that as a result of her assistance several hundred of her customers between 1975 and 1977 were able to handle their own divorce cases and successfully dissolve their own marriages. Without her assistance, she argued, most of them would have been unable to proceed at all.

In March 1977, Furman, doing business as the Northside Secretarial Service, was served with a petition, filed by the Florida bar, and a rule to show cause, issued by the Supreme Court of Florida, why she should not be enjoined from engaging in the practice of law. Her pro se answer denied that she was practicing law, raised a constitutional defense, and sought dismissal of the petition. On August 1, 1977, in accordance with its standard practice in cases of this type, the Florida Supreme Court appointed a retired trial judge as a referee to take testimony and report his factual findings. The bar then filed an amended petition on September 23, 1977. Furman by then had obtained counsel: Alan Morrison, a well-known litigator of consumer issues, former assistant to Ralph Nader, and practicing attorney with the Public Citizen Litigation Group in Washington, D.C. Morrison filed an answer contending, among other grounds, that to prohibit Furman from assisting indigents would violate their constitutional right to obtain a divorce by requiring them to pay for the services of an attorney that they could not afford.

While discovery was proceeding, the Supreme Court of Florida issued an opinion in *The Florida Bar* v. *Brumbaugh*, 355 So.2d 1186 (1978), which altered some of the rules governing what lay persons could do in assisting individuals seeking to obtain a divorce. The court in *Brumbaugh* at 1194 stated:

> We hold that Ms. Brumbaugh, and others in similar situations, may sell printed material purporting to explain legal practice and procedure to the public in general and she may sell sample legal forms.... Further, we hold that it is not improper for Marilyn Brumbaugh to engage in a secretarial service, typing such forms for her clients, provided that she only copy the information given to her in writing by her clients.... However, Marilyn Brumbaugh must not, in conjunction with her business, engage in advising clients as to the various remedies available to them, or otherwise assist them in preparing those forms necessary for a dissolution proceeding. More specifically, Marilyn Brumbaugh may not make inquiries nor answer questions from her clients as to the particular forms which might be necessary, how best to fill out such forms, where to properly file such forms, and how to present necessary evidence at the court hearings.

According to Morrison, Furman initially attempted to conform her practices to *Brumbaugh* by developing detailed forms and instructions to try to handle as much as possible in writing. She eventually concluded that she could not provide adequate services in this way, since both she and the bar viewed the *Brumbaugh* opinion as precluding her from even correcting mistakes, clarifying ambiguities, eliminating contradictions or providing any assistance whatsoever when the client was unable to read and write.

On July 18, 1978, the referee for the Florida bar's suit against Furman heard testimony in the case after the parties had stipulated to many of the facts, "including that no client of [Furman's] had ever suffered any harm from her services." After the hearing and without benefit of briefs, the referee issued a lengthy report, most of which consisted of quotations from the record. According to Morrison, the referee's findings reflected a "plain distaste for lay assistance, as demonstrated by his assertion that [Furman's] practices were creating 'a grave danger to the citizens of Florida' even though he adopted the parties' stipulation that none of [Furman's] customers had suffered any harm as a result of her services." The referee did recognize that there were many individuals who could not afford needed legal services, and he urged the court and the bar to correct the matter immediately. He also urged that Furman be "prohibited from typing legal papers of any kind, [or] filling blanks on any legal forms," precluding what the Florida Supreme Court had specifically authorized only seven months before in *Brumbaugh*. Moreover, he recommended that Furman be held in contempt of court even though the bar had not sought such relief in its petition.

The case then went to the Supreme Court of Florida for a decision on the merits. Briefs were filed, and oral argument held on February 9, 1979. Once again, Furman defended against the bar's charges by seeking modifications and/or clarifications of *Brumbaugh*, and by asserting that the state's unauthorized practice rules could not constitutionally be applied to preclude her from assisting indigents seeking divorce.

On May 10, 1979, the court issued its opinion, in which it concluded that Furman had been engaged in the unauthorized practice of law. In response to her request for clarification or modification of *Brumbaugh*, the court repeated what it had said in *Brumbaugh* and added, "Our directions could not have been clearer." The court did not address Furman's constitutional arguments at all, but found Furman in contempt of court and directed the parties to submit further briefs addressing punishment to be meted out. Because the petition and rule to show cause had sought only an injunction, Furman filed a motion for rehearing in which she objected on due process and fairness grounds to the contempt finding and to any punishment against her, since the cases had been tried under a civil injunction. Her submission also included a further request for clarification of the scope of *Brumbaugh*, pointing out that the Florida bar itself had made a similar request in its petition for rehearing in *Brumbaugh*. Furman also sought rehearing on her constitutional claim. Almost six months after the original opinion, the court issued a brief order granting a limited rehearing, but making no changes in its opinion other than removing the references to contempt and eliminating any punishment.

On November 16, 1979, Morrison filed a notice of appeal to the United States Supreme Court on Furman's behalf. Written briefs were filed by Furman and the Florida bar. On February 19, 1980, in a memorandum decision, the appeal was dismissed for want of a substantial federal question, *Furman* v. *The Florida Bar*, 444 US 1061 (1980). Based in part on this experience, Morrison wrote that "... the bottom line is that states are by and large free to decide what constitutes the [authorized] practice of law at least as far as federal law is concerned." And the body in most states that made those decisions, in the first instance, was the bar.

Discussing the problem after his appeal to the Supreme Court had been turned down, Morrison suggested that the bar should not take on the task of defining the boundaries of legal practice because of its own conflict of interest and economic self-interest in the issue. Although the bar contended that in developing policy governing this question it was most concerned with injury to the public, in a study conducted by Deborah Rhode in 1981, only two percent of bar committees' inquiries, investigations and complaints about unauthorized practice in the entire United States arose from an injured consumer's complaints. Rhode commented:

> In a culture where law plays so dominant a role in dispute resolution, broad constraints on the ability of laymen to give and receive assistance raise substantial... concerns. When the individuals construing and enforcing those restraints have a direct financial stake in their application, questions of due process arise.

For Rhode, as for Morrison and others, it is clear that the real issue in the unauthorized debate is not consumer protection but rather the bar's self-protection. "[A]nalysis of the lawyer's role in uncontested divorces offers no convincing basis for granting them a monopoly over document preparation and advice. Completion of the necessary forms requires no esoteric legal skills, a point frequently noted by courts and commentators."

EPILOGUE

The referee in the Furman case stated:

> The only way to protect the public from the hazards of unauthorized practice of law is for the Florida bar to provide legal service to everyone who is in need. The supreme court could exercise its administrative and rule making power to stop this dangerous and insidious movement which, under the guise of a small fee,

is leading many innocent people's future into mudholes and quicksand.

In response, the Florida Supreme Court directed the Florida bar to "begin immediately a study to determine better ways and means of providing legal services to the indigent."

The bar commissioned a comprehensive study of the Center for Governmental Responsibility at the University of Florida. The report made an assessment of the legal needs of the poor and near-poor in Florida, and then examined a number of ways of meeting that need, through simplification, paralegals, legal clinics, and a host of other devices.

In 1981, the bar urged the court to implement a program whereby attorneys could contribute the interest on clients' trust accounts to the Florida Bar Foundation, a large part of whose resources go to support legal services for the indigent. Such a program was subsequently adopted by the court.

More recently, the bar urged the court to establish by rule a summary procedure (requiring no attorney and no court appearance) for certain types of simple divorces (e.g., cases involving no children, no substantial property, and where the parties had been married less than five years.) Some sections of the Florida Bar Association (e.g., the Family Law Section) opposed this suggestion on the ground that the service of attorneys is essential in all cases in order properly to protect the clients. At the same time the bar reiterated its earlier request that Rosemary Furman be held in criminal contempt. This latter action led Alan Morrison to file a 1983 class action in federal court on behalf of all indigents who are illiterate and hence unable to handle their own divorces by filling in the necessary forms.

A group of fifty-seven private attorneys made a separate proposal to the Florida Supreme Court. They argued that the court should adopt a rule requiring a mandatory *pro bono* obligation for all licensed Florida attorneys. This obligation could be fulfilled in either of two ways: (1) by doing twenty-five hours of *pro bono* work each year; or (2) by contributing $500 to the Florida Bar Foundation. Alternatively the group asked the court to adopt a rule *requiring* all attorneys to turn over the interest in their clients' trust accounts to the Florida Bar Foundation.

As of March 1983, these petitions are still pending before the Florida Supreme Court.

[Chronology:]
Rosemary Furman and
the Florida Bar

1975 Rosemary Furman founded the Northside Secretarial Service in Jacksonville, Florida. With thirty years experience as a legal secretary, Furman operated Northside alone. For a minimal fee averaging $50, Furman typed legal forms for indigents who could not afford an attorney. Though most procedures related to divorce, Furman assisted in matters of child custody and name-change. Furman worked with "self-filers," men and women using simple pro se processes. Simple in principle, these matters overwhelmed Furman's often illiterate and usually poor customers. During the time of Northside's operation, the average attorney in the Jacksonville area charged $350 for an uncontested divorce.

1977 The Florida Bar Association (bar) filed petitions with the Supreme Court of Florida (the court) alleging that in 1976 and 1977 Furman had engaged in the unauthorized practice of law by giving legal advice and by rendering legal services in connection with adoptions and marriage dissolutions. Specifically, the bar alleged that Furman prepared legal pleadings for customers solicited by publicly advertising her expertise in family law. These actions allegedly violated Florida law.

In March, the court summoned Furman to show cause why she should not be enjoined from the unauthorized practice of law. Furman answered *pro se* that (1) she was not practicing law; (2) the Constitution protected her activities; and (3) the court should dismiss the petitions.

On August 1, the court appointed a retired judge as referee to receive evidence, to make findings of fact and conclusions of law, and to dispose of the case.

In the fall, the bar filed an amended petition and Furman contacted Alan Morrison, an attorney with the Public Citizen Litigation Group in Washington, D.C. Through Morrison, Furman answered that an injunction would violate the constitutional right of indigents to obtain a divorce because they could not pay the average attorney's fee.

1978 The court issued *The Florida Bar v. Brumbaugh*, 355 So.2d 1186 (1978). *Brumbaugh* set the standard for the "unauthorized practice of law." This standard allowed Furman to type forms from information provided by customers and to sell pamphlets with general explanations of court proceedings. On the other hand, *Brumbaugh* prohibited Furman from advising her customers in any way. Specifically forbidden, Furman could not discuss ways to fill out the forms or how to present evidence in the court hearings.

On July 18, the referee issued his report. The referee recommended two restrictions beyond *Brumbaugh*. He urged the court to forbid even the typing of legal forms. Although the bar had not sought this relief, the referee further urged the court to hold Furman in indirect criminal contempt.

1979   On February 9, the court heard the case. In its opinion issued May 10, the court held Furman in indirect criminal contempt. It did not address the constitutional issues which Furman had raised. Furman moved for a rehearing on grounds of due process and fairness. She argued that criminal contempt inappropriately punished her for what originated as a civil injunction. She further argued that she had a right to trial by jury.

Approximately six months later, the court granted a limited rehearing, removing the references to contempt.

On November 1, the court issued a permanent injunction prohibiting Furman from the unauthorized practice of law.

On November 16, Furman appealed to the U.S. Supreme Court.

1980   On February 19, the Supreme Court dismissed Furman's appeal because it lacked a substantial federal question. *Furman* v. *The Florida Bar*, 444 U.S., 1060 (1980).

1982/1983   On September 28, 1982 and March 9, 1983, the bar filed petitions alleging six and ten instances, respectively, when Furman continued the unauthorized practice of law in contempt of the court's order. On November 30, 1982 and March 21, 1983, the court issued rules to show cause and appointed a referee to receive evidence and make findings of fact, conclusions of law and recommendations. The referee conducted the pretrial hearing, consolidated the rules and set the evidentiary hearing for June 20 and 21, 1983.

1983   On June 20, the court denied Furman's motions for a stay of the proceedings and for a trial by jury. Furman did not testify at the evidentiary hearing because, as Furman and Morrison explain,

her testimony belonged only in a jury trial. Therefore uncontradicted, the testimony of Furman's former customers established on the record that Furman urged them to falsify and conceal information in marriage dissolution petitions.

With the evidentiary hearing completed, the referee scheduled briefing. The case was orally argued on August 18.

On September 28, the referee set another hearing date and requested that both parties submit proposed orders. The hearing took place on October 10. At the hearing, the referee distributed draft copies of his prospective order and asked for arguments in aggravation or mitigation. The draft recommended that Furman be held in indirect criminal contempt and be sentenced to an unspecified prison term. After arguments, the referee entered the draft which, in its final form, recommended concurrent four-month sentences in a state prison.

Furman raised five objections to the referee's reports:

(1) She was entitled to a jury trial under both the Sixth Amendment and the due process clause of the Fourteenth Amendment.

(2) The referee upheld an erroneous legal standard in determining whether she violated the court's injunction; that is: the *Brumbaugh* standard is unclear about which activities are enjoined and the referee adopted an unreasonably expansive reading.

(3) The referee improperly rejected the defense of laches regarding alleged instances of the unauthorized practice of law.

(4) The referee erred in failing to discuss the second rule to show cause of procedural irregularities; that is: there were irregularities in follow-

ing the procedures which govern the investigation of the unauthorized practice of law. The Florida Bar Integration Rule, Article XVI.

(5) As established by his draft, the referee had actually decided the sentence before Furman could present evidence in mitigation.

1984   On April 26, the court held Furman in contempt of court but rejected the referee's recommendation that Furman be imprisoned for two concurrent four-month terms. Rather, the court sentenced Furman to the Duval County jail for a single term of 120 days. The court suspended 90 days of this term so long as Furman did not violate the court's injunction. The court conditioned this upon two years compliance with the injunction. *See Florida Bar* v. *Furman*, 451 So.2d 808 (Fla. 1984).

The U.S. Supreme Court refused to hear an appeal saying no substantial federal question was involved. *Furman* v. *The Florida Bar*, No. 84-196.

On November 14, the day before Furman was to be jailed, Florida Governor Bob Graham granted Furman a thirty-day reprieve.

On November 27, Governor Graham met with his clemency board. On the same day, he commuted Furman's thirty-day jail sentence on the condition that she comply with the court's injunction for two years.

1985   Furman closed her business and has refrained from the activities prohibited by the court. She has announced that she will travel throughout the nation to force a definition on the practice of law and to share her message that lawyers are "like hungry sharks in bloody waters."

◆

LAWYERS AND LEGAL CONSCIOUSNESS: LAW TALK IN THE DIVORCE LAWYER'S OFFICE
Austin Sarat and William L.F. Felstiner

THE SIGNIFICANCE OF RULES

How do lawyers describe the law, particular laws, or legal processes to their clients? What characteristics are attributed to law and the legal system? Before addressing these question it is important to note that there is a rather regular progression in law talk — a constant narrative structure. Almost all divorce cases start with the lawyer's brief explanation of divorce procedures as they are laid out

in statutes. This law talk is full of explicit references to rules. Lawyers begin, if you will, with formalism. They describe the *rules* that frame the process, establish its limits and provide alternative routes. However, the written law is only a starting point. Formalism fades rather quickly as the interaction progresses. Descriptions and characterizations of the legal system now occur mainly when clients ask why a particular result occurred or what results might be predicted. In re-

Austin Sarat and William L.F. Felstner, "Lawyers and Legal Consciousness: Law Talk in the Divorce Lawyer's Office," *Yale L.J.* vol. 98, 1989, pp. 1663, 1671, 1674, 1682–1684 (edited).

sponse to these unsolicited inquiries, lawyers rarely make explicit reference to rules. Rules and their relevance are taken for granted by lawyers who generally act as if clients already shared their empirical understanding of the legal process. As a consequence, at this point in the interaction, lawyers do not take the time to introduce their clients to the subtle manner in which rules penetrate and permeate the legal process.

Lawyers often talk about what can or cannot be done or what is or is not likely to happen without explicitly noting that their views are shaped by statutes or court decisions, although the trained ear would recognize that their formulations are clearly rooted in an understanding of rules. Typical of such implicit rule references is the response of a lawyer to a client's inquiry about what would happen to child support if his income were reduced:

> You should keep in the back of your mind... that if your financial situation changes in the future the judgment can be modified. That's not a problem. It is not etched in stone.... Anything to do with a child is always modifiable by the court.

How and why judgments in court "can be modified" is not explained. The client is not told whether that possibility is a result of the ease with which lawyers escape from earlier agreements, or of the sympathy that judges display toward children, or of the rules governing support, custody, and visitation. This failure to identify rules and highlight their relevance prevents clients from having access to law's public discourse and the resources for argument provided by an understanding of rules. In addition, it helps

lawyers maintain a monopoly of those resources and focuses client concerns on the professional skills and capacities of their particular lawyer.

Lawyers, in fact, talk to clients in much the same way that they talk to each other. There is no acknowledgment that clients may not already understand the salience of rules. The normal conventions of lawyer-to-lawyer discourse are not translated for divorce clients, who most often bring an incomplete and unsophisticated understanding to their encounters with the legal process. There is no concerted effort to bridge the gap between professional and popular culture.

Even when rules are explicitly noted, there are few references to or discussions of their determinate power. Lawyers do not describe the legal process of divorce as rule driven or rule governed. Nor do they usually provide an explicit evaluation of the rules themselves. However, when rules do at times emerge as part of the explicit conversational foreground, they are generally disparaged; contrary to the assumption of both the organized bar and critical scholars, lawyers rarely defend the rationality, importance, or efficacy of legal rules.

For instance, it is common for lawyers to mock rules as irrelevant or useless in governing the behavior of legal officials involved in the divorce process. Rules, according to one California lawyer, do not give "clear-cut answers. If they did we wouldn't even have to be talking." A Massachusetts lawyer spoke more generally about the irrelevance of rules in describing the way the local court system operated: "There really are no rules here, just people, the judge, the lawyers, the litigants." Another maintained that the scheduling of cases reflected the virtually unchecked power of the bailiff:

When you get heard is up to the court officer... he's the one who controls the docket. They don't have a list prepared and they don't start at the top and work down. They go according to his idea of when people should be heard.

Other lawyers extended the argument about the ambiguity or irrelevance of rules to more important aspects of the legal process of divorce. Several suggested that judges refuse to be guided by rules of evidence and that such rules therefore have no bearing on the way hearings are conducted. One Massachusetts lawyer explained that he would not be able to prevent the opposing spouse from talking about his client's alleged adultery even though such testimony would be technically inadmissible according to the literal rules:

I think we just have to realize that it is going to come out. We just have to take that as a given. You know, they teach you in law school about how to object to that kind of testimony: "I object, irrelevant," "I object, hearsay." But when you start to practice you realize that judges, especially in divorce cases, don't pay any attention. They act as if there were no rules of evidence.

Other lawyers expressed frustration about the ineffectiveness of rules governing filing periods, establishing times in which responsive pleadings are to be submitted or governing the conduct of discovery.

Moreover, statutes concerning property division are, as lawyers tell it, often irrelevant to actual outcomes. Lawyers in both Massachusetts and California regularly criticized judges for failing to pay attention to those statutes or to the case law interpreting them. As one Massachusetts lawyer told her client in a case involving substantial marital property,

[i]n this state the statute requires judges to consider fifteen separate things, things like how long you were married, what contributions you and Tom made, whether you have good prospects. It is a pretty comprehensive list, but I've never seen a judge make findings on all of those things. They just hear and then divide things up. Things generally come out roughly even, but not because the rules require it.

Thus, what lawyers do make visible as they respond to their clients' questions are the personalities and dispositions of actors within the legal process and the salience of local norms rather than legal rules. Emphasizing people over rules, law talk acquaints clients with a process in which judges exercise immense discretionary power. The message to the client is that it is the judge, not the rules, that really counts. What the judge will accept, what the judge will do is the crucial issue in the divorce process. With respect to property settlements, Massachusetts clients are reminded that since all agreements require judicial approval there is, in effect, "nothing binding about them. The judge will do what he wants with it." Another lawyer explained that in dividing the marital property, "the judge can do with it as he chooses to do." Still another lawyer informed his client of what he called the "immense amount of power and authority" which judges exercise and suggested that the particular judge who would be hearing his case would use that power "pretty much as he deems fit."

JUSTICE AND THE LEGAL ORDER

What do lawyers say to clients about the efficiency, fairness, and social utility of law in general, and about the legal process of divorce in particular? Again one begins by noting the relative absence of positive characterizations. Lawyers, at least in the divorce context, do not defend the legal order in which they participate as either the critics would predict or the organized bar would prescribe. Instead, law talk suggests distance between lawyer and legal order, with the former portrayed as struggling valiantly within the confines of a process that seems neither equitable nor just. In numerous instances, moreover, lawyers suggest that their clients are being "victimized" rather than being well-served by the legal process. Here, the goal of law talk is to initiate the client into a jaded professional world, disabused of the illusion of formalism.

Money, clients are advised, is the chief determinant of legal results. Legal rights are "absolute" to the extent that clients "want to invest the time, effort, energy and money" necessary to assert or defend them, but, at the same time, clients are often advised that they cannot afford to do so. As a result, lawyers suggest that clients should settle for less than the client initially perceives as fair. As one Massachusetts lawyer explained to a client in a hotly contested divorce in which the wife's wealthy family was paying her lawyer.

> I'm not just making this up. I'm telling you very frankly it appears as though he's (the wife's lawyer) doing a $10,000 case. That's just the way it is. Your — no matter who you go to — you can't afford a $10,000 case. Can't do it. And that's part of the injustice of the American legal system but I'm not going to do

as much work as he is at the moment. I can't... I'm just not equipped to do it. If you were to give me $10,000 I would drop everything, drop everything, and work 40 hours a week, but I can't based on what you can afford.

This lawyer attributes the "injustice" of the "American legal system" to the law's inability to compensate for economic differences. At the same time, he shifts responsibility for any possible failure from his own performance to the client's limited means while he both suggests the wisdom of putting more money into the case and disclaims an interest in having the client do so.

A costly, slow, and painful process might be justified if it were fair, reliably protected important individual rights, or responded to important human concerns. Law talk is, however, full of both lawyer and client doubts about whether the legal process even aims at meeting those goals:

> *Client:* Sure. I mean, that's as much as can be expected, I believe. Am I right in that?
> *Lawyer:* I think so, too. I think that that effects a good settlement. Well, it effects an equal division. I don't know — is a legal settlement, a fair settlement? It gets the legal aspects of the case over.

Here the lawyer notes that a "legal settlement" entails an "equal division" while questioning whether such a result, or a settlement that deals only with the "legal aspects of the case," is "fair."

This exchange represents another example of the discourse in which lawyers teach clients about the distance between law and society, not just because of the limited efficacy of legal rules, but because of the law's tightly limited concerns. This indoctrination is especially important because there is frequently a clash between the client's ultimate objectives and the lawyer's description of what the law can actually do; typically, the client's agenda is broader than the law's alleged competence. Lawyers readily point out the limited nature of legal justice:

> *Client:* Well, I mean, I'm a liberal. Right? A liberal dream is that you will find social justice, and so here was this statement that it was possible to fight injustice, and you were going to protect me from horrible things like judicial abuse. So that's uh, it was really nice.... But as you

say, if you want justice in this society, you look somewhere other than the court. I believe that's what you were saying to Bob.
> *Lawyer:* Yeah, that's what I said. Ultimate justice, that is.

Juxtaposing legal and "ultimate" justice, this California lawyer implies that any person seeking such a final accounting is clearly not going to be fully satisfied by a system with more narrow concerns. Law talk encourages clients to come to terms with this reality by lowering their expectations and by implicitly directing them to look elsewhere for consolation.

◆

PRO SE DIVORCE: A STRATEGY FOR EMPOWERING WOMEN
Emily Joselson and Judy Kaye

I.

As third-year law students commencing the day-to-day work of low-income client advocacy at the Legal Service Institute, we subscribe to the basic tenets of progressive or "political" lawyering: That the law can and should be used instrumentally to effect social and political change; that an integral part of this process is the demystification of the legal system; and that one end result must be the empowerment of disenfranchised groups and individuals. However, as we struggled to connect these political theories with our daily legal practice, we discovered that such often-used terms as "demystification" and "empowerment" elude our attempts to define them.

As such, we were hard-pressed to recognize their achievement, either in the context of our interactions with clients or in any other aspect of our work. In an effort to understand these concepts and the assumptions upon which they were based, we turned our attention to the Institute's *Pro Se* Divorce Clinic, a "self-help" project designed to enable legal services-eligible women to do their own uncontested divorces.

Only after listening to and analyzing hours of taped discussions did we set about to formulate working definitions of empowerment and, within that, of legal demystification. To a large extent our definitions, although born of our original assumptions

Emily Joselson and Judy Kaye, "Pro Se Divorce: A Strategy for Empowering Women," *Journal of Law and Inequality*, vol. 9, 1983, pp. 239–247, 269–270 (edited).

and orientations, are firmly rooted in the women's experiences, for we attempted to incorporate within the definitions the most positive ways in which the women had been changed by the *pro se* process. On the other hand, our definitions also look to what we see as the unrealized potential for a more profoundly feminist experience, were the clinic to undergo a significant shift in emphasis. Finally, we note that our definition of empowerment is presented as a series of stages, or "levels," in order to connote a gradual, incremental process, rather than a static state of being.

What follows, then, are the four "levels" in our working definition of empowerment. They are offered not only as goals toward which clinic participants might strive, but also as guideposts for those seeking to structure the clinic experience of others.

Level One: Control and Confidence
Acquiring sufficient skills and information concerning the substantive and procedural aspects of divorce law so that the woman feels in control of the process and satisfied with her performance. Such mastery breeds confidence in herself as a person.

Level Two: Legal Demystification
Through reflection and discussion about her *pro se* experience, the woman is able to view the legal system critically; that is, to develop insights into the ways the system facilitates or discourages access, influences social outcomes, and otherwise maintains itself as the powerful social institution that it is.

Level Three: Connecting With Other Women Opening up and sharing her experiences as a woman with the other clinic participants and, as a result, discovering the degree to which their life experiences are similar to hers. This leads to recognizing and valuing other women as a source of support and strength.

Level Four: Feminist Consciousness-Raising Progressing beyond the realization that individual women share important life experiences, to an understanding that such experiences reflect the myriad and subtle ways in which society fosters the subordination of women as a class. This, in turn, can lead to developing strategies for change.

The first two levels of empowerment set out the definitional objectives most commonly shared by those involved in developing *pro se* divorce programs, as we will discuss below. We will argue, however, that these objectives, when not explicitly acknowledged, too often elude achievement. Moreover, in our view, *pro se* clinics which seek to achieve no more than these first two levels fall short of their full political potential. Thus, in the second two levels of empowerment we stretch the meaning of that term in explicitly feminist directions, based on our belief that the feminist consciousness-raising model can and should be incorporated into the *pro se* divorce clinic structure.

The clinic at the Institute was specifically designed to enable women to master the divorce process, to foster their growth of confidence, and to encourage their exposure to the legal system.

II.

Those women who derived the most satisfaction from their clinic experience attributed it to the following aspects of the clinical experience: they *themselves* were in control of the legal process which eventually led to their divorce decree; the process was neither as complicated nor as mysterious as they had imagined; and, as a result of having mastered this relatively straightforward legal task, they felt better about themselves and more competent in other areas of their lives as well. From these reflections we formulated the first two levels in our definition of empowerment. Thus, a woman was empowered in the "level one" sense if she felt she had actually controlled the divorce process herself, understanding each procedural step well enough to feel relatively autonomous as she executed it, rather than feeling overly dependent on the clinic staff for direction. As a result of the successful achievement of these legal tasks, she gained more confidence in herself as a social actor and, consequently, took more control over other aspects of her life.

If "level one" empowerment meant successfully following the rules of a system to which the woman had just gained limited access, "level two" meant questioning those rules, discovering and testing the assumptions upon which they are based, and challenging efforts to make the relatively simple and straightforward procedures involved in obtaining an uncontested divorce appear mysterious, complex and beyond the ability of non-lawyers. Admittedly, we hold very definite views about the law and legal institutions which form these definitions, and this should be fully acknowledged here. Simply stated, we believe that, in order to maintain its role, retain its authority and ensure its legitimacy within the social structure, the American legal system shrouds itself in mystery, symbolism, and complicated ritual, enhancing the need for legal expertise and justifying the role of abstract reasoning as the basis for legal decision-making. Laws, both statutory and judge-made, are not neutral entities which exist by supernatural fiat; rather, they are promulgated by people in positions of power, whose values and interests necessarily influence their ultimate content. Further, while such laws are frequently cumbersome and often outmoded, for the most part they are comprehensible and predictable.

In the same vein, we believe that lawyers have, over time, exerted ever more control over human interactions, and now perform some tasks which their clients could easily perform for themselves. Moreover, lawyers are generally overcompensated, often for fairly routine jobs, and as a result they are overly protective of their position and power. Finally, we maintain that court personnel are so used to dealing exclusively with lawyers that they overestimate the importance of a law degree and underestimate the extent to which lay people can often solve their own legal problems. Consequently, they are frequently rude and intimidating to *pro se* litigants, and thereby impede people's right to act legally on their own behalf.

Thus, by legal demystification we mean the process whereby clinic participants take advantage of their firsthand legal experience — however limited — and begin to question and scrutinize the subtle ways in which the system limits access and fosters expensive lawyer domination and control. Such an awareness is important for several reasons. First, given reduced funding for legal services, poor women will find it increasingly difficult to retain lawyers on a full-representation basis; thus, the more willing and able they are to handle relatively simple legal problems *pro se*, the more likely they will be to assert such rights. Second, if and when they are represented by counsel, they will be more equal participants in the relationship, and may be less likely to approach their lawyers with the inflated awe, unquestioning deference, or even active distrust, which clients too often bring to such relationships. Finally, in the unlikely event that they never have another legal problem, it is an important lesson to learn that even such a powerful and accepted social institution as the legal system should be subjected to scrutiny and challenge.

As the clinic at Legal Services Institute was structured at the time of our study, participants were empowered in the "level one" sense described in Section II — namely, they handled the divorce process themselves, and saw a net gain in confidence as a result. While most people who run *pro se* and other community legal education projects tend to assume that their work also encourages critique and demystification of the legal system in a larger sense, we discovered that this process is not automatic. During the interviews the women did have insights into the role of law and lawyers in society, but the clinic would have to be structured more deliberately to explore and develop such insights in order to encourage significant "level two" empowerment.

Such conscious planning is even more crucial if participants are to be empowered in a feminist sense, what we define in levels three and four. Significant consciousness-raising did not occur at the Legal Services Institute clinic, not because the clinic staff rejected CR as a valuable activity or ultimate goal, but because consciousness-raising does not occur simply by bringing women together to go through a common process. Without a commitment on the part of the staff and the participants to take time in the clinic to discuss, share, and examine the women's feelings and experiences, and without a structure to facilitate such work, feminist consciousness is unlikely to emerge by itself. Rather, any growth in confidence or consciousness will occur, if at all, on an *ad hoc* basis, depending more on the individual woman's personality and prior experience than on the clinic's format.

Based on our research and interviews, and despite the legitimate concerns we have raised, we believe that *pro se* divorce clinics can and should be structured more explicitly to allow talking, sharing, and consciousness-raising. Women would thereby be empowered not only in terms of personal confidence and competence in dealing with legal and other technical systems, but also in terms of developing bonds with other women, and gaining a feminist outlook and identity.

FIVE

Alternatives to Court, Alternatives to Law, Alternatives to Family Law

Lawyers, psychologists, socialworkers and other professionals often advocate the use of mediation, negotiation, and arbitration as alternatives to court for resolving divorce and custody disputes. Some also advocate these techniques for other family matters, including spouse abuse, child abuse, and parent-child conflicts. When should these alternatives be available? When should they be preferred? When should they be required before the individuals can gain access to a judicial hearing? These questions in turn prompt more basic inquiries, such as: (1) what is the relation between these procedural alternatives and likely outcomes; (2) what relative importance should be placed on party satisfaction and sense of control during the process compared with formal legal rights, and do these alternatives promote greater control or introduce new kinds of manipulation; (3) what professional competencies besides adversarial lawyering can help parties handle the emotional and psychological dimensions of their family disputes, and do those competencies complement or replace the skills of adversarial lawyering?

The search for alternatives should not respond merely to the drawbacks of courts. There are larger issues. For example, how can the stresses and conflicts in and about families be located within communities? What social conditions promote or undermine intimate human connection? Should family law, to address the real difficulties of family law, look outward to these larger issues? A deep issue arises from a central ambivalence in legal treatment of families. The law sometimes seems to protect the family from the state, and sometimes it aims to protect individuals from the family. It is as if the legal system, predicated on liberal assumptions, produces a game board with only two positions: the role for the individual and the role for the state. When an entity, such as the family, presents a legal issue, the courts, legislatures, and agencies have available only the two positions — one for the individual and one for the state. So sometimes, the family gets the position of the individual, poised against the state; sometimes the family gets the position of the state, poised against the individual. Are there alternative ways to think about the relationships among individuals, families, and governments?

This book began by asking how images of the family as either a haven or a hell, or both, might explain legal discourse about families. Can family law pursue utopian visions or would that mission simply disguise the ways that the law itself can injure families and the individuals within them? Or must the family, as constituted by legal practices, impose patterns of powerlessness on individuals, substitute abstractions for human relationships, and impose bureaucracies between people and the ones they love — or hate? Can family law, as a set of activities and debates, instead provide a framework for affirming human dignity and renewing possibilities for human connection? Or are some issues of family law intractable, at least until other dimensions of social practice change.

♦

THE NEW MEDIATORS
Marilyn Stasie

Steven Sykes is a Manhattan lawyer who had been earning $200,000 a year from his business-law practice when Janet, his wife of twenty-three years, decided to leave him. Because of new developments in his specialty, Steven's income suddenly dropped by half, a fact that Janet couldn't accept. For two years, she spent nearly $10,000 going from one matrimonial lawyer to another, fighting for a maintenance settlement that her husband insisted was unrealistic.

"I felt as if I was being torn apart limb from limb," said Steven, who had spent a fortune on his own lawyers. "Then one day, I saw an ad in *Newsday* for a divorce-mediation center on Long Island."

Divorce mediation is a new social service that has emerged in the past few years, partly in response to the public desire for more humane and non-adversarial methods of making divorce and separation agreements and partly in an attempt to free up the courts through alternative means of resolving disputes. Although New York State lags behind many others in the practice of divorce mediation, it is catching up fast.

"Everybody's becoming a divorce mediator," said Adele Lerman Janow, a Westchester speech-and-language teacher who has just completed a twelve-week course in divorce-mediation training at the Family Institute of Westchester. "Things will be much better when mediators have to be licensed."

"These people are not professionals," warned Irvin H. Rosenthal, whose New York law firm, Rosenthal & Shays, specializes in matrimonial law. "They have no license, no degree, no training, and no criteria. Anybody can call himself a divorce mediator."

Does mediation work? It did for Steven and Janet Sykes. They went to Lenard Marlow, a former matrimonial lawyer who now operates five offices of Divorce Mediation Professionals in the metropolitan area. "It was like dragging her to the dentist," Steven recalled, "but she was reassured because the mediator was so obviously competent. He cut through that reach-for-the-moon attitude we had gotten from our lawyers and came up with much more reasonable figures."

The crux of the settlement — reached after a series of consultations that cost $2,500 — involved an escalation clause

From Marilyn Stasie, "The New Mediators," *New York Magazine,* Oct. 8, 1984, p. 38.

that increased the amount of Janet's maintenance as Steven's income rose. Sounds simple.

"Sometimes the issues *are* simple," said Marlow. "But a couple often can't see that, because every time they sit down and try to talk rationally, their personal hurt, disappointment, anger, and fear get in the way. Mediation helps resolve these emotional problems so they can get to the issues."

John M. Haynes — whose *Divorce Mediation: A Practical Guide for Therapists and Counselors* is considered by many mediators to be the definitive handbook on the subject — suggests that mediation begin with a one-hour orientation meeting, followed by a series of two-hour sessions to help couples draw up budgets for their future needs; identify, evaluate, and divide their assets; and decide parenting issues. At his Family Mediation Services, an average mediation takes twelve to fifteen hours, at $100 per hour.

"Mediation is private and non-adversarial," said Haynes. "It helps restructure the two families that will emerge from the divorce."

Mediators agree that children usually cause the most emotional stress in divorce. Barbara and John Whelan, a Long Island couple, had no trouble dealing with the division of their modest assets. But they were deeply divided over the welfare of their fourteen-year-old daughter, whose drug and alcohol problems were exacerbated by her parents' custody battle.

"It was a real dogfight," said Barbara, who maintained that her husband refused to acknowledge their daughter's problems. But he suggested they consult a mediator, who helped them reach a decision to place the girl in a drug-rehabilitation program.

While divorce mediation spares many couples some of the time, money, and anguish of adversarial legal procedures, it is very controversial. As matrimonial lawyers are quick to note, mediation is *not* a legal service. Responsible mediators acknowledge that the new approach is still so unstructured that anyone, regardless of qualifications, can practice it. Fees are arbitrary. Mediators tend to be better trained in psychology than law. "The mediator is primarily interested in getting an agreement," said lawyer Rosenthal, "not necessarily one that is fair, just or in the best interests of the parties."

But, said Lorraine Marshall, an officer of the newly formed New York State Council on Divorce Mediation, "we're working hard to establish credentials, set minimum standards, and establish training programs."

When Helen and Colin Hardwick, a professional couple from New York, went into mediation, they had already agreed that because of the uncertain nature of Helen's work as a free-lance designer she would remain in the co-op that both would continue to own. The mediator, however, strongly suggested a three-to five-year limit on Helen's residency, advising Colin that "no attorney would file divorce papers" on a settlement that set no such parameters.

"The mediator was *forcing* me to sell the apartment and give up my only security," said Helen, claiming that with her small fluctuating income she could never buy Colin out at escalating real-estate prices.

Helen and Colin broke off negotiations with the mediator and went to their accountant. He showed Colin how he could raise money against his share of the apartment without having to force Helen to sell before she was ready. He solved their problem in forty-five minutes for the price of a cup of coffee.

Lawyer Earl Nemser said he saw so much "pain and acrimony" in the matrimonial cases he handled for his Manhattan firm of Cadwalader, Wickersham & Taft that he devised his own informal system of mediation. In some cases, he hires separate lawyers, invites them to present five-page briefs and an hour's argument and then delivers his own binding decision within a week. In one recent case, which involved issues such as alimony, child support, and the division of more than $1 million in assets, Nemser delivered his decision in two days, and the couple's legal fees were under $2,000.

"People are never happy with divorce settlements, whether they're made in court or in my office," said Nemser, who had spent more than $20,000 and suffered great personal anguish over his own divorce — without mediation. "But in my experience, the decision of a mediator is usually no more than ten percent off what a judge would decide — and look at the time, money, and pain you save. I think it's unfortunate that people have to fight."

♦

DIVORCE MEDIATION: A CRITICAL OVERVIEW
Kenneth Kressel

While I am an enthusiastic student of the mediation process, my understanding of mediation in other domains of conflict has convinced me that mediation is a vehicle of social influence which is not inherently superior to any other method of conflict resolution. Like the others, it has its own decided liabilities as well as assets. The polemical claims of its proponents and critics notwithstanding, my study of divorce mediation has done nothing to dissuade me from this view. Indeed, my reading of the record is that divorce mediation, for all its promise, is a complex and stressful social role with difficulties that are remarkably similar to, and, in certain respects, perhaps even worse than, those I have described earlier in considering the headaches of the divorce attorney. In sum, I have attempted to describe divorce mediation with an open but critical eye and to delineate the unique problems which it poses for professional intervention.

THE ROLE OF THE MEDIATOR

Within the divorce mediation community there are important differences of opinion regarding the precise nature of the mediator's role. Some of these differences reflect the very different settings in which divorce mediation occurs, others reflect philosophic or conceptual differences of a more profound nature. (We shall examine some of these matters shortly.) In spite of the disagreements and differences, however, it is possible to give an overall characterization which is shared by nearly all schools of divorce mediation.

Divorce mediation refers to a process in which divorcing spouses negotiate some or all of the terms of their settlement agreement with the aid of a neutral and trained third party. Some of the negotiating sessions may involve separate meetings between the mediator and each of the parties, but the emphasis tends to be on face-to-face sessions in

From Kenneth Kressel, "Divorce Mediation: A Critical Overview," in *The Process of Divorce* (New York: Basic Books, 1985), pp.178–182, 183–185 (edited).

which the parties deal with each other directly. The mediator's overarching objective is the establishment and maintenance of a cooperative, problem-solving orientation between the spouses (as opposed to the competitive "I win-you lose" orientation said to surround the adversary use of lawyers). Within this broad objective the mediator's attention is directed to two principal areas: establishing a productive negotiating climate and addressing the substantive issues.

With regard to the negotiating climate, the mediator's principal functions include facilitating accurate and honest communication; seeing to it that anger and hostility are kept within manageable bounds; promoting in each party a feeling of confidence in the process and in their respective abilities to use it to attain their most significant objectives; reminding the parties of the needs and perspective of their children; and inculcating in each side at least the rudiments of a constructive negotiating style — principally in the form of a recognition of the need for compromises and trade-offs and the value of attention to the other's needs as well as to one's own.

On the substantive side, the mediator's activities include the development of an orderly agenda; the fostering of open and productive sharing of relevant information; providing legal, economic, or psychological information; helping each side identify objectives of greater and lesser importance; making suggestions for settlement; pressing recalcitrant or unrealistic parties to move toward agreement; and translating the agreements reached into a written document.

Typically, lawyers are not directly involved in the negotiating sessions but serve the parties as consultants. This may occur in the form of a single advisory attorney who serves both spouses and the mediator as a source of neutral legal expertise, or each party may be encouraged to retain outside legal counsel, particularly for final advice regarding the settlement document drawn up by the mediator.

THE SETTING

Divorce mediation is either arranged for privately by the parties or is provided to them by a public agency, usually one with direct ties to the court. Pearson, Ring, and Milne (1983) have conducted a useful national survey of mediation service providers in both these areas. Their results suggests that there are important differences between the two sectors. The data that follow are drawn from their report.

Private sector mediation is much more likely than public sector mediation to involve the negotiation of all the issues, including economic ones such as child support, spousal maintenance, and division of marital property, all of which have traditionally been the domain of attorneys. This form of mediation is sometimes referred to as *comprehensive* divorce mediation. For the most part, public sector mediators restrict themselves (or are restricted by the terms of their court sponsorship) to the resolution of custody and visitation disputes. This narrower focus reflects both the court's formal role as ultimate guardian of the children's interests and the much greater willingness of bench and bar to acknowledge the limits of their expertise in matters affecting children.

Private sector mediation is also likely to last longer and to be more expensive than mediation in the public sector. Thus, the average private sector mediation takes almost nine hours and costs about $440 (exclusive of any legal fees which the parties may incur). Public sector mediation averages slightly more than six hours with an average cost of $156.

Private sector mediation is also much more likely to be a voluntary process — one is almost tempted to say a "word of mouth" process. Thus, private mediators report that more than half (fifty-six percent) of their clients are self-referred, with less than a third entering mediation at the suggestion of another professional such as an attorney or a therapist. Fewer than ten percent of all private mediations involve a referral from the court. In the public sector the situation is reversed, with eighty-two percent of all referrals coming directly from the court and only sixteen percent by self-referral.

The two sectors also orient themselves somewhat differently regarding the involvement of attorneys in the mediation process. Although very few mediation services of either type by-pass the attorneys completely, this is slightly more likely to occur in the private sector than in the public one. Eleven percent of private mediators have no contact with lawyers during mediation compared to five percent in the public sector. On the other hand, with specific regard to the draft settlement agreement, which is the usual product in all but a very small percentage of cases in both sectors, it is the public sector mediators who are more likely to eschew any role for the attorney in looking things over (thirty-nine to twenty-six percent).

The overwhelming majority of mediators in the private sector are mental health professionals, principally socialworkers (forty-two percent) and psychologists (twenty-two percent). Approximately fifteen percent of private sector mediators are lawyers. By contrast, in public sector mediation socialworkers constitute nearly seventy-five percent of all practitioners and lawyers do hardly any public sector work (one percent). Few practitioners in either sector make mediation their exclusive area of practice. Private practice mediators spend about a third of their professional time doing mediation; public sector mediators about half of their time.

One final difference of note: by virtue of their built-in referral base from the courts, public sector mediators are more likely to be experienced at mediation than their counterparts in the private sector. Thus, nearly all (ninety-three percent) of the private sector mediation services polled by Pearson and her colleagues reported handling fewer than fifty cases a year in 1981, and about one-half conducted fewer than ten. In the public sector, by contrast, fifty-four percent of the services conducted more than one hundred mediations per year, a figure matched by only two percent of the private sector services.

To date there are no uniform standards for the training of divorce mediators. It is generally felt that mediators should be well versed in both the psychological, economic, tax, and legal aspects of divorce. The precise knowledge required and the relative weight of knowledge desirable in each of these areas are matters of uncertainty and disagreement.

The criticisms of the traditional legal approach to divorce negotiations are founded on what is widely believed to be its overall poor record of performance. The critics, many of whom come from within the legal community, point to the increasingly long and vexing backlogs of cases awaiting adjudication because the parties and their lawyers have been unable to resolve matters. The quality and durability of the settlement agreements have also been found wanting in the aggregate, with noncompliance common, especially in regard to child support and visitation, and with the parties frequently remaining at each others throats emotionally, if not legally, long after the "final" settlement is reached.

In contrast to this plaintive list stand the numerous virtues attributed to mediation — virtues thought to flow more or less inevitably from the cooperative ethos on which all models of mediation are built; from the mediator's training and sophistication in matters practical and psychological; and from the structural arrangement which allows the mediator simultaneous access to both parties. Thus, mediation is said to result in a more open and complete sharing of information; a more positive negotiating climate; more flexible and creative agreements; enhanced ability to clarify the priorities of each side; the ventilating of emotions which might otherwise block constructive problem solving; the preservation of a working relationship between the parties, including the development of much needed communication and problem-solving skills; the avoidance of blame; the more rapid recovery from the emotional trauma of divorce; the fostering of a greater feeling of mutual power and psychological ownership of the agreements reached, and hence the production of more durable agreements; and a savings in time and money as the result of a more efficient, less destructive negotiating process. This list of mediation's putative virtues is not necessarily exhaustive. A more complete catalogue may be complied by consulting any of the leading expositions of the process. The basic thrust is that the legal system is built on coercion and mediation is built on consent.

The polemical, not to say adversarial quality reflected in these anti-lawyer, pro-mediation arguments is understandable — perhaps even inevitable. To make their way against entrenched ways of doing things and to develop the necessary internal cohesion and esprit de corps, the proponents of new modes of social activity often state their case in an extreme, one-sided fashion. It is merely an ironic note that this well-established social phenomenon is so easily discernible in the divorce mediation movement, whose fundamental premise is the ultimate destructiveness of the adversarial mode.

On the other hand, it is important to distinguish reality from polemics. Research on the effects of divorce mediation is in its infancy. The results to date are promising, but far from conclusive. Moreover, on analytic grounds there are good reasons to suspect that the complexities and headaches of the mediator's role are no less severe, and in certain ways very similar to those of the divorce attorney.

◆

DOMINANT DISCOURSE, PROFESSIONAL LANGUAGE, AND LEGAL CHANGE IN CHILD CUSTODY DECISION-MAKING
Martha Fineman

This article explores how the rhetoric used by socialworkers and mediators has been successful in appropriating the business of child custody decision-making. An integral part of this process has been an attack on the nature of existing rules and decision-making institutions, a phenomenon that can be viewed metaphorically as

From Martha Fineman, "Dominant Discourse, Professional Language, and Legal Change in Child Custody Decision-making," *Harv. L. Rev.*, vol. 101, 1988, pp. 727, 728, 746–768.

the claiming by the helping professions of the custody decision-making terrain through the rhetoric of reform.

OPPORTUNITY SEIZED: THE RHETORICAL WAR

As their involvement with divorce cases through conciliation counseling and court-ordered custody evaluations increased, socialworkers rejected the lawyer/socialworker partnership that they had initially espoused. Within the context of divorce generally — and disputed custody cases particularly — helping professionals challenged central aspects of legal ideology. With the elimination of fault-based divorce and the advent of their crisis theory of divorce, helping professionals began to assert that adversarial concepts and procedures were inappropriate for resolving divorce and custody cases. Socialworkers objected to the very nature of the adversarial process, asserting that it was unnecessary, inappropriate, and indicative of the outmoded notions of "winning" or "losing" custody. Divorce was a crisis to be worked through; conflict was to be recognized and managed. Spouses (with the aid of a socialworker) were to be self-determining and exercise their responsibility to each other and their children to settle their differences so they could function as post-divorce parents. There simply was no room for such growth in the traditional adversarial system. Lawyers' use of adversarial procedures was especially criticized for its effect on children. In essence, socialworkers' attacks questioned both the appropriateness of the representation ideal and adversariness of a process by which fact-finding and decision-making occur.

The helping professions tend to distinguish two aspects of divorce — the emotional divorce, which involves "feelings," and the legal divorce, which involves a division of property, a determination of support, and a decision about custody. Socialworkers view the legal divorce as secondary to the emotional divorce. Thus, once an emotional divorce has occurred, the legal divorce is pro forma; conversely, without an emotional divorce, no true separation can or will occur and the parties will continue to battle throughout and after the legal divorce. Some form of counseling, therapy, or mediation is seen as essential to a resolution of these emotional issues, with post-divorce shared parenting as the optimal goal.

In this regard, socialworkers argued that an adversarial role was unnecessary — lawyers were not needed to prove grounds for divorce as they had been under the fault-based system. Similarly, socialworkers viewed lawyers as unconcerned with, and incompetent to perform, the needed therapeutic function. Lawyers could not be discarded altogether, however, as some issues still needed legal resolution. The social work literature explicitly expressed the competition between the professions, with legal personnel cast as inappropriate decision-makers in custody cases due to their lack of training in child development and psychology.

Although it was initially thought that no-fault divorce would eliminate conflict, socialworkers' involvement with the system convinced them that this legal change had no such transformative effect. In the custody area, in particular, conflict was still apparent. Moreover, the mental health worker, philosophically geared toward cooperation and compromise, experienced great frustration working within a legal system that required the choice of one parent over another and promoted one relationship while "terminating" another. In the task of performing custody evaluations, for example, even the most carefully expressed adverse recommendation might produce pain and anger.

Socialworkers' criticisms of the existing no-fault system formed the basis of calls for an alternative system, reflecting even more procedural and substantive changes, such as mediation and the establishment of a shared parenting norm. These reforms were urged in rhetoric that embodied their view of litigation, conflict, and what is desirable in the post-divorce family.

The calls for change were accompanied by assertions about what was "really" happening in the divorce context. That reality was psychological, not legal, in its focus. According to mental health professionals, the desire to litigate divorce issues, particularly custody, is the product of unresolved feelings about the termination of the marriage. Intervention by a helping professional is necessary to assist a couple in resolving these feelings so that they do not engage in protracted litigation as the extension of their emotional battles. The helping professionals' view is that litigation is harmful to all, particularly children, and that it is usually undertaken without any true legal or factual justification.

Moreover, results achieved under a sole custody legal doctrine were objectionable from the viewpoint of socialworkers' "family-systems" theory. Rather than focusing on the best parent, the socialworker concentrated on how to "restructure" the family. Restructuring meant allowing both parents to continue their parental relationship with the children. When forced to choose between parents, helping professionals preferred the parent who would most freely allow the child access to the other parent. The notion of "the most generous parent" became synonymous with the determination of who was the better parent.

Given socialworkers' assumptions, their criticisms of the legal system, and their characterization of the divorce, it is no surprise that mediation by those trained in the helping professions emerged as the logical procedural solution. If disputed custody was really an emotional event, and the legal system and lawyers had no ability to address the problems, then a new process and new personnel were necessary. Socialworkers' criticisms of legal decision-makers, processes, and results were essential to the formulation of the mediation ideal.

Language has played a critical role in the reform process that has shifted decision-making authority to mediators and the helping profession. The rhetoric employed criticized the traditional system and established an alternative that called for skills possessed by the helping professionals. Yet the rhetoric has occasioned more than a transfer, formal or informal, of responsibility for making the ultimate decision in contested cases. More importantly, it has invoked changes in the substantive rules by which cases are resolved. The domination of socialworker ideology and rhetoric now appears complete. It is inconceivable that one could seriously discuss custody policy and practice today without both using the rhetoric and addressing the concepts and values of the helping professions.

THE MANNER OF APPROPRIATION: THE USE OF NARRATIVE STRATEGIES AND THE INTERSECTION OF OTHER INTERESTS

I believe that the rhetoric and strategy of the helping professions have been successful for two related reasons. First, the helping professions have presented their arguments in the form of "stories" that contain powerful images that are readily understood by those not familiar with the custody decision-making process. Second, the images that they project intersect and are compatible with the interests of significant societal groups that have facilitated the changes suggested by the stories.

Narrative Strategies

One of the significant methods by which the helping professions' ideals became dominant in the custody area was through the construction and manipulation of rhetorical visions or narratives. I call these rhetorical devices narratives because they are stories with a beginning, a middle, and an end. There is competition and drama — tension and resolution — in these narratives. Their "morals" are ways of legitimating one type of substantive and procedural result to the exclusion of others. In describing or illustrating a "problem," they also suggest the "solution." This form of presentation makes the professional standards of the helping professions and the legal system concrete, understandable, and susceptible to positive action. This rhetorical strategy operates by presenting simplistic dichotomous images: negative images or "horror stories" regarding the existing (lawyer-controlled) divorce practice, and corresponding positive images or "fairy tales" of an idealized (socialworker-controlled) process for purer and better decision-making.

These narratives had an additional characteristic that operated to the helping professions' advantage in securing changes. They were cast in terms of mere substitution of decision-makers rather than of alteration of results. They focused on divorce as a discrete event that had to

be made less volatile through the use of trained mediators. These narratives either assumed or ignored and obscured the desirability of the substantive goal of shared parenting. The narratives confined the discussion to the desirability of a change in procedure without revealing that this would also produce a change in substance compatible with the new decision-makers' professional ideology and norms.

The use of rhetorical devices serves the institutional interests of those in the mediation business who wish to stake out an area for their own control. Their language, which is cast as neutral and professional, is political. This fact has been obscured, however, because their rhetoric has confined the debate to a procedural level.

The Horror Story   The image of the legal system constructed by the helping professions is adversarial, combative, and productive of divisions, misunderstandings, and hostility. These negative characterizations are understood to be the inevitable product of a system controlled by attorneys and the judiciary. Socialworkers assert that lawyers focus on rights, claims, due process, and other things "peripheral" to the real issues.

Those who flock to mediation as the ideal decision-making mechanism accuse lawyers and the adversary system of increasing trauma, escalating conflict, obstructing communication, failing to perceive the need for negotiation and counseling, and generally interfering with the development of a process that could help the parties. In their vision, the adversarial system, with its emphasis on conflict and rationality, is inherently unresponsive to the "emotions" and "feelings" associated with the divorce process, which socialworkers believe are more important and worthy of concern.

Lawyers in general and judges in particular are viewed as poorly trained to deal with the psychological aspects of divorce. Because they employ what is described as "militant tunnel-vision advocacy" as a result of their "temperament and training," lawyers cannot possibly make a "success of... divorce." Lawyers and judges are seen as acting on their own biases and values in determining what is in the best interest of the child. A related criticism is that lawyers replace the parties in the negotiation process and thereby fail to enhance the conflict management skills of the parties and to produce agreements to which the parties are committed. Lawyers are criticized for dwelling on the past, laying blame, finding fault, and failing to focus on future conduct as do mediators. In this way, socialworkers' rhetoric lays the basis for their claim to control of the process.

Even socialworkers and mediators who are friendly to lawyers cannot seem to avoid a negative, stereotypical characterization of them. In a recent article advocating a close working relationship between the professions, one author described how lawyers are committed to "rationality, rights, and conflict solution," whereas socialworkers are concerned with "feelings, needs, and growth through relationship." In the socialwork world, of course, to accuse some one of rationality or intellectualism is a criticism, implying an insensitivity to more important emotional concerns.

The generic horror story therefore involves a husband, wife and child(ren) who enter the divorce process, employing two lawyers (his and hers). There is escalating bitterness, pain, and suffering. More and more money is expended. The child(ren) is(are) particularly hurt by the process, particularly since he/she(they) lose(s) a parent in the process (the "non-custodial" parent). It is a process in which there are "winners" and "losers." In other words, it seems inevitable that there will be an unhappy ending to this narrative.

The Fairy Tale   In contrast to the negative images embodied in the horror stories describing the legal process, the helping professions present themselves as a distinct and preferable alternative. The ideal is established rhetorically.

Socialworkers view divorce as occasioning the birth of an ongoing, albeit different, relationship, with mediators and socialworkers as its midwives and monitors. "Let's talk about it" seems to be the ideal, and the talk is envisioned as continuing for decades. The continued involvement is not only with each other but with the legal system as well. This ideal is obviously very different from the traditional legal system, which seeks an end or termination of a significant interaction at divorce: a division, distribution, or allocation of the things acquired during marriage — an emancipatory model — and with its "ending," the permission for a "new life" for the participants and the withdrawal of active legal interference in their relationship.

The helping professions' ideal process "avoids" or "reduces" conflict and is typified by mediation. Helping professionals believe that mediation, employing a therapeutic process, is within their exclusive domain because lawyers, unlike socialworkers, ignore the underlying causes of divorce and give little regard to the "real reason" for the split-up. Therapeutic skills can facilitate acceptance of the divorce and foster a positive approach to the crisis.

Lawyers' skills are downgraded and socialworkers' and mediators' skills are mystified and reified:

Lawyers or others with legal experience have much to offer, but skills in behavioral science are lacking. It is generally easier for one trained in behavioral sciences to acquire legal and other knowledge required for mediation, than for the legally trained person to gain knowledge and a feel for behavioral science and counseling skills.

In this way, socialworkers and mediators set apart the concerns of the adversarial system and subordinate them to the more important concerns of their own professions. Caring, sharing, mental health, and concern for future functioning, they assert, are their exclusive preserve and cannot be attained through the adversarial process.

In this contrasting generic fairy-tale narrative, husband, wife, and child(ren) consult not two lawyers but one mediator; only one is necessary because the process is nonadversarial. The process is characterized by cooperation, caring and acceptance. It costs less money and produces a fairer result. This is obviously a narrative with a happy ending.

Intersection With Other Interests

Also significant in regard to the success of the transformation of custody decision-making is the fact that the rhetoric of socialworkers and mediators intersected with and incorporated the concerns and assumptions of several other groups concerned with custody policy. This overlap assisted the mediators' discourse in gaining dominance. The helping professions' views on mediation, for example, have empowered fathers and fathers' rights groups. The rhetoric has offered fathers' groups a legitimate way to argue for their political goal of removing custody cases from the courts, which they view as favor-

ing women. Fathers' rights groups see mediators as more malleable than judges and attorneys, who are concerned with laws and rights. They also see mediators as less powerful and exacting and less likely to focus on embarrassing child support issues when custody and visitation problems exist. Thus, within the fathers' rights discourse, mediators are the preferred decision-makers.

Some of the nonprocedural implications of the change in process may begin to emerge in the political use of various groups of the helping professions' concepts. There is still no careful or developed assessment of the shared parenting norm, however. Rather, the shared parenting norm is presented as the solution to identified problems. For example, fathers' rights groups have pushed for mediation and joint custody because they claim these innovations will encourage men, who now default in alarming numbers, to pay their child support orders. These groups indicate that the legion of fathers who never bother to visit their children will flock to see them if they are empowered with unilaterally exercisable rights with regard to their children. Ironically, the failure of divorced fathers is used as one of the major arguments for giving men more control and power over children and, through them, over their mothers' lives. Joint custody or shared parenting, however, empowers fathers as a group without requiring any demonstration of responsibility. I consider this inappropriate. In no other area does the law reward those who have failed in their duties as an incentive for them to change their behavior.

The rhetoric of mediators also intersects with and complements the concerns of members of the legal profession. This convergence is probably one of the most significant factors in the success of the helping professions' reforms. Mediators have been empowered by judges and court administrators who dislike custody decision-making under the best interest test, or who believe that such cases clog up the system. The substantive implications may be lost and the discussion focused merely on the transfer of troublesome custody issues to an "alternative" system. This is particularly true when the alternative system is characterized as "more humane and caring" and appears to resolve everyone's problems.

Further, family law attorneys who are uncomfortable in courtroom settings or bored with their profession may find it attractive to envision themselves as mediators, employing a whole new set of mechanisms that will enhance their prestige, their self-worth, and the quality of what they do on a day-to-day basis. There is a mystique about mediation that many find compelling. Mediators do not choose sides but are counsel for the situation. Mediators are disinterested advisors whose only role is to assist the family in making nonadversarial decisions. Family lawyers have a bad image in the press, in the eyes of the public, and in their own eyes; mediation may be a way of rehabilitating that image.

Legislatures also have found the reallocation of decision-making power attractive. The reallocation can be accomplished by using existing court-associated personnel — the socialworkers who previously performed custody investigations can now try their hand at mediation. Further, it has symbolic appeal. Because the goal of shared parenting leads to equal division or joint custody, it is consistent with the recent trend in all of family law toward mathematical formulas for decision-making.

To those uncertain about or upset with the function of the present family law system, the mediators' vision presents a more coherent and more encompassing ideal referencing deeply held beliefs and assumptions. In the procedural context, it offers a process free of conflict. In the substantive context, it appeals to ideals of equality, sharing, and caring. The mediators' view is also one that seems distinctly utopian. Its underlying premise is that one can seek personal happiness and fulfillment by terminating a marriage relationship, yet not lose any of the benefits that marriage provides. The hidden message is that divorce can be painless. One can retain one's children, even one's "family," although the family structure may be slightly altered. It is a grand dream: everybody wins, nobody loses.

PRACTICAL CONSEQUENCES

The issue arises why anyone (except those involved) should care about the rhetorical "competition" I have described between lawyers and socialworkers in this area. In fact, some lawyers join the mediators and fight for the very reforms that will take divorce and custody decision-making out of the legal system. The rhetorical "competition" I have described has important implications for many people who are or will be involved in the family law process, particularly custodial mothers. The ideological shifts described may in fact result in a process that produces bad decisions for many women and children. Joint custody can be a disaster if parents are unwilling or unable to cooperate. Such an arrangement may give a man continued control over his children (and through the children, control over his ex-wife's life), yet not result in increased assumption of responsibility on his part. Anecdotal evidence indicates that many women view joint custody as "losing" — whereas many men view it as "winning" —

the divorce wars; as a result, many women bargain away needed property and support benefits to avoid the risk of "losing" their children. The negative implications of the shift to a therapeutic model and mediation remain largely unexplored.

Proponents of the therapeutic model have defused possible political controversy and opposition to these changes by casting themselves as neutral, disinterested professionals in their advocacy of mediation and the substantive goal of shared parenting. But they are *not* neutral. They have an institutional and professional bias for certain procedural and substantive results that promote their own interests and that will produce changes designed to enhance and ensure their continued centrality in custody decision-making.

Assessing the Narratives

The discourse of the helping professions has created rather than reflected reality. In part, helping professionals have been successful in appropriating the divorce business for themselves because, in the abstract, they offer hope to those who have been hurt by divorce and custody battles. The "reality" that they construct through their rhetoric is one that many want to believe exists.

The realistic assessment of the "fairytale" narrative, however, is that there will be no happy endings; in fact, there will be no ending at all. The narrative assumes an ongoing relationship between the spouses — not an ending — a fact that is not apparent in the presentation of the typical adversary system versus mediation.

The costs associated with such non-endings are also hidden. Traditional divorce was an emancipatory process that terminated the relationship and freed lives for rebuilding. The socialworkers' ideal of an ongoing co-parental relationship may leave little room

for the formation of new relationships by parents or by children. Children may, in fact, suffer more from these non-endings. They may never be able to overcome the quite typical fantasy that mommy and daddy will get back together. It is not clear that non-endings will in fact be "happy" in any significant number of family situations.

Non-endings do benefit mediators, however, who assert that only they can achieve reorganization of families (the process that produces happy non-endings). In the view of the socialworker, mediation is in the first instance designated as a superior *process* — one based on informality that can therefore give full protection to the privacy and autonomy of the parties by allowing them to make important decisions for themselves. The ideal process takes place within a context of open communication and protects against the parties having issues decided for them through lawyers' adversarial tricks.

Yet the supposed benefits of mediation are not all process related. It is also argued that the purpose of mediation — to reorient the parties toward one another — is substantially different from, and superior to, the legal ideal. Mediation discourages the focus on legal rights and seeks to help the divorcing parties achieve a new and shared post-divorce relationship, in which they redirect their attitude and disposition toward one another for post-divorce shared parenting. The ideal product of the process, in the rhetoric of the helping professions, is a *restructuring* of the relationship of the adults, rather than its termination.

Some processes, according to the helping professions, facilitate the adjustment of the "family system" for post-divorce parenting; others, such as adversarial processes, interfere with it. The professions believe that the process for awarding sole custody, for example, is indicative of the win/loss mentality that socialworkers seek so desperately to purge from the system. Implicitly, within the helping professions' rhetorical framework, the mediator-socialworker is the appropriate, preferred decision-maker, who dispenses the appropriate, preferred result. The socialworker's old role as dispenser of "treatment" to deter divorce or, failing this, of advisor to the court about what placement would be in the "best interest of the child," has evolved into a new role. Socialworkers are now in charge of reordering and maintaining the family system. Their role has evolved into one that begins by managing the initial trauma, then attempts to achieve acceptance of the changes caused by the divorce, and ultimately seeks to restructure the family from "married couple with children" to "divorced co-parents."

Although "system stability" has remained a constant goal under early and contemporary socialwork practice, the new ideal focuses on building the post-divorce relationship between both parents, rather than ensuring that there is one "custodial parent" with whom the children have a primary relationship. In this process, the relationship of the "noncustodial" parent to his or her children has assumed great importance, and facilitating continual contact between children and "noncustodial" parents is the paramount pragmatic goal.

The implications of this approach are enormous. Not only does this represent a serious decision about who it is that ultimately makes custody decisions — judge, attorney, or mediator-socialworker — but, because of the inherent nature of the mediator/shared parenting ideal, adoption of this approach represents a significant opportunity for continuous and substantial intervention by socialworkers or other court-associated personnel. The goal of the helping professions are at odds with

the traditional legal goal of divorce. Nothing is "terminated," except the formal marital bond between the adults. Because the family unit theoretically continues, it may often be in need of the services and communication skills provided by the mediator alternative to the adversarial system. Potentially, therefore, the legal system's involvement will not end either, at least until all the children reach adulthood. Coercive and continuous supervision of the restructured unit is compatible with this view. There are no legal or doctrinal impediments to reactivating the mediation system. If things are not operating to the satisfaction of one ex-spouse, the mediation mechanism can be reengaged to work things out.

This narrative non-ending has been uncritically incorporated into reform rhetoric concerning the legal system. Recent changes in custody rules, particularly those setting forth presumptions of joint custody, are consistent with the rhetoric and the non-ending it advocates. The acceptance of this nontermination ideal is also associated to some extent with the imposition of other ideals onto family law, including the goals of equality, gender neutrality, and social restructuring. Concern with these abstract goals may overtake the desire to reach workable and practical decisions upon divorce. The entire area is permeated with symbolism that relates only tangentially to the realities of divorce.

Ultimately, the helping professions' discourse has encompassed and absorbed traditional legal dialogue concerning custody. "Sharing" became identified as the public and political language of the escalating debate over the appropriate concept and process for resolving custody disputes. The political victory of the helping professions is manifested by the conferring of legally significant rights and obligations, through the explicit delegation of decision-making

authority to the socialworkers and mediators. Legislatures and the judiciary have delegated this power both on an institutional
level, as with the creation of mandatory
mediation or counseling services staffed
with socialworkers and connected to the
court system, and in individual cases, in
which judges seek and accept the advice of
"experts" in the helping profession. This
formal recognition of the helping
professions' role places the state's im-
primatur on their appropriation of custody
decision-making.

The Politics of Rhetoric

The rhetorical symbolism employed by
socialworkers and mediators is politically
powerful. It empowers the helpers and may
allow them to eclipse the interests of those
who are designated as the very ones to be
helped. For example, although the helping
professions' vision portrays mediation as
allowing custody decisions to be made with
sharing and caring rather than with conflict
and contention, mediation may in fact
merely hide rather than eliminate conflict,
allowing the stronger of the two parents to
dominate and control the weaker.

The adoption of the mediators' image
has important substantive implications
with significant political and social rami-
fications. One of the most harmful assumptions underlying socialworkers'
discourse is that a parent who seeks sole
custody of a child has some illegitimate
motivation. Mediators may acknowledge
exceptions to this generalization in situations in which one parent is a drunkard or
drug addict or in which a child is abused,
but the general assumption is that the parent who is willing to live up to the ideal of
shared custody and control is the one with
the child's real interest at heart.

Mediation advocates often characterize opposition to shared custody as

pathological. The assumption in the
socialworkers' discourse is that the parent
who rejects the shared parenting ideal and
seeks sole custody of his or her child has
an illegitimate motive. A mother who resists sharing her child with her ex-husband
is characterized as having "issue overlay";
she protests too much. Such women may
be characterized as clinging or overly dependent on the role identification as wife
and mother, socialworkers and mediators
assert that these women can be helped
through the mediation process only if they
are cooperative. Other women are seen as
greedy, merely using the children in order
to get larger property settlements; it is
claimed that an "effective" mediator can
block these women from achieving their
evil ends. A third stereotype focuses on
vindictive mothers who use the children to
get back at their ex-husbands; it is perceived that these are the type of women
who should be punished by having their
children taken away and sole custody
awarded to the fathers.

Lost in the rhetoric of the socialworker
are real concerns. There is little or no
appreciation of the many real problems
that joint custody and the ideal of sharing
and caring can cause. The prospect of a
continued relationship with an ex-spouse
may be horrifying to contemplate, but the
sharing ideal assumes that a relationship
between the noncustodial parent and the
child cannot proceed without it. Also unsettling is the extent to which allegations
of mistreatment, abuse, or neglect on the
part of husbands toward either their wives
or children are trivialized, masked, or lost
amid the psychological rhetoric that reduces mothers' desires to have custody
and control of their children to pathology.

We should be deeply skeptical of
these views of women and mothers. They
are not accurate and the visions they present are deeply misogynous. Most mothers

love their children and would not willfully deprive them of contact with a caring and responsible father. In fact, if the children are old enough to assert their own interests, it is unlikely that mothers could deprive them of contact with their fathers even if they wanted to. By making these observations, I do not mean to suggest that abuses never occur, but rather to point out that they are not typical, or even common, and that it is irrational to base custody policy on the deviant than the typical post-divorce situation.

Because socialworkers and others sympathetic to mediation have created and controlled the presentation of both narratives, the real nature of the competition between the legal and therapeutic models has been hidden. Notably, there are no parallel scenarios involving vindictive or greedy husbands in the mediation literature. No alternative narrative, sympathetic to single parent or sole custody and control, has gained any credibility in the literature. Nor do many stories assign different characters to the stock "victim" and "villain" roles.

Further, by branding opposition to mediation and joint custody as the manifestation of a psychological problem to which mediation is itself the solution, mediation rhetoric forecloses any effective expression of women's legitimate concerns. As things now stand, the cries of protest over the imposition of a joint custody or shared parenting solution from mothers who will be assuming primary care for their children (but sharing control) are attributed to the fact that these mothers have not accomplished an "emotional divorce." As soon as they are able to get over "their issues" they will be able to begin "rational problem solving" and will cooperate agreeably.

The socialworkers' discourse accepts without criticism the superiority of "rational decision-making" within the new, reconstructed family structure. Through this method, the "vindictive" woman is thwarted, the "victimized" man allowed to continue to operate as *paternal familius* (in an altered form, of course) by being given "equal rights" without the formal imposition of responsibility. The helping professionals believe this approach remedies the pro-mother imbalance that has existed in custody decision-making.

♦

THE ANTI-SOCIAL FAMILY
Michele Barrett and Mary McIntosh

TWO GENERAL AIMS

In our view there are two general aims for political strategy on the family: (1) We should work for immediate changes that will increase the possibilities of *choice* so that alternatives to the existing favored patterns of family life become realistically available and desirable; (2) We should work toward collectivism and away from individualism in the areas at present allocated to the sphere of family life, especially income maintenance, the work of making meals, cleaning and house-

From Michele Barrett and Mary McIntosh, *The Anti-Social Family* (London: NLB, 1982), pp. 134–159.

keeping, and the work of caring for people such as children, the old and the sick or disabled.

Before we can discuss what these principles mean in practice for the various aspects of the politics of the family, it is necessary to say a little about the philosophical problems involved in concepts of "collectivism" and "choice." A good way into this is to look at feminist and socialist debates about abortion rights.

To speak of extending people's right to choose smacks of the bourgeois individualism for which feminism has often been derided. It is said that to demand the right to choose between pursuing a profession and staying at home to care for children is all very well for the bourgeois woman, but meaningless for the working-class woman who must in any case work herself to exhaustion, both inside and outside the home and for whom employment is a necessary evil rather than personal fulfilment. Or it is said that the demand for "a woman's right to choose" to have an abortion or not is fine for the bourgeois woman who can afford to have either the abortion or the baby as she chooses, but is inadequate for the poorer woman who needs access to free abortion, not merely the legal right to choose, and who needs time, money, help and house-room if the choice to have a baby is to be a real one. As Denise Riley has put it: " 'The right to choose' must imply the right to choose to have (not merely *not* to have) children, and this right is a very metaphysical assertion in a situation where provisions for the myriad needs for bringing up those children in a human way are thin on the ground. And, of course, conspicuously thinner for some than for others. To follow through the 'positive' aspect of the right to choose would entail a many-faceted campaign, a generalizing of the issue which linked it to a wider context of agi-

tation for the reforms necessary to give more plausibility to the notion of choice." But she continues: "Nevertheless, it seems to me to be wrong to criticize an essentially defensive slogan, so heavily marked by its necessary strategic location, on the grounds of its incompleteness." Clearly, when we talk of choice, we must mean something more than purely formal legal freedom; we mean viable possibilities as well.

But there is a more fundamental risk of bourgeois individualism in the simple demand for the "right to choose" in private life: that is, acceptance of the bourgeois distinction between public and private, between production and reproduction. Writing again of the campaign to retain abortion rights, Sue Himmelweit asked: "Are we accepting that under socialism, or whatever name we give the society we are working for, production will be planned, ever so democratically, but planned for the benefit of all, but reproduction will remain a private individual decision and right?" She, like Denise Riley, goes on to say, "I raise these questions not because I believe that under the present climate and the present threats we have any choice but to wage a defensive struggle to claim the little areas of freedom that the present system has partially granted us and now threatens to take away." Even if we accept Marx's critique of Malthusian population theories, we must believe that a socialist society might wish to control its population growth or size. At its best this could involve collective decision-making by local groups of women as has been claimed for the anti-natalist policies of Maoist China. At its worst it could involve the peremptory removal of access to abortion, as in the pro-natalist Romanian policy of 1966. In between, it can involve structuring economic incentives, welfare and nursery provision or whatever in such a way as to attempt to influence what women choose. But in one way or another, socialism is bound to give a positive value to collective rather than individual concerns in questions of reproduction. What socialists must do is not *deny the existence* of individual rights, for these will surely exist and even flourish in socialist society, but *challenge the private content* attributed to such rights in bourgeois thought.

So political philosophy alerts us to the limited nature of demands for freedom of choice and the dangers of resting our analysis on a pure liberal individualism. And the philosophy of mind may alert us to deeper problems in any ultimate conceptualization of what a pure choice could be or what the implications of positing a freely choosing subject might be. Yet again, as Denise Riley has written, "it is nevertheless the case that the uncertain speech of the philosophy of 'rights' is the chief inherited discourse — whatever its deficiencies — for the framing of *any* demands for social reform or revolution. And demands for rights and choices are the expression of a critical refusal to leave the powers of decision to external authorities, be they doctors or government. The political significance of this refusal must override objections to the 'right to choose' which are based only on the slogan's apparent implications of a free individual operating on an uncircumscribed terrain, in an idealism of isolated 'choice.' For while 'choice' is obviously a complex concept, and while the right in law and in social policy to 'make a choice' is by no means the whole story, nonetheless that right, minimal enough, is of a critical importance."

The theories of Michel Foucault have been used to deflate simplistic views of sexual liberation which depend upon a notion of a sexual being subjected to external repression. As Athar Hussain puts it: "The lofty and noble projects of linking sexual liberation with political revolution — a not uncommon theme in left writings on sexuality — come in for withering mockery. Sexual liberation, Foucault claims, is an illusory horizon created by a mistaken view of power which comes to bear on sexuality." The workings of power are more complex than this; they cannot be understood as repression versus freedom or repression versus some rebellious, polyvalent sexual instinct. Nevertheless, the notion of liberation needs to be defended. The idea of repression may indeed be merely a way of talking of sexuality that has developed in the last two centuries, but some situations are more repressive and others more free. The attribution of, say, homosexuality as a personal identity may well be a phenomenon of those cultures often called "anti-homosexual," but homosexual liberation, the right to claim that identity and engage in those activities, is still an important freedom to be won.

PERSONAL POLITICS — MAKING CHOICES

There are many changes in law and institutions that we should fight for to give us a context of greater choice. But first we need to examine what we should do within the choices available to us now. For "lifestyle politics" and the struggle to develop prefigurative forms of cooperative activity in the bosom of an often hostile society have long been an important strand of our political tradition, and rightly so. Time and again, feminist thought has rejected life-long monogamy, especially as imposed by marriage laws. Drawing on ideas that go back at least as far as the bohemians of the 1920s but came most immediately through the hippies of the 1960s, early women's liberationists set up households that rejected the conventions of bourgeois morality and sought to revalorize personal life by breaking down the boundaries of public and private. In the early 1970s there were feminist households where all doors had been removed, where people slept in whichever room had spare bed-space, and wore whichever clothes were at hand. More recently some feminists, despairing of transforming their relations with men, have turned to separatism, living as far as possible without the help or company of men. Most of us would not want to live in this way and do not accept the arguments in its favor. But we should defend the right of these women to do so.

Unfortunately, also, such projects have often been sustained by a moral righteousness that makes them distasteful to others. Separatists accuse women who live with men of "loving their enemy." People who believe in multiple relationships deride as politically backward those who feel the need of a primary partner. Life-style politics has fallen into disrepute partly because it so often claims to be *the* way; it claims that everyone should adopt the new way of life to bring about the revolution and it claims that this change in everyone's practice is all that is required. The Red Collective in London was one of the few groups to reject these claims quite explicitly. A group of five women and men who each had some sexual relationships within the group, they sought to change the form of their relationships and to break down their one-to-one character. But they did not expect to inaugurate a new way of living just by an act of will. "The particular structures of relationships that we have in the group are... not seen as an end which we have been trying to achieve as such, but as a context in which we have been trying to carry out changes in the way we relate." They recognized

that the patterns of intimate relations are deep within us, that they are not just a habit of conformity to an alien bourgeois morality but involve needs and defences that are set up in childhood. At the same time they recognized that the isolation of families and the form of the couple relationship are structured by their place in a wider society. They expressed this in general terms by saying: "Because capitalism imposes a separation between the sphere of commodity production and the sphere of consumption and the domestic economy, economic relations coincide with emotional ones in a very particular way within the family." But they also saw that changes in such things as housing provision, abortion law, child-care arrangements, and women's chances to earn good wages would open up more possibilities for changing the domestic economy and sexual relations. Even the existing social institutions do not determine unalterable family forms. The nuclear family, they argue, is an untheorized practice which emerged in the context of capitalist development. A conscious, theorized practice that would challenge the personal and the social relations of capitalism is a possible and necessary part of broader mass struggles.

If we must avoid the counterproductive stance of self-righteous moralizing, we must also avoid the defeatist stance of colluding with existing family morality on the grounds that it is too hard to change or cannot be changed on its own. It is important to work at the development of shared ideas toward a better way of living together. Perhaps one of the best of the varied meanings of the slogan "the personal is political" is the idea of public discussion about personal life. This does not mean that our intimate relationships must be enacted on a public state, but that the principles on which they are conducted and the conditions surrounding them should be a regular part of general political discussion. It is in this spirit that we propose some basic principles of daily political struggle in personal life.

Encourage Variety

Shulamith Firestone, who saw the oppression of women as rooted in the "tyranny of reproductive biology" and fed by the economic dependence of women and children on a man and their isolation from the wider society, argued for flexibility in life styles, for a program of multiple options existing simultaneously, so that people could choose what suited them at different periods of their lives. She thought there should be more possibilities for being single, which she rather quaintly associated with "single professions," more ways of "living together" without marriage, whether in sexual or non-sexual arrangements, and a developed system of larger "households" where children could grow up. Her blueprint for these households involves shared child-care, shared chores, full membership rights for children, no ownership of children, a limited contract with the possibility of transfer to another household. Such households would exist alongside the single and group non-reproductive life styles giving a range of choice. Though her households are very similar to what are usually known as "communes," she would clearly not accept the goal of many involved in British communes of transforming the whole of society into a federation of communes.

It is easy, perhaps, to dream up a variety of alternatives to the family or ways of eliminating the oppressive aspects of family life, such as the "open marriage," or the "open family." It is even easier to ridicule other people's dreams. Women separatists cannot cope with men and are living in a cozy regressive nursery. Communes have done little to transform gender relations and nothing to break down the mother-child bond. The open family boasts of children's rights, but at the whim of the parents. Homosexual couples either become purely domestic, seeking sex outside, or else ape marriage (or sometimes both). Experimentation with new ways of living is a form of petty-bourgeois protest against alienating occupations and the suburban nuclear family.

But sneering at what others are trying to do is too easy. They are bound to be idealistic, infantile, crypto-reactionary or insufficiently radical. What purpose does such criticism serve? It can be constructive and a valuable part of a political commitment to change. Or it can be a justification for settling down, after some youthful experimentation, into a conventional family mode. The thoughtful article that Philip Abrams and Andrew McCulloch wrote about "Women, Men and Communes" is often invoked to dismiss all attempts to transcend the family. Yet if the commune movement is a form of petty-bourgeois protest, then socialists should be glad their protest has taken this progressive direction. We should welcome it, engage with it, try to understand its class nature, but also help it to develop beyond that.

Many of us in and around the women's liberation movement choose to live alone or else in households that are not formed on the family model. There is by now a wealth of experience of the many problems involved. Sharing housework, cooking or child-care is not easy, especially for people brought up in families where all this was controlled by one women. The loss of control and absence of established norms and patterns of trust can engender a sense of insecurity. The decision to have children may have to be made in the context of uncertainty about who will enjoy rights and who will shoulder responsibilities. Households can break up amidst resentment and recrimination. Yet living in these various ways that challenge the family is often rewarding and enjoyable. Children brought up more collectively are at least as sane and independent as their peers. Friendships and love relationships are less clearly demarcated and can be enduring and remarkably supportive. Heterosexual and homosexual ways of life merge and learn from one another. We may not ourselves wish or feel able to be radically innovative in our personal lives. But we should encourage variety by supporting others who do. If others work at communal living, shared child-care, shared housework, celibacy, non-parenthood (how strange we have nothing but clumsy words for it: childlessness?), homosexuality that does not mirror heterosexual patterns, the least we can do is support them. We should not undermine their efforts, but engage with them constructively.

Avoid Oppressive Relationships

The idea of love has a lot to answer for. In its name, people who are otherwise rational and socially perceptive walk as if spellbound into traps and prisons. How often has a male lecturer having a relationship with a student, or a doctor with a nurse, or a manager with a typist, been heard to say, "our relationship is not like that; she is really a strong, mature person; we are breaking down status barriers; we are absolutely equal?" Of course. In love the partners are equal. But in every other aspect of their relationship — at parties, in discussions, in money, in arguments — they are inevitably unequal, gender being reinforced by hierarchy. How often have people succumbed to the argument, "if

you really loved me you wouldn't mind marrying me, despite your theoretical and principled objections to marriage; what harm can a bit of paper do to a relationship between people? It only sets a seal on what we feel anyway?" Of course. But is also endows the relationship with respectability and social privilege and thereby devalues all other relationships. It is the end of the woman's economic independence as far as tax, social security and a pattern of welfare benefits are concerned. And when love is over, the shell of the relationship endures, and to break out of it a whole machinery of law must be invoked. How often have mothers (though seldom fathers) said, "I am enjoying the new baby so much, I don't think I'll go back to work straight after my maternity leave?" Of course, caring for a baby can be a delight. But such women usually also take over the housework and cooking from that time on. And when they do look for a job again they can only find one that is less good than the one they left. How often have women said, "My husband's career means he has to work long hours, so I have a part-time job and look after the house;" or, "I gave up my job when his father had a stroke and came to live with us; that was twelve years ago?" Of course, loving care for a partner and his family are fine. But in its name women became trapped in the household and unable to support themselves. Sometimes there is no choice open to us, but too often we take the easy conforming path without considering where it leads.

As well as being clear-eyed about what we are doing and trying to rethink our own relationships and households, we should be aware of the social impact of what we do. Each woman who is coquettish with men and each mother who indulges her child with excessive attention and toys makes it harder for other women to resist the pressures from men and children. "No man is an island," despite the cultural view that personal life is a purely private matter of consequence only to those involved.

Marriage is an oppressive institution for both the married and the unmarried, and provides the major legal support for the current family form. We believe that socialists and feminists should not get married themselves and should not attend or support the marriages of any who can be convinced of our critique of the family. "Paper" marriages designed to get round immigration restrictions may perhaps be an exception. But savings to be made on income tax or death duties are no excuse: that is a form of collusion, not of subversion. Distress to older relatives is scarcely ever an excuse; only twenty years ago such distress would have been acute in most sections of British society, yet many young people were courageous enough to follow their own beliefs and marriage is a weaker institution in consequence. There are very few cultures within British society where the young should not be beginning to take this stand. As Diana Leonard Barker put it: "For a 'companionate,' sexually libertarian couple to undergo the [wedding] ceremony is, at the very least, a recognition of the continuing power of their parents, the community, the church and socially structured sex roles.... Our feminist ire should not be aroused by the apparent anachronism of the rituals but by what they confirm and tell us about the continuing characteristics of marriage as an institution." Of course, just resisting formal marriage itself does not guarantee that we escape from a marital type of relationship. In Sweden, for instance, cohabitation has become common among younger couples. Yet it is said that their relations often give them household presents when they set up home together, and

they seem to have become assimilated to the old patterns. Similarly, even swapping roles between a man and a woman can produce a mirror-image couple that does more to confirm the recognized pattern than to challenge it.

Nobody should have a housewife. Nobody, man, child, invalid, or woman, needs a long-term "housewife" or has the right to have one. Unpaid domestic service is in principle inferior to social provision. For those who can afford it, paying someone to clean the house or cook meals is preferable to making it the duty of one household member. Many socialists have qualms about this, without being very clear about why. What is wrong with it is not that someone else is doing your dirty work — after all, if you believe it should be socialized, you believe that it is not eternally *your* private responsibility. What is wrong is that someone, usually a woman, is being paid an abysmally low wage and that the relation is one of mistress-and-servant. It should be more like engaging a plumber and less like having a skivvy. As long as we must all do our own housework on the same scale, women are essentially no more capable of housework than men. Men have deskilled themselves in order to get out of it and women have colluded in order to gain some pride in compensation for a disadvantaged situation.

By the same token, women are no more innately fitted for intensive child-care than men. So child-care should be shared between men and women. And it should not be shared on the basis of contrasting styles: when men care for children they should do it in the warm, intimate way that only women usually have — allowing children to show their vulnerability, comforting and cuddling, rather than just romping and joking, as men have so often done. Women, too, should feel able to have fun with children, rather than only "looking after" them. Men should also recognize that being involved with children means being responsible: you cannot make plans to go out without considering what will happen to them. Such responsibility need not be the burden it is for isolated little families at present. This is why feminists have long campaigned for more social forms of care. We cannot rely on redistributing existing tasks within existing households, important though this is; we must also try to socialize them and find alternative ways of carrying them out. The problem with this at present is that these alternatives are often not available or are unappealing or too expensive.

The women's movement has articulated the resentment underlying women's, often graceful, resignation to the role of housewife and mother; more and more women are aware of what a sacrifice it is. Men who have housewives have more energy to devote to their careers or to working odd hours or overtime. They get on well, but at the expense of others and women who have no houseperson.

These are not ideas that will make life miserable, but ideas for happier living. Though they are mainly aimed at undermining the guarantees of male privilege, they also pave the way for forming new kinds of household that are more rewarding for all involved.

Beware of Domesticity

The Red Collective wrote of one unreconstructed relationship that it was "a basis from which the man can act on the outside world but which absorbs the woman into the couple." A danger may be that in reconstructing our relationships, in devoting ourselves to the politics of the personal, we may all become absorbed into the couple or into the household. This is more likely to happen where a couple live together without other adults. One simple antidote is that each person should have their own space within the household — a "room of one's own." Cramped housing makes this impossible for most people. Yet many who have the space, and can afford to heat it, still seem to use it in such a way that they live in each other's pockets. The television that the children watch is in the only comfortable living room. The woman does her sewing at the dining-table, though there is a whole room upstairs designated as a "spare bedroom." The sharing of a marital bedroom is considered essential, despite snoring, sickness or insomnia. The open-plan living space enhances family "togetherness" and demands a high level of involvement in family life. Anyone who has friends in must share them with the whole family.

We are not arguing against personal life, or against privacy, but for a better balance between private and public and a private life that is not so demanding and draining and not so all-important. For many people, work is so unrewarding that they center their lives around the home. Decorating the home, furnishing it, equipping it with gadgetry become major activities. Family leisure and a child-centered life style become the sources of their deepest satisfaction. Public spaces become shopping precincts where people go only to stock up on the goodies they consume in private. As every socialist knows, it becomes almost impossible to attract a decent crowd to a public meeting.

To some extent the solution must involve changing the nature of work, and "revitalizing public life." As Alexandra

Kollantai wrote, "the stronger the collective, the more firmly established becomes the communist way of life. The closer the emotional ties between the members of the community, the less the need to seek refuge from loneliness in marriage." Nevertheless there is much that we can do in our own lives to resist pressures toward cozy domestic self-sufficiency and the privileging of home life. This is not without its problems, since the less conventional our household arrangements the more we become cut off from ordinary people and thrown back on each other. But we can at least beware of the Scylla of home improvements, domestic comforts and security without getting psychologically wrecked by the Charybdis of squalor, isolation and impersonality.

We have presented these three principles — encourage variety, avoid oppressive relationships, beware domesticity — in a spirit of opening up discussion. We have put forward our own views, but we do not intend to preach a rigid pattern of moral rectitude to everyone else. We do, however, believe that changes in our own lives are possible and that everyone should be working on the kinds of questions we have outlined.

SOME CHANGES TO FIGHT FOR

It is in the light of the two guiding aims of greater freedom of choice and the move toward collectivism that feminist and socialists should judge current proposals on social policy as they affect the family. At present all of us, and especially the poor, are constrained to forms of personal life that are privatized in families. There are few available alternatives, and the alternatives that do exist are inferior and stigmatized. Those who have managed to

choose and establish other ways of living have tended to be better off, or else willing to put up with considerable material privation. A key strategy, then, must be to change all the state policies that currently privilege "the family" at the expense of other ways of living.

This does not mean attacking families or people who live in them. But it does mean cutting through the common political cant about the family as "the basic unit of society" and the need to "strengthen the stability and quality of family life." In practice, those who most fervently preach the organic role of the family do least when in power to help family members. For what they are defending is precisely a family that will look after itself, whose members will not turn elsewhere for care or support, self-sufficient, self-contained, selfish.

Wages

As long as we live in a system where the wage is the main way in which people's needs are met, wages should be large enough to support those who work for them. This means that women and young people should be able to earn a wage that does not assume they live as a dependant in someone else's household. For women, this means a great deal more than "equal pay for equal work": it means some kind of positive action to change the whole way work is organized. Women should not be confined to "women's jobs," and women's jobs should not be defined as less skilled and demanding than men's. Women should have equal chances of training and promotion and equal chances of working overtime or obtaining other perks. Time off to care for children should not condemn anyone to the worst and least secure jobs. Maternity leave should be extended to cover anyone caring for small babies during the day. None of this can be done without changing men's situation. They will lose some privileges; they will also gain the opportunity to take a period off paid work for childcare, or to work shorter hours so that they can shop and cook, without spoiling their career. They will lost the right to assume they should earn a "family wage" to support a wife and children; they will also gain freedom from the obligation to be a breadwinner.

If young people or women can earn a living wage as individuals they are not bound to their parents or their husband by financial need. They are free to come and go and to form relationships that are not mercenary and in which they have more of a say. A man who is no longer the main breadwinner will begin to lose some of his power as father and husband.

Social Security

Not everyone can earn a wage: children cannot and, for the foreseeable future, women will spend more time out of employment than men. They should not have to be dependent on their husbands. Social security provision should not be based on the assumption that family members will support each other. This leads to gross inequalities. Families with children are in general poorer than those without; so are families with only one person earning. Yet it is when children are young that their mothers find it hardest to work outside the home. Clearly an adequate child benefit is needed, at a level commensurate with what it costs to keep a child. In Britain a universal child benefit already exists in principle, but so far it has not begun to match what children actually cost. Then we need an adequate income for women whether or not

they are in employment and whether or not they are living with a man. In Britain at present women have similar National Insurance rights to men (though it will not be until 1984 that they will be able to claim benefits for their dependent children on the same basis as men). But as far as non-insured benefits are concerned (and once insured sickness or unemployed benefits have run out), married and cohabiting women are treated as their husband's dependant. They cannot have an invalidity pension unless they are incapable of housework as well as paid work; they cannot claim an allowance to stay at home and care for an invalid dependent relative; for means-tested benefits their resources and needs are "aggregated" with those of their husband so that if he is earning they probably get no benefit. We need to move toward "disaggregation," so that married women have independent rights to social security on the same condition as anyone else. The same principle should apply to income tax (and to capital transfer tax, where there should be no exemption for husbands and wives). The "aggregation" of husband and wife in means-tested social security and in tax is the most important way that the state bolsters the marriage system; yet it does so quite often by putting married people at a disadvantage. Disaggregation would have immense effects on women's dependence. Many unemployed women become housewives, relying on their husbands for support. If they could claim a benefit in their own right, they would become unemployed people, seeking work and living on supplementary benefit meanwhile.

But means-tested benefits were originally intended as a residual safety net; they are not appropriate for providing support for people whose earning capacity is cut by responsibility for caring for children or other dependants. Time out of paid work for such care should be a risk covered by the ordinary National Insurance scheme. There has been dispute among feminists as to whether women should be paid an allowance for child care. Some have even gone so far as to say all women should get "wages for housework." Others argue for a "home responsibility payment" for anyone, man or woman, who stays at home to care for small children or for the old or disabled. The advantage here is that this is hard work that is seldom recognized as important and useful, and that, if it were paid for, many women would be released from economic dependence. The disadvantage is that they might become more firmly trapped, instead, in "womanly" duties to home and family, as the proposal effectively privileges individual family child care. If the allowance were really enough to live on, it would scarcely be worthwhile for such a woman to take a paid job, especially as she would then have to pay for some other form of child care. One possibility that has been canvassed is that every preschool child (or set of children) should have a child care allowance which could be paid either to a parent staying at home or to a nursery or child minder. This would mean that nurseries and child care would not, as the women's liberation movement has demanded, be provided free; yet everyone would be able to afford them. The payment would be a way of creating choice, and there is little doubt that we would find many more mothers opting for their children to be cared for in some collective way. The payment would also open up the possibility for all sorts of new nurseries and nursery schools, developing non-sexist and democratic styles.

A scheme like this might also be adapted to the care of the dependent disabled, with cash allowances covering either home or day-care centres or spells in residential care. In Britain, at least, the principle of a state "attendance allowance" has been established; it needs to be extended.

Caring

Paying for the care of young children and the disabled drives a coach and horses through the old idea of the self-sufficient family. It recognizes caring as a collective responsibility and as a real social contribution, not just a natural expression of love and duty. But even more important is that such caring should become collectively organized and, as much as possible, take place in a lively and sociable setting, not shut away in isolated flats and houses. We need more and better nurseries and after-school play facilities, not only to help harassed mothers but also because they are more efficient and socially more stimulating and enriching. We need a better health service that can look after the chronically ill and the convalescent as well as acute hospital cases. We need day centers and residential care for everyone who cannot be left alone to look after themselves. The people who use these services should have a major say in deciding how they are run, so that they can really meet their needs.

But we also need collective provision to cover a lot of the everyday caring that women do within the family: housework, cooking, washing. Proper meals should be available at school and at work. There should be communal social centers where people can eat out and enjoy their leisure without spending a fortune. Pubs and restaurants should be more welcoming to people with children. There should be shared facilities for laundry and dry cleaning and shared machinery like industrial vacuums, sewing machines and lawnmowers, making household work and gardening easier.

Housing

More modern housing can reduce the amount of drudgery and make housework easier. There is a danger that it can also raise standards and offer opportunities for even more elaborate arrangements for home-centered living. But at least it can offer people greater choice about the way they live. At present too much of the good housing is geared to nuclear-family living. Housing managers tend to allocate the best council housing to "good" families with a stable breadwinning father and relegate the single parents and other "undesirables" to poorer-quality dwellings. Building societies are reluctant to give mortgages except to heads of families; they are not keen on households of unrelated adults, or even on dual-career couples. Housing cooperatives and associations, which in recent years have provided some accommodation for single people, are being squeezed financially, though the "single homeless" are at last being recognized as a serious housing problem. The policy of increasing the amount of owner-occupation, at the expense of private and public rented accommodation, is specifically designed to bolster the family and the commitment to domestic life. In the present housing market, owning your own house is the best form of security; but it involves a great investment of money and time and ties you emotionally to the home. It gives residents greater control, but it tends to give that control to the man in the household, the one who can get a mortgage and afford to make the repayments. On divorce, for instance, the wife can now often claim the right to the home even if she did not pay

for it, but she will often not be able to afford to go on living in it. In the private rented sector, socialists have long fought for security of tenure — yet it can be double-edged in a context of acute housing shortage, when you are secure only as long as you remain in the same family group. A woman who just chooses to leave her husband is not considered a priority for rehousing even if she has children; her husband, as the tenant, has security of tenure in their house or flat, so the council is reluctant to be responsible for housing both partners separately. Getting housed after separation or divorce has never been easy, but the new Housing Act may have made it even more difficult. So security of tenure must not be a socialist shibboleth; it must go alongside policies that make for greater freedom and flexibility in setting up and changing households.

Family Law

The increasing amount of divorce and single parenthood is making the whole field of family law a newly problematic one. some notable advances have been made in Britain in recent years. The Domestic Violence Act (1976) gives women much better protection against violent husbands; it has even — at last — been recommended that rape in marriage should be treated *as* rape and be punishable as a crime. Since 1969 divorce can be obtained by mutual consent, or after separation, without the idea of one party being innocent and the other guilty of a matrimonial offence of adultery, cruelty or desertion. This reform has thrown into question the obligation of one partner (almost always the husband) to maintain the other after a divorce or separation. There is a lobby on behalf of divorced men arguing that "in these days of women's liberation" women should not expect marriage to be a "bread ticket for life." On the other hand, some feminists argue that since the husband has used his wife for unpaid labour during the marriage and she is disadvantaged in the labour market, he should pay her maintenance after divorce. Official opinion is very divided and the Law Commission recently produced a report in which the pros and cons of seven different possible models for financial settlement on divorce were aired; one thing they seem fairly clear about is that a man ought to support his ex-wife if she would otherwise have to turn to the state for support. The problems are far from simple and are, of course, further complicated where there are young children.

Discussions in this area are too often couched in terms of abstract moral principles and do not take account of the realities of post-marital life. For instance the Supplementary Benefits Commission did a study which found that many women were claiming benefit because the maintenance order granted by the Court was below the state benefit level, and furthermore that "payment of forty percent of the maintenance orders fell into the category of less than ten-percent degree of regularity." It is no good ordaining that maintenance shall be paid if husbands cannot or will not pay and women have to turn to the state for support anyway. There is no way that justice can be achieved between people who are so often fundamentally unequal. Nevertheless, our view is that the law should not simply assume married women's dependence — to do so would be to reinforce it — but should do everything to ease divorce and the formation of new households. So we favor the "clean break" model of divorce where any property is divided as soon as possible and there is no continuing obligation to provide maintenance, except for children until they start work. However, this would

need to be tempered by a recognition that women often are unable to support themselves, especially after a long period of marriage when they have kept house and worked outside only intermittently or part-time. The courts should be given guidelines on making protective settlements in such cases. Also, disposal of the marital home presents rather different problems from maintenance, though at present the two tend to be considered together. But in general principle we do not think that the inequality between men and women — differential wages and job opportunities — can be corrected by individual women, such as the "chivalrous" ones for which Lord Denning was famous, are not necessarily in the interests of women as a whole. As *The Cohabitation Handbook* puts it: "Desirable as it is to improve matters, this is not the way to do it."

The same sort of thinking must guide us in disputes about the custody of children. But here the balance seems to us to fall the other way at present. Ultimately we are aiming to create a society in which men and women are equally involved in childcare, which will be in any case much less centred on parents. So a father, or indeed anyone else, who has really been equally involved in caring for a child has as much right to custody as a mother has. Nevertheless, we think that the usual current practice of the courts of awarding custody to the mother is the right one, simply because women nearly always have been the main parents and because the ideology of motherhood is so strong that they feel far more bereft, feel a greater sense of failure, if they are parted from their children. We do not accept the usual considerations that judges are guided by: that young children are naturally better off with their mother, that if the father has a new wife or lives with his mother his claim is stronger because he can offer a substitute mother, that a woman who is a lesbian has a weaker claim because she cannot provide a "normal" environment. But we do not think we have yet reached the stage where it would be helpful to ignore the sex of the parent and take only "sex-blind" considerations into account. So, for the immediate future at least, each father must justify his claim to custody against a strong presumption of the mother's right. Anyone, whether a blood relative or not, should be able to claim custody on the basis that they have actually done the work of caring for the child.

Parents' Rights

We have already discussed some of the problems in the politics of abortion and contraception and argued that, at present, it is very important to defend parents' (and particularly mothers') right to choose whether or not to have children. For at present it really is parents who 'have' them and who must take on most of their support, care, rearing, training, as a private responsibility and more or less on their own. The time to start questioning whether bringing children into the world should be a purely individual decision will be when childrearing is a much more collective enterprise.

To some extent, the same argument can be applied to parental rights over children. In principle, children are not the private property of their parents, so we should favor social rather than individual prerogatives over their lives. but this does not mean that the existing local authority children's departments should have the right to whisk children off into care whenever they disapprove of the way a mother runs her home, or that the existing schools have the right to make children abandon

the clothing of their ethnic minority or submit to corporal punishment. The political problem at present is that these debates are, always couched in terms of parental rights versus state rights. In reality, the idea of parents' rights has grown up alongside the idea of parental responsibility for rearing the children the state needs. So parents are held responsible for preparing infants to start school, for ensuring the attendance and motivation of school children, for preventing delinquency and drug taking and generally for turning out hard-working and law-abiding citizens. Miriam David has argued that state policy relies upon a "family-education couple" to reproduce the social and sexual division of labour. In this context we should be striving to shift the parameters of the debate away from rights and towards responsibilities, away from *whose* responsibilities and toward responsibilities *to do what*.

Take for instance the right-wing argument for the "right to choose" in education, which means that parents should be able to choose what sort of state school system there is and whether to send their children to private school. Firstly, it is worth pointing out that this "right to choose" is often presented as opposition to outside interference: in fact it means parental control over children instead of social control. Then, the debate should properly not be about parental rights versus state rights but about whether it is better for the children of rich and ambitious parents to be sent to the "best" schools while the children of the poor go to the nearest, or for the local education department to plan things so that each school has a mixture of background and ability and offers everyone the best possible opportunities.

Similarly, the debate about corporal punishment should not be over whether the school has the right to cane *my* child but it over whether the use of the cane is a good thing, in school or out. Teachers should feel that they are responsible, not to parents, but to the community as a whole, for the way they treat the children. The recent ruling in the European Court, that a parent can insist on their child not being punished physically, will have the effect of abolishing corporal punishment in British schools. Although we agree with the end result, it would have been more progressive for this to have been achieved as a social decision rather than through the individualist rhetoric of parents' rights over the bodies of their children.

The issue of child-neglect and the role of the socialworker raises perhaps more thorny questions. Even when it is suspected that young children are being battered by their parents, local authority social services departments are reluctant to remove the child from the home. The logic of our collectivist position might seem to be that the child may not be best off staying with its parents and that children should more often be taken into the care of the local authority. Yet social-work also represents an intrusion into people's lives — and especially work-ing-class lives. Through socialworkers and other professionals the state regu-lates family life, and the threat of the compulsory care order is only one instru-ment of control. Here again, then, we meet the problem of the rebarbative char-acter of the existing class forms of col-lectivity. Yet here again we would argue that we must not retreat into the individ-ualism of "the family," but must fight for better kinds of collectivism. So we should recognize that at present we would often want to defend a parent's right to keep her child. But at the same time we should be working to improve the quality of children's homes, to open them up so that teenagers unhappy at home might actually *choose* to go to them or parents choose to send their younger children to them for a while without fear or stigma.

WHAT WOULD YOU PUT IN ITS PLACE?

Any critique of the family is usually greeted with, "but what would you put in its place?" We hope that by now it will be clear that we would put nothing in the place of the family. Anything *in its place*, with the world around it unchanged, could probably be little different from the house-hold patterns and ideology that we know as "the family" at present. A society that offers few other sources of psychic secu-rity and little other means of material sup-port is likely to throw people together into little defensive groups and to leave those who do not form such groups isolated and deprived. A male-dominated society is likely to produce a form of private life in which men are privileged and powerful. What is needed is not to build up an alter-native to the family — new forms of household that would fulfil all the needs that families are supposed to fulfil today — but to make the family less necessary, by building up all sorts of other ways of meeting people's needs, ways less volatile and inadequate than those based on the assumption that "blood is thicker than water."

It is the belief that kinship, love and having nice things to eat are naturally and inevitably bound up together that makes it hard to imagine a world in which "fam-ily" plays little part. This mythologized unity must be picked apart, strand by strand, so that we can understand its power and meet the needs of each of its separate elements more fully. In part, this can be done by analysis and discussion, as we have tried to do here. But it must also be done by experiments in new ways of living and by political campaigns to transform not the family — but the society that needs it.

◆

LOVE IS NOT THE PROBLEM
June Jordan

In between classes and in the middle of campus, I met him on a very cold day. He stood, without shivering, behind a small table on which an anti-McCarthy petition and pages of signatures lay, blowing about. He wore no overcoat, no gloves, no scarf, and I noticed that his cheeks seemed almost bitterly red with the wind. Although that happened some twenty-eight years ago, I remember that he wore a bright yellow Oxford cloth button-down shirt, open at the neck, and no tie. He explained the petition to me. But I wanted to do something else. I wanted to excuse myself and find him a cup of coffee so he'd keep warm enough to continue standing out there, brave against Senator Joe McCarthy and the witchhunts that terrorized America. He looked like a hero to me. It really was cold. He really didn't care. He stood there, by himself, on purpose. I went away to bring him back a cup of coffee, and, as I recall, that same afternoon I told a couple of my friends that I had met the man I would marry.

That was 1954. He was a twenty-year old senior at Columbia College. I was eighteen and a sophomore at Barnard College, across the street. It would be hard to say which one of us was younger or more ignorant of the world beyond our books, our NAACP meetings, school parties,

ping-pong, running hikes through Van Cortlandt Park, or our exhaustively romantic letter-writing at the rate of two or three letters a day. But he was taller and stronger, and he was white. We were not the same.

In 1954, the United States Supreme Court ruled, in *Brown* vs. *Board of Education*, that "separate" was not "equal," that segregated schools delivered an inferior education to the children of the dominated. The court found that black children needed to integrate with the children of the dominating American groups — white children — in order to secure a decently acceptable education.

Although this decision did not arrive with trumpets sounding, it surely prefigured the revolutionary nature of the next twenty years of American history. "Separate but unequal" became the gathering outcry of millions of black people as everything imposed upon us, all forms of hatred and discrimination, because coherently recognizable inside that single concept. Integration with the powerful became the tactic and the strategy for equal rights.

I happen to believe that analysis was off. Rather than struggling to share in a patently evil kind of power, the power of people who will demean and destroy those who are

Fomr June Jordan, "Love Is Not the Problem," in *On Call, Political Essays*, 1985, pp. 51–54.

weaker than they, I think we might, more usefully, have sought to redefine that meaning of power, altogether.

But I was not thinking about law or theory of any kind when, in 1955, I married my young man from across the street. My parents utterly opposed the marriage. His parents opposed the marriage. Our friends (an unruly mix of black and white students) thought we must be kidding: Why get married? Nobody thought either of us was old enough to do anything so serious as that. (And I would have to agree with them, at this remove.) But our friends came. The Episcopal minister came. At the last minute, my parents came. His parents did not. And we got married to the accompaniment of wedding presents that included the four-volume *Social History of Art* and a snakebite kit for camping.

Now I look back on those two kids who fell in love and went ahead and married each other, he wearing an awkwardly fitted but spotless tuxedo and she wearing the highest spike heels and the best $35 wedding gown from Brooklyn, and both of them, in every sense, obvious virgins in a cruel land. From that moment in 1955, where, I wonder, should the cameras cut? To the white mothers screaming invectives at fifteen-year-old Elizabeth Eckford as she approached the schoolyard in Little Rock, Arkansas? To the mutilated bodies of the black and white SNCC volunteers found below the Mississippi highway? To the Birmingham police and the police dogs and that white violence that killed the four black children in the Birmingham church?

■ ■ ■

Thinking only about what to wear, exactly, or what reading to pack on the honeymoon trip they couldn't afford and about brand new sleeping bags, those two kids quietly did something against the law, against every tradition, against the power arrangements of this country; they loved each other.

Apparently, this is where the rest of us get into the story. When two people do something the rest of us don't like or some of us feel real nosy about, then the rest of us interpose ourselves in any way we can. We call out the law. We produce experts. We maintain an attitude. We ostracize. We whisper. We develop jargon such as interracial marriage, or sleeping white, or niggah lover, or identity conflict, or acting out, or patterns of rebellion. And if possible, we kill them, the ones who love each other despite sacrosanct rules of enmity and hatred.

Well, my marriage to that young man from across the street lasted ten and a half years, which is, of course, longer than many. And I think ours was more interesting in some ways. And I know that in America, one out of two marriages fails nowadays: the institution itself is not well, evidently. And I know that I do not regret my marriage. Nor do I regret my divorce.

Hardly anyone talks about love anymore, but I know that I did love that particular young man and that he loved me. And I know that despite the varieties of racist resistance to such love, the number of men and women entering black and white interracial marriage more than doubled from 1970 to 1980. And, on the campus where I teach, I see an increasing number of young people who are interacting with each other, as black and white friends and lovers.

But as a university teacher for the past sixteen years, I have also learned how extremely few of anyone's children are either happy or clear or confident. Most of our children suffer from an agonizing lack of self-respect and a critical absence of faith in anyone or anything.

I think that the children of love between somebody black and somebody white will probably know burdens beyond the enormous "normal" difficulties of growing up in a rather insane, internecine society. As my own son puts it, "There is a disjuncture between your personal identity, which is both black and white, and your social identity, which is black; it takes some time and some doing to work it out for yourself."

It seems to me that such a burden carries with it possible privileges of vision and strength as well as possible disabilities of personal clarity. But you do have to work it out for yourself.

When my son was still an infant, a friend of mine invited me to a join a freedom ride to Baltimore, Maryland. I had seen the burned and overturned buses of the freedom riders. I had seen the bleeding and bandaged heads of the freedom riders after white vigilantes attacked. And as I watched my son asleep in his crib, under the bluebird mobile, I resolved that I would go. To be sure, I was not remotely interested in traveling to Baltimore, but I thought, in the most literal-minded way, that my son might someday want to drink a cup of coffee while he drove through his country. I felt responsible for his future.

His father was furious: How could I risk my life like that? Didn't I care about what would happen to our son?

I went on that freedom ride as the wife of a white man and the mother of a black child. None of it was easy. I was working out a disjuncture between my personal life and my social situation, for myself.

None of this means that any marriage is a great idea or a terrible thing. All I'm saying is that *love* is not the problem.

May, Elaine Tyler, "Epilogue: The Pursuit of Happiness," in *Great Expectations: Marriage and Divorce in Post-Victorian America*, pp. 156–163. Copyright © 1980 University of Chicago. All rights reserved. Reprinted by permission of the Chicago University Press.

Munro, Alice "Royal Beatings." From *The Beggar Maid* by Alice Munro. Copyright © 1977, 1978 by Alice Munro. Reprinted by permission of Alfred A. Knopf, Inc.

Neckerman, Katheryn, Robert Aponte, and William Julius Wilson, "Family Structure, Black Unemployment and American Social Policy," in *The Politics of Social Policy in the United States*, 397, pp. 415–419. Copyright © 1988 by Princeton University Press. Reprinted by permission of Princeton University Press.

Nelson, Barbara, *Making an Issue of Child Abuse*, pp. 1–18. Copyright © 1984 by the University of Chicago. All rights reserved. Reprinted by permission of the University of Chicago Press.

Excerpted from Susan Moller Okin, *Justice, Gender, and the Family*. Copyright © 1989 by Basic Books, Inc. Reprinted by permission of BasicBooks, a division of HarperCollins, Publishers Inc.

Olsen, Francis, "The Politics of Family Law," 2 *Journal of Law and Inequality*, (1984), pp. 1–19. Reprinted by permission.

Olsen, Francis "The Myth of State Intervention in the Family," 18 *University of Michigan Journal of Law Reform* 835 (1985) (edited).

Olsen, Tillie "I Stand Here Ironing," from *Tell Me A Riddle* (New York: Delacorte, 1981), pp. 9–21. Copyright © 1956, 1957, 1960, 1961 by Tillie Olsen. Used by permission of Delacorte Press/ Seymour Lawrence, a division of Bantam Doubleday Dell Publishing Group, Inc.

Painter, Pamela, "New Family Car," a short story. First appeared in the Spring 1992 issue of *Story Magazine*. Reprinted in *The Graywolf Annual Eight: The New Family*, Scott Walker, ed., 1991 Graywolf Press, pp. 241–250.

Peacock, Carol, *Hand Me Down Dreams* (New York: Schocken Books, 1981), pp. 65–66. Copyright © 1981 by Carol Antoinette Peacock. Reprinted by permission of Regina Ryan Publishing Enterprises, Inc.

Pogrebin, Letty Cottin. Reprinted with permission of the author from the book, *Family Politics: Love and Power on an Intimate Frontier*. Copyright © 1983 by Letty Cottin Pogrebin, published by McGraw-Hill, Inc.

Pritchard, Robert, "A Market for Babies," 34 *University of Toronto Law Journal* 341 (1984). Copyright © University of Toronto Press. Reprinted by permission of University of Toronto Press.

Rich, Adrienne. "Night-Pieces: For a Child" is reprinted from *The Fact of a Doorframe, Poems Selected and New*, 1950–1984. Reprinted with permission of W. W. Norton & Company, Inc., and by Adrienne Rich. Copyright © 1984 by Adrienne Rich; copyright © 1975, 1978 by W.W. Norton & Company, Inc.; Copyright © 1981 by Adrienne Rich.

Sarat, Austin and Felstiner William L.F., "Lawyers and Legal Consciousness: Law Talk in the Divorce Lawyer's Office." Reprinted by permission of the Yale Law Journal Company and Fred B. Rothman & Company from *The Yale Law Journal*, vol. 98, pp. 1663–1668.

Sarton, May. Pages 56–59 are reprinted from *A Reckoning*, a novel by May Sarton, by permission of W.W. Norton & Company, Inc. Copyright © 1978 by May Sarton.

Schorr, Nanette, "Foster Care & The Politics of Compassion," *Tikkun*, May/June 1992, pp. 19–22, 80–83.

Sidel, Ruth, "But Where Are the Men," pp. 101–114. From *Women and Children Last* by Ruth Sidel, Copyright © 1986 by Ruth Sidel. Used by permission of Viking Penguin, a division of Penguin Books USA, Inc.

Simon, Rita J., "Comment on Where Do Black Children Belong?" in 1 *Reconstruction*, no. 4 (1992), p. 51.

Stack, Carol, "Cultural Perspective on Child Welfare" 12 *New York University Review of Law and Social Change*, pp. 539–547. Copyright © 1983–84 by Carol B. Stack. Reprinted by permission of Carol B. Stack.

Stack, Carol, "Personal Kindreds" from *All Our Kin: Strategies for Survival in a Blck Community* pp. 45–361. Copyright © 1974 by Carol B. Stack. Reprinted by permission of HarperCollins Publishers, Inc.

Thompson, Sharon, "Pregnant on Purpose." Reprinted by permission of the author and *The Village Voice*.

Timmons, Bonnie "The New Family." Appeared in *Anxiety*, Ballentine 1991. Reprinted by permission of Bonnie Timmons.

Wasserman, Dan, "Pregnancy Leave Discriminates Against Men," *Boston Globe*, Tuesday, Jan. 27, 1987. Copyright © 1987, Boston Globe. Distributed by Los Angeles Times Syndicate. Reprinted with permission.

Wooden, Kenneth, "No Name Maddox: Case History of Charles Manson" from *Weeping in the Playtime of Other*, pp. 45–57 (1976). Reproduced with permission from McGraw-Hill Publishing Co.